# Technology and Testing

From early answer sheets filled in with number 2 pencils, to tests administered by mainframe computers, to assessments wholly constructed by computers, it is clear that technology is changing the field of educational and psychological measurement. The numerous and rapid advances have immediate impact on test creators, assessment professionals, and those who implement and analyze assessments. This comprehensive new volume brings together leading experts on the issues posed by technological applications in testing, with chapters on game-based assessment, testing with simulations, video assessment, computerized test development, large-scale test delivery, model choice, validity, and error issues.

Including an overview of existing literature and groundbreaking research, each chapter considers the technological, practical, and ethical considerations of this rapidly changing area. Ideal for researchers and professionals in testing and assessment, *Technology and Testing* provides a critical and in-depth look at one of the most pressing topics in educational testing today.

**Fritz Drasgow** is Professor of Psychology and Dean of the School of Labor and Employment Relations at the University of Illinois at Urbana-Champaign, USA.

------------------------------------------------

*Technology and Testing: Improving Educational and Psychological Measurement*
Edited by Fritz Drasgow

------------------------------------------------

Forthcoming:

*Meeting the Challenges to Measurement in an Era of Accountability*
Edited by Henry Braun

*Testing the Professions: Credentialing Policies and Practice*
Edited by Susan Davis-Becker and Chad W. Buckendahl

*Fairness in Educational Assessment and Measurement*
Edited by Neil J. Dorans and Linda L. Cook

*Validation of Score Meaning in the Next Generation of Assessments*
Edited by Kadriye Ercikan and James W. Pellegrino

# Technology and Testing
Improving Educational and Psychological Measurement

**Edited by Fritz Drasgow**

Routledge
Taylor & Francis Group

NEW YORK AND LONDON

First published 2016
by Routledge
711 Third Avenue, New York, NY 10017

and by Routledge
2 Park Square, Milton Park, Abingdon, Oxon, OX14 4RN

*Routledge is an imprint of the Taylor & Francis Group, an informa business*

*Library of Congress Cataloging-in-Publication Data*
Technology and testing : improving educational and psychological measurement / edited by Fritz Drasgow.
    pages cm. — (Ncme applications of educational measurement and assessment book series)
    Includes bibliographical references and index.
  1. Educational tests and measurements.   2. Educational technology.   I. Drasgow, Fritz.
    LB3051.T43 2015
    371.26—dc23   2015008611

ISBN: 978-0-415-71715-1 (hbk)
ISBN: 978-0-415-71716-8 (pbk)
ISBN: 978-1-315-87149-3 (ebk)

Typeset in Minion
by Apex CoVantage, LLC

Printed and bound in the United States of America by
Edwards Brothers Malloy on sustainably sourced paper

# Contents

# Contributors

**Malcolm I. Bauer** is a senior managing scientist in the Cognitive Science group at the Educational Testing Service. His research has two main foci: game-based assessment for complex problem solving and non-cognitive skills, and learning progressions for assessment in STEM areas.

**Randy Elliot Bennett** holds the Norman O. Frederiksen Chair in Assessment Innovation at Educational Testing Service in Princeton, New Jersey. His work concentrates on integrating advances in the learning sciences, measurement, and technology to create new approaches to assessment that measure well and that have a positive impact on teaching and learning.

**Daniel Bolt** is Professor of Educational Psychology at the University of Wisconsin, Madison and specializes in quantitative methods. His research interests are in item response theory (IRT), including multidimensional IRT and applications. He teaches courses in the areas of test theory, factor analysis, and hierarchical linear modeling, and consults on various issues related to the development of measurement instruments in the social sciences. Dan has been the recipient of a Vilas Associates Award and Chancellors Distinguished Teaching Award at the University of Wisconsin.

**Krista Breithaupt**, Ph.D., has 25 years of experience with modern psychometric methods and computerized testing, including assessment in clinical epidemiology, nursing, and population health. Krista served for 10 years as a psychometrician and then as Director of Psychometrics at the American Institute of CPAs (AICPA). She guided research and development to computerize a national licensing exam for CPAs, contributing innovative research in test development, assembly, scoring, and delivery technologies for the national licensing exam administered to 250,000 examinees annually. Krista held the position of Director, Research and Development (retired) at the Medical Council of Canada. In this post, Krista defined and led national studies to determine the skills, knowledge, and attitudes required for licensure as a physician in Canada. Krista developed and guided studies to validate and streamline the delivery, scoring, and comparability of certification examinations for Canadian and internationally trained physicians in Canada.

**Oleksandr S. Chernyshenko** received his Ph.D. from the University of Illinois at Urbana-Champaign in 2002 with a major in industrial organizational psychology and minors in quantitative methods and human resource management. He is currently an Associate

Professor at Nanyang Technological University in Singapore, conducting research and teaching courses related to personnel selection. Dr. Chernyshenko is an Associate Editor of the journal *Personnel Assessment and Decisions* and serves on the editorial board of the *International Journal of Testing*.

**Brian E. Clauser** has worked for the past 23 years at the National Board of Medical Examiners, where he has conducted research on automated scoring of complex assessment formats, standard setting, and applications of generalizability theory. He led the research project that developed the automated scoring system for a computer-simulation-based assessment of physicians' patient management skills. The simulation is part of the licensing examination for physicians. Brian is also the immediate past editor of the *Journal of Educational Measurement*.

**Jerome C. Clauser** is a Research Psychometrician at the American Board of Internal Medicine. His research interests include standard setting, equating, and innovative item types.

**Linda L. Cook** is recently retired from Educational Testing Service. While employed by ETS, she served in a number of roles including Executive Director of the Admissions and Guidance area, Vice President of Assessment, and Director of the Center for Validity Research. Linda is a past member of the NCME Executive Board and Past President of NCME. She has also served as Vice President of AERA Division D, Measurement and Research Methodology and was a member of the Joint Committee for the Revision of the Standards for Educational and Psychological Testing. Her primary research interests are the fairness and accessibility of assessments for examinees with disabilities and linking academic assessments. Cook has published numerous articles and several edited volumes on these topics.

**Seth Corrigan** is the Research Scientist for Learning Analytics at GlassLab Games where he uses psychometrics, educational data mining, and principled design to create responsive game-based assessments and simulations. He is also a member of the Embodied Design Research Laboratory at University of California, Berkeley, using dynamic models to "turn touch into knowledge" about embodied cognition in mathematics. Seth has more than 10 years of experience contributing to and directing national, regional, and local projects in measurement, assessment, and evaluation.

**Laurie L. Davis** is Director of Solutions Implementation for Pearson and is currently responsible for supporting next generation assessment practice and implementation of research in applied assessment settings. Dr. Davis additionally leads Pearson's research efforts in the area of Digital Devices with the goal of establishing best practice for fairly assessing students on touch-screen tablet devices. Dr. Davis holds a Ph.D. in Educational Psychology with a specialization in Quantitative Methods and Psychometrics from the University of Texas. Her current research interests include the incorporation of technology to enhance assessment and measurement.

**Kristen DiCerbo** is a Principal Research Scientist and lead of Pearson's Center for Learning Science and Technology. Her research program centers on the use of interactive technologies in learning and assessment, investigating how to use evidence from learner activity in games and simulations to understand what learners know and can do. Dr. DiCerbo has also engaged with teachers to understand how to best communicate information about student performance to inform instructional decisions.

**Fritz Drasgow** is Dean of the School of Labor and Employment Relations and Professor of Psychology at the University of Illinois at Urbana-Champaign. His research focuses on psychological measurement, computerized testing, and modeling. His recent psychometric work examines the use of ideal point models for personality assessment. Drasgow is a former chairperson of the U.S. Department of Defense's Advisory Committee on Military Personnel Testing and the American Institute of Certified Public Accountants' Psychometric Oversight Committee. He is a former President of the Society for Industrial and Organizational Psychology and received their Distinguished Scientific Contributions Award in 2008.

**Michael Fetzer** is the Global Director of Advanced Assessment Technologies at CEB. In this role, he is responsible for leading teams of I-O psychology and simulation/multimedia experts that design and develop leading-edge simulations and multimedia-based assessments that are utilized across many industries around the world. In addition, Dr. Fetzer is responsible for developing and implementing new and innovative methods for multimedia-based talent measurement, including serious games and other cutting-edge technologies. Dr. Fetzer holds a doctoral degree in I-O psychology and is a contributing member of the Society for Industrial and Organizational Psychology (SIOP), the Association of Test Publishers (ATP), the International Test Commission (ITC), the International Association of Applied Psychology (IAAP), and the American Psychological Association (APA).

**David Foster** currently serves as the CEO and President of Caveon Test Security. Dr. Foster introduced a number of testing and security innovations during his career. He graduated from Brigham Young University in 1977 with a Ph.D. in Experimental Psychology and completed a biopsychology post-doctoral fellowship at Florida State University in 1982.

**Karen Fung** is a Ph.D. student specializing in the area of Measurement, Evaluation, and Cognition in the Department of Educational Psychology at the University of Alberta. Her research interests include automatic item generation, automatic essay scoring, test translations and adaptations, educational and psychological measurement, and differential item and bundle functioning. She is also a psychometrician currently residing in Toronto, Canada.

**Kurt F. Geisinger** is the W.C. Meierhenry Distinguished University Professor and Director of the Buros Center for Testing at the University of Nebraska-Lincoln. He is editor of *the APA Handbook of Testing and Assessment in Psychology, Psychological Testing of Hispanics* (two editions), several *Mental Measurements Yearbooks*, and numerous other volumes and has edited the journal *Applied Measurement in Education* for approximately 10 years. His professional interests include testing members of special populations, fairness, validity, admissions testing, and licensure and certification testing.

**Mark J. Gierl** is Professor of Educational Psychology and Director of the Centre for Research in Applied Measurement and Evaluation at the University of Alberta. His research interests include assessment engineering, including cognitive modeling, automatic item generation, automated test assembly, and automatic essay scoring. He holds the Canada Research Chair in Educational Measurement.

**Robin A. Guille** holds a Ph.D. in Educational Psychology and an M.S. in Computer Science. She is Vice President of Cognitive Assessment Research and Development at the American Board of Internal Medicine, focusing on operations research, psychometrics, and project management.

**Edward Haertel** is Jacks Family Professor of Education, Emeritus, at Stanford University. His most recent research has centered on policy uses of achievement tests, validity arguments for high-stakes testing, the logic and implementation of standard setting methods, and trend comparisons across different tests. He is a past president of the National Council on Measurement in Education, a former member of the National Assessment Governing Board, a past chair of the National Research Council's Board on Testing and Assessment, and a member of the National Academy of Education.

**Donovan Hare** divides his time as an Associate Professor, Department of Mathematics, University of British Columbia Okanagan, and as a discrete optimization consultant to industry in the U.S. and Canada, specializing in CPLEX for more than 20 years.

**Michael John** is the Game Director at GlassLab Games where he oversees the development of game-based assessments and core technologies. Prior to joining GlassLab, he had 20 years of commercial game design experience, working with Sony, Electronic Arts, and many other game development companies large and small.

**Leslie Keng** is a Principal Research Scientist for Pearson and is currently the lead psychometrician for the Partnership for Assessment of Readiness for College and Careers (PARCC) assessment project. Dr. Keng has more than a decade of operational experience in comparability research in assessments, starting with traditional paper-and-pencil to computer-based testing, to comparability between traditional and nontraditional computing devices, such as touch-screen tablet devices. Dr. Keng holds a Ph.D. in Educational Psychology with a specialization in Quantitative Methods and Psychometrics from the University of Texas.

**Hollis Lai** is an Assistant Professor at the Faculty of Medicine and Dentistry, University of Alberta. He is the director of assessment and evaluation of the MD program. His research interests are in item generation, educational measurement, and medical education.

**Cara C. Laitusis** is a Senior Research Director in the Research Division at Educational Testing Service (ETS). She currently leads the K12 Research Center and has published numerous articles on testing accommodations and computer-based assessments.

**Richard M. Luecht** is a Professor of Educational Research Methodology at the University of North Carolina at Greensboro. His research interests include developing computer-based testing models, large-scale systems design, innovative item design, and the application of design engineering principles to assessment.

**Melissa J. Margolis** is a Senior Measurement Scientist at the National Board of Medical Examiners. Over the past 20 years, her main areas of research have focused on automated scoring of complex performance tasks, performance-based assessment, workplace-based assessment, and standard setting. She also has authored and co-authored more than 100 scholarly publications and professional conference presentations on a variety of medical education, assessment, and measurement-related topics. Her recent interests are in the areas of assessment and instrument design, competency-based assessment, validity, and standard setting.

**Robert J. Mislevy** is the Frederic M. Lord Chair in Measurement and Statistics at ETS, and Emeritus Professor of Measurement and Statistics at the University of Maryland. His research applies developments in technology, statistics, and cognitive science to practical problems in assessment.

**Jaison Morgan** is the CEO of Common Pool, a company responsible for the design, development, and management of scientific trials and online competitions, intended to spur innovative breakthroughs in science, education, and technology. He completed graduate studies at the University of Chicago and worked with a team to establish a lab at MIT in 2007, to study the use of incentives for accelerating advances in engineering. He remains a lifelong learner and lectures regularly on the topic of "incentive engineering."

**Andreas Oranje** is lead psychometrician for the NAEP program at Educational Testing Service and works on design and analysis aspects of digitally based assessments, including simulation, scenario, and game-based tasks. He received his master's degree and doctorate in psychological methods at the University of Amsterdam and serves on the editorial board of the *Journal of Educational Measurement*.

**Cynthia G. Parshall** holds a Ph.D. in Educational Measurement and Research and an M.Ed. in Instructional Computing. Dr. Parshall works as a consultant at CBT Measurement, focusing broadly on the intersection of technology with assessment, especially innovative item types. She has authored approximately 40 publications and presentations on the topic of innovative item types and she is the lead author on the book *Practical Considerations in Computer-Based Testing*.

**Eric C. Popp** directed the selection process for an international nonprofit organization for 10 years before attending the University of Georgia where he received his Ph.D. in Industrial-Organizational Psychology. He is currently a Managing Research Scientist with CEB where he has worked for nine years. His work at CEB has included validation studies, localization of assessment content for international markets, and the development of a series of animation-based situational judgment tests.

**Mark D. Reckase** is a Distinguished University Professor Emeritus at Michigan State University where he specializes in psychometric theory and the practical aspects of educational measurement. He is the author of *Multidimensional Item Response Theory*, and his recent work focuses on the design of item pools to support computerized adaptive testing. Professor Reckase has been the editor of two measurement journals and the president of the National Council on Measurement in Education.

**Mark D. Shermis** is Dean and Professor at the University of Houston–Clear Lake. He has worked extensively in the field of automated essay scoring and was the principal investigator of the Hewlett Trials that examined machine scoring for long- and short-form constructed responses to determine whether or not the technology might be applied to scoring the new assessments associated with the Common Core State Standards.

**Stephen G. Sireci**, Ph.D. is Professor of Educational Policy, Research, and Administration; and Director of the Center for Educational Assessment at the University of Massachusetts Amherst. His areas of specialization include test development, test evaluation, content validity, cross-lingual assessment, measurement invariance, standard setting, and computer-based testing.

**Stephen Stark** is a Professor of Psychology at the University of South Florida, where he teaches psychometrics and personnel selection courses and conducts research on topics, such as differential item and test functioning, aberrant response detection, forced choice IRT models, and personality measurement. He received his Ph.D. from the University of Illinois at Urbana-Champaign in 2002 with a major in industrial organizational psychology and a minor in quantitative methods after earning a B.S. in physics from the University of New Orleans. He is a Fellow of the American Psychological Association and the Society of Industrial and Organizational Psychology, co-editor of the *International Journal of Testing*, and he currently serves on the editorial boards of *Applied Psychological Measurement*, *Journal of Applied Psychology*, and the *Journal of Business and Psychology*.

**Elizabeth Stone** is an Associate Research Scientist in the Research and Development Division of Educational Testing Service. Since joining ETS in 1998, her work has included time as a statistical analyst and statistical coordinator for two major operational computerized adaptive testing programs; related research focused on item- and person-parameter estimation; and investigation of validity and fairness issues for students with learning disabilities, visual impairments, and hearing impairments on standards-based assessments. Evaluation of computer-based accommodations and of computerized adaptive testing of students with learning disabilities are focuses of her current research

**Ellen Strain-Seymour** currently designs assessment development technologies at Pearson. Prior roles at Pearson included spearheading a technology-enhanced item design initiative, researching device comparability, designing online accommodations, and conducting usability testing and cognitive laboratories related to online assessment. In the years preceding her move to Pearson, Strain-Seymour founded and managed an eLearning software development company, directed a user-centered design group at Harcourt, and taught usability engineering as a member of the Georgia Institute of Technology faculty.

**Jonathan Templin** has a joint appointment as an Associate Professor in the Research, Evaluation, Measurement, and Statistics (REMS) Program in the Department of Educational Psychology and as an Associate Scientist in the Achievement and Assessment Institute, both at University of Kansas. The main focus of Dr. Templin's research is in the field of diagnostic classification models—psychometric models that seek to provide multiple highly reliable scores from psychological tests. Dr. Templin's research program has been funded by the National Science Foundation and has been published in journals such as *Psychometrika*, *Psychological Methods*, *Applied Psychological Measurement*, and the *Journal of Educational Measurement*. Dr. Templin is a coauthor of the book *Diagnostic Measurement: Theory, Methods, and Applications*, which won the 2012 American Educational Research Association Division

D Award for Significant Contribution to Educational Measurement and Research Methodology. For more information, please visit his website: http://jonathantemplin.com.

**Kathy Tuzinski** is a Principal Research Scientist in the Measurement Capabilities group at CEB, where she develops new products for talent assessment. She specializes in translating customer requirements into face-valid and predictive assessments and extending psychometric methods of test development into new forms of measurement. In her previous role as a Principal Consultant at CEB, she provided high-end consulting by advising new and prospective customers on assessment/talent measurement offerings and best practices. She has an M.A. in Industrial/Organizational Psychology from the University of Minnesota.

**Alina von Davier** is a Senior Research Director and leader of the Center for Advanced Psychometrics at ETS. She also is an Adjunct Professor at Fordham University. At ETS, von Davier is responsible for developing a team of experts and a psychometric research agenda in support of next generation of assessments. Machine learning and data mining techniques, Bayesian inference methods, and stochastic processes are the main set of tools employed in her current research.

**Walter D. Way** is Vice President of Assessment Solutions and Design at Pearson. Dr. Way has more than 25 years of assessment experience in a variety of settings. He is a nationally known expert on computer-based testing and has worked on testing programs in higher education, licensure and certification, and K-12 assessment. Dr. Way received his Ph.D. in Educational Measurement and Statistics from the University of Iowa.

**Mo Zhang** is a Research Scientist in the Research and Development Division at Educational Testing Service. Her research interests lie in the methodology of measurement and validation for automated scoring.

**Bin Zheng** is the Endowed Research Chair in Surgical Simulation, Director of Surgical Simulation Research Lab (SSRL) in the Department of Surgery of the University of Alberta. He collaborates with surgeons, clinical educators, psychologists, and computing scientists to develop simulation and simulation-based programs for surgical training. His long-term goal is to promote the use of innovative technologies for improving education outcomes and patient care quality.

# Foreword

The Editorial Board is pleased to introduce the National Council on Measurement in Education (NCME) Applications of Educational Measurement and Assessment Book Series with the first volume, edited by Fritz Drasgow, titled *Technology and Testing—Improving Educational and Psychological Measurement*. It is fitting to initiate the series with a volume on the use of technology that has become central to a wide range of aspects of tests and assessments, including item and test development, delivery, scoring, analysis, and score reporting. Fritz Drasgow has been at the forefront of the use of technology in tests and assessments since the late 1970s and has substantial experience in developing books in the measurement field. We anticipate that readers of the volume will appreciate the impressive lineup of chapter authors and the excellent content of the volume.

The NCME Applications of Educational Measurement And Assessment Book Series was launched during Wayne Camara's 2010–2011 year as NCME president. The primary purpose of the book series is to increase understanding and inform research-based applied educational measurement and assessment. Secondary purposes include increasing NCME's impact, visibility, member engagement, and advancement of science. Intended audiences include NCME members, graduate students in measurement and assessment, and professionals in related fields engaged in measurement and assessment (e.g., psychology, educational leadership, educational and learning policy, curriculum and instruction, learning sciences, and certification and licensure).

**NCME Book Series Editor Board**
Michael J. Kolen, The University of Iowa, Editor
Robert L. Brennan, The University of Iowa
Wayne Camara, ACT
Edward H. Haertel, Stanford University
Suzanne Lane, University of Pittsburgh
Rebecca Zwick, Educational Testing Service
*February 2015*

# Preface

Fritz Drasgow

These are exciting times for people interested in testing. Rapid advances in computing power, steep reductions in cost, and great improvements in software have created remarkable opportunities for innovation and progress. This book documents many of these new directions and provides suggestions for numerous further advances. It seems safe to predict that testing will be dramatically transformed over the next few decades—paper test booklets with opscan answer sheets will soon be as outdated as computer punch cards.

This book is organized into four sections, each with several related chapters, followed by comments from a leading expert on testing. In this era of rapid innovation, it is appropriate that the book begins with a chapter on managing change. Cynthia Parshall and Robin Guille discuss an approach for rapid development and deployment of assessment innovations. It is based on the Agile method for software development, which aims for accelerated creation, flexible response to needed adjustments, and continuous improvement. The ensuing three chapters describe new approaches to assessment. Robert Mislevy and colleagues address game-based assessment; wouldn't it be remarkable if testing was fun? The underlying framework is Mislevy's evidence-centered assessment design. In the next chapter, Brian Clauser and colleagues review a variety of assessments using simulations, with Clauser's work on the United States Medical Licensing Examination patient management simulation providing an outstanding example. New technology plays an even bigger role in Eric Popp and colleagues' chapter "Actor or Avatar." They describe issues and considerations for video-based assessment and, specifically, the decision on whether to use actors or animation. In the old days, animation was excruciatingly labor intensive; now software can create avatars quickly and efficiently. In fact, the software can create avatars that are so realistic that a phenomenon termed the "Uncanny Valley" is now a concern. Stephen Sireci provides some integrative comments on these first four chapters.

The next set of chapters describes the use of technology to create items, assemble items into test forms, and provide scores. There is a growing demand for testing programs to make their assessments available on a nearly continuous basis, which in turn creates the need for many items and many forms. In regard to the need for very large item banks, Mark Gierl has been a leader in using technology to create items. In this chapter, he and his colleagues review his earlier work on generating items in a single language and then extend the approach to multiple languages. In regard to creating many test forms, manual assembly becomes prohibitively time consuming; Krista Breithaupt and Donovan Hare describe automated test assembly, which can create myriad test forms subject to user-imposed constraints. Another important trend in testing is the growing emphasis on constructed responses. However, scoring constructed responses with human graders is very expensive for programs that may test hundreds of thousands of examinees. Randy Bennett and Mo Zhang begin their chapter with a review of automated scoring. They then address a number of critical issues related to the validity of automated scoring. Mark Reckase provides a number of comments on this set of chapters.

The third group of chapters addresses some issues of growing importance due to new technology. Richard Luecht provides an overview of the system of systems required by a state-of-the-art computer-based testing program. This includes the data structures and repositories, the processes of transmission, the test delivery models, and psychometric systems. In the next chapter, Oleksandr Chernyshenko and Stephen Stark review a new direction in testing: assessment via smart phones and other handheld devices. A variety of issues arise with tests delivered via such small form factors; they are described in the context of several ongoing mobile testing applications. Test fairness, the focus of the next chapter, has long been a concern, but it has gained increasing attention of late. For example, the 2014 *Standards for Educational and Psychological Testing* now includes fairness as one of its three foundational chapters (the other two being validity and reliability). Elizabeth Stone and colleagues describe how technology can help provide test takers with an unobstructed opportunity to demonstrate their proficiency in the content of the test by minimizing construct irrelevant variance. While on the one hand, technology can be used to improve test fairness, on the other hand, technology has created threats to test security. David Foster reviews a variety of such threats (e.g., unauthorized online distribution of test materials) and describes a variety of approaches test programs can take to thwart test compromise. Following these chapters, Kurt Geisinger provides some thoughts and insights.

The final set of chapters considers issues and opportunities provided by our growing technological capabilities. Walter Way and colleagues tackle a thorny problem created by uneven availability of this technology. Although technology-enhanced assessments may be improvements over their paper-and-pencil alternatives, not all schools and school districts have the requisite hardware and software infrastructure. Thus, students may take varying versions of a test, which leads to questions about the extent of comparability of scores across versions. This chapter reviews research on score comparability and then presents some strategies for addressing these issues. The next chapter, by Jonathan Templin, considers the longstanding problem of tests generally assessing multiple skills but only reliably yielding an overall score (with subscores too unreliable for meaningful interpretation). He reviews the emerging field of diagnostic classification models (DCMs), which can provide important insights into a test taker's multidimensional profile of skills. For most of the history of computer-based testing, the logistic item response theory (IRT) models have been predominant (with DCMs a notable exception). In the next chapter, Daniel Bolt reviews a variety of alternative IRT models that are customized for particular applications. For example, he reviews various models that can play roles in item generation, understanding response times, and identifying test compromise. The final chapter, by Mark Shermis and Jaison Morgan, implicitly addresses how to continue progress in testing and even enhance lagging areas. They compare computer adaptive testing, which has been an active area of research with substantial innovation and development, to automated essay scoring, which has seen far less progress. They then describe the use of prizes (specifically, the William and Flora Hewlett Foundation's Automated Student Assessment Prize), which seems to have fostered important progress for automated essay scoring. Finally, the book is concluded with comments by Edward Haertel on the final set of chapters.

In sum, these chapters illustrate the many directions in which testing experts are making rapid and important progress. New technology is changing almost everything about testing, ranging from the materials to which test takers respond, to how scores are created from the test taker's actions. Better hardware, better software, better psychometric models, and better conceptual frameworks are leading to new directions in testing. I predict that over the next few decades, many of the innovations described in this book will be widely implemented and thereby profoundly change testing for the better.

# 1

# Managing Ongoing Changes to the Test
## Agile Strategies for Continuous Innovation

**Cynthia G. Parshall and Robin A. Guille**

## Introduction

When an exam program is delivered via computer, a number of new measurement approaches are possible. These changes include a wide range of novel item types, such as the hot spot item or an item with an audio clip. Beyond these relatively modest innovations lie extensive possibilities, up to and including computerized simulations. The term *innovative item type* is frequently used as an overarching designation for any item format featuring these types of changes (Parshall, Spray, Kalohn, & Davey, 2002). The primary benefit that these new item types offer is the potential to improve measurement. When they are thoughtfully designed and developed, novel assessment formats can increase coverage of the test construct, and they can increase measurement of important cognitive processes (Parshall & Harmes, 2009). A further advantage provided by some innovations is the opportunity to expand the response space and collect a wider range of candidate behaviors (e.g., DiCerbo, 2004; Rupp et al., 2012).

However, the potential benefits offered by innovative item types are not guaranteed. Furthermore, to successfully add even a single new item type to an exam may require substantial effort. When an exam program elects to add several innovations, the costs, complexities, and risks may be even higher. Part of the challenge in adding innovative item types is that so much about them is new to testing organization staff and stakeholders. And while the standard approaches for processes and procedures serve an exam program well in the development of traditional item types, it fails to meet the needs that arise when designing new item types. A more flexible approach is needed in these cases, ideally one that provides for "experimental innovation" (Sims, 2011), in which solutions are built up over time, as learning occurs. Looking to the future, a likely additional challenge with test innovations is that the measurement field and all aspects of technology are going to continue to advance. Testing organizations may need to begin thinking of innovation and change as an ongoing, continuous element that needs to be addressed.

The research and development team at the American Board of Internal Medicine (ABIM) sought a strategic approach that would help them manage the task of continuous change in their exam programs. The methods presented in this chapter enable their goal for a strategic and sustainable process. The heart of the process is an *Agile* implementation philosophy (Beck et al., 2001) coupled with a semistructured *rollout plan*.

These approaches, individually and in combination, are presented in this chapter as useful strategies for managing ongoing assessment innovation. They are also illustrated through a case study based on one of ABIM's recent innovations. It is hoped that these methods will also be useful to other organizations that anticipate the need to strategically manage continuous innovations.

## Background on Innovative Item Types

The primary reason for including innovative item types on an assessment is to improve the quality of measurement (Parshall & Harmes, 2009). The ideal innovative item type would increase construct representation while avoiding construct irrelevant variance (Huff & Sireci, 2001; Sireci & Zenisky, 2006). Potential benefits of innovative item types include greater fidelity to professional practice (Lipner, 2013), the opportunity to increase measurement of higher-level cognitive skills (Wendt, Kenny, & Marks, 2007), the ability to measure broader aspects of the content domain (Strain-Seymour, Way, & Dolan, 2009), and the possibility of scoring examinees' processes as part of the response as well as their products (Behrens & DiCerbo, 2012).

The term "innovative item types" has been used most often to describe these alternative assessment methods, though in the field of educational testing, the term "technology-enhanced items" has also become common (e.g., Zenisky & Sireci, 2013). Both phrases are broadly inclusive terms that have been used to encompass a very wide range of potential item types and other assessment structures. In general, any item format beyond the traditional, text-based, multiple-choice item type may be considered to be an innovative item type, though the most complex computerized assessment structures are more typically referred to as *case-based simulations* (Lipner et al., 2010). Item formats that are possible but rarely used in paper-based testing are often included in the category of innovative item types, because the computer platform may mean they are easier to deliver (e.g., an item with a full-color image or an audio clip) or to score (e.g., a short-answer item, a drag-and-drop matching item).

The range of innovative item types that could be created is so great that various compendia and taxonomies have been produced in an effort to help define the field. For example, Sireci and Zenisky (2006) present a large number of item formats, including extended multiple choice, multiple selection, specifying relationships, ordering information, select and classify, inserting text, corrections and substitutions, completion, graphical modeling, formulating hypotheses, computer-based essays, and problem-solving vignettes. Multiple categorization schemas for innovative item types have also been proposed (e.g., Scalise & Gifford, 2006; Strain-Seymour, Way, & Dolan, 2009; and Zenisky & Sireci, 2002). For example, in Parshall, Harmes, Davey, and Pashley's (2010) taxonomy, seven dimensions are used to classify innovative item types. These dimensions are assessment structure, response action, media inclusion, interactivity, complexity, fidelity, and scoring method.

The extensive lists of innovative item types provided in compendia and taxonomies typically include a fair number that have never been used operationally. In some cases, an item type was developed as part of the preliminary research a testing organization devoted to new item types. As such, even the incomplete development of an alternative item type might have been a valuable learning experience for the organization. In other cases, intractable problems (e.g., a scoring solution) were uncovered late in the development process, and the novel item type was forced to be abandoned.

For the first decade or more of operational computer-based tests (CBTs), if an exam program wanted to implement any nontraditional item types, custom software development was required. In fact, all the early CBTs required custom software development, even to deliver the traditional multiple-choice item type, since there were no existing CBT applications. Nevertheless, expanding beyond multiple-choice items required further effort, and most exam programs continued to deliver tests using that sole item type. Only a handful of exam programs pursued customized item type development (e.g., Bejar, 1991; Clauser, Margolis, Clyman, & Ross, 1997; O'Neill & Folk, 1996; Sands, Waters, & McBride, 1997). It was an expensive and time-consuming process, as extensive work was needed to support the underlying psychometrics, as well as the software development, and the effort did not always result in an item type that could be successfully used.

Over time, wide-scale changes in the CBT field occurred. These changes included the development of commercial CBT software, such as item banks and test-delivery applications. Testing organizations are now able to contract with a commercial firm for applications such as these rather than undertaking proprietary software development. In a related development, measurement-oriented interoperability specifications such as the Question and Test Interoperability standard (QTI; IMS, 2012) were established. The QTI specification represents test forms, sections, and items in a standardized XML syntax. This syntax can be used to exchange test content between software products that are otherwise unaware of each other's internal data structures. As a result of these technological developments, all testing organizations have become much less isolated. There is much greater integration and communication across software systems, as well as more standardization of the elements included in different software applications.

Under these newer, more integrated software conditions, the development of customized assessment innovations is relatively streamlined in comparison to the past. In some cases, the IT department at a testing organization may develop a plug-in for an item type feature that will then work within the larger set of CBT software for delivery and scoring. In other cases, a testing organization may work with a third-party vendor that specializes in CBT item/test software development to have a more elaborate innovation custom developed (e.g., Cadle, Parshall, & Baker, 2013). These technological changes have undoubtedly made the development of customized item types more achievable, though substantial challenges, including potentially high costs, remain.

One area of interest requiring customization is the development of multistep, integrated tasks or scenarios. Behrens and DiCerbo (2012) refer to this approach as the shift from an item paradigm to an activity paradigm. One goal often present when these task-based assessments are considered is the opportunity to focus on the examinee's process as well as the end product (e.g., Carr, 2013; DiCerbo, 2004; Mislevy et al., this volume; Rupp et al., 2012). In some cases, though the task may be designed to be process oriented, the outcome is still product oriented (Zenisky & Sireci, 2013). The response formats in these cases often include traditional approaches such as the multiple-choice and essay item types (e.g., Steinhauer & Van Groos, 2013). Other response formats use more complex approaches (e.g., Cadle, Parshall, & Baker, 2013; Carr, 2013; Steinhauer & Van Groos, 2013). When researchers and developers are interested in the examinee's process, they may also seek ways to score *attributes* of the examinee's response set, either in addition to or instead of the response's *correctness* (Behrens & DiCerbo, 2012). Examples of assessments that can score attributes of the examinee's response include interactive tasks in the National Assessment of Educational Progress (NAEP) Science Assessment; student responses to these tasks can be evaluated to determine if they were efficient and systematic (Carr, 2013). In addition, children's task persistence has been investigated in a game-based assessment (DiCerbo, 2004), while users' effectiveness and efficiency in responding to computer application tasks has also been considered (Rupp et al., 2012).

As some of these examples suggest, a "digital ocean of data" (DiCerbo, 2004) may be available for analysis. Potential data sources can include computer log files (Rupp et al., 2012), the user's clickstream, resource use pattern, timing, and chat dialogue (Scalise, 2013). Determining which elements to attend to in these cases can be a challenging problem (Rupp et al., 2012). Luecht and Clauser (2002) describe this as the need to identify the "universe of important actions."

Scoring these types of assessments is often a challenging problem to resolve. Use of a much larger examinee response space and evaluation of multiple attributes naturally suggests a need for new analysis methods (Behrens et al., 2012 ; Gorin & Mislevy, 2013; Olsen, Smith, & Goodwin, 2009; Way, 2013; Williamson, Xi, & Breyer, 2012). As new analysis methods are developed for novel types of assessments, investigations are also needed into the types of response analysis and feedback that item writers find most useful in their task of item review and revision (Becker & Soni, 2013).

At the same time as interest in this new wave of customized innovations has been growing, several modestly innovative item types have been incorporated into many popular CBT applications. Depending on the specific CBT applications, these built-in innovative item types can include the multiple-response (also referred to as the multiple-answer–multiple-choice); items with graphics, audio, or video clips; the hot spot; the short-answer item type; and the drag-and-drop item. Several of these item types have a potential utility across a fairly large number of content areas, and have in fact been used on a considerable number of operational exams.

In some cases, the availability of these built-in, or off-the-shelf, item types within an application can mean that their inclusion on an exam is fairly easy. However, it is still not unusual for software support of these built-in item types to be incomplete across the full set of applications needed to deliver an exam (from item banking through test delivery and on to scoring and reporting). And because exam programs are so dependent on standardized measurement software and delivery vendors, whether the exam includes off-the-shelf or customized innovative item types, it is essential that all these elements interface seamlessly with each other.

The future of measurement is likely to include more novel item types and customized tasks. Testing organizations are increasingly likely to need strategies to help them manage the process of continuous innovation.

## Strategies for Continuous Innovation

The recommended process for an exam program to follow when initially considering innovative item types is to begin with the test construct and to identify any current measurement limitations in the exam that innovations could help address (e.g., Parshall & Harmes, 2008, 2009; Strain-Seymour, Way, & Dolan, 2009). Through this analysis, a list of desirable new item types is often developed; this list might include both item types that are provided within a CBT vendor's software and one or more that require custom development. At the same time, other exam innovations may also be on the table (e.g., some form of adaptive testing). In a short while, these possible improvements to the exam may be in competition with each other, and staff may be overwhelmed by the decisions needed and the work required.

In addition to potential software development challenges, every exam program has multiple stakeholders, and these stakeholder groups may have very different or even conflicting opinions regarding the value of a potential innovation. New materials for communicating with these stakeholder groups will be needed, just as new materials will be needed to support the work of the item writers and staff. Furthermore, new procedures for a host of test-development activities are often important in the development and delivery of an innovative item type.

At ABIM, this set of challenges led the research and development team to seek out a flexible yet consistent approach for the overall development of a broad set of potential innovations. The goal was to utilize the flexible and iterative nature of Agile software development methods, while at the same time including a standardized framework to ensure that the full assessment context would always be considered. ABIM anticipates that these methods, use of Agile principles and the innovation rollout plan, will be useful for many years into the future. These methods can support the current set of planned innovations and should also be robust enough to be helpful in years to come, even given the ongoing changes in medicine, technology, and measurement that will occur.

The strategies we propose for managing ongoing change are illustrated throughout this chapter via one specific innovation ABIM recently undertook. This case study involves the inclusion of patient–physician interaction video clips within standard multiple-choice items.

### Case Study—Introduction

ABIM certifies physicians in the specialty of internal medicine and, additionally, in the 18 subspecialty areas within internal medicine, such as cardiovascular disease and medical oncology. Its multiple-choice examinations largely measure medical knowledge, which is but one of six competencies assessed by the certification process. In order to best manage the research and development of innovations, ABIM formed a cross-departmental innovations team, with content, psychometric, and computing backgrounds.

Many of the innovations considered by this cross-departmental research team seek to improve the multiple-choice examinations by enhancing fidelity to practice, both in enhanced look and feel of case presentation and in improved alignment of the thinking required to answer the test questions with the thinking required in practice. The use of video clips showing patient–physician interactions was one of these potential innovations.

The use of video was selected for the case study because it provides an example that is likely to be familiar to most readers. However, the strategies proposed in this chapter would generally be even more valuable and more critical when the innovation under development is less familiar or more elaborate. Under these conditions, where risk is higher, a flexible and iterative approach offers the greatest opportunity to develop a successful solution.

### The Agile Method

The Agile method of project management grew out of the software development business. The method was defined in 2001 by a group of 17 academic and industry leaders in the field (Beck et al., 2001). It quickly became a generic project management method, not limited to software projects. In 2012, it was recognized by the Project Management Institute (PMI) as an alternative approach to the traditional method (known informally as the "waterfall" method), with a recognized training pathway and certification (Project Management Institute, 2013).

Key Agile principles that make it very different from the waterfall method—and arguably more appropriate for innovations research and development—are:

1. Being more person oriented than process oriented [i.e., valuing "Individuals and interactions over processes and tools" (Beck et al., 2001, line 4)];
2. rapid, iterative development.

Iterative development is what mainly distinguishes Agile from the "waterfall" method, which transitions through its development phases without the possibility of repetition, as if moving steadily down the steps of a waterfall. Agile development, on the other hand, repeats small loops of "design–build–test" phases.

Workers collaborate in pairs or in teams using daily face-to-face communication. High team motivation is fostered. They begin delivering valuable information (in the form of components or a prototype) early in the development timeline and continue to expand the information base or strengthen the prototype at frequent intervals thereafter. Continuously making the prototype more sound (a process known as "refactoring") is important in Agile. It is never viewed as "rework" to strengthen an already working prototype (Wellington, 2007, pp. 12–14).

This idea of continuously making the prototype more sound is what makes Agile development a good fit for the development of innovative assessments. It is possible that the final prototype will be somewhat different from the version originally conceived, as new possibilities present during development. Changes to the original concept can be tried out and easily reverted if unsuccessful.

## The Use of Agile for Prioritizing Innovations

Just as the design of each innovation can change during the course of development, so too can change the organization's sense of the relative importance of the innovations in the full collection under consideration. A key principle of Agile is that development should be in the interest of adding *value* to the organization or its stakeholders. Innovations are not explored simply because they are interesting "bells and whistles." As a rule of thumb, an Agile convention is that the innovations that add the most value should be undertaken first, when there are several potential innovations to explore. Rank ordering potential innovations and possibly deleting some, based on value estimates, is an important, ongoing activity in Agile, referred to as "grooming the product backlog" (Pichler, 2010).

What makes the rank ordering tricky is that *risk* and *complexity* must also be taken into account in addition to value. Some of the most valuable innovations can also be very complex or risky. Despite their high value to the organization, these innovations may need to be tackled after the "low-hanging fruit"—innovations of lower risk and complexity—are explored first.

In Agile methodology, the risk, complexity, and value of each innovation are carefully assessed to prioritize the set of potential innovations for development. This Agile assessment involves the steps of:

1. Identify the risks, opportunities (the inverse of risks), complexities, and values of each innovation
2. Obtain ratings on all of these factors for each potential innovation
3. Recode the ratings into just three variables (opportunities are combined with risks)
4. Produce a visual display of the ratings for the full set of innovations

In the first step, the risks, opportunities, complexities, and types of value potentially added by each possible change are identified by key personnel. For an exam program considering a specific innovation, one risk might be related to technical challenges, while an opportunity might be stakeholder appreciation. A complexity could be the additional Americans with Disabilities Act (ADA) accommodations that the innovation might require. And the value of the innovation could be related to its potential to increase content coverage.

In the second step, people having expertise or experience with the innovation are asked to provide a Likert rating, estimating the magnitude of the risks, opportunities, complexities, and value for that innovation. These ratings can be obtained by individual surveys, distributed on paper or online. Alternatively, the ratings can be collected in a single meeting, using a Delphi method called "Planning Poker" (Cohn, 2006, pp. 90–93), which is similar to the method of collecting ratings during an Angoff standard-setting session.

Next, the ratings are recoded so that only a single rating for risk, a single rating for complexity, and a single rating for value remain. Typically, opportunities are combined with risk. The magnitude of a risk or opportunity is usually a combination of a rating on how likely the event is to happen and a rating of the impact it would have if it did happen. Additionally, in some instances, *cost* is included in the earlier steps as another factor that raters consider. When cost has been included in the ratings, it can be combined with complexity at this point, so that only three variables remain.

Finally, the ratings of risk, complexity, and value are visualized in the aggregate. One of the best tools for doing this is the bubble chart. With a bubble chart, ratings for risk and complexity can be plotted on the X and Y axes, with the size of the bubble representing value.

This Agile approach to prioritization clearly has direct implications for exam programs considering a large number of potential changes. Furthermore, given the Agile goal of continual refinement, the steps described here could naturally be retaken at periodic intervals. In this way, as data continues to come in, long-term planning can evolve, and a well-informed reprioritization may occur. This process would thus continue to be a valuable tool to an exam program interested in managing an ongoing process of changes to the test.

### Case Study—Prioritizing Innovations

#### Classifying Innovations

At ABIM, the initial set of potential innovations under consideration was quite large—too large to undertake all of them at one time. Goals for these various innovations included improving fidelity to practice, as well as improving test design (e.g., exploring adaptive administration) and content development (e.g., exploring improved automated test assembly, assessment engineering item-generation methods, and automated item pool management). To make the best long-term plan, all of these potential innovations were first categorized and then prioritized.

Each of the possible innovations was classified according to a four-category schema that ABIM developed to subsume all of the possibilities (Lipner, 2013). (The first three of these comprise elements that might all fall under the rubric of "innovative item types," but the fourth is clearly distinct.)

ABIM's classification schema defines innovations as:

- Those that affect the *item presentation* to examinees (e.g., adding an element that is presented to examinees, such as video exhibits)
- Those that affect the *item design* (e.g., changing from single best answer to multiple correct response)

- Those that affect *lookup resources* accessed from within an item (e.g., a searchable medical database)
- Those that affect *examination design* (e.g., multistage testing)

ABIM finds classifying innovations helpful because it allows staff to build on commonalities and to gain an economy of scale. This process capitalizes on similarities between innovations rather than treating every one as unique. And staff members can often specialize in certain categories, working on two simultaneously if they are extremely similar.

### Prioritizing Innovations

Once the full set of potential innovations had been classified, ABIM staff utilized Agile methods for prioritizing the development of exam innovations, implementing the series of steps listed. The risks, opportunities, complexities, and values of each potential innovation were identified by key staff members. Then a broader set of stakeholders with relevant experience rated each innovation in terms of these risks, opportunities, complexities, and values. The resulting ratings were recoded and a bubble chart was produced.

Figure 1.1 displays the results of this analysis. Each numbered bubble represents a specific innovation under consideration at ABIM. The size of the bubble reflects the overall value, and the shade of each bubble reflects its classification within ABIM's four categories of innovations.

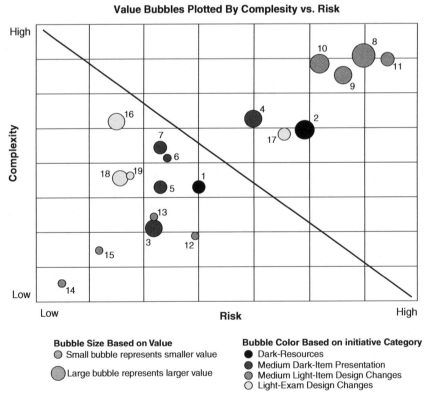

**Figure 1.1.** Bubble Chart of Prioritized Innovations

This chart has proven to be a highly useful summary of a substantial amount of data, and ABIM stakeholders have responded positively to this tool. The bubble chart reveals that there are a number of low-risk and low-complexity items in the lower left corner that might easily be implemented. Some innovations that would add great value, in the upper right corner, are also complex and risky. From this bubble chart, a rank ordering of innovations was produced and put to an initial schedule. Work began on the first series of innovations, including patient–physician interaction videos (bubble #4 on this chart).

These methods have enabled us to prioritize the initial list of potential innovations so that we could begin development, using an order that will deliver optimal value and opportunity, with minimal cost, complexity, and risk.

Over time, as new information is obtained about these potential innovations, and as other possible innovations are proposed, Agile methods provide for periodic reuse of the prioritization steps. This offers valuable insight for managing ongoing change.

### Principles of Agile Development

In addition to the basic element of iterative prioritization, there are several other important principles of Agile. A few of these with particular implications for assessment innovations are welcoming change, making "no go" decisions early, deferring risky design decisions to the "latest responsible moment," and taking advantage of the benefits of teamwork.

#### *Welcoming Change*

The iterative nature of Agile development makes it possible to change plans as new information is learned in each iteration. The waterfall method, on the other hand, encourages a more complete and detailed design up front before beginning any development or testing. Change becomes an exception to the design under the waterfall paradigm, not something to be expected and even welcomed, as it is in Agile.

When undertaking the development of something as novel as an innovative item type, building an expectation for change into the development plan seems warranted. And, with each successful Agile iteration, confidence in the feasibility of the innovation increases as more is known, and so risk decreases. Midcourse corrections to the original design can be made after any iteration, but over time, they become less likely to occur as more is known. When changes do occur at later points in time, they are typically modest refinements rather than substantial changes in direction.

Viewing development as a series of month-long or even 2-week-long Agile time-boxes (also known as "sprints") is conducive to frequent reflection on the progress of development, which is also strongly encouraged in Agile methods. In fact, if we think of each sprint as a mini research study, Agile is like any other research method: Each study builds upon the previous, and our knowledge base expands by assimilating the results of each.

This Agile philosophy of welcoming change will be helpful to testing organizations that choose to develop a process for managing ongoing change. This attitude recognizes that new, potentially worthwhile elements are going to continue to be available, within the measurement field, in technology, and often in the content of the exam subject as well. And the Agile method provides for quick responsiveness when a new opportunity occurs.

The philosophy of welcoming change proved effective at ABIM when one exam committee made an unanticipated request for changes to a computerized tool that was embedded within their exam. The research team responded by quickly setting up and carrying out a mini practice analysis within a local physician's practice. This field observation provided a rich set of data that the larger team was able to rapidly review as they considered changes to the online tool.

### Case Study—Welcoming Change

At ABIM, we categorize videos into three types: those produced by diagnostic medical equipment (e.g., endoscopes), those with low production requirements (physician-shot videos of patient gaits or conditions), and those with high production requirements (professionally shot videos of dialog between actors). We had prior experience with the first two of these video types; however, videos of patient–physician interactions had not previously been included on the secure exams.

The Agile principle of welcoming change is important to our goal of continuous innovation, and we began investigations into high-production videos using actors in response to exam committee's request. Then, when one of the physicians said that he required an additional category—one with patient–physician dialog, while using a real patient—we were able to get a team working on this idea right away. Because of our openness to change, we were able to see this modification of our plans as a good change. It hadn't occurred to us that there might be some physical symptoms that an actor can't realistically portray. In this case, a real patient speaking the dialog would be a better option. We were able to combine our teams to shoot the hybrid category of real patient dialog, even though this approach would not be frequently used going forward. It didn't cause us to have to go back to the drawing board and rethink our entire approach. We simply treated it as an uncommonly seen exception to our plans.

### Making "No Go" Decisions Early

Few would consider it wise to heavily invest resources early in the development timeline before feasibility can be assured—or at least considered to be likely. Although it is reasonable in the research environment to expect that some ideas will not pan out, it is important to spot infeasibility early in the development process so that resources can be rapidly redirected to more promising innovations.

The lengthy design stage of the traditional approach is replaced in Agile by short bursts of design throughout the development timeline. So, too, the lengthy build and test stages are replaced by short bursts, or "time-boxed iterations."

For example, the traditional approach to a typical 1-year project might be: 4 months of design followed by 4 months of building and finally 4 months of testing. Using the Agile approach instead, there might be a series of—say—12 smaller design–build–test iterations. Each of these 12 iterations corresponds to a 1-month time-box. The same amount of overall designing, building, and testing is being performed during the course of the year using either method. It's just that the frequency and duration of the design–build–test loops are radically different when using the time-boxed iterations of Agile. The innovation prototype is shaped like clay after each iteration.

Because the testing or evaluation of a new feature doesn't wait until month 8 (i.e., after 4 months of designing and 4 months of building), infeasibility might be spotted as early as month 1 using the Agile method. Because of this, when a "no go" decision is needed, it can be made quickly.

At ABIM, this Agile principle is heavily emphasized early in the research into a potential innovation. An innovation is investigated in a series of iterations, each one of which provides further information. That information may be used to make a "no go" decision, or, in more promising cases, it's used to refine and shape the innovation as it is further investigated and developed.

This Agile principle can be helpful to any testing organization concerned about ongoing change; it provides a way to get started early, learn as you go, and change course as new data are obtained. These benefits mean that Agile will be most useful to measurement organizations when they are invested in the concept of test innovations. The Agile principle related to "no go" decisions means that an organization can try out a concept, and if it proves to be intractable, a change in direction can be made very quickly. For example, an exam program might consider adding a new item type, but if an initial feasibility analysis shows that there are current technical limitations (such as insufficient bandwidth to deliver video files), then a decision could be quickly made to defer that item type for a couple of years or until a technical solution is available.

### Case Study—Making a "No Go" Decision Early

We've learned that high-quality medical videos can best be produced when there is close collaboration among physicians, videographers, and testing professionals. Simply handing off storyboards from physicians to videographers doesn't work as well as having a physician present during the filming to direct action and pay attention to details of the patient presentation. Likewise, film editing works best when a physician's eye oversees the cutting and sequencing. This change in our procedures helps us catch any problems early on and make a "no go" decision about them before extensive resources have been expended.

The iterative nature of Agile development also allows the team of physicians, videographers, and testing staff to become acquainted and grow increasingly more cohesive with each iteration. Mistakes made in the early iterations can be refilmed once the team begins to work more effectively together. With each iteration, the team should become more cohesive and efficient. If cohesiveness does not happen to be building, then another early "no go" decision can be made: The team can be scrubbed at an early stage and a new one assembled before much money has been invested.

### Deferring Risky Design Decisions to "Latest Responsible Moment"

The iterative nature of Agile development also makes it possible to defer some decision making until later in the development timeline, when risk is lower. By definition, risk is lower at these later points, since more is known. For this reason, whenever members of the team have experience in building similar innovations, the manager can leverage that experience by postponing certain decisions until the "latest responsible moment"—the point when progress will halt if the decisions are not made.

Of course, senior management who hear "we'll cross that bridge when we come to it" may find it a bit discomfiting! But in fact, making a decision too early can be highly problematic. It can force a project down an inferior developmental path when a design decision is made before it is possible to obtain sufficient information. Furthermore, it is reasonable to delay certain decisions when the experience of staff is being leveraged. When some on staff have experience in building a similar innovation, there are fewer unknowns in the development of the new one. Deferral of decisions is not recommended when all members of the team are inexperienced. But when a series of innovations is conducted across time, the team as a whole gains experience, meaning that each sequential project is less daunting and there is an overall reduction in risk.

### Case Study—Deferring Risky Decisions

Since high-quality digital cameras are inexpensive nowadays, the use of video in itself wouldn't be considered a risky innovation, and we wouldn't likely make a "no go" decision on the innovation itself. On the other hand, for a video project that spans more than a year, certain design decisions would be beneficially delayed. For example, it may be wise to defer technological decisions, such as which codec and bit rate to use when generating the final digital file, until more is known about what the capabilities of the display technology will be in a year's time. Deferring these decisions until the latest responsible moment might permit exploiting new technological features for an improved viewing experience.

### Taking Advantage of the Benefits of Teamwork

Under both the waterfall and Agile methods, workers are selected for membership in teams based on their special skills. The difference in Agile is the emphasis on using all of a person's relevant skills, even if they don't necessarily align with his or her formal role on the team. For example, a staff member could initially be added to the development team in the role of content specialist. But if this person also happens to know a lot about audio by virtue of being a musician hobbyist, he or she might be encouraged to work on audio innovations within the team in addition to content. In other words, there aren't necessarily distinct nonmanagerial developer roles in an Agile project.

Crossover work and a high degree of collaboration are encouraged in Agile. A team works best whenever the total amount of work produced is greater than the sum of the work each member would have produced working in isolation. Workers should be empowered to brainstorm new ways of approaching the problems as a team; and they should never be treated as interchangeable human resource units.

In Agile, teams should meet briefly each morning in "stand ups" to touch base and identify any roadblocks to successful development that may be cropping up. It is then the manager's responsibility to remove or suggest ways to work around the roadblocks.

ABIM has a number of remote employees. For teams with members working remotely, meeting as few as two mornings per week via videoconferencing tools (such as Skype or Connect) seems to work as well. The important point is to have face-to-face contact in Agile, whether that is via in-person meeting or videoconferencing.

The Agile process, with its iterative approach and its emphasis on the appreciation of people, progressively builds an experienced team that can handle change (Guille, 2013). This can be a permanent team within the testing organization. And once the team has handled one innovative development project, they can more easily do another.

### Case Study—The Benefits of Teamwork

Implicit in the fostering of teamwork is the belief that the group is greater than the sum of its parts. In the case of video production, reaching the point where all members get excited about the project and propose new ideas for filming and editing is a major benefit of the process. The new ideas may even be about broader issues. For example, the video team might envision new video-related test design innovations or methods of scoring. Working well collaboratively benefits more than just the team itself.

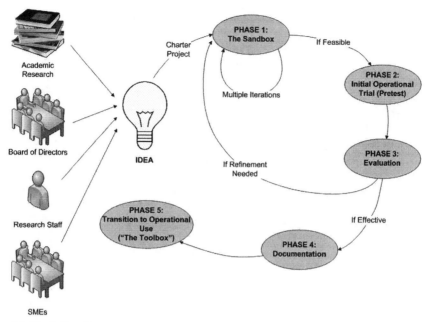

**Figure 1.2** The Rollout Plan

## The Rollout Plan

The rollout plan is implemented as each innovation, in the overall prioritized set, is investigated. This offers a standardized approach that can be used in the research and development of any innovation while retaining as many of the iterative, flexible features inherent in Agile methods as possible. Thus, the rollout plan is intentionally a semistructured approach. The structure is apparent in the five phases, designed to address major test development needs, while Agile flexibility is evident particularly in iterative loops that allow developers to try out early versions, collect data, and refine the item type accordingly (see Figure 1.2).

### Phase 1—A Potential Innovation Is Considered ("The Sandbox")

Phase 1, as the first phase in the rollout plan, is the stage where a proposed innovation is initially considered for possible development. Within ABIM, the Agile principle of welcoming change is clearly evident in this phase, as innovations may be proposed through a variety of channels, including physicians on any of the exam committees, staff members, and even exam candidates through their comments on posttest surveys.

The initial consideration of a proposed innovation often takes the form of a preliminary feasibility analysis. This would typically include a review of the technological and scoring feasibility, along with an identification of potential risks. If the innovation is not fully supported by one or more of the software applications in use, this could be a feasibility challenge. In this situation, the innovations team could investigate potential short-term workarounds, such as manual support by key staff. The team might also investigate the options for software development; further software support for a built-in innovation might be provided by internal IT staff for one innovation, while a custom software plug-in might be developed by an external vendor for another. Other feasibility challenges could occur when a new item type requires new item analysis or scoring procedures, or when the candidate response data takes a new form. For example, since candidates give more than a single response to the multiple-response item type (e.g., "Select two of the following"), existing data storage and analysis procedures may need to be modified for this built-in item type.

In addition to these areas of potential difficulty, other possible risks are identified. The broader set of possible risks includes stakeholder reactions, challenges for ADA candidates, and any impact on test assembly or timing. If the efforts needed to support an innovation are reasonable, and if the innovation seems to be potentially valuable, then the novel assessment option is considered to be feasible and further investigations are conducted. If not, then a "no go" decision can be made well before expensive development steps have been taken.

All of the efforts in this stage are referred to as "sandboxing" at ABIM. This term is derived from the software development field, where new programming code may be tried out in a "sandbox" that is isolated from the regular operational application. In a similar fashion, the term "sandboxing" is used at ABIM to refer to any investigations of a potential assessment innovation that are conducted separately from operational administrations.

The types of investigations conducted during Phase 1 vary depending on features of the specific innovation being considered. While any innovation will need some types of research and refinement, the specific types will vary. For example, media-related innovations are likely to need investigations into technical specifications, while innovations that call for alternative scoring models will need psychometric analyses. Wherever possible, risky design decisions are initially deferred, as all of these iterative investigations build on each other and additional information is collected.

In many cases, the innovations team will seek out published research on the specific assessment innovation. In the past, the literature on innovative item types has been relatively sparse in terms of any type of psychometric findings, though this may be changing (e.g., Becker & Muckle, 2013; Becker & Soni, 2013; Hess, Johnston, & Lipner, 2013; Jodoin, 2003; Maniar, Adams, & Smith, 2013; Muckle, Becker, & Wu, 2011; Olsen, Smith, & Goodwin, 2009; Parshall & Becker, 2008). Also, when the innovation has been used by other exam programs, especially other medical exam programs, staff at ABIM may reach out directly to staff at the other program and ask them for the benefit of their experience. The lessons learned from others with operational experience are then used to help shape the development of the innovation.

If the evidence so far confirms that the innovation has merit, then further research is conducted. Oftentimes another activity at this stage is the development of a nonfunctional prototype. These visual prototypes may be used for discussions, both internally and, at times, with various external stakeholder groups. In some cases, the prototypes may be evaluated and revised by consulting physicians. The prototypes may also be used in focus group sessions or in think-aloud usability studies, especially when the innovation has a marked effect on the user interface.

Specific implementation issues of the potential innovation are considered throughout this stage. For example, the multiple-response item type can be implemented with instructions that either state "Select all that apply. . ." or that specify a required number of responses (e.g., "Select *two* of the following. . ."). Issues like this, with both content and psychometric implications, are likely to be written up and discussed at length with appropriate stakeholders before a decision is made.

All of the work throughout this stage is conducted in an iterative fashion, with each research finding informing the next step. As the first stage in the investigation of a potential innovation, Phase 1 is intentionally the most flexible, and it most clearly reflects Agile principles. Some innovations that are considered by the team will never pass out of Phase 1. Others will be deferred until technological hurdles have been overcome. However, if the research and development in this stage is promising, then plans are put in place to move an innovation into Phase 2.

### Phase 1—Case Study

Our first step in the feasibility analysis of video was determining the level of software support currently available. No issues were found for the item bank, test delivery, or scoring applications. We had prior experience using all of these applications with other types of video, but the much longer video clips in the patient–physician interaction type have an impact on file size. We considered the potential effect of multiple videos on the overall test file size; if certain limits are exceeded, then the test publishing timeline must be extended, and additional costs to ABIM are incurred. The greater file size of these videos could also require additional server space.

We considered whether a new method for item writers to submit/access/review items would be needed. And we considered whether the longer video clips, across multiple video items, could have a meaningful effect on overall test timing. We also investigated the features and functions of the media player in the CBT delivery application to determine whether they were an appropriate match to the ways in which candidates would want to view these videos.

We then held preliminary discussions with the exam committee to determine how they envisioned that video would best address their exam content. For example, would they want to use the video clips solely within the item stem, or would they sometimes want to use video clips as multiple-choice response options as well? Would they ever want candidates to respond by selecting/identifying a frame within the video clip as the key?

These discussions, along with other information about video production gathered by the team, informed the development of draft item writing materials. Writing scripts for video items is very different from that of traditional multiple-choice items, and most item writers need targeted training and support as they undertake this new activity. A video storyboard template was prepared to guide item writers in providing all the necessary information (e.g., the practice setting, any medical equipment needed, patient demographics, the number of camera angles needed). Item writers were also advised about the need to avoid measuring trivial content; a rare patient condition might make an interesting video script but a poor exam item. Several iterations of these materials were needed to make them as helpful as possible.

Once the majority of these issues were considered and decisions made, then plans for an operational pretest began.

## Phase 2—Trial Run and Pretesting With a Single Exam Program

At ABIM, physician feedback and input are sought throughout the research and development process. By the second stage, the innovations team may be working with one of the subspecialty exam committees in a concentrated fashion, and once item type design decisions have been made, the exam committee writes a set of items using the innovation.

Initial pretesting is typically only conducted on this single exam program, and usually only a limited number of items on the exam include the innovation. These decisions are part of the overall iterative process, as they provide the best opportunity for obtaining feedback and further refining an innovation before broader deployment.

At this early point in the use of a new item format or feature, manual processes are often necessary, either pre- or post-administration. For example, the inclusion of a third-party executable within an item type may require hand-coding of the QTI code underlying item display. Alternatively, new psychometric procedures may need to be developed to address distractor analysis (e.g., hot spot items) or scoring (e.g., multiple response), depending on the innovation (e.g., Becker & Soni, 2013). Given the likelihood that additional staff effort will be needed for the first administration of an innovation, part of ABIM's rollout plan includes tracking the overall set of innovations so that, across exam programs, only a limited number of innovation trials are implemented at one time. Within an exam program, the number of innovations is also typically limited at a single administration out of consideration for the candidates.

Another important issue at this first operational use of an innovation is the need to communicate with stakeholders regarding the innovation. At ABIM, the primary stakeholder groups that need to be informed at this stage include candidates and program directors, and a series of communication strategies might be needed. For example, communication with candidates might include information about the innovation within a letter, in one or more email blasts, in announcements on the ABIM webpage, and/or in additional screens within the online exam tutorial. If an innovation may affect the exam administration for ADA candidates, then communication to these candidates about the innovation and their options must also be prepared. If the innovation may be seen as relating to the candidates' instructional needs, then further communication to medical college program directors is prepared. All of these materials are planned and disseminated in a timely fashion so that candidates have the opportunity to be fully prepared and so that any anxiety a new test feature might otherwise cause is mitigated.

Phase 2 intentionally has less flexibility than the first phase due to the impact on examinees when an innovation is placed on an operational exam. While changes in direction due to better knowledge are still possible, they are deliberately limited during this stage. "No go" decisions are much less likely, and most design decisions have been made, though a few refinements might still occur in Phase 3.

### Phase 2—Case Study

Since some ABIM exams already included the diagnostic equipment type of video, the tutorial already introduced the concept of video in items, and so only minor revisions to the instructions were needed when patient–physician interaction videos were pretested. However, a feature new to this type of video is the use of audio. This had important implications for ADA candidates with hearing impairments and needed to be addressed.

Operational decisions for the initial pretest included the number of new video items to be pretested, their location within the test form, and whether a dedicated candidate survey should be deployed. An important decision at this stage is whether to cluster items featuring the innovation in a test section or to randomize their appearance within the exam. Innovations that require the examinee to "switch gears," either physically (e.g., putting on headphones) or cognitively (e.g., switching from single-best-answer item type to multiple-correct-response item type) lend themselves to clustering in an independent test section.

### Phase 3—Evaluation

After the initial administration of a new item type or feature, a thorough evaluation is conducted, and an *Evaluation Report*, tailored to specific features of the innovation, is produced. For example, if a new technological element (e.g., audio, embedded clinical calculator) is used, then the evaluation would include a review of any "incident reports" by the CBT vendor to determine whether any reports of technical problems during an exam administration were made. If technical problems had occurred, they would be further investigated, and solutions for the future would be proposed.

As a standard feature of the ABIM secure exams, a survey is administered to all candidates at the conclusion of their exams. The relevant responses to this preset survey may be reviewed as part of an innovation's evaluation. When more extensive candidate feedback to an innovation is sought, a more targeted survey is developed and then administered via email a day or so after the exam administration. This approach allows for more comprehensive questions regarding the candidate experience when a new item feature warrants it.

A statistical analysis of the innovation is also included in the evaluation. This typically includes item performance data (e.g., item difficulty, discrimination, and timing). In some cases, a comparison of items with and without the new feature is possible. For example, if a set of multiple-response items had been adapted from existing multiple-choice items, then a comparison of the item's performance in both formats might be informative. As another example, existing items may have described heart sounds in text, while the items' innovative forms could include audio clips instead.

More novel innovations are likely to require more extensive evaluations, addressing both the construct validity and performance. In some cases, new psychometric methods will be needed (Gorin & Mislevy, 2013; Olsen, Smith, & Goodwin, 2009; Way, 2013). Additionally, innovative item types sometimes require more candidate testing time than a typical multiple-choice question, and an analysis of the average relative information contributed could be warranted. If the innovation appropriately expands the test construct or otherwise enhances the fidelity of the test, then the additional per-unit time may be a valuable trade-off. In this case, a variety of solutions can be considered, from limiting the number of that type of item placed on each test form to adjusting the scoring weight for that item type.

Another aspect of the evaluation phase consists of seeking input from staff who worked closely on the development or delivery of the innovative item type, whether exam developers, media specialists, or production staff. These staff members are asked if they noted any problematic aspects of the innovation that ought to be addressed before more extensive deployment.

Finally, the exam committee members and other physicians who were involved in the item-development stages are asked to provide their feedback as to what aspects of the item type are working well and where further refinement may be needed. Ideally, a brief report, summarizing all of the evaluation findings to date, is provided to the physicians so that they can offer their feedback about these results in conjunction with their experience in writing items of the new type.

The intentional flexibility of the rollout plan can be seen in the various types of evaluations that may be utilized. In addition, if the results of the evaluation suggest that further refinement is needed, the innovative item type will be modified. In some cases an additional iteration of Phases 1 through 3 is undertaken to fully improve the innovation before expanding it to ABIM's other exam programs.

### Phase 3—Case Study

Psychometric analyses of the new video items include standard item analysis methods such as difficulty, discrimination, distractor analysis, and timing. With a very different item-writing task such as video scripts it might be expected that some of the pretest items would display poorer performance in the initial use of this new item type. A basic question at this stage is whether the video was understandable to the candidates and if it was effective. A full analysis could help identify trends in the video or item features that were most effective; this information could feed back to improvements in the video storyboard or other item-writer training materials. At ABIM, item writers are encouraged to write multiple items for a given video clip (for reasons of both test security and cost effectiveness). One analysis procedure considers how the video performs in multiple contexts.

The longer video clips in these items would also be expected to have an effect on item timing. After the pretest, the extent of this effect could be accurately determined and then used to make ongoing test assembly decisions such as the number of patient–physician interaction videos to include on a test form.

Since video items are a technological change, an important part of the evaluation of this innovation is to consider whether there were any technical problems during test delivery. The CBT vendor incident reports could be reviewed, along with candidate survey comments about any technical difficulties they may have experienced. Candidate responses to the remaining targeted survey questions are also analyzed, including their perception of the medical relevance and importance of the content in the new video items.

ABIM media specialists and other targeted staff would also be consulted to identify any challenges to the use of this innovation that ought to be further addressed at this stage. For example, if some video clips were of insufficient display quality, then minimum technical specifications might be changed.

The physicians who have been involved with the development of the patient–physician interaction video items would also be consulted. Their feedback on the item-writing process is sought, along with their input on the item analysis and other evaluation findings.

All of these data would be used to decide whether the item type is ready for more wide-scale deployment across ABIM exam programs or if any further refinements are needed first.

## Phase 4—Document and Automate Specifications and Usage Guidelines

Once an innovative item type has undergone a successful evaluation, then the innovation can move to Phase 4. In this stage, a set of tasks is undertaken to ready the innovation for widespread use across the ABIM subspecialty exams. This set of tasks includes both documenting the innovation and ensuring that it is fully automated.

In addition to the evaluation report produced in the previous phase, in Phase 4, the innovations team at the ABIM prepares a *Developer Guide*. This document will contain all the specifications and usage guidelines related to the new item type. Like the evaluation report produced earlier, the developer guide will be tailored to specific features of the innovation. For example, if the innovation concerns audio or video, then relevant technical specifications, such as file format and maximum length, are included.

Additionally, resources to support the future item writers are offered. An important aspect of these resources is the provision of any item-writing guidelines that might be specific to the new item type (see Parshall & Harmes, 2009). Specific item-writing guidelines are used to document any decisions made about how the new item type will be implemented (e.g., a multiple-response guideline might state that no item should have more than eight response options), as well as any other instructions that may be helpful to new item writers. As such, these tailored item-writing guidelines improve the quality and consistency of items written to the new item type. A further approach, used at some testing organizations, is to develop enhanced test blueprints. This type of blueprint can include specifications for item types within explicit content/subcontent areas.

In many cases, the item type development undertaken in earlier phases includes work with exam committee members to prepare draft item-writing guidelines. The committee members then try those guidelines out as they first undertake writing items of the new type. In Phase 4, their feedback about the utility of the draft guidelines is sought, and a final version of the item-writing guidelines is prepared and documented. Whenever possible, the initial item-writing efforts are also used as sources of further material for the developer guide such as content-relevant examples (and, in some cases, non-examples) of the innovative item type. Any other item-writing training materials that may be helpful to exam committees are prepared.

The second component of Phase 4 is determining whether any manual efforts required initially have since been automated. Before an innovation can be used with large numbers of items or deployed across multiple exam programs, it is important that the need for manual staff effort in support of the innovation be as limited as possible. This goal is an important part of the rollout plan, both out of due consideration for hardworking staff and because manual efforts are, in the long run, potentially more error prone. The risk of errors occurring in manual efforts may be most likely when the innovation includes changes to scoring and/or item presentation.

By the end of Phase 4, the innovation should be fully supported by the complete set of software applications used throughout the test-development process, from item banking to score reporting. In some cases, software development will have been needed to automate tasks such as QTI coding for proper display of an innovative item type. In other instances, such as items that include video clips, additional hardware support may be necessary to store the large files that will be used. Any new psychometric analyses needed for the innovation should, by this stage, have been developed and tested to verify their accuracy and ease of use.

### Phase 4—Case Study

For the new video item type, the most important element of documentation that we produced in Phase 4 was the video storyboard. This template encapsulates all the essential instructions and guidance that future item writers will need when they have video item-writing assignments. A preliminary version of this storyboard was developed for use by the first exam committee that wrote video scripts; their experience provided a set of lessons learned that, along with the results of the pretest evaluation, were used to iteratively refine the initial storyboard. This Agile feedback loop supports good-quality future item-development efforts.

### Phase 5—Transition to Operational Use ("The Toolbox")

Once an innovation has been through all of these stages detailed, it can become a standard ABIM offering. At this stage, the innovation transitions out of the research-and-development process and into regular operational test use. ABIM refers to this stage as the innovation "moving out of the sandbox and into the toolbox."

The goal at this point is for an exam committee to see each available item type as a tool in an assessment toolbox (K.A. Becker, personal communication, 2009). When a particular item-writing assignment in a targeted content area would be best served by a specific item type, then that tool is selected. If another item type, including the traditional multiple choice, is the best tool for the item at hand, then that item type is selected.

*Phase 5—Case Study*

For the innovation of patient–physician interaction video items to be ready for the toolbox, all documentation needed to be finalized, and all technological considerations need to have been addressed. Finally, since video files can have a substantial effect on the size of the overall compiled test file, a modification to the operational test production timeline must be made for a given exam program if a considerable number of videos will be included on a test form.

Throughout all five stages, the rollout plan provides a framework for investigating and implementing new assessment features. The plan has structure by design; however, it also includes clear Agile elements. An innovation can always be modified if the team recommends the change based on new information. In addition, though the full rollout plan can easily take 18 months or more to fully investigate an innovation before implementing it operationally, it is also possible to fast-track a given innovation if there is a high demand or need for that adaptation. Putting an innovation on the fast track may require additional feasibility considerations and is likely to involve a reprioritization of competing innovations (i.e., one or more other innovations may be delayed in consequence).

## Summary

Innovative item types offer the potential to improve an exam program in meaningful ways, whether they are custom made for the exam program or off-the-shelf options within CBT item banking and test delivery software. While the standard procedural planning approach serves an exam program well when developing traditional item types, it fails to meet the need that designing new item types presents. When novel elements are being considered for an exam, then Agile methods, which have particular value when much is unknown and risk may be high, have clear benefits. And the rollout plan offers a series of assessment-related steps, each of which is controlled and sensible.

In this chapter, a video item type was used as a case study to illustrate how Agile methods and the rollout plan can be used in the design of a single innovation; implications for managing continuous innovations have also been given. While there are challenges to the development and implementation of any item type that is new to an organization, the video item type is not as novel as some that are in development at ABIM and elsewhere. As ABIM investigates more innovative possibilities, the same general principles of Agile methods apply. The team starts with the construct, considers critical aspects of feasibility (serious issues are more likely), and conducts extensive sandboxing (more iterations are expected). Numerous iterations and more wide-ranging investigations are common under these more challenging conditions, and some innovations will not move into later phases if they prove to be unfeasible. Nevertheless, the combination of Agile principles and a semistructured rollout plan appears to be an optimal strategy for finding and solving the problems in truly novel item development—before operational testing.

There is good reason to anticipate that new innovative item types will continue to be created in the years to come. Both technology and the field of measurement are continuing to develop and change, and this state of ongoing change is likely to mean that testing organizations will continue to have new assessment options available for their consideration. Many testing organizations have already begun to think of continuous change as the new normal. When ongoing change is likely, then efficient, long-term planning needs a process that has both flexibility and structure. We hope that the strategies offered here will be helpful to other organizations as they transition into managing that new process of ongoing innovation.

## Note

We thank Dr. Rebecca Lipner, Senior Vice President of Evaluation, Research and Development at the American Board of Internal Medicine, for her advice on the draft of the manuscript and allowing us to include the prioritization chart.

## References

Beck, K. M., Beedle, M., van Bennekum, A., Cockburn, A., Cunningham, W., Fowler, M., Grenning, J., Highsmith, J., Hunt, A., Jeffries, R., Kern, J., Marick, B., Martin, R., Mellor, S., Schwaber, K., Sutherland, J., & Thomas, D. (2001). *Manifesto for Agile software development*. Retrieved July 31, 2013 from http://agile manifesto.org

Becker, K. A., & Muckle, T. J. (2013). *Scoring and analysis of innovative item types*. Presented at the annual meeting of the Association of Test Publishers, Ft. Lauderdale, FL.

Becker, K. A., & Soni, H. (April, 2013). *Improving psychometric feedback for innovative test items*. Paper presented at the Annual Meeting of the National Council on Measurement in Education, San Francisco, CA.

Behrens, J. T., & DiCerbo, K. E. (2012). *Technological implications for assessment ecosystems: Opportunities for digital technology to advance assessment*. Paper written for the Gordon Commission on the Future of Assessment in Education.

Behrens, J. T., Mislevy, R. J., DiCerbo, K. E., & Levy, R. (2012). An evidence centered design for learning and assessment in the digital world. In M. C. Mayrath, J. Clarke-Midura, & D. Robinson (Eds.), *Technology-based assessments for 21st century skills: Theoretical and practical implications from modern research* (pp. 13–54). Charlotte, NC: Information Age.

Bejar, I. I. (1991). A methodology for scoring open-ended architectural design problems. *Journal of Applied Psychology, 76*, 522–532.

Cadle, A., Parshall, C. G., & Baker, J. (2013, February). *Development of a new item type: The drag and place item*. Presented at the annual meeting of the Association of Test Publishers, Ft. Lauderdale, FL.

Carr, P. (September, 2013). *NAEP innovations in action: Implications for the next generation science standards*. Presented at the Invitational Research Symposium on Science Assessment, Washington, DC.

Clauser, B. E., Margolis, M. J., Clyman, S. G., & Ross, L. P. (1997). Development of automated scoring algorithms for complex performance assessments: A comparison of two approaches. *Journal of Educational Measurement, 34*, 141–161.

Cohn, M. (2006). *Agile estimating and planning*. Upper Saddle River, NJ, Prentice Hall.

DiCerbo, K. E. (2004). Game-based assessment of persistence. *Journal of Educational Technology & Society, 17*(1), 17–28. Retrieved from: http://www.ifets.info/journals/17_1/3.pdf

Gorin, J. S., & Mislevy, R. J. (September, 2013). *Inherent measurement challenges in the next generation science standards for both formative and summative assessment*. Paper presented at the Invitational Research Symposium on Science Assessment, Washington, DC.

Guille, R. A. (2013). *Strategies to stimulate organizational change*. Presented at the annual meeting of the Association of Test Publishers, Ft. Lauderdale, FL.

Hess, B. J., Johnston, M. M., & Lipner, R. S. (2013). The impact of item format and examinee characteristics on response times. *International Journal of Testing, 13*, 294–313.

Huff, K. L, & Sireci, S. G. (2001, Fall). Validity issues in computer-based testing. *Educational Measurement: Issues and Practice, 20*, 16–25.

IMS. (2012). *IMS question & test interoperability specification*. Retrieved September 2, 2013, from www.imsglobal.org/question/

Jodoin, M. G. (2003). Measurement efficiency of innovative item formats in computer-based testing. *Journal of Educational Measurement, 40*, 1–15.

Lipner, R. S. (2013). *Rationale behind test innovations*. Presented at the annual meeting of ATP, Ft. Lauderdale, FL, February 3–6.

Lipner, R. S., Messenger, J. C., Kangilaski, R., Baim, D., Holmes, D., Williams, D., & King, S. (2010). A technical and cognitive skills evaluation of performance in interventional cardiology procedures using medical simulation. *Simulation in Healthcare, 5*(2), 65–74.

Luecht, R. M., & Clauser, B. E. (2002). Test models for complex computer-based testing. In C. Mills, M. Potenza, J. Fremer, & W. Ward (Eds.), *Computer-based testing: Building the foundation for future assessments* (pp. 67–88). Mahwah, NJ: Erlbaum.

Maniar, T., Adams, B., & Smith, R. (2013, February). *Developing the Cisco Certified Design Expert Practical (CCDEP) examination—a case study in developing an IT performance test*. Presented at the annual meeting of the Association of Test Publishers, Ft. Lauderdale, FL.

Muckle, T. J., Becker, K. A., & Wu, B. (2011, April 9–11). *Investigating the multiple answer multiple choice item format*. Presented at the annual meeting of NCME, New Orleans, LA.

Olsen, J. B., Smith, R. W., & Goodwin, C. (2009). *Using a performance test development & validation framework*. Retrieved December 12, 2013, from www.alpinetesting.com/presentations-and-publications.htm

O'Neill, K., & Folk, V. (1996, April). *Innovative CBT item formats in a teacher licensing program*. Paper presented at the annual meeting of the National Council on Measurement in Education, New York, NY.

Parshall, C. G., & Becker, K. A. (2008, July). *Beyond the technology: Developing innovative items*. Presented at the bi-annual meeting of the International Test Commission, Manchester, UK.

Parshall, C. G., & Harmes, J. C. (2008). The design of innovative item types: Targeting constructs, selecting innovations, and refining prototypes. *CLEAR Exam Review, 19*(2), 18–25.

Parshall, C. G., & Harmes, J. C. (2009). Improving the quality of innovative item types: Four tasks for design and development. *Journal of Applied Testing Technology, 10*(1), 1–20.

Parshall, C. G., Harmes, J. C., Davey, T., & Pashley, P. (2010). Innovative items for computerized testing. In W. J. van der Linden & C. A. W. Glas (Eds.), *Elements of adaptive testing* (pp. 215–230). Norwell, MA: Kluwer Academic Publishers.

Parshall, C. G., Spray, J. A., Kalohn, J. C., & Davey, T. (2002). *Practical considerations in computer-based testing*. New York: Springer-Verlag.

Pichler, R. (2010). *Agile project management with SCRUM*. Upper Saddle River, NJ: Addison-Wesley.

Project Management Institute. (2013). *PMI Agile Certified Practitioner (PMI-ACP) Handbook*. Newtown Square, PA: Project Management Institute.

Rupp, A. A., Levy, R., DiCerbo, K. E., Sweet, S. J., Crawford, A. V., Calico, T., Benson, M., Fay, D., Kunze, K. L., Mislevy, R. J. & Behrens, J. T. (2012). Putting ECD into practice: The interplay of theory and data in evidence models within a digital learning environment. *Journal of Educational Data Mining, 4*(1), 49–110.

Sands, W. A., Waters, B. K., & McBride, J. R. (1997). *Computerized adaptive testing*. Washington, DC: APA.

Scalise, K. (2013, September 24–25). *Virtual performance assessment and games: Potential as learning and assessment tools*. Presented at the Invitational Research Symposium on Science Assessment. Washington, DC.

Scalise, K., & Gifford, B. (2006). Computer-based assessment in e-learning: A framework for constructing "intermediate constraint" questions and tasks for technology platforms. *Journal of Technology, Learning, and Assessment, 4*(6). Retrieved July 24, 2013, from www.jtla.org

Sims, P. (2011). *Little bets: How breakthrough ideas emerge from small discoveries*. New York: Simon & Schuster.

Sireci, S. G., & Zenisky, A. L. (2006). Innovative item formats in computer-based testing: In pursuit of improved construct representations. In S. M. Downing & T. M. Haladyna (Eds.), *Handbook of test development* (pp. 329–347). Mahwah, NJ: Lawrence Erlbaum Associates.

Steinhauer, E., & Van Groos, J. (2013, September 24–25). *Presentation of a Program for International Student Assessment (PISA) Science 2015 task variant*. Presented at the Invitational Research Symposium on Science Assessment. Washington, DC.

Strain-Seymour, E., Way, W. D., & Dolan, R. P. (2009). *Strategies and processes for developing innovative items in large-scale assessments*. Pearson Education. Retrieved July 29, 2013, from www.pearsonassessments.com/hai/images/tmrs/StrategiesandProcessesforDevelopingInnovativeItems.pdf

Way, W. D. (2013, April 28–30). *Innovative assessment and technology*. Presented at an Invited Session at the Annual Meeting of the NCME, San Francisco, CA.

Wellington, C. A. (2007). *Refactoring to Agility*. Upper Saddle River, NJ: Addison-Wesley.

Wendt, A., Kenny, L. E., & Marks, C. (2007). Assessing critical thinking using a talk-aloud protocol. *CLEAR Exam Review, 18*(1), 18–27.

Williamson, D. M., Xi, X., & Breyer, F. J. (2012). A framework for evaluation and use of automated scoring. *Educational Measurement: Issues and Practice, 31*, 2–13.

Zenisky, A. L., & Sireci, S. G. (2002). Technological innovations in large-scale assessment. *Applied Measurement in Education, 15*(4), 337–362.

Zenisky, A. L., & Sireci, S. G. (2013, April 28–30). *Innovative items to measure high-order thinking: Development and validity considerations*. Presented at the Annual Meeting of the NCME, San Francisco, CA.

# 2

# Psychometrics and Game-Based Assessment

Robert J. Mislevy, Seth Corrigan, Andreas Oranje, Kristen DiCerbo,
Malcolm I. Bauer, Alina von Davier, and Michael John

This chapter discusses psychometric considerations when an assessment context is some form of educational game. "Psychometrics" literally means measuring psychological attributes, but its practice in educational assessment can be viewed as methodology to identify, characterize, synthesize, and critique evidence in arguments about examinees' capabilities in light of the purpose and the context of assessment use. We will address psychometric topics such as models and validity, but we first situate the discussion in the rather broad arena of game-based assessment (GBA). We will examine assessment arguments in GBAs and implications for design to arrive at a position to discuss GBA psychometrics. The goal is to connect the concepts and methods of assessment and psychometrics with those of games. Designers may choose to exploit all, various parts, or none of the machinery as suits the purposes of different games.

Section 1 provides background on game-based assessment: its nature, potential use cases, the design challenge, and some concepts from game design. Section 2 walks through the layers of an evidence-centered design framework to see how assessment arguments play out in an artifact that is at once a game and an assessment, and Section 3 discusses in more detail some roles that psychometric methods can play in identifying and modeling evidence. Section 4 highlights some particular psychometric challenges in GBA. Section 5 discusses reliability, generalizability, and validity in the GBA use cases.

## 1.0 Introduction

After a broad overview of theoretical views, examples, and definitions, Salen and Zimmerman (2004) defined a game as "a system in which players engage in an artificial conflict, defined by rules, that results in a quantifiable outcome" (p. 80). There could be one player or many, and multiple players might compete, collaborate, or both. Football, poker, and charades are certainly games, but our focus will be digital games. We will focus further on so-called serious games, which emphasize some educational or professional capabilities, such as touch typing (the Car Racer game in Mavis Beacon Teaches Typing®), land use management (Urban

Table 2.1 Use Cases of Games for Assessment

| Use Case | Description |
|---|---|
| Information for internal game purposes | Many recreational games already assess players, at least implicitly. They gather information about what players are doing well and what they are not to adjust the pace or difficulty to optimize engagement. A GBA can similarly allow adaptation or provide feedback to optimize learning or information about players. |
| Formative assessment: Information for students | A GBA can provide information to students as they play or at the end of challenges. Some information could be organized around details of players' actions and their results or, in serious games, around standards or learning objectives. |
| Formative assessment: Information for teachers | Teachers working with multiple students can be provided with summaries of students' progress with respect to challenges or learning objectives so as to keep a class on pace, lead classroom discussion on key concepts, or trigger follow-up with certain students. |
| Information for designers | If many students are playing a game, information about aspects of play such as feature usage, heightened or decreased engagement, sticking points, and pacing can be gathered and explored to improve play and improve learning. |
| End-of-course assessment | End-of-course assessments might use performance data from games as a source of information to evaluate learning in a course. |
| Large-scale accountability assessment | In large-scale accountability tests, states administer assessments based on grade-levels standards. Stakes for students, teachers, and/or schools might be attached to the results. Game-based tasks could be contemplated for such assessments. |
| Large-scale educational surveys | Educational surveys such as the National Assessment for Educational Progress administer samples of tasks to samples of students in order to provide a snapshot of what students in a population are able to do. Game-based tasks could also be contemplated for these assessments. |

Science; Shaffer, 2006), network engineering (the Cisco Networking Academy's Aspire®), and systems thinking (GlassLab's Pollution Challenge[1] game). Finally, by game-based assessment, we will mean explicitly using information from the game or surrounding activities (what Gee, 2008, calls the small-g and big-G game, respectively) to ground inferences about players' capabilities. Table 2.1 lists a number of characteristic ways that such information might be used, or "use cases" for GBAs.

## 1.1 Design Across Domains

A successful game-based assessment must "work" in several senses. To the outside observer, playing a GBA is a phenomenon in the here and now: one or more students acting in an environment, perceiving situations, interpreting them, acting, seeing consequences, acting again, perhaps continuously, perhaps in cycles, quickly or deliberatively. But the designers are trying to achieve different purposes from this activity: for game design, engagement; for instructional design, developing key concepts and capabilities in the target domain; for assessment design, evoking evidence of those capabilities for the intended use case(s) (Mislevy, Behrens, DiCerbo, Frezzo, & West, 2012).

All three domains have their own languages for describing the goals and the design-under-constraints challenges they regularly face. They have their own methods for evaluating the tradeoffs and crafting solutions to balance them. GBA designers must tackle all three jointly in the same artifact. This is particularly challenging when goals, constraints, and solutions conflict across domains.

The game perspective focuses on creating a player's experience: to use skills and knowledge, to make choices, to learn, to take on challenges, and to achieve goals. There may be a narrative line, drawing on cultural themes and dramatic situations. The paragraphs that follow on game elements summarize some of the techniques game designers use to construct the narratives, challenges, affordances,[2] and rewards that create engaging play spaces.

The learning perspective focuses on the target domain and what people do to acquire and use capabilities. The elements of a game situation can draw meaning from their connections to ideas, representations, and practices of a disciplinary community. This perspective connects with the game perspective as features of the game situations, actions, and challenges match up with features of domain situations, actions, and challenges. Ideally, doing well in the game means learning to think and act in the ways that people act and think in the domain.

From the assessment perspective, elements and activities take on meaning through their roles in assessment arguments and, as a result, support the elicitation, interpretation, synthesis, and use of evidence about students' capabilities. Assessment arguments connect the game perspective with how the features of situations, actions, and challenges provide clues about aspects of students' domain thinking and acting, with what evidentiary value. Assessment and measurement methods can help shape the situations, the challenges, and the actions to support reasoning from the resulting evidence and to examine the qualities of the evidence and the reasoning—in a word, its validity.

## 1.2 Elements of Game Design

Game designers have developed practices and "mechanics" to engage players (Salen & Zimmerman, 2004). These game design concepts will connect with assessment and psychometrics.

The elementary particles of a game are objects, rules, connections, and states. Rules define what the connections between objects are (i.e., how they behave and interact). Together they provide an account of the current state of the game and changes to that state. Sets of particles can form higher-order game play elements.

The basic structure of most games revolves around *rules* that define how the game reacts to player behavior (including inaction), given the current state of the game. In its most basic form, a rule is a function

$$y_{t+1} = f(x_t | a_t, b_t, c_t), \tag{1}$$

where $y_{t+1}$ is the reaction of the game at time $t+1$, which is a function of the user behavior $x$ at time $t$, given conditions at time $t$ of features (i.e., objects with attributes in environments) $a_t$, $b_t$, and $c_t$ that reflect the current state of the game at time $t$. Subsequently, $a,b$, and $c$ are updated to reflect the fact that $y_{t+1}$ happened. A vector of game condition variables (just a few in a simple game, thousands in more complicated games), in conjunction with rules that govern possible actions, interactions, and behaviors of objects is called a *state machine*.

*Objects* are things in the game environment that have attributes and rules about how they interact with players and other objects. *Connections* are relationships among all the objects and their attributes and therefore indicate how the rules work synchronously. Connections are the building blocks for creating the game experience and are further supported by the narrative, goals, feedback, and rewards. The vast complexity of connections and game play emerge from the rules and objects (Salen & Zimmerman, 2004, p. 150). Patterns of actions under certain game states are also the source of evidence for the assessment aspect of a GBA. These are in most cases either sequences of actions in states with particular features or attributes of an object the player has interacted with. An example of a sequence in Pollution Challenge is building a replacement green power plant before bulldozing a coal plant. An example of an attribute in Aspire is whether the security settings the player set will block or allow the right messages to the PC in the student lounge.

A *game mechanic* combines the rules, objects, affordances, and environment to produce configurations of kinds of actions that players can take in recurring situations in a game, with certain kinds of outcomes on the game state, to advance play. The video game Angry Birds® uses the mechanic of sling-shotting birds. In GBAs, a designer wants the kind of thinking that game mechanics evoke to advance play to also promote the targeted thinking in the domain. In Aspire, for example, players configure, replace, and connect network devices.

Engagement is central to the argument for using GBA. Increasing freedom or allowing wider control within the game mechanics frequently increases engagement but can also decrease the comparability of evidence across players. Engagement also depends in part on creating situations, challenges, rules, and affordances that will keep players near the leading edge of what they can do (Gee, 2007). This is one finding where game design, instructional design, and assessment design roughly agree: It is around the cusp of their capabilities that people experience what Csíkszentmihályi (1975) called "flow," what Vygotsky (1978) called the zone of proximal development in learning, and what Lord (1970) called "maximum information" in computerized adaptive testing.

### 1.3 Where Is the Assessment?

There are three places to locate assessment and psychometrics in GBA. We will focus on the second and third, although a given GBA can employ any combination of them.

One way is for assessment to take place in the big-G Game. The small-g game is for exploration, play, learning, and problem solving. Assessment is based on evidence outside the course of play—for example, students' final solutions, their rationale as produced in a presentation or write-up, or the connections they make to other topics. Psychometrics from performance assessments can be applied. Minimal coordination is needed between game coding and assessment, but the game and assessment designs must work together to draw out the targeted capabilities and capture pertinent evidence.

A second possibility is assessment inside the game, with prespecified work products. As part of play, students must carry out certain actions or complete certain products, often at a specified time or place in the game, such as the zoning plan in Urban Science (Bagley & Shaffer, 2009). Like familiar assessment tasks, they are designed up front, elicit evidence in known ways, and come with evaluation strategies. In game terms, there are objects that players must, through their actions, create or enter attribute values. At best, they are integral to game play, like the zoning plan in Urban Science. At worst, they are experienced as very restricted or interrupting game play.

A third possibility is evidence inside the game from work processes as captured in data streams (Shute, 2011). In more complex and interactive games, players choose how to move through the game space, investigate situations, and meet goals. Features of sequences and partial solutions can provide evidence about their understanding of the context, strategy use, and metacognitive skills. (Section 3.2 will discuss dynamic evidence in the forms of log files and so-called contingent work products.) Identifying and interpreting such data is an exciting challenge to assessment designers and psychometricians. We can build from experience in performance assessment. For example, the National Board of Medical Examiners designs computer-simulated patient-management cases, identifies key features of candidates' widely varying solution paths, and creates scoring algorithms that combine expert judgment and psychometric modeling (Margolis & Clauser, 2006).

## 2.0  An Assessment Design Framework

This section uses the evidence-centered assessment design framework (ECD; Mislevy, Steinberg, & Almond, 2003) to sketch out the elements of assessment arguments in GBAs and the roles psychometric methods play in assessments that operationalize those arguments (also see Levy, 2012; and Shute, Ventura, Bauer, & Zapata-Rivera, 2009).

Assessment is argument from evidence. Messick (1994) says "we would begin by asking what complex of knowledge, skills, or other attributes should be assessed. . . . Next, what behaviors or performances should reveal those constructs, and what tasks or situations should elicit those behaviors?" (p. 16). ECD distinguishes layers at which different kinds of activity take place to instantiate an argument:

- Domain Analysis. Research, experience, documentation of information needed to ground the argument—for example, standards, research studies, previous assessments, theory.
- Domain Modeling. Assessment argument structures, design patterns.
- Conceptual Assessment Framework (CAF). Student, evidence, and task models.
- Assessment Implementation. Detailing scoring routines, fitting models, authoring, etc.
- Assessment Delivery. Activities processes, messages, in implemented assessment.

Development is generally iterative, feeding back and refining thinking across layers as designers brainstorm, implement, test, and learn in cycles.

Domain analysis for a GBA addresses the targeted proficiencies—the kinds of knowledge and activities involved, the situations and ways people use them, the representations and the interactions that learning, assessment, and game play will build around. Pollution Challenge, for example, draws on the Next Generation Science Standards' (NGSS; Achieve, 2013) cross-cutting concept of systems and systems modeling: Students are expected to demonstrate an understanding of how to delineate the components and boundaries of systems as well as how to represent systems in order to understand and test ideas or claims about them.

Actual psychometric machinery is specified in the CAF, is built in Assessment Implementation, and runs according to the structures developed in Assessment Delivery—but its meanings are developed in Domain Modeling.

## 2.1  Domain Modeling

Domain modeling is about arranging situations for students to act in that draw on targeted knowledge and skills and say or do something that evidences their capabilities and supports inferences about them. The ideas and the representations are meant to be accessible to all the members of a design team whose expertise must come together to design a GBA, such as game designers, subject matter experts, psychometricians, and teachers. They all have their own language and tools, but in Domain Modeling, they can talk about goals, constraints, and approaches that cut across their areas. The results will be implemented in more specialized machinery, but this is where we figure out what the pieces need to do and how they need to work together to serve the goals of learning, assessment, and game experience.

Messick's quote is a good start for understanding assessment arguments, but Figure 2.1 adds detail using Toulmin's (1958) schema for arguments that is useful for designing assessments and interpreting results (see Mislevy, 2006, for a fuller discussion). A GBA can have feedback loops at different grain sizes for different purposes. This diagram focuses on the argument for a given chunk of evidence. The claim refers to a target of assessment. It might be an educational competency such as a level in a learning progress or a narrower inference such as whether a student is floundering. Claims and the data to support them depend on who needs what information in which feedback loops. A step in reasoning from data to a claim requires some justification—in Toulmin's terms, a warrant. In assessment arguments, a warrant is generally of the form that a student who has some understanding or capability is likely to use it in a situation where it is applicable.

Alternative explanations are especially important in assessment arguments because they are central to validity. We want to make inferences about students' capabilities based on their actions in a game, but are there other ways they can do well without understanding the substantive concepts at issue? The same feature of a GBA can produce an alternative explanation with respect to one inference—a threat to validity—but strengthen evidence for another. Solving a Pollution Challenge mission requires understanding and manipulating a jobs-and-pollution system. A player's actions in this particular system might be good evidence for her

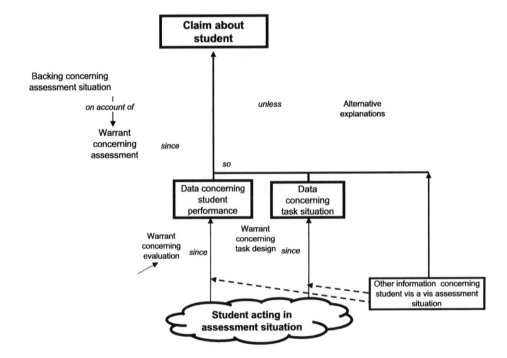

**Figure 2.1** An assessment design argument

systems thinking with this system, but the embedding causes weaker evidence for a broader claim about "systems thinking," because her understanding and performance might be quite different with other systems.

The assessment argument structure depicts three kinds of data. The first is features of students' actions (i.e., data concerning the performance). In Pollution Challenge, for example, we can observe a player bulldoze a coal-fired power plant and build a new one that runs on different fuel. But just as important are the features of the situation the student is acting in, representing the second kind of data or the data concerning the situation. Observable Variables in assessments actually involve both: they are evaluations of actions in situations with certain features. Key features of situations are designed into traditional assessment tasks. A GBA can contain preconstructed tasks, but we can also seek patterns of performance in situations that arise as players work through a less constrained environment.

The third kind of data that an argumentation perspective highlights is "what else is known" (i.e., other data concerning students vis-à-vis assessment situation). It affects whether potential alternative explanations can be ruled out—for example, if a user knows whether the student is familiar with some aspects of the content and the reasoning challenges in a GBA but not others. Knowledge and skills that are not germane to the assessment's purpose yet are required for successful performance need to be either supported so they are known or included as nuisance variation in psychometric models. This is why using a GBA as part of instruction simplifies the assessment modeling challenges and provides more useful information to students and teachers. A substantial amount of the "what else is known" is directly available to these users. The more distant users are from that context, the less of this additional information they have, the more alternative explanations they must entertain, and the less evidentiary value the same data hold.

## 2.2  The Conceptual Assessment Framework (CAF)

The conceptual assessment framework (CAF) contains specifications for the objects that instantiate an assessment. The three main ones are student, evidence, and task models (see Figure 2.2). Their internal structures can be detailed in various ways (e.g., Gierl & Lai, 2012; Mislevy, Steinberg, & Almond, 2003; Riconscente et al., 2005). The psychometric machinery is specified in the student and evidence models, embodying arguments developed in Domain Modeling. The following paragraphs sketch the kinds of things they contain and look ahead to their roles in GBA.

The Student Model contains student model variables (SMVs) to express claims about targeted aspects of students' capabilities. Their number and character depend on the

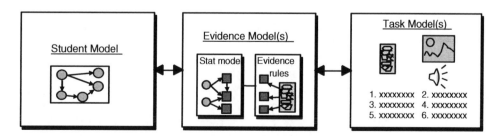

**Figure 2.2** The central models of the conceptual assessment framework

purpose(s) of the assessment, or, in some interactive assessments like GBAs, purpose(s) at a given level in a hierarchy of purposes. GBAs may track multiple aspects of proficiency, which may be involved in different ways in different situations and which may change as students interact with the system (e.g., they learn). The situated meanings of SMVs will be determined by patterns in the students' actions in the situations we design for them to act in.

The Task Model at the right describes salient features of assessment/game situations, in terms of task-model variables that can take on different values. In familiar assessment, these are forms and descriptors of distinguishable, well-defined, tasks. In GBAs, tasks need not be predefined and encapsulated in this way but can be recognized as instances of recurring evidence-evoking situations that arise as players interact with the game. Task design in GBA thus takes the form of building features into game situations that evoke the targeted thinking and providing players affordances that capture traces of that thinking as they play. Task models also include specifications of work products, or what is captured of what students say or do. In familiar assessments, these are things like discrete responses, essays, and problem solutions. These can be required of GBA players as well, but GBA work products can include detailed traces of game states and students' actions (variously called log files, click streams, slime trails, and transaction lists). From the player's point of view, she uses affordances to make things happen in the game world. From the assessment point of view, these actions produce evidence about her capabilities.

Evidence models bridge between what we see students do in situations (as described in task models) and what we want to infer about their capabilities (as expressed in SMVs).

- The *evaluation component* specifies how to identify and evaluate the salient aspects of work products, expressed as values of *Observable Variables* (OVs). These can be as simple as 1/0 dichotomous variables. More complex features may be gleaned from more complex work products (e.g., efficiency, systematicity, in what order actions are taken). Carrying out such evaluations can require the use of metadata (what else is known about the student and the tasks) or paradata (features about the situations and the consequences of the student's previous interactions with the system, as in Equation 1). This component is the reasoning in the assessment argument from performance to features of performance. It contains the information to implement *Evidence Identification* processes in the delivery system layer.
- The *measurement model component* contains statistical models that synthesize evidence across situations, in terms of updated belief about student model variables. The simplest measurement models are classical test theory models, in which scores based on observable variables are added. More complicated measurement models such as item response theory or Bayes nets can be assembled modularly (Almond & Mislevy, 1999). This component contains the information needed to implement *Evidence Accumulation* processes in the delivery system layer.

The next ECD layer is Implementation, where the actual elements of an operational assessment are created. We will skip directly to Delivery but refer the reader to Luecht (2003) on reusable structures for modular assessment design. Where feasible, reusable assessment design elements should be integrated with reusable game design elements for modular construction of GBA elements, around the integrated conceptual elements of the two domains (Riconscente & Vattel, 2013).

## 2.3 Assessment Delivery: The Four-Process Architecture

This layer concerns the processes and messages that take place when students interact with the GBA situations, their performances are evaluated, and the GBA reacts. Almond, Steinberg, and Mislevy's (2002) four-process assessment delivery architecture is adapted here to GBAs. The four assessment processes described above interact in a pattern determined by a test's structure and purpose. In a GBA, they act and communicate through the state machine described in Section 1, as shown in Figure 2.3. The messages are assessment/game data objects specified in the CAF (e.g., parameters, task/game situation features) or objects and values produced by the student or other processes in data structures that are also specified in the CAF (e.g., work products, values of OVs).

The *activity selection process* concerns what to do next. In a GBA, it is operationalized as rules in state machines that govern game interactions and now also assessment functioning and can use current knowledge about the student as variables being tracked.

The *presentation process* controls interaction with the student. This process is incorporated in the game finite state machine, where rules that depend on game-state variables determine how to react to player actions and what to capture as work products.

*Evidence identification processes* evaluate work products using methods specified in Evidence Models to produce values of OVs. OVs can be used to provide more immediate feedback based on what the student has done, such as hints or comments, and by *evidence accumulation processes* to update beliefs about SMVs.

*Evidence accumulation processes* use measurement models to summarize evidence about the SMVs for inferential feedback and score reports. The θs in Figure 2.3 indicate that point estimates or full distributions can be available to the other processes to condition their actions.

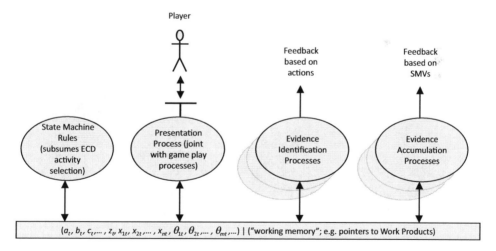

Figure 2.3 The four assessment delivery processes and a GBA finite state machine. $(a_t, \ldots, z_t)$ are variables for current and relevant past game state features at Time $t$; $(x_{1t}, x_{2t} \ldots, x_{nt})$ are variables for current and relevant past player action features at Time $t$; $(\theta_{1t}, \theta_{2t} \ldots, \theta_{mt})$ are variables for current and relevant past player latent variables at Time $t$; final (. . .) represents any other game or player variables that are needed to manage game play or assessment.

## 3.0 Psychometric Methods in GBA

In common usage, "psychometrics" addresses activities ECD addresses in evidence identification and evidence accumulation. This section provides an overview of the roles of psychometrics in GBA, then looks more closely at work products, observable variables, and measurement models.

### 3.1 Orientation to Psychometric Methods in GBA

Evidence Identification concerns reasoning from particular observed performances to values of observable variables—that is, identifying features of the performance or product that are data for an assessment argument as nuggets of evidence about students' capabilities. The reasoning runs in one direction: from particular realized work products to particular values of OVs that characterize the salient features of the performance.

Evidence Accumulation involves modeling probability distributions of OVs as functions of aspects of students' knowledge, skill, strategy-use propensities, and so on. These are expressed as unobservable, or latent, variables in psychometric models—the SMVs in ECD. They, rather than specific performances, are targets of learning and of assessment. There are several reasons to consider using probability-based psychometric models in GBAs for at least some inferences. (Immediate feedback based on specific performances is useful for hints and observations.)

The key idea is that student model variables express tendencies or capabilities that can be used to model patterns in performance across multiple situations, actual or hypothetical. We make inferences about them based on the particular things students do. Their values might be assumed to remain constant over some period of observation, as in familiar large-scale tests, or they might be expected to change as an activity unfolds, as in instructional systems.

Psychometric models transform data about specific performances into evidence for beliefs about capabilities of students in terms of SMVs. They can synthesize evidence from disparate forms of data in terms of more underlying aspects of students' capabilities.

The SMVs are of more persistent interest than particular actions. They can be defined to connect directly to standards and learning progressions. The same student model can be used with different forms of a game, with different situations students work themselves into and new OVs or game situations added in later.

The way psychometric models are built—conditional probability distributions for OVs given configurations of SMV values—affords all the tools and methods of probability-based reasoning. We know how to characterize weight and direction of evidence. It can be expressed in terms of indices for reliability, standard error of measurement, and classification accuracy. This gives GBA designers metrics to evaluate the effects of design alternatives with respect to evidence.

We know how to build models that account for complexities such as multiple aspects of proficiency being involved in various mixes for different aspects of performance, dependencies introduced by time and problem structures, different forms of data, and changing values of SMVs as students learn. Not to say that this is easy in any given application, but there are well-understood logics and models to do it.

Once the models are in place, we know how to update beliefs about a student's SMVs as evidence arrives (through Bayes's theorem). Probability models for different kinds and sources of evidence can be modular, assembled in real time as situations evolve, and adapted to design changes for parts of a GBA without revamping the evidence-handling framework.

## 3.2 Work Products

From the game perspective, we see many things that players do in various situations in a GBA as they act to achieve their goals. From the assessment perspective, we now think of captured forms of this activity in terms of the work products—such as structured objects students create or properties of those objects, problems they solve or steps by which they solve them, places they visit, how they get there, and in what orders they do things at what times. We can design some *predetermined work products* into a GBA to produce data objects that are like work products from familiar assessments (e.g., answering a question posed by an agent in the game or producing a configuration file for a faulty computer network). We can recognize instances of recurring situations that emerge in less constrained activity, or *contingent work products* (i.e., a particular kind of recurring situation that provides evidence about some capability, which players may or may not work themselves into). In Aspire, for example, one player's choices may lead him to troubleshoot five networks with faulty configurations, while another player only works himself into such a situation once. And we can capture *log files* that contain information from which a wide variety of patterns that constitute evidence can be gleaned.

### 3.2.1 Predetermined and Contingent Work Products

Designers can draw on a wide range of "constrained response task forms" (Scalise & Gifford, 2006) for both predefined and contingent work products in GBAs. A predetermined work product could range from answering multiple-choice questions during a pause in game action to naturally constructing a plan, an artifact, a model, a report, or a representation in the course of pursuing a game goal. Elegant uses of predetermined work products have tight assessment arguments (by controlling conditions, they reduce alternative explanations for performance and reduce construct-irrelevant sources of variance) but feel integral to game play. Predetermined work products are like standard assessment tasks in that the key contextual features that are relevant to the assessment argument (the second kind of data) have been explicitly designed into the game context and affordances. In Urban Science, for example, players are required to produce project reports, iterative planning diagrams, and a final zoning proposal.

In contrast, contingent work products arise when key contextual features are recognized in game play through agents that monitor the values of the pertinent variables in the state machine. An example of contingent work products is space-splitting situations in the Hydrive coached practice system for troubleshooting aircraft hydraulics systems (Gitomer, Steinberg, & Mislevy, 1995). In some situations, a judicious test can rule in or rule out a large portion of the problem space. This is space-splitting, an effective troubleshooting strategy. Different students work themselves into space-splitting opportunities at different times and different ways (and may not be aware of it). Hydrive computes the effect of their ongoing actions on the active path, and when it detects the conditions of a space-splitting opportunity, it records the next sequence of actions as a work product. An evidence-identification process is activated to evaluate the sequence to produce a value for an observable variable as space-splitting, serial elimination, remove-and-replace, redundant, or irrelevant.

Note that the contingent work product schema allows us to recognize the lack of action as an important piece of evidence. We are not simply recognizing those occasions when players space-split but the distribution of actions they take in all the occasions when space-splitting is possible. Understanding and monitoring key contextual variables is essential to doing this. We will see that the same variables can play important roles in measurement models for these observables.

### 3.2.2 *Log Files*

A log file captures, at some level of detail and in some organized form, salient features of the status and activity in a game or simulation and could embed multiple work products. Log files generally begin from unstructured records of player actions, or click streams. These often take the form of a time stamp, an identifier, an indicator of location or place in the environment, an indicator of an action, and sometimes detail about that action. More parsimonious log files consist of low-level semantically relevant sequences of actions.

Because evidence inevitably depends on actions in situations, log files are generally supplemented with key contextual game-state variables. In Pollution Challenge, a "heartbeat" was established in the log files. Every 30 seconds of game time, the levels of primary measures (e.g., level of pollution, jobless rate, number of citizens) in the city were captured and stored. With this information, it was determined that sufficient context could be established to evaluate actions not just as they contribute to game play but as they must be interpreted for assessment—for example, "bulldoze in low-pollution scenario" versus "bulldoze in high-pollution scenario." They are data about the situation that are critical to interpreting data about the player's performance.

## 3.2 Evidence Identification

This section addresses how to identify and characterize aspects of work products that hold evidence about what students know and can do. They concern semantic and pragmatic aspects of performance, expressed in terms of values of observable variables. Evidence identification is the center of the bridge from performances to inferences about students' capabilities (see Figure 2.2).

### 3.2.1 *Evidence Identification for Predetermined and Contingent Work Products*

For more constrained work product forms, possible actions produce only semantically meaningful patterns by design. For less constrained work products, even though we know where to look and what they are supposed to bear evidence about, the patterns that constitute evidence can be less clear cut. A fair amount of tuning, exploration, and data mining can be required to extract meaning.

Once a work product has been defined, it is possible to revise the definitions of observable variables or add new ones. With a data set containing many players' game play and auxiliary information, we can empirically search for functions of features that correlate well with other indicators of the target competency, such as degree of success on that competency for the final state of the game. When work products are complicated, even if they are predetermined, we can use data mining techniques such as the ones discussed in the following sections to discover additional evidence (and, in the process, gain insights to improve the design of situations and affordances).

### 3.2.2 *Evidence Identification for Log Files*

Much excitement about game-based assessment is generated from being able to capture fine-grained data about player activity. The hope is that these data will provide evidence about complex knowledge, skills, and capabilities. A primary challenge in fulfilling the potential of log files for making inferences about students thus lies in evidence identification. What are the important features of the work product, and how do we apply scoring rules?

The problem of evidence identification in log files is frequently tackled by combining *a priori* hypotheses about the relationships between observables and constructs with exploratory data analysis and data mining (Mislevy, Behrens, DiCerbo, & Levy, 2012). When there are hypotheses about particular actions that are related to the SMVs of interest, expert tagging of events can be used to train "feature detectors" for these patterns (Gobert, Sao Pedro, Baker, Toto, & Montalvo, 2012). These are the basis of observable variables. Exploratory data analysis and educational data mining techniques can also be used to uncover patterns that provide information about targeted constructs, or newly revealed ones. Rupp and colleagues (2012) demonstrate how four different indicators in the log files were used to create a measure of the efficiency of a solution to a computer networking problem. The indicators included time, number of commands, proportions of different types of commands, and amount of switching between computer devices. Kerr and Chung (2012) conducted exploratory cluster analyses to identify salient features of student performance in an educational video game targeting rational number addition. DiCerbo and Kidwai (2013) used classification and regression tree (CART) analysis to build a detector of whether game players were pursuing a goal of completing quests (as opposed to other potential goals) in a game environment.

In early Pollution Challenge development, for example, the relationship between the first action taken and final levels of pollution was examined. Players whose first action was to bulldoze coal plants or dezone residential areas both ended up with low final pollution scores, which was one of the players' goals in the GBA. These results suggest the importance of the first actions to ultimate success in the scenario. Bulldozing other buildings suggested a misunderstanding of the causes of pollution in the city or a lack of understanding of the goals of the game. Data visualization served as an impetus to begin forming hypotheses about the relationship between early actions in the game and both causal understanding and game comprehension.

As with exploratory analyses of patterns in complex predetermined and contingent work products, we can expect to both improve a GBA in two ways through these processes. We can extend the sets and sharpen the definitions of observables at a given point in design, and we can use the insights we gain to improve the situations, affordances, and challenges to better focus the evidence.

## 3.3 Measurement Models

This section addresses using measurement models to synthesize nuggets of evidence (in the form of values of OVs) across observations in terms of SMVs. As noted, this is not the only way that observable features of game situations and players' actions can be used in GBAs for either game or assessment purposes. But using measurement models is a way to accumulate information across multiple sources of evidence, expressed as belief about characteristics of players whether transitory or persistent, and it provides tools to sort out evidence in complicated circumstances, quantify its properties, and flexibly assemble evidence-gathering and evidence-accumulating components. We first say a bit about these qualities generally then look at some particular models.

Reasoning is bidirectional in probability-based measurement models. Their basic structure models distributions of observables conditional on SMVs—that is, reasoning from student characteristics to what we can observe. In such models, the probability machinery enables us to reason back the other way, from seeing a student's OV values to updating beliefs about the values of her SMVs via Bayes's theorem (Mislevy & Gitomer, 1996). These updated beliefs can then be the basis of selecting activities, modifying features of game situations, providing feedback to students, and reporting summaries to teachers.

The nature and the grain size of SMVs depends on their use—generally more detailed and qualitative for the tight feedback loops that monitor and guide play, more global for characteristics that change more slowly or pertain to broader proficiencies. A GBA can be using multiple feedback loops to synthesize information at different levels of detail or time spans. For example, in a GBA that has multiple levels that reflect different progressions of a target competency, we can apply a single (unified) or different psychometric model(s) both within and across levels and use summary results within levels to update an across-level model.

### 3.3.1 Observed Score Models (aka Classical Test Theory)

Many games already use counts and timing data. We can apply methods from classical test theory (CTT; Lord & Novick, 1968) to more rigorously examine the qualities of evidence that result. The basic premise is that an observed score is the sum of a true score and random error, that is, the count or proportion correct that is actually observed arises from a conditional distribution given the true score. This simple conception generates a surprisingly large array of useful tools for practical work to characterize evidence (Gulliksen, 1950/1987).

In practical terms, an average or sum across several OVs is taken to approximate the true score. "Reliability" quantifies the amount of true score relative to random error. The more closely multiple measures of a construct are related, the more reliable the score is, and multiple measures that tend to point in the same direction are more reliable than ones that conflict. When there are multiple opportunities to get information about a player's proficiency for a certain kind of task, even simple calculations of reliability can be used to gauge the quality of evidence.

CTT works well when the multiple measures at issue are similar nuggets of evidence about the same thing—in GBAs, independent attempts at similar problems, when learning is negligible across those attempts. It doesn't work as well when the evidence comes in different forms, has dependencies among its pieces, depends on different mixes of skills in different combinations, proficiencies change over the course of observation, or different players contribute different kinds or amounts of evidence. Latent variable models were invented to deal with such features.

### 3.3.2 Latent Variable Models

Latent variable models posit unobservable variables $\theta$ denoting the construct of interest and model the relationship between OVs $x$ and $\theta$ (both can be vector valued): for Situation $j$, the conditional probability or link function $h_j(x_j|\theta)$ (Moustaki & Knott, 2000). Under appropriate conditions, we can estimate these conditional probability distributions; further, given a person's observed $x$s, we can make inferences back about her $\theta$. The forms of the $\theta$s, the $x_j$s, and the links are determined by the nature and grain size of the inferences about players that are needed, the forms of the observables, and the relationship between them. These are determined in turn by the design of the tasks, the conceptualization of how performance depends on the posited proficiencies, and data to the extent they are available. The latent variable model posits conditional independence among the OVs across $J$ situations, or $h(x\,|\,\theta) = \prod_j h_j(x_j\,|\,\theta)$. Ultimately our interest lies in what can be said about $\theta$ given $x$, given by Bayes's theorem as $g(\theta|x) = g(\theta)h(x|\theta)/f(x)$, where $g(\theta)$ is a prior distribution for $\theta$, based on background information for a student or previous play.

When link functions are specified by parameters $\theta$ that in turn depend on features $y_j$ of the situations, we can write $h_j(x_j | \theta, \beta_j(y_j))$. These $y_j$s are "data concerning the task" in the assessment argument. Incorporating features of situations into latent variable models can be useful to improve modeling in predetermined work products, but the move is critical for modeling observable variables from contingent work products: A vector of situation features is used both to (1) identify a situation where an instance of a preidentified class of evidence-bearing situations occurs, and (2) indicate the probability model that applies, as to what the observables will be, which student model variables they depend on, and the nature and strengths of the relationship (Adams, Wilson, & Wang, 1997; Geerlings, Glas, & van der Linden, 2011).

The conditional independence structure of latent variable models is well suited to interactive assessments like GBAs that allow students to work down different paths. The student model variables $\theta$ in a given student model are of interest for some period of time, perhaps a level or the game as a whole. The link functions for observations are used to update beliefs about $\theta$ as new data $x$ arrive via Bayes's theorem. This procedure holds even when different players have different sets of observables and when the assessment situations have been presented based on a player's previous actions, such as presenting more challenging situations to players who are doing well and easier challenges to players who are struggling. The process takes the form of docking appropriate link functions to the student model and carrying out Bayesian updating (Almond & Mislevy, 1999; Mislevy, Steinberg, Breyer, Johnson, & Almond, 2002). Figure 2.4 suggests this modular model construction and updating machinery using a multivariate measurement model.

A number of measurement models have these properties. Although it is convenient to describe three of them as separate models, one can mix model fragments for different kinds of SMVs, OVs, and link functions (De Boeck & Wilson, 2004; M. von Davier, 2005).

*Item response theory* (IRT; Yen & Fitzpatrick, 2006) was originated for scoring students and modeling item-level performance on achievement tests. Extensions support a wide variety of

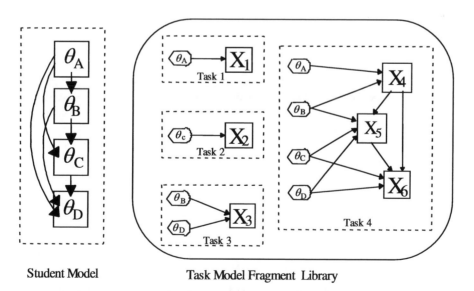

Student Model      Task Model Fragment Library

**Figure 2.4** The student model and a set of link functions that are used to update beliefs about its variable when various forms of evidence arrive.

observable variables that might occur in GBAs, such as counts, response times, ordered and unordered categorical variables, and sets of conditionally dependent responses. Multidimensional IRT models (Reckase, 2009) accommodate multiple aspects of proficiency that are required in different mixes in different situations as in Figure 2.4. Structured IRT models use task features $y$ to model item parameters (De Boeck & Wilson, 2004).

*Diagnostic classification models* (DCMs) involve multiple categorical latent variables and OVs that by virtue of task design (or discovery, in the case of contingent work products) depend on one or more of the latent variables (Rupp, Templin, & Henson, 2010). The dependence is indicated by a so-called Q-matrix whose rows indicate which task (situation) features are associated with a given OV. An agent that monitors the situation features in a GBA state machine for contingent work products is in effect looking for patterns to appear that match a row in the Q-matrix of an available DCM evidence-accumulation process.

*Bayesian inference networks*, or Bayes nets for short, are a broad class of models for interrelationships among categorical variables. They can be applied as psychometric models by operationally defining observable variables that depend on unobservable student model variables (Almond & Mislevy, 1999; Mislevy & Gitomer, 1996). Shute (2011) illustrates the use of Bayes nets in GBA, using an ECD design framework.

## 4.0 "Interesting Factors" for Psychometrics in Game-Based Assessment

This section discusses a number of factors that arise in psychometrics that GBA designers will often need to consider. On the surface, psychometrics is about measuring latent variables. For GBAs, it helps to view them more broadly as information-managing tools. From this perspective, we can see how design choices about psychometrics interact with design choices about learning and game play.

## 4.1 The Situated Meaning of Student Model Variables in GBAs

The meanings of SMVs in any assessment application are grounded in the particulars of the observational settings and the persons whose performances are used to fit the model. Interpretations of scores in the form of summary statistics of student model variables have this sense of meaning by construction. Whether they support inferences about other situations and/or other people is an empirical question.

A situative perspective on learning would urge caution and would strongly advise against extrapolations based simply on the label attached to the SMV. The idea is that learning occurs in terms of resources developed in specific situations and is initially tied to those situations (Greeno, 1998). Whether underlying concepts or capabilities would be activated in other situations depends on features of the new situations and whether the initial learning happened in ways that make that activation more likely—quite apart from parallels an expert would see.

## 4.2 Who Needs What Information, When, and Why, and in What Form?

Assessments should address users' purposes. Diagnostic tests need finer-grained student models to give students or teachers focused feedback. End-of-course tests need fewer student model variables, often just one to capture an overall proficiency in a sample of challenges across what students have been studying. A GBA can have multiple users interested in different questions that need information at different grain sizes and different time scales.

As noted, observable variables support some feedback to players and the GBA itself directly. OV values can also be passed to evidence-accumulation processes. They convert information from performances to evidence about players' capabilities at some time scale as sums or counts in observed-score models or as posterior distributions over SMVs then post it to the state machine for conditioning game play. Summary feedback can reported out continuously to the player in a dashboard or as a final report to a player at the end of a challenge or at the end of the full game. Summaries of SMV information across students can also be reported to teachers to monitor students' progress.

When there are hierarchies of delivery-process interactions, say within challenge and cross game, the form of the models and SMVs can differ across levels. The SMVs at inner levels can be of use only during that phase of play to provide feedback and adjust game situations at just that level. At the end of that phase, their values might have no further use, or their ending values can be used to update coarser-grained SMVs at a higher level.

## 4.3 Adaptivity

Adaptive testing selects tasks or material based on students' performance thus far (Wainer et al., 2000). Adaptive procedures for multidimensional item response theory (MIRT) models (Segall, 2010) make it possible to select (or construct or modify) tasks for a student that become more challenging in one aspect but easier in another if this is what performance thus far suggests will keep her at the cusp of her capabilities.

A game designer sees a player as a learner continuously trying to level up, mastering skills through play. Being consistently in either a state of anxiety or of boredom turns a player away, while incremental accomplishments motivate. A good game adapts constantly to the skill level of the player without making it too hard or too easy for very long. As long as these adaptations are based on observable information, the values of OVs that are not observed are missing at random, and Bayesian inference proceeds through the measurement model correctly (Mislevy, in press). A GBA can adapt play based on players' actions and accomplishments, as entertainment games do, but also with respect to knowledge about players' status on SMVs—for example, with challenges explicitly at higher levels of a learning progression, explained to the player as such, or by focusing on thus-far-underrepresented content.

## 4.4 Learning

Most assessments presume that the capabilities being assessed are constant over the course of observation and use measurement models that embody this assumption. GBAs that mean to help students learn must accommodate values of unobservable SMVs that may change over time.

*Recency-weighting of evidence* uses models that do not accommodate change but fade the influence of past data. An advantage is that simpler models can be used. A disadvantage is that as the value of the SMV changes, the current estimate lags behind the current true value. Stronger fading makes the current estimate closer to the current true value in expectation but noisier. Two implementations are (1) reestimating a statistic using weights $w(t)$ for each data point that decrease over time, and (2) using Bayesian updating but flattening the prior distribution some each time.

*Bayesian model tracing* (Baker, Corbett, & Aleven, 2008; Corbett & Anderson; 1995) is used in several cognitive tutors. It evolved from power-law learning curves and reinforcement models in mathematical psychology. Its most basic form concerns a learner's repeated attempts on equivalent dichotomously scored problems. There is an unobservable probability (an SMV) that she has "mastered" the skill in question, with guessing and slip probabilities for OVs, an initial probability for the mastery state, and a probability that a nonmaster moves to the mastery state on an attempt. Further extensions would be required for broader use in GBAs such as Pollution Challenge, where there are not always crisply defined tasks, situations can differ in their difficulties, and different combinations of knowledge and skill may be required. Theory and task design (or task discernment, in the case of contingent work products) would indicate which SMVs are involved, how they combine, and how much demand there is for each and for their combinations, and a learning model would be overlaid to move from one situation to the next.

*Dynamic Bayes nets* with latent student model variables are hidden Markov models (HMMs). OVs at time $t$, $x_{tk}$, depend on the unobservable value of the SMV at time $t, \theta_t$. Additionally, the value of the SMV can change from one point to another and is dependent on the previous value through the transition probabilities. It is further possible to condition the transition matrix on intervening experience, such as whether a player doing poorly at a given level chooses to decline or to take advantage of help that the system suggests. Ting, Phon-Amnuaisuk, and Chong (2008) illustrate dynamic Bayes nets in their exploratory learning environment for learning physics.

*Periodically updating higher-level models* is appealing when student modeling takes place in hierarchies. During a phase of play, a static student model and evidence-accumulation process can be used to synthesize capabilities within that phase and adapt play or provide feedback. When the segment is completed, the fact of its completion, the degree of success, or number of attempts is used to update beliefs about coarser SMVs in a higher-level model. Kimball's (1982) calculus tutor was an early application of this approach.

### 4.5 Collaboration

In some games, players collaborate with one another. How does this impact psychometric modeling? One possibility is to model at the level of a team. The foregoing discussion about modeling an individual's capabilities applies directly to the modeling of a team *as a unit*. This may suffice when the team is of interest in its own right. Discussions among the players of team-level feedback and of individuals' actions within scenarios can still help individuals learn.

Modeling the contributions and capabilities of individuals in collaborative units is harder. It is possible to have distinct models for individuals, but it must be noted how each player's actions influence the situations of the other players. The techniques for identifying contingent work products apply, with aspects of other players' actions as variables in the state machine.

Researchers and game designers have devised methods for managing collaborative action (O'Neil & Chuang, 2008), which sharpen evidence for assessing collaboration in GBAs. Jigsaw problems provide collaborators with predetermined parts of information that is needed jointly to solve a problem, so we know what a solution looks like and what individuals have to do. Interactions can be restricted to controlled patterns or communications limited to a designated set of messages (Hsieh & O'Neil, 2002). Players can have assigned roles or designated responsibilities for creating specific objects (Avouris, Dimitracopoulou, & Komis, 2003).

Tasks can require noncollaborative work as well as collaborative work to provide information about players' capabilities as individuals and thus highlight emergent characteristics of joint work.

The familiar game feature of nonhuman characters, or avatars, is suited to assessing collaboration in digital GBAs (Zapata-Rivera & Bauer, 2011). Avatars appear in the environment as characters to interact with, but their behavior, while displaying some adaptivity, has known styles, knowledge bases, and behavioral patterns—all designed to evoke targeted collaborative capabilities from the human player.

In collaborative problems, pertinent aspects of log file data can be considered as interacting time series for the players involved. They share situational features. The resulting multivariate time series can be analyzed with a number of modeling strategies used in other fields, such as dynamic linear models, differential equation models, social network analysis, Bayes nets, machine learning methods, neural networks, and point processes, which are stochastic processes for discrete events. A. von Davier and Halpin (2013), for example, describe an extension of IRT in which the probability of a student's response at time $t$ is a function of her $\theta$, but also the event history of the entire process, which includes the actions of the other individuals in the collaborative task. Independent work following local-independence IRT models is a baseline against which to evaluate the degree, the nature, and the impact of collaboration.

Collaboration is an engaging aspect of games and learning, and the capabilities that collaboration requires are of current interest in substantive domains. A psychometrics for collaboration, however, is only beginning. A route for further development will be continued development along formal modeling lines and low-stakes implementations starting with schemas for which both design configurations and analytic methods have been worked out.

## 5.0  Psychometric Properties

Reliability, generalizability, comparability, and validity have familiar meanings in large-scale, high-stakes testing, but they can be viewed more broadly as qualities of assessment arguments. The common issue is the quality of inferences and decisions made from fallible and finite information. A creative developer could certainly design a great GBA without drawing on psychometric machinery, and the GBA might provide excellent evidence about students to support inference. But it doesn't provide evidence about the evidence: how much, for what decisions, how alternative design choices affect it, and how the design choices affect learning.

## 5.1  Reliability

Reliability concerns the weight of evidence in assessment data for an inference about what a student can do, understands, or has accomplished. More data generally provide more evidence, and data that point in different directions provide less evidence than data that point in a similar direction. For OVs that are sums or averages of similar things that all players do, standard reliability coefficients like KR-20 and Cronbach's alpha still work. When different players have different amounts or forms of evidence, the model-based approaches can be used to characterize evidence (e.g., posterior variance for continuous SMVs, entropy for categorical SMVs).

An approach to quantifying evidence that applies to both observed-variable and latent-variable methods is to divide data into parts and use variation among the parts to characterize its precision (Mosteller & Tukey, 1977). Such resampling measures can work well even when model assumptions are violated and often when there is no model. They can be applied when the parts differ in form, source, or data type, as long as there is a defined way to combine them.

Examples of ways GBA designers can use reliability metrics are to (1) see how much evidence there is in the collection of all the observables we might obtain for a given challenge, (2) compare how much evidence is obtained for players who use different strategies or follow different paths through a challenge, (3) see how much evidence is added with observable variables in the form of new "detectors" constructed for patterns in log files, and (4) compare different methods of combining information across features of performances in log files using A/B testing or experiments embedded in fielded games (e.g., which features to retain, whether to combine them with neural nets or logistic regressions or weighted sums).

## 5.2  Generalizability

Whereas reliability focuses on the weight of evidence from the data actually gathered from individuals, the extension to generalizability theory (Cronbach, Gleser, Nanda, & Rajaratnam, 1972) and further extension to psychometric models more generally addresses questions of how much inferences could vary under different design alternatives.

For example, posterior standard deviations for a Pollution Challenge player would tell us how much we knew about her level of systems-thinking capability as displayed with the jobs-and-pollution system in the SimCity environment. But what would it tell us about what her systems thinking might have been with wolves and moose on Isle Royale? How about in a hands-on, real-world investigation? Generalizability helps us study how much performance varies across conceivable circumstances and thus see how well performance in particular circumstances supports inferences across the contemplated possibilities. This is a key issue for 21st-century skills, like systems thinking, and others such as communication and collaboration. We can surely build uses of such skills into a GBA and obtain reliable evidence for formative feedback *in that context*. But to what degree does this evidence support inferences about other contexts and other contents, or about a more decontextualized sense of the skill in question?

The results from generalizability studies carried out in the performance assessment movement in the 1980s are sobering: The particulars of format, context, content, and occasion matter a lot (Dunbar, Koretz, & Hoover, 1991; Linn, 1994; Ruiz-Primo & Shavelson, 1996). Yet it is precisely in in-depth, interactive, engaged experiences, with particular content in particular contexts, that students learn best, and it is the application to such situations that a more general education needs to help prepare students for.

The generalizability properties of GBAs are critical for understanding when they can be used for different use cases. The task depth and specificity serve learning well and are matched nicely with formative assessment uses that help students understand concepts in particular contexts. Extended game-based tasks might also be suited to large-scale educational surveys, where interest lies in capabilities in populations rather than in making precise inferences about individuals. But assessments that must support high-stakes uses for individuals *and* must obtain direct evidence about capabilities for acting in complicated situations have to observe performance in many tasks in order to overcome the low generalizability problem.

## 5.3 Comparability

High-stakes assessments are meant to accurately compare the capabilities of examinees across different times and places for purposes that hold substantial implications such as grades and licensure. If students are administered different forms of an assessment, considerations of fairness demand that the different forms are comparable with respect to their difficulty, content coverage, and accuracy. Achieving comparability in the classical sense is achieved by designing equivalent tasks and imposing standard testing conditions. Statistical test equating can be used to fine-tune the relationship (Kolen & Brennan, 1995).

For the reasons discussed, we may not expect this degree of comparability in GBAs. There are sources of difficulty related to background knowledge, for example, that can vary substantially from one student to the next. Even within the same GBA, different students (a) may be following different paths, (b) will be differently familiar with interfaces and representations, and (c) feel more or less engagement due to narrative structures and game pressures.

Requirements for comparability vary with use cases. When comparisons among individuals are required, requirements for comparability are stricter—and, with GBAs, more difficult to attain if play considerations require contextual depth, interaction, and engagement. When the purpose is learning, comparability is less important with respect to forms of challenge and amount of information, but it is still essential in the sense that learning goals be addressed no matter how the GBA adapts to different players. Fairness across various groups that differ in their experience with games, in general and with respect to particular genres, will have to be addressed in the development of the GBA.

## 5.4 Validity

Validity speaks directly to the extent to which inferences and actions about students, based on assessment data, are justified (Cronbach, 1989; Messick, 1989). Establishing validity entails making the reasoning that justifies inferences from scores, such as the warrant, explicit, examining the beliefs and evidence it relies on, and testing its strength and credibility. Because validity pertains to inferences and actions, validation studies take different (though in some cases overlapping) forms for different GBA use cases.

For all GBA use cases, the background research in domain analysis provides construct-representation evidence for validity. The ECD framework helps make explicit how this research is embodied in its elements and the processes. Failing to evoke some aspects of the targeted capabilities is a threat to validity that Messick (1989, 1994) called "construct under-representation." GBAs can improve construct representation by including interaction, an array of actions and representations, and open-ended spaces for assembling and carrying out strategies.

Messick identified another threat to validity, "construct irrelevant variance": Capabilities other than the targeted ones are required for good performance, and these demands hinder some students. Even as GBAs allow for greater construct representation, they introduce potential for construct-irrelevant variance. Lacking background knowledge, not knowing how to use the interface, and not knowing what is expected are all factors that can cause some students difficulties. Tutorials, help, and support from outside the small-g game help reduce the impact of construct-irrelevant demands. However, the very factors that can make games engaging—narrative lines, competition, time pressure—can also work against some students. This is not a problem if using a GBA is a choice for learning and students who don't like the GBA have alternatives. It is a serious problem when students must use them and results are high stakes.

*Information for internal game purposes.* Using information for game play means adjusting game situations and affordances based on SMVs. Using it for assessment means using it to adapt difficulty or focus evidence gathering. Validity evidence can be gathered in A/B testing (i.e., experiments) in which different versions of a game use different rules for adaptation, or no adaptation at all, in certain portions of play. The validity criteria are reliability metrics for evidence, and engagement and enjoyment metrics for play.

*Formative assessment: information for students.* A GBA can also provide information to a student as they play or at the end of sessions or challenges. This information, based on patterns gleaned from their play and their work products, is meant to give them better insight into their progress and how they might enhance it. Examples of validity evidence in the small-g setting are again better performance (in comparable groups) and quicker advancement. Validity evidence from outside the game could include students' use of terminology, concepts, and representations in the feedback and reports as they tackle other assessments outside the game, in the same substantive area or different substantive areas, or discuss the game and related topics with peers.

*Formative assessment: information for teachers.* In addition to whatever information a GBA may provide to students themselves, a GBA can also provide information to teachers to support learning. There are two levels at which one can gather evidence to evaluate the effectiveness of formative assessment information with teachers as users. At the student level, the techniques discussed in connection with information to students are again relevant. At the teacher level, in what ways do the information and affordances the GBA provides the teacher impact classroom practice? Herman, Osmundson, and Silver (2010) distinguish impacts on *practices and activities* that teacher-level formative assessment information brings about and the *quality of teacher inferences* that are based on the information.

*Information for designers.* Reliability metrics in play testing are meant to help designers improve evidence gathering. Sources of confusion and construct-irrelevant variance can be decreased. Additional actions or work products can be incorporated to capture information that can become additional evidence. Data exploration can lead to improved evidence identification for existing work products, development of additional contingent work products, and discovery of additional OVs in log files. Validity evidence consists of designer behavior and its consequences: Do they use such data to improve the GBA's assessment properties? What do they do with reliability data, and how does it fit with ongoing improvements to game play? What is the effect of the resulting modifications on reliability and validity measures?

*End-of-course assessment.* End-of-course assessments usually attach medium-high stakes to results. To validate this use case requires converging evidence about the capabilities we want students to develop by working through the game (both small and big G): Performance by alternate assessment means, both addressing the targeted skills in the content of the GBA and in different areas so as to reveal transfer.

*Large-scale accountability assessment.* It is possible to include one or more focused game experiences as part of state large-scale accountability tests. The reasons for doing so are the potential for increased engagement and obtaining direct evidence about interactive and constructive capabilities. High-stakes uses heighten the importance of reliability and generalizability. Validation would include a psychometric component, determining the contribution of such data to the variables being measured in the assessment system, and a qualitative component, through observation and postexperience interviews, the levels of increased engagement on the one hand and difficulties and frustration on the other. Particular attention would focus on potential sources of construct-irrelevant variance, such as prior knowledge, expectations, usability, interaction with cultural backgrounds, and confounding assessment goals with game goals.

*Large-scale educational surveys.* A large-scale *survey*—as opposed to a *test*—could also include a game segment like Pollution Challenge to obtain information about distributions of capabilities in populations. The same considerations noted above apply, such as provoking engagement versus nonengagement and construct-irrelevant sources of variance. Psychometric considerations such as reliability are also a concern but at the level of providing useful information about populations rather than about individuals. This is a more forgiving environment, although the value of the information trades off against the time it uses.

## 6.0 Conclusion

Game-based assessment is an exciting opportunity for educational measurement. There are issues of reliability, generalizability, comparability, and validity, all long-standing psychometric values, which the field has developed insights and methods to address in familiar kinds of assessments. They may need to be extended, augmented, and reconceived to play analogous roles in GBA. GBA will proceed with or without the insights of psychometrics. If it is without, the underlying evidentiary principles will need to be rediscovered and tackled anew.

## Notes

1  Pollution Challenge is a formative GBA produced by the GlassLab project, addressing systems modeling, in the SimCity® environment. See http://glasslabgames.org/.

2  The psychologist John Gibson (1977) defined an "affordance" as an action possibility formed by the relationship between an agent and its environment. Examples of affordances in the Pollution Challenge game are bulldozing buildings and zoning land tracts.

## References

Achieve, Inc. (2013). *Next generation science standards.* Washington, DC: Achieve, Inc.

Adams, R.J., Wilson, M., & Wang, W.C. (1997). The multidimensional random coefficients multinomial logit model. *Applied Psychological Measurement, 21*(1), 1–23.

Almond, R.G., & Mislevy, R.J. (1999). Graphical models and computerized adaptive testing. *Applied Psychological Measurement, 23,* 223–237.

Almond, R.G., Steinberg, L.S., & Mislevy, R.J. (2002). Enhancing the design and delivery of assessment systems: A four-process architecture. *Journal of Technology, Learning, and Assessment, 1*(5). Downloaded May 8, 2015, from http://citeseerx.ist.psu.edu/viewdoc/download?doi=10.1.1.198.5129&rep=rep1&type=pdf

Avouris, N., Dimitracopoulou, A., & Komis, V. (2003). On analysis of collaborative problem solving: An object-oriented approach. *Computers in Human Behavior, 19,* 147–167.

Bagley, E., & Shaffer, D.W. (2009). When people get in the way: Promoting civic thinking through epistemic gameplay. *International Journal of Gaming and Computer-Mediated Simulations, 1,* 36–52.

Baker, R.S.J.D. Corbett, A.T., & Aleven, V. (2008). *More accurate student modeling through contextual estimation of slip and guess probabilities in Bayesian knowledge tracing.* Paper 6. Pittsburgh: Human-Computer Interaction Institute, Carnegie-Mellon University. Available online at http://repository.cmu.edu/hcii/6

Corbett, A.T., & Anderson, J.R. (1995). Knowledge tracing: Modeling the acquisition of procedural knowledge. *User Modeling and User-Adapted Interaction, 4,* 253–278.

Cronbach, L.J. (1989). Construct validation after thirty years. In R.L. Linn (Ed.), *Intelligence: Measurement, theory, and public policy* (pp. 147–171). Urbana: University of Illinois Press.

Cronbach, L. J., Gleser, G. C., Nanda, H., & Rajaratnam, N. (1972). *The dependability of behavioral measurements: Theory of generalizability for scores and profiles.* New York: Wiley.

Csíkszentmihályi, M. (1975). *Beyond boredom and anxiety.* San Francisco, CA: Jossey-Bass.

De Boeck, P., & Wilson, M. (Eds.). (2004). *Explanatory item response models: A generalized linear and nonlinear approach.* New York: Springer.

DiCerbo, K. E. & Kidwai, K. (2013). *Detecting player goals from game log files.* Poster presented at the Sixth International Conference on Educational Data Mining, Memphis, TN.

Dunbar, S. B., Koretz, D. M., & Hoover, H. D. (1991). Quality control in the development and use of performance assessments. *Applied Measurement in Education, 4,* 289–303.

Gee, J. P. (2007). *What video games have to teach us about learning and literacy* (2nd ed.). New York: Palgrave.

Gee, J. P. (2008). Learning and games. In K. Salen (Ed.), *The ecology of games: Connecting youth, games, and learning* (pp. 21–40). Cambridge: MIT Press.

Geerlings, H., Glas, C. A., & van der Linden, W. J. (2011). Modeling rule-based item generation. *Psychometrika, 76*(2), 337–359.

Gibson, J. J. (1977). The theory of affordances. In R. Shaw & J. Bransford (Ed.), *Perceiving, acting, and knowing* (pp. 67–82). Mahwah, NJ: Erlbaum.

Gierl, M. J., & Lai, H. (2012). The role of item models in automatic item generation. *International Journal of Testing, 12,* 273–298.

Gitomer, D. H., Steinberg, L. S., & Mislevy, R. J. (1995). Diagnostic assessment of trouble-shooting skill in an intelligent tutoring system. In P. Nichols, S. Chipman, & R. Brennan (Eds.), *Cognitively diagnostic assessment* (pp. 73–101). Hillsdale, NJ: Erlbaum.

Gobert, J. D., Sao Pedro, M., Baker, R.S.J.D., Toto, E., & Montalvo, O. (2012). Leveraging educational data mining for real time performance assessment of scientific inquiry skills within microworlds. *Journal of Educational Data Mining, 5,* 153–185.

Greeno, J. G. (1998). The situativity of knowing, learning, and research. *American Psychologist, 53,* 5–26.

Gulliksen, H. (1950/1987). *Theory of mental tests.* New York: Wiley. Reprint, Hillsdale, NJ: Erlbaum.

Herman, J. L., Osmundson, E., & Silver, D. (2010). *Capturing quality in formative assessment practice: Measurement challenges.* CRESST Report 770. Los Angeles: University of California, National Center for Research on Evaluation, Standards, and Student Testing (CRESST).

Hsieh, I.-L., & O'Neil, H. F., Jr. (2002). Types of feedback in a computer-based collaborative problem solving group task. *Computers in Human Behavior, 18,* 699–715.

Kerr, D. & Chung, G.K.W.K. (2012). *Using cluster analysis to extend usability testing to instructional content.* CRESST Report 816. Los Angeles: University of California, National Center for Research on Evaluation, Standards, and Student Testing (CRESST).

Kimball, R. (1982). A self-improving tutor for symbolic integration. In D. Sleeman & J. S. Brown (Eds.), *Intelligent tutoring systems* (pp. 283–307). London: Academic Press.

Kolen, M. J., & Brennan, R. L. (1995). *Test equating: Methods and practices.* New York: Springer.

Levy, R. (2012, May). *Psychometric advances, opportunities, and challenges for simulation-based assessment.* Princeton, NJ: K-12 Center at ETS. Retrieved from www.k12center.org/rsc/pdf/session2-levy-paper-tea2012.pdf

Linn, R. L. (1994). Performance assessment: Policy promises and technical measurement standards. *Educational Researcher, 23*(9), 4–14.

Lord, F. M. (1970). Some test theory for tailored testing. In W. H. Holtzman (Ed.), *Computer-assisted instruction, testing and guidance* (pp. 139–183). New York: Harper & Row.

Lord, F. M., & Novick, M. R. (1968). *Statistical theories of mental test scores.* Reading, MA: Addison-Wesley.

Luecht, R. M. (2003). Multistage complexity in language proficiency assessment: A framework for aligning theoretical perspectives, test development, and psychometrics. *Foreign Language Annals, 36,* 527–535.

Margolis, M. J., & Clauser, B. E. (2006). A regression-based procedure for automated scoring of a complex medical performance assessment. In. D. W. Williamson, I. I. Bejar, & R. J. Mislevy (Eds.), *Automated scoring of complex tasks in computer-based testing* (pp. 123–168). Mahwah, NJ: Lawrence Erlbaum.

Messick, S. (1989). Validity. In R. L. Linn (Ed.), *Educational measurement* (3rd ed., pp. 13–103). New York: American Council on Education/Macmillan.

Messick, S. (1994). The interplay of evidence and consequences in the validation of performance assessments. *Educational Researcher, 23*(2), 13–23.

Mislevy, R. J. (2006). Cognitive psychology and educational assessment. In R. L. Brennan (Ed.), *Educational measurement* (4th ed., pp. 257–305). Phoenix, AZ: Greenwood.

Mislevy, R. J. (in press). Missing responses in item response theory. In W. J. van der Linden & R. K. Hambleton (Eds.), *Handbook of modern item response theory*, (2nd ed., Vol. 1). Chapman & Hall/CRC Press.

Mislevy, R. J. Behrens, J. T., DiCerbo, K. E., Frezzo, D. C., & West, P. (2012). Three things game designers need to know about assessment. In D. Ifenthaler, D. Eseryel, & X. Ge (Eds.), *Assessment in game-based learning: Foundations, innovations, and perspectives* (pp. 59–81). New York: Springer.

Mislevy, R. J., Behrens, J. T., DiCerbo, K., & Levy, R. (2012). Design and discovery in educational assessment: Evidence centered design, psychometrics, and data mining. *Journal of Educational Data Mining, 4*, 11–48. Available online at www.educationaldatamining.org/JEDM/images/articles/vol4/issue1/MislevyEtAlVol4Issue1P11_48.pdf

Mislevy, R. J., & Gitomer, D. H. (1996). The role of probability-based inference in an intelligent tutoring system. *User-Modeling and User-Adapted Interaction, 5*, 253–282.

Mislevy, R. J., Steinberg, L. S., & Almond, R. A. (2003). On the structure of educational assessments. *Measurement: Interdisciplinary Research and Perspectives, 1*, 3–67.

Mislevy, R. J., Steinberg, L. S., Breyer, F. J., Johnson, L., & Almond, R. A. (2002). Making sense of data from complex assessments. *Applied Measurement in Education, 15*, 363–378.

Mosteller, F., & Tukey, J. W. (1977). *Data analysis and regression: A second course in statistics*. Reading, MA: Addison-Wesley.

Moustaki, I. & Knott, M. (2000). Generalised latent trait models. *Psychometrika, 65*, 391–411.

O'Neil, H. F., Jr., & Chuang, S. H. (2008). Measuring collaborative problem solving in low stakes tests. In E. L. Baker, J. Dickieson, W. Wulfeck, & H. F. O'Neil (Eds.), *Assessment of problem solving using simulations* (pp. 177–199). Mahwah, NJ: Lawrence Erlbaum Associates.

Reckase, M. D. (2009). *Multidimensional item response theory*. New York, NY: Springer.

Riconscente, M., Mislevy, R., Hamel, L., & PADI Research Group. (2005). *An introduction to PADI task templates* (PADI Technical Report 3). Menlo Park, CA: SRI International. Available online at http://padi.sri.com/downloads/TR3_Templates.pdf

Riconscente, M. M., & Vattel, L. (2013, April). Extending ECD to the design of learning experiences. In M. M. Riconscente (Chair), *ECD from A to Z: Applying evidence-centered design across the assessment continuum*. Invited session presented at the National Council on Measurement in Education, San Francisco, CA.

Ruiz-Primo, M. A., & Shavelson, R. J. (1996). Rhetoric and reality in science performance assessments: An update. *Journal of Research in Science Teaching, 33*, 1045–1063.

Rupp, A. A., Nugent, R., & Nelson, B. (2012). Evidence-centered design for diagnostic assessment within digital learning environments: Integrating modern psychometrics and educational data mining. *Journal of Educational Data Mining, 4*(1), 1–10. Available online at www.educationaldatamining.org/JEDM/images/articles/vol4/issue1/IntroVol4Issue1P1_10.pdf

Rupp, A. A., Templin, J., & Henson, R. A. (2010). *Diagnostic measurement: Theory, methods, and applications*. New York: Guilford Press.

Salen, K., & Zimmerman, E. (2004). *Rules of play: Game design fundamentals*. Cambridge: MIT Press.

Scalise, K., & Gifford, B. (2006). Computer-based assessment in e-learning: A framework for constructing "intermediate constraint" questions and tasks for technology platforms. *Journal of Technology, Learning, and Assessment, 4*(6), Retrieved July 16, 2013, from http://ejournals.bc.edu/ojs/index.php/jtla/article/view/1653

Segall, D. O. (2010). Principles of multidimensional adaptive testing. In W. J. van der Linden & C. A. W. Glas (Eds.), *Elements of adaptive testing* (pp. 57–75). New York: Springer.

Shaffer, D. W. (2006). Epistemic frames for epistemic games. *Computers and Education, 46*(3), 223–234.

Shute, V. J. (2011). Stealth assessment in computer-based games to support learning. In S. Tobias & J. D. Fletcher (Eds.), *Computer games and instruction* (pp. 503–524). Charlotte, NC: Information Age Publishers.

Shute, V. J., Ventura, M., Bauer, M. I., & Zapata-Rivera, D. (2009). Melding the power of serious games and embedded assessment to monitor and foster learning: Flow and grow. In U. Ritterfeld, M. Cody, & P. Vorder (Eds.), *Serious games: Mechanisms and effects* (pp. 295–321). Mahwah, NJ: Routledge, Taylor and Francis.

Ting, C.-Y., Phon-Amnuaisuk, S., & Chong, Y.-K. (2008). Modeling and intervening across time in scientific inquiry exploratory learning environment. *Educational Technology & Society, 11*, 239–258.

Toulmin, S. E. (1958). *The uses of argument*. Cambridge: Cambridge University Press.

Von Davier, A. A., & Halpin, P. F. (2013, May). *Modeling the dynamics in dyadic interactions in collaborative problem solving*. Paper presented at an invited symposium at the annual meeting of the National Council of Measurement in Education, San Francisco, CA.

Von Davier, M. (2005). *A class of models for cognitive diagnosis*. Research Report RR-05–17. Princeton, NJ: ETS.

Vygotsky, L.S. (1978). *Mind and society: The development of higher psychological processes*. Cambridge, MA: Harvard University Press.

Wainer, H., Dorans, N.J., Flaugher, R., Green, B.F., Mislevy, R.J., Steinberg, L., & Thissen, D. (2000). *Computerized adaptive testing: A primer* (2nd ed.). Hillsdale, NJ: Lawrence Erlbaum Associates.

Yen, W.M., & Fitzpatrick, A.R. (2006). Item response theory. In R. Brennan (Ed.), *Educational measurement* (pp. 111–153). Portsmouth, NH: Praeger/Greenwood.

Zapata-Rivera, D., & Bauer, M. (2011). Exploring the role of games in educational assessment. In M.C. Mayrath, J. Clarke-Midura, & D. Robinson (Eds.), *Technology-based assessments for 21st century skills: Theoretical and practical implications from modern research* (pp. 149–172). Charlotte, NC: Information Age.

# 3

# Issues in Simulation-Based Assessment

Brian E. Clauser, Melissa J. Margolis, and Jerome C. Clauser

This chapter examines the use of simulations in assessment. Consistent with the volume's focus on technology, the emphasis will be on computer-based simulations, although some of the central issues will be common to other simulation settings. The chapter begins with an introduction that provides examples of the range of computer simulation systems that have been developed. Emphasis is given to those simulations that have been well documented in the scientific literature. The second section considers issues relevant to producing scores on simulation-based assessments. The third section examines validity issues for simulation-based assessment, and the final section considers some of the practical issues related to developing and administering simulations for assessment.

In a sense, any task that is presented in an assessment setting might be viewed as a simulation. Multiple-choice questions are at one end of the simulation continuum in that they represent a low-fidelity replication of the real-world situation in which the proficiency of interest is to be displayed. Essay questions may be a step toward higher fidelity, but they are still a somewhat artificial approximation of the criterion behavior. At the far end of the continuum would be seamless virtual reality simulations; high-fidelity flight simulators might come close to this extremely realistic assessment method. Between the extremes of multiple-choice questions and virtual reality fall a wide range of constructed-response formats and complex simulations. These formats are intended to simulate specific—typically critical—aspects of a cognitive challenge without (re)creating all aspects of the natural environment. For example, the patient-management simulations implemented as part of the United States Medical Licensing Examination (USMLE) are designed to assess physicians' decision-making skills in the context of patient management (Margolis & Clauser, 2006). No effort is made to simulate the full complexity of the patient-care environment, which would include communication with the patient and other members of the healthcare team, procedural skills, and many other important proficiencies. Similarly, HYDRIVE, a computer-based simulation for training technicians to troubleshoot problems with the hydraulic system on jet aircraft, focuses on decision making and ignores hands-on mechanical skills, which certainly are important (Mislevy & Gitomer, 1996). Though it is tempting to create the most complete simulation possible, technology and practicality argue against this approach. The challenge is aptly summarized by a statement that has been attributed to Einstein: Everything should be made as simple as possible, but not simpler. The simulation must include the aspects of the real-world task that are essential for assessing the proficiency of interest. Cognitive models, theoretical models, or empirically derived models might provide guidance in determining what aspects are essential. Beyond that, validity research will be needed to determine if test-development decisions introduced construct-irrelevant variance (e.g., the assessment measures familiarity with the interface) or whether limitations in the model led to construct underrepresentation.

It is not the intention of this chapter to provide a how-to guide for test developers who are interested in implementing a simulation-based assessment. Such an effort is well beyond the scope of this chapter; a complete practical guide certainly would require an entire volume. Instead, the purpose of this chapter is to introduce the reader to the general issues that must be considered in using simulations for assessment and to provide useful information about how previous researchers have dealt with these issues. The potential appeal of simulations is self-evident: They provide an opportunity to use technology to more fully and directly assess the real-world proficiencies of interest. What may be less evident is how difficult it is to use simulation technology to create valid test scores. For this reason, the majority of the chapter focuses on the challenges of simulation-based assessment. The remainder of this section will provide examples of simulations that currently are being used as part of operational assessments as well as research projects that provide insight into what works and what does not. Many of these examples will be used throughout this chapter.

## Computer Simulations in Assessment

### USMLE Step 3 Patient-Management Simulations

One of the best known simulation-based assessments is the patient-management simulation assessment used as part of the USMLE. The USMLE sequence is the required licensure pathway for medical school graduates with an MD degree seeking a license to practice medicine in the United States; it consists of three Steps, each of which is composed of one or more examinations. The final hurdle in the USMLE battery is the 2-day Step 3 examination, which includes 480 multiple-choice items along with 12 patient-management simulations (Federation of State Medical Boards & National Board of Medical Examiners, 2013). These simulations require examinees to manage virtual patients in an unprompted patient-care environment.

Each case simulation presents the examinee with a brief scenario describing a virtual patient who has arrived for treatment. Figure 3.1 provides a screen shot of the simulation interface that includes a sample scenario. Following this case introduction, the patient's current vital signs and medical history are presented; examinees then are left to manage the case independently by selecting one of four main categories of actions (as shown in Figure 3.1). They can (1) request the results of targeted physical examinations (e.g., Chest/Lungs, Abdomen, Rectal), (2) enter orders (e.g., tests, consultations, treatments) using free text entry, (3) set a time to see the patient in the future, or (4) change the patient's location (e.g., from the emergency department to the ward or home).

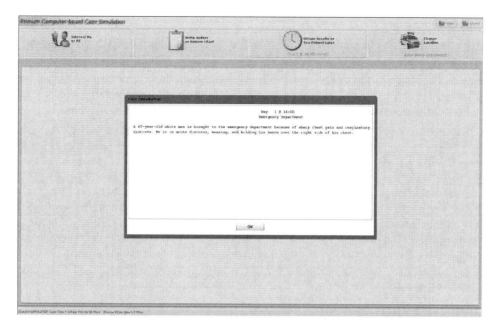

**Figure 3.1** Screen shot of the interface from the patient-management simulation included as part of Step 3 of the USMLE

To direct patient care, the examinee is able to order a wide range of diagnostic and therapeutic management options by typing orders into an order sheet. The order sheet recognizes nearly 9,000 different terms pertaining to more than 2,300 different tests and treatments, including common abbreviations. Examinee input is unprompted, and at any time, the examinee can order virtually any test or procedure. The patient care takes place in "simulated time" where results for each test and the effect of each treatment become available only after the appropriate amount of simulated time has passed. The examinee is able to advance the simulated time to view test results or the impact of their treatment decisions. Throughout the patient-management process, the virtual patient's condition evolves in simulated time as a result of both the original underlying condition and the actions taken by the examinee. This process of entering orders into the order sheet and viewing the results of these actions continues until the system terminates the case because the assessment objective has been completed or because the testing time has expired.

The scoring of the patient-management simulations is based on the sequence, timing, and type of actions ordered by the examinee. The goal of this assessment is to focus on process rather than outcome. For example, a patient's condition might improve even though the examinee received a relatively low score for failing to rule out a potentially dangerous diagnosis that might be associated with the presented symptoms. When the simulation originally was launched, it was scored using a regression-based procedure designed to approximate the scores that would have been provided by expert judges (Margolis & Clauser, 2006). More recently, a transition has been made to a rule-based scoring approach. (The next section of this chapter presents a complete treatment of both regression and rule-based scoring procedures.)

### Architect Registration Examination

The Architect Registration Examination (ARE) is a computer-based licensure examination developed by Educational Testing Service (ETS) on behalf of the National Council of Architectural Registration Boards (NCARB). The ARE is composed of seven divisions covering broad content areas such as site planning, schematic designs, and building systems. Each division includes one to three interactive graphical simulations, known as vignettes, targeted at a specific content area. In total, the exam battery includes 11 graphical simulations utilizing roughly half of the 28 hours of testing time (National Council of Architectural Registration Boards, 2013). For a typical vignette, the examinee is presented with an architectural task with a series of requirements. For example, the examinee may be asked to design a firehouse for a small town, expand a local school, or make site alterations to improve drainage. Each task carries with it a series of specific requirements, such as the placement of the building relative to geographic features, the number of rooms in the building, and specific requirements for each room. The examinee is presented with a site map and simplified computer-aided design (CAD) interface through which s/he can design a structure that will meet the requirements (see Figure 3.2; Bejar & Braun, 1999). These graphical simulations allow examinees to demonstrate their abilities as they work through a series of real-world architectural tasks.

The quality of the examinee's solution is assessed based on both the form and the functionality of the design. A feature's form is assessed when the task requires the examinee to place elements in a specific geometric orientation. For example, if the task requires that the cafeteria allow for easy access to the playground, this feature would be assessed by judging the

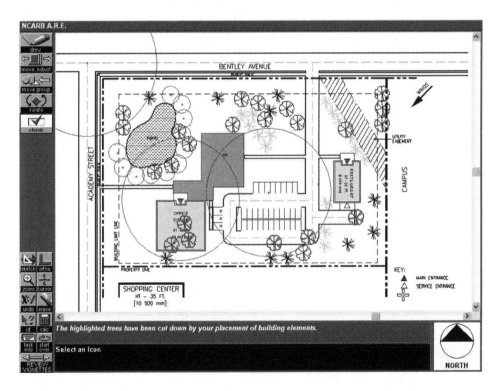

**Figure 3.2** Screen shot of the interface from the ARE Site Simulation design task

relative placement of each of those elements in the design. A feature's functionality is assessed when the task requires that the structure serve a specific purpose. For example, the task may require that rain water effectively drain away from the structure. This can be assessed by simulating a rainstorm and judging the efficacy of the drainage system. These methods allow the automated scoring system to judge both the form and the function of individual site features.

The Architect Registration Examination employs a hierarchical rule-based scoring system for its interactive simulations (Braun, Bejar, & Williamson, 2006). This means that the score on a given vignette is the result of individual site features aggregated into a multitiered hierarchy of clusters. For example, a simple cluster may be composed of two or three observable tasks. That cluster could be combined with other clusters and more tasks to create the score for the next tier of the hierarchy. Each element of the scoring process can be weighted to reflect its relative importance. This allows a high score on critical features to overwhelm any mistakes on minor elements. All levels of the hierarchy are scored as Acceptable, Intermediate, or Unacceptable based on the scores of the subcomponents beneath it. This hierarchical scoring system provides a flexible method for scoring complex tasks based solely on distinct quantified site elements.

### Uniform CPA Exam

The Uniform CPA examination is a battery of tests that must be successfully completed by any person with an accounting degree who wants to become a certified public accountant (CPA) in the United States. The complete testing sequence consists of four examinations that can be completed in any order. Three of these examinations include short task-based simulations that require examinees to perform accounting functions commonly conducted by certified public accountants. Although several variations on these task-based simulations exist, the two primary simulation types are *Realistic Data Entry and Manipulation* and *Research within Authoritative Literature* (Stopek, 2012).

The *Realistic Data Entry and Manipulation* items allow examinees to enter their answers to test items using an embedded spreadsheet or tax form. For example, an examinee could be presented with an item and asked to "Record the necessary year 2 adjustments" based on a sale of inventory and a realized profit. The examinee then is able to name spreadsheet rows by selecting account names from a predefined list and input appropriate values in the corresponding cells (see Figure 3.3; Breithaupt, Devore, Brittingham, & Foreman, 2005). The spreadsheet interface allows candidates to embed formulae and functions into each cell to calculate values by referencing other cells within the spreadsheet. This simulation design gives examinees many different ways to arrive at the correct answer while providing the structure needed for effective automated scoring.

The scoring for these items is handled through the development of an elaborate scoring rubric. When the item is developed, content experts define the parameters of a correct response for each cell. These may include different content types, such as numbers, text, and formulae, in addition to allowing for a tolerance around the target values (Stopek, 2012). The rubrics even are capable of determining target values based on references to other cells, thus preventing an error in one cell from necessarily creating errors in other cells. Although these rubrics must be designed for each item, many of the principles apply across many items of the same type.

The second task-based simulation common to the Uniform CPA exam is the *Research within Authoritative Literature* simulation format (see Figure 3.4). These items allow

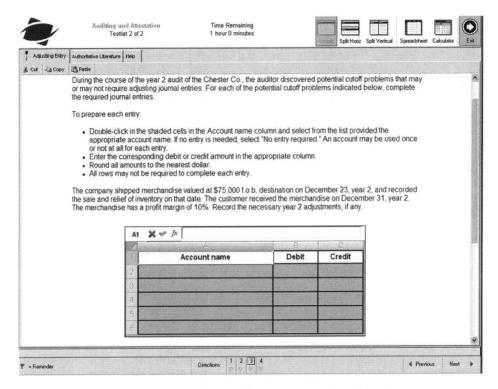

**Figure 3.3** Screen shot of the interface from the Uniform CPA Spreadsheet Simulation

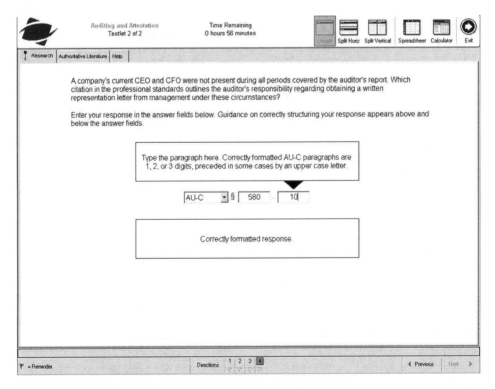

**Figure 3.4** Screen shot of the interface from the Uniform CPA *Research within Authoritative Literature* Simulation

examinees to demonstrate their ability to conduct research within a broad set of relevant accounting documents. These items typically ask examinees to provide a citation to justify a specific action. For example, the items may ask the examinee to identify the citation in the professional standards that outlines the auditor's responsibility in a given situation. The examinee is able to search and review sources from a database of authoritative literature to determine the correct citation. When the examinee has identified the appropriate citation, s/he enters the citation through a dynamic set of data-entry fields. These fields include a drop-down list to select the source followed by a dynamic number of text fields to enter the section, subsection, and finally the specific paragraph where the reference can be found. For each field, the interface indicates the types of inputs that are appropriate (e.g., the number of numerical digits in the citation) to ensure that data are properly entered (Breithaupt et al., 2005). These items provide the flexibility to test skills not readily addressed by multiple-choice items while maintaining the data-entry structure required for scoring.

### Cisco Packet Tracer

The three simulations described previously are in operational use with high-stakes tests; several other simulations are being used in formative and low-stakes summative assessments. Packet Tracer is a computer networking simulation used for both training and low-stakes summative assessment. The software was developed by Cisco Systems in collaboration with Educational Testing Service (ETS) and the University of Maryland and is used as part of the Cisco Networking Academy (a four-semester course offered primarily to students in high school, community college, and vocational schools). The purpose of the Networking Academy is to teach students to design, implement, and maintain large-scale computer networks. Although the primary purpose of Packet Tracer is as an instructional tool, the software supports the creation and administration of instructor-developed assessments (Advancing Assessment with Technology, 2012).

Packet Tracer allows students to arrange and configure networking hardware through a simple drag-and-drop interface (University of Greenwich at Medway, 2014; see Figure 3.5). Students are free to select from a wide variety of modems, routers, switches, and PC hardware

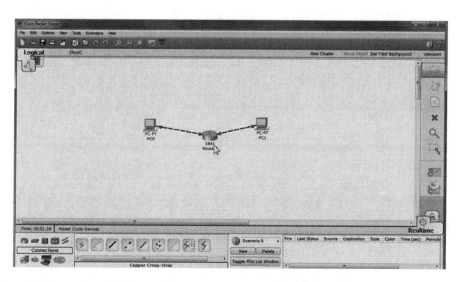

**Figure 3.5** Screen shot of the Packet Tracer interface showing the Physical Network Layout

to develop networks of almost any complexity. They also must select the appropriate cables to connect the hardware as well as the appropriate physical port for the connection. After building the "physical" layout of the network hardware, students are given the opportunity to configure each hardware component. For high-end routers and switches, the configuration is handled through a command line text interface (see Figure 3.6). The command line allows students to configure hardware through free-text entry using the Cisco IOS syntax just as they would in practice. For configuration of PC hardware, the students use a graphical user interface (see Figure 3.7). This interface mimics a traditional Microsoft Windows environment in which students point and click to configure PC hardware on the network. Together, these dual interfaces allow students to practice configuring networking hardware in a realistic unprompted environment.

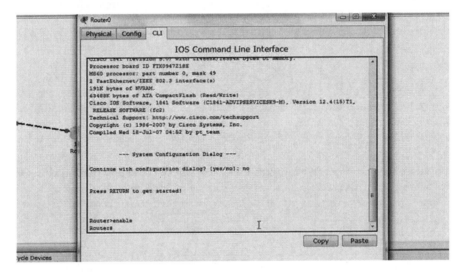

**Figure 3.6** Screen shot of the Packet Tracer interface showing the Command Line Configuration

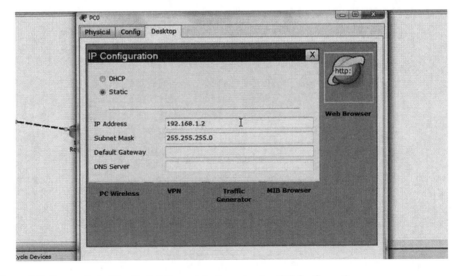

**Figure 3.7** Screen shot of the Packet Tracer interface showing GUI Configuration

Although Packet Tracer primarily has been used as an instructional tool, a related project called Packet Tracer Skills Assessment allows for the creation of instructor-developed assessments. Cisco Networking Academy teachers can select from hundreds of existing networking activities or author their own using the built-in activity wizard. The instructor-developed assessments provide the examinee with a scenario and an initial network configuration. From there, students can modify the initial network to address a problem or to accommodate some new desired functionality. This solution can be scored automatically through the creation of an answer network, which is an instructor-created diagram of the properly configured network and is considered the ideal solution. The activity wizard identifies all the features that are different between the initial network and the answer network and allows the instructor to identify which of these differences should be scored. For example, the instructor may decide that the computer's specific IP address is not important but that use of the appropriate router is. In addition to design and configuration of the network, instructors also can score students' work based on connectivity tests. For these scoring rules, Packet Tracer will determine if a packet can successfully be transferred from one point on the student's network to another. The instructor can include this information in the scoring to determine if the examinee's network works for an intended purpose. These scoring procedures allow the instructor to assess both the form and the function of an examinee's solution network.

Prior to the development of Packet Tracer, Cisco developed a prototype known as NetPASS. NetPASS served a similar purpose and was intended for use in instruction and assessment for the Cisco Networking Academy; the simulation used an elaborate scoring system based on Bayesian networks (Williamson et al., 2006). Although considerable research was devoted to the possibility of scoring simulation tasks using Bayesian networks, the approach was not adopted for operational scoring in Packet Tracer. (A more complete discussion of Bayesian networks is presented in the next section of this chapter.)

### HYDRIVE

HYDRIVE is a computer-based simulation developed on behalf of the U.S. Air Force for the assessment and training of aircraft hydraulics technicians. The system has been designed to assess examinees' ability to troubleshoot malfunctioning hydraulics systems in the F-15 fighter jet. The simulation begins when the examinee is presented with a video recording in which a pilot describes an aircraft malfunction to the hydraulics technician. For example, the pilot might explain that the landing gear failed to retract during his flight. The examinee then is able to troubleshoot the problem by reviewing videos of aircraft components and acting on aircraft components in the computer interface. In addition, at any time, the examinee is able to review technical material and schematic diagrams (Mislevy & Gitomer, 1996). Although considerable research went into the development of this system, it is not clear whether HYDRIVE was used operationally, and the system has not been updated since it originally was developed (D.H. Gitomer, personal communication, July 29, 2013).

Research was conducted on scoring the HYDRIVE encounters using Bayesian networks (Mislevy & Gitomer, 1996). Bayesian networks are particularly well suited to scoring interactions with these sorts of deterministic mechanical systems. The authors found that Bayesian networks were effective in modeling examinee behavior at different levels of mastery. For the final version of the simulation, however, HYDRIVE utilized rule-based scoring to identify examinees' weaknesses and provide feedback.

### English and Math Assessment-Based Learning Environment

In addition to the process-oriented simulations described earlier, researchers have begun to experiment with the use of video games as a form of simulation for instruction and assessment. The goal of this type of assessment is to provide greater engagement for examinees while measuring higher-order thinking that cannot be assessed easily using traditional multiple-choice items. One such example is the English and Math Assessment-Based Learning Environment, better known as EM ABLE, that has been developed by ETS as part of its CBAL Initiative (Cognitively Based Assessment of, for, and as Learning). CBAL is focused on creating future assessments that not only measure what the student currently knows but also adaptively provide instruction tailored to the student's needs (Bennett, 2010). As part of CBAL, EM ABLE attempts to meld instruction and assessment in an immersive gaming experience (Zapata-Rivera & Bauer, 2012).

EM ABLE begins by allowing examinees to create and customize an avatar that they will guide around a virtual environment known as EM City. As the character moves from place to place, s/he is invited to participate in various activities that provide an integrated learning and assessment experience. For example, the virtual character may be invited to a pizza party. In preparation for this party, the character will be asked to perform a number of tasks that will demonstrate facility with fractions. S/he may be asked to express pizza preferences in the form of a fraction, reduce those fractions to determine how much pizza to buy, and add fractions to determine how much pizza is left at the end of the party. Based on the examinee's performance on these tasks, the game provides customized feedback through conversations that the avatar has with other game characters about what took place during the task.

EM ABLE uses Bayesian networks to continually revise estimates of examinee ability (Zapata-Rivera, 2007; Zapata-Rivera & Bauer, 2012). As the examinee completes additional tasks, the Bayesian student model is updated to incorporate this information. The estimate of the examinee's current ability is used to customize the instructional feedback provided throughout the game. Furthermore, the examinee's current ability estimate is reflected in the game as a cell phone power meter. This helps examinees to see how their ability has grown as they move through tasks in EM City. Although EM ABLE is still in the early development stages, initial studies reported that examinees found the game play instructional and motivating (Zapata-Rivera & Bauer, 2012).

### High-Fidelity Training Simulations

Although the focus of this chapter is on computer-based simulations used in assessment, significant work has been devoted to the development of immersive high-fidelity simulations for use in professional training contexts. Due to lack of published information about the assessment properties of these high-fidelity simulations, we can address them only briefly here.

One of the most frequently mentioned examples of high-fidelity simulations is flight simulators used for the training of aircraft pilots. These can range from relatively simplistic instrument simulators to fully immersive cockpit simulators. At the extreme end of the scale are flight simulators that not only mimic the interior of the cockpit but also replicate pitch, roll, yaw, and g-force by attaching the simulation chamber to a centrifuge. The primary purpose for all of these simulators appears to be pilot training. The authors are not aware of any flight simulators being used in high-stakes assessment, although time in a simulator can in some instances be substituted for actual flight time as a qualification for a pilot's license, and performance of defined tasks in a simulator may be required for certification to fly specific aircraft (Adams, 2013).

Medical procedural simulators are another commonly used high-fidelity simulation technology. These simulators allow physicians and other medical professionals to conduct procedural tasks on an anatomically accurate model. These models can range from a single body part designed for a single procedure to a more complete manikin designed to accommodate a wide array of procedures. Physicians can work individually or in groups to perform the procedure and receive feedback from both the anatomic model and an instructor. These systems are increasingly used in training, but relatively little research has been done to support their use in high-stakes assessment, and scoring models tend to be relatively simplistic.

The simulations discussed here exhibit a wide range of complexity and are useful for illustrating a variety of common measurement challenges. This discussion, however, has necessarily been limited to simulations with published accounts of their development and scoring. Table 3.1 provides a list of other simulations used in assessment and training. Although this list is by no means exhaustive, it serves to demonstrate the diversity of simulations in development for both students and professionals.

Table 3.1  Additional Simulations Currently Used in Assessment and Training

**K–12 Simulations**

| Simulation | Affiliated Organization | Simulation Type | Simulation Description |
|---|---|---|---|
| SimScientists | WestEd | K–12 Science | Allows students to make observations and conduct experiments to solve problems in a 2-dimensional environment. |
| SimCityEDU: Pollution Challenge! | GlassLab | K–12 Science | Places students in the role of city planner and asks them to improve their city's environment while maintaining employment levels. The simulation uses the Electronic Arts SimCity game engine. |
| Virtual Performance Assessment | Harvard University | K–12 Science | This simulation allows students to collect evidence and utilize the scientific method to solve mysteries in a 3-dimensional environment. |
| PhET Simulations | University of Colorado–Boulder | K–12 Science and Mathematics | Provides a wide variety of 2-dimensional simulations that provide representations of a lab environment where students can conduct simple experiments. |
| Molecular Workbench Simulations | Molecular Workbench | K–12 Science and Mathematics | Provide a series of 2-dimensional simulations that allow students to manipulate variables to understand scientific phenomena. |
| Gizmos | Explore Learning | K–12 Science and Mathematics | Series of 2-dimensional simulations that provide representations of a lab environment where students can conduct simple experiments and explore mathematical concepts. |

*(Continued)*

Table 3.1  (Continued)

**Medical Simulations**

| Simulation | Affiliated Organization | Simulation Type | Simulation Description |
|---|---|---|---|
| Clinical Performance Vignettes | Qure Health Care | Medical Decision Making | Presents a scenario and asks physicians to manage the patient encounter. The simulations are text based and delivered over the Internet. |
| Interactive Medical Case | *New England Journal of Medicine* | Medical Decision Making | Presents a scenario and asks physicians to manage the patient encounter. Responses are selected from multiple-choice options, and feedback and explanatory materials are provided throughout. |
| ClinSim | American Board of Family Medicine | Medical Decision Making | Presents a scenario and asks physicians to manage the patient encounter. Responses are selected from multiple-choice options, and feedback is provided dynamically based on these selections. |
| Dental Implant Training Simulation | Medical College of Georgia | Dental Decision Making | Allows students to manage a patient and practice surgical dental procedures in a 3-dimensional environment. |
| Pulse!! Virtual Clinical Learning Lab | Texas A&M University—Corpus Christi | Clinical Health-Care Skills | Allows physicians to practice clinical skills in a 3-dimensional patient-care environment. |

**Military and Professional Simulations**

| Simulation | Affiliated Organization | Simulation Type | Simulation Description |
|---|---|---|---|
| VPR (Virtual Role-Players) MIL | U.S. Department of Defense | Military Mission Rehearsal | Allows military personnel to realistically train for foreign missions in a 3-dimensional recreation of a location's language, culture, and environment. |
| 24 Blue | U.S. Naval Education Training Command | Flight Deck Operations Training | Provides students with 3-dimensional training on aircraft carrier flight deck operations. |
| Incident Commander | U.S. Department of Justice | Homeland Security Training Tool | Trains Homeland Security personnel in National Incident Management Protocol by requiring players to coordinate efforts from multiple first-responder organizations. Trainees respond to a wide variety of natural and manmade disasters in a 2-dimensional environment. |
| FlightSafety Simulation | FlightSafety International | Flight Simulator | Trains pilots in the operation of a wide variety of aircraft under a variety of 3-dimensional simulated flying conditions. |

**Military and Professional Simulations**

| Simulation | Affiliated Organization | Simulation Type | Simulation Description |
|---|---|---|---|
| vBank | Federal Deposit Insurance Corporation | Fraud Detection and Auditing | Allows players to examine bank records and interview bank employees in a 3-dimensional environment to uncover evidence of wrongdoing by senior bank officials. |
| Aspire | Cisco Systems | Computer Networking | Provides a 3-dimensional environment in which players interact with virtual customers to understand problems and provide networking solutions. |

## Scoring Issues

As the previous section suggests, simulations typically are complex and have the potential to produce large amounts of scorable data. This raises two important questions: (1) Which of these data are important in the context of the intended score interpretation? and (2) How should the data be aggregated to produce a usable score? Despite the fact that computers have been used to score complex response formats (e.g., essays) for more than half a century (Page, 1966), surprisingly little is known about how to answer these questions. This section provides insight into how previous researchers have answered these questions. The section begins with a short discussion of conceptual approaches to constructing and scoring examinations; this is meant to provide context for the more detailed consideration of scoring that follows. We begin by discussing evidence-centered design principles and contrasting them to other more *ad hoc* approaches.

### Conceptual Approaches to Test Development

Evidence-centered design principles (Mislevy, Steinberg, Almond, & Lukas, 2006) provide one way of conceptualizing the problem of structured test development. Broadly speaking, this approach begins with a careful specification of the inferences that the test scores are intended to support. Evidence that would support these inferences then must be identified, and tasks must be developed that allow for collection of that evidence. After these initial steps, statistical frameworks can be constructed to combine and summarize the observed evidence to create scores or classifications. Because the specifics of the evidence were identified in advance, there is no question about what should be viewed as scorable information or how that information should be combined to yield the resulting score(s). In practice, however, it often is impossible to implement the evidence-centered design approach in any strict sense because the cognitive models required to support test construction decisions do not exist. When a system is well understood, as is the case with the hydraulic system on a jet aircraft, for example, it may be possible to develop an assessment to evaluate jet technicians based on evidence-centered design and specify in advance the types of evidence to be collected, the types of tasks to be used, and how that evidence should be combined for scoring. Other areas such as persuasive writing or patient management may not have such well-understood frameworks supporting mechanical relationships between evidence and inferences. In these cases, test development is an approximation of the approach represented by evidence-centered design. Intended inferences may be clearly specified, but the details of the evidence that would support those inferences may be lacking. There are no widely accepted and empirically verified cognitive models for how expert clinicians make diagnostic decisions, and in many cases, best practices are based on expert opinion rather than a body of empirical evidence or an accepted theoretical framework. Without being able to make precise statements about the evidence required, the tasks cannot be precisely specified, and the way evidence is collected from task performance and combined to support inferences is similarly approximate. At the far end of this continuum is the situation in which the simulation is constructed to approximate the real-world task of interest, and scoring becomes an afterthought. Clearly, "scoring as an afterthought" leaves a lot to be desired, and an approach in which inferences, evidence, and task design can be specified clearly in advance may be unrealistic. Instead, both designing the simulation and developing the scoring procedure are likely to be iterative processes in which approaches are evaluated and modifications are made as part of what might be viewed as an ongoing program of validity research. Evidence is gathered to support or refute the reasonableness of the intended score interpretations, and the tasks as well as the scoring procedures may be modified in light of the new evidence. It may well be that the originally specified inferences are shown to be too ambitious and must be scaled back or that evidence that seemed pertinent cannot be gathered from the tasks that have been developed without the influence of damaging construct-irrelevant variance.

### Identifying Variables

In many assessment contexts, the lack of precise knowledge about both the evidence that should be collected and the specifics of the tasks that will elicit that evidence means that the test developers will build tasks that they believe will capture the relevant evidence. If such precise knowledge is available, it may be possible to create highly effective assessment tasks. Precision in this area is more likely to be the exception than the rule, at least for complex proficiencies such as those that are apt to be assessed in credentialing examinations. As Mislevy and Gitomer (1996) comment in the context of constructing the HYDRIVE system:

> Unlike bridge hands and coin flips, few real world problems present themselves to us in terms of natural "random variables." Random variables are not features of the real world, but features of the patterns through which we organize our thinking about the real world. From unique events, we must create abstractions which capture aspects we believe are salient but neglect infinitely many others. . . . conceptualizing our problem in terms of variables amenable to probabilistic inference (particularly "observable variables") was one of the toughest challenges we faced!
>
> (p. 258)

One difficulty in constructing simulation tasks designed to provide evidence in the form of random variables is that the process will be unique to the context. Although there are a limited number of approaches available for aggregating evidence, the problem of creating the variables will be heavily dependent on the assessment context. Content experts will provide important guidance, but there also are some theoretical and practical questions that can shape the process. First, it is important to begin by asking about the purpose of the simulation. The choice of variables may be different depending on whether the primary purpose of the simulation is education or assessment. For example, proxy variables (such as word count and language complexity) have been shown to be useful in scoring essays. They may be less useful for providing feedback; telling a student to write longer sentences or longer essays is a limited instructional strategy. By contrast, a simulation such as Packet Tracer, which was designed to allow students to experiment with the behavior of computer networks, needs to provide accurate feedback about the functioning of the simulated network, but there may be little concern for collecting evidence that directly reflects student proficiency or maps performance into levels of expertise.

Another important question is: What aspects of the real-world task/environment are necessary to meet the goals of the simulation? This is in keeping with the admonition that everything should be made as simple as possible, but not simpler. The assessment tasks must reflect those aspects of the real-world setting that are essential to support score interpretation; that is, the task must reflect the cognitive (or other) task of interest. Beyond that, extending the bounds of the simulation may lead to (1) increased expenses for test development, (2) increased assessment time requirements to allow the examinee to consider potentially unimportant aspects of the simulated environment, and (3) the introduction of construct-irrelevant variance. Consider, for example, a simulation designed to assess physicians' patient-management skills. In many real settings, a patient presenting with a new symptom will have extensive health records reflecting previous visits. A simulation might or might not include such records. Including such records certainly would be realistic. It also would add substantially to the amount of time required to complete the simulation. Additionally, lengthy records could contain information that would complicate the task and lead some particularly proficient examinees to consider actions that were not intended by the test developers but might be appropriate.

A third question is: What aspects of the real-world task can be simulated seamlessly with high fidelity? Limitations of the simulation may lead to construct underrepresentation or construct-irrelevant variance. For example, the use of standardized patients—laypeople trained to portray real patients—has become a popular methodology for evaluating physicians' clinical skills. Though this methodology provides a potentially valuable means of assessing skills such as the ability to collect a patient history and the ability to communicate with the patient, it is limited because it often is difficult (or impossible) to simulate abnormal physical findings. This limitation restricts the range of problems that can be presented and also may create an assumption on the part of the examinee that unusual physical findings will be absent. This in turn may reduce the likelihood that the examinee will check for those findings—even though s/he would have in the real world—and it also may lead examinees to record that those findings were absent despite the fact that they did not check for them.

The complexity of the problem of developing tasks and creating variables makes it clear that a lengthy program of test development and refinement is likely to be necessary before optimal solutions can be found for the problem of variable identification. As those solutions are identified, it is hoped that generalized strategies will emerge; for the time being, however, answers are likely to remain context specific.

### Aggregating Scoring Data

As noted previously, scoring simulations requires that (1) the relevant data resulting from an examinee's interaction with the simulation are collected and coded, and (2) the data are combined—or otherwise aggregated—to produce a score. As should be clear from the previous paragraphs, the approach to identifying the appropriate data will be highly dependent on the specifics of the assessment. By contrast, the aggregation step is likely to follow one of a few general procedures: (1) Linear or tree-based regression procedures might be used to approximate the judgments that would have been made by content experts (Margolis & Clauser, 2006), (2) logical rules can be developed that directly operationalize the decision processes used by content experts (Braun, Bejar, & Williamson, 2006), or (3) statistical models such as Bayesian networks (Williamson, Almond, Mislevy, & Levy, 2006) or cognitive diagnostic models might be used to identify an examinee's level of mastery within an established framework.

### Regression-Based Procedures

If essays are included under the heading of simulation, it is clear that the most widely used approach for automated scoring of simulations is regression based. Page's work from nearly a half century ago used this approach, and it has continued to remain popular (Page, 1966; Shermis & Hamner, 2012). Regression models also have been used to score patient-management simulations designed to measure physicians' patient-management skills (Margolis & Clauser, 2006) and to score patient notes created as part of clinical skills assessments (Cook, Baldwin, & Clauser, 2012; Swygert et al., 2003). The basic approach is that characteristics of the performance are quantified and used as the independent measures in a regression, with expert judgments acting as the dependent measure. The dependent measures typically have been counts, nominal variables representing whether a characteristic is present, or ordinal variables representing the quality of some aspect of the response. Nonlinear transformations of counts also are common. Examples of counts include number of words in an essay, number of "if" clauses in the essay, and the number of tests or treatments ordered in a patient-management simulation that were identified as beneficial in the context of the specific case. Nominal variables might include "ordered a chest x-ray within the first 2 hours of simulated time" in a patient-management simulation or recorded the concept "cough has persisted for 2 weeks" in a patient note. Ordinal variables might include measures representing the complexity of the vocabulary used in an essay or variables representing whether the antibiotic ordered as part of a patient-management simulation likely would have been optimal, suboptimal, or ineffective in the context of the case. The number of independent variables may vary widely depending on the application. The basic models used for scoring patient-management simulations had as few as six or seven variables; models for scoring essays may have 20 to 50 (or more).

Regression-based procedures have a number of potential advantages: They are conceptually simple, they have a long history showing that they perform well across a number of applications, and they do not require the content experts to be able to clearly articulate the specific logic behind their judgments. Nearly a century ago, Henry Wallace (Secretary of Agriculture, later to become vice president under Roosevelt) suggested that such models could be used in place of expert judgments of the quality of corn (Dawes & Corrigan, 1974). Well over half a century ago, Paul Meehl (1954) demonstrated that regression procedures could outperform clinicians in making diagnostic judgments. Since then, numerous other studies have shown that linear models are useful for approximating expert judgment (Meehl, 1986). Page and Petersen (1995), Swygert and colleagues (2003), and Margolis and Clauser (2006) all have shown that these models are useful for scoring assessments. In general, regression-based scores have modestly higher correlations with scores produced by human judges than the score produced by a single judge would have with the same independent human judgments. Regression-based procedures also have compared favorably to other approaches for automated scoring. Clauser, Margolis, Clyman, and Ross (1997) provided a direct comparison between regression-based models and rule-based models for scoring patient-management simulations. Their results showed that the regression-based scores had generally higher correlations with human ratings than the rule-based scores had with those same ratings.

Regression-based approaches do, however, have limitations. Ironically, one of the strengths of regression-based approaches also can be the source of difficulties. Regression-based approaches allow for building models based on what content experts do rather than on how they do it. These approaches allow for modeling judgments by optimizing statistical relationships, not by understanding the logic underlying expert judgment; in effect this approach allows for scoring by proxy. Writing experts are unlikely to judge an essay based on its length or the average number of words in a sentence. Nonetheless, a good writer—at least a good writer in elementary or secondary school—likely is a fluent writer. Such a writer typically will write longer essays and longer sentences. Thus length can become a proxy for the actual attributes that characterize good writing. The use of proxies can be valuable when content experts have difficulty articulating the logic of their judgment process or when it is difficult to quantify the actual attributes of interest. At the same time, the use of regression procedures creates potential threats to score validity. First, the regression procedure applies weights to variables in ways that may make it a "black box" from the perspective of content experts. This may seriously limit the extent to which they can confirm that the resulting scoring algorithm is consistent with their intentions. Additionally, the use of proxies may introduce construct-irrelevant variance into the scores (Clauser, Kane & Swanson, 2002). Again, longer essays are not necessarily better essays, so some examinees may receive unwarranted credit for a rambling and inarticulate composition.

Potential difficulties aside, regression-based procedures remain popular and effective. The choice to use these procedures should, however, not be taken as evidence that test developers prefer indirect approaches to capturing expert judgment. The simple truth is that more direct modeling of the cognitive process used by experts in evaluating performance generally has remained elusive; as Camerer and Johnson (1991) noted, in general, the study of how experts make decisions has been much less productive than the study of how to approximate expert judgments. Although they made that statement more than two decades ago, it remains accurate.

### Rule-Based Procedures

As implied by the discussion of regression methods, scoring based on rules that can be coded as logical if/then statements has the obvious advantage that the mechanism producing the resulting scores is transparent. These rules can be affirmed or challenged by content experts, and the rules can be refined by identifying the characteristics of performances for which the logic coded in the scoring engine leads to scores that differ meaningfully from those produced by expert judges. In some cases, the logic to support the scoring rules will follow from the mechanical nature of the problem. Again, assessing the approach a technician takes to diagnosing a problem in the hydraulic system of a jet aircraft may be reduced to rules because the system literally is mechanical. Similarly, strictly mechanical rules may be used to evaluate the grading of the landscape in an architectural design problem; the computer can verify that the ground level is constant or decreasing as the distance from the building increases. Mechanical rules also can be used if expert opinion can be reduced to a set of logical statements if all of the characteristics of the performance that the expert considers can be quantified. For example, even without a mechanical model for how the human body responds to treatment, expert judgment might lead to the statement: if "ordered chest x-ray before hour 4" = 0 then score ≤ 3. A series of such statements can be used to create a scoring algorithm (see Clauser et al., 1997, or Margolis & Clauser, 2006, for more complete examples).

Whether based on a mechanical model, a strong theoretical framework, or expert opinion, this approach to scoring will be attractive—and may even be viewed as theoretically optimal—as long as three requirements are met. First, it must be feasible to quantify all of the characteristics of the performance that figure into the judgments. As already noted, given the present state of technology, such quantification is not likely to be possible for some complex tasks such as persuasive writing. The second requirement is that it must be possible to elicit the rules from the content experts. This step may be facilitated by the presence of a model or strong theoretical framework that supports scoring decisions, but expert policies still will be needed to support the modeling of rules. The final requirement is that the expert opinion must be able to be credibly viewed as the gold standard. These final two requirements may be problematic. Eliciting the policies of experts may require considerable skill on the part of the facilitator. Clauser, Margolis, and colleagues (1997) reported higher correlations between ratings and automated scores based on regression approaches than between those same ratings and scores developed using rule-based algorithms. However, more recent research showed little difference between the performance of the two approaches; the correlations for the rule-based algorithms had risen to be similar to those for the regression-based procedures (Harik, Clauser, & Baldwin, 2010). The authors speculated that the improved results followed from changes in the procedures used to elicit the policies of the content experts. The improved correspondence between rule-based scores and ratings is evidence that the rules effectively capture (or at least approximate) what those same content experts do when rating examinee performance. Unfortunately, subsequent research called into question the stability of expert policy across equivalent panels of experts. Harik, Clauser, Murray, and colleagues (2013) reported only moderate correlations between scores produced for the same tasks but based on the elicited policies of different groups of experts. It is impossible to be sure whether these modest correlations resulted from actual differences in expert policy or from artifacts of the elicitation process. These results are in stark contrast to those reported by Clauser and colleagues (2000). That paper reported a high level of correspondence between regression-based scores modeled from ratings provided by independent panels of content experts.

Results from a small number of studies do not provide a basis for generalization. Nonetheless, it may be that regression-based approaches are more forgiving of minor differences in the implicit policies of different groups of experts or variations in the elicitation process. Dawes and Corrigan (1974) make the case that models often will produce similar results provided there are no differences in the signs associated with the independent measures. Similarly, Wainer (1976) demonstrated that over a range of circumstances, unit weights perform as well as individually estimated weights. These studies make a strong argument for the potential of regression-based approaches to provide robust estimates. The results also suggest that regression-based procedures might be a reasonable first step in the development process; an assessment program might rely on regression-based procedures until a level of sophistication is achieved in understanding the relationship among the inferences, evidence, and tasks that supports rule-based scoring. This level of sophistication may come very quickly in the case of simple and well-defined proficiencies (e.g., adding fractions), or it may be extremely challenging (e.g., persuasive writing). It should be remembered that in many cases, the actual model will be a combination of rules and statistical aggregation. Variables may be defined based on rules and aggregated based on regression weights. For example, the score on a variable from a patient-management simulation might equal 1 if a bacterial culture is ordered, the order is made within the first 8 hours of simulated time, and the order is made before an antibiotic is administered; this rule-driven variable score then may be weighted and added into the final score based on a regression algorithm. The same combination of rules at the level of constructing variables and statistical aggregation for making inferences based on variable scores has been described with scoring approaches based on Bayesian networks (Mislevy & Gitomer, 1996).

### Bayesian Networks

Rule-based and regression-based procedures typically are designed to model expert judgment about the quality of a product or performance. Although it is possible to use these approaches to create scores based on empirical or theory-based models, this has been the exception.

In the absence of models based on expert judgment, constructing automated scoring algorithms will require a cognitive model that provides some framework for differentiating between the approaches taken by experts and novices or, at least, a means of separating the proficiency of interest into component parts and evaluating the level of (or probability of) mastery for each component. This approach allows for diagnostic feedback and is particularly useful for tutoring systems, for providing formative feedback to examinees, or for providing feedback to teachers to help in formulating the next step in instruction. Conceptually, Bayesian networks are similar to cognitive diagnostic models in that they represent an explicit effort to interpret performance based on a cognitive model and place examinees into mastery/nonmastery classifications. Bayesian networks are supported by a structure based on deductive relationships (e.g., relating an examinee's skills and knowledge to observable behavior). If this structure is sound, the Bayesian approach to probability allows for inferential reasoning that reverses the direction of the inference to allow for inductive conclusions about the examinee's skills and knowledge based on observed behavior (Mislevy & Gitomer, 1996). Given this structure, the Bayesian system allows for updating probability estimates based on examinee responses. The potential advantages of this type of system are obvious. The complex structural relationship between mastery of component skills and examinee behavior allows for detailed diagnostic feedback. In the case of an intelligent tutoring system, this allows for selecting the most appropriate learning module for the specific examinee. Within the tutoring framework, the probability of mastery for each component skill can be updated based on both examinee behavior and the learning modules that have been completed.

Several research projects have provided examples of how Bayesian networks can be implemented. These include HYDRIVE (Mislevy & Gitomer, 1996) and NetPASS (Williamson, Almond, Mislevy, & Levy, 2006). As with other approaches that fall under the general heading of cognitive diagnostic models, validity of the resulting inferences requires strong evidence about the appropriateness of the cognitive model; if this requirement can be met, these approaches have very considerable potential.

The preceding pages describe three approaches to scoring computer-delivered simulations. This is not an exhaustive taxonomy. For example, artificial neural networks offer an approach to creating frameworks for mapping observed performance to scores (Stevens & Casillas, 2006). It also is worth noting that a number of operational programs use approaches that might be described as "adding up the number of points the examinee received." The choice of a scoring procedure in part will be driven by practicality, but it should be driven primarily by issues related to the intended score interpretations; this choice will have direct implications for the validity of the interpretations. The next section examines issues of validity in more detail.

## Validity Issues

The question of validity for simulations that are administered and scored by computer often is reduced to evidence of a correspondence between scores produced by the computer and scores from the same task scored by trained judges (Clauser et al., 1995; Clauser et al., 1997; Shermis & Hamner, 2012). This is important evidence, but it is far from the whole story. In this section, Kane's (2013) four-part framework for validity as a structured argument is used to focus on validity issues for simulation-based assessments. Kane's framework emphasizes that the credibility of a proposed score interpretation depends on the strength of the chain of evidence leading from collection and scoring of assessment data to the ultimate interpretation or use of the scores. This chain of evidence is only as strong as its weakest link. The use of computer-delivered simulations is likely to strengthen some aspects of the validity argument and possibly weaken others; the specific effects will depend on the context. The following subsections will provide more detail about validity considerations with simulation-based assessments within the four components of Kane's framework: (1) scoring, (2) generalization, (3) extrapolation, and (4) decision/use.

### Scoring

The use of computer simulations may enhance the scoring component of the argument because the stimulus can be delivered uniformly and the scoring will not be subject to the errors that would be introduced by human judges. For example, the patient-management simulations currently used as part of USMLE might be viewed as replacing bedside oral examinations. The oral examination was problematic because the questioning was based on a real patient and each patient presentation was different. Additionally, the examiner did not necessarily ask the same questions of all examinees; instead, the examiner might ask what conclusions the examinee would draw or what next steps the examinee would take given some hypothetical test result or change in the patient's condition. By contrast, computer simulations allow a group of patient scenarios to be developed to meet the specifications of a predetermined test blueprint. The patient scenarios then can be programmed to unfold in a manner that is consistent with the patient's underlying condition, contingent on the specific actions taken by the examinee and, perhaps most importantly, uniform across any examinees who take the same actions in the same order. This uniform delivery eliminates a potentially serious source of measurement error that could significantly impact the scores of some examinees.

The use of computer-delivered simulations also allows for mechanically accurate recording of the examinee response and scoring of that response: Two identical performances will be scored identically. This mechanical replicability typically will be a great asset, but it should be remembered that it can cut both ways; any errors in programming will be replicated perfectly for each examinee performance.

### Generalization

The question of generalizability for scores from computer simulations is in essence no different than the issue in any other assessment context; the researcher must ask what constitutes a replication of the assessment procedure and assess the level of variability across replications. The simplest conception of a replication likely will involve repeating the procedure with a new set of tasks sampled to meet the same content specifications. This is an appropriate starting point, because variability across samples of tasks may be the biggest source of measurement error. The problem is not unique to simulations. In educational assessment, variability across tasks is a major source of error. Simulations, like other performance assessments, have the added complication that they tend to be more time consuming than selected-response items. This means that fewer samples of performance can be collected in a fixed amount of time allocated for assessment. Numerous studies have reported generalization across tasks as an issue for performance assessments (Swanson, Clauser, & Case, 1999).

Replication across samples of tasks is important, but it is not the only factor that might sensibly be varied across replications. For example, the specific interface might be considered fixed, but it also might be appropriate to consider scores from other interfaces with the same functionality but slightly different presentation. If there is one universally accepted tool that is used in practice (e.g., CAD software for architects, spreadsheets for accountants), the use of that tool may be mandated. If practitioners select their own tool, the variability in scores associated with the choice of the tool (incorporated into the simulation) reasonably might be viewed as a source of measurement error. Similarly, because the computer will implement the scoring rules with mechanical accuracy, it also may be attractive to think of the scoring procedure as fixed across replications. Realistically, however, we are unlikely to be interested in the specific scoring rules created by a specific group of content experts; we are more likely to view variation across equivalent groups of experts as a source of measurement error. Consider the case in which we are interested in scoring short essays. Setting aside the fact that these typically will be scored by identifying proxies for good writing (e.g., longer and more unusual words, longer sentences, more complex sentence structure), imagine that we were able to directly implement the evaluation criteria that actually are used by writing experts. It is reasonable to believe that these criteria generally would agree about which essays were excellent and which were substandard. It also is clear that individual experts would have differences of opinion. Operationalizing their specific criteria would lead to at least minor differences in the ranking of essays. Although there may be some instances in which we have a specific interest in the opinion of "Professor Smith," generally we would want the consensus of experts, and the consensus (or average) of a sample of experts would be used to approximate this value. Kane (2006, 2013) noted the importance of this source of variability in the context of valid score interpretation, but generally the issue has received relatively little attention. Clauser, Harik, and Clyman (2000) presented generalizability analyses based on a study in which three independent groups of content experts were used as the basis for building regression-based scoring algorithms for computer simulations used in medical licensing. The results indicated that the group effect had only a modest impact on measurement error. More recently, Harik, Clauser, Murray and colleagues (2013) presented correlational results for scores developed by independent groups of content experts using rule-based procedures to score tasks from the same examination. The results suggested that when rule-based procedures are used, the impact of the group effect may be substantial. The implications of this source of measurement error are neither trivial nor ignorable.

## *Extrapolation*

Simulations and other forms of performance assessment typically are used because it is thought that they measure the constructs of interest more directly than simpler selected-response items. What simulations may sacrifice in generalizability is thought to be compensated for with a more direct extrapolation to the real-world constructs of interest. Unfortunately, this direct extrapolation often is supported with good intentions and the appearance of similarity to real-world tasks rather than with empirical evidence. If the task closely approximates the real-world task of interest, it is assumed that scores from the task will extrapolate to the real world. To provide support for the extrapolation component of the validity argument, various types of empirical evidence might be gathered. These would include (1) correlations (or consistent mastery/nonmastery classifications) between simulation scores and direct evaluation of performance in the setting of interest and (2) evidence that the cognitive processes that were required for the simulations are the same as those that are used in the real-world task. When this more direct evidence cannot be collected, a potentially weaker but credible argument might be based on the overall similarity of the task posed in the simulation to the real-world setting and a careful effort to demonstrate that the simulation scores are not substantially impacted by sources of construct-irrelevant variance and not unduly limited by construct underrepresentation. To be persuasive, such an argument likely will require the support of an extensive program of research; all credible sources of potential construct-irrelevant variance will need to be considered. The approach that is best likely will depend on the specific context, but the appearance of similarity should not be viewed as compelling evidence for extrapolation. Inevitably, the simulation will fail to completely mimic the real-world challenge of interest. Consider simple essays administered and perhaps scored by computer. These essays provide a simulation of academic and perhaps professional writing. Clearly there are similarities with the real world; there also are easily overlooked differences. One obvious difference is that real academic and professional writing rarely calls upon the individual to write a short essay on an assigned topic—often a topic where no prior content knowledge is needed—within a tightly constrained time limit. This is not to say that scores from such writing tasks cannot be extrapolated to other settings, but it certainly does not go without saying that they can.

As with the generalization step in the argument, it is easier to make suggestions about the type of studies that should be carried out than to point to published results. A recent paper by Winward, Lipner, Johnston, Cuddy, & Clauser (2013) provides an example of a study in which scores from a simulation are compared to judgments made about the examinees in a workplace setting. Scores representing examinees' communication skills were collected as part of the USMLE Step 2 Clinical Skills Examination and were compared to subsequent ratings of communication skills that were provided by the directors of the residency programs where the examinees were participating in postgraduate training. The results showed a modest but significant relationship after accounting for other relevant examinee characteristics. The relatively weak relationship between the scores and the ratings was in part a function of the fact that neither of the measures is highly reliable. Kane (2006, 2013) has noted that this approach to collecting validity evidence is far from straightforward because the validity of the criterion remains open for question. It may be that this is why there are relatively few studies of this sort; it also may be that the studies are difficult to conduct.

Another important consideration with respect to extrapolation (based on the similarity between the assessment task and the real-world challenge) is the fact that examinees do not necessarily view the test situation as an opportunity to behave the way that they would in a more typical academic or work setting. Two of the present authors recently conducted think-aloud studies to better understand how examinees would interact with a simulation interface designed to assess the ability to write hospital admission orders. A number of the participants expressed the view that they would have no trouble using the interface to complete the task but that they would need to know how it would be scored—their behavior would be dictated by the scoring criteria, not by what they would do in an actual hospital setting. It is, of course, natural for examinees to want to maximize their scores. To the extent that this leads examinees to practice an important skill that might be given less attention if it were not assessed with the simulation, it *may* even be desirable. However, it also is possible that examinees will practice aspects of the simulation that are unimportant or even counterproductive in the real-world setting. For example, in medical education and licensure testing, it has become common to use standardized patients to assess the ability of physicians to communicate with patients, collect a patient history, and complete a focused physical examination. Typically, these assessments are at least in part scored using checklists to document the information collected as part of the patient history (e.g., examinees receive a point for each of the important pieces of information on the checklist that they elicit from the patient). Until recently, this approach was used for scoring several components of the USMLE Step 2 Clinical Skills Examination. More recently, however, the history checklist was dropped from that examination because it was becoming clear that rather than engaging the patient and conducting hypothesis-driven interviews to reach a diagnosis, examinees were preparing for the test by memorizing lists of questions and then asking as many as time permitted in the hope of maximizing their test scores. Professionally developed test-preparation materials supported the use of this approach (e.g., Le, Bhushan, Sheikh-Ali & Shahin, 2012). The history-taking component of the test now is scored based on the elements of the patient history that are recorded by the examinee after completing the encounter. This shifts the scoring away from information gathered as part of rote lists and toward identifying the information that is important to support diagnostic reasoning.

The point is that although a simulation may approximate the real-world setting, the specifics of scoring or other aspects of the test setting may result in examinees displaying behaviors that do not support extrapolation. Considerable attention has been given to efforts to "game the system" for writing tasks that are scored by computer. Higgins (2013) and Bejar (2013) both examined the extent to which construct-irrelevant strategies can impact scores on computer-scored written responses. The strategies include arbitrarily increasing the length of the response, including words from the prompt, and including nonrelated academic words in the response. The results showed that—depending on the specifics of the scoring system—these approaches could meaningfully impact scores. These two papers demonstrated that the strategies could impact scores; they did not speak to the question of how frequently these strategies are used by actual examinees. A previous paper by Bridgeman, Trapani, and Attali (2012) did, however, report that examinees from mainland China performed better on e-rater scores than on human ratings and speculated that the difference might be attributable to the effects of test-preparation courses. These courses encourage examinees to memorize "large chunks of text that can be recalled verbatim on the test" (p. 37). Clearly, such behavior would not support generalization of performance to real-world academic or professional writing contexts.

The examples provided in the previous paragraphs focus on circumstances in which characteristics of the scoring systems motivate examinee behavior that may not generalize to real-world situations. In these instances, the examinees could, in principle, display the behaviors of interest, but they use different strategies and, in some cases, entirely different cognitive processes to maximize their scores. In other cases, the sources of construct-irrelevant variance may be related to characteristics of the simulation itself. Simulations are by definition not the real-life activity of interest. As noted previously, even writing tasks only approximate real academic writing challenges. If nothing else, computer-delivered tasks almost always are administered with time limits that may impact performance. Ramineni and colleagues (2007) presented results showing how scores change across the examination day for examinees completing the USMLE Step 2 Clinical Skills Examination. Again, this is a simulation in which physicians interact with a series of trained actors portraying patients with specific problems. The approach used for administration results in all cases being administered in each sequence position, with examinees randomly assigned to sequences. The results show nontrivial score increases across the first several encounters of the day for the communication and interpersonal skills score, the data-gathering score, and the documentation score. The results suggest that familiarity with the simulation experience led to increased performance; clearly, the examinees were not improving their clinical skills throughout the day. Similar results have been reported for the USMLE Step 3 computer simulations described previously (Clauser, Harik, & Margolis, 2011). With this simulation, each examinee completes 12 cases. For any given test form, the same cases are administered to each examinee, but the order of administration is randomly selected for each examinee. The results of this research show a decrease in the mean amount of time used across the first several sequence positions and an increase in scores across the initial positions. Again, the proficiencies being assessed have not improved during the test day; instead, familiarity with the simulation interface and/or improved pacing appears to have led to improved performance.

### Decision/Use

One final validity-related issue for simulations is that of consequences. It frequently is asserted that such assessment tasks are important because they have the consequence of focusing attention on important skills (e.g., writing) that otherwise might be given less attention by teachers interested in maximizing test scores for their classes. Whether such "consequences" appropriately fall under the heading of validity might be debated (Kane, 2013), but either way, such assertions that assessment tasks of this sort lead to better educational outcomes deserve critical attention. Clearly, all test preparation activities do not lead to improved educational outcomes. Memorizing "large chunks of text that can be recalled verbatim on the test" does not result in better writing, and memorizing lists of questions that can be asked as part of collecting a patient history does not teach diagnostic problem solving. Preparing for simulations actually may take time away from other more important educational activities. Spending time in the classroom practicing writing short essays under time constraints—because such essays will be on statewide assessments—may represent increased time allocated to writing, or it may represent a diversion of time from other more salient writing activities. When such logic is part of the decision to introduce simulation-based assessment, evidence should be collected rather than relying on anecdotes and good intentions.

The issue of consequence as a driving force in the use of performance assessments is not new, but there are aspects that may come into play in the context of computer-delivered (and scored) simulations that deserve particular attention. Computers score performance based on attributes that may be proxies for the characteristics that experts actually value.

This is obvious in the case of scoring essays, but it is true in other contexts as well. Even if we set aside deliberate efforts to game the scoring engine (such as inserting memorized but off-topic text or lengthening the essay by copying and pasting the same text into the response multiple times), aspects of the computer scoring approach are likely to impact teaching. If students will be assessed using an automated scoring engine that values longer essays or longer and less common words, teachers will be hard pressed to teach students to follow the advice provided by Strunk and White (2000), who said that a "sentence should contain no unnecessary words, a paragraph no unnecessary sentences" (p. 23) and "Do not be tempted by a twenty-dollar word when there is a ten center handy, ready and able" (p. 77). Students with better writing skills may write longer essays and use more diverse vocabulary, but these are characteristics associated with better writing skills and not characteristics that produce better writing. Once again, the intended consequences of an assessment system may be quite different than the actual consequences.

As noted previously, Kane's framework for validity focuses on identifying the weakest links in the argument that supports score interpretation. The use of technology-based simulations in assessment has considerable promise, and excitement about the possibilities that technology creates may distract attention from the importance of carefully considering potential threats to validity. Many of these threats to validity have been considered in the previous pages, but in addition to these psychometric challenges, there also are practical challenges to successful implementation of simulation-based assessment related to the fact that simulations often are resource intensive. The next section describes some of these practical challenges and offers some possible solutions.

## Practical Issues and the Next Generation of Simulations for Assessment

### Resource Issues

The use of computer-delivered simulations for assessment raises some practical issues with respect to test development and delivery. Perhaps the most important consideration in this regard is that the simulation tasks and accompanying scoring algorithms often are expensive to produce. This has limited their use in some settings. For example, patient-management simulations have been used as part of licensing for physicians for more than a decade, but there is relatively little related use in either credentialing of health-care professionals or as part of assessment within medical schools. Each task and the associated scoring algorithm requires many hours of effort by test-development and content experts. Efforts to simplify the process by developing more general scoring procedures that can be applied across tasks have shown that although more general procedures can be used, they come at the cost of producing scores that have weaker correspondence to those that would be assigned by content experts (Harik, Baldwin, & Clauser, 2013). Attali, Bridgeman, and Trapani (2010) reported on a similar study comparing generic and prompt-specific scoring algorithms for e-rater. They found only modest differences and concluded that for some—but not all—applications, the generic procedures would provide an efficient alternative.

Limiting the scope of the simulation also may be a useful approach for controlling complexity and cost for simulation-based assessments. Much of the cost results from the need to model possible outcomes over a wide range of pathways that an examinee might use to solve a problem. Constraining the problem may limit this range. For example, the USMLE Step 3 patient management simulations require the physician to order diagnostic tests and treatments sequentially. Constraining some cases to focus on diagnosis and others to focus on treatment may substantially limit the simulated time span in which the case plays out. This could simplify programming for the task and simplify the scoring algorithm. The potential advantages of this type of strategy will be specific to the assessment. For example, Packet Tracer creates a logic-based model of the simulated computer network. This eliminates the need to program specific logic for each task and so there is little efficiency associated with simplifying the task. A similar model describing how the human body will respond to tests and treatments may well be practical in the future. Of course, limiting the scope of the simulations does not only impact the cost and complexity of scoring; this type of change also may impact both the generalization and extrapolation of the resulting scores.

In addition to the cost of production, simulations typically require a significant amount of testing time. The USMLE Step 3 examination, for example, devotes 4 hours—or nearly 30% of the allotted time—to the patient-management simulations. The ARE goes even further, with more than half of the testing time across the seven-test battery devoted to the 11 simulations. This additional time in testing centers comes at a significant financial cost, but it also may come at the expense of test score reliability. Although simulations may offer relatively more test information than multiple-choice items do, this information typically does not offset the time required to complete the task. Jodoin (2003) found that the information per unit time for multiple-choice items was more than double that offered by the more informative but ultimately more time-consuming innovative items. These results suggest that an exam developer with a fixed amount of testing time may be best served by using the more efficient multiple-choice items. This view is consistent with the results reported by Wainer and Thissen (1993) in a study that compared the relative contribution to reliability for the multiple-choice components and constructed-response sections of several Advanced Placement tests. This result may not hold for all exams, however. For examinations with large numbers of items like Step 3 of the USMLE (which contains 480 multiple-choice items), adding more multiple-choice items will yield a relatively modest increase in score precision. Alternative item types that are capable of capturing a different dimension of examinee proficiency have the potential to contribute substantively to measurement quality. Clauser, Margolis, and Swanson (2002) showed that substantial time could be productively allocated to computer simulations on a test as long as the Step 3 examination. Their analyses showed, however, that the same conclusion would not hold if the total testing time were substantially reduced. Balancing these factors may be as much a policy decision as it is an empirical one, but a reasonable person certainly is justified in wondering how the addition of simulations into a fixed amount of testing time will impact score precision and the accuracy of resulting inferences.

The expense associated with item creation, scoring algorithm development, and examinee seat time also may have ripple effects through the test-delivery system. This expense may lead to relatively small pools of simulation tasks. The simulations also may be relatively memorable, and the memorability may raise problems with reusing simulation tasks—at least for high-stakes assessments. Small item pools coupled with limitations on the ability to reuse individual tasks has the potential to significantly impact the settings in which simulations can be used; many testing programs will not have the financial resources needed, and others will be limited by the potential security risks.

The problems described in the previous paragraphs are not new. Performance assessments in general suffer from being (1) expensive to develop, deliver, and/or score, (2) time consuming, (3) relatively unreliable, and (4) susceptible to memorization or other threats to security. Efforts over the last two decades have shown that simulations can have a sustained and important place in assessment, and technical advances including natural language processing and voice recognition are likely to open new areas for simulation in assessment. But in spite of these successes and the promise of future possibilities, these practical issues remain, and short-term advances in computer technology are not likely to provide solutions. In this context, it is important to consider strategies that might mitigate these practical problems.

### Strategies for Efficiency

One approach to minimizing cost is to plan for production from the outset. At least two strategies are available. First, simulations can be restricted to areas in which cognitive or logical models make development and scoring more straightforward. When it is possible to construct a mechanical or logical structure such as that used in Packet Tracer, the original development costs may be high, but the marginal cost of developing or scoring additional tasks may be substantially reduced. Alternatively, in areas where such models are not practical, there may be possibilities for creating economy of scale by planning for modular task development and/or scoring components. For example, in the case of the USMLE Step 3 patient-management simulations, one approach is to build each task as if it were unique. This may be appropriate for proof of concept or early piloting efforts. It is likely, however, that both from the perspective of how the case progresses and from the perspective of scoring, there is likely to be considerable redundancy. It may be, for example, that for a range of cardiovascular cases, the patient's progression may be similar. This might minimize the programming required for subsequent tasks and, similarly, may provide a template for content experts to use for mapping the specifics of how the case will play out both with and without appropriate treatment and for defining scoring criteria.

Another strategy that may reduce cost—as well as potentially shortening the time requirements and increasing reliability—is to simplify the tasks. Focusing the simulation only on the components of the task that are essential to support the intended score interpretation may reduce the "face validity" of the task, but it may allow for a simpler and less expensive simulation that can be completed in less time. This allows for more tasks to be presented in a fixed amount of testing time. Because the relatively low reliability of many simulation-based assessments results from the relatively small number of tasks, this is a potentially appealing strategy from multiple perspectives. Similarly, reducing the scope of the simulation may reduce cost and testing time and increase reliability. Again, to consider patient-management simulations as an example, individual tasks could focus on diagnosis or treatment rather than including both.

One possibly obvious issue with controlling the amount of time that is spent on completing simulations is to have time allocation be empirically based. Experimental evidence is important. The specifics of how examinees use time is likely to vary across contexts, but in licensing and certification contexts examinees view the stakes as high and are likely to use most—if not all—the time available even if they could have completed the task more quickly with comparable accuracy. An empirical study of the USMLE Step 3 patient management simulations revealed that the timing allowed for individual tasks could be reduced by between 20 and 40% without impacting scores (Margolis, Clauser, & Harik, 2004).

One final strategy that may be useful in some settings is to integrate assessment into teaching/training activities. Although this does not necessarily help with the fact that simulation-based assessments often are expensive, devoting substantial amounts of examinee time to completing simulations may be viewed as more acceptable if the students are learning while they are being assessed. Simulations commonly are used for training (e.g., procedural simulators in medicine, flight simulators in aviation), and as described previously, they are used as part of formative assessment procedures in intelligent tutoring systems. In some restricted settings in which the inference of interest is directly related to the examinee's ability to demonstrate mastery in the simulation setting, these systems designed for training may provide a sufficient basis for summative assessment. For example, an examinee may be considered to have mastered the defined task/content if s/he successfully completes all components of the tutoring system, successfully logs the prescribed number of hours in the flight simulator, or completes the simulated medical procedure to criterion on several separate occasions. In effect, each of these outcomes simply represents the successful conclusion of the training process. In other circumstances, where a measure of achievement (rather than a classification of mastery) is required, the approaches described by Mislevy and Zwick (2012) for reporting scores based on through-course summative assessment may be appropriate. These latter procedures require continued research and evaluation, but they do represent a potentially promising strategy.

## Conclusions

Serious work on technology-based simulations and automated scoring systems has now been going on for nearly half a century. The recent rapid growth of computer technology and availability has made these efforts even more attractive, and certainly the potential to assess a range of complex proficiencies will grow as this work continues. Nonetheless, it is important to remember that the potential to construct technologically impressive simulations does not directly translate to valid measurement. Many practical problems remain. Improvements in technology will solve some of them, but it is important to remember that the perennial issues associated with constructing assessments to support valid score interpretation are not eliminated by the use of simulations; they may be made even more complex.

## References

Adams, C. (2013, September). *Measurement of practices and procedural knowledge in professional licensure exams.* Paper presented at the Invitational Research Symposium on Science Assessment, Washington, DC.

Advancing Assessment with Technology. (2012). A Cisco Networking Academy point of view. Retrieved from www.cisco.com/web/learning/netacad/index.html

Attali, Y., Bridgeman, B., & Trapani, C. (2010). Performance of a generic approach in automated essay scoring. *Journal of Technology, Learning, and Assessment, 10*(3). Retrieved from http://www.jtla.org

Bejar, I. I. (2013, April). *Gaming a scoring engine: Lexical and discourse-level construct irrelevant response strategies in the assessment of writing.* Paper presented at the annual meeting of the National Council on Measurement in Education, San Francisco, CA.

Bejar, I. I., & Braun, H. I. (1999). *Architectural simulations: From research to implementation.* (Research Memorandum RM-99–2). Princeton, NJ: Educational Testing Service.

Bennett, R. E. (2010). Cognitively based assessment of, for, and as learning (CBAL): A preliminary theory of action for summative and formative assessment. *Measurement: Interdisciplinary Research and Perspectives, 8*, 70–91.

Braun, H., Bejar, I. I., &Williamson, D. M. (2006). Rule-based methods for automated scoring: Application in a licensing context. In D. M. Williamson, R. J. Mislevy, & I. I. Bejar (Eds.), *Automated scoring for complex tasks in computer based testing* (pp. 83–122). Hillsdale, NJ: Lawrence Erlbaum Associates.

Breithaupt, K., DeVore, R., Brittingham, P., & Forman, L. (2005, March). *Examinees do the darnedest things: Lessons learned from the computerization of the CPA Examination.* Invited seminar presented at the annual meeting of the Association of Test Publishers, Scottsdale, AZ.

Bridgeman, B., Trapani, C., & Attali, Y. (2012). Comparison of human and machine scoring of essays: Differences by gender, ethnicity, and country. *Applied Measurement in Education, 25*, 27–40.

Camerer, C. F., & Johnson, E. J. (1991). The process-performance paradox in expert judgment: How can experts know so much and predict so badly? In K. A. Ericsson & J. Smith (Eds.), *Toward a general theory of expertise: Prospects and limits* (pp. 195–217). Cambridge: Cambridge University Press.

Clauser, B. E., Harik, P., & Clyman, S. G. (2000). The generalizability of scores for a performance assessment scored with a computer-automated scoring system. *Journal of Educational Measurement, 37*, 245–262.

Clauser, B. E., Harik, P., & Margolis, M. J. (2011, May). *Computer-based case simulations in high-stakes medical assessment.* ETS Seminar on Technology-Enhanced Assessments, Princeton, NJ.

Clauser, B. E., Kane, M. T., & Swanson, D. B. (2002). Validity issues for performance based tests scored with computer-automated scoring systems. *Applied Measurement in Education, 15*, 413–432.

Clauser, B. E., Margolis, M. J., Clyman, S. G., & Ross, L. P. (1997). Development of automated scoring algorithms for complex performance assessments: A comparison of two approaches. *Journal of Educational Measurement, 34*, 141–161.

Clauser, B. E., Margolis, M. J., & Swanson, D. B. (2002). An examination of the contribution of the computer-based case simulations to the USMLE Step 3 examination. *Academic Medicine (RIME Supplement), 77*(10), S80–S82.

Clauser, B. E., Ross, L. P., Clyman, S. G., Rose, K. M., Margolis, M. J., Nungester, R. J., Piemme, T. E., Pincetl, P. S., Chang, L., El-Bayoumi, G., & Malakoff, G. L. (1997). Developing a scoring algorithm to replace expert rating for scoring a complex performance based assessment. *Applied Measurement in Education, 10*, 345–358.

Clauser, B. E., Subhiyah, R., Nungester, R. J., Ripkey, D. R., Clyman, S. G., & McKinley, D. (1995). Scoring a performance-based assessment by modeling the judgments of experts. *Journal of Educational Measurement, 32*, 397–415.

Cook, R., Baldwin, S., & Clauser, B. (2012, April). *An NLP-based approach to automated scoring of the USMLE® Step 2 CS patient note.* Paper presented at the annual meeting of the National Council on Measurement in Education, Vancouver, BC.

Dawes, R. M., & Corrigan, B. (1974). Linear models in decision making. *Psychological Bulletin, 81*, 95–106.

Federation of State Medical Boards & National Board of Medical Examiners. (2013). Step 3 content description and general information. Retrieved from www.usmle.org/step-3

Harik, P., Clauser, B. E, Murray, C., Artman, C., Veneziano, A., & Margolis, M. (2013, April). *Comparison of automated scores derived from independent groups of content experts.* Paper presented at the annual meeting of the National Council on Measurement in Education, San Francisco, CA.

Harik, P., Baldwin, P. A, & Clauser, B. E. (2010, April). *Comparison of alternative scoring methods for a computerized performance assessment of clinical judgment.* Paper presented at the Annual Meeting of the National Council on Measurement in Education, Denver, CO.

Harik, P., Clauser, B. E., & Baldwin, P. (2013). Comparison of alternative scoring methods for a computerized performance assessment of clinical judgment. *Applied Psychological Measurement, 37*, 587–597.

Higgins, D. (2013, April). *Managing what we can measure: Quantifying the susceptibility of automated scoring systems to gaming behavior.* Paper presented at the annual meeting of the National Council on Measurement in Education, San Francisco, CA.

Jodoin, M. G. (2003). Measurement efficiency of innovative item formats in computer-based testing. *Journal of Educational Measurement, 40*, 1–15.

Kane, M. T. (2006). Validation. In R. L. Brennan (Ed.), *Educational measurement* (4th ed., pp. 17–64). Westport, CT: American Council on Education/Praeger.

Kane, M. T. (2013). Validating the interpretations and uses of test scores. *Journal of Educational Measurement, 50*, 1–73.

Le, T., Bhushan, V., Sheikh-Ali, M., & Shahin, F. A. (2012). *First aid for the USMLE Step 2 CS.* New York, NY: McGraw-Hill.

Margolis, M. J., & Clauser, B. E. (2006). A regression-based procedure for automated scoring of a complex medical performance assessment. In D. M. Williamson, R. J. Mislevy, & I. I. Bejar (Eds.), *Automated scoring for complex tasks in computer based testing* (pp. 123–167). Hillsdale, NJ: Lawrence Erlbaum Associates.

Margolis, M. J., Clauser, B. E., & Harik, P. (2004, April). *The impact of differential time limits on scores from a complex computer-administered performance assessment.* Paper presented at the annual meeting of the National Council on Measurement in Education, San Diego, CA.

Meehl, P. E. (1954). *Clinical versus statistical prediction.* Minneapolis: University of Minnesota Press.

Meehl, P. E. (1986). Causes and effects of my disturbing little book. *Journal of Personality Assessment, 50*, 370–375.

Mislevy, R. J., & Gitomer, D. H. (1996). The role of probability-based inference in an intelligent tutoring system. *User Modeling and User-Adapted Interaction, 5*, 253–282.

Mislevy, R. J., Steinberg, L. S., Almond, R. G., & Lukas, J. F. (2006). Concepts, terminology, and basic models of evidence centered design. In D. M. Williamson, R. J. Mislevy, & I. I. Bejar (Eds.), *Automated scoring for complex tasks in computer based testing* (pp. 15–47). Hillsdale, NJ: Lawrence Erlbaum Associates.

Mislevy, R. J., & Zwick, R. (2012). Scaling, linking, and reporting in a periodic assessment system. *Journal of Educational Measurement, 40*, 148–166.

National Council of Architectural Registration Boards, Architect Registration Examination Guidelines. (2013). Retrieved from www.ncarb.org/en/ARE/Preparing-for-the-ARE.aspx

Page, E. B. (1966). Grading essays by computer: Progress report. *Notes from the 1966 invitational conference on testing problems.* Princeton, NJ: Educational Testing Service.

Page, E. B., & Petersen, N. S. (1995). The computer moves into essay grading. *Phi Delta Kappan, 76*, 561–565.

Ramineni, C., Harik, P., Margolis, M. J., Clauser, B., Swanson, D. B., & Dillon, G. F. (2007). Sequence effects in the USMLE® Step 2 Clinical Skills examination. *Academic Medicine (RIME Supplement), 82*(10), S101–S104.

Shermis, M. D., & Hamner, B. (2012, April). *Contrasting state-of-the-art automated scoring of essays: Analysis.* Paper presented at the annual meeting of the National Council on Measurement in Education, New Orleans, LA.

Stopek, J. (2012, February). *Objectively scoring innovation.* Paper presented at the annual meeting of the Association of Test Publishers, Palm Springs, CA.

Stevens, R. H., & Casillas, A. (2006). Artificial neural networks. In D. M. Williamson, R. J. Mislevy, & I. I. Bejar (Eds.), *Automated scoring for complex tasks in computer based testing* (pp. 259–312). Hillsdale, NJ: Lawrence Erlbaum Associates.

Strunk, W., & White, E. B. (2000). *The elements of style* (4th ed.). Boston, MA: Allyn and Bacon.

Swanson, D. B., Clauser, B. E., & Case, S. M. (1999). Clinical skills assessment with standardized patients in high-stakes tests: A framework for thinking about score precision, equating, and security. *Advances in Health Science Education, 4*, 67–106.

Swygert, K., Margolis, M., King, A., Siftar, T., Clyman, S., Hawkins, R., & Clauser, B. (2003). Evaluation of an automated procedure for scoring patient notes as part of a clinical skills examination. *Academic Medicine (RIME Supplement), 78*(10), S75–S77.

University of Greenwich at Medway. (2014). Packet Tracer Tutorials. Retrieved from http://engweb.info/cisco/Packet%20Tracer%20Tutorials.html

Wainer, H. (1976). Estimating coefficients in linear models: It don't make no never mind. *Psychological Bulletin, 83*, 312–317.

Wainer H., & Thissen, D. (1993). Combining multiple-choice and constructed-response test scores: Toward a Marxist theory of test construction. *Applied Measurement in Education, 6*, 103–118.

Williamson, D. M., Almond, R. G., Mislevy, R. J., & Levy, R. (2006). The application of Bayesian networks in automated scoring of computerized simulation tasks. In D. M. Williamson, R. J. Mislevy, & I. I. Bejar (Eds.), *Automated scoring for complex tasks in computer based testing* (pp. 201–257). Hillsdale, NJ: Lawrence Erlbaum Associates.

Winward, M. L., Lipner, R. S., Johnston, M. M., Cuddy, M. M., & Clauser, B. E. (2013). The relationship between communication scores from the USMLE Step 2 Clinical Skills Examination and communication ratings for first year internal medicine residents. *Academic Medicine, 88*(5), 693–698.

Zapata-Rivera, D. (2007). Indirectly visible Bayesian student models. In K. B. Laskey, S. M. Mahoney, & J. A. Goldsmith (Eds.), *Proceedings of the 5th UAI Bayesian Modeling Applications Workshop, CEUR Workshop Proceedings, 268* (online). http://sunsite.informatik.rwth-aachen.de/Publications/CEUR-WS/Vol-268/paper11.pdf

Zapata-Rivera, D., & Bauer, M. (2012). Exploring the role of games in educational assessment. In M. C. Mayrath, J. Clarke-Mirdura, D. H. Robinson, & G. Schraw (Eds.), *Technology-based assessments for 21st-century skills* (pp. 149–172). Charlotte, NC: Information Age Publishing Inc.

# 4

# Actor or Avatar?
## *Considerations in Selecting Appropriate*
## *Formats for Assessment Content*

Eric C. Popp, Kathy Tuzinski, and Michael Fetzer

## Introduction

For several generations, paper-and-pencil–based assessments were the only practical option for any large-scale testing program. The development of computers with fast processor speeds and large memory capacities coupled with the emergence of the Internet changed the landscape of testing forever by making possible the delivery of test content directly to individuals on personal computers. Another radical shift occurred with the proliferation of wireless connectivity, portable computing devices, and increased connection speeds, which allowed for streaming of video with remarkable quality. The impact of these new technologies on the testing industry cannot be overstated. Paper-and-pencil testing may quickly become a relic of the past, more of a curiosity, a look back to the "old days" for new generations raised on portable devices. Multimedia content is also being introduced into the testing experience. Twenty years ago, "multimedia testing" referred primarily to the inclusion of video content using real actors in a test that was either administered via a television monitor (and stopped at appropriate moments to allow for applicant responses) or via a computer on a local network (McHenry & Schmitt, 1994). Today, multimedia testing can occur without proctoring, be administered "on the go" via mobile devices, and may include not only video but animation and gamelike interfaces. Testing has gone from a static, single-sensory experience to a dynamic, multisensory experience.

As advancements in technologies create new test format options, the formats previously available do not necessarily become obsolete. Thus, the test developer is faced with an expanding list of formats that can be used for an assessment. Deciding on the optimal format to use can be difficult, particularly when research on the new format is limited. This chapter will explore issues the test developer should consider when determining which format to adopt. In this chapter, we consider three formats: text, video (in which the characters are actors), and animation (in which the characters are computer-generated avatars). We chose these formats because they are the most commonly used in testing. The differences between text and the other two formats are obvious—mainly because text is considered a non–multimedia format, whereas video and animation are both considered multimedia formats. However, it may come as a surprise that there are differences that go beyond mere appearance between the animation and video formats, differences that will be explored in depth in this chapter.

## Formats Considered

### Text

The text format is familiar to most test developers and includes text, tables, and diagrams. A wide variety of content can be delivered in this format. Content types include simple trait statements, deductive reasoning items, reading comprehension items, mathematical word problems, and attitude statements. Text formats may be used for low-fidelity situational judgment tests (SJTs; Motowidlo, Hanson, & Crafts, 1997) where individuals are given a description of a situation and asked to respond with either the best response (the knowledge format) or the response they are most likely to exhibit if placed in the situation (the behavioral format). We focus on SJTs in this chapter in particular because they are the one test type that can be equally effective as a text-, video-, or animation-based assessment and, for that reason, serve as a great example for comparing the relative merits of different media formats. SJTs have also been shown to be very predictive of job performance. In a comprehensive meta-analysis conducted by McDaniel and colleagues (summarized in Whetzel & McDaniel, 2009), the overall validity of SJTs across 118 coefficients was .26 ($N = 24,756$). Research conducted by CEB on our SJTs shows similar positive relationships between supervisor ratings of job performance and SJTs designed specifically for roles such as bank tellers, retail store associates, call center agents, managers and professionals. SJTs have been developed for measuring constructs as varied as cognitive ability and personality (McDaniel, Hartman, Whetzel, & Grubb, 2007), integrity (Becker, 2005), teamwork (Mumford, Morgeson, Van Iddekinge, & Campion, 2008), supervisor judgment (McDaniel, Morgeson, Finnegan, Campion, & Braverman, 2001), conflict-resolution skills (Olson-Buchanan, Drasgow, Moberg, Mead, Keenan, & Donovan, 1998), emotional abilities (Roberts, Matthews, & Libbrecht, 2011), and tacit knowledge (Wagner & Sternberg, 1991).

### Video

With the video format, actors and/or objects are the subjects of the scenario content. The assessment stimulus is delivered through an acted-out scenario that is recorded either on a set designed for that purpose or on location. For example, actors could play the roles of victims or perpetrators of crime in situations that a law enforcement officer candidate may encounter while on duty. Knowledge-based topics can be presented in this way with the actor writing a problem on a whiteboard. This format may also be used to assess social skills by presenting a social situation and asking the test taker how he or she would respond in that situation. Mechanical reasoning content could be delivered in this format, with the test taker being presented with videos of different machine components and given questions about how the machine would operate.

Increased interest on the part of organizations, government, and learning institutions in assessment of interpersonal or "soft skills" such as empathy, flexibility, learning orientation, and collaboration (e.g., 21st-century skills; Stuart & Dahm, 1999) has contributed to the rise in popularity of video-based SJTs, because this test type is particularly amenable for showing (rather than just describing) various interpersonal situations. This interest is not limited to the video format only. With the increase in the access to animation technology, SJTs are also incorporating simulated avatars and environments as the test stimuli.

## *Animation*

With animation, avatars and virtual objects are used to present the content. The visual content is created entirely through the use of computer animation software. If voice-over narration or dialogue is included in the animation, this is obtained by recording voice talent in a sound studio. Additional sound effects such as background noise may be included to increase realism. The quality of animation differs depending on the amount of pixilation and the realism of the settings, characters, and motions. High pixilation coupled with photorealistic animation results in scenes that are most similar to video.

Within animation, there are three subcategories: (1) two-dimensional, (2) stylized three-dimensional, and (3) photorealistic three-dimensional. In two-dimensional animation, avatars, objects, and settings tend to be simple representations of their real world counterparts rather than lifelike images. In stylized three-dimensional animation, avatars, objects, and settings are more realistic in appearance and motions compared to two-dimensional animation but do not approach looking lifelike. In photorealistic three-dimensional animation, the avatars, objects, and settings can approach a lifelike appearance. Examples of each animation format are shown in Figure 4.1.

## Importance of a Framework

We propose a framework by which to judge the appropriateness of the various formats (i.e., text, video, or animation) for a given assessment. Advances in technology can carry a certain "wow" factor, and newer formats are attractive simply due to their novelty. The most visually rich formats developed for the entertainment industry (e.g., Pixar and EA Games) have become familiar to the general public. This can drive (or lure) the test developer toward using a particular technology without full consideration of the implications. A hasty and

**Figure 4.1** Examples of animation formats

ill-considered decision to adopt a new format may produce negative consequences that may include poor psychometrics, low validity, unnecessary expense, and delays in production schedules.

On the other hand, older formats do not include some of the benefits of newer formats. These benefits include the ability to collect more detailed data on the behavior of test takers (Sydell, Ferrell, Carpenter, Frost, & Brodbeck, 2013), a reduction in the influence of confounding constructs such as reading ability on the measurement process (Chan & Schmitt, 1997), a higher level of engagement on the part of the test takers and increased face validity and user acceptance of the test (Bruk-Lee, Drew, & Hawkes, 2013; Richman-Hirsch, Olson-Buchanan, & Drasgow, 2000; Tuzinski, Drew, Bruk-Lee, & Fetzer, 2012), and potentially higher psychological fidelity via verbal and visual cues (Olson-Buchanan & Drasgow, 2006).

We have found it helpful to establish our own framework in which to evaluate the benefits and limitations of formats in particular situations. This topic was explored extensively quite a few years ago by Motowidlo, Hanson, and Crafts (1997), where the relative merits of written, interview, and video formats for delivering low-fidelity simulations were explored. It is from their chapter that we expand on the issues surrounding newer forms of multimedia technology for delivering situations.

This framework is based on four areas that test developers will need to keep in mind when developing a new simulation: (1) psychometric, (2) applied, (3) contextual, and (4) logistical. The framework has a multidisciplinary focus, as each area draws from different sources. For the psychometric considerations, we look to research studies and existing literature for direction. For applied considerations, direction can be taken from rational evaluation or survey-oriented research. For contextual considerations, environmental conditions can provide clues. And for logistical considerations, the test developer's own experience or that of others can be brought to bear on the situation. While these categories of considerations overlap, with some issues fitting into multiple categories, the issues are grouped to help the reader think through the various areas. The nature of these categories is expanded on in what follows.

*Psychometric considerations* address the fundamental question of whether psychometric integrity (reliability and validity) can be achieved using the format in question. The test developer must consider the most appropriate way to estimate reliability and validity for content delivered in a particular format. The possibility that using one format over another will enhance or degrade reliability and/or validity through the removal or introduction of contaminants must be considered.

*Applied considerations* center on the unique benefits each format offers. These include how well a format fits the construct of interest, available scoring options, user engagement and acceptance, possible distractions, accommodation needs, ease or difficulty in developing and modifying the content, and impact on test security.

*Contextual considerations* center on the environment in which the proposed assessment will be used. These include representation of demographic diversity, desired organizational image, the expectations of test takers, the level of test taker access to and familiarity with technology, and the types of devices the assessment will be taken on (desktop computers, laptop computers, or mobile devices). While this category of considerations may go beyond what test developers typically consider, these factors can significantly impact how much the assessment is used.

*Logistical considerations* are practical in nature and center on the production of an assessment. Test developers tend to get academic training on test development for traditional test formats. Test developers may wonder how to adjust the process when working with a new format. Questions here can be very pragmatic in nature and include sourcing content writers who have experience in writing for a given format and the process for producing the assessment.

The test developer must weigh information obtained from all four categories to determine the optimal format to adopt in a particular situation. This chapter will not attempt to prescribe which format should be used in various circumstances but will discuss and compare key considerations from each of the four areas (Table 4.1).

Full information on these topics may not be easily available because the extant literature is not complete, but there are areas in which existing research from psychology and education can inform decisions. The test developer is encouraged to explore the most recent research on the formats and test types of interest when developing an assessment. For areas in which information cannot be found, we encourage the reader to conduct additional investigations before implementing decisions on format choice, particularly in high-stakes testing situations, and to contribute research findings and observations to the literature. We now turn to a more detailed treatment of the four key considerations.

Table 4.1 Categories of Considerations

| **Psychometric Considerations** | |
| --- | --- |
| | Reliability |
| | Validation efforts |
| | Impact of nonrelevant constructs |
| | Biasing of responses |
| **Applied Considerations** | |
| | Construct–format match |
| | Test taker perspective |
| | Data available for scoring |
| | Face validity |
| | Test taker engagement |
| | Test taker distraction |
| | Accommodations |
| | Content development |
| | Content modifications and expansions |
| | Test security |
| **Contextual Considerations** | |
| | Diversity representation |
| | Organizational image |
| | Test taker expectations |
| | Test taker access to technology |
| | Test taker familiarity with technology |
| | Target devices |
| **Logistical Considerations** | |
| | Content writer experience and availability |
| | Production |

## Psychometric Considerations

### Reliability

As paper-and-pencil assessments migrated to computer-based formats, considerable attention was given to comparing the reliability and validity of the two formats. Researchers found that the computerized versions of text assessments had acceptable levels of reliability (Alkhadher, Anderson, & Clarke, 1994). Less attention has been given to assessing the reliability for multimedia formats. Therefore, when choosing a multimedia format, the test developer should plan to establish an estimate of reliability using a method appropriate for the type of content in the assessment. For many simulations, including multimedia SJTs, test–retest reliability may be the most appropriate metric to use given the heterogeneity of most item content (e.g., most SJTs assess multiple constructs at the item level, Whetzel & McDaniel, 2009), but for other multimedia assessments, such as measures of skills or personality, coefficient alpha may be the most appropriate.

More research on the reliability of the multimedia formats is needed. We predict that greater attention in this area would result in assessments that are tighter and more reliable as test developers learn which content is critical and which is irrelevant for providing candidates the information required to respond to the items.

### Validation Efforts

Tests should be validated for the purpose for which they will be used. Additionally, validity evidence can be accumulated in a number of ways (AERA/APA/NCME, 1999). With text, content validation procedures are well established. Strong validity evidence (construct, criterion-related, and content) has been found for assessments in video format as well (Olson-Buchanan & Drasgow, 2006). However, the format used to deliver content may complicate or simplify the validation process.

For text assessments, validation efforts are typically conducted on the items as the test developer intends them to appear in the final assessment. Based on data from the validation process, items might be dropped or redesigned and revalidated. However, dropping multimedia items can be expensive, as generally the costliest aspect of multimedia production starts where the text format development ends. Thus, if final versions of multimedia items are dropped from an assessment, considerable time and monetary resources may be lost. With multimedia assessments, several stages of validation efforts may be prudent. Once the scripts and responses have been written, the test developer may seek to conduct an initial content or criterion-related validation study on the scripts. This allows for revisions to be made to the materials before they are developed into the multimedia format. While there is some initial research that indicates the validity of text versions is replicated in multimedia versions of situational judgment tests (Ablitt, Vaughan, Lee, & Fix, 2013), additional validation efforts should be made on the final multimedia versions if feasible. Additional validation may be particularly important if the text version requires a level of reading comprehension not needed in the multimedia version (Chan & Schmitt, 1997).

### Impact of Nonrelevant Constructs

The format chosen should minimize the impact on test scores of test taker characteristics not directly relevant to the construct of interest and maximize the impact of the characteristics most relevant.

Performance on text assessments may be influenced by the test taker's reading speed and comprehension. Chan and Schmitt (1997) found an interaction effect of test method (text vs. video) and reading comprehension on test performance. Reading comprehension was found to influence performance on an SJT when delivered in text format but not when delivered in a video format. When the assessment is intended to predict performance where the test takers will be working in the context of written language, this influence of reading ability might not be problematic and may even be desirable. However, if performance on the construct is going to be in the context of either spoken language or physical actions, the influence of reading ability on assessment scores could create significant noise in the measurement. Multimedia assessments may reduce the reading speed and comprehension requirements by relaying content verbally or visually. Items containing elaborate descriptions of scenes or actions may require extensive reading when presented in a text format. Situations in which it is desirable to minimize the influence of reading ability (for example, to limit adverse impact) may call for a multimedia format. For longer assessments, the use of multimedia rather than text may also help reduce test taker fatigue.

Conversely, multimedia could introduce undesirable factors. Actor/avatar demographic details not normally present in a written description may become salient. A text item could simply refer to a "fellow student" without mentioning race, gender, age, hair color, or style of dress. In multimedia assessments, the required inclusion of these demographic details may activate either implicit or explicit attitudes or biases on the part of the test taker. A test taker may implicitly associate a characteristic with a demographic group due to early experiences, affective experiences, cultural biases, or cognitive consistency principles (Rudman, 2004). These attitudes or biases may influence the way that test taker responds to the material (McNamara, Muldoon, Stevenson, & Slattery, 2011; Sadler, Correll, Park, & Judd, 2012). For example, if the item required the test taker to choose an option on how he or she would respond to a mistake a coworker made, a test taker may choose a more gracious response if the actor or avatar is from the test taker's own demographic group.

In some situations, using multimedia rather than text to present an assessment could significantly change the construct being measured by providing additional context that is not present in the other format. For example, a text presentation of a geometry problem might require the test taker to first recognize the problem as one that requires geometry and then know which geometric principle(s) to apply to solve the problem. Showing a teacher drawing the problem on the board while describing the problem might provide additional clues that could alter the properties of the problem.

### Biasing of Responses

Various factors apart from the construct of interest can influence test takers to respond in a certain manner that contaminates the measurement process. These factors include social desirability (Moorman & Podsakoff, 1992), demand characteristics (McCambridge, De Bruin, & Witton, 2012), and response formats (Sriramatr, Berry, Rodgers, & Stolp, 2012).

The format chosen should be one that is unlikely to bias a test taker's responses. Some formats may increase the salience of a content feature, prompting test takers to consider information they would not have considered if viewing the content in another format. For example, a text item could simply have the test taker rate the statement, "I like going to parties" to measure extraversion. Using multimedia where an actor or avatar invites the test taker to a party, the appearance of the actor or avatar (gender, attractiveness, age, clothing style, etc.) could influence the test taker's response. Conversely, multimedia allows for the subtle introduction of features of interest without bringing undue attention to those features. In a customer service scenario, the test developer may be seeking to assess the influence of a customer's race on the level of service offered. A written description in which the customer's race is explicitly stated may cause the test taker to focus on race more than if the situation were presented visually. Researchers who study the effects of race on impressions have already grasped the positive aspects of multimedia for advancing their research programs.

## Applied Considerations

### Construct–Format Match

Some constructs may be a more natural fit for one format than for another. The text format is clearly a good fit for constructs related to some aspect of reading ability, such as speed or comprehension. Text is also appropriate when detailed information needs to be presented in a concise form, such as an item that involves interpreting data from a table. Knowledge-based constructs that can clearly be communicated in written language, such as information on historical events, also fit well with the text format.

When the content involves the extensive description of a scene or situation that would take a large amount of text to describe, the multimedia formats allow for quick presentation of the information. Multimedia also allows the information to be presented globally rather than constraining information to a sequential presentation, as required in a text format.

Measuring constructs primarily related to information not normally communicated in written format may be enhanced using the multimedia formats. Constructs related to interpreting nonverbal cues such as voice intonation, body posture, or facial expressions fall into this category. While this information could be communicated with descriptions in a text assessment, doing so may place undue focus on the feature. For example, a social skills item designed to measure one's preferred personal distance in relation to others could be described in text format. However, describing the distance between individuals may draw attention to this distance when the test taker would not have attended to it otherwise. Describing the distance without communicating a judgment on the appropriateness of the space would be a challenge. Would the test developer say the one individual stood "close to the other," "too close to the other," "inappropriately close to the other"? Describing the distance in a measurement unit such as inches would introduce the influence of the person's ability to translate measurement units into perceived distances. With multimedia, the distance would not have to be mentioned or described at all. The actors or avatars could simply be placed at the required distance.

Videos have an advantage over stylized animation in communicating subtleties in expressions and movements. However, three-dimensional photorealistic animations allow for detailed facial expressions and movements that can also be fine-tuned as necessary. This permits the test developer to pilot items and to make adjustments as needed. Making this type of modification to a video requires reshooting the scene. If vocal tone, pace, or pitch is integral to the content, no multimedia format provides a clear advantage over another, but any multimedia format is favored over text, especially if additional nonverbal cues are important. For knowledge-based content where nonverbal cues are less important, the use of 2D avatars may be adequate and save the additional time and expense involved in creating photorealistic avatars.

Multimedia may also be desired in assessing constructs involving quick processing of a situation. Unless presented in a timed administration (which may introduce an unwanted reading speed element in the measurement), text allows the test taker to read the material at his or her chosen pace, processing information along the way. Multimedia, on the other hand, can present information at a pace set by the test developer.

### Test Taker Perspective

There are two basic perspectives from which the multimedia formats can be designed. In the third-person perspective, the test taker is given the standpoint of an observer who does not have direct involvement in the scenario. In the first-person perspective, the test taker is given the standpoint of a direct participant in the scene. Both perspectives will be explained via an example involving an interaction between a teacher and a student. In the third-person perspective, the test taker would observe the interaction between a student and her teacher, and select the response he/she believes is the most effective way for the teacher to respond to the student. In the first-person perspective, the test taker assumes the role of the teacher, with only the student appearing in the video and is given options on ways to respond directly to the student. The third-person perspective offers the advantage that background information can be provided through the conversation between the observed characters. In the student–teacher scenario, the teacher might mention to the student the particulars of a school policy. In the first-person perspective, the policy information would have to be provided another way such as a separate conversation with a colleague or as sidebar text. The use of the first-person perspective may help to engage the test taker more quickly; however, this still needs to be explored with research.

If the third-person perspective is used, it is important to consider if at any time during the assessment the test taker is expected to identify with one of the characters. For example, after viewing an interaction among the members of a team, the test taker may be asked, "What would you do in this situation?" It is important to be clear which character is representing the test taker.

If the first-person perspective is used and the assessment is localized for multiple cultures, the possibility of demographically oriented language conventions must be considered. In some cultures, the way a person is addressed may depend on his or her age or gender. In this case, the use of the first person perspective may be difficult. Demographically based language differences may also impact how response options should be worded.

### Data Available for Scoring

When assessments are administered in a paper-and-pencil format, little information beyond the test taker's final response is available for evaluation. With computer administration, it is possible to collect data on process-related behaviors, such as how long the test taker spends on any particular item and if one response was selected and then changed to another. Time spent on particular items can be collected in both text and multimedia. However, with text assessments, it may still be unclear what test takers are doing with that time. They could be rereading the question, considering their response, or simply be distracted. Multimedia formats may be designed to provide additional information on how the test taker is spending his or her time. Recording if the test taker replays the media could provide additional construct-relevant information for those jobs for which repeating information would reflect poorly on performance. For example, consider the job of a contact center agent in which asking for repeat information from the caller could be frustrating for the caller and reflect poorly on customer satisfaction. While the possibility exists that the test taker is just distracted while the media replays, the number of times the media is replayed becomes a data point. If the assessment is designed to allow the test taker to replay selected portions of the media or to cue the media to a desired location, data could be available on the specific portions of the media that the test taker was attending to more closely. For recent discussions on the ways in which multimedia assessments can be expanded to capture information on hidden thought processes, we refer the interested reader to two chapters that give more in-depth treatment to the topic (i.e., Sydell, Ferrell, Carpenter, Frost, & Brodbeck, 2013 and Guidry, Rupp, & Lanik, 2013).

### Face Validity

Face validity is the extent to which the test appears relevant to the outside observer. A test may have high criterion-related validity but low face validity. The test developer needs to consider which format will be best perceived as face valid by three groups: those making the final decision to use a test, those administering the test for making decisions based on test performance (for admission, hiring, or promotion), and those who are taking the test. If the first group does not perceive the test as being relevant, they will be less likely to adopt the test. If those administering the test do not see its relevance, they may disregard the results or deemphasize their role in decisions. If the test takers do not perceive the relevance of the assessment, their motivation for taking the assessment may be lowered (Chan, Schmitt, DeShon, Clause, & Delbridge, 1997), or they may develop a poor impression of the organization and choose not to pursue an association with it (Ekuma, 2012), possibly resulting in the loss of a high-quality student or employee. Test takers may also have a lowered perception of procedural and distributive justice regarding the outcome of the assessment (Hausknecht, Day, & Thomas, 2004).

Both test type and test format have been found to be related to face validity (Chan & Schmitt, 1997; Hausknecht, Day, & Thomas, 2004). While well-written text situational judgment tests can carry face validity, research has indicated that perceived face validity is significantly higher when such tests are delivered in a video format (Chan & Schmitt, 1997; Richman-Hirsch, Olson-Buchanan, & Drasgow, 2000). Some early research has shown that animation-based assessments may not show the same level of perceived job relevance as video-based assessments. Tuzinski, Drew, Bruk-Lee, and Fetzer (2012) had test takers rate the same situational judgment item presented in text, video, and two- and three-dimensional animation on job relevance and engagement. Video was rated higher than the three other formats on both job relevance and engagement. In rankings that directly compared the three formats, video received the highest average ranking on level of information, positive impression, realism, and general preference. The three-dimensional animation format was the second most preferred based on a composite of all ratings and rankings.

The "uncanny valley" may play a role in test takers' preferences for video over photorealistic three-dimensional animation. The idea of the uncanny valley was first presented by the Japanese roboticist Masahiro Mori in 1970 (Misselhorn, 2009). The concept states that people's perceptions of the pleasantness of an artificial human face increase as the representation becomes more realistic up to a point. However, people develop unpleasant impressions if the representation becomes almost but not perfectly realistic. More recent research indicates that this negative perception may involve more factors than the degree of realism in the image

(Seyama & Nagayam, 2007). Seyama and Nagayam found that viewers reacted more negatively to slight visual abnormalities (such as eyes being slightly larger than average) in realistic faces than they did in more artificial-looking faces. If photorealistic three-dimensional animation is used, the test developer should pilot the content and gather test taker reactions. A negative reaction to the avatars could impact the manner in which the question is answered, which in turn could impact reliability and validity of the assessment. Currently, more research is needed. This highlights the importance of validating not only the text version of the content but also of the multimedia version where feasible.

Multimedia formats may enhance face validity of personality assessments, which may have lower face validity than work samples, interviews, and cognitive tests (Hausknecht, Day, & Thomas, 2004). For example, an employer interested in assessing a tendency for cooperation could use a text-based personality measure, but the applicant might not see a connection between the test and the job. However, if the applicant is presented with multimedia scenarios in the workplace context and given a range of responses reflective of different levels of a personality construct, then the connection to the employment situation may be clearer.

### Test Taker Engagement

If the outcome of the test matters to them, test takers may be fully engaged in a test regardless of the format used. This may not be the case if the test taker's motivation is less. While the research on test taker engagement with multimedia assessments is limited, there is evidence that the inclusion of motion, audio, and video in presentations can elicit greater audience attention (Berk, 2012). It is reasonable to expect these principles to apply to engagement with assessments. In our own unpublished surveys on applicant reactions to a contact center simulation, test takers reported by a wide margin that they enjoyed taking the assessment and that time seemed to move quickly during the assessment. The test developer needs to find an optimal balance between the increased engagement offered by multimedia assessments and increased test time required.

To maximize test taker engagement, multimedia assessments need to be thoughtfully designed. Lowe and colleagues (2010) identified several features that increased student engagement with multimedia learning tools. The use of text should be kept to a minimum (including in the instructions) and should be replaced or supplemented with graphics, animations, and audio where possible. When video or animation is used, the clips need to be distinct and easily interpreted. Finally, animation is preferred over video when important features need to be enhanced that cannot be easily emphasized with video.

### Test Taker Distraction

The test developer should consider which format is least distracting to the test taker. Research indicates that when text passages or lectures include "seductive details" (highly interesting material only tangentially related to the core topic), students perform more poorly on the core topic than when these details are omitted (Harp & Maslich, 2005). Including environmental details in the multimedia formats could have a similar impact. Even when multimedia is the preferred format, the test developer must be aware that details designed to enhance realism and engagement may actually increase distraction. For example, in a retail store scene, inclusion of background sounds such as muted conversations could draw attention away from the main action. In the stylized two-dimensional and three-dimensional animation formats, the test developer needs to be careful that the avatars are not too cartoonish or that the mouth motions are not roughly done. Furthermore, audio not properly synched with lip movements or background sounds not synched with actions may introduce distractions.

### Accommodations

In the interest of promoting fairness, diversity, and compliance with relevant laws, the test developer must consider what modifications may need to be made to the assessment to accommodate individuals with disabilities. The purpose of modifications is to minimize the impact of test characteristics that are not germane to the construct of interest while not changing the construct that is being assessed (AERA/APA/NCME, 1999). It is not possible to build all accommodations that might be needed directly into an assessment. However, the more accommodation features that are integrated into an assessment, the easier it is for the end users to utilize the assessment.

For visual impairments, accessibility concerns for text assessments can often be addressed by the use of large fonts, screen magnifiers, or screen readers. The dynamic nature of the multimedia formats may make these accommodation tools less effective. Using a screen magnifier to view a video or animation may allow the test taker to view only a portion of the material at a time, altering how the test is experienced. Multimedia may lose the sharpness of detail when viewed with a screen magnifier. The audio associated with multimedia may help address some visual impairment accommodations; however, with this format, descriptions of the scene and of major actions may need to be provided. If any text boxes or text responses are used with the multimedia, audio files may need to be associated with them to allow the test taker to listen to the text, as a screen reader may not function with the multimedia.

For hearing impairments, the inclusion of audio in the multimedia creates accessibility considerations. The multimedia formats should include the option to view closed captioning of the dialogue for this accommodation.

### Content Development

In comparing the process of content development for text and for multimedia assessments, it is useful to break the content into two aspects. First is the core concept of the content. The core concept is the basic stimulus that will be presented to the test taker to elicit a measureable response. In personality assessments, this may be a statement such as, "I do not often initiate conversations with people I do not know." For knowledge tests, this may be a statement like, "When rotating tires, the first step is to determine the appropriate rotation pattern." For a situational judgment test measuring customer service, this may be a description of a sales clerk interacting with an angry customer. The process of designing the core concepts depends on the construct being assessed and the type rather than the format of the test being used.

The second aspect of the content is the manifestation of the core concepts. Manifestation refers to how the core concepts and the responses are presented to the test taker. The core concept "When rotating tires, the first step is to determine the appropriate rotation pattern" could be manifested in several ways. A text format could include the stem "When rotating tires, the first step is to:. . ." along with four possible responses. A multimedia format might depict a vehicle in a service center along with several objects sitting alongside it, such as a tire pressure gauge, an impact wrench, a chart illustrating the rotation patterns, and a car jack, with the test taker having to select the correct object to start the rotation process.

With the text format, the transition from the core concept to the manifestation of the concept is usually straightforward. Often the core concepts can be directly written in the manifestation form. With the multimedia formats, the process of transforming the core concepts into the manifestation is a more complicated process. The test developer needs to be able to bring a vision to life through multimedia, considering the time, effort, and resources that may be required to create the manifested content. The test developer must determine the details of the visual content of the multimedia, describe the nature and timing of any actions, and transform written narratives into natural-sounding dialogue for the actors or avatars. In situations where extensive dialogue would be needed to convey background information or where the first-person perspective would make inclusion of the material difficult (see section on test taker perspective), the use of voice-over by a narrator can communicate a large amount of information quickly.

We already discussed pitfalls, such as response bias and test taker distraction, that can be inadvertently caused by different multimedia elements. Another thing to consider is how to represent the content as a holistic scene that pulls the elements together in a meaningful way, considering the setting or background in which the action is to take place, along with furniture, tools, and other props. In many cases, animation may be more flexible and less expensive than video. Animation is superior for settings that are difficult to replicate in real life. For example, filming in a factory may require a section of the factory to stop production for the duration of the filming, which may not be practical. However, animators could create a factory scene based on a few photo images. Animators can also remove objects that might interfere with a clear shot of the scene in video. The advantage of this flexibility increases when the settings are complex or dangerous, as in representing an industrial accident or a military operation.

The format can dictate the required skills, experience, and time needed of the test developer. Test developers who work mostly with text-based content may find it challenging to put content into concise and natural dialogue and actions. Spoken dialogue tends to be less formal and terser than text content. Dialogue may include contractions, sentence fragments, or idioms not used in a written format. We suggest that the recorded audio be reviewed to make sure it sounds natural as well as effectively communicating the core concept.

Background information that is included in a text format may need to be converted into an action or conversation in multimedia. If the core concept of the content is a sales clerk interacting with an angry customer, in the text format, the material can just state that the customer is angry. In the multimedia formats, the test developer must decide how the anger will be displayed physically. The actor or avatar could be in a more aggressive posture, scowling, or have agitated movements. The anger could be communicated with a statement or just with the tone of voice.

### Content Modifications and Expansions

Content may need to be refreshed or adapted after its initial development. A rapidly changing construct such as knowledge of computer networking systems may drive modifications. Assessments may also be part of a suite of tests developed over time. For example, a test developer may develop a set of assessments to cover an exhaustive competency framework where it is not possible to develop all of them simultaneously. In these situations, consistency may be desired across multiple tests that are developed over a several-year period. Modifications may be needed as assessments are localized for multiple cultures. Organizational-specific customizations such as branding with a company logo may also require assessments to be modified.

Text assessments provide the greatest ease in expansion and modifications, whereas multimedia formats can be more challenging. If actors were used in a video assessment, the same actors may need to be used for updates. Depending on the availability of the acting talent initially used, this may become difficult. If consistency in settings is important, the same recording locations would need to be available unless a green screen was used. Animation assessments allow more flexibility in this area than do the video assessments. Avatars do not age or relocate and can easily be used for new content. While securing the same voice talent is desirable, skilled voice actors can adjust their voices to match characteristics of earlier recordings. While localization of an assessment for use in another culture is an involved process for all formats, text is generally the easiest and fastest to localize. Cultural subject matter experts can review the written material for cultural relevance and make recommendations for changes, and once the material is modified, the translation, review, and local validation process (if needed) can be started.

For multimedia formats, the localization process is more involved. In addition to adaptation of the core content, the visual aspects must be judged for their cultural appropriateness. Dialogue may have more culturally specific idioms than text content. Adapting these idioms may present the test developer with unique challenges, so it is best to avoid idioms from the beginning.

If video was used, then all scenes would have to be reshot in the target language. If animation was used, then new narration and dialogue could be recorded in the target language and applied to the existing animation. However, this process is not automatic and requires a rework of the lip synchronization of the characters. If differences in the source and target languages make the audio files in the target language considerably longer or shorter than in the source language, the timing of the avatars' actions may also have to be reworked. Avatar characteristics including skin tone, hair color and style, and type of clothing may need to be modified. In some cases, just the heads of avatars can be swapped to provide different facial features. Changes in the avatars' gender and body type/size are more involved, as these changes can also impact the movements associated with the avatar. Changes in the avatars' appearances may allow for the reuse of large portions of animated scenes, particularly where no dialogue is used.

If the ability to change surface aspects of the material is important (as in the case of customizing an assessment to match an organization's brand), animation provides a unique advantage. To be sure, a text format may be changed to include the company name and incorporate company-specific vocabulary, such as "associate" rather than "employee." However, companies may wish to see their brand enhanced by the assessment. An organization's logo can be placed in the background or on an object (such as a coffee cup or a wall calendar) in a video or animated scene. They may also prefer to have characters in the scene outfitted in a company's uniform or have a logo appear on their shirts. For video, this would generally require reshooting the content, with the associated time and costs. If the original video was shot in front of a green screen, the background could be changed less expensively, but changes in the characters' appearances would still require reshooting of the material. Animation allows for the relatively inexpensive inclusion of custom logos in the scene or of customized outfits for the avatars. If the original animation is properly designed, logos in multiple locations could be changed by changing a single linked graphics file.

### Test Security

With online delivery, particularly in unproctored and high-stakes settings, test security is an important consideration. Tests that have high exposure rates may require large item pools to ensure they are not compromised. Two basic types of threats to test security are piracy and cheating (Foster, 2010). Cheating denotes efforts to achieve a higher score on an assessment than would normally be deserved. Piracy refers to capturing test content in order to distribute it to others and to provide them with a means of cheating. Foster (2010) highlights seven main types of piracy, which we have grouped into three categories: (1) obtaining a copy of the content by intercepting a test file during download or via collusion with a test administration insider; (2) capturing the content with a camera, video recorder, screen capture program, or transcription to an audio recorder; and (3) memorization of the content during test administration to be transcribed later (sometimes performed as a coordinated effort among several individuals). For piracy to be a threat to assessment integrity there must be an avenue for the stolen content to be distributed to future test takers, and these future test takers must have a means of associating the previewed material with the content they encounter on the assessment. Creating parallel forms of items (Oswald, Friede, Schmitt, Kim, & Ramsay, 2005) that are rotated over time reduces item exposure and makes it difficult for a potential cheater to know what content will be encountered on an assessment.

One method of creating parallel forms is to separate an item into its radicals and incidentals (Lievens & Sackett, 2007). Radicals are structural elements that drive an item's difficulty. Incidentals are surface elements that do not impact the item difficulty or the construct assessed. By modifying only the incidentals rather than the radicals, it may be possible to create parallel forms without altering the test properties, such as validity, reliability, and difficulty. Although early results indicated that altering even the most surface elements of an assessment may affect test properties, this is a promising technique that warrants further investigation; see Gierl et al. (this volume) for more information on automatic item generation.

The multimedia formats confer some advantages where piracy is concerned. First, capturing images of multimedia content is more difficult than capturing text content. While screen captures or digital imaging of multimedia is possible, the process is involved and requires more data storage. Second, multimedia content may be more difficult for test takers to reproduce from memory after the assessment. Not only must the core content be remembered, but descriptions of the scenes (specifically where the key content appeared) must also be recounted faithfully.

By permitting the scene in which the action and dialogue occurs to be changed, the multimedia formats allow for the introduction of an abundance of incidental content without adding any additional time to the assessment. A scenario depicting students having a discussion could be staged in three different settings: a hallway, classroom, and cafeteria. The radical content would be delivered via dialogue or actions, with some aspects of the dialogue earmarked as incidental content that could be changed for each setting. For example, small talk unrelated to the radical content can be included to alter the appearance of the scenario. Inclusion of this type of dialogue-focused incidental content fits naturally in the multimedia formats. Even when dialogue delivers radical content, it may not have to be spoken by the same character each time. An item could be changed by using different characters to present the same information in parallel forms. These types of changes should make it more difficult for potential cheaters to link assessment content with material they have previewed, even though the radical content is unchanged.

Animation allows for easier manipulation of incidentals compared to video. If extensive modification of content is expected over time, animation provides some flexibility and cost advantages. In terms of video, if settings are changed, the use of green-screen technology may allow the scene to be recorded once and then different backgrounds introduced, but if there is much actor movement or if many props are included, the usefulness of this approach is limited. If a green screen is not used, the actors must travel to the locations, or sets must be created at a central location and the scene refilmed multiple times, which may introduce unintended differences in the tone and intonation of the dialogues. Also, it multiplies the need for retakes, as described in the production section. With animation, the same audio files can be used for creating scenes with consistent dialogue across multiple settings. With careful planning, animated action can also be reused across settings. Two different settings, say a conference room and a break room, could be designed with chairs located in identical positions, allowing the same avatar actions to be used.

Refreshing content by replacing an existing avatar with a new avatar is easily achievable with animation. To do this, only one additional voice talent needs to be recorded. In determining the time and resources required to make these various changes in animation, it is important for the test developer to consult closely with the animators, as some changes require more effort than others.

In addition, voice talent can perform multiple incidental dialogue lines with only a minimal increase in costs. As described in the production section, dialogue lines are recorded separately for avatars and later pieced together into a conversation. These incidental lines can be then be swapped in the conversations across multiple settings. If placed correctly, this can be done without having to reanimate the entire scene. By combining the various settings and incidental dialogue lines, multiple versions of an item can be created with only one recording session per character. If three virtual settings were created with three incidental dialogues, nine versions of an item could be created with the same radical content. Having different characters present radical background content can be achieved the same way in animation. At the time of the initial video or voice recordings, alternate material or scenarios could be recorded and held in reserve. Clearly, this requires forethought on the part of the test developer, to think ahead about how future modifications to multimedia can be made quickly and economically.

## Contextual Considerations

### Diversity Representation

It may be desirable to have an assessment reflect a diverse demographic. For items presented in a social context such as math word problems or situational judgment tests, representing the demographic of the target population may help reduce social identity threat. Social identity threat occurs when an individual recognizes that he or she may be devalued in a situation because of one of his or her social identities such as race or gender (Murphy, Steele, & Gross, 2007). Murphy and colleagues found that numerical underrepresentation of females in a video promoting a math, science, and engineering conference was associated with women reporting a lower sense of belonging and a lower desire to participate in the conference when compared with women who viewed the video with a balanced representation. Similar dynamics appear in virtual environments. Minorities reported a lower sense of belonging and a lower desire to participate in a virtual world when white avatars were numerically dominant than when the ethnic diversity of the avatar population was more balanced (Lee & Park, 2011). This lower sense of belonging and intent to engage could impact performance on an assessment.

While diversity may be accomplished in any of the three formats, the ease of achieving diverse representation differs. In the text format, diversity can be implied with the use of names characteristic of different groups. This can be effective for communicating diversity of gender and national origin but is limited in presenting other aspects of diversity such as age or style of dress. Text assessments can also reflect diversity through direct reference to the demographic characteristics of individuals. However, this may bring both an unwanted and unnatural focus to the demographic features. With the multimedia formats, demographic diversity can be included without any explicit reference to it. This can be achieved with the video format by securing actors with a range of demographic characteristics. The advantage with video is that the diversity is directly represented without an animator's interpretation of what physical characteristics reflect a particular demographic. Animation provides an advantage in communicating a wider range of diversity with a limited number of voice talents. Skilled voice actors can represent characters from a range of ages and ethnicities, so one talent could provide the audio for two or three characters. Animation also permits updating clothing styles without having to reengage the voice talent. Animation allows for the easy addition of diversity by including a range of avatars in the background. For example, an avatar could pass two other avatars having a discussion in a hallway. While this background diversity is possible in the video format, it is more expensive, as separate actors must be employed.

In representing diversity in animation, animators need to be careful not to default to stereotyping in creating the avatars. Unless stock characters are used, avatars are designed from core elements, involving decisions on details of facial structure, hair color, skin tone, and body form. It is advisable to have a diverse group of reviewers evaluate the appropriateness of the avatars. In regard to stereotyping, particular caution must be used in representing diversity in stylized two-dimensional and three-dimensional forms. With the stylized forms, the details available to the animators to represent the diversity are more limited than with the photorealistic three-dimensional form. Thus, the depiction of demographic features may be more of a caricature than a positive representation.

### Organizational Image

Organizations often devote substantial resources to creating and maintaining a carefully crafted public image. An organization's image can impact its attractiveness to potential employees (Tsai & Yang, 2010). The test developer should be cognizant that the format chosen may influence how test takers perceive the image of the administering organization. Leaders in an organization may prefer one format over another because they believe it better fits the image they are seeking to project. Here are just some of the possible associations stakeholders may make about the different formats: text assessments project an image of being boring or out of date (or alternatively, text assessments project an image of stability and professionalism); multimedia formats show that the company is at the leading edge of technology (or alternately, that they are unnecessarily extravagant with their money); video productions may project an image of sophistication; stylized animations may project a more casual image. If an assessment is being developed for a particular organization or for a particular target sector, it is wise to actively seek out information from leaders regarding their perspective on the image conveyed by text or multimedia assessments.

Regardless of the favored medium, keep in mind that poorly produced multimedia will certainly deflate any hopes an organization has about the potential for the assessment to promote a positive image of its company, and it could even lead to a rejection of an assessment based on looks alone. Our culture has become accustomed to high-quality video-based news and entertainment productions, and also high-quality animation material in entertainment. As few assessment providers (or organizations) have the type of budget available to hire major multimedia production companies, it needs to be determined if adequate funding is available to create an acceptable product using the chosen multimedia.

### Test Taker Expectations

Test takers may have expectations about which format an organization should use. This is different from the concept of face validity. While face validity is concerned with the perception that the assessment is relevant, test taker expectations address what individuals expect in an assessment format. These expectations may be driven by cultural trends, individual differences, target roles/careers, or perceptions of the organization utilizing the test. The amount of time young people from ages 8 to 18 years old in the United States spent with electronic visual media increased about 21% from 2004 to 2009, reaching an average of about 8 hours and 36 minutes a day (The Henry J. Kaiser Family Foundation, 2010). During some of this time, they were multitasking with media viewing or listening to multiple sources at one time. This extensive exposure to media may increase the expectation of the use of multimedia in assessments. Also, individuals who are early adopters of technology may expect potential employers to also stay on the forefront of these developments. If someone is applying for employment at a small locally owned business, he or she might not expect more than a simple paper-and-pencil–based assessment of the basic knowledge of the product/service the business offers. However, if that same individual is applying for employment at a large technology-related business, he or she may expect a more media-rich assessment.

### Test Taker Access to Technology

Text, video, and animation have different technical requirements for administration. The data transfer requirements are greater for video and animated assessments than for the text format. If the assessment is to be administered in an unproctored setting on test takers' personal computers, it is important that the target group has a connection to the Internet with adequate bandwidth. It should be kept in mind that not all members of the target group may have equal access to the required technology. In the United States, this digital divide initially referred to differences in access to technology and the Internet based on demographic factors. But now with rapid gains in accessibility to technology and Internet connectivity, the term primarily refers to the differences in the intensity and nature of information technology use (Jackson et al., 2008). However, in other parts of the world, access to information technology is not as evenly distributed (Ayanso, Cho, & Lertwachara, 2010). These differences in access may result in unintended discrimination or bias favoring a particular group.

When the assessment is to be administered at central locations, technology capabilities of the administering locations need to be considered. Corporate IT parameters may need to be modified to allow for the viewing of video files over the Internet. If the assessment is administered in a group setting, adequate bandwidth must be available to handle the peak data transfer load. Video and animation assessments typically have content that requires audio capabilities on the computer. In a group setting where test takers are working through the assessment at their own pace, headsets will be required to prevent to test takers from being distracted by the audio of their neighbors. The support software required, such as a media player, is also a consideration. It cannot be assumed that all devices will have this software preloaded, so the capacity to download support software needs to be considered.

Some test takers may either not have audio capabilities on their devices or may take the assessment in a noisy environment where it is difficult to hear the audio. If captioning (see section on accommodations) or subtitles are available, test takers may utilize these in lieu of the audio. This could lead to different response patterns. Assessing measurement invariance between the results of test takers listening to the audio, reading subtitles, or some combination of the two is an area needing research.

### Test Taker Familiarity With Technology

A factor closely related to but distinct from access to technology is familiarity with technology. Different demographic groups use information technology for different purposes and may have different familiarity with different formats. Adult females are more likely to use the Internet for communication, while adult males are more likely to use it for information, entertainment, and commerce (Jackson et al., 2008). Individuals who regularly use instant messaging and video-chatting platforms (such as Skype or Google Chat) may be more comfortable navigating a multimedia assessment and may be more at ease receiving content such as news and entertainment via short video clips, giving them an advantage with multimedia assessments. The test developer must consider the range of exposure in the target groups to the technology used in the assessment. If the range is wide, then the test developer may need to include training or practice questions.

### Target Devices

A variety of devices may be used for delivering assessments, and the test experience may vary greatly across these devices. Test takers could access an online test via a desktop computer, laptop computer, tablet, or smartphone. The small screen space provided by a smartphone may accommodate a text format nicely but may obscure important details such as facial expressions in the multimedia formats. If the assessment requires the test taker to respond by entering text, then the screen space consumed by virtual keyboards on mobile devices must be considered.

Not all devices may handle the required support software (e.g., Flash) for all of the formats. The test developer must plan accordingly if the test is deployed on multiple operating systems and devices. There may also be situations in which some types of devices should be blocked from displaying the assessment if the use of that device would put the test taker at a significant disadvantage (for example, in the case of a typing test).

## Logistical Considerations

### Content Writer Experience and Availability

Consideration should be given to the availability of enough experienced content writers. While most content writers are familiar with developing material for text assessments, fewer have had experience with developing multimedia content. As discussed in the Content Development section, multimedia content requires attention to visual details and dialogue. For large-scale multimedia assessment development, the test developer may need to budget time and resources to develop and deliver detailed training to the content writers. If common actors or avatars are used across multiple scenarios within the same assessment, content writers should be trained to maintain consistency in the roles and personalities of the characters.

If an avatar is an achievement-oriented supervisor in one scenario, he or she should not appear as a nonambitious new employee in another.

If a large amount of material is to be developed and the availability of experienced content writers is limited, one approach is to have writers focus on the different aspects of the content. As the development of the core concept material is similar for all of the formats, a larger group of writers could be utilized to develop this part of the material. Then a smaller group experienced in writing multimedia content could translate the core concepts into the multimedia format.

### Production Considerations

Unique issues associated with producing the content in the final format can play a role in determining the most appropriate format. This is distinct from content development, as it relates to the process of taking the content and creating it in the chosen format. The creation of content in the text format can be as straightforward as typing the test content into a proprietary assessment-builder program that delivers the content onto the testing platform. This generally gives the text format an advantage over the multimedia formats in regard to production time and cost. Although a number of variables will impact final cost, most multimedia productions will fall somewhere in the range of $1,000 to $15,000 per "finished minute" of animation or video, taking into account all of the costs associated with production and editing. Typically, 2D animation tends to fall at the lower end of this range, 3D animation in the middle, and video at the higher end. This is a general rule of thumb, as each project is different and requires sufficient scoping to provide an accurate estimate.

Production in the multimedia formats involves the use of specialized equipment and software requiring a specific skill set. Unless the test developer is experienced in the details of the production process of the chosen format, collaboration with production specialists will be required to determine what is feasible. Early in the test-development process, the test developer should start conferring with the appropriate specialists about design considerations.

### Securing Talent

The multimedia formats require the use of actors for video or for voice-overs. The availability of the required talent should be investigated as early as possible, particularly if the talent must meet specific demographic requirements. Production companies or talent agencies can be useful in securing the needed talent. Contractual details also need to be worked out to ensure that the final assessment product can be administered without usage restrictions or fees. Many vendors have contract templates that allow distribution without royalties or other restraints. The test developer should work with appropriate legal counsel in reviewing contract terms before committing to the contract.

### Recording Sessions

In video, one actor making a mistake may require the whole scene to be redone. As scenes increase either in length or in number of actors, opportunities for mistakes also increase. Recording sessions for the purposes of animation voice-overs are usually much shorter because they record audio for each character separately and in small segments. Then, during the animation process, audio files are associated with the appropriate avatar and built into the desired dialogue. This provides notable advantages over video recordings. First, the labor cost of the talent is reduced, as those characters with only a few lines are not required to be on location while the characters with more extensive roles in the same scenes are doing their lines. Second, not having to have all the talent available at the same time simplifies the scheduling of recordings. Third, the impact of mistakes by one voice talent on the production effort of the other talents is eliminated. When an individual makes a mistake, only his or her lines have to be redone. Fourth, the impact of a talent's mistakes on his or her own production efforts is reduced. With the dialogue from a scene broken into small segments, gaffes in one segment do not require all the segments from the scene to be rerecorded. Fifth, voice-only recordings permit the talent to read from a script, minimizing errors. One advantage of video over animation is that total production time is usually shorter. If extensive editing is not required, once the footage is shot, the final video file can be ready in a few days, whereas animation may take weeks or months to create.

It is advisable for the test developer to be present when the audio or video recordings are made to help ensure that performance is consistent with the intent of the material. For video production, this will require the test developer to be at the filming location. For voice-overs, it is feasible for the test developer to join the recording session via a phone call or video conference. If a video or audio production company is recording the talent, the company may also provide direction or coaching of the talent to help the test developer achieve the desired tone or affect from the actors.

It is particularly important to give detailed forethought before producing video. Once recording of the scene is complete, changes require both actors and production crew to return to the filming locations, increasing production cost and time. A fundamental decision is whether the scenes will be filmed on a studio set, in front of a green screen, or on location. Use of a studio set or a green screen set allows for greater control of lighting, background noise, and camera placement. Use of a set requires assembling the necessary props. While a set permits a good deal of movement in the scene, it may not be feasible to create all the settings required. Green screens allow for multiple backgrounds to be placed behind the actors after the video has been recorded. However, with a green screen, the actors' motions, particularly forward and backward in the scene, are restricted. Filming on location provides realistic settings but can complicate sound and lighting issues, as there is less control over these factors. Background noise that might not be noticed during shooting can become a distraction on the recorded video. The hum of a vending machine or the rush of air from a vent might not be noticeable in daily activities but, if present when filming, can impact the clarity of the actors' voices in the final product. Balancing the presence of natural and artificial light and placement of actors so that they will be readily visible to the camera are challenges for on-location filming. The aspect ratio and degree of definition of the video should be determined beforehand to ensure that they are compatible with the desired final format.

### Production Considerations Unique to Animation

For creating animation, there is a variety of software that ranges widely in cost, complexity of use, and capabilities (Hawkes, 2013). On the high end, there are suites of software that allow for the production of extremely detailed scenes. However, this software requires specialists in multiple areas such as motions, facial expressions, skin tones, and surface textures and requires a high level of computing power, leading to a high price tag and an extended production time. On the other end of the spectrum is user-friendly software that allows the production of scenes via "drag and drop" editing. This convenience generally comes with a limited selection of avatars, scenes, motions, and details. In the midrange is software which allows the creation of photorealistic scenes, custom avatars, and motions all within a single program. While specialist skills are required in using this program, the process is straightforward enough for a single individual to handle all the animation steps.

Several areas within animation might dictate decisions that the test developer is well advised to discuss very early on with the animators. The level of detail desired in the animation should be discussed, particularly when photorealistic animation is used. In three-dimensional animation, once the avatars and motions have been created, the scene must be rendered into a movie format. The inclusion of more details in the avatars, setting, and movements requires more memory and render time. Additional details in the avatars' facial expressions, clothing, and complexion all require additional animator involvement and computing power.

The length of the scenarios should also be discussed. Longer scenes require more animator time and computer power to process. Longer scenes will take longer to upload if the assessment is administered online. Scenes need to be written to balance the need for natural, incidental interactions like small talk with the need for succinct presentation of radical content. The number of avatars in each scene should also be discussed with animators. The software must keep track of the appearance, location, and movements of each avatar in the scene, often even after it leaves the scene. Each avatar included places additional demands on the software's capacities and should be discussed ahead of time with the animators, before characters are written into the scenes.

At times, animation may be used to convey activity that takes place over time. An animation of a situational judgment test may begin with a scene in which a manager gives a team a project assignment. A later scene may involve the manager meeting with the team to review how the project went. If the time lapse is more than one day, the need for multiple clothing outfits for the avatars needs to be considered. Depending on the software, the ease of changing various characteristics of the avatar clothing may vary and should be discussed with animators.

The effective synchronizing of audio with the lip movement is important in animation. Longer dialogue requires more synchronizing. Detail lip synchronizing can be time consuming for the animator, so this should be discussed prior to finalizing the audio script.

Finally, it may be necessary to limit the amount of motion to keep the required animator time and computer resources reasonable. A scene opening with the avatars entering a room and sitting down at a conference table requires more resources than a scene starting with the avatars already seated at the table. Three-dimensional animation software generally allows for the placement of multiple virtual cameras that determine the perspective on the scene from which the rendering will take place. Which camera angles to utilize should be decided early in the process so that the scenes can be written accordingly.

### Production Quality Assurance

For text formats, quality assurance is mainly focused on careful proofreading for spelling and grammatical issues. The multimedia formats require additional quality-assurance steps. Not only do the scripts need proofing, but the recorded audio or video needs to be compared with the written scripts. Attention needs to be given to details such as the use of contractions. When spoken, it is easy for "We will" to become "We'll." While the use of contractions may be appropriate in the spoken material, the decision to allow their use should be made ahead of recording. The text of any closed captioning should be proofed to confirm it matches exactly what is spoken, including the use of contractions.

The recordings should be reviewed for voice clarity and absence of unintended background noise. Again, the use of a video or audio production company can be helpful, as it can provide experience in detecting unclear pronunciation, background noises, or poor recording quality.

## Conclusion

The emergence of the feasible use of video and animated scenes in assessments has provided test developers with an expanded tool kit. These relatively new formats offer a number of potential benefits. However, in adopting these formats, the test developer needs to proceed deliberately to appropriately utilize them. There are a number of questions associated with these formats that have not been adequately informed by research. However, careful consideration of the issues raised in this chapter coupled with a thoughtful validation and research plan can help maximize the advantages and minimize the risks of adopting these new formats.

## References

Ablitt, H., Vaughan, C., Lee, E., & Fix, C. (2013). *Situational judgement tests: Made to measure?* Paper presented at E-ATP 2013 Conference.

Alkhadher, O., Anderson, N., & Clarke, D. (1994). Computer-based testing: A review of recent developments in research and practice. *European Work & Organizational Psychologist, 4*(2), 169.

American Educational Research Association, American Psychological Association, & National Council of Measurement in Education. (1999). *Standards for educational and psychological testing.* Washington, DC: AERA.

Ayanso, A., Cho, D. I., & Lertwachara, K. (2010). The digital divide: Global and regional ICT leaders and followers. *Information Technology for Development, 16*(4), 304–319. doi:10.1080/02681102.2010.504698

Becker, T. E. (2005). Development and validation of a situational judgment test of employee integrity. *International Journal of Selection and Assessment, 13,* 225–232.

Berk, R. (2012). How to create "thriller" PowerPoints in the classroom! *Innovative Higher Education, 37*(2), 141–152. doi:10.1007/s10755–011–9192-x

Bruk-Lee, V., Drew, E. N., & Hawkes, B. (2013). Candidate reactions to simulations and media-rich assessments in personnel selection. In M. Fetzer & K. Tuzinski (Eds.), *Simulations for personnel selection* (pp. 43–60). New York: Springer Science + Business Media.

Chan, D., & Schmitt, N. (1997). Video-based versus paper-and-pencil method of assessment in situational judgment tests: Subgroup differences in test performance and face validity perceptions. *Journal of Applied Psychology, 82*(1), 143–159.

Chan, D., Schmitt, N., DeShon, R. P., Clause, C., & Delbridge, K. (1997). Reactions to cognitive ability tests: The relationships between race, test performance, face validity perceptions, and test-taking motivation. *Journal of Applied Psychology, 82,* 300–310.

Ekuma, K. (2012). The importance of predictive and face validity in employee selection and ways of maximizing them: An assessment of three selection methods. *International Journal of Business & Management, 7*(22), 115–122. doi:10.5539/ijbm.v7n22p115

Foster, D. F. (2010). Worldwide testing and test security issues: Ethical challenges and solutions. *Ethics & Behavior, 20*(3/4), 207–228.

Guidry, B. W., Rupp, D. E., & Lanik, M. (2013). Tracing cognition with assessment center simulations: Using technology to see in the dark. In M. Fetzer & K. Tuzinski (Eds.), *Simulations for personnel selection* (pp. 231–257). New York: Springer Science + Business Media.

Harp, S. F., & Maslich, A. A. (2005). The consequences of including seductive details during lecture. *Teaching of Psychology, 32*(2), 100–103. doi:10.1207/s15328023top3202_4

Hausknecht, J.P., Day, D.V., & Thoms, S.C. (2004). Applicant reactions to selection procedures: An updated model and meta-analysis. *Personnel Psychology, 57*(3), 639–683.

Hawkes, B. (2013). Simulation technology. In M. Fetzer & K. Tuzinski (Eds.), *Simulations for personnel selection* (pp. 61–82). New York: Springer Science + Business Media.

The Henry J. Kaiser Family Foundation. (2010). *Generation m2 media in the lives of 8- to 18-year-olds.* Retrieved from http://kaiserfamilyfoundation.files.wordpress.com/2013/01/8010.pdf

Jackson, L.A., Yong, Z., Kolenic III, A., Fitzgerald, H.E., Harold, R., & Von Eye, A. (2008). Race, gender, and information technology use: The new digital divide. *Cyberpsychology & Behavior, 11*(4), 437–442. doi:10.1089/cpb.2007.0157

Lee, J., & Park, S. (2011). "Whose second life is this?" How avatar-based racial cues shape ethno-racial minorities' perception of virtual worlds. *Cyberpsychology, Behavior & Social Networking, 14*(11), 637–642. doi:10.1089/cyber.2010.0501

Lievens, F., & Sackett, P.R. (2007). Situational judgment tests in high-stakes settings: Issues and strategies with generating alternate forms. *Journal of Applied Psychology, 92*(4), 1043–1055.

Lowe, K., Lee, L., Schibeci, R., Cummings, R., Phillips, R., & Lake, D. (2010). Learning objects and engagement of students in Australian and New Zealand schools. *British Journal of Educational Technology, 41*(2), 227–241. doi:10.1111/j.1467–8535.2009.00964.x

McCambridge, J., de Bruin, M., & Witton, J. (2012). The effects of demand characteristics on research participant behaviours in non-laboratory settings: A systematic review. *PLoS ONE, 7*(6), e39116. doi:10.1371/journal.pone.0039116

McDaniel, M.A., Hartman, N.S., Whetzel, D.L., & Grubb, W.L., III (2007). Situational judgment tests, response instructions and validity: A meta-analysis. *Personnel Psychology, 60*, 63–91.

McDaniel, M.A., Morgeson, F.P., Finnegan, E.B., Campion, M.A., & Braverman, E.P. (2001). Predicting job performance using situational judgment tests: A clarification of the literature. *Journal of Applied Psychology, 86*, 730–740.

McHenry, J.J., & Schmitt, N. (1994). Multimedia testing. In M. Rumsey, C. Walker, & J. Harris (Eds.), *Personnel selection and classification* (pp. 193–232). Hillsdale, NJ: Lawrence Erlbaum Associates.

McNamara, N., Muldoon, O., Stevenson, C., & Slattery, E. (2011). Citizenship attributes as the basis for intergroup differentiation: Implicit and explicit intergroup evaluations. *Journal of Community & Applied Social Psychology, 21*(3), 243–254. doi:10.1002/casp.1090

Misselhorn, C. (2009). Empathy with inanimate objects and the uncanny valley. *Minds & Machines, 19*(3), 345–359. doi:10.1007/s11023–009–9158–2

Moorman, R.H., & Podsakoff, P.M. (1992). A meta-analytic review and empirical test of the potential confounding effects of social desirability response sets in organizational behavior research. *Journal of Occupational & Organizational Psychology, 65*(2), 131–149.

Motowidlo, S.J., Hanson, M.A., & Crafts, J.L. (1997). Low-fidelity simulations. In D.L. Whetzel & G.R. Wheaton (Eds.), *Applied measurement methods in industrial psychology* (pp. 241–260). Palo Alto, CA: Davies-Black Publishing.

Mumford, T.V., Morgeson, F.P., Van Iddekinge, C.H., & Campion, M.A. (2008). The team role test: Development and validation of a team role knowledge situational judgment test. *Journal of Applied Psychology, 93*, 250–267.

Murphy, M.C., Steele, C.M., & Gross, J.J. (2007). Signaling threat: How situational cues affect women in math, science, and engineering settings. *Psychological Science, 18*(10), 879–885. doi:10.1111/j.1467–9280.2007.01995.x

Olson-Buchanan, J.B, & Drasgow, F. (2006). Multimedia situational judgment tests: The medium creates the message. In J.A. Weekley & R.E. Ployhart (Eds.), *Situational judgment tests: Theory, measurement, and application* (pp. 253–278). Mahwah, NJ: Lawrence Erlbaum Associates.

Olson-Buchanan, J.B., Drasgow, F., Moberg, P.F., Mead, A.D., Keenan, P.A., & Donovan, M.A. (1998). Interactive video assessment of conflict resolution skills. *Personnel Psychology, 51*, 1–24.

Oswald, F.L., Friede, A.J., Schmitt, N., Kim, B.K., & Ramsay, L.J. (2005). Extending a practical method for developing alternate test forms using independent sets of items. *Organizational Research Methods, 8*, 149–164.

Richman-Hirsch, W.L., Olson-Buchanan, J.B., & Drasgow, F. (2000). Examining the impact of administration medium on examinee perceptions and attitudes. *Journal of Applied Psychology, 85*(6), 880–887. doi:10.1037//0021–9010.85.6.880

Roberts, R.D., Matthews, G., & Libbrecht, N. (2011). *Video-based SJTs to assess emotional abilities: Innovative approaches to examine the relation with social-emotional outcomes.* Paper presented at the Annual Conference of the Society for Industrial and Organizational Psychology.

Rudman, L.A. (2004). Sources of implicit attitudes. *Current Directions in Psychological Science, 13*(2), 79–82. doi:10.1111/j.0963-7214.2004.00279.x

Sadler, M.S., Correll, J., Park, B., & Judd, C.M. (2012). The world is not black and white: Racial bias in the decision to shoot in a multiethnic context. *Journal of Social Issues, 68*(2), 286–313. doi:10.1111/j.1540-4560.2012.01749.x

Seyama, J., & Nagayama, R.S. (2007). The uncanny valley: Effect of realism on the impression of artificial human faces. *Presence: Teleoperators & Virtual Environments, 16*(4), 337–351.

Sriramatr, S., Berry, T.R., Rodgers, W., & Stolp, S. (2012). The effect of different response formats on ratings of exerciser stereotypes. *Social Behavior & Personality: An International Journal, 40*(10), 1655–1665.

Stuart, L., & Dahm, E. (1999). *21st century skills for 21st century jobs.* United States Department of Commerce. Retrieved July 28, 2013, from http://digitalcommons.ilr.cornell.edu/?utm_source=digitalcommons.ilr.cornell.edu%2fkey_workplace%2f151&utm_medium=pdf&utm_campaign=pdfcoverpages/

Sydell, E., Ferrell, J., Carpenter, J., Frost, C., & Brodbeck, C. (2013). Simulation scoring. In M. Fetzer & K. Tuzinski (Eds.), *Simulations for personnel selection* (pp. 83–107). New York: Springer Science + Business Media.

Tsai, W., & Yang, I.W. (2010). Does image matter to different job applicants? The influences of corporate image and applicant individual differences on organizational attractiveness. *International Journal of Selection & Assessment, 18*(1), 48–63. doi:10.1111/j.1468-2389.2010.00488.x

Tuzinski, K., Drew, E.N., Bruk-Lee, V., & Fetzer, M. (2012, April). *Applicant perceptions of multimedia situational judgment tests.* Paper presented at the annual meeting of the Society for Industrial and Organizational Psychology, San Diego, CA.

Wagner, R.K., & Sternberg, R.J. (1991). *Tacit Knowledge Inventory for Managers: User manual.* San Antonio, TX: The Psychological Corporation.

Whetzel, D.L., & McDaniel, M.A. (2009). Situational judgment tests: An overview of current research. *Human Resource Management Review, 19*, 188–202.

# Commentary on Chapters 1–4:
# Using Technology to Enhance Assessments

Stephen G. Sireci

It is a pleasure to have the opportunity to comment on four chapters that address some of the most cutting-edge developments in contemporary educational and psychological assessment. It is impossible to be a psychometrician living in this 21st century and not be excited about the potential of technology to improve the validity and efficiency of our assessments. But how do we do it? As these four chapters illustrate, important developments have already been implemented in large-scale testing programs that have used computerized technology to transform the testing experience and expand the types of characteristics we can measure.

When I think about technology and its potential for improving assessment, I look to the gaming industry as the model for what is possible. As Mislevy and colleagues (this volume) indicate, we have much to learn from the gaming industry. I agree. I cannot get my children off their game consoles. They are completely engaged. Actually, engrossed is a better description. Moreover, I can see the games they play are adapting to their responses and are teaching them how to get better. They are *learning* as they play, and the games are *assessing* them. In essence, the video games my children play are tailoring the game to their current proficiency level and are integrating assessment with instruction. And they are doing it without item response theory (IRT)!

### Reactions to the Individual Chapters

The four chapters I had the pleasure of reviewing addressed different aspects of technology-enhanced assessments. The Parshall and Guille (this volume) chapter provides important insights about conceiving, designing, and implementing technology in a testing program. Product management and implementation are not topics covered in doctoral programs in measurement, yet they are critically important for successful measurement. Their chapter contains a wealth of information regarding how test construction must adapt to facilitate the incorporation of technology-enhanced items. In particular, the Agile product development method seems well aligned for testing programs that are new to implementing technology. As Parshall and Guille point out, "Agile methods . . . have a particular value when much is unknown and risk may be high" (p. 20).

The Parshall and Guille chapter was also helpful in understanding the difficulties in properly implementing technology into an assessment program. Psychometricians and test developers often come up with creative ideas for using technology to improve an assessment but are frustrated when the technology team tells them it is not possible or will take much longer than expected. Parshall and Guille helped me understand the realistic details of successful implementation of large-scale computerized innovations (e.g., bandwidth, accounting for software updates, etc.). The processes they described about considering and measuring risk, benefit, complexity, feasibility, and cost are likely to be very helpful to testing programs as they address the best ways to improve their assessments using technology. In short, this chapter should help us all get out of the "sandbox" and into the "toolbox."

Given my introductory remarks, you can imagine I was particularly interested in the game-based assessment chapter by Mislevy and colleagues (this volume). They also pointed out the adaptive nature of recreational games by stating,

> Many recreational games already assess players, at least implicitly. They gather information about what players are doing well and what they are not, to adjust the pace or difficulty to optimize engagement.

(p. 24)

Their chapter provides overviews of several models for developing and scoring game-based assessments. In so doing, they cover a wide terrain from evidence-centered assessment design to latent variable models for scoring examinees.

This Mislevy and associates chapter argues that game-based assessments need a psychometric foundation. I believe that is true at a fundamental level. That is, the same standards of reliability, validity, and fairness should apply. However, I think we have a lot more to learn from the recreational gaming industry than it has to learn from us. As I mentioned earlier, Sony, Nintendo, and others are engaging players (examinees?), assessing them, and adapting their games accordingly, and I do not think they have even heard of IRT. I am curious about the rules they use to present more- or less-challenging material to players and reward them. Such topics are beyond the scope of the Mislevy and associates chapter, but I believe if we look more to the gaming industry for ideas and solutions rather than try to impose 20th-century psychometrics on them, we will have a lot more to gain. Clearly, they are not using evidence-centered design, because their goals are different than those of an educational test. However, these games have goals and objectives—just as we do in education. Thus, I would like to know more about the design features of recreational games that allow them to engage players, assess them, adapt the games to them, and reward them before I think about psychometric design. The more we can make game-based assessments seem more like games than assessments, the more likely we are to engage examinees and improve our measurement of their proficiencies.

In considering "gamifying" assessments, it is important to note that when a player plays a recreational game, he or she is responding to hundreds of "items" in a relatively short period of time, and the player is likely to "retest" very soon. These are features that will be of great benefit in lower-stakes testing situations, and so the reliability of a provisional score is of little value. Of course, as we apply gaming to higher-stakes situations, the reliability of classification decisions will be of utmost importance.

The Clauser, Margolis, and Clauser (this volume) chapter provides a helpful overview of many important issues in implementing simulations in an assessment, and they provide several examples of programs that are successfully using simulations in both low- and high-stakes settings. I found their review of operational programs illuminating, as was their coverage of the validity issues involved in using simulations. They point out that although simulations are "complex and have the potential to produce large amounts of scorable data" (p. 61), little is currently known about which are the best data to gather and how they should be scored. What is known is reviewed in their chapter, which is one reason I found it so helpful.

Although all four chapters addressed validity issues to some degree, I liked that Clauser and colleagues explicitly connected validity issues in using simulations to construct representation and construct-irrelevant variance. As Messick (1989) pointed out, "Tests are imperfect measures of constructs because they either leave out something that should be included according to the construct theory or else include something that should be left out, or both" (p. 34). Messick introduced the terms "construct underrepresentation" and "construct-irrelevant variance" to refer to these threats to validity.

Like the avatars discussed in the Popp, Tuzinski, and Fetzer (this volume) chapter and the computerized innovations discussed in the other chapters, simulations should be used to *increase* construct representation, which will lead to increased validity. Much of the concerns raised across these four chapters focus on ensuring that increased is accomplished without introducing factors unrelated to the construct that will affect test performance. An excerpt from the conclusion of the Clauser and associates chapter is worthy of repeating here: "the potential to construct technologically impressive simulations does not directly translate to valid measurement" (p. 76).

The fourth chapter, by Popp and colleagues (this volume), provides a comprehensive review of formats for portraying situations to examinees, including the use of *avatars*. I appreciated their discussion of the three major presentation formats (text, video, animation) and the advantages and disadvantages of each. They provide helpful guidance regarding the factors that would suggest one format over another, and these factors include both practical issues (e.g., ease with which changes can be made to a scenario) and validity issues (e.g., improved construct representation). This chapter separates itself from other writings in this area in that the authors discuss many psychological variables that should be considered in presenting situations to examinees that have not gotten much attention (e.g., Is the examinee experience first person or third person? How do ethnic differences among actors in a video differentially affect examinees of different ethnicity? How realistic should we make the features of an avatar?).

Popp and colleagues also provide guidance regarding issues to consider in scoring situation-based assessments (e.g., If an examinee replays a situation multiple times, should that count against their score?) and adapting them for use across multiple contexts such as for use across different languages. Like the other chapters, it contains a wealth of practical information for enhancing assessments with a particular form of technology.

I will not comment further on the specifics of each chapter because I encourage you to read them. In the remainder of this invited commentary, I will identify a few themes across the chapters that warrant further discussion.

## Technological Enhancements and Validity

As mentioned earlier, all chapters touched on important validity and practical issues. The coverage of practical issues was very instructive across chapters, but I was disappointed that none of the chapters used or mentioned the five sources of validity evidence described in the *Standards for Educational and Psychological Testing* (American Educational Research

Association [AERA], American Psychological Association, & National Council on Measurement, 1999, 2014). Some of the discussion of validity was outdated. For example, in one chapter, the validity of a type of test was reported as a numerical value (.26), as if that were sufficient justification for test use. The Clauser and associates chapter used Kane's (2013) validity framework, which is laudable, but given the book you are reading is published by one of the organizations that cosponsored the *Standards*, it was surprising their value was not given more attention across the four chapters.

The frameworks provided by the authors for evaluating technological innovations were valuable in that they combined practical and psychometric issues. I believe explicitly focusing on the five sources of validity evidence would enhance the evaluation. For example, as all four chapters point out, the degree to which technology-enhanced assessments improve construct representation is one of the most important factors in considering or implementing technological innovations. At least four of the five sources of validity evidence—test content, response processes, internal structure, and relations to other variables—are extremely valuable in evaluating increased construct representation. Unfortunately, only validity evidence based on test content was covered at any length in the chapters. A much more powerful evaluation of technological enhancements on construct representation would involve cognitive labs, dimensionality studies, and criterion-related validity studies.

Another validity issue mentioned by all four chapters was the degree to which cheating or test preparation activities might introduce construct-irrelevant variance. A proper evaluation of that threat should involve validity evidence based on the consequences of testing (e.g., Do new test-preparation courses emerge, and what do they teach? Are examinees who cannot afford those courses at a disadvantage?). Thus, I encourage readers to consider the validity issues raised in these chapters alongside a close reading of the AERA and associates (2014) *Standards*.

One other issue touched on in some of the chapters that warrants further discussion is the degree to which technology can promote access to individuals with disabilities and to linguistic minorities who are not fully proficient in the language in which the test is administered. As Popp and colleagues pointed out, video can be a better way to better convey situations to linguistic minorities relative to text presentation. Computerized test administrations can also be used to facilitate read-aloud test administrations, increased size of text and graphics (perhaps using a larger screen), and building in *rewards* to keep students engaged.

## More Gamelike Than Testlike

In returning to the issue of gaming technology, it is clear recreational video games offer flexibility to players. They can choose their own avatars, pause the game to go off on quests or to get a tutorial, and they can start at the beginning, or in the middle, if they experience failure. Educational video games also offer much flexibility. Although they offer flexibility, these games are essentially standardized across players, but they adapt for each player. Contrast that flexibility with current assessments that must be taken one item at a time, in a specific order, without any opportunity to review previous items or pause for a break. Of course, high-stakes testing situations and large testing volumes offer challenges to offering such flexibility, but I remain hopeful we can move closer to what the gaming industry offers in a way that improves validity and fairness for all. Hopefully, we will read about that in the future, in volume 2 of this book!

## References

American Educational Research Association, American Psychological Association, & National Council on Measurement in Education. (1999). *Standards for educational and psychological testing.* Washington, DC: American Educational Research Association.

American Educational Research Association, American Psychological Association, & National Council on Measurement in Education. (2014). *Standards for educational and psychological testing.* Washington, DC: American Educational Research Association.

Kane, M. (2013). Validating the interpretations and uses of test scores. *Journal of Educational Measurement, 50*(1), 1–73.

Messick, S. (1989). Validity. In R. Linn (Ed.), *Educational measurement* (3rd ed., pp. 13–100). Washington, DC: American Council on Education.

# 5

# Using Technology-Enhanced Processes to Generate Test Items in Multiple Languages

Mark J. Gierl, Hollis Lai, Karen Fung, and Bin Zheng

## Introduction

Automatic item generation (AIG; Embretson & Yang, 2007; Gierl & Haladyna, 2013; Irvine & Kyllonen, 2002) is a rapidly evolving research area where cognitive and psychometric theories are used to produce tests that contain items created using computer technology. AIG serves as a technology-enhanced approach to item development that addresses one of the most pressing and challenging issues facing educators today: the rapid and efficient production of high-quality, content-specific test items. AIG can be characterized as the process of using models to generate items with the aid of computer technology. The role of the test development specialist is critical for the creative task of identifying the required content as well as designing and developing meaningful item models. The role of computer technology is critical for the algorithmic task of systematically combining large amounts of content in each item model to produce new assessment tasks. By combining content expertise with computer technology, testing specialists can produce models that yield large numbers of high-quality items in a short period of time.

## Multilingual Automatic Item Generation

There are practical reasons why large numbers of items are needed in modern 21st-century testing programs. A flexible and accommodating administration schedule has become a requirement in most programs because examinees have come to expect continuous, on-demand testing, while decision makers want timely access to information about these examinees. But with flexibility also comes risk and, hence, adequate item exposure controls are needed to ensure that the administration is secure so each test yields fair and accurate information about all examinees. Typically, a bank is developed that serves as a repository for the items as well as a database to maintain information about these items, including their content codes, psychometric characteristics, and usage rates. But with frequent testing, these banks must be continually replenished with new items to ensure that examinees receive a constant supply of unique, content-specific assessment tasks while, at the same time, limiting item exposure within the testing environment to maintain security.

For much of the 20th century, tests were developed and administered in the language specific to the culture for the regional exam. But profound global, technological, and economic changes occurring at the end of the 20th century have resulted in a dramatic increase in multilingual testing. Educational and psychological tests are now developed and administered to examinees in different languages across diverse cultures throughout the world (Hambleton, Merenda, & Spielberger, 2005). As a result, large numbers of items are not only required to promote flexible administration with adequate security but also must be developed in multiple languages. This multilingual requirement simply adds to the already costly, time-consuming, and challenging process of item development.

Take, for instance, the item-development challenges inherent in the international comparative achievement testing conducted by the Organization for Economic Co-Operation and Development (OECD) as part of the Programme for International Student Assessment (PISA). OECD member countries initiated PISA in 1997 as a way to measure the knowledge, skills, and competencies of 15-year-olds in the core content areas of mathematics, reading, and science. The results from these tests are intended to allow educators and policy makers to compare and contrast the performance of students from around the world and to guide future educational policies and practices. The broad scope and growing popularity of PISA is extraordinary. The first data collection began in 2000 with 32 countries. Since that time, the number of participating countries has only increased. The fifth and most recent data collection was in 2012. It included 66 participating countries with anywhere from 4,500 to 10,000 students being tested in each participating country. Paper-based tests are administered most frequently, with students writing both multiple-choice and constructed-response items as part of a 2-hour session. To cover a broad range of content, a sampling design is used in which students write different combinations of items. The outcome from this design is a basic knowledge and skill profile for a typical 15-year-old within each country. To accommodate the linguistic diversity among member countries, 101 different "national versions" of the PISA exam were created, validated, and then administered in 45 different languages (OECD, 2012).

Other equally formidable but not-so-obvious examples of multilingual item development can readily be found. The current testing practices in the European Personnel Selection Office (EPSO) serve as an example. The EPSO is responsible for selecting the staff required for a wide range of high-profile governmental agencies throughout the European Union (EU), including the European Commission, the European Court of Justice, and the European Parliament. EPSO evaluates approximately 100,000 candidates per year using a three-stage testing process. The first stage is a computer-based preselection test administered in each EU country. The computer-based component is a two-part exam in which the first part contains multiple-choice items designed to evaluate the candidates' knowledge of the EU, and the second part focuses on numeric and verbal reasoning skills. Currently, the first-stage computer-based preselection Part 1 knowledge test contains 25 items distributed across 100 unique forms. It is administered in the three core languages of English, French, and German. The first-stage computer-based preselection Part 2 skills test contains a variable number of items administered adaptively. EPSO maintains a bank containing tens of thousands of items for the first-stage computer-based skills test. It is administered in all 23 official EU languages. The second stage of the selection process requires the candidate to write a paper-based exam containing both multiple-choice and constructed-response items designed to evaluate the specialized knowledge particular to their job competition. The specialized paper-based exams each have different item lengths, specific to each content area. This exam is administered in 23 different languages. Candidates who successfully complete the first two stages are then invited to the EPSO headquarters in Brussels for the third-stage oral examination, conducted in one of the three core languages (Stefan-Hermann Meyer, personal communication, February 13, 2013).

These OECD and EPSO examples are but two from a list of many that help highlight the daunting multilingual item-development challenges facing many testing organizations today. If we look into the future, the requirements for multilingual testing are only expected to increase as global development, technological changes, and economic expansion continue virtually unabated. One way to address the challenge of creating more items in multiple languages is to hire a larger number of developers and translators to work with the traditional, one-item-at-a-time content-specialists approach. But this option is costly and time consuming as well as riddled with complex item development and translation challenges (see, for example, chapter 5, "Translation and Verification of the Test and Survey Materials" in the *PISA 2009 Technical Report*, 2010). An alternative method for item development that may help address the growing need to produce large numbers of new multilingual test items is through the use of AIG. In the next section, we describe and illustrate a technology-enhanced three-step process for AIG that could prove useful in producing new multilingual items in an efficient and cost-effective manner.

## Generating Items Using an Automated Three-Step Process

Gierl, Lai, and Turner (2012; see also Gierl & Lai, 2013a) described a three-step process for generating test items in a single language. In step 1, the content required for the generated items is identified by test-development specialists. In step 2, an item model is developed by the test-development specialists to specify where content is placed in each generated item. In step 3, computer-based algorithms are used to place the content specified in step 1 in the item model developed in step 2.

### Step #1: Identify Content for Generated Test Items

To begin, test-development specialists identify the content required to produce new test items. Gierl, Lai, and Turner (2012) introduced the concept of a *cognitive model for AIG* in the area of medical testing. Figure 5.1 contains a cognitive model for AIG required to diagnose and treat complications with hernias. This cognitive model was created by two medical content specialists, thereby serving as a representation of how they think about and solve problems related to hernias. The content specialists, who were both experienced medical examination item writers and practicing physicians, were asked to describe the knowledge and clinical reasoning skills required to diagnose hernia-related medical problems. Their knowledge and skills were identified in an inductive manner using a verbal reporting method when the content specialists were given an existing multiple-choice item and asked to identify and describe the key information that would be used to solve the problem specified in the item. This representation was documented as a cognitive model.

The cognitive structure in Figure 5.1 highlights the knowledge and skills required to make medical diagnostic inferences in order to treat the problem. It is presented in three panels. The top panel identifies the problem and its associated scenarios. Four different

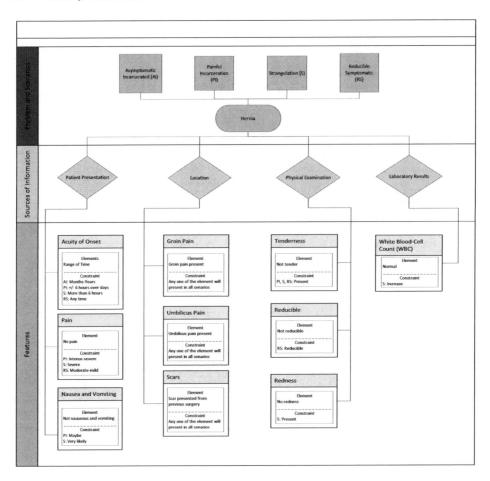

**Figure 5.1** Cognitive model for AIG using hernia example

hernia scenarios are used in this example: asymptomatic incarcerated (AI), painful incarcerated (RI), strangulation (S), and reducible symptomatic (RS). The middle panel specifies the relevant sources of information. Four sources of information are specified for this problem: patient presentation, location, physical examination, and laboratory results. The bottom panel highlights the salient features. Our example contains 10 features: acuity of onset, pain, nausea and vomiting, groin pain, umbilicus pain, scars, tenderness, reducible, redness, and white blood-cell count (WBC). In our example, the Location source of information, for instance, has three features: groin pain, umbilicus pain, and scars. Each feature, in turn, includes elements and constraints. The first component for a feature is the element. Elements contain content specific to each feature that can be manipulated for item generation. For the groin pain feature of Location, groin pain is either present or absent. The second component for a feature is the constraint. Each element is constrained by the scenarios specific to this problem. For example, strangulation (S) is associated with more than six hours in the acuity-of-onset feature for the patient presentation source of information (i.e., S: More than 6 hours at the top left side of the Features panel in Figure 5.1).[1]

### Step #2: Item Model Development

Once the content is identified in the cognitive model, it must be placed into the format required for functional item generation. Item models provide this functional format (Bejar, 1996, 2002; Bejar, Morley, Wagner, Bennett, & Revuelta, 2003; LaDuca, Staples, Templeton, & Holzman, 1986). Item models contain the components in an assessment task that require content. These components include the stem, the options, and the auxiliary information. The stem contains context, content, item, and/or the question the examinee is required to answer. The options include a set of alternative answers with one correct option and one or more incorrect options. Both stem and options are required for multiple-choice item models. Only the stem is created for constructed-response item models. Auxiliary information includes any additional content, in either the stem or option, required to generate an item, including text, images, tables, graphs, diagrams, audio, and/or video.

A sample parent item and the associate item model are presented in Figure 5.2. The item model contains the stem, which specifies the context, content, item, and/or the question the examinee is required to answer. The stem also highlights the sources of information that will be manipulated for item generation as well as the location of those sources in the model itself. For the Figure 5.2 example, the sources of information include age, gender, pain, location, acuity of onset, physical examination, and the white blood-cell count (WBC).

### Step #3: Item Generation Using Computer Technology

Once the content has been identified and the item models are created by the test development specialists, this information is assembled to produce new items. This assembly task must be conducted with some type of computer-based assembly system because it is often a large and complex combinatorial problem. We illustrate the use of technology for generating test items using the IGOR software described by Gierl, Zhou, and Alves (2008). IGOR, which stands for **i**tem **g**enerat**or**, is a JAVA-based program designed to assemble the content specified in an item model, subject to elements and constraints articulated in the cognitive model. The logic behind IGOR is straightforward: Iterations are conducted to assemble all possible combinations of elements and options, subject to the constraints. Without the use of constraints, all of the variable content would be systematically combined to create new items. However, some of these items would not be sensible or useful. Constraints therefore serve as restrictions that must be applied during the assembly task so that meaningful items are generated. Constraints are identified by test-development specialists using professional judgment. For instance, asymptomatic incarcerated hernias (AI) are constrained by time because this type of hernia—according to the physicians who developed the cognitive model—is only associated with months or years in the acuity-of-onset feature (i.e., AI: Months-Years at the top left side of the Features panel in the Figure 5.1 example). IGOR is character set neutral. As a result, characters from any language can be used to generate test items.

---

A 24-year-old man presented with a mass in the left groin. It occurred suddenly 2 hours ago while lifting a piano. On examination, the mass is firm and located in the left groin. Which of the following is the next best step?

A [AGE]-year-old [GENDER] presented with a mass [PAIN] in [LOCATION]. It occurred [ACUITYOFONSET]. On examination, the mass is [PHYSICALEXAMINATION] and lab work came back with [WBC]. Which of the following is the next best step?

---

**Figure 5.2** Parent item (top) and the associated item model (bottom) used to measure examinees' ability to diagnose a hernia

**Types of Item Models: The Importance of *n*-Layer Modeling for Multilingual AIG**

Test development specialists have the critical role of identifying the required content and designing the item models for the generation task. The principles, standards, guidelines, and practices used for traditional item development (e.g., Case & Swanson, 2002; Downing & Haladyna, 2006; Haladyna & Rodriguez, 2013; Schmeiser & Welch, 2006) provide the foundational concepts necessary for creating item models. Some item model examples are also available in the literature (e.g., Bejar et al., 2003; Case & Swanson, 2002; Gierl & Lai, 2013b; Gierl et al., 2008). Gierl and Lai (2012) recently described two types of item models that can be created for AIG (see also Gierl & Lai, 2013a): 1-layer and *n*-layer item models.

*1-Layer Item Modeling*

The goal of item generation using the 1-layer item model is to produce new assessment tasks by manipulating a relatively small number of elements at one level in the model. This type of item model now dominates the practical applications in AIG described in the literature (e.g., Arendasy, 2005; Arendasy & Sommer, 2007; Bejar, 1990; Embretson, 2002; Embretson & Daniels, 2008; Sinharay & Johnson, 2013; Wendt, Kao, Gorham, & Woo, 2009). Typically, the starting point is to use an existing test item called a "parent." Parent items can be found by reviewing previously administered tests, by drawing on a bank of existing test items, or by creating the parent item directly. The parent item highlights the underlying structure of the model, thereby providing a point of reference for creating alternative items (see Figure 5.2). Then an item model is created by identifying elements in the parent item that can be manipulated to produce new items.

One drawback of using a 1-layer item model for AIG is that relatively few elements can be manipulated because the number of potential elements is fixed to the total number of sources of information and/or features in the stem. By restricting the element manipulations to a small number, the generated items may have the undesirable quality of appearing too similar to one another. An example of a 1-layer item model for the hernia example is presented in Figure 5.3. In this example, 7 of the 10 elements presented in the Features level from the bottom panel of Figure 5.1 are manipulated. These elements include age, gender, pain, location, acuity of onset, physical examination, and white blood-cell count.

| | |
|---|---|
| *Stem* | A [AGE]-year-old [GENDER] presented with a mass [PAIN] in [LOCATION]. It occurred [ACUITYOFONSET]. On examination, the mass is [PHYSICALEXAMINATION] and lab work came back with [WBC]. Which of the following is the next best step? |
| *Elements* | [AGE] (Integer): From 25.0 to 60.0, by 15.0 |
| | [GENDER] (String): 1: man 2: woman |
| | [PAIN] (String): 1: 2: and intense pain 3: and severe pain 4: and mild pain |
| | [LOCATION] (String): 1: the left groin 2: the right groin 3: the umbilicus 4: an area near a recent surgery |
| | [ACUITYOFONSET] (String): 1: a few months ago 2: a few hours ago 3: a few days ago 4: a few days ago after moving a piano |
| | [PHYSICALEXAMINATION] (String): 1: protruding but with no pain 2: tender 3: tender and exhibiting redness 4: tender and reducible |
| | [WBC] (String): 1: normal results 2: elevated white blood-cell count |
| *Options* | exploratory surgery; reduction of mass; hernia repair; ice applied to mass |

**Figure 5.3** 1-layer item model for the hernia example

### n-Layer Item Models

The second type of item model can be described as *n*-layer. The goal of AIG using the *n*-layer item model is to produce items by manipulating a relatively large number of elements at two or more levels in the model. Much like 1-layer item modeling, the starting point for the *n*-layer model is to use a parent item. The *n*-layer model permits manipulations of a nonlinear set of generative operations using elements at multiple levels, unlike the 1-layer model, in which the manipulations are constrained to a linear set of generative operations using a small number of elements at a single level. As a result, the generative capacity of the *n*-layer model is often quite high. The concept of *n*-layer item generation is adapted from the literature on syntactic structures of language, where researchers have found that sentences are organized in a hierarchical manner (e.g., Higgins, Futagi, & Deane, 2005). This hierarchical organization, where elements are embedded within one another, can also be used as a guiding principle to generate large numbers of meaningful test items. The use of an *n*-layer item model is therefore a flexible rendering for expressing different syntactic structures that permit the development of different but feasible combinations of embedded elements. The *n*-layer structure can be described as a model with multiple layers of elements, where each element can be varied simultaneously at different levels to produce different items.

A comparison of the 1-layer and *n*-layer item model is presented in Figure 5.4. For this example, the 1-layer model can provide a maximum of four different values for element A (see left side of Figure 5.4). Conversely, the *n*-layer model can provide up to 64 different values by embedding the same four values for elements C and D within element B. That is, 4 values embedded within 3 elements, or $4^3$, yields 64 outcomes (see right side of Figure 5.4).

An *n*-layer hernia item model is presented in Figure 5.5. This example helps illustrate how the structure of the item can be manipulated to produce more generated items. In addition to manipulating the elements for the 1-layer example in Figure 5.2, we now embed the elements within one another to facilitate the generative process. That is, by embedding elements within elements, different question prompts, test findings, and situations can be used, thereby

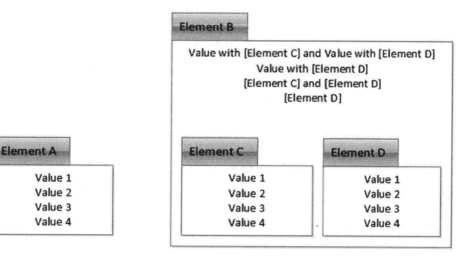

Example of a 1-layer element      Example of an *n*-layer element, with two layers

**Figure 5.4** An comparison of the elements in a 1-layer and *n*-layer item model

| | |
|---|---|
| *Stem* | [SITUATION] [TESTFINDINGS] [QUESTIONPROMPT] |
| Elements: | |
| *Layer 1* | QUESTIONPROMPT (Text): 1: What is the best next step? 2: Which one of the following is the best prognosis? 3: Given this information, what is the best course of action? |
| | TESTFINDINGS (Text): 1: On examination, the mass is [PHYSICALEXAMINATION] and lab work came back with [WBC]. 2: Upon further examination, the patient had [WBC] and the mass is [PHYSICALEXAMINATION]. 3: With [WBC] and [PHYSICALEXAMINATION] in the area, the patient is otherwise normal. 4: There is [PHYSICALEXAMINATION] in the [LOCATION] and the patient had [WBC]. |
| | SITUATION (Text): 1: A [AGE]-year-old [GENDER] presented with a mass [PAIN] in [LOCATION]. It occurred [ACUITYOFONSET]. 2: Patient presents with a mass [PAIN] in [LOCATION] from [ACUITYOFONSET]. The patient is a [AGE]-year-old [GENDER]. 3: A patient complains of a mass [PAIN] in [LOCATION] which has been a problem since [ACUITYOFONSET]. 4: A [GENDER] was admitted with pain in the [LOCATION] from [ACUITYOFONSET]. |
| *Layer 2* | [AGE] (Integer): From 25.0 to 60.0, by 15.0 |
| | [GENDER] (String): 1: man 2: woman |
| | [PAIN] (String): 1: 2: and intense pain 3: and severe pain 4: and mild pain |
| | [LOCATION] (String): 1: the left groin 2: the right groin 3: the umbilicus 4: an area near a recent surgery |
| | [ACUITYOFONSET] (String): 1: a few months ago 2: a few hours ago 3: a few days ago 4: a few days ago after moving a piano |
| | [PHYSICALEXAMINATION] (String): 1: protruding but with no pain 2: tender 3: tender and exhibiting redness 4: tender and reducible |
| | [WBC] (String): 1: normal results 2: elevated white blood-cell count |
| *Options* | exploratory surgery; reduction of mass; hernia repair; ice applied to mass |

**Figure 5.5** *n*-layer item model for the hernia example

generating more heterogeneous items. For the *n*-layer example in Figure 5.5, two types of layers are used. The first type is sentence presentation. The last sentence of the item stem, for instance, can serve as an element by rewording the phrase, "Which of the following is the next best step?" to "Which one of the following is the best prognosis?" or "Given this information, what is the best course of action?" The second type is sentence structure. Four alternative sentence structures can be used to present the information in the original sentence from the 1-layer item model "On examination, the mass is [PHYSICALEXAMINATION] and lab work came back with [WBC]." Three alternative structures are "Upon further examination, the patient had [WBC] and the mass is [PHYSICALEXAMINATION]", "With [WBC] and [PHYSICALEXAMINATION] in the area, the patient is otherwise nominal", and "There is [PHYSICALEXAMINATION] in the [LOCATION] and the patient had [WBC]." In short, by introducing new layers of elements such as sentence presentation and structure, more hernia items can be generated with *n*-layer item models compared to the 1-layer approach.

### Multilingual AIG and n-Layer Item Modeling

The *n*-layer model is a flexible structure for item generation, thereby permitting many different but feasible combinations of embedded elements at multiple levels. And, as we illustrated,

**Figure 5.6** *n*-layer hernia item model with language as a layer

the *n*-layer models can accommodate a wide range of elements, producing larger numbers of generated items. In addition to generating more items, another application of *n*-layer modeling is in generating multilingual test items, where language is added to the model as an explicit layer. Because different languages require different grammatical structures and word orderings, a 1-layer model cannot easily or readily accommodate this type of variation, because the generative operations are constrained to those elements at a single level. However, with the use of an *n*-layer model, the generative operations are expanded dramatically to include a large number of elements at multiple levels. Language, therefore, can serve as an additional layer that is manipulated during item generation. Figure 5.6 shows an *n*-layer structure that could be used to generate items in English, Chinese, and French for our hernia item model. Next, we describe how *n*-layer item modeling can be used to generate tasks in multiple languages by adding language as an additional layer in the model.

### Linked Elements and Multilingual AIG

Using the Gierl, Lai, and Turner (2012) three-step process, items are created through systematic replacement, where different plausible values are iteratively replaced in models using computer algorithms. These replacement values are organized as elements. As item models become more complex due to the requirements specified in cognitive models and/or the linguistic complexity required for adapting items into different languages, the number of elements used for item generation dramatically increases. The increase in the number of elements is problematic because it affects the programming task required to run IGOR by making it more challenging, and it affects the computation time required to generate new items with IGOR by causing it to dramatically increase. In this section of the chapter, we introduce the concept of a *linked element* as a way to facilitate the IGOR programming task and to increase IGOR's computational speed.

Recall that the use of layered elements permit content to be embedded within content in an item model (see Figure 5.4). Layered elements, therefore, have a "vertical" function for item content (i.e., content within content). Linked elements also expand the capabilities of item modeling by permitting content to be transformed within an item model. In our case, the transformation is from one language to another. Linked elements, therefore, have a "horizontal" function for item content (i.e., content in form 1 is transformed to content in form 2). The linked elements used for language transformations can function in four different forms: words, key phrases, single sentences, and multiple sentences. These four forms are then used to adapt words, phrases, and sentences from one language to another to permit multilingual AIG.

In our current example, we generated hernia surgical items in English. Using linked elements, we demonstrate how these items can be generated simultaneously in Chinese and French. These examples were created with the help of two bilingual medical content specialists. The Chinese-speaking content specialist was an experienced surgeon who was fluent in both English and Chinese. His bilingual competence was established and continually practiced through his additional role as a surgery textbook translator. The French-speaking content specialist was an experienced editor who was fluent in both English and French. Her bilingual competence was established and continually practiced through her role as a full-time medical item developer and translator. Working with our two bilingual content specialists, four types of linked elements were identified and used for multilingual AIG in our example. For the sake of brevity, we focus our description on the challenges inherent in the English-to-Chinese translations and adaptations, but we provide the results for all three language outcomes throughout our example.

First, linked elements were specified in the form of a *word*. These elements require the direct translation or adaptation of a single word between languages. These translations or adaptations can be challenging and often warrant both linguistic and content expertise. For example, the Chinese word "patient" can be translated into the phrase "ill person" (病人), but a more formal and appropriate Chinese medical expression for "patient" is required in medical testing (患者). Hence, each word in the *n*-layer hernia item model (Figure 5.5) must be translated or adapted for a medical testing context. A summary of two word-level adaptations in Chinese and French is provided in Table 5.1.

Second, linked elements can be specified in the form of a *key phrase*. These elements require the direct translation or adaptation of key phrases between languages. Again, challenges abound with the translation and adaptation process when considering a medical education context. For example, the term "vitals" can be translated directly to produce 命脈. Unfortunately, "vitals" could also be interpreted in a "fortunetelling" setting and, hence, this phrase may be confusing for some examinees. To avoid ambiguity, a more context-specific medical phrase is required, which, in our study, is 生命體徵. A summary of two key phrase-level adaptations is provided in Table 5.1.

Third, linked elements can be specified in the form of a *single sentence*. These elements require the direct translation or adaptation of words and key phrases as well as the coordination of these elements to produce a coherent sentence. Because the literal or direct combination of words and key phrases can produce awkward expressions, some linguistic refinement may be required to produce a more precise sentence. For example, the translation of the sentence "What is the best next step?" (那最佳的下一步是應該怎樣?), which is expressed as "Then what should be the best next step?" can be presented more precisely and succinctly as 下一步最佳處治是哪一個, which literally means "which one is the best next form of treatment?" A summary of two single-sentence–level adaptations is provided in Table 5.1.

Table 5.1 Four Types of Linked Elements Required for Multilingual AIG in English, Chinese, and French

| Level of Analysis | Medical Expression | Chinese Adaptation | French Adaptation |
|---|---|---|---|
| Word | Patient | 患者 | La patiente/Le patient |
| | Mass | 包塊 | la masse |
| Key Phrase | tender and exhibiting redness | 稍有充血但柔軟的 | sensible et rougeâtre |
| | Normal vitals | 生命體徵正常 | des résultats normaux |
| Single Sentence | What is the best next step? | 下一步最佳處治是哪一個? | Quelle est la prochaine étape de la prise en charge? |
| | Given this information, what is the best course of action? | 基於上述的信息，以下哪一樣是最佳的處治 | Compte tenu de cette information, quelle est la meilleure mesure à prendre? |
| Multiple Sentences | A 25-year-old woman presented with a mass in the left groin. It occurred a few months ago. | 一名25歲的女患者在左側腹股溝出現一個包塊. 徵狀已持續了幾個月. | Une femme de 25 ans présente une masse du côté gauche de l'aine. Elle est apparue il y a quelques mois. |
| | Patient presents with a mass and mild pain in an area near a recent surgery from a few days ago after moving a piano. The patient is a 34-year-old woman. | 一名患者的手術的切口附近從數天前，自搬動鋼琴後出現一個有輕微痛感的包塊. 患者牲別女，34 歲 | Une patient été hospitalisé en raison d'une douleur dans la région d'une opération récente apparue il y a quelques jours après avoir déménagé un piano. La patiente est une femme de 34 ans. |

Fourth, linked elements can be specified in the form of *multiple sentences*. This type of linked element can include multiple sentences such as, "Patient presents with a mass and mild pain in an area near a recent surgery from a few days ago after moving a piano. The patient is a 34-year-old woman." A multiple-sentence linked element could also be the entire test item. Because words, key phrases, and single sentences have been carefully adapted prior to assembling multiple sentences, only small adjustments should be required for this linked element transformation. However, as with the linked elements at the single-sentence level, care must be taken to coordinate these elements so a coherent whole is produced. And, again, because the literal combination of words and key phrases can produce awkward expressions, some refinement from the bilingual content specialists was required to produce a more precise test item. For example, a translation of the sentence, "Patient presents with a mass and mild pain in an area near a recent surgery from a few days ago after moving a piano. The patient is a 34-year-old woman." These sentences can be translated into 一名病人的手術的傷口附近從數天前，自剛剛搬移鋼琴後出現一團帶有微痛的組織. 病人牲別女，34 歲, which means, "Since moving a piano from a few days ago, a mass has appeared on the patient near the wound from a surgery. The patient is a female/woman, 34-year-old." But a more precise and succinct translation for a medical context would be 一名患者的手術的切口附近從數天前，自搬動鋼琴後出現一個有輕微痛感的包塊. 患者牲別女，34 歲. In this translation, medical terminology for "wound," "patient," and "mass" is included. A summary of two multiple-sentence–level adaptations is provided in Table 5.1.

Taken together, linked elements specify content in four different forms that provide the translation or adaptation necessary to program IGOR so item generation can occur in multiple languages. Our example is constrained to three languages, but four or more languages can be developed using the same linked element logic to permit simultaneous multilingual item generation. Once the four-level linked elements are completed, a map is produced. Figure 5.7 contains the linked-element map required to generate English, Chinese, and French items using the $n$-layer model in Figure 5.5. The map summarizes the necessary links for words, key phrases, single sentences, and multiple sentences across the three languages. Then IGOR is programmed using the item model content in Figure 5.5 as well as the linked element map in Figure 5.7 to produce new items.

**Elements (Word and Key-Phrase Level):**

| Variable | English | Chinese | French |
| --- | --- | --- | --- |
| Age | 25–60 Step 15 | 25–60 Step 15 | 25–60 Step 15 |
| Gender | man | 男 | homme |
| | woman | 女 | femme |
| Location | the left groin | 左側腹股溝 | du côté gauche de l'aine |
| | the right groin | 右側腹股溝 | du côté droit de l'aine |
| | the umbilicus | 臍部 | au nombril |
| | an area near a recent surgery | 手術的切口附近 | dans la région d'une opération récente |
| AcuityofOnset | a few months ago | 幾個月前 | il y a quelques mois |
| | a few hours ago | 幾個小時前 | il y a quelques heures |
| | a few days ago | 數天前 | il y a quelques jours |
| | a few days ago after moving a piano | 數天前，自搬動鋼琴後 | il y a quelques jours après avoir déménagé un piano |
| PhysicalExamination | protruding but with no pain | 突出而不疼痛 | saillante, mais indolore |
| | tenderness | 不剛硬的 | sensible |
| | tender and exhibiting redness | 若有沖血但柔軟的 | sensible et rougeâtre |
| | tender and reducible | 軟而可回復的 | sensible et réductible |
| WBC | normal vitals | 生命體微正常 | des résultats normaux |
| | elevated white blood-cell count | 白血球上升 | une numération leucocytaire élevée |
| Pain | and intense pain | 有強烈痛感的 | et une vive douleur |
| | and severe pain | 有明顯痛感的 | et une douleur intense |
| | and mild pain | 有輕微痛感的 | et une légère douleur |
| Key | ice applied to mass | 在包塊上冷敷 | application de glace dans la région de l'aine |
| Distractor | hernia repair | 疝氣修補手術 | réparation immédiate de la hernie |
| | reduction of mass | 手法回復包塊 | réduction de la masse |
| | exploratory surgery | 腹腔探查術 | chirurgie exploratoire |

**Figure 5.7** Summary of linked elements at the word, key-phrase, single-sentence, and multiple-sentence levels required for English, Chinese, and French item generation using the $n$-layer item model in Figure 5.5

**Elements (Single-Sentence Level):**

|  | English | Chinese | French |
|---|---|---|---|
| Sentence 1 | Patient complaints of a mass [ENG.PAIN] in [ENG.LOCATION] which has been a problem since [ENG.ACUITYOFONSET]. | 一名患者主訴[CH.ACUITYOFONSET]在[CH.LOCATION]出現的一個[CH.PAIN]包塊 | Un patient se plaint d'une masse [FR.DOULEUR] [FR.RÉGION] qui est apparue [FR.APPARITION]. |
| Sentence 2 | A [ENG.GENDER] was admitted with pain in [ENG.LOCATION] from [ENG.ACUITYOFONSET]. | 一名[CH.GENDER]子因[CH.ACUITYOFONSET][CH.LOCATION]出現疼痛而入院。 | Un [FR.SEXE] a été hospitalisé en raison d'une douleur [FR.RÉGION] apparue [FR.APPARITION]. |
| Sentence 3 | On examination, the mass is [ENG.PHYSICALEXAMINATION] and lab work came back with [ENG.WBC]. | 經檢查後，那包塊是[CH.PHYSICALEXAMINATION]，化驗結果顯示[CH.WBC]。 | À l'examen, la masse est [FR.EXAMENPHYSIQUE], et les analyses de laboratoire sont [FR.NUMÉRATION LEUCOCYTAIRE]. |
| Sentence 4 | Upon further examination, the patient had [ENG.WBC] and the mass is [ENG.PHYSICALEXAMINATION]. | 經身體檢查後，患者[CH.WBC]，而那包塊是[CH.PHYSICALEXAMINATION]。 | À la suite d'examens supplémentaires, les résultats étaient [FR.NUMÉRATION LEUCOCYTAIRE], et la masse est située [FR.EXAMENPHYSIQUE]. |
| Sentence 5 | With [ENG.WBC] and [ENG.PHYSICALEXAMINATION] in the area, the patient is otherwise normal. | 患者[CH.WBC]，除了影響範圍是[CH.PHYSICALEXAMINATION]，患者基本正常。 | Mis à part [FR.NUMÉRATION LEUCOCYTAIRE] et [FR.EXAMENPHYSIQUE] dans la région, le patient ne présente aucune autre anomalie. |
| Sentence 6 | There is [ENG.PHYSICALEXAMINATION] in [ENG.LOCATION] and the patient had [ENG.WBC]. | 在[CH.LOCATION]上感覺到[CH.PHYSICALEXAMINATION]，而患者的[CH.WBC] | Il y a [FR.EXAMENPHYSIQUE] à [FR.LOCATION], et le patient avait [FR.NUMÉRATIONLEUCOCYTAIRE]. |
| Sentence 7 | What is the best next step? | 下一部最佳處治是那一個? | Quelle est la prochaine étape de la prise en charge? |
| Sentence 8 | Which one of the following is the best prognosis? | 以下那一個預測是正確的? | Quel est le meilleur pronostic? |
| Sentence 9 | Given this information, what is the best course of action? | 基於上述的信息，以下那一樣是最佳的處治? | Compte tenu de cette information, quelle est la meilleure mesure à prendre? |

**Elements (Multiple-Sentence Level):**

|  | English | Chinese | French |
|---|---|---|---|
| Sentences 1 | A [ENG.AGE]-year-old [ENG.GENDER] presented with a mass [ENG.PAIN] in [ENG.LOCATION]. It occurred [ENG.ACUITYOFONSET]. | 一名[CH.AGE]歲的[CH.GENDER]患者在[CH.LOCATION]出現一個[CH.PAIN]包塊。微狀已持續了[CH.ACUITYOFONSET]。 | Un [FR.SEXE] de [FR.ÂGE] ans présente une masse [FR.DOULEUR] [FR.RÉGION]. Elle est apparue [FR.APPARITION]. |
| Sentences 2 | Patient presents with a mass [ENG.PAIN] in [ENG.LOCATION] from [ENG.ACUITYOFONSET]. The patient is a [ENG.AGE]-year-old [ENG.GENDER]. | 一名患者的[CH.LOCATION]從[CH.ACUITYOFONSET]出現一個[CH.PAIN]包塊. 患者牲別[CH.GENDER],[CH.AGE] 歲 | La patiente présente une masse [FR.DOULEUR] [FR.RÉGION] apparues [FR.APPARITION]. La patiente est une [FR.SEXE] de [FR.ÂGE] ans. |

**Figure 5.7** Continued

## *Combining the "Art" and "Science" of Item Development*

Using the three-step approach for AIG, a total of 1,824 hernia items was generated—608 English, 608 Chinese, and 608 French items. The IGOR run time for item generation was approximately 1 minute and 15 seconds using a Asus laptop with a Core i7 processor and 8 GB of internal memory. The combinatorial challenges for a relatively simple item-modeling problem, as demonstrated in the current example, are noteworthy. The three-language hernia model produced 221,184 combinations (i.e., items) from 11 elements[2] (each element contains multiple values) and four constraints (some constraints contain single values and others contain multiple values). In total, 221,184 unconstrained item combinations were initially produced, but, after imposing the constraints, 1,824 feasible item combinations were created. A random sample of four items in English, Chinese, and French is presented in Tables 5.2, 5.3, and 5.4, respectively.

Our example also demonstrates how AIG, which is a new approach to technology-enhanced item development, helps focus the roles and refine the responsibilities of the test-development specialist. We noted in the introduction to our chapter that AIG can be described as the

Table 5.2  A Random Sample of Four English Items Generated Using the Hernia Cognitive Model

14. Patient presents with a mass in right groin from a few months ago. The patient is a 25-year-old man. Upon further examination, the patient had normal vitals and the mass is protruding but with no pain. What is the best next step?

1. ice applied to mass*
2. exploratory surgery
3. reduction of mass
4. hernia repair

85. A 25-year-old man presented with a mass and intense pain in an area near a recent surgery. It occurred a few hours ago. On examination, the mass is tender and lab work came back with normal vitals. What is the best next step?

1. ice applied to mass*
2. exploratory surgery
3. reduction of mass
4. hernia repair

301. A 40-year-old man presented with a mass in the umbilicus. It occurred a few months ago. On examination, the mass is protruding but with no pain and lab work came back with normal vitals. What is the best next step?

1. ice applied to mass*
2. exploratory surgery
3. reduction of mass
4. hernia repair

521. A 55-year-old man presented with a mass and mild pain in the left groin. It occurred a few days ago after moving a piano. On examination, the mass is tender and reducible and lab work came back with normal vitals. What is the best next step?

1. ice applied to mass*
2. exploratory surgery
3. reduction of mass
4. hernia repair

* = correct option

Table 5.3  A Random Sample of Four Chinese Items Generated Using the Hernia Cognitive Model

33. 一名25歲的女患者在左側腹股溝出現一個包塊。徵狀已持續了幾個月。 經檢查後，那包塊是突出而不疼痛，化驗 果顯示生命體徵正常。下一部最佳處治是哪一個？

1. 在包塊上冷敷*
2. 腹腔探查術
3. 手法回復包塊
4. 疝氣修補手術

111. 一名患者的手術的切口附近從數天前，自搬動鋼琴後出現一個有輕微痛感的包塊。患者牲別女，25歲。經身體檢查後，患者生命體徵正常，而那包塊是柔軟而可回復的。下一部最佳處治是哪一個？

1. 在包塊上冷敷*
2. 腹腔探查術
3. 手法回復包塊
4. 疝氣修補手術

199. 一名男子因幾個小時前右側腹股溝出現疼痛而入院。在右側腹股溝上 稍有充血但柔軟的，而患者的生命體徵正常。以下哪一個預測是正確的？

1. 在包塊上冷敷*
2. 腹腔探查術
3. 手法回復包塊
4. 疝氣修補手術

322. 一名女子因幾個小時前右側腹股溝出現疼痛而入院。在右側腹股溝上 稍有充血但柔軟的，而患者的生命體徵正常。基於上述的信息，以下哪一樣是最佳的處治？

1. 在包塊上冷敷*
2. 腹腔探查術
3. 手法回復包塊
4. 疝氣修補手術

* = correct option

Table 5.4  A Random Sample of Four French Items Generated Using the Hernia Cognitive Model

105. Une nulligeste de 25 ans présente une masse et une douleur intense du côté gauche de l'aine. Elle est apparue il y a quelques jours. À l'examen, la masse est sensible et rougeâtre, et les analyses de laboratoire révèlent une numération leucocytaire élevée. Quelle est la prochaine étape de la prise en charge？

1. Application de glace dans la région de l'aine.*
2. Aspiration à l'aiguille.
3. Réduction de la masse.
4. Réparation immédiate de la hernie.

508. La patiente présente une masse et une douleur intense du côté droit de l'aine, qui sont apparues il y a quelques jours. La patiente est une nulligeste de 55 ans. Des examens supplémentaires révèlent une numération leucocytaire élevée, et la masse est sensible et rougeâtre. Quelle est la prochaine étape de la prise en charge？

1. Application de glace dans la région de l'aine.*
2. Aspiration à l'aiguille.
3. Réduction de la masse.
4. Réparation immédiate de la hernie.

(Continued)

## Table 5.4 (Continued)

---

557. Une nulligeste de 40 ans présente une masse et une douleur intense du côté gauche de l'aine. Elle est apparue il y a quelques jours. À l'examen, la masse est sensible et rougeâtre, et les analyses de laboratoire révèlent une numération leucocytaire élevée. Compte tenu de cette information, quelle est la meilleure mesure à prendre?

1. Application de glace dans la région de l'aine.*
2. Aspiration à l'aiguille.
3. Réduction de la masse.
4. Réparation immédiate de la hernie.

721. Une nulligeste de 25 ans présente une masse du côté droit de l'aine. Elle est apparue il y a quelques mois. À l'examen, la masse est saillante mais indolore, et les analyses de laboratoire sont normales. Quelle est la prochaine étape de la prise en charge?

1. Application de glace dans la région de l'aine.*
2. Aspiration à l'aiguille.
3. Réduction de la masse.
4. Réparation immédiate de la hernie.

---

* = correct option

process of using models to generate items with the aid of computer technology. The role of the test-development specialist is critical for the creative task of identifying the knowledge and skills required to think about and solve problems, organizing this information into a cognitive model, designing meaningful item models, and adapting the models and content for use in other languages. These responsibilities will not be replaced any time soon by computer technology because they require judgment, expertise, and experience. The role of computer technology is critical for the algorithmic task of systematically combining large amounts of content in each model to produce new test items. This task warrants computing power and efficiency, as our example helps demonstrate, because it is a complex combinatorial problem that is not easily or readily solved by test-development specialists. But, by combining content expertise with computer technology, testing specialists can produce meaningful cognitive and item models that can be programmed in multiple languages to yield large numbers of high-quality items in a short period of time. That is, AIG represents a merger between the "art" and "science" of item development where well-defined responsibilities that adhere to specialized skills according to the appropriate division of labor contribute to the production of test items in multiple languages.

### Conclusions

Many testing agencies now require large numbers of high-quality items that are produced in a cost-effective and timely manner. Increasingly, these agencies are also required to produce their items in different languages. One way to address this challenge is by increasing the number of content specialists and test translators who are assigned the task of developing multilingual items. But this option is expensive, tedious, and slow. An alternative approach is to combine content expertise with computer technology to systemically produce multilingual test items using AIG. AIG is the process of using item models to generate test items with the aid of computer technology. We described a three-step AIG approach in which test-development specialists first, identify the content that will be used for item generation, then create item models to specify the content in the assessment task that must be manipulated, and, finally, manipulate the elements in item models using computer-based algorithms. With the use of *n*-layer item models generation capacity is high because this approach provides a flexible structure that accommodates a wide range of elements at multiple levels. Language is added as an additional layer in the model to permit multilingual AIG. Hence, multilingual AIG can be considered a specific case of *n*-layer item modeling where language serves as one layer. One consequence of adding layers is that item models become more complex, and, as a result, IGOR programming time and processing run time increase. To address this challenge, we introduced the concept of a linked element in this chapter. Linked elements facilitate the IGOR programming task and increase IGOR's computational speed. Whereas layered elements permit content to be embedded within content (i.e., vertical function), linked elements permit content transformations (i.e., horizontal function). For multilingual AIG, the transformation is across languages. Test translators used the linked elements to adapt words, phrases, and sentences from one language to another to permit multilingual AIG. An example of multilingual AIG was presented using a hernia problem in which 1,824 items were generated simultaneously across three different languages.

We presented a general method for creating large numbers of multilingual items. But the psychometric properties (e.g., item difficulty) and the quality of these items must still be evaluated. Psychometric properties are often determined through a field testing process in which each item is administered to a sample of examinees so the item statistics can be calculated. Item quality is evaluated using judgments from content specialists through which the guidelines, conventions, and standards of practice form the basis of scrutinizing the items. Unfortunately, studies designed to collect data on these types of indicators using the method presented in this chapter have not yet been conducted.

### Technology and the Future of Item Development

There is a growing view that the science of educational assessment will prevail to guide the design, development, administration, scoring, and reporting practices in educational testing. For instance, in their seminal chapter on "Technology and Testing" in the fourth edition of the handbook *Educational Measurement*, Drasgow, Luecht, and Bennett (2006, p. 471) begin with this statement:

> *This chapter describes our vision of a 21st-century testing program that capitalizes on modern technology and takes advantage of recent innovations in testing. Using an analogy from engineering, we envision a modern testing program as an integrated system of systems. Thus, there is an item generation system, an item pretesting system, and examinee registration system, and so forth. This chapter discusses each system and illustrates how technology can enhance and facilitate the core processes of each system.*

That is, Drasgow and colleagues present a view of educational measurement in which integrated technology-enhanced systems govern and direct all testing processes. In the current chapter, we presented a concrete example of how we envision an item-generation system by describing a three-step AIG process and then illustrating how this process can be used to generate thousands of medical items across multiple languages. But it is important to also emphasize that the technology-enhanced AIG system we described does not replace test-development specialists. Rather, it helps focus their role on the task of identifying, organizing, and adapting the content needed to develop test items. Computer technology also has an important role to play. Algorithms are used for the generative task of systematically combining the information identified by the test-development specialists in each item model. By merging the outcomes from the content-based creative task with the computer-based generative task, AIG can serve as a new technology-enhanced approach for developing test items in multiple languages.

## Acknowledgments

We would like to thank Vasily Tanygin and the Medical Council of Canada for their contributions to this research. However, the authors are solely responsible for the methods, procedures, and interpretations expressed in this study.

## Notes

1  Age and gender are unconstrained elements that can be applied to each hernia problem. Hence, they are not represented as elements in the model under "Patient Presentation" in order to simplify our description.
2  The example we initially presented for Figure 5.3 is based on 10 elements. The current example adds one new element to the problem, which is language (English, Chinese, and French).

## References

Arendasy, M.E. (2005). Automatic generation of Rasch-calibrated items: Figural matrices test GEOM and endless loops test E$^c$. *International Journal of Testing, 5*, 197–224.

Arendasy, M.E., & Sommer, M. (2007). Using psychometric technology in educational assessment: The case of a schema-based isomorphic approach to the automatic generation of quantitative reasoning items. *Learning and Individual Differences, 17*, 366–383.

Bejar, I.I. (1990). A generative analysis of a three-dimensional spatial task. *Applied Psychological Measurement, 14*, 237–245.

Bejar, I.I. (1996). *Generative response modeling: Leveraging the computer as a test delivery medium* (ETS Research Report 96–13). Princeton, NJ: Educational Testing Service.

Bejar, I.I. (2002). Generative testing: From conception to implementation. In S.H. Irvine & P.C. Kyllonen (Eds.), *Item generation for test development* (pp. 199–217). Hillsdale, NJ: Erlbaum.

Bejar, I.I., Lawless, R., Morley, M.E., Wagner, M.E., Bennett, & R.E., Revuelta, J. (2003). A feasibility study of on-the-fly item generation in adaptive testing. *Journal of Technology, Learning, and Assessment, 2*(3). Available from www.jtla.org.

Case, S.M., & Swanson, D.B. (2002). *Constructing written test questions for the basic and clinical sciences* (3rd ed.). Philadelphia, PA: National Board of Medical Examiners.

Downing, S.M., & Haladyna, T.M. (2006). *Handbook of test development*. Mahwah, NJ: Erlbaum.

Drasgow, F., Luecht, R.M., & Bennett, R. (2006). Technology and testing. In R.L. Brennan (Ed.), *Educational measurement* (4th ed., pp. 471–516). Washington, DC: American Council on Education.

Embretson, S.E. (2002). Generating abstract reasoning items with cognitive theory. In S.H. Irvine & P.C. Kyllonen (Eds.), *Item generation for test development* (pp. 219–250). Mahwah, NJ: Erlbaum.

Embretson, S.E., & Daniels, R.C. (2008). Understanding and quantifying cognitive complexity level in mathematical problem solving items. *Psychological Science Quarterly, 50*, 328–344.

Embretson, S.E., & Yang, X. (2007). Automatic item generation and cognitive psychology. In C.R. Rao & S. Sinharay (Eds.), *Handbook of statistics: Psychometrics, Vol. 26* (pp. 747–768). North Holland, UK: Elsevier.

Gierl, M.J., & Haladyna, T. (2013). *Automatic item generation: Theory and practice*. New York: Routledge.

Gierl, M.J., & Lai, H. (2012). Using automatic item generation to create items for medical licensure exams. In K. Becker (Chair), *Beyond essay scoring: Test development through natural language processing*. Paper presented at the annual meeting of the National Council on Measurement in Education, Vancouver, BC.

Gierl, M.J., & Lai, H. (2013a). Using automated processes to generate test items. *Educational Measurement: Issues and Practice, 32*, 36–50.

Gierl, M. J., & Lai, H. (2013b). Using weak and strong theory to create item models for automatic item generation: Some practical guidelines with examples. In M. J. Gierl & T. Haladyna (Eds.), *Automatic item generation: Theory and practice* (pp. 26–39). New York: Routledge.

Gierl, M. J., Lai, H., & Turner, S. (2012). Using automatic item generation to create multiple-choice items for assessments in medical education. *Medical Education, 46,* 757–765.

Gierl, M. J., Zhou, J., & Alves, C. (2008). Developing a taxonomy of item model types to promote assessment engineering. *Journal of Technology, Learning, and Assessment, 7*(2). Retrieved fromwww.jtla.org

Haladyna, T. M., & Rodriguez, M. C. (2013). *Developing and validating test items.* New York: Routledge.

Hambleton, R. K., Merenda, P. F., & Spielberger, C. D. (2005). *Adapting educational and psychological tests for cross-cultural assessment.* Mahwah, NJ: Erlbaum.

Higgins, D., Futagi, Y., & Deane, P. (2005). *Multilingual generalization of the Model Creator software for math item generation.* Educational Testing Service Research Report (RR-05–02). Princeton, NJ: Educational Testing Service.

Irvine, S. H., & Kyllonen, P. C. (2002). *Item generation for test development.* Hillsdale, NJ: Erlbaum.

LaDuca, A., Staples, W. I., Templeton, B., & Holzman, G. B. (1986). Item modeling procedures for constructing content-equivalent multiple-choice questions. *Medical Education, 20,* 53–56.

OECD. (2010). *PISA 2009 results: What students know and can do—student performance in reading, mathematics and science* (Volume I). http://dx.doi.org/10.1787/9789264091450-en

OECD. (2012). *PISA 2009 technical report.* OECD Publishing. http://dx.doi.org/10.1787/ 9789264167872-en

Schmeiser, C. B., & Welch, C. J. (2006). Test development. In R. L. Brennan (Ed.), *Educational measurement* (4th ed., pp. 307–353). Westport, CT: National Council on Measurement in Education and American Council on Education.

Sinharay, S., & Johnson, M. S. (2013). Statistical modeling of automatically generated items. In M. J. Gierl & T. Haladyna (Eds.), *Automatic item generation: Theory and practice* (pp. 183–195). New York: Routledge.

Wendt, A., Kao, S., Gorham, J., & Woo, A. (2009). Developing item variants: An empirical study. In D. J. Weiss (Ed.), *Proceedings of the 2009 GMAC Conference on Computerized Adaptive Testing.* Retrieved April 1, 2011, from www.psych.umn.edu/psylabs/CATCentral/

# 6

# Automated Test Assembly

**Krista Breithaupt and Donovan Hare**

## Introduction

Automated test assembly is the use of information processing available via computer programming solutions to select test questions or tasks from an eligible item bank (or subpool) onto one or more test forms. The completed test forms may be presented either on paper or via computerized delivery, and the test taker experience can be adaptive or fixed in terms of their interaction with the assembled test content (van der Linden, 2005). This discussion of automated methods of test assembly is not limited to only computerized delivery or paper publication of forms for paper-and-pencil tests. Any test program might make use of either manual selection of test content or a computerized (automated) item selection method for test production. It may be useful, however, to note that when the selection of test items depends on the performance of the test taker during the administration (for adaptive or tailored tests), the selection of test items must occur dynamically at testing time and will take into account the prior performance of the candidate. This adaptive mode of testing has become popular with the introduction of computerized delivery and must make use of some automated selection mechanism using logic included in the test delivery system. When test content is prepared in advance of the test event and does not depend on prior performance of examinees, the test developer has a choice of either traditional manual test construction, a computerized or automated solution, or some combination of these two methods.

Interest and research on automated test assembly (ATA) has increased in recent decades for a variety of reasons. As computerized adaptive testing (CAT) models of delivery became popular in the last two decades, many comparable subpools of test items were required to ensure fairness of test presentation to a large number of test takers and security of undisclosed item banks during any administration period. Manual assembly of item subpools for CAT becomes impractical and quality assurance impossible when test committees have to consider thousands of potential test questions and create hundreds of CAT pools in order to support long and frequent CAT administrations for large numbers of test takers.

Also, modern technology has vastly enabled easy and immediate communication among test takers, which increases our concern with test security. As a result of these forces, researchers have focused a great deal of attention on CAT item subpool construction and on resolving problems related to item overexposure when item banks are limited and simple heuristics are the basis for item selection (e.g., Stocking & Lewis, 2000). Some operational programs have identified benefits to preconstructing CAT item subpools using linear programming (LP) and to creating shadow test forms to define CAT item pools (e.g., Van der Linden & Glas, 2010). Also, research into computer-adaptive multistage tests (MSTs) for adaptive administration has led to operational implementation of automated assembly of modules or testlets and adaptive panels for administration in large-scale testing programs using large item banks (e.g., Breithaupt & Hare, 2007).

As described, adaptive administration models via computer require subpool or MST panel construction prior to real-time presentation of items or testlets that are selected based on prior performance of the test taker during the administration appointment. This preconstruction of CAT pools or testlets (or both) allows the test developer to preserve some of the benefits that can be derived from adaptive test administration, including increased precision in test scores and a greater number of unique forms, while reliably covering the essential domains of the test blueprint with greater control over exposure of items and yielding comparable scores for examinees (e.g., a computerized adaptive multistage test model is described by Luecht, this volume). The MST is a multistage or testlet-based model that has been adopted by several high-stakes testing programs (e.g., tests for physicians, CPAs, and graduate admissions examinations in the last decade).

In order to preassemble modules, pools of items, or shadow tests for CAT, it is necessary to solve a complicated multivariable optimization problem. Traditionally, heuristic- or algorithmic-based solutions have been used for preassembly of test forms by computers and for selection of items during adaptive administrations (Swanson & Stocking, 1993). Of course, traditional manual preconstruction is possible for linear paper or computerized delivery when only a few forms are needed and small volumes of candidates are tested, when test administrations are infrequent, or when test forms are routinely disclosed (e.g., not secure).

The manual process involves experts selecting test items from a pile of available questions described on separate cards and sorting these into sets representing comparable forms to satisfy content coverage and other specifications for each test form. However, as computerized administrations have made more frequent or continuous test scheduling possible, and as security problems proliferated in high-stakes testing programs with large populations of test takers, an automated assembly system became necessary to meet the need for rapid construction of equivalent forms, testlets, shadow tests, or item subpools in an efficient and predictable process.

The automation of the test assembly process can be expressed as a linear programming (LP) discrete optimization problem of applied mathematics (e.g., van der Linden, 2005). A simple statement of the assembly problem as an LP problem expresses rules of selection as a set of summation statements (e.g., choose items such that a fixed number of items covers each required content category, or choose items so that a fixed number of forms of $N$ items are created).

When item response theory (IRT) is used to express statistical constraints based on item properties, it is possible to describe desired test information functions in the summation. The LP now includes both integer and binary variables, and the discrete optimization version of this LP model uses real variables to optimize the test information targets using IRT parameters. It is the presence of binary decision variables that model the selection of items, which forces the LP model to be a mixed-integer program (MIP) model. When modeled efficiently and appropriately, sophisticated mathematical optimization software called "solvers" can be used to select items for multiple pools, forms, and testlets to produce a large variety of test designs and even complex test specifications (Breithaupt & Hare, 2007; Breithaupt, Ariel, & Veldkamp, 2005; van der Linden, 2005). An example of the discrete optimization solution for a test assembly problem is provided in the next section.

This chapter provides an overview of some popular solutions to the automated assembly of test forms and item pools for computerized administration. Each of these methods has a well-publicized literature available to interested scholars. Here we seek to describe some key features of the most popular methods and to discuss unsolved issues in operationalizing automated assembly and to propose future directions for research and development of automated assembly systems.

## Overview of Assembly Methods

Traditional manual preconstruction for linear delivery is not easily scalable and may not be the most effective use of the time from subject-matter experts or SMEs (e.g., Luecht; Gierl, this volume). Often this manual process requires a panel of SMEs to meet well in advance of test publishing to review draft test forms or to actually build test forms from scratch given the available items in an item bank. Item records (in hard copy or in an electronic database) describe the content and/or skill, as well as relevant statistics used in the test assembly. Initial, manual test-form assembly may range from sorting item records or cards into discrete sets representing unique forms to simple database queries to filter and sort possible test questions based on various fields representing features of items (e.g., content covered). When each draft form has the required number of items to cover the content and other specifications for a test form, the forms may be published and reviewed by an independent policy committee, who are often empowered to replace or reorder items prior to approving completed draft test forms. Next there may be a step in which a design or publishing team arranges the content, including any instructions, figures or response options and input fields, into an attractive and logical presentation on paper booklets or on the computer screen. Finally, there may be calculations of form properties using statistical parameters of items to evaluate or adjust forms for uniform difficulty and projected score precision (reliability). Traditional methods have many variations and are described by Downing and Haladyna (2006). What is common to all manual processes is that they are time consuming and expensive, particularly as the size of item banks grows to allow secure rotation of the items for large-volume testing programs (Way, Steffen, & Anderson, 2002).

Often we need many comparable pools for frequent or continuous administration of tests—especially for nearly continuous computer-based testing. Within a single test administration period, we also need to assemble large numbers of test forms and do so to satisfy increasingly more complex specifications for adaptive test designs—including using innovative item types. These modern test-assembly requirements have spurred a productive body of research on operationally efficient solutions to the assembly process that do not rely solely on expert and manual selection and reviews of subpools, forms, or modules for paper or computerized administration of examinations.

## Automated Test Assembly Models

A review of some fundamental concepts and applications of integer programming and optimization methods from manufacturing is appropriate to the assembly of items into CAT pools, modules, or test forms for a variety of administration modes. There are many industrial problems whose solutions require decision variables to have one of a set of discrete choices to be made (e.g., a yes-or-no decision is one of two choices). These choices might take the form of the number of widgets of a given type that could be made and a schedule for the group of machines that make them. The choices usually have natural dependencies that constrain the idealized solution. Perhaps there is an order for some of the machines that build a type of widget or a time delay for a machine to paint widgets with differing colors. These situations are analogous in many respects to our test construction and inventory planning and assembly problems. Breithaupt, Ariel, and Hare (2010) describe a discrete optimization solution for item bank management and preassembly for a computer-adaptive MST. Van der Linden (2005) also describes in detail a variety of linear optimization models applied to a range of test design problems.

## Discrete Optimization Assembly Solutions

Generally, to build a test form of traditional multiple-choice questions (MCQs), a viable MIP solution will require us to choose a number of questions from a bank of potential questions as a series of discrete choices (yes or no for each test item for any form). Selection for test forms is ordinarily guided by or constrained by content specifications and other design or business rules, such as form length and item exposure restrictions. In the case that there are many forms to create and a large bank of items, our objective is to choose items for forms so that the total solution of all modules, forms, or CAT subpools created is optimal with respect to some design metric. That is, the set of forms will be optimal according to some established set of metrics and a criterion, given the items available. When assembling modules for test delivery, it may be desirable to maximize some function of statistical properties of items to ensure optimal score precision or to allow for adaptive subtest designs based on the difficulty of test questions.

One example of the importance of statistical properties of items for test and inventory designs is the popularity of IRT for ensuring equivalence across test forms (Hambleton & Swaminathan, 1985), or in building adaptive subtests or modules in CA-MST design (Luecht & Nungester, 1998). The use of statistical properties of test questions, in addition to the discrete selection variables in the problem, introduces complexity in the overall assembly problem. In the mathematical literature, these kinds of choice decision problems are modeled as "discrete optimization" problems.

Discrete optimization problems range widely in their difficulty to solve efficiently and in their solution techniques. One example of a solution technique for discrete optimization problems is the greedy approach (e.g., Stocking & Swanson, 1993). Here the next choice is made by selecting the item that is optimal for that step without regard for whether the choice will lead to an overall optimal selection of all choices. The greedy approach can be shown to be an optimal solution strategy to solve the problem of finding the cheapest way to pave the fewest roads to connect all the towns of a road network (the minimum-weight-spanning tree problem). In general, however, a greedy approach is called a heuristic whereby the selections will lead to local minima of an objective function and not the global minimum. For

MIPs, the solution strategies use a branch and bound tree (or, more recently, branch and cut tree) where at each node a relaxed LP is solved and new branches of the tree are provided by integer-constrained variables whose current values are fractional. LPs have been solved efficiently for many years now. MIPs are guaranteed to find a globally optimal solution that satisfies all the constraints but may not do so efficiently.[1]

The structure of the discrete optimization problem solved in assembly of subtests and forms for CA-MST has made use of mixed integer programming where globally optimal solutions were found efficiently (e.g., Breithaupt & Hare, 2012). Mixed-integer programming has been used extensively in a variety of problems in the research literature ranging from CAT item subpools to optimal linear test designs and long-term inventory planning (van der Linden, 2005). In an applied setting, each organization must weigh the potential benefits of alternative administration designs and goals for automated assembly. Some typical considerations in deciding on a preferred approach include the following:

- equivalence of forms within administrations and across time;
- flexibility for updating content specifications;
- efficient and effective use of expert judgment in form creation and approval;
- need for quality control, review, and audit opportunities for individual test forms prior to use;
- minimum item and form exposure within and across test administration periods;
- uniform or prescribed use of the subpool or bank of test items;
- complete coverage of the required knowledge and skills as defined in the test specifications;
- uniform experiences for test takers (fixed-length tests and adequate appointment times);
- seeding of sufficient numbers of pilot items for field testing or calibration;
- high precision in the range of decisions made using the total test score (e.g., decision accuracy at the pass/fail decision point or where any classification decisions are made);
- support for the security of form development and administration schedules (e.g., minimize predictable inventory rotation or real-time item presentations to deter "gaming" or foreknowledge of test questions).

The theory of how to solve LPs and MIPs has evolved since the subject was introduced in the 1950s. As computer interfaces in general have changed dramatically during this time period, so has how one describes an MIP model to a computer. Early versions required posing the problem using a matrix formulation. The maximum amount of computer memory and slow processor speed limited the size of the problems that could be tackled. Software engineering approaches helped in this evolution to provide languages that describe these models to computers without using the matrix formulation. These descriptions have been implemented in efficient ways so that memory is conserved, thus enabling the loading of larger problems into a computer.

Specifying an appropriate optimization model in terms of constraints, decision variables, and objective functions is only part of the solution. Software is also required to solve the model. Much of the early ATA work required customized programs (e.g., Theunissen, 1985). More recently, commercially available solvers were introduced (e.g., LPSOLVE); however, these still required complex interfacing software. Other heuristic implementations like the weighted deviation method (WDM) and normalized weighted absolute absolute deviation heuristic (NWADH) were programmed by their inventors for specific ATA applications (e.g., Stocking & Swanson, 1993). Foundational research on LP solutions for constrained discrete optimization used traditional programming languages in a DOS or Windows environment (an excellent review of software useful for integer LP solutions is given by van der Linden, 2005). Recently, some powerful solvers such as CPLEX (available from IBM 2013) have been packaged with a mathematical programming interface to simplify problem specification, streamline analysis, and allow for troubleshooting and preprocessing of input data representing the test items.

An example of an evolved discrete optimization programming language is Optimization Programming Language (OPL) of the popular CPLEX solver from ILOG (© IBM, 2011; an academic version is available). Other tools are also commercially available (e.g., Frontline Solvers™, 2013, and others; Ariel & Veldkamp, 2005). These solvers are useful to set up and then solve linear programming problems where integer and noninteger variables must be represented. As noted, a simple function for optimization suitable for small pools or short tests is available from Microsoft with the Excel© suite (Cor, Alvez, & Gierl, 2009).

In the interactive developer environment, the CPLEX solver tool can be used to describe the objectives of the assembly of items into CAT pools, test modules, or forms according to the quality goals of the individual testing organization (Breithaupt & Hare, 2012). The CPLEX solver uses linear programming to examine alternative feasible solutions where different combinations of test items are constructed. Some advantages of this approach to the test assembly problem include the ability to compare feasible solutions or test forms with the unconstrained "optimal" problem solution. The software can run on a typical desktop computer with moderately large memory and processing speed and produces multiple test forms in only a few minutes.

An optimal solution for the selection of test items onto test forms is possible when all forms are created simultaneously so that there is a globally optimized result for all forms (or subpools or testlets). The example that follows describes summation statements appropriate for optimizing $T$ test forms composed of $n$ items (items indexed by $i$), where maximal precision is defined at a set of desired IRT ability levels on the theta metric ($\theta$). An optimized test information function (TIF) for all test forms is described by a set of ability targets ($\theta_k, k=1,\ldots,K$), each with a specified weight ($w_k$). The goal of obtaining maximum measurement accuracy for all test forms is expressed by minimizing the difference between their weighted maximums at the target theta values. The relative objective function and some simple constraints can be expressed in the following way:

Maximize $y$ subject to: (1)

$$\sum_{i=1}^{I} x_{it} I_i\left(\theta_k\right) \geq w_k y, \quad t = 1,\ldots,T, and\ every\ \theta_k\ value, \tag{2}$$

$$\sum_{i=1}^{I} x_{it} = n, \quad t = 1,\ldots,T \tag{3}$$

For each test form $t$ and item $i$, the binary decision variable $x_{it}$ encodes whether item $i$ is selected for test form $t$. Expression 1 defines the quantity that will be maximized as $y$. In our example, $y$ is defined as the weighted minimum information obtained at the target over all $T$

tests. Expression 2 defines the total information as the sum of item information, $I_i$, across all selected items at a target theta value, $\theta_k$, in test form $t$. This information value is divided by the weight, $w_k$, given for each target $\theta_k$ for the test. Equation 3 is a simple constraint on the number of selected items, $n$, in each test.

In a formulation similar to the constraint on the number of items per test, the bounds on content constraints can be easily expressed. In addition, it is possible to specify enemy rules and other content-balancing rules within and across tests. The automated assembly LP solutions from OPL Studio for this example with 40 tests of 25 items each from a subpool of 1,000 items applied approximately 50,000 constraints and 60,000 variables. Using a common desktop computer (1.2 GHz), the solution time varied from less than 5 minutes to up to 30 minutes to create all the required tests. Case studies of optimization solutions for more complex MST designs, subpool creation and assignment of items to test forms including development schedules and piloting of new items for long-term inventory scheduling are described in Breithaupt and Hare (2007, 2012).

As we noted in the introduction, real-time selection of items for adaptive computerized delivery relies on heuristics (e.g., Luecht & Hirsch, 1992; Stocking & Swanson, 1993). This is a necessary assumption because neither the candidate's final score nor the true ability level can be known during an adaptive test while the next test question is being selected. Thus, any CAT or MST is by definition relying on heuristic rules for item selections. Item exposure remains an issue of concern in high-stakes testing (Way, Steffan, & Anderson, 2002). The test assembly problem expands dramatically with continuous test delivery on computer and larger item banks, more numerous pools and administrations, and greater security risks accompany 21st-century advances in communication technologies (e.g., D. Foster, this volume). A variety of linear optimization models has been proposed for preassembly of forms (e.g., van der Linden, 2005). However, the size of available computer memory, software costs, and slow processing speeds had delayed adoption of the technology for many large-volume testing programs. Until recently, infeasibility of solutions and slow processing speeds on workplace computers made operationalizing this solution difficult. These problems no longer pose significant obstacles, and several case studies have been published as proof of concept that automated assembly using discrete optimization of LPs is now an efficient and appropriate alternative to manual or heuristic-based assembly of tests and item pools for a variety of test administration modes (Breithaupt & Hare, 2012).

Discrete optimization methods for preconstructed CAT pools and automated assembly for linear or adaptive delivery became practical with mathematical programming interfaces and efficient solvers becoming available in the last decade. Breithaupt and Hare (2007) described simultaneous assembly of optimal testlets for a large number of MST forms and the creation of optimally comparable pools from a large bank of possible items on a typical desktop computer system as requiring only a few minutes. However, in some case studies where an assembly problem required a large number of equivalent forms and many constraints from a large item pool, the MIP model did not return a globally optimal solution in a reasonable amount of time. For example, Breithaupt, Veldkamp, and Ariel (2005) describe days required for some solution times, and infeasibility problems. To help solve this problem, the MIP model can be used to create two equivalent subpools for which the original MIP model for testlet or form assembly can be applied (e.g., Breithaupt & Hare, 2012). This solution strategy was successful in producing a large number of equivalent testlets and assembling MST panels from separate optimal pools in just a few minutes (Breithaupt & Hare, 2012). In this study, we showed how subdividing the item pool using optimization resulted in exactly comparable results for unique forms when forms were later assembled using these separate subpools and a discrete optimization assembly solution for MST testlets. Design rules used in the constraints for the assembly included:

1. Total testlet length in items
2. Number of testlets of each difficulty level
3. Target ability levels ($\theta$s) and weights for maximizing total score precision and profile of testlet difficulty
4. Number of testlets per stage
5. Restrictions on items that should not appear together in a testlet
6. Available typical pool size
7. A feasible number of modules, given pool size and content coverage of items
8. Number of unique panels composed of testlets

## Future Directions in Test Assembly

Significant problems remain to be solved in the automation and improvement of selection of test questions into complete tests for delivery. Our discussion will focus on high-stakes, large-volume testing programs for which innovations in technology which advance measurement theory and practice will require proof of concept. Issues include the following general themes. What follows are our observations on issues receiving attention in global discussions of computerized test administration. The final section of this chapter will discuss how these relate to future evolution in automated assembly of tests. Issues of current interest in international research forums on CBT for high-stakes testing programs include:

- Limitations associated with publishing pools or forms for CBT in dedicated secure test centers
- Lack of inter-operability across software tools for item development, pool management, and test publication and delivery
- Difficulties in incorporating novel item formats, reference materials, and assistive technologies in our tests
- Batch or just-in-time workflows for item development and test publication versus more comprehensive, longer-term inventory-management planning
- Effective use of computer-assisted item development and scoring technologies to increase item banks and expedite score reporting
- New approaches to updating rest plans and batch methods for item calibration (traditional approaches may be inadequate to keep pace with a rapidly evolving global business environment in credentialing examinations)

Some practical challenges exist with secure test delivery in dedicated test centers for high-stakes examinations. Some promising directions in the assembly of tests include dynamic updating of item exposures, scoring information, or exclusion of previously seen content on an examinee-by-examinee or administration event basis. Currently, CBT delivery channels have long lead times for the publication and distribution of content. For example, if some test questions become compromised, it is not usually possible to immediately remove these from the subpool currently in rotation in the test centers.

Similarly, while empirical counts of item usage can be collected along with responses to items on a daily basis, there is no mechanism to immediately include this information, so it might be considered in the selection of items any time prior to the publication of a future subpool for test events in the (somewhat distant) future. The use of ongoing data collected during test events (including evidence that test content may be compromised) is not compatible with the fairly rigid batch publication and delivery cycles for CBT in dedicated test centers. Synchronization of results data and test administrations is feasible only when synchronous communication is possible among results processing, developer specifications for selection rules, and test administration systems.

A related set of issues emerges from the traditional batch approach to the test development, publication, and scoring workflows more generally. When paper tests are published and delivered to large numbers of candidates on just a few occasions annually, opportunities for quality assurance are tied to the test event date itself (e.g., changes to content or scoring rules are possible up to administration time or score report publication). When continuous testing is available on computer and scoring immediate, quality-assurance (QA) activities must be built into the workflow and changes heavily controlled. This is because it is common to draw subpools from the same bank so that the same items might simultaneously be at very different points in the item development, QA, publication, and scoring workflows. The coding of items in item banks used with automated test assembly must include accurate meta-data relevant to high-quality test form creation. This includes accurate and exclusive content or skill coding, item exposure, item enemy information, history of prior usage, and the status of items as operational or pilot and pending scoring or calibration information.

Some practical technical limitations exist with our familiar model of dedicated test centers. Connectivity and bandwidth limitations prohibit the use of sophisticated linear programming (LP) solvers with commercial test drivers for real-time assembly (Drasgow, Luecht, & Bennett, 2006; Luecht, 2012). This is certainly true for smaller testing programs that lack the market influence to inspire delivery vendors to develop customized systems or to improve server-based test administrations.

It seems inevitable that even our smaller testing programs will soon demand interoperability for item banking software, assembly, and scoring systems. Drasgow, Luecht, and Bennett (2006) describe a vision for interoperability in testing programs as a system of systems for comprehensive inventory planning, test development, publishing, delivery, and scoring.

System interoperability might just mean use of a common markup language for test content to allow data to be easily loaded into systems needed to manage the development, storage, publication, review, and assembly of tests or tasks and items on computer. As described in Drasgow and colleagues (2006), many vendor-provided systems for item banking and test delivery software use extensible markup language, XML; others have proprietary language for their test delivery systems. Many test developers also rely on commercial word processing or publishing applications for authoring and revisions to test questions, and few content management systems allow the test developer to see the questions exactly as they will be presented to the test taker during test delivery.

The "heirloom" nature of our custom-built applications is evident in even our largest testing programs, where disparate custom systems are created separately for key functions in the workflows, and these are often supplemented by commercial software tools. In these workflows, many file hops and manual intervening steps are common. For example, different systems and applications are usually used for item authoring, rubric management, item banking, response processing, scoring, item calibrations, and the production of score reports.

Inadequate change control, vulnerability to security breaches for test content and results, and opportunities to introduce errors threaten the accuracy of our test results when programs lack adequate preventive and detective controls in these workflows. The issue of system compatibility becomes even more complicated when developers use complex content, innovative item formats such as graphics or audio or video files, or searchable reference materials as components of the test questions.

Attempts to standardize systems supporting computerization have been only partly successful (e.g., International Guidelines for Computer-based or Internet-based testing, ITC, 2005); Performance Testing Council Standards and Best Practices, PTC, 2004). However, some programs have begun to adopt open-source applications available from Accessible Portable Item Protocol (APIP) and Question and Test Interoperability (QTI; e.g., IMS GLOBAL, 2012).

An extension of the idea of interoperability would allow relevant data to be transmitted easily between systems so that metadata needed for the management of item pools and assembly of tests can be frequently or even automatically updated as test results are received and scored. Updating item metadata during test administration periods would allow for automated assembly to incorporate empirical item exposures and updated calibration or item parameter estimates for pilot items (IRT chapter, this volume). User-configurable classification systems for content stored in item banks are available from most commercial vendors; however, it is rare to find flexibility to include additional metadata for items useful in the future for ATA. For example, it would be important to include in the relational database structure for item banking the ability for developers to code and list information about test questions generated using a semiautomated process such as described by Gierl and associates (this volume), and it may be useful to track and consider in item selection the existence of approved automated scoring models or rubrics.

The demand for more fidelity in the test taker experience, service to a cross-cultural population, and accommodations for a variety of special needs has forced testing programs to consider technologies that stretch the boundaries of automated assembly. Translation of test content is now possible during test administration with the availability of a variety of translation engines, and access to online dictionaries or libraries of searchable literature is sometimes justified. How is the test developer to consider implications of the option to view content in one of a variety of languages when assembly rules are defined? Implications for time required on items and for the comparability of scoring rules (e.g., item calibrations using IRT) will require additional research as we make these resources available in our examinations. Studies of response data from exams offering these resources or tools will inform new constraints to be provided for future assembly of tests.

Adaptation of tests for persons with disabilities is a requirement in many jurisdictions in North America where standardized tests are offered and by many regulatory authorities offering credentialing examinations. Software solutions are now readily available to assist with disabilities of many kinds (e.g., Landmark College, 2010). These include voice-to-text and text-to-audio in addition to concept mapping tools to aid reading comprehension and also aids for numeracy comprehension. Implications exist should testing programs wish to include this flexibility in our testing programs, and new item selection rules may have to be considered if we are to preserve comparable test experiences for all examinees and fairness in our scoring of tests.

Innovative item formats and delivery models are arising from use of handheld technologies and from natural language recognition in response capturing or scoring (e.g., Parshall, this volume; Stark & Chernychenko, this volume). We will require a more comprehensive solution to the assembly problem that considers the availability and cost of automated and manual scoring methods for our items and tasks. As test administrations become more flexible, and possibly without group administration-based proctoring, larger item banks will be needed to ensure security of content. Also, batch or manual scoring becomes infeasible in conditions of rapid or continuous score reporting; therefore, it seems inevitable we will need to take advantage of more efficient item writing, automated scoring and precalibration, or real-time calibration of pilot items. These developments will lead test assembly to incorporate provisional calibrations for items and/or real-time calibration of pilot items to drive more subtle test and item pool designs in future assessments.

The popularity of cloud- or Internet- based delivery of high-stakes examinations is already causing the development of even larger item banks to assure secure item bank rotations for flexible scheduling of many unique test forms across time zones and continents (Breithaupt, Mills, & Melican, 2006).

The need for larger item banks means shorter item development timelines and some mechanisms to improve and automate the steps in the test development, delivery, and scoring process workflows. It may be fair to note that the needs of the largest testing programs typically drive development and innovation among the commercial providers of systems supporting computerized test delivery. As more of our influential large-volume testing programs incorporate innovative items and demand greater control over pool rotation and content updates to ongoing test administrations, we will begin to see effective solutions in which a range of vendors compete with greater interoperability across systems and where automation in test assembly is supported seamlessly by item banking and by test publishing and delivery system designs and workflows.

There exist several case studies in the literature to illustrate the practical use of discrete optimization for distinct models of computer-delivered high-stakes examinations. It is our belief, however, that real progress in future may exist in research on the broader problems of large item pool planning, inventory management, and deliberate long-term supply-chain analyses where banking, assembly, and inventory management are fully integrated.

Large investments in research and test development occur whenever test plans are updated to reflect changes in the knowledge and skills for a given testing program. These updates to content are carefully controlled to balance currency of content and the response from educators, who must prepare our test takers adequately for standardized testing. Often, shifts in the educational programs (e.g., Raymond & Neustel, 2006) drive such changes. Any assembly methodology must be flexible enough to accommodate periodic changes in test plans. For credentialing exams, it may be desirable to update test specifications more often and to obtain and update statistically calibrated item data for pilot items so we can easily meet the needs of rapidly changing professional practices. For global test administrations, our scoring methods may have to consider cross-lingual assessment and translations of test content with equated or rescaled scoring to ensure comparability across and within diverse populations. This vision can be realized only if we are able to carefully impose subtle design in the composition of test forms and also in the development and scoring of our test items via computer (e.g., Gierl, this volume).

While these issues are practical concerns for the quality, security, and cost of program delivery, we also forecast that more effective management of item banks will be essential to program management in the future. This deliberate management of large item banks may include the ability to "layer" item pools so that the selection of test questions for CAT subpools or on preconstructed forms or testlets is built in. The class to which an item belongs might indicate the degree of similarity an item has to a unique model or template used in the automatic item generation process. It may be necessary to limit the appearance of several items when only surface features differ. In contrast, it may be desirable to allow several items with different cognitive skill steps or knowledge needed for solutions or different "deep" structures to be selected together on test forms. This status of the item, described here as an item "class," could be input to an assembly problem in addition to the content or skill coding and the statistical properties of the items (e.g., IRT difficulty and discrimination). All data relevant to high-quality test design and scoring would need to be considered throughout the test development process and be supported by the procedures, systems, and applications we use (e.g., exposure data, word count, reading level, item enemy status, identifiers of common exhibits for linked tasks, and skill and content codes, author ID, and date of creation). Benefits from computer-assisted item writing may be most evident when test and pool design includes class and variant and family- related rules (Gierl, this volume) for item selection onto test forms and for inventory management.

LP solutions can be used to plan and implement the writing and use of these larger item banks in order to produce comparable tests over time (e.g., van der Linden, 2005). This kind of deliberate item authoring is already needed to supply item banks over a longer planning horizon in order to meet the need for more frequent testing in high-stakes examinations.

Given the promise of cost-effective and rapid item production from computer-assisted item generation (Gierl, this volume), it makes sense to anticipate a need for more efficient ways to replace pilot item statistics with the results of calibrated and banked IRT item parameters used for scoring. Commercial vendors can return results from test administrations on a daily or immediate basis. As we have noted, most operational testing programs use separate processes and software applications to score candidates and to calculate IRT item parameter estimates for pilot items. Separate steps are needed to provide this item data to the test delivery system, often in a complex transfer of packaged data that may require republishing the electronic data file supplied to the test delivery system in the test centers. It can require weeks or even months of lead time in order to effectively administer and score a new counting (operational) test question for the first time. This long cycle time must become shorter if we are expected to routinely update the content and skills we are assessing or refresh our item pools or test forms without interrupting test delivery for long periods.

### Discussion

Some progress has been made on these issues, and our investment in research programs will ensure we remain viable and continue to meet the need for secure and valid assessment. Research feeds innovation, and stakeholder demands drive business strategies where innovation can be piloted. A more collaborative future waits, with strong links between academic and industry researchers working toward solutions to these and to other emerging assessment problems. Cross-disciplinary collaboration holds promise, and our interactions with innovators in telecommunications, mathematical programming, cognitive psychology, education, virtual reality, gaming, and the professions in which simulation has been integrated into learning and assessment (medicine and military training are examples) are already lighting the way to a new era in measurement.

Some of our colleagues are already adopting open-source test content management and delivery solutions (e.g., TAO, 2013). Open-source essay scoring systems have also been shown to be at least as accurate as commercial products (Mayfield & Rose, 2012; Shermis et al.,

2012). These examples showcase the potential of open-source solutions that promise greater interoperability potential and may help to overcome the barriers imposed by intellectual property protections in the commercial vendor market for assessment systems. The integration of a sophisticated solver within an open-source relational database for test content could support inventory planning and assembly needs for operational testing programs.

Traditional practices and the technological issues related to automated assembly of tests are not insurmountable, and good case studies have shown practical optimization solutions can work efficiently in large-volume high-stakes programs (e.g., Zhang & Hare, 2011). Evidence is accumulating to indicate testing programs and the technologies we depend on are also evolving to meet these challenges (e.g., Gierl & Haladyna, 2013). This volume also offers some encouraging examples of automation in item generation and appropriate models for calibration and scoring equivalent unique forms for computer-delivered test questions. As our stakeholders raise their standards for service delivery, our testing programs will look to the evidence from research on innovations, and commercial vendors will revisit their business strategies to enable our assessment programs to realize the potential of higher fidelity and richer assessment in a technologically supported global community. The quality of operational testing programs depends on our ongoing support for research and development in academia and in industry. Both are essential to the defensible and valid use of tests in our society.

## Note

1  The general problem of asking for an optimal solution to an MIP is NP-hard, a category of algorithmic complexity for which no known efficient solution strategy has yet been found.

## References

Breithaupt, K., & Hare, D. (2012). *Test assembly and delivery models for a national examination of medical knowledge.* Annual meeting of the Association of Test Publishers, Palm Springs, CA.

Breithaupt, K., Ariel, A., & Hare, D.R. (2009). Assembling an inventory of multi-stage adaptive systems. In W. van der Linden & C.A.W. Glas (Eds.), *Computerized adaptive testing theory and practice* (2nd ed.). Norwell, MA: Kluwer.

Breithaupt, K., Ariel A., & Hare, D.R. (2010). Assembling and inventory of multi-stage adaptive testing systems. In van der Linden & Glas (Eds.), *Elements of adaptive testing* (pp. 247–266). New York: Springer.

Breithaupt, K., Ariel, A., & Veldkamp, B.P. (2005). Automated simultaneous assembly for multistage testing. *International Journal of Testing, 5,* 319–330.

Breithaupt, K., & Hare, D.R. (2007). Automated simultaneous assembly of multistage testlets for a high-stakes licensing examination. *Educational and Psychological Measurement, 67*(1), 5–20.

Breithaupt, K., Mills, C., & Melican, J. (2006). Facing the opportunities of the future. In D. Bartram & R.K. Hambleton (Eds.), *Computer-based testing and the Internet: Issues and advances* (pp. 219–251). West Sussex, UK: John Wiley & Sons, Ltd.

Cor, Alvez, & Gierl, M.J. (2009). Three applications of automated test assembly within a user-friendly modeling environment. *Practical Assessment, Research & Evaluation, 14,* 1–9. http://pareonline.net/pdf/v14n14.pdf. Accessed Dec. 14, 2012.

Downing, S.M., & Haladyna, T.M. (2006). *Handbook of test development.* Mahwah, NJ: Lawrence Erlbaum Associates.

Drasgow, F., Luecht, R.M., & Bennett, R.E. (2006) Technology and testing. In R. Brennan (Ed.), *Educational measurement* (4th ed., pp. 471–515). Westport, CT: American Council on Education and Praeger.

Frontline Solvers. (2013). www.solver.com/premium-solver. Accessed June 26, 2013.

Gierl, M.J., & Haladyna, T.M. (2013). *Automatic item generation: Theory and practice.* New York: Routledge.

Hambleton, R.K., & Swaminathan, H. (1985). *Item response theory: Principles and applications.* Boston, MA: Kluwer-Nijhoff.

IMS Global Learning Consortium. (2012). *IMS Question and Test Interoperability Assessment Test, question and item information.* www.imsglobal.org/question/qtiv2p1/imsqti_infov2p1.htmlModel. Accessed November 21, 2013.

International Testing Commission. (2005). *International guidelines for computer-based and internet-delivered testing.* www.intestcom.org/Downloads/ITC%20Guidelines%20on%20Computer%20-%20version%202005%20 approved.pdf. Accessed November 21, 2013.

Landmark College. (2010). Assistive technologies for everyone. https://intranet.landmark.edu/tls/TechnologyResources.cfm. Accessed November 25, 2013.

Luecht, R.M., & Hirsch, T.M. (1992). Computerized test construction using average growth approximation of target information functions. *Applied Psychological Measurement 16*, 41–52.

Luecht, R.M., & Nungester, R.(1998). Some practical examples of computer-adaptive sequential testing. *Journal of Educational Measurement, 35*, 229–249.

Luecht, R.M. (2012). Operational CBT implementation issues: Making it happen. In R. Lissitz & H. Jiao (Eds.), *Computers and their impact on state assessments: Recent history and predictions for the future.* Baltimore, MD: Information Age Publishers.

Mayfield, E., & Rose, C.P. (2012). *LightSide text mining and machine learning users' manual.* Pittsburgh, PA: Carnegie-Mellon University.

Performance Testing Council. (2004). *Standards and best practices.* www.performancetest.org/uploads/resources/ Standards%20and%20Best%20Practices.pdf. Accessed November 21, 2013.

Raymond, N.R., & Neutsel, S. (2006). Determining the content of credentialing exams. In S.M. Downing & T. Haladyna (Eds.), *Handbook of test development* (pp. 181–223). Mahwah, NJ: Lawrence Erlbaum Associates.

Shermis, M., Hammer, B., & Kaggle (2012). *Contrasting state of the art automated essay scoring systems.* Paper presentation at the annual meeting of the National Council on Educational Measurement, Vancouver, BC.

Stocking, M.L., & Lewis, C. (2000). Methods of controlling the exposure of items in CAT. In W.J. van der Linden & C. Glas (Eds.), *Computer-adaptive testing: Theory and practice* (pp. 163–182). Boston, MA: Kluwer.

Stocking, M.L., & Swanson, L. (1993). A method for severely constrained item selection in adaptive testing. *Applied Psychological Measurement, 17*, 277–292.

TAO. (2013). Open-source assessment tools. www.taotesting.com/. Accessed May 21, 2013.

Theunissen, T.J.J.M. (1985). Binary programming and test design. *Psychometrika, 50*, 411–420.

van der Linden, W.J. (2005). *Linear models for optimal test design.* New York, NY: Springer.

van der Linden, W.J., & Glas, C. (2010). *Elements of adaptive testing.* New York, NY: Springer.

Way, W.D., Steffan, M., & Anderson, G. (2002). Developing, maintaining, and renewing inventory to support CBT. C.N. Mills, M.T. Potenza, J.J. Fremer, & W.C. Ward (Eds.), *Computer-based testing: Building the foundation for future assessments* (pp. 143–164). Hillsdale, NJ: Erlbaum.

Zhang, O., & Hare, D.R. (2011). *Automated systems and algorithms used in the assembly of MST.* Paper presented at the annual meeting of the International Association for Computer-Adaptive Testing, Monterey, CA.

# 7
# Validity and Automated Scoring

Randy Elliot Bennett and Mo Zhang

This chapter concerns the automated scoring of answers to constructed-response items as seen through the lens of validity. That lens was chosen because scoring and validity cannot be meaningfully separated (Bennett, 2011; Bennett & Bejar, 1998). Attempts to treat automated scoring without a central focus on validity have too often led to a misunderstanding of what the technology can and cannot do. In essence, what this chapter is about is how to do automated scoring with validity considerations at the forefront—where they belong.

The chapter is organized as follows. First, a definition of automated scoring is offered, the types of tasks that have been scored in the English language arts and mathematics are listed, and the process involved in carrying out one type of scoring, that for essays, is detailed. Second, several assertions about validity and automated essay scoring are made, with examples offered in the K–12 context and in graduate admissions testing. Third, suggestions for implementation in operational settings are given. Finally, the chapter's main points are summarized.

## An Introduction to Automated Scoring

### A Definition

By automated scoring, we mean the machine grading of constructed responses that are generally not amenable to exact-matching approaches because the specific form(s) and/or content of the correct answer(s) are not known in advance. That definition covers a large collection of grading approaches that differ dramatically depending upon the constructed-response task being posed and the nature of the answers expected from a given population of examinees. Those approaches vary enough that, even within a broad content domain like the English language arts, a single characterization of the "state of the art" for a domain would be misleading (Bennett, 2011).

### Types of Tasks That Have Been Scored Automatically

In the English language arts (ELA), including English as a foreign language, approaches have been developed for scoring essays (Shermis & Burstein, 2013), short text responses ranging from a few words to a few sentences (Brew & Leacock, 2013), predictable spoken responses

(Versant, 2008), and unpredictable speech (Higgins, Xi, Zechner, & Williamson, 2011). A brief description of example tasks, target competencies, and scoring approaches associated with these categories can be found in Bennett (2011, p. 7).

In mathematics, approaches have been created for scoring equations and expressions (Bennett et al., 1997); instances from an open set in numeric, symbolic, or graphical form (Bennett et al., 1999); symbolic work leading to a final answer (Sebrechts, Bennett, & Rock, 1991); and short text responses (Sandene et al., 2005, pp. 31–36). See Bennett (2011, p. 10) for additional description.

Within each of ELA and mathematics, the extent to which the cited response types can be effectively scored automatically varies widely. As a consequence, only some of those task types have been used in operational testing programs.

Without question, as of this writing, the greatest operational use—in terms of both the number of testing programs and number of examinees—is for essay scoring. For consequential assessments, automated essay scoring can be found in postsecondary admissions (GRE revised General Test, Graduate Management Admission Test, Test of English as a Foreign Language iBT, Pearson Test of English), professional licensure and certification (Uniform Certified Public Accountants Examination), postsecondary placement (ACCUPLACER, COMPASS), and K–12 state assessment (Utah Direct Writing Assessment, West Virginia WESTEST 2). Automated essay scoring is also used in formative and instructional systems, including Criterion (ETS), MyAccess (Vantage Learning), MyWritingLab (Pearson), and Writing Roadmap (CTB/McGraw-Hill).

For consequential assessment purposes, there has been little use to date for other types of ELA tasks. Among the few exceptions are for short text responses in the Hawaii State Assessment and Minnesota Comprehensive Assessments (J. Cohen, personal communication, February 25, 2013) and for predictable spoken responses in the Pearson Test of English.

In mathematics, use has been considerably more limited than in ELA. One example involves tasks calling for the scoring of instances from an open set in numeric, symbolic, or graphical form. Such tasks are automatically scored in the Delaware Comprehensive Assessment System, Hawaii State Assessment, Minnesota Comprehensive Assessments, and Oregon Assessment of Knowledge and Skills (J. Cohen, personal communication, February 25, 2013).

### A High-Level Overview of the Automated Essay Scoring Process

As noted, the most widely used application of automated scoring is for essay responses. Understandably, those systems are also the most developed and researched, with a history dating to Page (1966). To score a task or similar group of tasks, a "model" must be created, or trained and calibrated. Figure 7.1 gives an overview of that process.

First, a task, or essay prompt, is selected from a pool representing a universe of prompts ("task domain") created to elicit examinee processes and produce a result aligned with some construct definition (the undergirding foundation at the bottom of the figure). That construct definition—and the associated prompts—may vary widely depending upon the purpose of the test, ranging from an emphasis on low-level fundamentals (as in the NAEP writing assessment) to advanced skills like argumentation (as expected in the PARCC and Smarter Balanced assessments of the Common Core State Standards). Second, examinees respond to that prompt in a computer interface having a set of affordances and constraints, producing a performance artifact or, in this case, an essay. The affordances may include such tools as cut and paste, spellcheck, and outlining templates; the constraints may entail a time limit that the interface enforces. Third, a suitable training and calibration sample of responses is drawn from the population on which the system is to be used. Fourth, human judges are trained to score the responses in keeping with a rubric and exemplars aligned to the construct definition. Exemplars may illustrate each score point ("benchmarks"), as well as boundaries between score points ("rangefinders"). Fifth, features are automatically extracted from each essay. Depending upon the modeling method and the predilection of the model developers, the number of features extracted may run from a handful to thousands. Sixth, the features of the essays in the training and calibration sample, on their own or in conjunction with the human scores, are used to create a scoring model—essentially, a selection of features and combination rules. Many modeling methods are possible but, among the disclosed essay-scoring systems, multiple linear regression of the human scores on the feature scores has been the method most frequently used. Seventh, that model can then generate scores for as-yet-unseen essays.

Using those as-yet-unseen essays, the model is evaluated and, if suitable, put into operation. An overview of the operational process is shown in Figure 7.2. In operational use, essays with aberrant features (e.g., too few words) may be automatically filtered by a predetermined process associated with the scoring model and may be routed to receive only human scores. Operational deployment may involve the sole use of automated scores (with human scoring as quality control), the use of automated scoring as a check on human scores, or the use of automated scoring in combination with human scores (Zhang, 2013a). However produced, the essay scores may be employed on their own to generate a reported score via some measurement model or scaled with responses from other items to create that reported score. Finally, the reported score will have some intended interpretation and use.

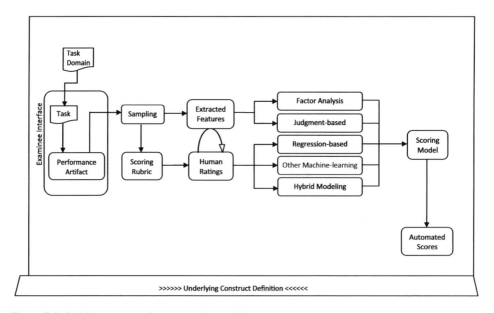

**Figure 7.1** Deriving automated essay scoring models

*Note:* The semi-circular arrow between "human ratings" and "extracted features" denotes the potential joint use of human ratings and extracted features in producing the scoring model as in, for example, regressing ratings on features.

*Source:* Copyright by Educational Testing Service, 2015. All rights reserved.

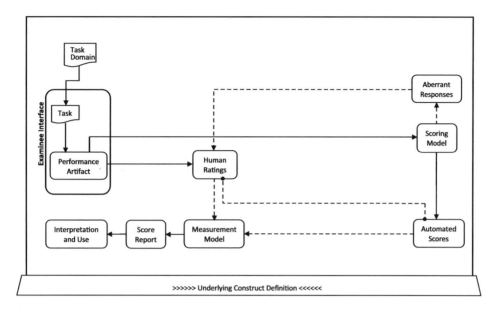

**Figure 7.2** Automated essay scoring in operational use

*Note:* Dashed lines indicate that a connection is optional.

*Source:* Copyright by Educational Testing Service, 2015. All rights reserved.

It should be noted that this operational process diagram is broad enough to cover the automated scoring of most of the ELA and mathematics tasks listed earlier. The model training and calibration diagram in Figure 7.1 is less general. For some approaches to the scoring of short text responses, in particular ones based on regression and other machine-learning approaches, the depicted training and calibration process might well stand as is. In the case of predictable or unpredictable speech, however, the process would require the addition of a recognition step prior to feature extraction.

### Seven Assertions About Validity and Automated Essay Scoring

If nothing else, the model-creation and operational-scoring diagrams should make clear that, even at a very high level, these processes involve multiple steps, assumptions, and decisions. That level of complication raises significant validity issues. To frame the issues, we make seven assertions.

#### It's Not Only the Scoring

Automated scoring should be designed as part of a construct-driven, integrated system because the interplay among system components is complex and that complexity must be accounted for in scoring-program design and validation (Bennett, 2006; Bennett & Bejar, 1998). As an example, the automated grader must be able to process what the interface allows. On the one hand, a minimally constrained interface might allow for the most naturalistic problem solving but make scoring more difficult. An essay-response interface that included tools for creating figures, tables, and bulleted lists and for underlining, bolding, and italics would have many of the knowledge representations that students use in school and that professionals use in their daily writing. However, the resulting essays would be hard to score automatically if those interface affordances were to be accounted for directly. On the other hand, constraining the interface may make scoring easier but narrow the measured construct to its basic elements, elements that in the test situation are substantially less than what students do in their classroom writing. This interplay among computer-based test components—and particularly the interplay between automated scoring and the intended construct—is a theme we will come back to repeatedly in this chapter, because that interplay is key to any validity argument for such scoring, as well as to understanding potential rebuttals to it (e.g., NCTE, 2013).

### Automated Scoring Is Becoming More Important

An example in support of this second assertion can be found in the ELA Common Core State Standards (Common Core State Standards Initiative, 2012), some of which cannot be measured meaningfully without the use of essay tasks. As a consequence, the Common Core State Assessments (CCSA) include such items (Measured Progress/ETS Collaborative, 2012; PARCC, 2013), as typically do the tests of other states adhering to substantively similar standards. Consider this hypothetical but plausible scenario. Approximately 24 million students will be tested annually, with each student producing at least one essay. If scored as in common practice, each of the responses would be read by two human raters. Those raters would disagree substantially some of the time, which might require ~ 5% of the responses to be read again. In this scenario, the total number of human essay readings would approach 50 million.[1] To put that figure in context, ETS processed something on the order of 26 million essay readings in 2011 across all of its testing programs (Personal communication, P. Matthew, June 12, 2012). Under such demand conditions, the motivation to use automated scoring is substantial because, without it, including essays for all students taking these tests may simply not be sustainable.

Not surprisingly, demand creates availability, so currently, many organizations—nonprofit and for-profit alike—offer automated essay-scoring services. Among those organizations are AIR; ETS; CTB/McGraw Hill; Measurement, Inc.; Pacific Metrics; Pearson; and Vantage Learning. Automated essay scoring programs can also be assembled from off-the-shelf components. The Carnegie-Mellon University (CMU) LightSIDE tool box is an example that is open source and free (Mayfield & Rose, 2012).

### Automated Scoring Methodology Is Becoming More Obscure

Coincident with its increased importance, the methodology has become less transparent. Three factors underlie this change. First, the technology itself is continuously advancing, with a level of sophistication and complexity far greater than that employed in the field's early years (e.g., Page, 1966). A second reason for diminished transparency, which interacts with the first, is that the technology increasingly brings to bear areas of expertise well outside of educational measurement. To be sure, educational measurement has also advanced markedly, but testing program directors have well-established ways to access the necessary expertise, including through their own training or through technical advisory committee (TAC) members. Few testing directors or TAC members are familiar, however, with the intricacies of the natural language processing and machine-learning methodologies used in state-of-the-art automated scoring systems. Finally, with multiple vendors offering these services, the competition has become intense. To maintain competitive advantage, vendors have tended to keep their methods proprietary and confidential. As a consequence, exactly how most commercial programs work is not known.

Increased sophistication, contributions from other fields, and competition among vendors are valued by testing program directors because those factors promise technological improvements. Those improvements may, in turn, reduce the cost and time associated with human scoring, which may make it possible to include tasks that both measure and exemplify important standards. On the other hand, these same factors simultaneously make the technology harder to understand substantively and, as a consequence, challenging for program directors to explain and publically defend.

Under such conditions, singular and simple metrics become very appealing because they appear to offer a direct, easily understandable indicator of quality. For automated scoring, the accuracy of predicting operational human scores has become that direct indicator, as both development goal and evaluation criterion (Attali, 2013; Bridgeman, 2013). The disclosed approaches generally regress operational human scores on essay features, while some other approaches are reputed to use other, more complicated, and potentially less understandable machine-learning techniques. Those latter techniques induce regularities from essays that may predict human scores but that might not be readily explainable or necessarily have substantive meaning. The implications of this choice of metric and its consequences for validation will shortly become apparent.

In 2012, the Hewlett Foundation, in collaboration with the two main Common Core State Assessment Consortia, sponsored the Automated Student Assessment Prize Phase I (ASAP I; Shermis & Morgan, 2013). This competition facilitated a comparison of performance across vendor systems on a common dataset and also attracted new developers to the field of automated scoring. The details of the competition deserve further discussion because they raise issues at the very center of validity and automated scoring.

In the words of the Foundation, the goal was ". . . to begin to solve the problem of the high cost and the slow turnaround resulting from the time consuming and expensive task of hand scoring thousands of essays for standardized tests" (Hewlett Foundation, 2012). The design called for separate vendor and public competitions, with a cash prize for the public contest. The vendor competition included nine entrants: the testing companies (AIR, ETS, CTB/McGraw Hill, Measurement, Inc., Pacific Metrics, Pearson, Vantage Learning), CMU with its open toolbox, and MetaMetrics with its Lexile technology. The public competition, in contrast, had 159 entrants.

The dataset consisted of eight essays from six state assessments (Shermis & Hamner, 2013). The essays covered several genres and had been taken by 7th-, 8th-, or 10th-grade students. The average length of the responses ran from 94 to 622 words, with the median of averages equal to 163 words, or about half a double-spaced, typewritten page. Six of the eight essays had been responded to by students on paper and were subsequently transcribed to digital form. One essay was scored on two trait scales and treated as two separate essays, making nine rather than eight prompts in the data set. Each response was operationally scored by two human raters on score scales ranging from 4 to 31 points, where the longest scales came from summing across trait scores to create a composite score.

The student response data were divided into training and blind cross-validation sets, with the former set including both response text and human scores, and the latter having only the response text.[2] Cross-validation sample sizes ranged from 304 to 601. In those samples, the human–human exact percentage-agreement values ran from 28% to 76%, where the lowest values were understandably associated with the longest score scales. The sole evaluation criterion was agreement with operational human ratings.

For the vendor competition, the means, standard deviations, percentages agreement, Pearson correlations, kappa, and quadratic weighted kappa were reported. For the public competition, only quadratic weighted kappa was released. For readers unfamiliar with quadratic weighted kappa, that index weights disagreements nonlinearly by their size, so larger discrepancies receive a disproportionately greater penalty than do smaller ones. As a consequence, for datasets having frequent but small discrepancies, quadratic weighted kappa will suggest a much more positive picture of interrater consistency than will exact agreement, kappa, or linearly weighted kappa.

Before discussing the results, one additional methodological detail deserves mention. The quality of human rating was evaluated by computing agreement between Human 1 and Human 2. However, instead of then computing machine agreement with each of Human 1 and Human 2, as is common practice (Attali, 2013, p. 189; Williamson, 2013, p. 153), that agreement was evaluated against a "resolved score," which itself differed depending on the prompt. For two essay questions, the resolved score was only Human 1. For three essay questions, it was Human 1 plus Human 2, and for four essay questions, the resolved score was the higher of Human 1 or Human 2. This double inconsistency in agreement computation—that is, different criteria for human and for machine, *and* different criteria for the machine depending on the prompt—makes the interpretation of results less clear than it might otherwise have been.

The results of the vendor competition were widely reported. There was coverage in *USA Today*, the *New York Times*, National Public Radio, *TIME* magazine, and in many other media outlets. Some of that coverage was quite balanced, but some was more like that given in Table 7.1.

Of particular importance in Table 7.1 is the tendency among some of those describing the results to conclude that machine and human scores were essentially interchangeable. What, in fact, were the results? If one considers only the differences in the overall score distributions between the machine and the human ratings, the quotes in Table 7.1 might be reasonable.

Table 7.1 The Results of the Automated Student Assessment Prize Phase 1 Vendor Competition as Reported in a Press Release, News Article, and Blog

| Source | Quotation |
| --- | --- |
| Man and machine: Better writers, better grades (University of Akron, 4/12/2012) | "A direct comparison between human graders and software designed to score student essays achieved *virtually identical* levels of accuracy, with the software in some cases proving to be more reliable, a groundbreaking study has found." |
| Hewlett automated-essay-grader winners announced (*EdWeek*, 5/9/2012) | "The William and Flora Hewlett Foundation . . . found automated essay-graders capable of *replicating* scores of their human counterparts." |
| OpenEd project demonstrates effectiveness of automated essay scoring (OpenEd Blog, 5/13/2012) | "The demonstration showed *conclusively* that automated essay scoring systems are fast, *accurate*, and cost effective . . ." |

*Note*: Italics added.

But that judgment is, strictly speaking, uncertain because no statistical test of the human and machine means was reported.

Table 7.2 gives the exact agreement deltas—that is, exact machine–human agreement minus exact human–human agreement—taken from Shermis and Morgan (2013), with the addition of a column of median values and of shading. Light shading indicates instances for which the difference is bigger than .10 in favor of the machine, where .10 is an arbitrary but noticeable difference. There are two such instances in which the machine agrees more highly with the human "resolved score" than the two human raters agree themselves. Shown in dark shading are the instances that favor human–human agreement (i.e., < = −.10). As can be seen, automated scoring is not as equivalent to human rating, at least in terms of exact agreement, as the quotes in Table 7.1 would suggest.

Table 7.3 gives the results in terms of unweighted kappa, which attempts to account for chance agreement, penalizing all discrepancies equally. As should be obvious, these values also do not support the case for the equivalence of machine and human scores either.

With quadratic weighted kappa, the situation is certainly better. As shown in Table 7.4, the medians now are more evenly distributed around zero. But, even so, the results still favor human scoring. Excluding the medians, there are 18 entries in the table smaller than or equal to −.10 and only 2 in the opposite direction. A similar story emerges when examining the deltas for the correlations (not shown).[3]

The fact that there are fewer highlights in Table 7.4 than in Table 7.3 (unweighted kappa) suggests that, relative to human–human agreement, the humans and machines disagree with one another more often over smaller differences than over larger ones. Said another way, the humans appear to be more reliable than the machine at distinguishing these smaller differences. But note that these "smaller" differences are not always so small. On the 4-point scales

Table 7.2  Cross-Validation Exact-Agreement Deltas From the ASAP I Vendor Competition

| Essay (Scale) | Vendor | | | | | | | | | |
| | 1 | 2 | 3 | 4 | 5 | 6 | 7 | 8 | 9 | Mdn |
|---|---|---|---|---|---|---|---|---|---|---|
| 1 (6) | −0.20 | −0.20 | −0.20 | −0.22 | −0.18 | −0.33 | −0.21 | −0.21 | −0.17 | −0.20 |
| 2a (6) | −0.08 | −0.12 | −0.06 | −0.07 | −0.06 | −0.21 | −0.12 | −0.08 | −0.06 | −0.08 |
| 2b (4) | −0.05 | −0.14 | −0.07 | −0.04 | −0.07 | −0.18 | −0.07 | −0.06 | −0.04 | −0.07 |
| 3 (4) | −0.04 | −0.02 | −0.06 | −0.03 | 0 | −0.09 | −0.11 | −0.03 | −0.03 | −0.03 |
| 4 (4) | −0.11 | −0.08 | −0.12 | −0.10 | −0.04 | −0.28 | −0.16 | −0.12 | −0.05 | −0.11 |
| 5 (5) | 0.12 | 0.08 | 0.09 | 0.06 | 0.09 | −0.12 | 0.09 | 0.06 | 0.12 | 0.09 |
| 6 (5) | 0.04 | −0.02 | 0 | −0.01 | 0.06 | −0.12 | 0.01 | 0.05 | 0.06 | 0.01 |
| 7 (13) | −0.18 | −0.13 | −0.16 | −0.16 | −0.11 | −0.21 | −0.19 | −0.16 | −0.16 | −0.16 |
| 8 (31) | −0.17 | −0.03 | −0.06 | −0.11 | −0.12 | −0.20 | −0.14 | −0.09 | −0.19 | −0.12 |

*Note:* Adapted from Table 19.9 of "Contrasting state-of-the-art automated scoring of essays" by M. D. Shermis and B. Hamner, 2013. In M. D. Shermis & J. Burstein (Eds.), *Handbook of automated essay evaluation: Current applications and new directions* (pp. 313–346). New York: Routledge. Values are exact machine–human agreement minus exact human–human agreement, where machine–human agreement is the concurrence between the machine and the human "resolved score," and human–human agreement is the concurrence of Human 1 and Human 2. Dark shading indicates difference of < = −.10 in favor of humans. Light shading indicates difference of > = .10 in favor of machine.

Table 7.3  Cross-Validation Unweighted-Kappa Deltas From the ASAP I Vendor Competition

| Essay (Scale) | Vendor | | | | | | | | | |
|---|---|---|---|---|---|---|---|---|---|---|
| | 1 | 2 | 3 | 4 | 5 | 6 | 7 | 8 | 9 | *Mdn* |
| 1 (6) | −0.16 | −0.16 | −0.20 | −0.17 | −0.12 | −0.29 | −0.16 | −0.18 | −0.13 | −0.16 |
| 2a (6) | −0.16 | −0.18 | −0.13 | −0.11 | −0.11 | −0.32 | −0.19 | −0.14 | −0.12 | −0.14 |
| 2b (4) | −0.10 | −0.21 | −0.14 | −0.07 | −0.10 | −0.29 | −0.13 | −0.11 | −0.08 | −0.11 |
| 3 (4) | −0.05 | −0.01 | −0.07 | −0.03 | 0.02 | −0.12 | −0.14 | −0.02 | −0.04 | −0.04 |
| 4 (4) | −0.16 | −0.09 | −0.15 | −0.12 | −0.05 | −0.35 | −0.21 | −0.15 | −0.07 | −0.15 |
| 5 (5) | 0.15 | 0.11 | 0.11 | 0.07 | 0.12 | −0.16 | 0.10 | 0.07 | 0.15 | 0.11 |
| 6 (5) | 0.04 | −0.01 | −0.05 | −0.01 | 0.10 | −0.14 | 0.02 | 0.06 | 0.06 | 0.02 |
| 7 (13) | −0.13 | −0.09 | −0.11 | −0.10 | −0.06 | −0.15 | −0.13 | −0.11 | −0.11 | −0.11 |
| 8 (31) | −0.10 | −0.03 | −0.05 | −0.08 | −0.06 | −0.12 | −0.07 | −0.05 | −0.12 | −0.07 |

*Note:* Adapted from Table 19.13 of "Contrasting state-of-the-art automated scoring of essays" by M.D. Shermis and B. Hamner, 2013. In M.D. Shermis & J. Burstein (Eds.), *Handbook of automated essay evaluation: Current applications and new directions* (pp. 313–346). New York: Routledge. Values are unweighted kappa for machine–human agreement minus unweighted kappa for human–human agreement, where machine–human agreement is the concurrence between the machine and the human "resolved score," and human–human agreement is the concurrence of Human 1 and Human 2. Dark shading indicates difference of < = −.10 in favor of humans. Light shading indicates difference of > = .10 in favor of machine.

Table 7.4  Cross-Validation Quadratic Weighted Kappa Deltas From the ASAP I Vendor Competition

| Essay (Scale) | Vendor | | | | | | | | | |
|---|---|---|---|---|---|---|---|---|---|---|
| | 1 | 2 | 3 | 4 | 5 | 6 | 7 | 8 | 9 | *Mdn* |
| 1 (6) | 0.05 | 0.06 | −0.03 | 0.09 | 0.09 | −0.07 | 0.07 | 0.03 | 0.06 | 0.06 |
| 2a (6) | −0.12 | −0.10 | −0.11 | −0.06 | −0.08 | −0.18 | −0.10 | −0.08 | −0.10 | −0.10 |
| 2b (4) | −0.09 | −0.13 | −0.12 | −0.06 | −0.06 | −0.21 | −0.11 | −0.07 | −0.08 | −0.09 |
| 3 (4) | −0.05 | −0.03 | −0.08 | −0.05 | −0.02 | −0.12 | −0.12 | −0.04 | −0.04 | −0.05 |
| 4 (4) | −0.10 | −0.04 | −0.09 | −0.04 | −0.03 | −0.18 | −0.10 | −0.08 | −0.05 | −0.08 |
| 5 (5) | 0.07 | 0.07 | 0.05 | 0.06 | 0.09 | −0.10 | 0.05 | 0.03 | 0.08 | 0.06 |
| 6 (5) | 0.02 | 0.03 | −0.10 | 0.01 | 0.07 | −0.09 | 0.01 | 0.04 | 0.02 | 0.02 |
| 7 (13) | −0.05 | 0.06 | 0.03 | 0.09 | 0.12 | −0.14 | 0.05 | 0.08 | 0.09 | 0.06 |
| 8 (31) | 0.07 | 0.03 | −0.01 | 0.09 | 0.12 | 0 | 0.08 | 0.07 | 0.07 | 0.07 |

*Note:* Adapted from Table 19.15 of "Contrasting state-of-the-art automated scoring of essays" by M.D. Shermis and B. Hamner, 2013. In M.D. Shermis & J. Burstein (Eds.), *Handbook of automated essay evaluation: Current applications and new directions* (pp. 313–346). New York: Routledge. Values are quadratic weighted kappa for machine–human agreement minus quadratic weighted kappa for human–human agreement, where machine–human agreement is the concurrence between the machine and the human "resolved score," and human–human agreement is the concurrence of Human 1 and Human 2. Dark shading indicates difference of < = −.10 in favor of humans. Light shading indicates difference of > = .10 in favor of machine.

of essays 2b, 3, and 4, one point off is arguably nontrivial, but it is these 1-point differences that quadratic weighted kappa only minimally considers.

In sum, the claim in Table 7.1 that machine and human scores had "virtually identical levels of accuracy" would seem to be debatable.

In contrast to the vendor competition, the results for the public competition are harder to evaluate because only quadratic weighted kappa was reported. Further, that index was computed across all nine prompts rather than for each prompt separately.[4] Results for the top ten competitors were reported to five decimal places and ranged from a mean quadratic weighted kappa of 0.81407 to 0.78391 (Kaggle, 2012).

*Education Week* (Quillen, 2012) described the public competition as follows:

> Three teams split the $100,000 in prize money . . . The 11 contestants comprising the first-, second-, and third-place teams have backgrounds in particle physics, computer science, data analysis, and even foreign service work. But none have educational backgrounds, a departure from the [vendor-competition] report, in which participants were companies or nonprofits with experience in the educational market.

Should the fact that these teams didn't include educators be of concern? Could that omission have implications for validity? One reason the public competitors might have done as well as they did is that some entrants reportedly employed machine-learning algorithms that search among hundreds, sometimes thousands of text features, to find the ones most associated with human scores, regardless of the substantive value of those features (e.g., Preston & Goodman, 2012). Here is an excerpt from a Reuters report (Simon, 2012), done in the course of the competition, about the sixth-place entrant, whose mean quadratic weighted kappa was almost .80, less than two hundredths of a point below the winning team's value.

> Martin O'Leary, a glacier scientist at the University of Michigan, has been working on the contest for weeks. Poring over thousands of sample essays, he discovered that human graders generally don't give students extra points for using sophisticated vocabulary. So he scrapped plans to have his computer scan the essays for rare words. Instead, he has his robo-grader count punctuation marks. "The number of commas is a very strong predictor of score," O'Leary said. "It's kind of weird. But the more, the better."

This quotation may or may not be indicative of the preponderance of scoring methods used in the ASAP I competition, so the substantive meaningfulness of those methods cannot be fairly evaluated. In fact, other than this quotation, very little is known about how the top performers in that competition optimized their scoring systems to the one indicator on which they were judged.

The fact of obscure methodology and unitary indicators aside, the competitors' main concern was with the predictor side of the equation. Of equal concern should be the criterion (Gulliksen, 1950).

### We Don't Fully Understand How Humans Score

Though perhaps surprising, this fourth assertion has been made many times before (Attali, 2013; Bennett, 2011; Bridgeman, 2013; Lumley, 2002). Consider what is commonly done in operational K–12 testing practice. We develop rubrics to identify the features of responses that denote different levels of quality. Next, we train (nonexpert) raters to implement those rubrics.[5] Last, we qualify those raters and monitor their performance by measuring agreement with benchmarks and with other raters, including rating managers. But high inter-rater agreement does not necessarily indicate consensus on the intended aspects of the construct. That is why, of course, it is called "interrater agreement" and not "interrater validity." To make the job easier, some disingenuous raters may intentionally be awarding scores that hover around the scale midpoint, which would produce high agreement by chance alone. Alternatively, some raters might simply be using features that they can quickly evaluate, that they can judge with high agreement, and that are correlated with the intended construct. Essay length (or the number of commas!) would be examples that, while relevant, by themselves significantly underrepresent modern conceptions of writing skill (e.g., Deane, 2013).

What do raters actually do when they score operationally? Unfortunately, we do not really know, at least not for the K–12 state assessment programs that were the focus of the ASAP I study. Although there is a research base on rater cognition (Bejar, 2012; i.e., the processes used by human judges in scoring and the features to which they attend), much of the recent work appears to center on contexts considerably different from K–12 state assessment—for example, assessment systems in other countries (Crisp, 2007, 2012; Suto & Greatorex, 2006, 2008a, 2008b), English-as-a-foreign-language testing programs (Cumming, Kantor, & Powers, 2002; Eckes, 2012; Lumley, 2002)—or on contexts that cannot be clearly identified with K–12 state assessment (Wolfe, 2005).

Anecdotal reports, however, suggest that, at least in some K–12 testing programs, the implemented rubric may not always be the intended one (Farley, 2009a, 2009b, 2009c; Lussenhop, 2011). Because these reports are anecdotal, their claims should not be broadly generalized. However, those claims should probably not be dismissed out of hand, either. They suggest strategies being used by at least some operational raters that are essentially the construct-irrelevant short-cuts just described.

Given our limited understanding of operational human rating, it would seem sensible to invoke Bejar's (2012) concept of *first-order validity argument* if we wish to use those ratings as the sole validation criterion.[6] That is, in addition to stipulating and gathering evidence about the relationship between predictor and outcome, stipulate and gather evidence to support the meaning of the outcome.

What evidence should be gathered? We offer a comprehensive answer that few testing programs will have the wherewithal to do. Even so, as with any validation, in general, the more clearly specified the claim and the more evidence available to support it, the stronger the basis for interpretation and use.

Going back to first principles, we start with a set of basic evidentiary sources and questions about those sources. For one, do the processes in which examinees engage align with the construct definition? If the text entry interface, for example, is very different from the one most examinees use, they may spend more time and cognitive resources on the mechanics of entry and editing than on composition. As a consequence, the human scores being used as the validation criterion would then reflect not just writing skill but also interface familiarity. Second, does the rubric fully capture the construct definition? If the rubric, as communicated, drives human raters toward some subset of that definition, then it is only that subset that will constitute the criterion. Third, do the processes in which raters engage when operationally judging performances align with the rubric? As noted, the intended rubric may not always be the implemented one, with significant negative consequences for the modeling and validation of automated scores. Fourth, do raters agree highly with one another in terms of both group-level measures (mean, variance) as well as in terms of multiple individual-level measures (correlation and percentage-agreement-related indices, including those with appropriate corrections for chance)? Multiple measures are critical because they are sensitive to different aspects of agreement and have different underlying assumptions. If raters do not highly agree with one another, are there many raters and/or many tasks per examinee over which to balance out random error and thereby prevent modeling and validation against noise? Fifth, do raters accurately score responses that are atypically creative or, alternatively, that attempt to game their way into higher scores than deserved? If raters are insensitive to these two types of unusual responses, developers will be modeling and validating against a contaminated criterion. Sixth, do human ratings on one task predict performance on other tasks from the task universe? In most assessment programs, the intention is not to measure "a performance" but instead a construct that is marked by an instance sampled from some task domain. If the human ratings taken across tasks are not significantly and consistently correlated, there is no construct being measured. Seventh, are human ratings related in theoretically predictable ways to other indicators, including of similar and of different constructs? Human ratings should be significantly correlated with other indicators of writing (e.g., grades in courses that depend heavily on composition). At the same time, those ratings generally ought to have significantly lower correlations with indicators of constructs that are not the essence of writing, like keyboarding skill. Finally, do the listed characteristics hold across important population groups? If those characteristics are not invariant, the meaning of human ratings may differ for some groups, an outcome which might affect our automated scoring in unanticipated ways.

Figure 7.3 graphically summarizes the interconnected elements of the first-order validity argument. If the answers are "No" or are not known, for too many of the associated questions, human ratings will not be a suitable "sole criterion" either for automated scoring validation or for modeling.

By way of example, Table 7.5 lists some published studies and results that might be relevant to evaluating the first-order validity argument for the GRE Analytical Writing (GRE-AW) measure.[7] GRE-AW is used here because there is no U.S. K–12 state assessment program with a relevant, published research base of any scope.

Table 7.5 is a useful example for at least two reasons. First, it suggests that, to be meaningful, the evidence base needs to focus on a particular testing program, including its purpose (and claims), task types, and population(s). Generalizing the meaning of human rating from one program, purpose, task type, or population to a different program, purpose, task type, or population would seem unjustified in the absence of evidence. Second, the table shows that, even for a program as well researched as the GRE-AW measure, some components—like agreement and external relations—appear to have gotten far more attention than others—like rater processes and the treatment of unusual responses. In addition, some results suggest concerns regarding the meaning of human ratings for some population groups.

If a careful evaluation of the first-order validity argument were to find that all questions were answered "Yes" and that automated scores agreed close to perfectly with human ratings, then the automated scores would appear to be exchangeable with the human scores for that testing program. In reality, however, the answers to those questions are not very likely to be unequivocally "Yes" (as evident from Table 7.5), if the answers are known at all, precluding the use of human rating as the sole (or, arguably, even the primary) validation criterion.

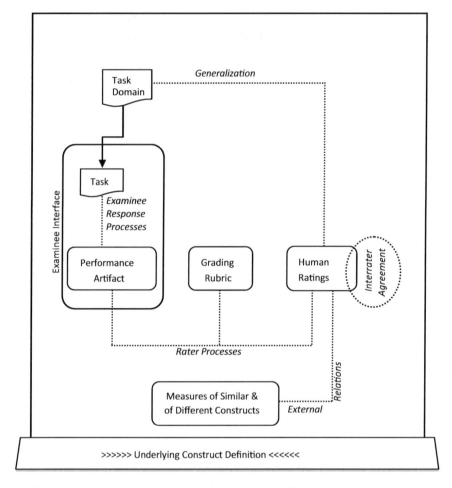

**Figure 7.3** Some components of the first-order validity argument (for human rating as the sole criterion for automated scoring)

*Note:* Invariance of the above relationships across population groups is not shown.

*Source:* Copyright by Educational Testing Service, 2015. All rights reserved.

### We Can't Critically Evaluate Automated Scoring Without Methodological Details

Consider this potentially problematic combination:

- a highly complex scoring technology,
- in many cases using undisclosed proprietary methods,
- typically built to emulate the (not-so-well-understood) operational behavior of (non-expert) human raters,
- providing operational rater agreement as the primary and sometimes only validity evidence.

Table 7.5 Some Published Studies and Relevant Results for the First-Order Validity Argument: GRE Analytical Writing Measure

| Evidentiary Source | Validation Question | Study | Result |
|---|---|---|---|
| Examinee Response Processes | Do the processes in which examinees engage align with the construct definition? | Powers & Fowles, 1996 | Additional time had no effect on score relationships with other indicators, did not interact with advanced prompt disclosure or interact with self-reported ability to write quickly, but did improve score level. (experimental design, $n \sim 300$, $p = 4$, $n$ of raters per essay = 2) |
| | | Powers & Fowles, 1997a | Advanced disclosure of prompts had no effect on essay score or score relations with other indicators. (experimental design, $n \sim 300$, $p = 4$, $n$ of raters per essay = 2) |
| | | Powers & Fowles, 1998 | Although examinees rated their ability to produce a strong essay as being related to prompt characteristics, their ratings were only weakly and inconsistently related to actual essay performance. ($n = 253$ participants from institutions enrolling significant numbers of minority students and 268 GRE General Test registrants, $p = 78$, $n$ of raters per essay not reported) |
| | | Powers, 2005 | Size of predisclosed prompt pool unrelated to examinee use of pool in preparing for the test. (experimental design, $n$ range = 11 to 65, focus $p = 27, 54, 108$, $n$ of operational raters per essay = 2) |
| Grading Rubric | Does the rubric fully capture the construct definition? | Powers & Fowles, 1997b | Most graduate school staff satisfied that scoring guide covered writing skills important for first-year grad students. ($n$ of survey respondents = 347) |
| | | Rosenfeld, Courtney, & Fowles, 2004 | Scoring rubric criteria were judged by test developers as aligned to almost all writing tasks considered important by surveyed graduate faculty. ($n$ of faculty completing survey responses = 861, $n$ of test developers = 5) |
| Rater Processes | Do the processes in which raters engage when operationally judging performances align with the rubric? | Attali, 2011 | Operational rater scores positively but very weakly related to scores awarded by the same rater on closely preceding essays. ($n \sim 526,000$, $p = 113$ Issue and 139 Argument prompts, $n$ of operational raters per essay = 2 of 326) |
| Rater Agreement | Do raters agree *highly* with one another (mean, variance, correlation, percentage-related indices)? | Powers & Fowles, 1996 | Agreement between two ratings was $r = 0.77$–$0.80$. ($n \sim 300$, $p = 4$, $n$ of raters per essay = 2) |

(*Continued*)

Table 7.5 (Continued)

| Evidentiary Source | Validation Question | Study | Result |
| --- | --- | --- | --- |
| Rater Agreement (con't) | Do raters agree *highly* with one another (mean, variance, correlation, percentage-related indices)? | Attali, Lewis, & Steier, 2012 | Grouping essays according to length had no effect on rater agreement. Rubric focusing on higher-order skills had inconsistent effects. (experimental design using extended 18-point rating scale, $n = 200$, $p = 4$ prompts, $n$ of raters per essay = 2 out of pool of 32) |
| | | Powers, Fowles, & Boyles, 1996 | Agreement between two ratings for Issue topics was $r = 0.77$–$0.80$. ($n = 470$, $p = 4$, $n$ of raters per essay = 2) |
| | | Powers et al., 2000 | Agreement between two ratings was $r = 0.85$ for Issue prompts and $r = 0.83$ for Argument prompts. Across Issue and Argument prompts, percentage exact agreement = 68. ($n = 101$–$149$ per essay prompt, $p = 20$ Issue and 20 Argument prompts, $n$ of raters per essay = 2) |
| | | Attali, 2007 | Agreement between two operational ratings was $r = 0.89$, $k = 0.68$, and percentage exact agreement = 76. ($n = 496$, $p = 1$ Issue prompt, $n$ of operational raters per essay = 2) |
| | | Attali, Bridgeman, & Trapani, 2010 | Agreement for Issue essays between two operational ratings was $r = 0.74$, $wk = 0.74$, and $|SMD| = 0.02$. Agreement for Argument essays between two operational ratings was $r = 0.79$, $wk = 0.78$, and $|SMD| = 0.02$. ($n$ range = 750 to 3,000 per essay prompt, $p = 113$ Issue and 139 Argument prompts, $n$ of operational raters per essay = 2) |
| | | Ramineni et al., 2012 | Average agreement for Issue essays between two operational ratings was $r = 0.74$, $k = 0.42$, $qwk = 0.74$, and percentage exact agreement = 59. Agreement for Argument essays between two operational ratings was $r = 0.78$, $k = 0.44$, $qwk = 0.78$, and percentage exact agreement = 58. (average $n = 2,070$ per prompt, $p = 113$ Issue and 139 Argument prompts, $n$ of operational raters = 2) |
| Treatment of Unusual Responses | Do raters accurately score responses that are atypically creative or that attempt to game their way into higher scores than deserved? | Powers et al., 2001 | For essays intentionally written by experts to receive either higher or lower (automated) scores than deserved, agreement between two human ratings was $r = 0.82$, $k = 0.42$, and percentage exact agreement = 52. ($n$ of writing experts = 27, $p = 2$ Issue and 2 Argument prompts, $n$ of raters per essay = 2) |

| | | | |
|---|---|---|---|
| | | Bejar et al., 2013 | Extent of irrelevant "shell language" unrelated to difference between operational rating and rating by scoring leaders under nonoperational conditions. ($n = 24$ essays per prompt, $p = 2$ Issue and 2 Argument prompts, $n$ of raters per essay = 2) |
| Generalization | Do human ratings on one task predict performance on other tasks from the task universe? | Powers, Fowles, & Boyles, 1996 | For two Issue essays written by the same examinees (but having different time limits and predisclosure conditions), cross-prompt agreement between ratings was $r = 0.55$. ($n = 470$, $p = 4$, $n$ of raters per essay = 2) |
| | | Schaeffer, Briel, & Fowles, 2001 | For two essays written by the same examinees, cross-prompt agreement between ratings was $r = 0.62$ for Issue and $r = 0.51$ for Argument. ($n = 618$ for Issue essays and 558 for Argument essays, $p = 20$ Issue and 20 Argument prompts, $n$ of raters per essay = 2 out of pool of 18) |
| External Relations | Are human ratings related in theoretically predictable ways to other indicators, including measures of similar and of different constructs? | Powers, Fowles, & Willard, 1994 | Graduate staff satisfaction with writing ability as indicated by essay responses increased monotonically with raters' essay scores. ($n$ of graduate staff = 231, $p = 18$, $n$ of raters per essay = 2) |
| | | Powers, Fowles, & Boyles, 1996 | Scores on each of two issue-based essays correlated with nontest composite indicators (median $r = 0.27$–0.53). Median $r$ over both essays with GRE verbal, quantitative, and analytical scores = 0.53, –0.01, and 0.30, respectively. ($n$ range = 71 to 470, $p = 4$, $n$ of raters per essay = 2) |
| | | Powers & Fowles, 1997b | $r = 0.88$–0.94 between analytical essay score means (taken across raters) and mean satisfaction ratings of graduate staff. ($n$ of graduate judges = 231, $p = 15$, $n$ of raters per essay = 4) |

*(Continued)*

Table 7.5 (Continued)

| Evidentiary Source | Validation Question | Study | Result |
|---|---|---|---|
| External Relations (con't) | Are human ratings related in theoretically predictable ways to other indicators, including measures of similar and of different constructs? | Powers, Fowles, & Welsh, 1999 | For combined scores on Issue and Argument, $r = 0.38$ with the combination of two student-submitted, course-related writing samples when graded by trained raters, 0.34 with UGPA in writing courses, 0.20 with overall UGPA, 0.11 with major field UGPA, 0.29 with self-comparison with peers' writing skills, 0.26 with success with various kinds of writing, 0.20 with success with writing activities, and 0.07 with writing-related accomplishments. ($n = 847$, $p = 20$ Issue and 20 Argument prompts, $n$ of raters per essay = 2 out of pool of 18) |
| | | Powers et al., 2000 | Between GRE Writing Assessment scores (average of Issue and Argument ratings, two ratings per prompt) and each of nine nontest indicators of writing and of general academic accomplishment, $r = 0.07$–0.38. ($n = 721$ to 890, $p = 20$ Issue and 20 Argument prompts, $n$ of raters per essay = 2) |
| | | Schaeffer, Briel, & Fowles, 2001 | Depending on administration order, $r = 0.54$ and 0.46 between Argument and Issue prompts. ($n = 598$ for Issue–Argument order and 552 for Argument–Issue order, $p = 20$ Issue and 20 Argument prompts, $n$ of raters per essay = 2 out of pool of 18) |
| | | Powers, 2005 | $r = 0.01$–0.32 between operational essay scores and other indicators of writing and reasoning skills, and $r = 0.12$–0.36 between total operational writing scores and the same indicators. ($n$ range = 182–199, $p = 120$ Issue and 120 Argument prompts, $n$ of operational raters per essay = 2) |
| | | Attali, Bridgeman, & Trapani, 2010 | For one operational Issue rating, $r = 0.51$ with GRE verbal, 0.07 with GRE quantitative, 0.15 with UGPA, and 0.60 with Argument essay score. For one operational Argument rating, $r = 0.55$ with GRE verbal, 0.22 with GRE quantitative, 0.19 with UGPA, and 0.62 with Issue essay score. ($n$ range = 750 to 3,000 per essay prompt, $p = 113$ Issue and 139 Argument prompts, $n$ of operational raters per essay = 2) |
| | | Attali, Lewis, & Steier, 2012 | Mean $r = 0.57$–0.58 between ratings of Issue and Argument essays written by the same examinees. ($n = 200$, $p = 4$ prompts, $n$ of raters per essay = 2 out of pool of 32) |
| | | Ramineni et al., 2012 | For one operational Issue rating, $r = 0.51$ with GRE verbal, 0.07 with GRE quantitative, 0.13 with UGPA, 0.15 with undergraduate major GPA, and 0.27 with English-as-best-language status. For one operational Argument rating, $r = 0.55$ with GRE verbal, 0.22 with GRE quantitative, 0.20 with UGPA, 0.18 with undergraduate major GPA, and 0.19 with English-as-best-language status. (average $n = 2,070$ per prompt, $p = 113$ Issue and 139 Argument prompts, $n$ of operational raters = 2) |

| Population Invariance | Do the above characteristics hold across important population groups? | Powers, Fowles, & Welsh, 1999 | Relationships of combined scores on Issue and Argument with various nontest criteria did not appear to differ in any consistent way for subgroups categorized by gender, ethnicity, English-as-best-language, and undergraduate major. ($n = 847$, $p = 20$ Issue and 20 Argument prompts, $n$ of raters per essay = 2 out of pool of 18) |
| | | Schaeffer, Briel, & Fowles, 2001 | No apparent subgroup interactions with prompt difficulty or prompt type identified for subgroups categorized by gender, ethnicity, and English-as-best-language. ($n = 32$–$508$, $p = 20$ Issue and 20 Argument prompts, $n$ of raters per essay = 2 out of pool of 18) |
| Population Invariance (con't) | Do the above characteristics hold across important population groups? | Broer, Lee, Rizavi, & Powers, 2005 | Using operational ratings, examination for differential item difficulty by gender, ethnicity, and English-as-best-language (EBL) status found no prompts warranting removal. ($n = 397,806$, $p = 109$ Issue and 117 Argument prompts, $n$ of operational raters per essay = 2) |
| | | Bridgeman, Trapani, & Attali, 2012 | For Issue prompts, the correlation between two ratings in most cases ranged minimally within groups categorized by gender, ethnicity, and gender-by-ethnicity. Exceptions included Whites ($r = 0.67$) vs. American Indians (0.76), White females (0.66) vs. American Indian females (0.76), and White males (0.69) vs. American Indian females (0.76). ($n$ range = 2,433 to 116,278, $p = 113$, $n$ of operational raters per prompt = 2.) For Argument prompts, the correlations were no more than 0.05 points different for any two population groups. ($n$ range not reported, $p = 139$, $n$ of operational raters per prompt = 2) |
| | | Ramineni et al., 2012 | For Issue and Argument essays, standardized mean differences between two operational ratings fell within an extremely narrow range across population groups categorized by gender, ethnicity, and domestic vs. international. Across all groups simultaneously, agreement indices also fell within relatively narrow ranges. For examinees taking the GRE in China, agreement was noticeably lower. For Issue essays, between two operational ratings, $r = 0.40$, $k = 0.16$, $qwk = 0.39$, and percentage exact agreement = 50. For Argument essays, $r = 0.44$, $k = 0.20$, $qwk = 0.43$, and percentage exact agreement = 47. (average $n = 12$–1,520 per prompt, $p = 113$ Issue and 139 Argument prompts, $n$ of operational raters = 2) |

*Note*: $n$ = number of examinees; $p$ = number of prompts; $k$ = kappa; $wk$ = weighted kappa; $qwk$ = quadratic weighted kappa; |SMD| = absolute value of the standardized mean difference; UGPA = Undergraduate GPA; GRE = Graduate Record Examinations.

As noted, one reason that methodological details are often undisclosed is that vendors wish to protect their intellectual property, for which some vendors use the mechanism "trade secret." One might ask whether trade secret is suitable for testing contexts in which individuals' life chances are at stake. Arguably, in such contexts, scoring methods need to be inspectable so that they can be evaluated and challenged, as appropriate, by those responsible for protecting the interests of students and teachers—testing program directors, technical advisory committee members, and knowledgeable members of the field and public. If those responsible for protecting the interests of students and teachers cannot get access to scoring-program details, how can they fully judge the fidelity of the resulting scores to the intended construct; the testing purposes, contexts, and populations for which automated scoring might not work and for which they had better gather sufficient empirical data; how the automated scoring might be gamed; and how the scoring might negatively impact learning and instruction? These are not minor issues because, for those cases in which we do know how the methodology works, that methodology tends to primarily target low- to mid-level text features (Quinlan, Higgins, & Wolff, 2009).[8] Reliance on those features, as well as on other undisclosed aspects of automated scoring methodology, may have important implications for the questions just enumerated.

### Validity Evidence Needs to Be Broadly Based

In honoring Harold Gulliksen, Messick (1989, p. 13) noted that ". . . if you do not know what predictor and criterion scores mean, you do not know much of anything in applied measurement." If developers do not disclose the details of their approaches and if the primary evidence for scoring quality is agreement with operational human raters, we are uncomfortably close to the state Messick described.

For automated scoring, as for score meaning generally, the validity argument should rest on an integrated base of theory and data that allows a comprehensive analysis of how effectively scores represent the construct of interest and how resistant they are to sources of irrelevant variance (Messick, 1989). Part of that comprehensive analysis must address plausible, competing interpretations for results. As Cronbach (1980, p. 103) said, "The job of validation is not to support an interpretation, but to find out what might be wrong with it. A proposition deserves some degree of trust only when it has survived serious attempts to falsify it." What are the practical implications of taking a comprehensive and—as Cronbach argues—*critical* approach toward the validation of automated essay scoring systems?

Figure 7.4 graphically summarizes the components of a validity argument for the use of automated scoring. First, we had better hope that, at the least, our analysis of the first-order validity argument supports the alignment of examinee response processes and the grading rubric to the construct definition. If not, the validity argument for automated scores will be immediately undercut, because those scores will be measuring something other than the intended construct (i.e., the construct reflected in the scoring of artifacts produced through off-target response processes and an off-target rubric). If grading-rubric and response-process answers are positive, we should next ask whether the automated scoring model was trained and calibrated on an appropriate sample of artifacts from the target population (Zhang, 2013b). If it was not so trained and calibrated, that model may encounter essays from a population it cannot properly evaluate. From a substantive point of view, are the model's features related to one another empirically in theoretically meaningful ways, and do the features and their weighting fully capture the rubric and construct definition? These analyses are critical to arguing that the model is a direct measure of writing skill, as opposed to simply a correlate of it. With respect to rater agreement, in the ideal case, we should be asking if the automated scores agree with the mean ratings taken across multiple experts who agree highly among themselves. The reason for this stipulation is that multiple expert raters who achieve consensus should make for a more reliable and nominally more valid criterion than only one or two raters grading under operational conditions. If collecting multiple ratings is not feasible, do the automated scores agree at least as highly with individual expert raters as expert raters agree among themselves? If we find that agreement is lower than desirable, are there many raters (human and automated) and/or many tasks per examinee over which to average the error, or dampen the bias, being observed?

Further sources of evidence come from asking how effectively automated scoring handles unusual responses, how well it predicts performance on other tasks from the universe, whether it relates to external criteria in the expected ways, and whether these functional characteristics are invariant across population groups. We should also ask about the intended and unintended impact of automated scoring on teaching and learning. That is, at its essence, writing is a communicative act, an intellectual and affective exchange between a composer and his or her audience. What is the effect on the composer's writing of knowing that the audience cannot, in any real sense, understand and react to it? Likewise, what is the effect on teacher knowledge and skill of removing the obligation to engage directly with and critique student work? Finally, we should ask how automated scoring compares on each of Figure 7.4's dimensions to the scores of expert human raters.

How scores are to be interpreted and used will dictate exactly how extensive the evidence base should be to support an assessment program's claims. Table 7.6 presents two general implementation approaches in order of required evidentiary support, holding constant the consequences attached to reported score. In the first case, A, the essay score is reported or has major impact on the final test score (e.g., as in GRE-AW, where each essay counts for half

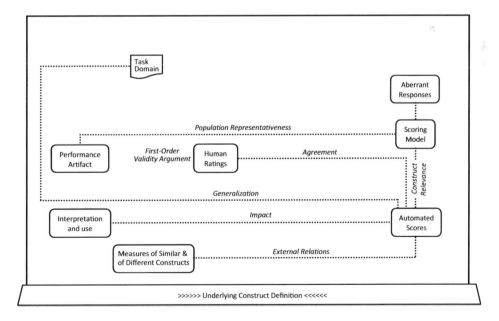

**Figure 7.4** Some components of a validity argument for automated scoring

*Source:* Copyright by Educational Testing Service, 2015. All rights reserved.

Table 7.6 Two General Implementation Approaches for Automated Scoring

A. Essay score is reported or has major impact on reported score

    1. Sole score

    2. Contributory score

    3. Check (confirmatory) score

B. Essay score is not reported and has limited impact on reported score

    1. Sole score

    2. Contributory score

    3. Check (confirmatory) score

*Source:* Copyright by Educational Testing Service, 2015. All rights reserved.

*Note:* A sample of responses may be graded by a human rater for quality control regardless of the approach.

of the total test score). In case B, the essay score is not reported and has only limited impact on the final score (e.g., as when it is combined with a lengthy set of more heavily weighted, multiple-choice questions). It should be obvious that the need for broad and deep evidentiary support is greater in case A than in case B. Also note that within each case, the uses would seem to imply decreasing levels of need for support; that is, more support is needed when automated scoring is the sole score than when it is employed as a check score.

By way of example, the implementation approach for GRE-AW was A3, check score, where the final essay rating has major impact on reported score. Something less than sole-score use seems consistent with the published evidence base, part of which is shown in Table 7.7.[9] For agreement and for external relations, considerably more is known than for the other evidence categories. Reading through the table, it is clear that the agreement findings more frequently favored human–human agreement over machine–human agreement, whereas the results for external relations showed the opposite pattern. For other evidence categories, far less work has been done—apparently none for generalization and impact—and that which has been done might not appear strong enough to unequivocally support claims beyond the quality-control level. Such is the case for questions related to the scoring model, treatment of unusual responses, and population invariance, which are at least partially negative. The use in the scoring model of features more attuned to the measurement of basic writing skills than analytical reasoning ability would seem to be especially relevant to the choice of implementation approach.

We should note that the presentation in Table 7.7 differs from the common vendor practice of reporting results for a scoring engine across applications (e.g., Foltz, Streeter, Lochbaum, & Landauer, 2013). To be sure, such results may be helpful in summarizing an engine's overall strengths and weaknesses, postulating the likelihood that it will perform acceptably in a new application, or evaluating that new application against past use. However, as with the first-order validity argument, for any given application, the validity argument for automated scoring should be particularized to the testing program in question (i.e., purpose and claims, task types, populations). In other words, that argument cannot be made *in general* for the scoring engine. That engine may not behave invariantly across task types or populations (Bridgeman, Trapani, & Attali, 2012; Zhang, 2013b); its performance may be simultaneously adequate for one purpose but not for others; and there will always be purposes, populations, and task types that differ significantly from past experience and for which sufficient evidence has not yet been gathered.

Table 7.7 Some Published Studies and Relevant Results Underlying the Validity Argument for the Use of Automated Scoring in the GRE Analytical Writing Assessment

| Evidentiary Source | Validation Question | Study | Result |
|---|---|---|---|
| Scoring Model | Was the scoring model trained and calibrated on an appropriate sample from the target population? | Quinlan, Higgins, & Wolff, 2009 | No published research located on appropriateness of sample for model training and calibration. |
| | Do the features and their weighting fully capture the rubric (and construct definition)? | | Qualitative analysis of the alignment of e-rater model features to the GRE Issue scoring rubric found only partial coverage, with most features capturing low-level aspects of essay quality that reflect basic writing skills. |
| | Does the internal structure of the automated scores substantially align with the construct of interest? | | No published research located on internal structure. |
| Agreement with Human Raters | Do automated scores agree, ideally, with the mean ratings taken across multiple experts who, themselves, agree highly with one another? | Powers et al., 2000 | Across all prompts, machine–human percentage exact agreement = 48, 20 percentage points lower than human–human agreement. ($n = 101–149$ per prompt, $p = 20$ Issue prompts and 20 Argument prompts.) Between e-rater scores summed across two prompts and the sum of four human ratings across the same two prompts, $r = 0.74$, in this sample considerably below the average correlation between two human ratings within prompt type (0.85 for Issue and 0.83 for Argument). ($n \sim 900$, $p = 20$ Issue and 20 Argument prompts) |
| | If not, do automated scores agree as least as highly with individual (expert) human ratings as human ratings agree among themselves? | Kelly, 2005 | For Issue essays, agreement between e-rater and operational human ratings was $r = 0.56$ to 0.75, $k = 0.26–0.41$, and percentage exact agreement = 48–55. For Argument essays, $r = 0.63–0.74$, $k = 0.37–0.48$, and percentage exact agreement = 38–66. ($n = 50–200$ for Issue prompts, 117–398 for Argument prompts, $p = 3$ Issue and 3 Argument prompts) |
| | If not, are there many raters (human and automated) and/or many tasks per examinee? | Attali, 2007 | Agreement between (optimal) e-rater scores and an operational human rating was $r = 0.83$, $k = 0.54$, and percentage exact agreement = 66, lower in this sample than human–human agreement by 6 points for correlation, 14 points for kappa, and 10 points for exact agreement. ($n = 496$, $p = 1$ Issue prompt) |

(Continued)

Table 7.7 (Continued)

| Evidentiary Source | Validation Question | Study | Result |
|---|---|---|---|
| Agreement with Human Raters (con't) | Do automated scores agree, ideally, with the mean ratings taken across multiple experts who, themselves, agree highly with one another? If not, do automated scores agree as least as highly with individual (expert) human ratings as human ratings agree among themselves? If not, are there many raters (human and automated) and/or many tasks per examinee? | Attali, Bridgeman, & Trapani, 2010 | For Issue essays, $r = 0.79$–$0.80$ between e-rater and one operational human rating, $wk = 0.76$–$0.77$, and $|SMD| = 0.03$ to $0.05$, slightly higher in this sample than operational human–human agreement for correlation and weighted kappa, but slightly worse for standardized mean difference. For Argument essays, the comparable ranges were $r = 0.76$–$0.79$, $wk = 0.72$–$0.76$, and $|SMD| = 0.02$ to $0.10$, in 7 of 9 comparisons values somewhat worse than operational human–human agreement. ($n = 750$–$3,000$ per essay prompt, $p = 113$ Issue and $139$ Argument prompts) |
| | | Attali, Lewis, & Steier, 2012 | For Argument essays, e-rater-human $r = 0.69$–$0.77$, noticeably lower in this sample than the human–human range of $0.78$ to $0.86$, regardless of differences in the type of rubric used. For Issue essays, in this sample, e-rater-human correlations were uniformly larger than human–human correlations when humans used a reduced, higher-order rubric but not consistently different from human–human correlations when humans used the regular rubric. (extended 18-point rating scale for all experimental conditions, $n = 200$, $p = 4$ prompts) |
| | | Ramineni et al., 2012 | For Issue essays, average $r = 0.79$ between e-rater scores and one operational rating, $k = 0.42$, $qwk = 0.76$, and percentage exact agreement = 59, comparable to or slightly higher than human–human agreement values. For Argument essays, average $r = 0.78$, $k = 0.37$, $qwk = 0.76$, and percentage exact agreement = 53 generally lower than the comparable human–human values of $0.78$, $0.44$, $0.78$, and $58$, respectively. (average $n = 2,070$ per prompt, $p = 113$ Issue and $139$ Argument prompts) |
| | | Zhang, 2013b | For Issue essays, median $r = 0.72$ between e-rater and one operational rating, $qwk = 0.66$, percentage exact agreement = 62, and SMD $= 0.08$ (weighted by the proportion of examinees in each examined country/territory group.) ($n \sim 14,000$–$115,000$, $p = 20$ Issue prompts) |

| | | | |
|---|---|---|---|
| Treatment of Unusual Responses | Do automated scores accurately treat responses that are atypically creative or that attempt to game their way into higher scores than deserved? Do they do so at least as well as expert human raters? | Powers et al., 2001 | For essays composed by writing experts to receive either higher or lower automated scores than deserved, $r = 0.42$ between e-rater and one human rater and 0.37 with the other human rater, $k = 0.16$ and 0.27, and percentage exact agreement ~34, values noticeably lower than the human–human $r = 0.82$, $k = 0.42$, and percentage exact agreement = 52. e-rater awarded notably higher scores than humans to well-formulated but substantively lacking essays. ($n$ of writing experts = 27, $p = 2$ Issue and 2 Argument prompts) |
| Generalization | Do automated scores on one task predict performance on other tasks from the task universe? Do they do so at least as well as expert human raters? | | No published research located. |
| External Relations | Are automated scores related in theoretically predictable ways to other indicators, including measures of similar and of different constructs? Is the pattern of relations similar to that for expert human raters? | Powers et al., 2000 | $r = 0.09$–0.27 between prompt-specific e-rater scores (averaged across Issue and Argument essays) with each of nine nontest indicators of writing and of general academic accomplishment, values generally lower than the corresponding correlations for human rating with the same indicators. Pattern of correlations was generally similar for e-rater and human scoring. ($n = 721$ to 890, $p = 20$ Issue and 20 Argument prompts) |
| | | Attali, Bridgeman, & Trapani, 2010 | For Issue essays, $r = 0.53$–0.55 between e-rater and GRE verbal, 0.11–0.14 with GRE quantitative, 0.18 with UGPA, and 0.65–0.66 with Argument essay score, in each case higher in this sample than the comparable correlations of one operational human rating with the same variables. For Argument essays, $r = 0.56$–0.59 with GRE verbal, 0.26–0.27 with GRE quantitative, 0.21 with UGPA, and 0.69–0.70 with Issue essay score, all values greater in this sample than the comparable correlations between one operational human rating and the same indicators. |

*(Continued)*

Table 7.7 (Continued)

| Evidentiary Source | Validation Question | Study | Result |
|---|---|---|---|
| | | Ramineni et al., 2012 | For Issue essays, $r = 0.51$ between e-rater and GRE verbal, 0.13 with GRE quantitative, 0.17 with UGPA, 0.17 with undergraduate major GPA, and 0.24 with English-as-best-language (EBL) status, values in this sample similar or somewhat higher in four cases, and slightly lower in one case (EBL status), than the values between one human rating and the same variables. For Argument essays, $r = 0.57$ between e-rater and GRE verbal, 0.24 with GRE quantitative, 0.22 with UGPA, 0.20 with undergraduate major GPA, and 0.20 with English-as-best-language status, values all marginally higher in this sample than the values between one human rating and the same external variables. (average $n = 2{,}070$ per prompt, $p = 113$ Issue and 139 Argument prompts) |
| | | Zhang, 2013b | The absolute differences in correlations for Issue essays between e-rater and one operational human rater were 0.06 with GRE verbal, 0.04 with GRE quantitative, and .08 with Argument essay score, suggesting a somewhat different pattern of external relations for human and e-rater scores. ($n \sim 14{,}000$–115,000, $p = 20$ Issue prompts) |
| Population Invariance | Do the above characteristics hold across important population groups? Are the characteristics similar in their invariance patterns to human rater patterns? | Bridgeman, Trapani, & Attali, 2012 | For Issue prompts, the correlation between e-rater and one human rating ranged minimally within groups categorized by gender, ethnicity, and gender-by-ethnicity, in each case slightly less than the comparable ranges for human–human agreement in the sample. The absolute value of the standardized mean difference between e-rater and human ratings was less than 0.10 for all groups except African American males (0.11) and American Indian males (0.12), for which e-rater awarded slightly lower scores than did human raters. For examinees testing in East Asia, e-rater awarded noticeably higher scores than did human raters for China ($|SMD| = 0.60$) and slightly higher scores for Taiwan ($|SMD| = 0.12$). ($n = 2{,}433$–116,278, $p = 113$) For Argument prompts, the correlations were minimally different within groups, very similar to the ranges found |

for human–human agreement. Human ratings were slightly higher than e-rater scores for American Indians overall (|SMD| = 0.11), Hispanic males (0.11), and American Indian males (0.15), but noticeably higher for African Americans overall (0.19), as well as for African American males (0.22) and African American females (0.18) separately. For examinees testing in China, e-rater awarded noticeably higher scores than did human raters (|SMD| = 0.38). (n range not reported, p = 139, n of operational raters per prompt = 2)

| | | |
|---|---|---|
| Population Invariance (con't) | Ramineni et al., 2012 | |

Do the above characteristics hold across important population groups?

Are the characteristics similar in their invariance patterns to human rater patterns?

For Issue essays, standardized mean differences between e-rater and one operational rating varied somewhat (−0.07 to 0.10) across population groups categorized by gender, ethnicity, and domestic vs. international. Across all groups simultaneously, other agreement indices fell within relatively small ranges: r = 0.72–0.80 between e-rater scores and one operational rating, k = 0.33–0.44, qwk = 0.69–0.76, and percentage exact agreement = 52–63. Compared to the general pattern of invariance for human–human agreement, the |SMD| values were sometimes larger, the qwk values were similar, and correlations somewhat higher. For examinees taking the GRE in China, however, e-rater scores were noticeably higher than operational human rating (SMD = 0.60). Other agreement indices for China were noticeably lower than the indices for other population groups, with r = 0.50 between e-rater scores and one operational rating, k = 0.14, qwk = 0.39, and percentage exact agreement = 41.

For Argument essays, standardized mean differences between e-rater and one operational rating varied somewhat (−0.18 to −0.02) across the same population groups, with the largest discrepancy for African American examinees who were scored lower by e-rater than by human rating. Across all groups simultaneously, agreement indices also fell within narrow ranges: r = 0.74–0.81 between e-rater and one operational rating, k = 0.32–0.37, qwk = 0.71–0.77, and percentage exact agreement = 49–55.

(Continued)

Table 7.7 (Continued)

| Evidentiary Source | Validation Question | Study | Result |
|---|---|---|---|
| | | | Compared to the general pattern of invariance for human–human agreement, the SMD values were always larger, with e-rater producing lower scores than human rating, the $qwk$ values were equal or slightly lower, and the correlations somewhat similar. For examinees taking the GRE in China, however, e-rater scores were somewhat higher than operational human rating (SMD = 0.23) and agreement was noticeably lower, with $r = 0.53$ between e-rater and one operational rating, $k = 0.19$, $qwk = 0.46$, and percentage exact agreement = 46. (average $n = 21$–1,520 per prompt, $p = 113$ Issue and 139 Argument prompts) |
| Population Invariance (con't) | | Zhang, 2013b | A simple random sampling procedure similar to that used in operational model training and calibration produced variation in agreement between e-rater and one operational human rater across population groups smaller than the average for all methods in only 38% of cases. In contrast, equal-stratification-by-language-group produced variation across groups that was smaller in 90% of cases. Simple random sampling minimized the difference across population groups between e-rater's correlation with relevant external variables and one operational human rater's correlation with those same variables in only 47% of cases. In contrast, equal-stratification-by-language-group produced variation across groups that was smaller in 58% of cases. ($n \sim 14{,}000$–115,000, $p = 20$ Issue prompts) |
| Impact | Do students and teachers change their learning and instructional behavior in intended or unintended ways?<br><br>Are learning outcomes affected? | | No published research located. |

*Note:* $n$ = number of examinees; $p$ = number of prompts; $k$ = kappa; $wk$ = weighted kappa; $qwk$ = quadratic weighted kappa; SMD = standardized mean difference; |SMD| = absolute value of the standardized mean difference; UGPA = Undergraduate GPA; GRE = Graduate Record Examinations. Questions and studies related to the first-order validity argument are presented in Table 7.5.

It is also important to note that the evidence base in Table 7.7 is not a validity argument itself but, rather, the raw material for it. That evidence base becomes a validity argument when it is coupled with a claim and used to demonstrate how each link is supported in the chain of reasoning that connects the interpretation and use of the essay score to that claim.

### Development Goals Need to Be Rethought

The last assertion is that development goals need to be rethought. First, until we better understand what we are modeling, we should stop developing and evaluating text features based primarily on their ability to predict the scores of operational raters. Second, we should consider targeting more modern (and expansive) construct definitions of writing (e.g., Deane, 2013). Such definitions are very intimidating because they highlight how limited our current scoring technologies really are. But being honest about those limitations is the first step toward improving that technology, which we can do by developing features to fill critical gaps in construct definition. Work being done on the development of argumentation, sentiment analysis, and other content scoring capabilities is an example (Burstein, Beigman-Klebanov, Madnani, & Faulkner, 2013). Finally, we might try alternatives to regression-based approaches. Potential options include having humans and machines score different dimensions, combining the scores accordingly (Attali, 2013; Bridgeman, 2013); using factor-based weights (Attali, 2013); and using expert weights rooted in the construct definition (Ben-Simon & Bennett, 2007).

### Suggestions for Implementation

The following suggestions are of the type that measurement advisors might offer to testing-program managers. First, design a computer-based assessment as an integrated system in which automated scoring is one in a series of interrelated parts. Among other things, that conceptualization will mean focusing attention on interface design and its interaction with the scoring system. In contrast, if the system is being added to an existing testing program, it will mean conducting a careful assessment design review. Second, encourage vendors to base the development of automated scoring approaches on construct understanding. The goal is to try to bring the features evaluated and the feature-aggregation rules into closer line with the views of domain experts. Third, strengthen operational human scoring by, for example, providing benchmarks, training samples, and qualification sets that force attention to higher-level features like argumentation by primarily varying those features, while holding other, more marginal features, like length, constant. Fourth, if the plan is to model automated systems on human rating or use human rating as a validation criterion, then sponsor studies to better understand the bases upon which humans assign scores. Cognitive labs, annotation studies, and perhaps eye-tracking investigations might help advance our state of knowledge in this regard. Fifth, stipulate as a contractual requirement the disclosure by vendors of those automated scoring approaches being considered for operational use. Disclosure can be facilitated and intellectual property protected through the mechanism of patent. We would hope that more vendors would use that mechanism instead of trade secret. Sixth, require a broad base of validity evidence similar to that needed to evaluate score meaning for any assessment. Last, unless the assembled validity evidence justifies the sole use of automated scoring, keep well-trained and carefully monitored human raters in the loop.

## Summary

In this chapter, automated scoring was defined as the machine grading of constructed responses generally not amenable to exact pattern-matching approaches. Although methods have been developed for scoring a wide array of English language arts and mathematics task types, the most frequent consequential operational use of those methods has been for the grading of essay responses. Automated essay scoring was defined as the machine extraction of (what are currently best classified as) low- to mid-level text features and their combination via a model.

Seven assertions were offered about validity and automated essay scoring. These assertions were offered because creating or employing automated scoring without a constant concentration on validation puts students and test users at risk. One of the most critical of those assertions was that validation should be broad based. Even though agreement with operational human raters is both very common and intuitively appealing, such agreement is generally insufficient as the sole or even primary validity evidence. Further, a broad-based validation should include attempts to falsify intended claims. Without those attempts, validation runs the risk of becoming more a sales and marketing activity than a scientific one. Last, suggestions for implementation were provided. Perhaps the most important was that, unless a broad base of validity evidence justifies the sole use of automated scoring, incorporate well-trained and carefully monitored human raters into the process. The main reason for incorporating human raters is that human raters can understand what they read. Computers, at least as yet, cannot.

## Notes

We thank Brian Clauser, Fritz Drasgow, Keelan Evanini, Michael Kane, and Nitin Madnani for their helpful reviews of an earlier draft of this section.

1   These figures were calculated as follows. At the time of this writing, 43 states had adopted the Common Core, accounting for approximately 41 million of the nation's public K–12 student enrollment in 2012 (http://nces. ed.gov/programs/digest/d14/tables/dt14_203.20.asp). If we assume that these 41 million students are equally distributed across grades and that essay tasks will be administered to all students in Grades 3–8 and one grade in high school, then 7/12 of the 41 million will be tested each year, or 24 million students. If read twice, one essay per student with 5% resolution will require ~50 million human readings.

2   For the public competition, an additional test set consisting of response text was provided so that entrants could repeatedly submit machine scores to the contest website and get an evaluation of the extent to which their machine scores agreed with the unreleased human scores for this test set's responses.

3   A similar outcome from the correlational comparison should not be surprising, as this index gives identical results to quadratic weighted kappa under some circumstances (Bridgeman, 2013).

4   The index was computed as the weighted mean of the quadratic weighted kappas (Kaggle, 2012).

5   We say "nonexpert" because teaching experience is not typically required. See, for example, Strauss (2013).

6   Bejar (2012, p. 7) uses the phrasing "comprehensive (first-order) interpretive argument . . . and the corresponding appraisal of the argument." Because Kane (2006) conceptualizes the validity argument to include the interpretive argument *and* the appraisal, for economy, we use the term "first-order validity argument."

7   GRE AW differs from the current GRE revised General Test Analytical Writing measure in that, for the revised test, the time for the Issue essay has been reduced from 45 minutes to 30 minutes, examinee choice between two Issue prompts has been eliminated, and the directions for both Issue and Argument now focus the examinee on a more structured writing task.

8   "Low-level text features" are generally basic and elemental, relating more to structural characteristics than to the semantics of the response. With respect to essay writing, low-level features might include word length, word frequency, grammatical errors, and essay length (or adaptations of it). "Mid-level text features" attempt to deal with rudimentary semantics. Such features might include overlap of words or word meanings among adjacent text segments and the similarity of words in an essay to the words in other human-scored essays on the same topic.

9   Only journal articles and peer-reviewed research reports are included. These articles span a time period during which the e-rater scoring engine was changed periodically, as were aspects of the human rating process.

# References

Attali, Y. (2007). *On-the-fly customization of automated essay scoring.* (Research report: RR-07–42). Princeton, NJ: Educational Testing Service.

Attali, Y. (2011). Sequential effects in essay ratings. *Educational and Psychological Measurement, 71,* 68–79.

Attali, Y. (2013). Validity and reliability of automated essay scoring. In M. D. Shermis & J. Burstein (Eds.), *Handbook of automated essay evaluation: Current applications and new directions* (pp. 181–198). New York: Routledge.

Attali, Y., Bridgeman, B., & Trapani, C. (2010). Performance of a generic approach in automated essay scoring. *The Journal of Technology, Learning, and Assessment, 10*(3), n.p.

Attali, Y., Lewis, W., & Steier, M. (2012). Scoring with the computer: Alternative procedures for improving the reliability of holistic essay scoring. *Language Testing, 30,* 125–141.

Bejar, I. I. (2012). Rater cognition: Implications for validity. *Educational Measurement: Issues and Practice, 31*(3), 2–9.

Bennett, R. E. (2006). Moving the field forward: Some thoughts on validity and automated scoring. In D. M. Williamson, R. J. Mislevy, & I. I. Bejar (Eds.), *Automated scoring of complex tasks in computer-based testing* (pp. 403–412). Mahwah, NJ: Erlbaum.

Bennett, R. E. (2011). *Automated scoring of constructed-response literacy and mathematics items.* Washington, DC: Arabella Philantropic Advisors. Available: www.ets.org/s/k12/pdf/k12_commonassess_automated_scoring_math.pdf

Bennett, R. E., & Bejar, I. I. (1998). Validity and automated scoring: It's not only the scoring. *Educational Measurement: Issues and Practice, 17*(4), 9–17.

Bennett, R. E., Morley, M., Quardt, D., Rock, D. A., Singley, M. K., Katz, I. R., & Nhouyvanisvong, A. (1999). Psychometric and cognitive functioning of an under-determined computer-based response type for quantitative reasoning. *Journal of Educational Measurement, 36,* 233–252.

Bennett, R. E., Steffen, M., Singley, M. K., Morley, M., & Jacquemin, D. (1997). Evaluating an automatically scorable, open-ended response type for measuring mathematical reasoning in computer-adaptive tests. *Journal of Educational Measurement, 34,* 163–177.

Ben-Simon, A., & Bennett, R. E. (2007). Toward more substantively meaningful automated essay scoring. *Journal of Technology, Learning and Assessment, 6*(1). Available: http://ejournals.bc.edu/ojs/index.php/jtla/issue/view/170

Brew, C., & Leacock, C. (2013). Automated short answer scoring: Principles and prospects. In M. D. Shermis & J. Burstein (Eds.), *Handbook of automated essay evaluation: Current applications and new directions* (pp. 136–152). New York: Routledge.

Bridgeman, B. (2013). Human ratings and automated essay evaluation. In M. D. Shermis & J. Burstein (Eds.), *Handbook of automated essay evaluation: Current applications and new directions* (pp. 221–232). New York: Routledge.

Bridgeman, B., Trapani, C., & Attali, Y. (2012). Comparison of human and machine scoring of essays: Differences by gender, ethnicity, and country. *Applied Measurement in Education, 25*(1), 27–40.

Broer, M., Lee, Y.-W., Rizavi, S., & Powers, D. (2005). *Ensuring the fairness of GRE writing prompts: Assessing differential difficulty.* (Research report: RR-05–11). Princeton, NJ: Educational Testing Service.

Burstein, J., Beigman-Klebanov, B., Madnani, N., & Faulkner, A. (2013). Sentiment analysis detection for essay evaluation. In M. D. Shermis & J. Burstein (Eds.), *Handbook of automated essay evaluation: Current applications and new directions* (pp. 281–297). New York: Routledge.

Common Core State Standards Initiative. (2012). *English language arts standards.* Retrieved from www.corestandards.org/ELA-Literacy

Crisp, V. (2007). Researching the judgment processes involved in A-level marking. *Research Matters, 4,* 13–17.

Crisp, V. (2012). An investigation of rater cognition in the assessment of projects. *Educational Measurement: Issues and Practice, 31*(3), 10–20.

Cumming, A., Kantor, R., & Powers, D. E. (2002). Decision making while rating ESL/EFL writing tasks: A descriptive framework. *The Modern Language Journal, 86*(1), 67–96.

Deane, P. (2013). An approach to automated essay scoring motivated by a socio-cognitive framework for defining literacy skills. In M. D. Shermis & J. Burstein (Eds.), *Handbook of automated essay evaluation: Current applications and new directions* (pp. 298–312). New York: Routledge.

Eckes, T. (2012). Operational rater types in writing assessment: Linking rater cognition to rater behavior. *Language Assessment Quarterly, 9,* 270–292.

Farley, T. (2009a, September 27). Opinion: Reading incomprehension. *The New York Times.* Retrieved from www.nytimes.com/2009/09/28/opinion/28farley.html?_r = 0

Farley, T. (2009b, October 28). Opinion: Standardized tests are not the answer. I know, I graded them. *Christian Science Monitor.* www.csmonitor.com/Commentary/Opinion/2009/1028/p09s01-coop.html

Farley, T. (2009c). *Making the grades: My misadventures in the standardized testing industry.* San Francisco: Berrett-Koehler.

Foltz, P. W., Streeter, L. A., Lochbaum, K. E., & Landauer, T. K. (2013). Implementation and applications of the Intelligent Essay Assessor. In M. D. Shermis & J. Burstein (Eds.), *Handbook of automated essay evaluation: Current applications and new directions* (pp. 68–88). New York: Routledge.

Gulliksen, H. (1950). Intrinsic validity. *American Psychologist, 5(10),* 511–517. doi: 10.1037/h0054604

Hewlett Foundation. (2012, January 9). *Hewlett Foundation sponsors prize to improve automated scoring of student essays.* Retrieved June 30, 2013, from www.hewlett.org/newsroom/press-release/hewlett-foundation-sponsors-prizeimprove automated-scoring-student-essays

Higgins, D., Xi, X., Zechner, K., & Williamson, D. (2011). A three-stage approach to the automated scoring of spontaneous spoken responses. *Computer Speech & Language, 25,* 282–306.

Kaggle. (2012). *ASAP: Public leaderboard.* Retrieved from www.kaggle.com/c/asapaes/leaderboard

Kane, M. T. (2006). Validation. In R. L. Brennan (Ed.), *Educational measurement* (4th ed., pp. 17–64). Westport, CT: American Council on Education/Praeger.

Kelly, P. A. (2005). General models for automated essay scoring: Exploring an alternative to the status quo. *Journal of Educational Computing Research, 33,* 101–113.

Lumley, T. (2002). Assessment criteria in a large-scale writing test: What do they really mean to the raters? *Language Testing, 19,* 246–276.

Lussenhop, J. (2011, February 23). Inside the multimillion-dollar essay-scoring business: Behind the scenes of standardized testing. *Minneapolis CityPages News.* Retrieved from www.citypages.com/2011–02–23/news/inside-the-multimillion-dollar-essayscoringbusiness/

Mayfield, E., & Rose, C. P. (2012). *LightSIDE: Text mining and machine learning user's manual.* Pittsburgh, PA: Carnegie Mellon University.

Measured Progress/ETS Collaborative. (2012). *Smarter Balanced Assessment Consortium: English language arts item and task specifications.* Retrieved from www.smarterbalanced.org/wordpress/wpcontent/uploads/2012/05/TaskItemSpecifications/EnglishLanguageArtsLiteracy/ELAGeeralItemandTaskSpecifications.pdf

Messick, S. (1989). Validity. In R. L. Linn (Ed.), *Educational measurement* (3rd ed., pp. 13–103). New York: MacMillan.

National Council of Teachers of English (NCTE). (2013). *NCTE position statement on machine scoring: Machine scoring fails the test.* Urbana, IL: Author. Retrieved from www.ncte.org/positions/statements/machine_scoring

Page, E. B. (1966). The imminence of grading essays by computer. *Phi Delta Kappan, 48,* 238–243.

Partnership for Assessment of Readiness for College and Careers (PARCC). (2013). *Grade ELA Literacy: Grade 7 summative assessment performance-based component.* Retrieved from www.parcconline.org/samples/english-language-artsliteracy/grade-elaliteracy

Powers, D. E. (2005). *Effects of preexamination disclosure of essay prompts for the GRE analytical writing assessment.* (Research report: RR-05–01). Princeton, NJ: Educational Testing Service.

Powers, D. E., Burstein, J. C., Chodorow, M., Fowles, M. E., & Kukich, K. (2000). *Comparing the validity of automated and human essay scoring.* (Research report: RR-00–10). Princeton, NJ: Educational Testing Service.

Powers, D. E., Burstein, J. C., Chodorow, M., Fowles, M. E., & Kukich, K. (2001). *Stumping e-rater: Challenging the validity of automated essay scoring.* (Research report: RR-01–03). Princeton, NJ: Educational Testing Service.

Powers, D. E., & Fowles, M. E. (1996). Effects of applying different time limits to a proposed GRE writing test. *Journal of Educational Measurement, 33,* 433–452.

Powers, D. E., & Fowles, M. E. (1997a). *Effects of disclosing essay topics for a new GRE writing test.* (Research report: RR-96–26). Princeton, NJ: Educational Testing Service.

Powers, D. E. & Fowles, M. E. (1997b). *Correlates of satisfaction with graduate school applicants' performance on the GRE writing measure.* (Research report: RR-96-24). Princeton, NJ: Educational Testing Service.

Powers, D. E., & Fowles, M. E. (1998). *Test takers' judgments about GRE writing test prompts* (Research report: RR-98–36). Princeton, NJ: Educational Testing Service.

Powers, D. E., Fowles, M. E, & Boyles, K. (1996). *Validating a writing test for graduate admissions.* (Research report: RR-96–27). Princeton, NJ: Educational Testing Service.

Powers, D. E., Fowles, M. E., & Welsh, C. K. (1999). *Further validation of a writing assessment for graduate admissions.* (Research report: RR-99–18). Princeton, NJ: Educational Testing Service.

Powers, D. E., Fowles, M. E., & Willard, A. E. (2004). Direct assessment, direct validation? An example from the assessment of writing. *Educational Assessment, 2(1),* 89–100.

Preston, D., & Goodman, D. (2012). *Automated essay scoring and the repair of electronics.* Retrieved from http://snap.stanford.edu/class/cs341–2012/reports/03-Preston_cs341__Dan_and_Danny_-_Final.pdf

Quillen, I. (2012, May 9). Hewlett Automated-Essay-Grader winners announced. *Education Week*. Retrieved from http://blogs.edweek.org/edweek/DigitalEducation/2012/05/essay_grader_winners_annonced.html

Quinlan, T., Higgins, D., & Wolff, S. (2009). *Evaluating the construct-coverage of the e-rater® scoring engine*. (Research report: RR-09–01). Princeton, NJ: Educational Testing Service.

Ramineni, C., Trapani, C. S., Williamson, D. M., Davey, T., & Bridgeman, B. (2012). *Evaluation of e-rater for the GRE issue and argument prompts*. (Research report: RR-12-02). Princeton, NJ: Educational Testing Service.

Rosenfeld, M., Courtney, R., & Fowles, M. E. (2004). *Identifying the writing tasks important for academic success at the undergraduate and graduate levels*. (Research report: RR-04-42). Princeton, NJ: Educational Testing Service.

Sandene, B., Bennett, R. E., Braswell, J., & Oranje, A. (2005). Online assessment in mathematics. In B. Sandene, N. Horkay, R. E. Bennett, N. Allen, J. Braswell, B. Kaplan, & A. Oranje (Eds.), *Online assessment in mathematics and writing: Reports from the NAEP Technology-Based Assessment Project (NCES 2005–457)*. Washington, DC: National Center for Education Statistics, U.S. Department of Education. Retrieved December 12, 2013, from http://nces.ed.gov/pubsearch/pubsinfo.asp?pubid=2005457

Schaeffer, G. A., Briel, J. B., & Fowles, M. E. (2001). *Psychometric evaluation of the new GRE writing assessment*. (Research report: RR-01–08). Princeton, NJ: Educational Testing Service.

Sebrechts, M. M., Bennett, R. E., & Rock, D. A. (1991). Agreement between expert system and human raters' scores on complex constructed-response quantitative items. *Journal of Applied Psychology, 76*, 856–862.

Shermis, M. D., & Burstein, J. (Eds.). (2013). *Handbook of automated essay evaluation: Current applications and new directions*. New York: Routledge.

Shermis, M. D., & Hamner, B. (2013). Contrasting state-of-the-art automated scoring of essays. In M. D. Shermis & J. Burstein (Eds.), *Handbook of automated essay evaluation: Current applications and new directions* (pp. 313–346). New York: Routledge.

Simon, S. (2012, March 29). *Robo-readers: The new teachers' helper in the U.S.* Reuters. Retrieved from www.reuters.com/article/2012/03/29/us-usa-schools-gradingidUSBRE82S0ZN20120329

Strauss, V. (2013, January 16). Pearson criticized for finding test essay scorers on Craigslist. *Washington Post*. Retrieved from http://www.washingtonpost.com/blogs/answer-sheet/wp/2013/01/16/pearson-criticized-for-finding-test-essay-scorers-on-craigslist/

Suto, W. M. I., & Greatorex, J. (2006). A cognitive psychological exploration of the GCSE marking process. *Research Matters, 2*, 7–10.

Suto, W. M. I., & Greatorex, J. (2008a). What goes through an examiner's mind? Using verbal protocols to gain insights into the GCSE marking process. *British Educational Research Journal, 34*, 213–233.

Suto, W. M. I., & Greatorex, J. (2008b). A quantitative analysis of cognitive strategy usage in the marking of two GCSE examinations. *Assessment in Education: Principles, Policies and Practices, 15*(1), 73–90.

Versant. (2008). *Versant English Test: Test description and validation summary*. Palo Alto, CA: Pearson. Retrieved November 17, 2010, from www.versanttest.co.uk/pdf/ValidationReport.pdf

Williamson, D. M. (2013). Probable cause: Developing warrants for automated scoring of essays. In M. D. Shermis & J. Burstein (Eds.), *Handbook of automated essay evaluation: Current applications and new directions* (pp. 153–180). New York: Routledge.

Wolfe, E. W. (2005). Uncovering rater's cognitive processing and focus using think-aloud protocols. *Journal of Writing Assessment, 2*, 37–56. Retrieved from www.journalofwritingassessment.org/archives/2–1.4.pdf

Zhang, M. (2013a). *Contrasting automated and human scoring of essays*. (RDC-21). Princeton, NJ: Educational Testing Service.

Zhang, M. (2013b). *The impact of sampling approach on population invariance in automated scoring of essays*. (Research report: RR-13-18). Princeton, NJ: Educational Testing Service.

# Commentary on Chapters 5–7: Moving From Art to Science

**Mark D. Reckase**

Test design, development, and scoring have often been considered more art than science. For example, Pandey (1992, p. 124) discusses "The Art of Questioning" and the "art of test construction." The invention of the multiple-choice item format was an attempt to make the scoring part of the test more objective and, in that sense, more scientific (Trewin, 2007). But the mere use of that item format tells us little about the cognitive processes that examinees use to get to the keyed answer—or any of the other answers they might choose. In recent years, cognitive labs have been used to gain greater insights into the processes that examinees use to respond to test items, but it is not clear whether the information gained from cognitive labs has been transferred to the item development process (i.e., Rupp, Ferne, & Choi, 2006). The same can be said for the way that items with open-ended responses are scored. Some cognitive labs have been done with the persons scoring the responses to determine the features that have the most impact (i.e., Wolfe, 2005), but it is not clear if this information has been used to refine scoring guides or to provide deeper insights into the quality of work produced by examinees.

The three chapters in this section of the book review and report some research on attempts to make the item development, test construction, and scoring of open-ended items more scientific—or at least more reproducible. Before delving into the details of these chapters, it is helpful to give an overall conceptual description of test design, development, and scoring as a scientific enterprise so that the contributions of these chapters can be better understood.

## Conceptual Overview of Test Design, Development, and Scoring

All tests are based on a premise that it is reasonable to order individuals on a continuum based on the responses to the test items. Often this continuum is formally labeled a hypothetical construct—the concept that is the target of the assessment. Test items are probes into the processes and knowledge stored in the brain of a person with the goal of gaining information about the location of the person on the hypothetical construct. Some test items are useful probes in that their use yields information that can be used to estimate the location on the continuum. Other test items may not give much useful information. From the perspective of educational and psychological measurement as a science, the construction of the test item should be done based on the best information available on how useful probes should be produced. When we use a thermometer to measure body temperature as an indicator of the hypothetical construct "health," the thermometer may be poorly constructed and inaccurate, yielding poor information about a person's location on the health continuum, or it can be a precise scientific instrument that gives accurate measures of temperature to the tenth of a degree. We want test items that are constructed to be precision instruments rather than poor indicators of the constructs.

One good test item is not sufficient to locate a person on the target continuum. Testing is based on the idea of aggregating information from multiple test items to get a good estimate of location. However, tests are complex devices akin to those for analyzing blood chemistry as a measure of health. The medical devices need detailed blueprints and careful assembly for them to function properly. The construction of a test also needs detailed blueprints, but test construction has the added challenge of having to construct the device using different kinds of parts each time. Uniform sets of prefabricated parts can not be used because they would be too memorable and would change the construct that is being assessed to one related to memory rather than the target continuum. Imagine creating a mosaic representing some picture using rocks of different colors. Recreating the same picture with a different set of rocks is challenging because the rocks have slightly different shapes and colors. It can be done if the rocks are fairly small and the mosaic is large. The same is true if the test is made up of many test items. The differences in items can be balanced so that the target construct remains the same. Use of computing processing power can make this process of balancing much more precise.

Of course, all of the items on a test must be scored to get the information that is used to determine the location of the examinees on the target continuum. For multiple-choice items, the scoring is straightforward. However, for items with unstructured open-ended responses, it has been typical for human readers to provide the scores, guided by scoring rubrics and training. The rubrics and the training are designed to focus the readers on important features of the open-ended responses that are related to the target continuum of interest. The creation of the rubrics and the training are also considered works of art more than scientific endeavors. It is also not clear what cognitive processes the readers are using when evaluating the open-ended responses. They may be using shortcuts, such as basing the score on the length of the response, rather than focusing on the intended evidence for the target continuum.

## Moving Art to Science

The three chapters in this section of the book directly address item development, test construction, and scoring of open-ended responses with the goal of moving them from art to more formal science. An important aspect of the chapters is that they describe computer processes and programs that are used to do tasks that had previously been human-only endeavors. Writing computer programs to do the task requires deep understanding of what the task is. As a result, these chapters provide interesting insights to these "artistic" parts of the development and scoring of tests that can lead to more scientific and rigorous processes for creating these types of instruments.

Chapter 5 in the set is about item development: "Using Technology-Enhanced Processes to Generate Test Items in Multiple Languages." While the major theme of this chapter is the computer generation of test items, it takes on the even more difficult task of developing items that function in the same way when presented in different languages. Building on the earlier mosaic example, this is like producing the same picture using rocks or shards of glass. It is not certain if the pictures that result will ever be totally equivalent even though they can be recognized as representing the same image.

The basic concept that is presented for computerized generation of items is the item model. The item model is essentially a template for the placement of component parts of the item. Creating this template is nontrivial, and it requires deep understanding of the target construct and the range of material that can be used to develop tasks that will give useful information about the target construct. The chapter describes a three-step process for developing and using the item model. Although useful examples are provided to show how the item model can be used to produce test items, and even test items in different languages, it is surprising that there is not more emphasis on the target construct for the assessment. It seems the approach is more focused on replicating items. It seems that there is an unstated assumption that the parent item provides good information about the target construct so that items produced according to the item model based on the parent item will also provide good information about the target construct.

A particular contribution of this chapter is an acknowledgment of the complexity of test items by adding complexity to the item model—the $n$-layer item model. The $n$-layer item model has a nested structure in which specific content can be placed within the context of other content decisions. The result is a very rich set of possibilities for generated test items.

The real purpose of this chapter is to show how the $n$-layer model can be used to generate test items in different languages. Language is considered a layer in the model. This is an important application given the number of international assessment programs and the desire to export testing programs from one country to another. However, for me, the interesting content in this chapter is the detailed analysis of parent items to produce item models. This is the part of the work that leads to the generalizable results that make the item generation closer to a science than an art. While being very excited about this work from a scientific perspective, I have not yet been sold on the practicality of this type of methodology for large-scale, high-stakes testing programs. It seems that a lot of refinement is needed before this methodology will become a standard component of large-scale testing programs.

Chapter 6 is about using computer technology to regularize the artistic endeavor of constructing test forms. The chapter titled "Automated Test Assembly" also gives the name for such procedures. Automated test assembly, or ATA, is a clear advance over human construction of tests. Past practice for test assembly has been for a person or a team of persons to select the set of items for use in a test based on formal test specifications. Usually, there would be a content-by-cognitive-level plan and possibly also target distributions for difficulty and discrimination statistics. This is about the maximum that the test constructors could manage. It is impossible to keep track of more item features without assistance. It might be possible to consider other things like item enemies and variation in the contexts for items in test form review after test construction.

The move to ATA has allowed the specifications for a test to be much more detailed, such as including word counts for the complete set of items, the gender references within items, the location of the answer choice for the items, and so on. The literature on ATA describes applications with tens or even hundreds of constraints on the test construction process (see van der Linden, 2005). The result is that test forms can have a much closer match to test specifications, and parallel test forms are much more similar than would be possible from the human judgment–based process.

This chapter does a nice job of summarizing the basic concepts of ATA and also give some perspective on how this technological area will progress in the future. As computer presentation of assessments becomes more widespread, the process of testing will likely become more distributed both over time and over testing sites. This implies that the schedule for building test forms/item pools will need to change to more flexibly accommodate the new realities of testing. For example, it will be helpful if information about item statistics can be input into the ATA system as it becomes available. This will require better communication between software systems.

There is also a lot of emphasis on new item types and the need for larger item pools. The ATA systems will need to be elaborated to respond to the new developments in test design. These changes do not require any conceptual or software breakthroughs. There is only the need to have the will and the resources to build the systems that will efficiently use ATA. In the future, it is likely that all formal testing programs will use ATA as a well-integrated part of the test design and development process.

The third chapter in the set, Chapter 7, "Validity and Automated Scoring," addresses another of those "artistic" parts of the testing process—the scoring of extended-response items. In recent years, there has been strong interest in the computerized scoring of these item types, both to increase the speed of reporting and to reduce the cost of the scoring process. Educators have touted the value of having students produce extended responses, but testing programs have often avoided such item types because of the cost of scoring them. Those costs include recruiting individuals to do the scoring, training them, distributing materials, collecting ratings, monitoring results, and so forth.

The process for computer scoring of open-ended questions is beginning to mature. There are many scoring engines available, and there is substantial information about how well the procedures work (Shermis & Burstein, 2013). The criterion for good computer scoring is usually a good match to the average score given by a set of well-trained human scorers.

This chapter shows the maturity of this technology by changing from a question of whether computerized scoring can be done with an acceptable level of match to human scoring to a question about what the scores produced by a computerized scoring engine really mean. The chapter has two main points. One is that there can be many different reasons computer-produced scores and human-produced scores are similar. Some of those are positive features that are related to the construct that is the target of the assessment, and some are negative features that are features of the writing that are correlated to the human score but that are not good targets for interpretation of the scores. For example, it may be that the number of commas in a piece of writing is related to the holistic rating of the writing task, but it would not make sense to report a "comma" score as meaningful. That type of score might encourage more disjointed writing that eventually leads to lower scores by humans and a lower correlation between this feature and the human score.

The second point made by this chapter is that those who produce the scoring software often keep the inner workings secret for business reasons. This makes it difficult to determine the features of the writing that have the greatest impact on the generated score and how those features change over time.

These are nuanced issues directly related to the validity argument for the scores produced by computers. I strongly concur with the authors in their call for a closer look at the outputs of computerized scoring processes and the need for a better understanding about how these procedures work. That greater understanding will move the scoring of extended open-ended responses to be more of a science than an art.

These three chapters are very valuable resources. In all three cases, they are showing how these difficult areas of test design, development, and implementation are moving more toward the ideal of measurement that is an objective process for determining the location of an entity on a target continuum. This is moving educational and psychological measurement further toward being a science rather than an art form.

## References

Pandey, T. (1992). Test development profile of a state-mandated large-scale assessment instrument in mathematics. In T.A. Romberg (Ed.), *Mathematics assessment and evaluation: Imperatives for mathematics educators* (pp. 100–127). Albany: State University of New York Press.

Rupp, A.A., Ferne, T., & Choi, H. (2006). How assessing reading comprehension with multiple-choice questions shapes the construct: A cognitive processing perspective. *Language Testing, 23*(4), 441–474.

Shermis, M.D., & Burstein, J. (2013). *Handbook of automated essay evaluation: Current applications and new directions.* New York: Taylor & Francis.

Trewin, S.A. (2007). Robert Yerkes' multiple-choice apparatus 1913–1939. *The American Journal of Psychology, 120*(4), 645–660.

van der Linden, W.J. (2005). *Linear models for optimal test design.* New York: Springer.

Wolfe, E.W. (2005). Uncovering rater's cognitive processing and focus using think-aloud protocols. *Journal of Writing Assessment, 2*(1), 37–56.

# 8

# Computer-Based Test Delivery Models, Data, and Operational Implementation Issues

Richard M. Luecht

## Introduction

Computer-based testing (CBT) has changed dramatically over the past two decades. In the 1970s and 1980s, CBT provided only limited test delivery options beyond standardized paper-and-pencil tests (e.g., immediate scoring). The 1990s saw increased adoption of CBT by large testing organizations and the first operational use of computerized adaptive testing (CAT) technology for both the Armed Services Vocational Aptitude Battery (ASVAB) and the Graduate Record Examination (GRE®). Dedicated testing centers also began emerging in the 1990s, offering near on-demand testing, and some organizations began routinely using automated test assembly technologies to produce large numbers of near-parallel test forms. The start of the new millennium ushered in Internet-based testing and the possibilities of ubiquitous testing—anytime and almost anyplace on Earth. Today, CBT is moving into large-scale adaptive and multistage testing applications, with testing organizations embracing the opportunities and promises of implementing innovative, technology-enhanced items and complex computerized performance exercises on a wider variety of operating systems and devices. Many technical and operational challenges remain before we can take full advantage of those opportunities and realize the promises.

CBT can require an elaborate system of systems (Drasgow, Bennett, & Luecht, 2006; Luecht, 2006a, 2012). Whether a testing organization elects to design and build its own CBT systems or contract for services, one thing is clear—it is never simple or inexpensive. In cases where organizations are migrating paper-and-pencil testing (PPT) to computer-based delivery, virtually all of the legacy systems designed for PPT will likely be replaced or at least significantly reengineered to support operational CBT. The following list describes just some of the key systems and support mechanisms needed for large-scale, operational CBT.

- Item and task prototyping and design to create and evaluate new item types
- Item authoring and editing to create the items, assessment tasks, and ancillary test materials that make up the "content" of the *item bank*(s)

- Item banking and content management software and data management structures to store all of the item-related data, exhibits, graphics, content, and statistical information
- Test specifications management software and data structures to create and maintain content and statistical test specifications
- Test assembly[1] and composition software to build test forms or test subunits (i.e., item selection)
- Examinee test registration and scheduling to assign CBT time slots to examinees at prescribed venues
- Test delivery software and hardware that actually administers CBTs to the examinees
- Digital data transmission channels and security systems for managing secure content, including authentication and encryption control
- Psychometric item and test analysis, including calibration and equating support to evaluate the quality of items and to establish the underlying scale(s)
- Score generation and reporting to prepare and disseminate score and interpretive information to examinees and other constituents
- Quality-control software and data management systems to ensure the integrity of all of the CBT systems and data, including version controls
- Communication and technical assistance to advertise, inform, and correspond with examinees and other stakeholders.

CBT development specifications such as the Assessment Interoperability Framework (AIF) have emerged using federal Race-to-the-Top Assessment (RTTA) grant funds that also funded the now well-known state assessment consortia: the Partnership for Assessment of Readiness for College and Career (PARCC) and the Smarter Balanced Assessment Consortium (SBAC). In particular, AIF specifies four general systems that need to share data—possibly across consortia, states, and other users: (1) the assessment creation and management system (ACMS), (2) the assessment delivery system (ADS), (3) the assessment score processing system (ASPS), and (4) the assessment score reporting system (ASRS). Interoperability can vary from coerced and tedious data exchanges to seamless processing that is invariant to the source of the data. Ideally, we would prefer seamless processing, but ultimately, even data restructuring and coercion are acceptable if they work.

Regardless of the frameworks or architectures adopted, the potential complexity of the overall enterprise may seem somewhat intimidating when jointly considering the many possible human–hardware–software interactions and data exchanges. There are also ancillary procedures that may or may not be part of the formal CBT architecture—for example, data forensics, accessibility support, and operational complexities that sometimes arise from an examination program maintaining dual modes of test administration (CBT and paper-and-pencil testing operating simultaneously). The measurement literature tends to conveniently ignore the scope and complexity of operational CBT enterprises: the software systems, data and database structures, the hardware infrastructures, and the human-level activity, technical expertise, decision making, and expense. For example, a literature search in the measurement journals on "computer adaptive testing" (CAT) will return articles about nuanced item-selection algorithms, score estimators, and various issues addressed using model-based simulations. The complex systems and operational support mechanisms needed to implement even the simplest CBT delivery recommendations coming out of the measurement literature are, unfortunately, often treated as trivial or ignorable.

This chapter discusses four classes of systems and processes that broadly cover most of the above CBT operations: (1) the data structures and repositories; (2) data transmission channels, infrastructure, and interactivity; (3) test delivery models and drivers; and (4) psychometric analysis and scoring. A final section addresses CBT issues and challenges that impact these systems and processes. Taken as a whole, this chapter serves (at least in part) as a *functional CBT-requirements specification* that testing organizations might wish to consider in their planning—a call for interoperability *by design*! The chapter also serves as a subtle call to measurement researchers to possibly expand their worldview and consider real costs and operational efficiencies before making ardent CBT design recommendations—such as to implement CAT or any other test delivery model based on largely the results of studies using model-based, computer-simulated examinees that show trivial changes in standard errors of estimated scores.

## Data Structures and Digital Repositories for CBT

Most people are somewhat familiar with terms like "files" and "databases." However, those terms can actually be limiting when talking more flexibly about data structures, storage, and access. A useful term is *digital repository*—that is, someplace where the digital CBT data is stored. Given modern distributed storage and high-speed transmission capabilities (e.g., distributed or "cloud storage"), a digital repository is not even required to be stored in a single location. Regardless of where and how the repository exists in the "cloud," most CBT systems require at least eight types of digital repositories: (1) the item bank; (2) test-form assembly specifications; (3) the test form/test unit database; (4) the CBT test administration and resource repository; (5) the primary data examinee database; (6) the examination results database; (7) interim psychometric analysis files; and (8) examinee scores and reported data. An in-depth discussion or specification for any of these repositories is far beyond the intended scope of this chapter. Nonetheless, it is possible to roughly indicate the types of data stored in terms of data structures and relationships among data structures.

Figure 8.1 contains a listing of the potential data that might be stored for items, test objects (sets, groups, testlets, modules, and forms), online tools and resources, item templates, examinee data, and examinee-by-item transactions. Each cluster of data can be considered a digital repository.

Although it is common to talk about digital repositories as simply storing data, it is important to realize that data need to be *structured* in particular ways to also facilitate high-integrity retrieval and processing—usually for multiple purposes. Dynamically created, unstructured data are not only difficult to manage but are quite likely to yield multiple answers to single, simple queries and misleading answers to complex questions. Poorly structured data may make it impossible to even access or process the data at an appropriate grain size. For example, storing test data as an examinee-by-item response matrix might seem reasonable for running certain types of analyses in software that uses that type of "flat file" (table-like) format. But flat file formats have many structural flaws (e.g., indirect referencing of the data by column position, limited manipulations of the data fields across columns, corrupted delimiters) that would preclude responsibly using them for most primary storage applications. Good data structures *promote* efficient storage, retrieval, and processing—including providing the on-demand flexibility to generate new and different *views* of the data (i.e., flexible queries, extract choices, transformations as needed, and formatting of the same data

| Item Data | Item Templates |
|---|---|
| Stimulus information (e.g., MCQ stem, a reading passage) | Template data model |
| Response display labels (e.g., distractors) | Template rendering form |
| Scripts for interactivity | Template scoring evaluator |
| Item template reference(s) | Display control properties |
| Content and other item attributes | Interactive control properties |
| Content category codes | Response capturing control properties |
| Cognitive and other secondary classifications | **Examinee Data** |
| Linguistic features | Examinee ID |
| Statistical item data | Name and other identification |
| Classical item statistics (p-values, biserial correlations, etc.) | Photo, digital signature, retinal scan information |
| IRT statistics (1PL, 2PL, 3PL, GPCM parameter estimates) | Address and other contact information |
| DIF statistics and other special indices | Demographic information |
| Operational data | Eligibility-to-test information |
| Reuse history | Jurisdiction |
| Exposure rates and controls | Retest restrictions |
| Equating status | Scheduled test date(s) |
| **Test Object Data** | Special accommodations required |
| Object list to include (e.g., list of item or other IDs) | Scores and score reporting information |
| Navigation functions (presentation, review & sequencing rules) | Testing history and exam blocking |
| Embedded adaptive mechanisms (score + selection) | Security history (e.g., previous irregular behaviors, flags) |
| Timing controls and other information | General correspondence |
| Title and instruction screens | **Examinee by Item Transactions** |
| Presentation template references | Examinee ID |
| Helm look-and-feel (navigation style, etc.) | Item ID |
| Functions (e.g., keyboard or mouse movement functions) | Sequence |
| **Tools and Exhibit Data** | Final responses |
| Calculators | Captured actions/inactions (state and sequencing of actions) |
| Hyperlink to other repositories | Cumulative elapsed time on "unit" |
| Custom exhibits available to test takers | Notes, marks or other captured during testing |

**Figure 8.1** Potential item, test, and examinee data

for various purposes). Multiple purposes for data should almost always be assumed from the onset; however, those purposes create some interesting challenges for data repository designers, who may not always understand all of the various demands on the data or necessarily be able to anticipate all future requirements.

All data repositories should adhere to the *single-source data* premise.[2] The single-source data premise implies a practice of building structured data models and schemas so every data element is stored exactly once and only once in a table. Single-source also implies that there is an uncorrupted, high-integrity, *master* version of every original data element. Multiple versions of the *same* data are not allowed to exist, except as interim or temporary instantiations of the data created from queries and other operations. Instead, modified data elements can evolve into new elements that are added to the digital master repository. A simple example involves considering how item answer key changes are handled for selected-response items. The answer keys should ideally reside in a master item repository. If an answer key changes, the single-source premise suggests that the change should first be made and locked down in the master item repository. Then any interim or auxiliary data files needed for item analysis or scoring purposes should be created or recreated to ensure that the appropriate key changes are propagated throughout all relevant data systems. If multiple (correct and incorrect) answer keys are allowed to reside in different versions or images of the item repository, there is definitely potential for scoring errors if the wrong version or image is inadvertently used.

The data need to be efficiently stored at a sufficiently small grain size or level of specificity so that all the data can be restructured as needed for many possible purposes. In addition, flexible structures and templates may be needed to ensure that the data can be faithfully formed into particular configurations or formats for all of those purposes (i.e., creating different data *views*). The term *metadata* is often used in database design to describe the structure of data (variable names, data types and properties, relations, etc.). There are two general metadata schemes used for most repositories: *relational database structures* and *object-oriented design*.

Relational database structures are typically defined to provide an efficient way to store data with minimal redundancy. For example, a typical examinee-by-item "transaction" can be recorded using four pieces of information:[3] (1) the examinee's identifier; (2) the item's identifier; (3) the serial position (sequence) in which the item was presented; and (4) the examinee's final response. It would certainly not be efficient to replicate the examinee's name and personal data for every examinee-by-item transaction record. Nor would it be efficient to include all of the item-related data such as the item text, content codes, and item statistics for every transaction. Instead, we can more efficiently use the examinee's assigned identification code and the corresponding item identification code as the minimum necessary relational information for each transaction. The more elaborate examinee data and all relevant item data can be respectively stored in different repositories and accessed as needed using only the corresponding identifiers. Formally, we use the word *entity* to describe a unique, implicitly or explicitly, structured data table. A given entity (table) can therefore have one of three types of explicit relationships with another entity: (1) hierarchical relationships with one entity as the parent data, with instantiated "children" or "cousins" in other tables; (2) one-to-one relationships by field or category reference (perhaps for entity tables merged across repositories); and (3) one-to-many relationships by identification, key field or category reference.

Figure 8.2 shows a relatively simple relational scheme where examinee-by-item transactions are stored in one entity table (lower box), examinee data in another (upper left), and item data in a third entity table (upper right). The relationship between the examinee entity table and the transaction table is one to many (each examinee linked with many transactions).

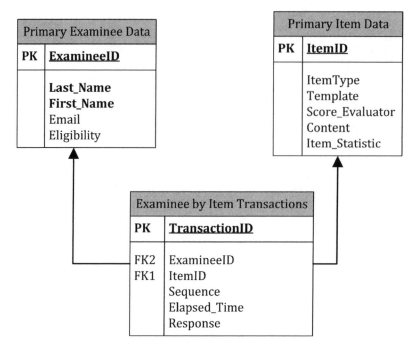

**Figure 8.2** A simple relational scheme for examinee and item records

A similar one-to-many relationship exists between the item entity table and the transaction table. More specifically, The *ExamineeID* and *ItemID* data fields link the transaction repository to the other two; there are as many unique *ItemID* transactions per *ExamineeID* as items on the test form. But there is only one *ExamineeID* for each examinee record in the Primary Examinee Data repository and only one *ItemID* per item in the Primary Item Data repository.

Careful and efficient planning and design of all of the repositories is essential to ensure that the data can be accessed and restructured for a variety of purposes within the testing systems enterprise. For example, if we query the Primary Examinee Data repository for examinees meeting a particular "eligibility" criterion (see Figure 8.1) and correspondingly query the Primary Item Data repository, we can create a specification for extracting the transactional responses for analysis or scoring purposes. Figure 8.3 demonstrates a relatively straightforward set of queries of examinees and items that culminates in a raw response data file (rows = examinees, columns = items) that might be used for item analysis or scored and used for other analyses.

The second metadata-related concept is called *object-oriented design* (OOD), an extremely versatile software and database design schema. With OOD, each "object" (item, examinee, etc.) is encapsulated and self-describing. OOD is actually fully compatible with relational database structures but adds scalable capabilities to combine objects to create other objects. As a simple example, we can create an item as an object, combine multiple items to form item sets, combine sets to form modules, and combine modules to form test forms. Each new object is uniquely defined, making it relatively straightforward to reference the data, further avoiding the need to predefine every possible "test object" in various repositories. OOD requires that the data follow certain rules and support "inheritance" of defined properties,

### Source: Primary Examinee Data

| ExamineeID | TestID | Eligibility | Exam_Date |
|---|---|---|---|
| 107555 | TST0183 | F | 8-Jan |
| 517101 | TST0181 | F | 1-Nov |
| 670048 | TST0181 | F | 19-Sep |
| 758735 | TST0183 | F | 20-Jul |
| 754364 | TST0183 | F | 29-Sep |
| 827960 | TST0183 | R | 14-Dec |
| 619834 | TST0183 | F | 30-Mar |
| 615233 | TST0182 | R | 11-Aug |
| 429336 | TST0182 | F | 19-Sep |

### Source: Primary Item Data

| TestID | ItemID |
|---|---|
| TST0181 | ITM020342 |
| TST0181 | ITM020920 |
| TST0183 | ITM020921 |
| TST0181 | ITM022222 |
| TST0181 | ITM023833 |
| TST0183 | ITM024519 |
| TST0183 | ITM028902 |
| TST0183 | ITM030102 |
| TST0183 | ITM030253 |
| TST0181 | ITM031935 |
| TST0181 | ITM035329 |
| TST0181 | ITM038632 |
| TST0183 | ITM038886 |
| TST0183 | ITM039981 |
| TST0183 | ITM040027 |
| TST0181 | ITM048392 |

### Source: Examinee by Item Data

| ExamineeID | TestID | ItemID | Sequence | Resp_Time | Response |
|---|---|---|---|---|---|
| 107555 | TST0183 | ITM020921 | 1 | 39 | B |
| 107555 | TST0183 | ITM030102 | 2 | 131 | D |
| 107555 | TST0183 | ITM028902 | 3 | 39 | C |
| 107555 | TST0183 | ITM038886 | 4 | 61 | B |
| 107555 | TST0183 | ITM024519 | 5 | 58 | D |
| 107555 | TST0183 | ITM039981 | 6 | 67 | A |
| 107555 | TST0183 | ITM040027 | 7 | 61 | A |
| 107555 | TST0183 | ITM030253 | 8 | 34 | B |
| 517101 | TST0181 | ITM020920 | 1 | 65 | C |

### Output: Examinee by Item Response Data Analysis Flat File

| ExamineeID | ITM020342 | ITM020920 | ITM020921 | ITM022222 | ITM023833 | ITM024519 | ITM028902 | ITM030102 | ITM030253 | ITM031935 | ITM035329 | ITM038632 | ITM038886 | ITM039981 | ITM040027 | ITM048392 |
|---|---|---|---|---|---|---|---|---|---|---|---|---|---|---|---|
| 107555 | | | B | | | D | C | D | B | | | | B | A | A | |
| 517101 | B | C | | A | D | | | | | C | C | B | | | | A |

```
107555   9919911019991009
517101   1190199990019991
```

Output: Examinee by Item Scored Data Analysis Flat File

**Figure 8.3** Relational database queries and extractions to obtain analysis files
The (usually unique) identifiers used for linking the data across multiple repositories are called relational data because they "relate" one data source (table) to another.

making it convenient to combine proven template objects to instantiate more complex templates and then generate new items as special cases—that is, instantiations of the template. This makes OOD highly useful for structuring repositories for items and test forms, as well as for housing complex examinee data.[4] Finally, OOD can be readily implemented using markup languages like XML.[5] Some assessment-relevant implementations of XML include the IMS Consortium's Question and Test Interoperability (QTI) specification and data model (www.imsglobal.org/question/qtiv1p2/) and the even more specific (and recent) Accessible Portable Item Protocol (APIP) data model for digital items and other assessment tasks (see www.imsglobal.org/apip and www.apipstandard.org/apip).[6]

Building robust, well-structured digital repositories can initially be quite complicated insofar as balancing efficiency in data storage with the likely need to support future, structural extensibility for new item types and scorable data, enhanced interoperability, and access across platforms and end-users, and supporting the multitude of possible end-user data requirements and export formats. But, by using relational databases and OOD—implemented using portable XML-based structures and content and combined with shared specifications like QTI and APIP—it should nonetheless be possible to painlessly reconfigure data, add new data structures and extract and format any of the data to meet many different assessment needs. Many limitations in interoperability and access stem from limited or short-sighted digital repository designs rather than unrealistic or inappropriate data requests by users.

### Data Transmission Channels, Infrastructure, and Interactivity

This section discusses some fundamental system requirements related to the movement of data between systems and the nature of the facilities and devices that make up the assessment infrastructure. Although it may seem as though data transmission for CBT is straightforward (i.e., an examinee sits in front of his or her computer and connects via the Internet to "the test"), the potential support networks, servers, possibly mainframe computers, and communications hardware and software systems needed can be incredibly complex. Figure 8.4 shows a conceptual infrastructure configuration with multiple Internet (web) servers handling the traffic across the Internet and background software applications and data servers, mainframe support (left side of figure). The examinees may be taking their tests on networked desktop computer workstations, notebooks, netbooks, tablet PCs, or other handheld digital devices. Network servers and proxy servers may also be layered between the test takers and the web servers. In short, there is usually a rather massive and complex digital communication system underlying even the simplest CBT delivery system.

Data-transmission channels provide the necessary digital linkages between systems. For example, an examinee sitting at a computer taking an Internet-based test may be linked via a router and modem to an Internet service provider's servers and ultimately, via the Internet, to a testing organization's central processing system thousands of miles away. The test takers should not have to wait for items or exhibits to appear or experience delays after submitting their responses. A fundamental requirement for CBT is therefore to minimize anything that creates any detectable delays in the exchange of data between their computer and the assessment delivery system. Although there are other very important types of intersystem data exchanges for analysis, archival needs, and so forth, seamless examinee-computer interactivity should always remain a primary goal.

Data-transmission channels are analogous to roads and traffic flow. Traveling a particular distance along a curvy, single-lane gravel or dirt road will typically take longer than traveling on a nicely paved, four-lane interstate highway—unless, of course, the interstate highway has lane closures or is crowded with rush-hour traffic. It is common to talk about speed and bandwidth when describing digital transmission channels; we talk less often about minimizing congestion. An interstate highway has higher bandwidth (multiple lanes versus a single lane) and usually allows vehicles to travel at higher speeds than on local roads. But, like a crowded highway during rush hour, heavy traffic or obstructions (accidents, construction, etc.) can clog the digital transmission channel. It may not always be cost or technically feasible to build/wait for higher bandwidth or acquire dedicated channels. So what are the obstacles to on-demand CBT anywhere and anytime?

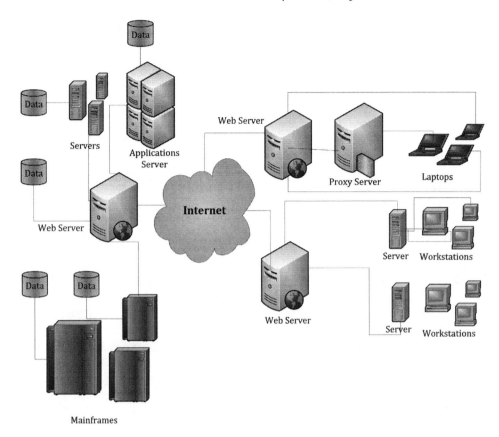

**Figure 8.4** A conceptual CBT digital communications infrastructure for Internet-based testing

With the rapid proliferation of wireless data-transmission capabilities, it seems safe to conclude that we will be able to have near-ubiquitous data transmission anywhere on the planet within the next 5 years. For example, Google's Project Loon (www.google.com/loon) is an experimental attempt to float algorithmically controlled, durable balloons in the stratosphere (approximately 20 km above the Earth) to form a massive network of antennas and high-speed routers capable of providing communications and wireless Internet access to even the most remote parts of the globe. Whether Google's project is a success is really not the point for purposes of this discussion. The important point is that Google and other large-scale Internet-centric organizations seem committed to providing ubiquitous wireless communication and data exchange; that fact makes the outcome (eventually) a *fait accompli*.

However, ubiquitous communications and Internet connectivity do not mean that we can necessarily offer assessments anytime or anyplace. We need a dramatically larger and better infrastructure of devices on which to deliver CBTs and ways to limit the data interactivity required so that available bandwidth and upload/download speeds can be effectively used despite high demands. The *de facto* standard for CBT for the past two decades has been the dedicated testing or assessment center (i.e., secure, permanent or temporary facilities with multiple testing workstations where examinees can schedule to take their examination of choice). Unfortunately, dedicated testing centers are not the solution; they simply will not scale up to meet the necessary capacity demands for CBT. If we only consider educational testing populations like high school students who typically take the SAT® and/or ACT®, we are looking at needing to securely test a combined total of about 3.3 million test takers each year (http://press.collegeboard.org/sat/faq and www.act.org/products/k-12-act-test/). Assuming 25 workstations per testing site on average, testing in 50 states and four U.S. territories would require more than 610 test centers per jurisdiction—assuming that testing was further spread over four windows. The number of testing centers could be reduced by offering the tests more frequently, but then substantially larger item banks would be needed. More broadly and based on 2009–2010 data, there are an estimated 77 million students enrolled in public and private education in the United States (www.census.gov), with an estimated 49.5 million students alone in K–12 public education. In contrast, an estimate the ratio of computers to K–12 students is about 1:4 (U.S. Census Bureau (Davis, J. & Bauman, K. (2013)) and the National Commission of Educational Statistics (2015)). If we add the qualifying condition of "CBT-capable" computers, the ratio of devices to students probably paints a far more dismal picture as to the *usable* CBT infrastructure.[7] We might amortize the examinees across time to spread out the demand given the limited capacity of our current CBT infrastructures, but then security, opportunity to learn, and other issues come into play.

Presently, one of the only viable ways to leverage creating the needed infrastructure is to put CBT-capable laptop, notebook, netbook, and tablet computers (or any viable handheld devices) into the hands of every K–12 student—devices that can be used for both educational applications and assessment. Luecht (2012) called this a "bring your own" (BYO) solution. We of course need better and more robust applications for presenting tests on handheld devices (see Chernyshenko & Stark, this volume). There are certainly important security challenges for high-stakes applications. But overcoming those technical challenges under the BYO paradigm is not all that complicated as long as the nature and scope of the problem are understood. For example, real-time authenticated packaging of encrypted test materials delivered over the Internet, remote proctoring and on-site proctoring, and modern data forensics are already being effectively used in high-stakes settings.

Beyond building the capacity for ubiquitous, on-demand testing, the anticipated digital *interactivity* is probably one of the most important overarching concerns for large-scale CBT implementation. Highly interactive adaptive assessments or assessments that require moving large amounts of digital data while an examination is "live" can tax even the best Internet routers and web servers. For example, complex performance exercises that require the examinees to engage in highly interactive Internet queries, moving high-resolution graphics or audio-video files, or even searches of large digital databases (e.g., the authoritative literature in a particular domain) may seem trivial. Considered as individual transactions, they are trivial. But, multiplied by millions of simultaneous, high-bandwidth demands, these can quickly create digital traffic jams that then need to be sorted out by network policy–determined protocols and optimization criteria that may not consider the most important criterion—making the CBT experience a seamless and hopefully engaging digital event for the examinee. As suggested earlier, this criterion needs to be given high priority in the overall infrastructure functional requirements.

### Operational CBT Delivery

Luecht and Sireci (2011) provided a fairly comprehensive summary and comparisons among various CBT delivery models (also see Folk & Smith, 2002; Luecht, 2012; van der Linden, 2006). Most of these models are distinguished by the type of test delivery model employed and, to a lesser extent, by the types of items used. Eight different types of CBT delivery models will be considered here: (1) preassembled linear tests (PLT); (2) linear-on-the-fly tests (LOFTs); (3) item-level computerized adaptive tests (iCAT), including constrained adaptive testing using shadow tests; (4) item-level stratified adaptive tests (iSAT); (5) item-level sequential mastery tests (iSMT); (6) testlet-based computerized adaptive tests (tCAT); (7) testlet-based sequential mastery tests (tSMT); and (8) computer-adaptive multistage tests (caMST).

These models differ from one another in some fundamental ways, but there are also some subtle and not-so-subtle commonalities. One of the commonalities is that almost any test delivery model involves the construction of a *test form* that is ultimately administered to the examinees. However, the concept of test form—that is, the collection of items administered to one or more examinees—can be difficult to apply in a concrete sense for certain types of CBT. Some test forms are static collections of items; others are dynamically created while the examinee is taking his or her test. Some models use an item or single assessment task as the basic test administration unit; others group the items or tasks together to form item sets, modules, or testlets. As Luecht (2012) noted, we can instead conceptualize a *test form list* (TFL) as a unique combination of items and/or assessment tasks drawn from an item bank and administered to an examinee. The TFL not only specifies a unique conglomeration of items, assessment tasks, item sets, modules, or testlets but can also present the units randomly or follow a prescribed presentation sequence. At a certain level of generalization, the eight test delivery models are variations in generating TFLs. A very brief description of the eight delivery models is presented in the context of building and administering TFLs to examinees.

Preassembled linear tests (PLTs) can be characterized as TFLs constructed using discrete items, item sets, and/or performance exercises. Preassembling the TFLs makes it possible to further carry out a wide range of quality control steps before they are released for active, operational use as CBT forms. The PLT TFLs can be assigned randomly as intact units—filtering out any previously seen test forms. Once assigned, item sequencing can be randomized or otherwise sorted to provide multiple "scrambles" of the TFL. In short, PLTs can be generated as one or more fixed TFLs, with items selected to match a *common* set of statistical and content-related test specifications. Historically, PLTs have been compared to paper-and-pencil test forms and viewed as a rather limited way to implement CBT. In practice, however, PLTs can (1) incorporate any of the myriad new item types available; (2) be generated in sufficiently large numbers with minimal item overlap to significantly ameliorate risks or concerns over item or test-form exposure; and (3) offer the advantage of most preassembled test units—namely, the possibility to carry out extensive quality-control checks on every item and test form before they are released for operational use.

Linear-on-the-fly tests (Folk & Smith, 2002) are similar to PLTs in design but move the entire assembly process to *real time*; that is, the TFLs are generated while or immediately before the examinees take their exams. LOFT is PLT-like insofar as including a common set of statistical and content specifications. But LOFT incorporates into the TFL generation process a randomization mechanism called *item exposure control* (cf. Sympson & Hetter, 1985) that works as a statistical buffer of sorts to prevent the most "popular" items—based on statistical and/or content-based criteria—from always being chosen for the TFLs. When properly implemented, LOFT mimics constructing the TFLs by essentially randomly choosing items from the item bank while also ensuring that each form meets the same content and statistical specifications.

Item-level computer-adaptive tests (iCATs) seem appealing to many testing organizations because they promise to create more efficient, possibly shorter tests by tailoring the item difficulty to each examinee's proficiency score and simultaneously maximizing the measurement precision of the scores (Wainer, 2000). There have been many variations on iCAT (Chang & Ying, 1999; Folk & Smith, 2002; Luecht, 1995; McBride, 1997; McBride, Wetzel, & Hetter, 1997; van der Linden, 2000; Weiss, 1974, 1983). Generically, a iCAT combines three mechanisms as part of the TFL-generation process—all applied in real time while the examinees are taking their tests. The first mechanism involves implementing a system of constraints that cover the test length and any content or other nonpsychometric test specifications. The constraints can be implemented by restricting the selection to content-grouped segments of the item bank (e.g., Kingsbury & Zara, 1991) or by formally building a series of adaptive test assembly models using a process that van der Linden (2000, 2005, 2006) calls a "shadow test." The constraints are imposed in iCAT to ensure that every TFL is "content balanced" according to some criterion established by the test developer (Stocking & Swanson, 1993). Note that these same types of nonpsychometric test specifications are also used to build PLTs and LOFTs. Second, an adaptive item-selection criterion is implemented so that the difficulty of each selected item is matched as closely as possible to the apparent proficiency of each examinee while also meeting the content and other specifications.[8] Finally, conceptually similar to its use in LOFT, an item exposure control mechanism (Hetter & Sympson, 1997; Sympson & Hetter, 1985) is employed to ensure that the same CAT-optimal items are not always chosen. Most iCAT implementations require complicated and sophisticated test delivery drivers because real-time scoring, adaptive item selection, and exposure controls must be simultaneously handled for every examinee-by-item transaction. iCAT also requires the most data at run time (answer keys, item parameter estimates, content attributes, and exposure control parameter estimates). These additional operational complexities need to be balanced against sometimes small theoretical gains in score precision and other operational costs (Luecht, 2005).

Item-level stratified adaptive testing or iSAT (Chang, Qian, & Ying, 2001; Chang & Ying, 1999) attempts to buffer the propensity of iCAT to choose the psychometrically "best" items[9] by forming strata or bins that group items by the relative difficulty of the items and/or by the amount of "measurement information" provided by each item. Stratifying only on item discrimination is called "$\alpha$-stratification" by Chang and colleagues. Stratifying only on item difficulty is called "$\beta$-stratification." Stratifying on the item characteristic makes better use of the entire item bank. Whereas iCAT always chooses the most informative items, relying on item exposure controls to buffer the tendency disproportionately to choose the same highly informative items, iSAT directly utilizes the less statistically informative items early in the test when we are still relatively uncertain about an examinee's proficiency score. The psychometrically "best" items are reserved for later in the test when we can more precisely match the statistical item characteristics to each examinee.

Item-level sequential mastery tests (iSMTs) present items or tasks one at a time and, during the interim, statistically evaluate the plausibility of three possible outcome decisions: (1) the examinee should clearly pass (i.e., probabilistically can be declared to have achieved "mastery"); (2) the examinee should clearly fail; or (3) there is insufficient statistical information to make a declaration of mastery, so testing continues. The NCLEX-PN and NCLEX-RN nursing examinations (National Council of State Boards of Nursing) are essentially hybrid iSMTs that employ iCAT for the item selections and iSMT to decide whether to stop testing beyond a fixed minimum number of items (Zara, 1994). The sequential mastery decision is typically carried out by evaluating a set of statistical hypotheses. Wald (1947) introduced the sequential probability ratio test (SPRT) as an optimally powerful way of evaluating outcomes #1 and #2 by controlling the size of an indifference region about the mastery cut score (see Reckase, 1983).

Testlet-based computerized adaptive tests (tCATs) are conceptually similar to iCATs but employ preconstructed item sets or small collections of items that Wainer and Kiely (1987) refer to as "testlets." Testlets are essentially item sets that include a common stimulus. They may also represent a problem series of items that must be solved together, with some answers dependent on other answers. Wainer, Bradlow, and Du (2000) subsequently introduced a hybrid item response theory model for use with testlets that had design-based or unanticipated dependencies among item response scores (within each testlet). The *testlet model* adds a parameter for each item test to statistically explain conditional residual covariances not fully accounted for by the usual IRT item parameters. The difference between tCAT and iCAT is apparent; instead of adapting at the item level, we adaptively select at the testlet level. Greater heterogeneity of the item characteristics within a testlet will tend to reduce some of the potential efficiency of adaptation. For example, in the degenerate case of every testlet having exactly the same joint distribution of item statistics, adaptive selection would be nonfunctional. The preassembly of the testlets offers some measure of quality control, although each TFL is generated in real time by adaptively combining the testlets.

Testlet-based sequential mastery tests (tSMTs) are the testlet-based counterparts to iSMT. The testlets can be constructed a priori according to any number of statistical and content-related test specifications. Testlets may, again, represent intact problem sets or simply a collection of items. The mastery decision hypotheses are merely reserved until after each testlet is "submitted" for scoring.

Computer-adaptive multistage testing (caMST) is becoming a popular test delivery model for implementing high-stakes adaptive testing. It has been adopted as the delivery model for the Uniform CPA Examination (American Institute of Certified Public Accountants and National Association of State Boards of Accountancy) and, more recently, for the Graduate Record Examination (Educational Testing Services). Fundamental to caMST is the notion of a *panel*—a highly structured assembly of multi-item modules, autonomously capable of adapting to each examinee's proficiency (Luecht, 2012, 2014; Luecht & Nungester, 1998). A module is a unique assembly of items that has its own statistical, content, and other relevant specifications. The modules are then further assigned to panels that have prescribed adaptive routes. Figure 8.5 shows eight possible two-, three-, or four-stage caMST panel configurations. Stage #1 has a moderate-difficulty module (M1). The modules then branch out at later stages (e.g., M1→E2 or M1→H2), with module difficulty denoted as E = easy, M = moderate, and H = hard. Each panel configuration allows test designers to target the measurement precision where it is most needed within different regions of the proficiency scale. More stages and more modules at different difficulty levels within stages imply more adaptive capability.

All of the modules and panels can be preassembled, implying that caMST has many of the same quality-control advantages of PLTs (e.g., allowing human review of panels for content and aesthetic audits before their activation) while still offering the adaptation options of iCAT, iSAT, and tCAT. Very accurate exposure controls can also be implemented within and across panels (Luecht, 2014; Luecht & Burgin, 2003). For example, under the simple 1–2 design (upper left configuration in Figure 8.5), we can use random assignment of panels to achieve 10% exposure in a given population by simply creating 10 panels, each with a unique Stage #1 module (M1.1,. . .,M1.10) and a uniform mixture of five content and statistically

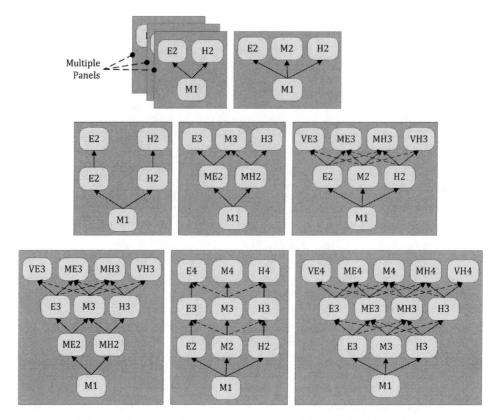

**Figure 8.5** Eight caMST panel configurations for two- (top row), three- (middle row), and four-stages (bottom row)

parallel modules for the E2 and H2 slots in the panel. The growing popularity of caMST is based on the model's strong quality-control capabilities, which minimize operational data and system processing loads, because the underlying data structures are specifically designed to be OOD compliant (see prior discussion) and minimize run-time data transmission and processing loads.

So where is the commonality among these CBT delivery models? Figure 8.6 provides a conceptual view of the TFL-generation process for all eight models. Items may be calibrated to an underlying scale and stored in an item bank—where *items* refers to any type of assessment task ranging from discrete selected-response (SR) items (e.g., multiple-choice items) to item sets and problem-based items to computerized performance exercises (CPEs). The item-selection mechanisms supported by any particular software test driver may vary greatly, from creating predefined lists to using unit-level randomization mechanisms to employing adaptive testing mechanisms that tailor the selections to maximize score precision or optimize some other defined statistical criterion. The TFLs may further be created and checked before the tests are administered to the examinees, or the process may take place in entirely real time, while the examinee is taking the test.

The *item bank* can be a rather complex data repository. It stores the item identifier(s), item text (stems, distractors, and prompts), graphics, interactive scripts, rendering/presentation

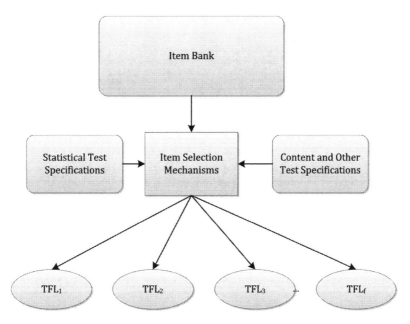

**Figure 8.6** Generating TFLs from an item bank

templates, content codes, cognitive codes, readability indices, lexical indices, item timing information, status (e.g., pretest or operational), item type indicators (multiple-choice, drag-and-drop, etc.), answer keys and/or scoring evaluators (e.g., rubrics), version controls, item usage statistics and dates, retest and jurisdictional usage controls, classical item statistics, and calibrated item response theory (IRT) statistics as reference materials (formula sheets, etc.), item-set references, indexes and sequencing/ presentation controls, reading passages and scrolling controls, and so on. The repository can consist of a single database or multiple databases with complex reference structures to link together the data for various uses. In short, accessing an item bank usually involves far more than a simple query or "lookup." In fact, entirely different types of data in the item bank often need to be extracted for test assembly, test administration, or scoring.

The *content and other test specifications* in Figure 8.6 reflect any content, cognitive, word count, reading load, or other nonpsychometric constraints on the items, item sets, or CPEs selected for particular TFL. It is common to refer to these as *test assembly constraints*, a label that stems from the use of optimization models for automated test assembly (ATA) and item-bank inventory control (Breithaupt & Hare, this volume). For example, when we specify that 10 to 12 algebra items must appear on every high-school mathematics test form, that implies a set of constraints with which the item-selection mechanism must contend. The test length, if specified,[10] can also be considered to be a test assembly constraint. Van der Linden (2005) provides an excellent overview of the mechanics of specifying and managing these types of constraints for ATA applications.

The *statistical test specifications* indicated in Figure 8.6 are usually used for one of two purposes: (1) to create TFLs with near-parallel psychometric properties or (2) to optimize the accuracy of score estimates or associated classification decisions (e.g., pass/fail). It is common to use fixed statistical *targets* for the first purpose.[11] The rationale behind using fixed targets is that if every test form more or less meets a common statistical target, the scores will be nearly parallel to one another, satisfying a goal of equating for exchangeable scores (Kolen & Brennan, 2010). The second purpose usually follows from a desire to create a psychometrically more efficient test—that is, one on which a desired level of score precision or decision accuracy can be achieved with as few items as possible or in a minimal amount of time, or where optimal accuracy can be achieved for a fixed-test-length TFL.

Statistical targets can range from target score means to using rather complex functions of a multidimensional IRT information matrix. A complete description of these functions is beyond the scope of this chapter. However, a generalized way of understanding the interplay between the item-selection mechanism, the item statistics in the item bank, and the statistical test specifications for TFLs can be obtained by borrowing some notation and concepts from the ATA and mathematical optimization literature (e.g., van der Linden, 2005; Breithaupt & Hare, this volume).

If we use the word *optimize* to broadly refer to some algorithmic or heuristic process that mathematically minimizes or maximizes to quantity of interest, we can generalize the item-selection process depicted in Figure 8.6. That is, we optimize the selection of items from the item bank such that some designated statistical function(s) of the items either matches a TFL-level target for the first purpose (achieving a target) or meets the optimization criterion such as minimizing the error variance of scores or maximizing the precision of scores. In the targeting context, we can generically express this optimization process as

$$minimize \left[ \sum_{i=1}^{I} x_{ig} f_i - T \right] \tag{1}$$

where $T$ is a target function such as a test information function, $f_i$ is the item-level function that is additive in the test form (e.g., an item information function), and $x_{if}$ is a binary selection coefficient specified so that $x_{if} = 1$ if the item, $i$ (for $I$ items in the item bank) is selected for form $g$, or $x_{if} = 0$ if it remains unselected on form $g$ at the completion of the item-selection process. The second purpose can be generically expressed as

$$optimize \sum_{i=1}^{I} x_{ig} f_i \tag{2}$$

where minimization or maximization is implied, depending on the criterion employed. Excluding the more complex case of optimization under a multidimensional model (Luecht, 1996; Segall, 1996; van der Linden, 2005), we can isolate four basic item functions that characterize most of the statistical optimization routines used in operational CBT: (1) item means, (2) item reliability indexes, (3) IRT item characteristics functions, and (4) IRT item information functions. I will briefly introduce each and then demonstrate how they apply under one of the two optimization functions in Equations 1 and 2 to distinguish our eight test delivery models.

One of the simplest statistical functions is an item mean, that, for $n$ items on a TFL, can be used to estimate total score mean in a specified population:

$$\mu(Y) \doteq \sum_{i=1}^{n} \bar{y}_i \tag{3}$$

which for dichotomously scored items resolves to the well-known item proportion-correct or *p-value*, $p_i$.[12] We can therefore specify a target mean and then select the items for each TFL that will match that target as closely as possible. Given a fixed target mean for a TFL, it is therefore relatively straightforward to use Equation 1 to formally specify the optimization process as

$$minimize \left[ \sum_{i=1}^{I} X_{ig} \bar{y}_i - \mu(Y_n) \right].$$ (4)

A mild variation of this same model is sometimes used to build a TFL so that the mean of the selected item means (item difficulty estimates) or, in an IRT context, the mean of the IRT item difficulty parameter estimates, matches a target mean. As noted earlier, test length, $n$, can be specified as a constraint with the optimization model. For example, we specify Equation 4 to meet a target mean, subject to:

$$\sum_{i=1}^{I} X_i = n$$ (5)

$$x \in \{0,1\}$$ (6)

as a binary numerical constraint on the decision variable.

We can also consider other types of statistical targets and item functions. For example, the item reliability index (Allen & Yen, 1979) can be used to meet a target total-score standard deviation by similarly indicating that we want to

$$minimize \left[ \sum_{i=1}^{I} X_{ig} r_{iY} s_i - \sigma(Y_n) \right].$$ (7)

where $s_i$ is the item standard deviation and $r_{iY}$ is the item-total point-biserial correlation (also see Gulliksen, 1950, p. 377). Although it might seem relatively simple to extend the association of $r_{iY} s_i$ to the standard deviation and $s_i$ to a reliability coefficient—that is,

$$\alpha \doteq \left( \frac{n}{n-1} \right) \left( 1 - \frac{\sum_{i=1}^{n} s_i^2}{S_Y^2} \right) = \left( \frac{n}{n-1} \right) \left[ 1 - \frac{\sum_{i=1}^{n} s_i^2}{\left( \sum_{i=1}^{n} r_{iY} s_i \right)^2} \right]$$ (8)

the summations in the numerator and denominator of the rightmost ratio of Equation 8 slightly complicate the optimization model and require either constraints, use of a composite, or other parameterization of the optimization model (see Sanders & Verschoor, 1998; van der Linden, 1998).

If we move into the realm of item response theory (IRT), the test characteristic function (TCF) is a useful way to indicate the desired expected number-correct scores at any value of the underlying proficiency score distribution, $\theta$,

$$T(\theta) = \sum_{i=1}^{n} \sum_{k=0}^{m} V_k P_{ik}(\theta)$$ (9)

where $P_{ik}(\theta)$ is the response category probability function under a particular IRT model for dichotomous or polytomous items and $V_k$ is a category scoring function (e.g., {0, 1, 2, etc.}). The TCF for dichotomously scored items simplifies to

$$T(\theta) = \sum_{i=1}^{n} P_i(\theta) \tag{10}$$

where the corresponding three-parameter logistic (3PL) probability function for a correct response is

$$prob(u_i = 1 | \theta; a_i, b_i, c_i,) \equiv P_i(\theta) = c_i + \frac{(1-c_i)}{1 + exp[-Da_i(\theta - b_i)]} \tag{11}$$

with $\theta$ representing the latent proficiency score and $a$, $b$, and $c$ respectively denoting the item response slope (discrimination), location (difficulty), and lower-asymptote (pseudo-guessing) parameters (Lord, 1980).

Given the additive relationship between the item response probability functions and the target TCF, it should be readily apparent that we can specify a target function TCF and reuse Equation 1 (with minor modifications) to give us a special case of the optimization model[13] so that we select exactly $n$ items for each TFL that satisfy that target. For the 3PL model, this revised model is:

$$minimize \left[ \sum_{i=1}^{I} X_i P_i(\theta) - T(\theta) \right] \text{ for all } \theta \tag{12}$$

$$\text{subject to: } \sum_{i=1}^{I} X_i = n, \ X_i \in \{0,1\} \text{ (see Equations 5 and 6).}$$

Perhaps the most popular functions for test assembly targets among psychometricians are the IRT item and test information functions. For most IRT models, an item information function (IIF) indicates each item's contribution to measurement precision at a particular value of $\theta$. This concept of conditional measurement precision allows us to design targets to place specific amounts of measurement information where it is most needed or to simply place the most measurement information possible at designated values of $\theta$. iCAT is a special case in which we choose the item that provides maximum information at the examinee's provisional estimated proficiency score. The examinee's score is then reestimated and a new score is used for targeting. In principle, and given a sufficiently large item bank, the provisional score estimates will converge to the examinee's true (but unknown) proficiency.

The relationship between item and test information functions (TIFs) and the precision of scores was first articulated in an IRT context by Birnbaum (1968), who demonstrated that conditional measurement error variance of the score estimates is inversely proportional to the test information function, $I(\theta)$,

$$var(\hat{\theta}|\theta) = [I(\theta)]^{-1} = \left[ \sum_{i=1}^{n} I_i(\theta) \right]^{-1} \tag{13}$$

where $I_i(\theta)$ is the item information function. More specifically, the item information function for the 3PL IRT model (Equation 11), can be written as

$$I_i(\theta) = \frac{D^2 a_i^2 \left[1 - P_i(\theta)\right]\left[P_i(\theta) - c_i\right]^2}{P_i(\theta)(1 - c_i)^2}.$$ (14)

Since the item information functions are additive in the test at specific values of $\theta$, we can define a target TIF to denote where and how much measurement precision we want along the $\theta$ scale. For example, to maximize our classical reliability, we would want to have the most information near the highest concentration of examinees—that is, near the mean of the population proficiency score distribution. For a mastery test, we might instead want to target the precision near the pass/fail cut score to optimize our decision accuracy.

Figure 8.7 shows four potential target TIFs. Each of these TIFs corresponds to a 50-item test form with items calibrated using the IRT three-parameter logistic model (see Equations 11, 13, and 14).

The three TIFs that peak near zero on the $\theta$ scale differ in two regards. The two highest peaked curves at the right differ in the average discrimination, $\mu(a)$, of the items to be selected. If used as a target, the flatter TIF curve to the right would produce a TFL with a large variation in the item difficulties, $\sigma(b)$—in fact, a somewhat uniform distribution of difficulty. The fourth potential TIF target peaked more to the left, near $\theta = -1.5$, would create a demand for 50 highly discriminating but relatively easy items with a relatively tight distribution of item difficulty. Luecht (2014) provides a description of some useful analytical procedures for generating target TIFs.

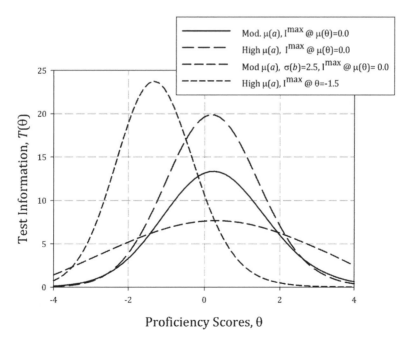

**Figure 8.7** Four Test Information Functions for a 50-Item Test

Again repurposing Equation 1 (with only minor modifications), our optimizing item-selection model becomes:

$$minimize \left[ \sum_{i=1}^{I} X_i I_i(\theta) - I(\theta) \right] \; for \; all \; \theta \qquad (15)$$

subject to: $\sum_{i=1}^{I} X_i = n, \; X_i \in \{0,1\}$ (again, see Equations 5 and 6).

For an adaptive test, we can repurpose Equation 2 to provide a model that selects the most informative items from the item bank at an examinee's provisional score estimate:

$$optimize \sum_{i=1}^{I} X_{ig} f_i \; : \; i_k \equiv \max_j \left\{ I_{U_j} \left( \hat{\theta}_{u_{i_1},...,u_{i_{k-1}}} \right) : j \in R_k \right\} \qquad (16)$$

where the function $max \{\}$ selects at cycle $k$ in the adaptive sequence ($k = 1,...,n$) the item with the maximum conditional information, computed at the examinee's provisional proficiency estimate, $\hat{\theta}$, based on his or her responses to the previous $k-1$ items.

This generalization implies that all eight of the CBT delivery models (PFT, LOFT, iCAT, iSAT, iSMT, tCAT, tSMT, and caMST) use essentially the same general item-selection process and merely vary the implementation of that process. This schema for item selection suggests different CBT models may not be so dramatically different when viewed from a functional perspective. However, there are differences. Table 8.1 presents 16 key features that distinguish

Table 8.1 Features and Attributes of Eight CBT Delivery Models

| Test Delivery Models | PLT | LOFT | iCAT | iSAT | iSMT | tCAT | tSMT | caMST |
|---|---|---|---|---|---|---|---|---|
| Fixed test length | X | X | X | X | X | X | X | X |
| Preassembled, intact "test forms" | X | | | | | | | X |
| Preconstructed modules | | | | | | X | X | X |
| Random presentation of items | X | X | | X | | X | X | X |
| Real-time adaptive ATA heuristic | | | X | X | X | X | X | X |
| ATA with absolute statistical targets | X | X | | | | | | X |
| Real-time interim IRT scoring needed | | | X | X | X | X | X | |
| Preconstructed module-adaptive panels | | | | | | | | X |
| Real-time adaptive by routing tables | | | | | | | | X |
| Real-time exposure controls | | X | X | | X | X | X | |
| Design-based exposure controls | X | | | X | | | | X |
| Review & answer changes allowed | X | X | | | | X | X | X |
| Decision-based stopping criterion | | | | X | X | X | X | X |
| Error-variance stopping criterion | | | | X | X | | X | | X |
| 100% test form QC capabilities | X | | | | | ? | ? | X |
| 100% reconciliation of test-forms | X | | | | | | | X |

the eight CBT delivery models. The utility that test developers assign to test-form quality controls is obviously a major consideration in choosing a delivery model. Only PLT and caMST provide the capability to fully review every test form. The question marks (?) for tCAT and tMST imply that "100% test form QC capabilities" is theoretically possible to the extent that the number of testlets employed for tCAT and tSMT is relatively small. That is, it is possible to mix and match testlets to generate all possible TFL combinations for review. For example, with three of 30 testlets selected for each tCAT or tSMT, there are 1,140 possible TFL combinations that would have to be reviewed for a 100% review.

## Psychometric Processing and Scoring

This section brings together aspects of the other three sections. For example, a consideration of data structures impacts how run-time scoring is handled for various types of adaptive tests as well as postadministration analysis such as item analyses and IRT calibration and linking analyses. Carrying out scoring during the active examinations likewise has implications as to the amount and speed of data transmission and interactivity necessary. Finally, most adaptive tests require provisional or interim scores of some type for use in test unit selection.

It may not always be apparent, but there are usually up to four levels of "scoring" required for CBT: (1) raw data capture (RDC); (2) discrete unit scoring (DUS); (3) aggregate unit scoring (AUS); and (4) aggregate score transformations (AST). Under an object-oriented design (OOD) paradigm, we can conceptualize these four scoring levels as one or more computational *agents*. OOD agents are software procedures that do a particular task in response to a message—the input data. For example, a simple multiple-choice item typically allows the test taker to click to select one of the distractor options. The marked box is actually represented as a Boolean state for that option. For example, given a generic "dot notation" syntax, "*item00001*" is the item identifier. Each distractor option checkbox or button has one of two *states*: on = *true* = 1 or off = *false* = 0. The response by the test taker can therefore be represented as *item00001.checkbox*[$k$] = *state* for $k = 1, . . ., m$ options. If the examinee chooses the third distractor option, the checkbox state representation becomes *item00001. checkbox*[$3$] = 1, with the states of the other option checkboxes set to zero (false). Although this multinomial selection format works well to record the examinee's action, it is not necessarily an efficient way to store the final response. Instead, we can convert the response to *item00001.response* = 3 (or "C" if we prefer letters). The RDC agent for multiple-choice items would therefore take as inputs the checkbox states of any item calling it and complete the response field for that item.

Scoring *agents* are important for two reasons. First, they allow us to clearly conceptualize the types of inputs (message and formats) to be supplied to each agent so that appropriately structured data can be prepared as needed. For example, the formatted "transactions" shown earlier in Figure 8.3 and quite appropriate for IRT item calibrations might need to be restructured for scoring purposes. Second, we can create a library of software scoring agents that are verified and accessible as needed.[14] The library reduces the likelihood of having different programs doing the same function produce different results. The "single-source" principle suggested earlier can be readily extended to apply to single-source agents (SSA) as well. For example, a SSA that generates maximum likelihood estimates (MLEs) of examinees' scores and associated standard errors of estimate would be called from the library whenever MLEs were needed, regardless of the context of use of the scores (e.g., for routing, for final scoring, etc.).

AUS agents process the relevant examinee actions or products to create what we more typically think of as "raw data." The example provided demonstrates how a multiple-choice or selected-response mouse click on an answer choice can be converted by an AUS agent to an integer, letter, or some other useful, compact representation of the examinees, response. For convenience, we can represent this type of agent by a functional form,

$$r.i = AUS.g(Inputs.i),$$

where the same AUS agent, $g$, can be called as often and whenever needed to process all relevant item inputs. Well-designed SSAs can even self-detect whether the incoming message (inputs) match expected formats from authorized sources or should otherwise be ignored (i.e., no response from the agent).

DUS agents apply rules and/or rubrics to the AUS outputs, $r.i$, to usually generate an integer score. A generic functional form can be written as

$$y.i = DUS.h,(r.i, a.i)$$

where the second input, $a.i$, denotes an answer key, scoring rule/rubric, or even parameters for a sophisticated artificial intelligence or neural net decision-making process. In addition to applying to handling simple pattern matches, like scoring a one-best-answer multiple-choice item, DUS agents can score distractors (Luecht, 2007), be human raters using scoring rubrics, or highly sophisticated software agents. New DUS agents can be added to the DUS repository as needed.

AUS agents generate the outputs that we typically think of as test scores. AUS scoring is typically performed using a vector or structured collection of DUS outputs and relevant scoring parameters (e.g., weights, IRT item parameter estimates). Weighted or unweighted number-correct SSAs, IRT scoring agents for various models, latent class scoring agents, and virtually any type of scoring operation that involves two or more inputs and optional parameters can be classified as AUS agents. A generalized expression for AUS agents is

$$t.n = AUS.j(\mathbf{y}.n, \mathbf{v}.n, \mathbf{d})$$

where $\mathbf{y}.n$ denoted a vector or array of DUS elements of size $n$ and $\mathbf{v}.n$ is a corresponding vector or matrix of weights, IRT parameters, etc., and $\mathbf{d}$ is an optional vector of auxiliary controls or parameters such as moments of a prior distribution used for Bayesian estimation. Table 8.2 lists six of the more common types of AUS agents used in CBT. Inputs are listed in the middle column and typical outputs are shown in the rightmost column. Note that some scoring estimation procedures can also compute error variances or standard errors (SE) without too much additional computational burden. The AUS agent would therefore return both the score and the associated error function.

Computational formulas and numerical routines for the IRT scoring functions are readily available (see, for example, Baker & Kim, 2004; Lord, 1980; Thissen & Wainer, 2001). It is important to realize that AUS scoring agents can be called when needed and not necessarily to just to get the final score for an entire test form. For example, tCAT and tCMT can pass interim testlet or combined testlet results and item parameters to the same scoring agent that is used for final scoring. Similarly, both EAP and MLE AUS agents can be called to score the same DUS response strings.

The final type of type of scoring agent can be used to compute one or more transformations of the AUS scores to reported categorical score such as "pass" or "fail" or to scale scores

Table 8.2 AUS Agent Types for CBT

| Description | Inputs | Outputs |
|---|---|---|
| Number-correct | **y**.$n$, **v**.$n$ = **1**, $d$ = null | $t$ = total score |
| Weighted-number correct | **y**.$n$, **v**.$n$ = vector of weights, $d$ = null | $t$ = weighted score |
| Weighted-composite | **y**.$n$ = vector of scores, **v**.$n$ = vector of scoring weights, $d$ = null | *[t.score,t.error]* = score & SE |
| IRT maximum likelihood estimates (MLEs) | **y**.$n$ = vector of scores, **v**.$n$ = vector of item param., **d** = convergence criterion and settings | *[t.score,t.error]* = score & SE |
| IRT expected a posteriori (Bayes EAP) estimates | **y**.$n$ = vector of scores, **v**.$n$ = vector of item param., **d** = prior distribution | *[t.score,t.error]* = score & SE |
| IRT maximum a posteriori (Bayes MAP) estimates | **y**.$n$ = *vector of scores*, **v**.$n$ = vector of item param., **d** = prior distribution | *[t.score,t.error]* = score & SE |

using linear or nonlinear transformations of the scores. Well-designed agents can even be combined to produce multiple transformations of the AUS scores. Categorical ATS conversions can typically be handled by a look-up table where the input value is evaluated relative to the minimum and maximum boundary values that define an interval. The returned value is a label or some other value associated with the interval that includes the input value. (Note: *Decision matrices* are relatively straightforward extensions of the look-up table concept where a vector of input values is compared to a multilevel two-way table and the returned value corresponds to label or value a cell in the matrix.)

Linear ATS transformations are also popular. A linear transformation takes the form: $u$ = ATS.$k(t.n, \mathbf{b}) = b_1 + b_2(t.n)$, where $b_1$ is an intercept constant and $b_2$ is a slope. The input vector **b** can also be expanded to in lowest obtainable scale scores (LOSS) and highest obtainable scale scores (HOSS). The LOSS and HOSS values are used to truncate the reported score scale to avoid extreme or negative values.

Nonlinear transformations can also be applied. For example, expected number-correct scores or expected percent correct can be computed for most of the standard IRT models for dichotomous and polytomous data by summing the score-weighted response functions over items. This type of nonlinear transformation function allows a *reference test* to be used for scoring all of the examinees—essentially computing what Lord (1980) called "domain scores." In addition to potentially providing content-based performance interpretations tied to the content of the reference test, these types of nonlinear transformation can also eliminate the need for arbitrary LOSS and HOSS values since the transformed scores are bounded by 0 and the maximum points on the reference test. As an example, to compute rounded expected percent-correct scores for $n$ items with polytomous scoring, we can use a ATS based on an AUS computed estimate of an IRT proficiency score, $\hat{\theta}$, as follows:

$$\text{ATS.EPC.PCM}\left(\hat{\theta}, n, \mathbf{X}_n^{max}, \xi_n\right) = ROUND_{int}\left\{100\left[\frac{1}{X_{total}}\sum_{i=1}^{n}\sum_{k=0}^{x_i}X_{ik}P_{ik}\left(\hat{\theta}\right)\right]\right\} \quad (17)$$

where $P_{ik}$ is the category response probability under a polytomous IRT model, $X_{ik}$ are the possible score points on each item, $n$ is the test length, $\xi_n$ is a matrix of item parameter estimates, and $\mathbf{X}_n^{max}$ is a vector of category counts (maximum points) for the $n$ items.

The final common type of ATS is a scoring look-up table. There is usually one scoring table for each test form. Scoring tables are commonly used in conjunction with certain IRT models—usually the family of Rasch models—in which the total raw score is a sufficient statistic for estimating the examinee's $\theta$ if the item parameters are assumed to be known (or are at least well estimated). The look-up table computes a number-correct score and then searches the table to locate the corresponding IRT estimated $\theta$ score and scale scores. The values in each score table are all precomputed. Other IRT models can also employ sum scores (Rosa, Swygert, Nelson & Thissen, 2001; Thissen & Wainer, 2001).

## Operational Issues and Challenges: The Possible Future of CBT

Despite the advances in computer technology, digitization, and connectivity via the Internet over the past few decades, CBT is still in its infancy, often using only slightly improved versions of "roll-out" software and hardware that may have been developed 10 or more years ago. A functional requirements specification for CBT Version 2.0 is needed. For example, many current test delivery architectures are simply too dependent on high-cost, low-capacity brick-and-mortar test centers that—while somewhat functional for organizations willing to pay the higher costs and put up with the rather severe constraints—will simply not work for making formative and summative tests available in every classroom—anytime and anywhere. We need new architectures and systems that support low-cost, high-capacity, high-bandwidth, high-speed, ubiquitous assessment capabilities.

It is likely that "bring your own" (BYO) solutions leveraged by both assessment and instructional/learning needs will be part of that new functional requirement. That means that we need to start planning now how to design the data structures, delivery channels, testing models, and assessment applications to effectively support BYO.

We also throw around the word "innovation" a lot in talking about assessment design—most commonly referring to using technology-enhanced items (e.g., drag and drop), computerized performance-based simulations, and computerized gaming. Automatic item generation (AIG) using computer-generated assessment tasks and various computerized scoring technologies would also fall under the heading of innovation (e.g., natural language processing and automated essay scoring, automated voice recognition). However, a strong caution seems necessary to stay faithful to the *intended* performance-based skill and knowledge claims as the primary drivers of our measurement information demands (Kane, 2006; Luecht & Clauser, 2002). Until we are clear about the nature of those claims, it makes little sense to design innovative uses of technology just for its own sake. In short, our assessment designs should follow from the integrated skills and knowledge claims we want to make rather than retrofitting validity arguments to those assessment design and scoring choices—regardless of whether technology is used.

A final comment concerns the CBT platforms of the future. Open-source solutions are also very likely to shape the CBT landscape in the future for several reasons. First, as an open-source platform matures and evolves, it typically becomes extremely robust with respect to operating systems and end-user requirements. Rather than coercing the types of items and assessments to fit a proprietary platform, we can expand the platform to accommodate and integrate new data structures, applications, item types, test designs, and delivery infrastructures. Second, the legal nature of software licensing for open-source solutions like TAO (www.taotesting.com/) implies that no one individual or group can constrain development or use of the platform. This does not imply that commercial CBT will be limited. For any entrepreneurial-supportive readers, it seems important to that customizable solutions can be added for a profit for open-source systems. However, the evolving open-source part of the system may not and is not legally required to support add-on capabilities that are not included in the open-source library. Technical implementation and hosting costs may also still apply—that is, paying an individual or company to use the open-ended architecture to build a CBT enterprise. But open source potentially becomes the ultimate way to guarantee interoperability by literally sharing the system across user platforms and designing robustness into the system.

It is an exciting and challenging time for CBT—a future that has many possibilities and easily as many potential pitfalls to consider. However, by focusing on robust assessment designs and making decisions that consider the data structures, infrastructures, and issues related to efficient data transmission and exchange, we can perhaps minimize the pitfalls. Ultimately, as stated earlier in this chapter, we need to realize that the ultimate functional requirement for CBT is to create an engaging, fair, and seamless assessment experience for every examinee.

## Notes

1 As noted further on, test assembly can occur in real time, while the examinee is taking the test.
2 This is also sometimes referred to as *single source of truth* (SSOT).
3 Other data can also be stored, including time on task and the number of answer changes.
4 Certain test delivery models discussed in the next section make direct use of OOD to create high-integrity adaptive tests (see discussion of *computer-adaptive multistage tests*).
5 XML = extensible *m*arkup *l*anguage
6 Another popular specifications project is the Common Education Data Standards (CEDS), a national collaborative effort involving many of the top assessment vendors and states to define common data standards and key education data elements (https://ceds.ed.gov/).
7 The distribution of access to technology and across the country is further NOT uniform given certain economic and political realities across states in the United States.
8 Item information at the examinee's provisional score (discussed further on) is more commonly maximized as a more general CAT item-selection criterion that incorporates both item difficulty and discrimination.
9 Items that are "located" nearest the highest concentration of examinees in a population and that have high statistical item discrimination will, without otherwise being constrained, have the greatest probability of being selected.
10 Test length may be specified as a minimum item count (e.g., for sequential tests) or replaced altogether by a different termination criterion. Some of those alternative criteria are discussed further on.
11 caMSTs actually use fixed statistical targets AND optimize decision or score accuracy. CAT likewise targets the item selection, but to a moving target—the examinee's provisional score estimate.
12 Note that *equated* item means can be used in place of the empirical item means or *p*-values.
13 Note that other parameterizations are possible—notably, reformulating the model as a mixed-integer programming model to incorporate the difference function in the system of model constraints and instead minimizing a *tolerance* variable on the deviation between the target and TCF for the selected items. See Breithaupt and Hare, this volume.
14 Human scorers or raters are also scoring agents, albeit neither inexpensive nor necessarily as consistent as the software variety.

## References

Allen, M. J., & Yen, W. M. (1979). *Introduction to measurement theory*. Monterey, CA: Brooks/Cole Publishing.
Baker, F. B., & Kim, S.-H. (2004). *Item response theory: Parameter estimation techniques* (2nd ed.). New York: Marcel Dekker, Inc.
Birnbaum, A. (1968). Some latent trait models and their use in inferring an examinee's ability. In F. M. Lord & M. R. Novick, *Statistical theories of mental test scores* (pp. 397–479). Reading, MA: Addison-Wesley.

Chang, H.H., Qian, J., & Ying, Z. (2001). A-stratified multistage computerized adaptive testing item b-blocking. *Applied Psychological Measurement, 25*, 333–342.

Chang, H.H., & Ying, Z. (1999). A-stratified multistage computerized adaptive testing. *Applied Psychological Measurement, 23*, 211–222.

Davis, J. & Bauman, K. (2013). *School Enrollment in the United States: 2011, Population Characteristics.* U.S. Census Bureau. (http://www.census.gov/prod/2013pubs/p20-571.pdf).

Dragsow, F., Luecht, R.M., & Bennett, R. (2006). Technology and testing. In R.L. Brennan (Ed.), *Educational measurement* (4th ed., pp. 471–515). Washington, DC: American Council on Education/Praeger Publishers.

Folk, V.G., & Smith, R.L. (2002). Models for delivery of CBTs. In C.N. Mills, M.T. Potenza, J.J. Fremer, & W.C. Ward (Eds.), *Computer-based testing: Building the foundation for future assessments* (pp. 41–66). Mahwah, NJ: Lawrence Erlbaum Associates.

Gulliksen, H. (1950). *Theory of mental tests.* New York: John Wiley & Sons.

Hetter, R.D., & Sympson, J.B. (1997). Item exposure control in CAT-ASVAB. In W.A. Sands, B.K. Waters, & J.R. McBride (Eds.), *Computerized adaptive testing: From inquiry to operation* (pp. 141–144). Washington, DC: American Psychological Association.

Kane, M.T. (2006). Validity. In R.L.Brennan (Ed.). *Educational measurement* (4th ed., pp. 17–64). Washington, DC: American Council on Education/Praeger.

Kingsbury, G.G., & Zara, A.R. (1991). A comparison of procedures for content-sensitive item selection in computerized adaptive tests. *Applied Measurement in Education, 4*, 241–261.

Kolen, M.J., & Brennan, R.L. (2010). *Test equating scaling, and linking: Methods and practices* (3rd ed.). New York: Springer.

Lord, F.M. (1980). *Applications of item response theory to practical testing problems.* Mahwah, NJ: Lawrence Erlbaum Associates.

Luecht, R.M. (1995, March). *Some alternative CAT item selection heuristics* (NBME Technical Report RES95031). Philadelphia, PA: National Board of Medical Examiners.

Luecht, R.M. (1996). Multidimensional computerized adaptive testing in a certification or licensure context. *Applied Psychological Measurement, 20*, 389–404.

Luecht, R.M. (2005). Some useful cost-benefit criteria for evaluating computer-based test delivery models and systems. *Journal of Applied Testing Technology, 7*(2). www.testpublishers.org/journal.htm

Luecht, R.M. (2006b). Operational issues in computer-based testing. In D. Bartrum & R. Hambleton (Eds.), *Computer-based testing and the Internet* (pp. 91–114). West Sussex, UK: Wiley & Sons Publishing.

Luecht, R.M. (2007). Using information from multiple-choice distractors to enhance cognitive-diagnostic score reporting. In J.P. Leighton & M.J. Gierl (Eds.), *Cognitive diagnostic assessment for education: Theory and applications* (pp. 319–340). London: Cambridge University Press.

Luecht, R.M. (2012). Computer-based and computer-adaptive testing. In K. Ercikan, M. Simon, & M. Rousseau (Eds.), *Improving large scale assessment in education: Theory, issues, and practice* (pp. 91–114). New York: Taylor-Francis/Routledge.

Luecht, R.M. (2014). Computerized adaptive multistage design considerations and operational issues. In D. Yan, A.A. von Davier, & C. Lewis (Eds.), *Computerized multistage testing: Theory and applications* (pp. 69–83). London: Taylor-Francis.

Luecht, R.M., & Burgin, W. (April, 2003). *Matching test design to decisions: Test specifications and use of automated test assembly for adaptive multi-stage testlets.* Paper presented at the Annual Meeting of the National Council on Measurement in Education, Chicago, IL.

Luecht, R.M., & Clauser, B. (2002). Test models for complex computer-based testing. In C. Mills, M. Potenza, J. Fremer, & W. Ward (Eds.), *Computer-based testing: Building the foundation for future assessments* (pp. 67–88). Mahwah, NJ: Erlbaum.

Luecht, R.M., & Nungester, R.J. (1998). Some practical applications of computerized adaptive sequential testing. *Journal of Educational Measurement, 35*, 229–249.

Luecht, R.M., & Sireci, S.G. (2011). *A review of models for computer-based testing.* New York., NY: The College Board. Research Report, 2011–12.

McBride, J.R. (1997). The Marine Corps exploratory development project: 1977–1982. In W.A. Sands, B.K. Waters, & J.R. McBride (Eds.), *Computerized adaptive testing: From inquiry to operation* (pp. 59–68). Washington, DC: American Psychological Association.

McBride, J.R., Wetzel, C.D., & Hetter, R.D. (1997). Preliminary psychometric research for CAT-ASVAB: Selecting an adaptive testing strategy. In W.A. Sands, B.K. Waters, & J.R. McBride (Eds.), *Computerized adaptive testing: From inquiry to operation* (pp. 83–96). Washington, DC: American Psychological Association.

Reckase, M.D. (1983). A procedure for decision making using tailored testing. In D.J. Weiss (Ed.), *New horizons in testing; latent trait test theory and computerized adaptive testing* (pp. 237–255). New York: Academic Press.

Rosa, K., Swygert, K., Nelson, L., & Thissen, D. (2001). Item response theory applied to combinations of multiple-choice and constructed-response items—scale scores for patterns of summed scores. In D. Thissen & H. Wainer (Eds.), *Test scoring* (pp. 253–292). Mahwah, NJ: Lawrence Erlbaum Associates.

Sanders, P.F., & Verschoor, A.J. (1998). Parallel test construction using classical item parameters. *Applied Psychological Measurement, 22,* 212–223.

Segall, D.O. (1996). Multidimensional adaptive testing. *Psychometrika, 61,* 331–354.

Stocking, M.L., & Swanson, L. (1993). A method for severely constrained item selection in adaptive testing. *Applied Psychological Measurement, 17,* 277–292.

Sympson, J.B., & Hetter, R.D. (1985). *Controlling item exposure rates in computerized adaptive tests.* Paper presented at the Annual Conference of the Military Testing Association. San Diego, CA: Military Testing Association.

Thissen, D., & Wainer, H. (2001). Overview of test scoring. In D. Thissen & H. Wainer (Eds.), *Test scoring* (pp. 1–19). Mahwah, NJ: Lawrence Erlbaum Associates.

U.S. Department of Education, National Center for Education Statistics. (2015). *Digest of Education Statistics,* 2013 (NCES 2015-011), Table 105.50 (nces.ed.gov)

van der Linden, W.J. (1998). Optimal assembly of psychological and educational tests. *Applied Psychological Measurement, 22,* 195–211.

van der Linden, W.J. (2000). Constrained adaptive testing with shadow tests. In W.J. van der Linden & C.A.W. Glas (Eds.), *Computer-adaptive testing: Theory and practice* (pp. 27–52). Boston: Kluwer.

van der Linden, W.J. (2005). *Linear models for optimal test design.* New York: Springer.

van der Linden, W.J. (2006). Model-based innovations in computer-based testing. In D. Bartram & R.K. Hambleton (Eds.), *Computer-based testing and the Internet: Issues and advances* (pp. 39–58). West Sussex, UK: John & Sons.

Wainer, H. (Ed.). (2000) *Computerized adaptive resting: A primer* (2nd ed.). Hillsdale, NJ: Erlbaum.

Wainer, H., Bradlow, E.R., & Du, Z. (2000). Testlet response theory: An analog for the 3-PL useful in testlet-based adaptive testing. In W.J. van der Linden & C.A.W. Glas (Eds.), *Computerized adaptive testing: Theory and practice* (pp. 245–269). Boston: Kluwer.

Wainer, H., & Kiely, G.L. (1987). Item clusters and computerized adaptive testing: A case for testlets. *Journal of Educational Measurement, 24,* 185–201.

Wald, A. (1947). *Sequential analysis.* New York: Wiley.

Weiss, D.J. (1974). *Strategies of adaptive ability measurement* (RR 74–5). Minneapolis, MN: Psychometric Methods Program, Department of Psychology, University of Minnesota. (NTIS NO. AD-A004 270).

Weiss, D. (1983). *New horizons in testing: latent trait test theory and computerized adaptive testing.* New York: Academic Press.

Zara, A.R. (1994, March). *An overview of the NCLEX/CAT beta test.* Paper presented at the meeting of the American Educational Research Association, New Orleans, LA.

# 9

# Mobile Psychological Assessment

Oleksandr S. Chernyshenko and Stephen Stark

The last decade has seen continuing advancement of computing technology. The development has shifted from increasing computing speeds to enhancing portability and connectivity. Market trends indicate that desktop computer purchases are declining as consumer preference shifts toward laptops, tablets, and smartphones for everyday browsing, word processing, gaming, and communication needs, and this shift is particularly evident for handheld mobile devices. According to the Pew Internet survey of computing device ownership (Pew Internet and American Life Project, 2013) in May 2013, 56% of U.S. adults owned smartphones, 34% owned tablets, and 26% owned e-readers. The use of these devices has been growing steadily at about 10% per year and is likely to continue into the foreseeable future.

The rapid adoption of smartphones and other handheld mobile technologies has brought unprecedented opportunities for the practice and science of psychological assessment. Now it is not only possible to conduct assessments at any time and at nearly any location, but also to instantly send and receive additional data about current and past performance for any number of examinees. Because most devices have GPS and wireless capabilities, assessments can interact with the outside physical and social worlds, thus opening myriad new measurement possibilities. In response, many testing applications are being developed, ranging from simple programs that merely provide connections to existing online assessments to complex programs that deliver customized assessments that fully utilize a device's technological capabilities. To support these applications, new psychometric research is needed.

The aim of this chapter is to help researchers, test developers, and test users navigate the seemingly uncharted waters of mobile testing. We describe what we see to be the three main avenues of mobile testing, namely mobile health (mHealth), mobile learning (mLearning), and mobile work (mWork). Each avenue is somewhat distinct in terms of the assessment goals, constructs measured, and measurement strategies. Consequently, each avenue has unique challenges and draws on different branches of psychometric theory and research. In subsequent sections, we discuss some current applications and practices and identify areas in need of further exploration.

## Defining Mobile Psychological Assessment

Although it is tempting to define a mobile device simply as any computing device that can be transported, in our view, the key considerations are *portability* and *ease of use* (see also Fallaw, Kantrowitz, & Dawson, 2012a). Portability means that a device can be used in virtually any environment, including when a person is walking. Ease of use means that a device can be held and operated with minimal effort. Thus, while small laptop computers (i.e., netbooks/ultrabooks) are often called mobile devices (e.g., Wikipedia, 2013), they are inconsistent with our definition, whereas mobile phones, personal digital assistants (PDAs), and pagers would be included, although they have limited multimedia, connectivity, and computing capabilities relative to more advanced mobile devices such as smartphones, tablets, or e-readers.

At the most basic level, mobile psychological assessment involves administering stimuli and collecting responses via a mobile device. Such a device might maintain a wireless connection with an external server that stores and scores collected responses and identifies additional stimuli to administer. Alternatively, if such a device has sufficient internal storage and computing capabilities, then assessment applications can be designed to run independently, that is without a live connection, and the data may be sent to a server at a later time at the discretion of an examinee.

Mobile psychological assessment has its roots in experience sampling, which is referred to, in some fields, as ecological momentary assessments methodology (see Beal & Weiss, 2003; Csikszentmihalyi & Larson, 1987; DeVries, 1992; Hektner, Schmidt, & Csikszemihalyi, 2007; Shiffman, Stone, & Hufford, 2008). Initially, mobile devices, such as pagers and wristwatches, were used to signal an examinee to complete a paper-and-pencil questionnaire (Alliger & Williams, 1993; Csikszentmihalyi & Larson, 1987). However, with the advent of PDAs, it became possible not only to signal but also to administer assessments (Shiffman et al., 2008). Mobile devices were perfectly suited for researchers and practitioners interested in experience sampling methodology because they provided the most straightforward means of tracking within-person changes, modeling temporal processes that connect independent and dependent variables, and reducing memory biases (Beal & Weiss, 2003).

Researchers in the fields of psychopharmacology and clinical and counseling psychology, where patients' real world improvements in response to treatments are of key concern, were among the earliest users of mobile devices for ecological momentary assessments (Shiffman et al., 2008). Organizational researchers also used mobile devices to gather data for examining the relationships among work events, affective states, and work outcomes (Miner, Glomb, & Hulin, 2005) and were among the first to evaluate the feasibility of a mobile device as an alternative to paper-and-pencil test administration (Overton, Taylor, Zickar, & Harms, 1996). Since then, the capabilities of mobile devices have improved exponentially and allowed assessment options to move well beyond recording answers to short survey questions. Consequently, much more vivid and dynamic mobile assessment applications have been created to measure a multitude of psychological variables in medical, educational, and work settings.

## Mobile Health (mHealth)

To be useful for a wide variety of health-related initiatives, mobile assessment systems must be sufficiently comprehensive in their coverage of various symptoms and outcomes, yet the measures must be fairly short and standardized for ease of use. Consequently, considerable resources and effort have been devoted to developing measures that can be delivered effectively via web applications. These efforts were spearheaded by the U.S. National Institutes of Health (NIH), which began funding these large-scale projects in 2005. Three interrelated projects of particular relevance to mobile health were the NIH Toolbox, the Patient Reported Outcomes Measurement Information System (PROMIS), and the Neuro-QOL (Nowinski, Victorson, Cavazos, Gershon, & Cella, 2010; Reeve et al., 2007). The NIH Toolbox is a multidimensional set of brief, royalty-free measures of cognitive, sensory, motor, and emotional functioning. More than 1,400 existing measures were identified and evaluated for inclusion by a team of about 300 scientists from nearly 100 academic institutions (Gershon et al., 2010a). A subset of measures was selected for psychometric research involving more than 16,000 participants ranging in age from 3 to 85. Measures that were designated for item response theory (IRT) applications were administered to large subsamples of participants to ensure adequate item parameter recovery. All measures were then normed using a large representative sample of the U.S. population ($N = 4,859$) to facilitate comparisons among age, ethnic, and gender groups (Gershon et al., 2010b).

PROMIS complements NIH Toolbox by focusing on physical, mental, and social well-being outcomes such as pain, fatigue, physical function, depression, and anxiety. PROMIS items ask patients to indicate how they have felt or what they have been able to do in the last 7 days using a 5-point Likert-type format. Healthcare practitioners may choose 3 to 10 items from various item banks, which are presented to patients using nonadaptive (fixed-form or static) or computerized adaptive testing (CAT) technology. CAT may be particularly useful in this context because the algorithms are designed to achieve adequate measurement precision with the fewest items, thus allowing quick diagnostic assessments, for example, just before examining a patient. These PROMIS measures are now being used in clinical studies of the effectiveness of various treatments, particularly chronic diseases (see Cella et al., 2010). In addition, the score reports can be used to design individualized treatment plans and improve communication between patients and physicians (PROMIS, 2013).

The Neurological Disorders and Stroke Quality of Life (Neuro-QOL) measurement system is a National Institute of Neurological Disorders and Stroke (NINDS)–funded initiative whose purpose was to provide a clinically relevant assessment for patients with chronic neurological diseases (Gershon et al., 2010b). From an initial item library of more than 3,000 items, IRT–calibrated item banks and scales were developed, normed, and validated to cover more than a dozen quality of life domains related to stroke, multiple sclerosis (MS), Parkinson's disease, epilepsy, and amyotrophic lateral sclerosis (ALS). Like PROMIS, Neuro-QOL measures can be used to facilitate comparisons across clinical trials and monitor treatment progress. Additional item banks are now being developed to cover bowel function, urinary/bladder function, sexual function, and end-of-life concerns.

The NIH Toolbox, PROMIS, and Neuro-QOL systems are administered by a unified browser-based research management software application called Assessment Center (Gershon et al., 2010a). Researchers and medical practitioners can create customized websites, choose instruments to administer using nonadaptive or adaptive testing modes, and securely link participants' responses to health information databases. The adaptive testing algorithm is based on a graded response model (Samejima, 1969), and the maximum information criterion is used to select items (Cella, Gershon, Lai, & Choi, 2007). Because the Assessment Center software runs from a central server, any mobile device with web browsing capabilities and sufficient screen resolution should be able, in principle, to access and run the application; however, at this point, only iPads are fully supported.

In addition to these large-scale development efforts, a number of stand-alone mobile health applications have been developed. One example is the Mobile Assessment and Treatment for Schizophrenia (MATS), which is a mobile phone intervention that sends 12 text messages per day to patients to monitor their medication adherence, socialization, and auditory hallucinations. More specifically, messages may contain multiple-choice questions, reminders, encouragements, and helpful suggestions that vary depending on patients' responses (Granholm, Ben-Zeev, Link, Bradshaw, & Holden, 2012). Another example is the PenScreenSix (see www.penscreen.com), which is a set of 14 psychomotor performance and cognitive tasks designed to run on 7-inch Android-based tablets. The battery has been used for a variety of purposes related to the assessment of neuropsychological functioning, such as driver impairment due to drug or alcohol use, recovery from the effects of anesthetics, and the effects of fatigue and sleep deprivation on cognition (Tiplady, 2011; Tiplady, Oshinowo, Thomson, & Drummond, 2009).

Research evaluating the benefits of mobile assessments has shown good convergent validities with respect to traditional ways of monitoring symptoms and treatment efficacy and similar compliance rates (Granholm, Loh, & Swendsen, 2008; Kimhy et al., 2006). Some other benefits include (1) less reliance on patient recall to describe the progression of symptoms, (2) the ability to customize assessments and palliative recommendations in real time, and (3) the capacity to collect psychological and physiological data during normal activities such as at work, at rest, and during exercise.

These benefits notwithstanding, there are also some psychometric challenges and opportunities that should be considered. First, although these early mHealth applications have utilized modern psychometric methods to create and administer short, standardized assessments, the use of traditional item formats does not take full advantage of the technical capabilities of current mobile devices. For example, rather than sending text messages containing multiple-choice questions to see how patients are doing, one might eventually design applications that use avatars to ask questions, record and encode responses using natural language processing technology, and provide tailored feedback and guidance. One might also create applications to run video-based assessments or interactive games that measure memory or complex cognitive skills impairment resulting from concussions, strokes, or dementia. The challenge, of course, would be how to obtain reliable scores for intra- and interindividual comparisons from these dynamic and often multidimensional assessments. Here, researchers and test developers may want to review earlier studies about the design and scoring of video-based situational judgment tests (Olson-Buchanan et al., 1998; Whetzel & McDaniel, 2009), simulation-based assessment (Mislevy, 2013), and serious gaming (Redecker & Johannessen, 2013; Ritterfield, Cody, & Vorderer, 2009).

The most significant methodological challenges facing mobile mHealth assessments, however, are associated with translating item-level data into information that is meaningful for both patients and physicians. Mobile assessments typically yield data for multiple constructs, different measurement formats (multiple choice, Likert, free response), and multiple time periods. Combining these data to improve diagnoses and monitor treatment progress requires complex statistical analyses, but they must be essentially invisible to the end user. In other words, these statistical analyses would need to be performed by automated scripts that ultimately produce user-friendly, personalized reports.

## Mobile Learning (mLearning)

In the past two decades, numerous computer-assisted systems have been developed to provide more flexible, person-centered learning environments (e.g., Huang, Lin, & Cheng, 2009; Yeh, Chen, Hung, & Hwang, 2010). Such systems are sometimes called adaptive learning systems because they customize the pace, breadth, and depth of the material that is presented to each learner. mLearning refers to the use of mobile devices for this purpose. Mobile devices provide two additional benefits, namely context embeddedness and immediate usability (Dillard, 2012; Park, 2011). With mobile technology, students can engage in "authentic activities" in real-world settings and apply their learning right away (Herrington & Oliver, 2000; Hwang, Chu, Shih, Huang, & Tsai, 2010).

The simplest and somewhat narrow use of mobile technology in mLearning focuses exclusively on real-time information gathering. For example, clickers became popular in the last decade for assessing individual and group learning outcomes in classroom settings. Instructors and students can receive instant feedback about understanding of a particular topic by answering one or more multiple-choice questions. Originally, information gathering was accomplished using dedicated hardware and software systems. However, these fully integrated systems are now being replaced by apps that can run on a variety of computing devices, including smartphones.

Another use of mobile assessments is to support adaptive learning and intelligent tutoring systems. A good example of this is a project, which was funded by the U.S. Army Geospatial Center, to develop a soldier-centered training system involving mobile, virtual classroom, and collaborative-scenario training environments (Murphy, Mulvaney, Huang, & Lodato, 2013). In the mobile environment, basic information about a piece of equipment is made available to trainees via applications that can be run on a variety of mobile devices. Trainees can peruse these instructional materials at their own pace, and when they feel they are sufficiently familiar with the equipment's basic features and functionality, they can take an adaptive test to qualify for the next phase of training in a virtual classroom. The virtual classroom presents more detailed information based on the trainee's current state of knowledge and uses an avatar to provide verbal and gestural cues aimed at building complex knowledge and skills, such as troubleshooting. When the virtual classroom training is complete, trainees are administered another adaptive test to assess their readiness for the final stage of training involving collaborative scenarios. In that phase, trainees are required to perform one or more roles in a collaboration exercise, which utilizes technology developed for massive multiplayer online gaming. In the end, a final assessment is administered to certify a trainee's readiness for fieldwork.

The most advanced mLearning applications, which feature both immediacy and context embeddedness, are location-aware mobile learning systems. Consider, for example, an application that was developed to improve learning outcomes in a fifth-grade botany course (Chu, Hwang, Tsai, &Tseng, 2010). PDAs equipped with radio frequency identifiers are used to guide learners to designated plants in school gardens, which serve as authentic learning environments. When a learner approaches a designated plant, a picture of the plant is presented along with a multiple-choice question. If a learner answers the question incorrectly, then a picture of a plant coinciding with the incorrect response is presented to highlight the difference with respect to the target plant, and the question is repeated. Alternatively, if the learner gets the first question correct, then a more difficult question is administered to assess depth of knowledge, and supplemental information is provided. Students who studied with this location-aware learning system scored .93 SD better on a posttest than those who simply browsed learning materials, completed quizzes, and received guidance via PDAs. There were also considerable differences in learning motivation between the two comparison groups; students who used the mLearning system expressed more interest in observing and learning about features of plants and other natural objects (Chu et al., 2010).

In our view, the key challenge for mobile assessments in mLearning contexts is in designing measurement systems with a sufficient degree of customizability to enable truly personalized, on-demand learning (Sharples, 2000). On one hand, as more mobile device capabilities are incorporated into instructional processes, more response formats and item types can be used to keep learners engaged. On the other hand, the size of item pools and corresponding content specifications are likely to grow dramatically and present challenges for item calibration and test scoring. Some possible solutions could include using subject matter expert ratings of item difficulty in place of IRT item parameter estimates (Stark, Chernyshenko, & Guenole, 2011) or using regression models to predict item difficulty based on encoded item features (Arendasy & Sommer, 2007; Irvine & Kyllonen, 2002). Generalized scoring methods might also be used to accommodate mixed item formats (Wilson & Wang, 1995), collateral information (de la Torre, 2009), and prior information about population characteristics.

## Mobile Work (mWork)

Mobile assessments are increasingly being utilized by organizations to conduct employee recruitment and selection initiatives. Typical mWork assessments administered on mobile devices include biographical data, personality, interests, and values questionnaires, social skills, situational judgment and cognitive ability tests. According to Fallaw, Kantrowitz, and Dawson (2012a), 9% of human resources (HR) practitioners worldwide in 2011 reported that candidates requested to fill in job applications and take selection tests via mobile devices. In 2012, that figure increased to 19%, and in fast-growing mobile-usage countries, such as China, the figure was as high as 35% (Fallaw, Kantrowitz, & Dawson, 2012b). In a U.S. study conducted by AON Hewitt involving approximately 12.9 million applicants, the percentage of applicants choosing to test on mobile devices increased from 3.1% in 2009 to 14.3% in 2013 (Golubovich & Boyce, 2013).

Clearly, mobile testing in the workplace is on the upsurge, and there are several likely reasons. First, once implemented, mobile assessment offers significant cost savings for initial personnel screening, as organizations do not need to dedicate employee hours and physical resources to testing and processing applicants. Second, having a mobile testing option can serve as a powerful recruitment tool, especially for young professionals who value flexibility and technology (Martin, 2005). Being able to attract, evaluate, and make offers to top applicants quickly provides an edge over competitors relying on traditional, on-site recruitment and screening. Finally, because minority and low-income applicants are less likely to own desktop and laptop computers than more affluent candidates (Zickuhr & Smith, 2012), organizations wishing to increase their outreach to those underrepresented groups must make the mobile assessment option available. In a study involving hourly hospitality industry workers, Impelman (2013) found that African Americans made up 50% of the mobile applicant pool, whereas they represented only 38% of nonmobile applicants. Golubovich and Boyce (2013) also reported African Americans being the largest mobile testing applicant group.

The key concern with mWork assessments is test fairness, meaning that testing on a mobile device does not disadvantage applicants relative to those who apply using a computer or in person. Although research indicates that reactions are generally favorable toward mLearning applications (Chu et al., 2010; Triantafillou, Georgiadou, & Economides, 2008), mWork research results have not all been as supportive. For example, Gutierrez and Meyer (2013) examined the perceived fairness of personality, situational judgment, and cognitive ability tests administered via mobile devices and personal computers. Overall reactions were comparable across testing platforms for the personality assessment, but mobile cognitive and situational judgment tests were seen as less fair. When asked whether testing on a device as part of the hiring process was fair to applicants, 100% of mobile respondents who took the situational judgment test and 63% who took the cognitive ability test disagreed, whereas only 17% and 37% disagreed in the personal computer condition.

One of the key reasons certain mobile assessments were perceived to be unfair was test difficulty. With assessments involving short stimuli and a limited number of response categories (e.g., interest and personality questionnaires), performance differences across delivery platforms are likely to be minimal. On the other hand, with tests involving reading passages or graphs that one must refer to when answering questions, the small screen sizes of mobile devices are clearly a disadvantage. The same could be true for tests requiring examinees to type extended answers. Results of several studies tend to support these conclusions. Doverspike, Arthur, Taylor, and Carr (2012) found that cognitive ability tests had lower means when taken on mobile devices, but there were no differences across mobile and nonmobile platforms for personality measures. Impelman (2013) found that applicants in some companies scored nearly .4 SD lower on timed cognitive ability tests taken on mobile devices, but no consistent differences were found for personality measures. Lawrence and colleagues (2013) compared means for seven noncognitive scales across very large samples of mobile and nonmobile test takers and found effect sizes near zero on all measures. Given that employment testing is highly scrutinized and subject to legal guidelines, these findings suggest that organizations should exercise caution when considering mobile testing. Organizations may have to develop item presentation and response formats that allow candidates with the same ability to perform equally well on mobile and nonmobile platforms. This might entail replacing some written content with multimedia alternatives and using speech-recognition software to capture free responses as an alternative to typing. Past research has shown, for example, that mixing auditory and visual modes of presentation for geometry items increases effective working memory and reduces cognitive load associated with reading comprehension questions (Mousavi, Low, & Sweller, 1995). At the very least, organizations should inform examinees that a mobile testing option is available for convenience, but differences in the size and speed of mobile devices, as well as distractions in the testing environment, could adversely affect test performance.

### Summary and Conclusions

In this chapter, we have discussed recent developments and research on mobile assessment. Although mobile devices have been used for research purposes since the early 1990s (Overton et al., 1996), field applications were relatively rare until recently due to limited device functionality. The emergence of reliable wireless networking technology, faster microprocessors, and high-resolution displays, which could be integrated into consumer-friendly handheld devices, has led to an explosion of mobile assessment applications in education, health, and workplace contexts. Keeping with emerging conventions, we designated mobile testing applications in these three mobile testing fields as mLearning, mHealth, and mWork, respectively, and pointed out that they appear to have fairly distinct assessment goals, strategies, and challenges (for a brief summary, see Table 9.1). The mHealth assessment initiatives have been largely driven by public health concerns, where efficient, comprehensive, and standardized assessments of patients' psychosocial symptoms and outcomes are seen as supportive of various diagnostic and treatment initiatives. In comparison, mLearning assessments are all about

Table 9.1 Assessment Goals, Strategies and Challenges for Three Main Mobile Testing Avenues

| Mobile Testing Field | Assessment Goals | Measurement Strategies | Main Challenges |
|---|---|---|---|
| mHealth | Efficient but comprehensive assessment of psychosocial health symptoms and outcomes | Royalty-free short scales and computer adaptive tests; standardized test administration via publicly funded test administration portals | Combining psychometric data from a multitude of assessments and occasions to improve diagnosis and to monitor treatment progress |
| mLearning | Person-centered assessments to support adaptive learning systems | Real-time information gathering and feedback using a range of mobile device capabilities (e.g., location services, video and audio recordings); assessments embedded within learning programs | Offering sufficient degree of assessment customizability and precision at a reasonable cost |
| mWork | On-demand and location-free recruitment, screening, and selection of employees | Presenting previously validated assessments on a mobile platform | Maintaining test fairness so applicants are not disadvantaged when taking test on mobile devices |

person-centered learning, where each assessment is uniquely designed to support the pace, breadth, and depth of a learner's journey. Finally, mWork assessments are motivated by organizations' desires to attract, evaluate, and make offers to applicants quickly and without the fixed costs associated with traditional recruitment and selection practices. The main challenge of mWork assessments is to make them maximally similar to traditional assessments so applicants are not disadvantaged by them.

In a narrow sense, a mobile device can simply be seen as a convenient option for administering measures that were developed for other modes of administration. The research questions surrounding the transition to mobile testing therefore parallel those that were asked when transitioning from paper-and-pencil to computerized assessments. For example, how do physical device limitations affect examinee performance (Bridgeman, Lennon, & Jackenthal, 2003)? Would the move to new technology disadvantage some groups of examinees? How can test security and score integrity be maintained in unproctored testing environments (Tippins et al., 2006)? Finally, are scores comparable across modes of administration (Beaty et al., 2011; Morelli, Illingworth, Moon, Scott, & Boyd, 2013) and, if not, what can be done to promote equivalence? We anticipate a number of future papers attempting to delineate specific factors influencing the amenability of assessments for mobile use. It may be the case that certain types of assessments (e.g., survey, noncognitive psychometric tests) are better suited for mobile test administration than others (e.g., general mental ability and performance tests). Or, perhaps, some item presentation formats lend themselves more naturally to mobile use. An example of such research is a paper by Isomursu, Tahti, Vainamo, and Kuutti (2007) that highlighted advantages and disadvantages of five methods for assessing emotions with mobile applications. Also, although the topic of high-stakes testing on mobile devices has not received much research attention to date, testing guidelines would likely be needed with regard to device types (e.g., research to address these issues is necessary, but may be seen by some as unexciting).

In a broader sense, mobile assessment can be seen as unique, because it provides unparalleled access to examinees in their natural environments. With mobile devices, one can now measure, for example, health symptoms and outcomes with more immediacy and less reliance on recall, which can improve understanding of disease states and lead to better treatments. Location services can be used to provide personalized, context-rich learning experiences that are more engaging and effective than traditional classroom-based instruction. Dynamic self- and other-reports about team interactions or transient phenomena, such as emotions, can also be collected to improve process models and ultimately the accuracy of inferences.

The research questions that arise from these and other likely applications go well beyond simple equivalence comparisons. They may even challenge many conventional notions about "good" measurement. Does the richness of mobile assessment data collected from multiple sources over multiple time points in multiple environments, outweigh concerns about standardization when it comes to predicting future behavior? What is more important, a person's normative standing or his/her personal trajectory for treatment or learning? Does mobile assessment blur the traditional lines between internal and external validity (Campbell & Fiske, 1959) and the veracity of inferences drawn from highly controlled experiments versus field studies? We believe that new psychometric and statistical methods may be needed to adequately account for the complexities of mobile assessment data, and as the number of applications increases, as they surely will, considerable changes to graduate educational curricula may be warranted.

Finally, the move toward mobile testing may influence who is involved in the test-development process. The new expectations with regard to test content display and brevity, the demands for continuous connectivity, and utilization of device technical capabilities (e.g., location services or instant messaging) may necessitate even closer collaborations among testing professionals and those in other fields or disciplines (e.g., computer science, human factors psychology, user experience research). Cross-disciplinary educational training may be required to instill a basic understanding of all the important criteria that must be satisfied for "next-generation" assessments to be as psychometrically sound as they may be engaging. Multidisciplinary development teams will be needed from the start to design assessments with reliability and validity goals in mind, and it is likely that expertise will be required from fields outside psychology and education to get the most predictive power from the vast amounts of data these assessments may generate.

## References

Alliger, M., & Williams, K. J. (1993). Using signal-contingent experience sampling methodology to study work in the field: A discussion and illustration examining task perceptions and mood. *Personnel Psychology, 46*, 525–549.

Arendasy, M., & Sommer, M. (2007). Using psychometric technology in educational assessment: The case of a schema-based isomorphic approach to the automatic generation of quantitative reasoning items. *Learning and Individual Differences, 17*, 366–383.

Beal, D. J., & Weiss, H. M. (2003). Methods of ecological momentary assessment in organizational research. *Organizational Research Methods, 6*, 440–464.

Beaty, J., Nye, C., Borneman, M., Kantrowitz, T., Drasgow, F., & Grauer, E. (2011). Proctored versus unproctored Internet tests: Are unproctored noncognitive tests as predictive of job performance? *International Journal of Selection and Assessment, 19*, 1–10.

Bridgeman, B., Lennon, M. L., & Jackenthal, A. (2003). Effects of screen size, screen resolution, and display rate on computer-based test performance. *Applied Measurement in Education, 16*, 191–205.

Campbell, D. T., & Fiske, D. W. (1959). Convergent and discriminant validation by the multitrait-multimethod matrix. *Psychological Bulletin, 56*, 81–105.

Cella, D., Gershon, R. C., Lai, J., & Choi, S. (2007). The future of outcomes measurement: Item banking, tailored short-forms, and computerized adaptive assessment. *Quality of Life Research, 16*, 133–141.

Cella, D., Rothrock, N., Choi, S., Lai, J.S., Yount, S., & Gershon, R. (2010). PROMIS overview: Development of new tools for measuring health-related quality of life and related outcomes in patients with chronic diseases. *Annals of Behavioral Medicine, 39*, 47.

Chu, H., Hwang, G., Tsai, C., & Tseng, J.C. (2010). A two-tier test approach to developing location-aware mobile learning systems for natural science courses. *Computers and Education, 55*, 1618–1627.

Csikszentmihalyi, M., & Larson, R. (1987). Validity and reliability of the experience-sampling method. *Journal of Nervous & Mental Disease, 175*, 526–536.

de la Torre, J. (2009). Improving the quality of ability estimates through multidimensional scoring and incorporation of ancillary variables. *Applied Psychological Measurement, 33*, 465–485.

DeVries, M. (Ed.). (1992) *The experience of psychopathology: Investigating mental disorders in their natural settings.* Cambridge, UK: Cambridge University Press.

Dillard, A. (2012). *Mobile instructional design principles for adult learners.* Master of Science in Applied Information Management. University of Oregon.

Doverspike, D., Arthur, W., Taylor, J., & Carr, A. (2012). *Mobile mania: Impact of device type on remotely delivered assessments.* Panel presentation at the 27th annual conference of the Society for Industrial and Organizational Psychology. San Diego, CA.

Fallaw, S. S., Kantrowitz, T. M., & Dawson, C. R. (2012a). *2012 Global Assessment Trends Report.* Alpharetta, GA: SHL.

Fallaw, S. S., Kantrowitz, T. M., & Dawson, C. R. (2012b). *2012 Global Assessment Trends Report: China.* Alpharetta, GA: SHL.

Gershon, R. C., Cella, D., Fox, N. A., Havlik, R. J., Hendrie, H. C., & Wagster, M. V. (2010a). Assessment of neurological and behavioural function: The NIH Toolbox. *The Lancet Neurology, 9*, 138–139.

Gershon, R. C., Rothrock, N. E., Hanrahan, R. T., Jansky, L. J., Harniss, M., & Riley, W. (2010b). The development of a clinical outcomes survey research application: Assessment center. *Quality of Life Research, 19*, 677–685.

Golubovich, J., & Boyce, A. (2013, April). *Hiring tests: Trends in mobile device usage.* Paper presented as a poster at the 28th annual conference of the Society for Industrial and Organizational Psychology, Houston, TX.

Granholm, E., Ben-Zeev, D., Link, P.C., Bradshaw, K., & Holden, J. (2012). Mobile Assessment and Treatment for Schizophrenia (MATS): A pilot trial of an interactive text-messaging intervention for medication adherence, socialization, and auditory hallucinations. *Schizophrenia Bulletin, 38*, 414–425.

Granholm, E., Loh, C., & Swendsen, J. (2008). Feasibility and validity of computerized ecological momentary assessment in schizophrenia. *Schizophrenia Bulletin, 34*, 507–514.

Gutierrez, S. L., & Meyer, J. M. (2013, April). *Assessments on the go: Applicant reactions to mobile testing.* Paper presented as a poster at the 28th annual conference of the Society for Industrial and Organizational Psychology, Houston, TX.

Hektner, J. M., Schmidt, J. A., & Csikszentmihalyi, M. (2007). *Experience sampling method: Measuring the quality of everyday life.* Thousand Oaks, CA: Sage.

Herrington, J., & Oliver, R. (2000). An instructional design framework for authentic learning environments. *Educational Technology Research and Development, 48*, 23–48.

Huang, Y.-M., Lin, Y.-T., & Cheng, S.-C. (2009). An adaptive testing system for supporting versatile educational assessment. *Computers & Education, 52*, 53–67.

Hwang, G.J., Chu, H.C., Shih, J.L., Huang, S.H., & Tsai, C.C. (2010). A decision-tree-oriented guidance mechanism for conducting nature science observation activities in a context-aware ubiquitous learning environment. *Educational Technology and Society, 13*, 53–64.

Impelman, K. (2013, April). *Mobile assessment: Who is doing it and how it impacts selection.* Paper presented as a poster at the 28th annual conference of the Society for Industrial and Organizational Psychology, Houston, TX.

Irvine, S. H., & Kyllonen, P. C. (Eds.). (2002). *Item generation for test development.* Mahwah, NJ: Lawrence Erlbaum Associates.

Isomursu, M., Tahti, M., Vainamo, S., & Kuutti, K. (2007). Experimental evaluation of five methods for collecting emotions in field settings with mobile applications. *International Journal of Human-Computer Studies, 65*, 404–418.

Kimhy, D., Delespaul, P., Corcoran, C., Ahn, H., Yale, S., & Malaspina, D. (2006). Computerized experience sampling method (ESM): Assessing feasibility and validity among individuals with schizophrenia. *Journal of Psychiatric Research, 40*, 221–230.

Lawrence, A., Wasko, L., Delgado, K., Kinney, T., & Wolf, D. (2013, April). *Does mobile assessment administration impact psychological measurement?* Paper presented as a poster at the 28th annual conference of the Society for Industrial and Organizational Psychology, Houston, TX.

Martin, C. (2005). From high maintenance to high productivity: What managers need to know about Generation Y. *Industrial and Commercial Training, 37*, 39–44.

Miner, A.G., Glomb, T.M., & Hulin, C. (2005). Experience sampling mood and its correlates at work. *Journal of Occupational and Organizational Psychology, 78*, 171–193.

Mislevy, R.J. (2013). Evidence-centered design for simulation-based assessment. *Military Medicine, 178*, 107–114.

Morelli, N.A., Illingworth, A.J., Moon, S.M., Scott, J.C., & Boyd, S. (2013, April). *Equivalence of assessments on mobile devices: A replication and extension.* Paper presented as a poster at the 28th annual conference of the Society for Industrial and Organizational Psychology, Houston, TX.

Mousavi, S.Y., Low, R., & Sweller, J. (1995). Reducing cognitive load by mixing auditory and visual presentation modes. *Journal of Educational Psychology, 87*, 319–334.

Murphy, J., Mulvaney, R., Huang, S., & Lodato, M.A. (2013). *Developing technology-based training and assessment to support soldier-centered learning.* Presentation at the 28th annual conference for the Society of Industrial and Organizational Psychology, Houston, TX.

Nowinski, C.J., Victorson, D., Cavazos, J.E., Gershon, R., & Cella, D. (2010). Neuro-QOL and the NIH Toolbox: Implications for epilepsy. *Therapy, 7*, 533–540.

Olson-Buchanan, J.B., Drasgow, F., Moberg, P.J., Mead, A.D., Keenan, P.A., & Donovan, M. (1998). Conflict resolution skills assessment: A model-based, multi-media approach. *Personnel Psychology, 51*, 1–24.

Overton, R.C., Taylor, L.R., Zickar, M.J., & Harms, H.J. (1996). The pen-based computer as an alternative platform for test administration. *Personnel Psychology, 49*, 455–464.

Park, Y. (2011). A pedagogical framework for mobile learning: Categorizing educational applications of mobile technologies into four types. *The International Review of Research in Open and Distance Learning, 12*, 78–102.

Pew Internet and American Life Project. (2013). Device ownership. Retrieved on October 20, 2013, from www. pewinternet.org/Trend-Data-(Adults)/Device-Ownership.aspx)

PROMIS Overview. (2013). Retrieved on October 20, 2013, from www.nihpromis.org/about/overview

Redecker, C., & Johannessen, O. (2013). Changing assessment—towards a new assessment paradigm using ICT. *European Journal of Education, 48*, 79–96.

Reeve, B., Hays, R.D., Bjorner, J., Cook, K., Crane, P.K., Teresi, J.A., Thissen, D., Revicki, D.A., Weiss, D.J., Hambleton, R.K., Liu, H., Gershon, R., Reise, S.P., Lai, J.S., Cella, D., & on behalf of the PROMIS Cooperative Group. (2007). Psychometric evaluation and calibration of health-related quality of life item banks: Plans for the Patient-Reported Outcome Measurement Information System (PROMIS). *Medical Care, 45*, 22–31.

Ritterfield, U., Cody, M.J., & Vorderer, P. (Eds.). (2009). *Serious games: Mechanisms and effects.* New York: Taylor and Francis.

Samejima, F. (1969). *Estimation of latent ability using a response pattern of graded scores.* (Psychometric Monograph No. 18). Iowa City, IA: Psychometric Society.

Sharples, M. (2000). The design of personal mobile technologies for lifelong learning. *Computers and Education, 34*, 177–193.

Shiffman, S., Stone, A.A., & Hufford, M.R. (2008). Ecological momentary assessment. *Annual Review of Clinical Psychology, 4*, 1–32.

Stark, S., Chernyshenko, O.S., & Guenole, N. (2011). Can subject matter expert ratings of statement extremity be used to streamline the development of unidimensional pairwise preference scales? *Organizational Research Methods, 14*, 256–278.

Tiplady, B. (2011). Mobile cognitive assessment: Validation of neuropsychological assessment administered on an android tablet. *Journal of Psychopharmacology, 25*, 31.

Tiplady, B., Oshinowo, B., Thomson, J., & Drummond, G.B. (2009). Alcohol and cognitive function: Assessment in everyday life and laboratory settings using mobile phones. *Alcoholism: Clinical and Experimental Research, 33*, 2094–2102.

Tippins, N., Beaty, J., Drasgow, F., Wade, M., Pearlman, K., Segall, D., & Shepherd, W. (2006). Unproctored Internet testing in employment settings. *Personnel Psychology, 56*, 189–225.

Triantafillou, E., Georgiadou, E., & Economides, A. (2008). The design and evaluation of a computerized adaptive test on mobile devices. *Computers and Education, 50*, 1319–1330.

Whezel, D.L., & McDaniel, M.A. (2009). Situational judgment tests: An overview of current research. *Human Resource Management Review, 19*, 188–202.

Wikipedia. (2013). Mobile device. Retrieved October 15, 2013, from http://en.wikipedia.org/wiki/Mobile_device

Wilson, M., & Wang, W. (1995). Complex composites: Issues that arise in combining different modes of assessment. *Applied Psychological Measurement, 19*, 51–71.

Yeh, Y.F., Chen, M.C., Hung, P.H., & Hwang, G.J. (2010). Optimal self-explanation prompt design in dynamic multi-representational learning environments. *Computers & Education, 54*, 1089–1100.

Zickuhr, K., & Smith, A. (2012). *Digital differences.* Pew Internet and American Life. Retrieved October, 15, 2013, from www.pewinternet.org/~/media//Files/Reports/2012/PIP_Digitaldifferences_041312.pdf

# 10
# Increasing the Accessibility of Assessments Through Technology

Elizabeth Stone, Cara C. Laitusis, and Linda L. Cook

## Standardized Testing and Individuals With Disabilities

Standardized testing was introduced in the United States in the 1800s by Horace Mann (Gallagher, 2003). Mann was interested in gaining information about the quality of teaching and learning in Boston public schools. The tests introduced by Mann in Boston were adopted by selected school systems throughout the United States. Most of these tests were written tests in spelling, geography, and math that were read and scored by teachers.

As early as the 1850s, children with disabilities were being identified, and attempts were made to provide them with an education. However, this education was more focused on functional life skills than academic skills. In addition, most children with disabilities were placed in separate institutions or separate sections of the public school and were not included in any academic assessments. It was not until the mid 1970s that education of individuals with disabilities began to be physically integrated into the general education classroom and more focused on the general classroom curriculum. The passage of legislation such as Section 504 of the Rehabilitation Act of 1973, the Education for All Handicapped Children Act of 1975 (EHA), the Individuals with Disabilities Education Act (IDEA) in 1990, the reauthorization of this act in 1997, and the passage of the No Child Left Behind Act (NCLB) in 2002 were significant milestones that led to the inclusion of children with disabilities in the K–12 education and assessment systems.

A particularly important milestone for children with disabilities was the enactment of EHA in 1975. Before the enactment of this legislation, the number of children with disabilities that were actually instructed in U.S. public schools was less than 20% of this population, with 80% of children with disabilities being confined to some type of institutional environment. Many states actually had laws specifically excluding children with disabilities from attending public school. Frequently, when children with disabilities were included in an "educational" environment, they were "warehoused" in inadequate facilities and hence received little or no appropriate educational instruction. The enactment of legislation such as Section 504 of the Rehabilitation Act, EHA, IDEA, and NCLB has had a profound impact on the education of children with disabilities over the course of the past three decades. As a result of these combined legislative efforts, the number of children with disabilities served by public education in the United States during the 2010–2011 school year was more than 13% of the total school population.

It is of interest to examine the legislation impacting the education and assessment of children with disabilities in a historical framework. Interest in the rights of individuals with disabilities and the educational opportunities for this population has its roots in the civil rights movement. The years that preceded, and to some extent precipitated, the EHA, were years when U.S. society was marked by the Vietnam conflict, the integration of public schools, and a plethora of protests and boycotts. Education became very important to many political agendas. Parents of children with disabilities joined together with organizations such as the Pennsylvania Association for Retarded Children and pushed for legislation. One of the results was the passage of EHA in 1975. Among other things, this act required all public schools accepting federal funds to provide equal access to education for children with physical and mental disabilities.

A slightly earlier piece of legislation that has had a profound impact on the education and assessment of children with disabilities is Section 504 of the Rehabilitation Act of 1973. This section is widely recognized as the first civil-rights statute for persons with disabilities and became effective in 1977. Section 504 provides equal access to all public school programs, services, and activities and requires programs receiving federal funding to provide accommodations. The Rehabilitation Act of 1973 was supplemented by the passage of the Americans with Disabilities Act (ADA) in 1990. The ADA extended Section 504 to much of the private sector and laid the groundwork for the rights of individuals with disabilities in all areas of society including education and assessment.

The EHA was replaced by the IDEA in 1990. This important legislation contained many improvements over the EHA, including a provision for educating children in their neighborhood schools rather than in separate schools for children with disabilities. The IDEA paved the way for the mainstreaming movement that has resulted in the inclusion today of almost all children with disabilities in general education classes in the U.S. public school system.

Very significant legislation impacting the education and assessment of children with disabilities was the reauthorization of the Elementary and Secondary Education Act (ESEA) in 2002, as the NCLB. The original ESEA was first authorized in 1965 as part of Lyndon B. Johnson's War on Poverty and is some of the most far-reaching federal educational legislation ever passed by Congress in terms of its scope and the increased role of the federal government in the education system. This act, which emphasized equal access to education and established standards for accountability, was reauthorized every 5 years since its enactment, with the latest version being NCLB. NCLB is significant for a number of reasons, most importantly for the fact that the standardized test scores of students with disabilities who have individualized education plans (IEPs) are counted for accountability purposes just as their nondisabled classmates' scores are counted. The National Council for Disabilities (NCD) reports in *No Child Left Behind: Improving Educational Outcomes for Students with Disabilities,* (www.aypf.org/publications/NCLB-Disabilities.pdf) that NCLB, in combination with IDEA, has resulted in both changed attitudes and changed expectations for the academic performance of students with disabilities. They found that as a result of this legislation, the scores of children with disabilities on academic assessments are finally being taken seriously by state assessment and accountability systems.

Now to turn specifically to technology and legislation that have impacted how technology is accessed and used by children with disabilities in the classroom and on assessments. An important act is the Assistive Technology Act (ATA) of 2004. One reason this act is important is that the 2004 reauthorization of IDEA references the use of universal design as defined in the ATA. The ATA (first passed in 1988 as the Technology Related Assistance for Individuals with Disabilities Act, updated in 1994 and 1998) was reauthorized in 2004 as S. 2595 and seeks to provide assistive technology (AT) to all persons with disabilities regardless of age or environment. The ATA specifically addresses the use of principles of universal design in the development of new technologies: Under this act, any emerging technology would always include planning for accessibility at the design phase. The passage of this legislation had a significant influence on both the education and testing of students with disabilities. It was the first clear statement about universal design and is frequently cited in subsequent laws on education, technology, and testing and, hence, laid the groundwork for many changes to come.

Earlier legislation that focused on technology and that is relevant to the topic of this chapter is the Section 508 amendment to the Rehabilitation Act of 1973 (29 U.S.C. § 794d) in 1986 designed to ensure that electronic and information technology developed by federal agencies is accessible to people with disabilities. To correct some shortcomings of Section 508, the Federal Electronic and Information Technology Accessibility and Compliance Act was proposed and became the new Section 508 in 1998. Another important component of legislation pertinent to this chapter was the National Instructional Materials Accessibility Standard (NIMAS; see http://idea.ed.gov/explore/view/p/%2Croot%2Cdynamic%2CTopica lBrief%2C12%2C), which outlines a set of consistent and valid XML-based source files created by K–12 publishers or other content producers. The source files can be used to create accessible specialized formats of print instructional materials. NIMAS was adopted as part of the Individuals with Disabilities Education Improvement Act of 2004, an update of IDEA. Finally, The Twenty-First Century Communications and Video Accessibility Act of 2010 outlines processes to ensure that new Internet-enabled telephone and television products and services are accessible to and usable by people with disabilities.

The most recent legislation pertinent to assessing children with disabilities that will be mentioned in this introduction is the Race to the Top (RTT) initiative enacted in 2009 as part of the federal American Recovery and Reinvestment Act (ARRA). RTT, which operates side by side with NCLB, provides funding for the development of assessments aligned to a common set of academic goals for K–12 education (Common Core State Standards, CCSS: www.corestandards.org/) as well as the development of tests to assess progress toward meeting these standards. The initiative helped to support a state-led movement to create the CCSS, which was sponsored by the National Governors Association (NGA) and the Council of Chief State School Officers (CCSSO). The RTT funding requires states to use a common set of standards in a consortium with other states and to develop assessments to measure student progress toward meeting the standards.

In their article, designed to provide recommendations to the states and state consortia who are working to implement testing for the RTT CCSS, Thurlow, Quenemoen, and Lazarus (2012) state that "Students with disabilities who receive special education services as required by the Individuals with Disabilities Education Act (IDEA) currently make up 13 percent of public school enrollment, with percentages in states varying from 10 percent to 19 percent" (p. 5). They make the point that there has been a strong three-decade movement by the states to include all students in the education system, and they are concerned ". . . that this commitment may now be challenged by questions about how best to include special education students as states move toward innovative approaches to assessments [and increased use of technology] through Race to the Top funding" (p. 4).

A key question that states must address as they develop assessments to measure the CCSS is how best to draw upon cutting-edge assessment methodology while not forfeiting any progress that has been made over the past three decades in inclusion and accessibility of assessments for students with disabilities. The challenge for both psychometricians and practitioners is how best to use advances in technology and psychometrics to provide accessible assessments to individuals with disabilities while maintaining the validity of inferences based on the scores from the tests they are developing.

In this chapter, we explore the use of technology to increase both the psychometric quality and the accessibility of assessments for individuals with disabilities. Most of the discussion focuses on the use of digital assessments. We discuss how digitizing assessments can help meet the challenges of assessing populations with diverse characteristics and needs (specifically, individuals with disabilities). We discuss applications of universal design and the design and use of digital assessments and other devices that increase accessibility of assessments for individuals with disabilities. Because we view accessibility as including the administration of tests with appropriate difficulty, and because the use of accessibility features may have an impact on item difficulty, we discuss the use of adaptive testing methods to tailor better test content and difficulty to individuals with different proficiencies. We also discuss the potential benefits and drawbacks of using technology, such as computers, to assess this population. The chapter concludes with a summary of the challenges that remain in each of these areas and recommendations for the use of technology in the design, development, and delivery of assessments that maximize accessibility for individuals with disabilities.

### Meeting the Challenges of Assessing Heterogeneous Populations

Approaches to meeting the challenges of assessing test takers with various proficiencies and ways of interacting with tests have, to date, fallen into several broad categories. In this section of the chapter, we discuss universal design of item content and accessibility initiatives for computer-based testing (CBT), including assistive technologies (AT) that can be integrated into an accessible testing environment, and the adaptive testing mode that allows for tailoring test content to individuals.

#### *Universal Design*

In this part of the chapter, we discuss the history of universal design and how it has impacted testing since it first appeared in federal legislation with regard to state- and districtwide assessments (IDEA, 2004; NCLB, 2001). In addition, we discuss how universal design has been incorporated into education in the form of universal design for learning (UDL) developed by the Center for Applied Special Technologies (CAST, 2011), which integrates the principles of universal design into an assessment context. Our discussion focuses on developments and legislation in the US; however, it should be noted that numerous contributions have occurred globally.

The concept of universal design comes from the field of architecture. More than 40 years ago, Ron Mace coined the term to describe his approach to the design of buildings and products that were both aesthetic and usable to the widest possible range of people. In his final speech, Mace (1998) attempted to differentiate three themes in accessibility at the time: barrier-free design, universal design, and AT. He defined barrier-free design as simply ensuring a building was accessible and met the requirements of federal mandates (e.g., ADA, 1990). Universal design was an approach that assumed all people had some sort of disability but that design should be focused on meeting the needs of broad groups of individuals rather than the specific needs of an individual. For example, many individuals might benefit from hearing content in addition to printed text (e.g., automobile drivers whose hands and eyes are busy and some English language learners, not just individuals with diagnosed print disabilities). Finally, he viewed AT as highly person oriented and tailored to meet the needs of one person rather than a broad group of individuals. For example, glasses are tailored to meet the vision needs of an individual and could not be used interchangeably by all people or even by other people who need glasses. At the time Ron Mace delivered this presentation, the idea of universal design had only begun to be integrated into education and assessment. In addition, many mainstream technologies today, such as talking GPS units, text to speech (TTS) for GPS systems, or predictive text entry and speech recognition on our smartphones, were originally highly specialized (and expensive) tools developed for individuals with disabilities. It is likely that today the integration of AT into assessment delivery would be viewed as a universal design feature.

Since Mace's introduction of universal design principles in architecture, the ideas of universal design have significantly influenced education of individuals with disabilities in the form of UDL and universal design for assessments. The CAST has trademarked their principles for UDL, including these three primary principles:

1. Multiple means of representation
2. Multiple means of action and expression
3. Multiple means of engagement

The first principle (multiple means of representation) recognizes that there are many different ways that individuals may have of perceiving information during instruction. For example, some students by nature of their disability (blind) are unable to learn when information is presented solely in a visual format. Likewise, audio presentation of information (e.g., lecture style) may be ideal for students with dyslexia or visual impairments but a poor match for visual learners, students with hearing impairments, and individuals with some language-based disabilities (e.g., auditory processing disorders).

The second principle (multiple means of action and expression) refers to how students demonstrate what they know and can do. This principle suggests that teachers allow students to show their work in ways that suit their own learning styles. For example, a student who struggles with writing may choose to give an oral presentation instead of a written report for a science project. Similarly, a teacher could allow students to respond orally to constructed-response test questions rather than writing their responses. This principle is the most challenging to implement in a large-scale standardized assessment context for both practical and psychometric reasons. One challenge is related to scoring: rubrics are typically constructed to respond to a standardized response format (e.g., text-based response or single correct answer in multiple-choice assessments) and do not lend themselves to students responding in another format (e.g., oral presentation or building a model). Another challenge is related to the comparability of difficulty level across multiple response modes. One example of differences in comparability across response formats was reported in research on the comparison of essays written on computer and by hand (Powers & Farnum, 1997; Powers, Fowles, Farnum, & Ramsey, 1994; Russell & Tao, 2004). If the response modes are not of comparable difficulty or have the potential to change the construct that the test is measuring, students using a particular response mode might be advantaged or disadvantaged when their scores are compared to those obtained by other students who took the test under standardized conditions.

The third principle (multiple means of engagement) is critical in a learning context and a strategy that good teachers have employed for generations (e.g., identify a genre of literature that appeals to an individual student or allow students to select which president they will write about for a history report). In an assessment context, student choice and individual preferences have largely been avoided. For example, passages selected for reading comprehension assessments are chosen to avoid the impact of prior knowledge on student performance because of the potential for introducing construct-irrelevant variance in the test scores. For many educators, however, there is a desire to allow students to select assessment tasks. Unfortunately, some research studies indicate that test takers may perform worse on the tasks they selected compared to the tasks assigned to them (Campbell & Donohue, 1997). The same cautions previously mentioned regarding choice of response format hold here. For example, students may not make the best choice when given options regarding which essay prompt they would prefer to write to. Also, it could be that not all possible choices presented to a student represent tasks that are of equal difficulty and, consequently, the student may be advantaged or disadvantaged by the choice made.

The National Center on Education Outcomes has taken the lead on developing seven elements of universally designed assessments (Thompson, Johnstone, & Thurlow, 2002). These include: "(1) Inclusive assessment population, (2) Precisely defined constructs, (3) Accessible, non-biased items, (4) Amenable to accommodations, (5) Simple, clear, and intuitive instructions and procedures, (6) Maximum readability and comprehensibility, and (7) Maximum legibility" (p. 7). While some of these elements include best practices for item writers (e.g., Precisely defined constructs or Simple, clear, and intuitive instructions and procedures), others rely on an interface with the delivery system. One of these elements (Amenable to accommodations), requires that the delivery system provide a variety of testing accommodations that can be delivered individually based on a student's need. Over the last decade, significant advances have been made in adding testing accommodations to CBT platforms. In the next section, we provide an overview of the challenges and potential for increased accessibility as assessments move to digital delivery.

### Accessible Computer-Based Testing

Computer-based testing has the potential to enhance accessibility but also presents new accessibility challenges. One advantage of moving away from paper-based testing is the potential for students who use AT to access digital text and information over the web to use these same tools in an assessment context. In addition, these same ATs can be embedded within the test platform to assist all students (not only students with disabilities) and reduce construct-irrelevant variance. For example, audio presentation of test content on a mathematics test could benefit an English learner who understands spoken English but struggles to read in English, struggling readers without disabilities, and students with print disabilities even if they do not use TTS as an instructional accommodation. However, CBT also has the potential to present new accessibility challenges for some individuals with disabilities. For example, some new item types may challenge a student's working memory if that student relies on audio presentation (TTS) alone. Other item types may present challenges for students who cannot see visual content. Highly interactive items requiring the mouse to make selections may pose challenges for students who have limited dexterity. Attempts to address these challenges of integrating AT into assessments have been made, in part, through additions to existing standards for the transfer of assessment data between standards organizations. One example of this is the recent integration of some web accessibility standards into the existing standard for exchanging accessible test content (i.e., the Accessible Portable Item Protocol, APIP; IMS Global Learning Consortium, 2013). However, future work is needed to expand web accessibility standards, which will be discussed subsequently, to include additional standards for the delivery of assessment content and to integrate the transfer of content to delivery systems.

The first generation of computer-based assessments attempted to integrate "paper-based" testing accommodations into the CBT platform. For example, large-print accommodations were provided via a variety of different forms of magnification and enlargement (e.g., magnifying glass, font enlargement with wrapping, and full-screen enlargement). Other accommodations such as read-aloud accommodations were more difficult to render in first-generation CBT platforms due to how the test items were formatted. For example, items were commonly stored as image files to allow for standardization of the size that the image would display on the screen regardless of the monitor used. This introduced a challenge when trying to provide audio presentation (read aloud) via TTS because the image file format did not include actual text that could be converted into speech but, rather, a picture of the text. Several organizations have attempted to address these challenges through the development or adoption of standards. There are several standards that address text books and e-readers (e.g., DAISY Consortium, www.daisy.org/, and NIMAS). However, the standards most commonly followed in an assessment context are APIP standards that focus on the transfer of accessible assessment content between the item author and item delivery vendor and on the standardized storage format for information on how test content should be delivered for specific individuals. For an example of the latter component, the Personal Needs Profile (PNP) for a student with dyslexia may indicate the need for audio presentation; likewise, a braille reader may have a PNP that documents the need for refreshable braille, audio navigation, and on-demand embossing.

In addition to these assessment-specific standards, the World Wide Web Consortium's (W3C) Web Content Accessibility Guidelines (WCAG) focus on standards for authoring of content in a format that both interoperates with AT and ensures that it is standardized across delivery platforms (e.g., web browsers). Additionally, the User Agent Accessibility Guidelines (UAAG: www.w3.org/TR/UAAG20/) provide guidance on how to make web browsers, media players, and other ATs themselves accessible to individuals with disabilities. The IMS and W3C standards are discussed in what follows.

*IMS Global Learning Consortium Standards.* In 2012, the IMS Global Learning Consortium published an accessibility extension to the already widely used Question and Test Interoperability (QTI) specifications that provide test-development and test-delivery vendors with standard XML language for describing questions and tests. In short, QTI provides a common language for authoring test items in a digital format. These accessibility extensions included both the APIP standard and the PNP standard. This work was spearheaded by states and test-development vendors interested in making sure accessibility markup (e.g., how elements of an item should be read aloud via TTS or how images should be described to students with visual impairments) was transferred with each test item and a uniform way for transferring information about students' needs to the test-delivery platform. In theory, this information will allow test items to be rendered in an accessible manner on an APIP–compliant test-delivery engine. Although APIP has not been put to the test operationally, many states and consortia are requiring that items be QTI/APIP compliant. Additional information on APIP is available from the IMS website.

*W3C accessibility standards.* Another important set of accessibility standards is the set of W3C accessibility standards for web-based content (WCAG and UAAG). The W3C is the main international standards organization for the World Wide Web and is widely accepted as the standards organization for digital accessibility. The WCAG documents explain how to make web content more accessible through code or markup that defines the structure or presentation of test content as well as the way in which information (text, images, and sounds) is stored. Additional information can be found on the W3C website.[1] Since most CBT platforms are web based, and most test takers with disabilities in the United States should have experience using accessible web-based content, these guidelines are essential to allowing students to use their own AT (e.g., TTS software) but have some drawbacks in that test content may not be standardized across AT. For example, one TTS engine may read 1924 as "nineteen twenty-four," while another TTS engine would read it as "one thousand nine hundred and twenty-four." These types of differences could have an impact on test takers and are some of the challenges that the previously mentioned APIP standards hope to overcome by standardizing the format in which test developers can transfer additional accessibility information (e.g., how text should be read aloud or how figures should be described) with test items. These types of standards are particularly important with the widespread use of numerous different types of delivery platforms for digital instructional materials (e.g., e-readers, tablets, smartphones, and traditional desktop and laptop computers).

*Assistive Technologies.* One important consideration when building a CBT platform is to ensure that the platform includes AT tools and/or interoperates with existing AT. AT includes a wide range of tools and software designed to improve accessibility. Under IDEA (2004), they are defined as "Any item, piece of equipment or product system, whether acquired commercially off the shelf, modified, or customized, that is used to increase, maintain, or improve the functional capabilities of children with disabilities." The definition encompasses both low-tech and high-tech tools ranging from a magnifying glass to software that translates speech to digital text. Table 10.1 includes descriptions of a wide range of AT that are currently used and/or are embedded in CBT platforms.

These types of AT (both hardware and software) can either be embedded within a CBT platform or used in conjunction with a CBT platform. While most test takers would prefer using their own AT (rather than learning to use those provided in the CBT platform), this presents test-security concerns by requiring that the testing engine be open to third-party software. In addition, the use of user-owned AT provides additional quality-control concerns (e.g., some screen readers may not recognize specific symbols), which is problematic in high-stakes assessments.

### Adaptive Testing

The previously described technologies used to test students with disabilities focus on the physical student–test interface in order to deliver a more individualized and accessible testing experience. However, there is another way in which tests can be made more individualized:

Table 10.1  List of Assistive Technologies and Other Embedded Support Tools

| Assistive Technologies | Description |
| --- | --- |
| Screen reader | Text-to-speech software that reads aloud the entire screen (including navigational elements, buttons, and image descriptions). In addition, screen readers generally incorporate keyboard substitutes for commands otherwise dependent on a mouse. |
| Text reader | Text-to-speech software that reads aloud only the text on the screen |
| Synchronized highlighting | Component of many text reader software apps that highlights text as it is read aloud to improve comprehension |
| Refreshable braille | External hardware that renders braille via pins that raise and lower to convey braille representation of digital text |
| Tactile embossers | External hardware that prints braille or tactile drawings |
| Speech recognition | Software that allows an individual to navigate or type via speech rather than a mouse or keyboard |
| Alternate pointing devices | Hardware that replaces a mouse (e.g., joystick, headwand) |
| Single switch | Hardware that replaces a mouse but uses tab and enter commands instead of mimicking a mouse |
| Magnification/Enlargement | Software for magnification include a variety of approaches such as a "magnifying glass," full-screen enlargements (may require scrolling side to side and up and down), and text enlargement (text rewraps). |
| Color changes | Component of many enlargement software programs or operating systems that allow an individual to change the color of the screen and or/text |
| Writing tools | Wide variety of software tools that allow for spellcheck, grammar check, cut and paste (within document), thesaurus, and word prediction |
| Memory/Focus tools | Embedded software tools that allow test taker to virtually highlight text, flag areas on the screen, take notes, block out (mask) content, or organize information |
| Language tools | Embedded software tools that provide pop-up glossary, dictionary (may include text definition in English, translation, or picture), side-by-side translation, or American Sign Language video or avatar translation |
| Math tools | Calculator, formula sheets, and virtual protractor or ruler |

by tailoring test content to individual test takers. This part of the chapter provides an overview of adaptive testing, in which test items are selected, in part, according to test taker proficiency. This mode of testing has been in operation for decades and has been shown to improve measurement precision, particularly for test takers in the tails of the proficiency distribution. Students with disabilities may be proficient on content but may not be able to demonstrate their proficiency due to accessibility obstacles. Ways to address this have been discussed in previous sections. However, students with cognitive or learning disabilities or students with disabilities that have impeded their opportunity to learn may perform in the lower tail of the proficiency distribution—even with the appropriate accommodations. This is where adaptive testing and tailored item selection can contribute to accessibility in addition to allowing better proficiency information to be obtained. Further, there is evidence that adaptive testing is more engaging than conventional linear testing for students who struggle to demonstrate proficiency and that adaptive tests may cause less anxiety for some test takers (with the exception of those in the upper tail of the proficiency distribution) because of the closer match of items to test taker proficiency (see, e.g., Betz & Weiss, 1976). Although adaptive testing has not been studied empirically for students with disabilities on a large scale, the method is hypothesized to hold similar benefits for these students (Stone & Davey, 2011).

Conventional tests are typically presented in a linear format, in which all test takers receive the same items. As is true for any test, linear tests are assembled to provide the most efficient measurement according to the goals of the test. Certification and licensure tests require the most precise measurement around the passing score, while other tests (e.g., admissions, aptitude, or accountability) are built for measurement precision that is greatest around the center of the proficiency distribution and tapers off toward the tails. Test takers with and without disabilities have, as groups, proficiency distributions that may span the range of proficiencies at each grade level. However, test takers with disabilities may have scores that fall toward the lower tail due to the inadequate accessibility of many large-scale assessments (i.e., a disconnect between observed and true proficiency) as well as the lack of opportunity to learn the subject matter that the test was designed to measure (i.e., true proficiency deficits, which can also occur for students without disabilities). For empirical evidence of this lower proficiency of test takers with disabilities, see recent data from virtually any K–12 large-scale assessment. For example, see California Department of Education (2006), in which only 23% of test takers with disabilities ("Special Ed Services") achieved at least proficient performance on the Grade 4 English language arts test, compared with 53% of students without disabilities ("No Special Ed Services"). The inaccessibility of the test content or due to student–test interaction limits the amount of information that can be gained about the test taker's ability. In contrast to the fixed-format tests just described, there are numerous approaches to assessing test takers adaptively. Adaptive testing better targets the test to a test taker based on individual test taker characteristics (e.g., proficiency). However, the issue of whether all students can be assessed reasonably against grade-level standards is one that could confound even the most flexible of delivery modes. One approach to addressing this challenge is to offer additional items that are off grade level to further refine the proficiency estimates of students who are advanced or who are below basic. This hybrid method has been employed in the Idaho Standards Achievement Tests (Idaho State Department of Education, 2013).

When we discuss adaptive testing in current educational contexts, we tend to think of item-level adaptive tests. In tests in which items are selected adaptively, selection of the next item is associated with the cumulative estimated proficiency after the current item. An alternative adaptive mode is the multistage test, in which each subset of items is selected based on the cumulative proficiency estimate after the last set. Despite the focus on CAT and the educational context, adaptive testing is not new, and these types of testing are used in many different contexts.

Histories of adaptive testing generally cite the Binet IQ test (Binet & Simon, 1905) as the first adaptive mental test. In that test, Binet attempted to administer items that were classified as being aligned with sequential mental ages. At each mental age, approximately half of children were expected to answer each item correctly. The trained psychologist administering the test would begin by choosing a level that appeared appropriate for the child (e.g., using chronological age as an initial estimate) and then administering items at each mental age level, scoring the items, and branching to a more-advanced or less-advanced level. The test would continue in this fashion until a basal (i.e., set of items that were answered correctly) and ceiling (i.e., set of items that were answered incorrectly) were discovered.[2] Binet's test-administration procedure illustrates the key feature of adaptive tests as previously stated: adaptive tests take individual test taker characteristics such as proficiency into account in order to select the full set of items on which a decision or final estimate is based.

An adaptive testing scenario familiar from educational assessment is that of an oral examination. For example, an oral thesis defense often consists of a panel of examiners asking a variety of questions designed to elicit information about the candidate's knowledge of the subject matter. In classroom-based question-and-answer dialogues between teacher and student, a similar adapting, or evolution, of the question difficulty takes place. There are some critical differences, however, between this example and the Binet procedure previously described. Binet used a scripted, step-by-step algorithm, or set of rules, for selecting subsequent items in the process. Further, Binet had placed the items on a (chronological-age) scale and used the subject's responses to locate the subject's position on that scale as well (van der Linden, 2008). In these ways, although Binet's procedure was not used for educational assessment, it is similar to the types of adaptive tests that are used today in the field of measurement.

Just as item (or item-subset) selection can take place adaptively, other test features can be adapted to the individual test taker. As previously described, new test platforms such as Computerized Assessments & Learning (CA & L)[3] allow the test administrator to implement accommodations (e.g., color filters, read aloud) that the student may use at the test and/ or item level. These platforms provide the opportunity for accommodations to be selected before the test starts according to disability profiles and used during the test if the test taker chooses. Another way to target the provision of an accommodation is to adapt the testing condition according to performance on a preliminary measure of the construct for which the accommodation may be useful. An example of a condition-adaptive test, in which the testing condition at the second stage of the test was determined by performance on a first, non-accommodated stage was the Designing Accessible Reading Assessments (DARA) field-test protocol described in Stone, Cook, and Laitusis (2013). For the test of reading comprehension administered in that research study, students were routed to either a nonaccommodated test or a test that had a read-aloud accommodation and an oral-fluency subtest. The goal was to increase score comparability between accommodated and nonaccommodated test takers by measuring masked component skills (e.g., decoding) when audio assistance was provided.

Adaptive testing on a large scale is implemented via computer using item response theory (IRT; Lord, 1980) to connect item and person characteristics. Rules for proficiency estimation, item selection, and content, overlap, and exposure constraints are executed algorithmically. These CATs can provide immediate scoring of many types of items, and accessible CBT platforms allow for a more accessible testing experience for all test takers.

## Integration of Universal Design, Assistive Technologies, and Adaptive Testing: What Challenges Remain

The focus on being able to assess a heterogeneous population of test takers adequately, accessibly, and appropriately has grown stronger over the past few decades. There have been numerous advances in technology-enhanced platforms, item types, and accommodations that better allow test takers with disabilities to perceive, respond to, and engage with the test content within a more universally designed environment. Developments such as CAT have enabled more tailored, individualized delivery of test content for test takers with disabilities. For example, accessibility-based item tagging could be used by a CAT algorithm to select versions of items that are of the appropriate format for the individual in accordance with that individual's IMS PNP or a similar profile. Further, some accessibility test changes or adjustments may change the difficulty of the item (e.g., allowing calculator use on a computation item). A CAT algorithm could use specific tagging, similar to the way that it incorporates content, exposure, and psychometric constraints, to administer items that are both accessible and at an appropriate level of difficulty for each test taker. However, while these technological features are the current state of the art in achieving better measurement and more appropriate testing conditions for test takers with disabilities, there are still some uses of technology that give rise to difficulties when they are implemented, meriting additional discussion.

In this section of the chapter, we provide recommendations for three areas that will require future work in order to maximize the potential of technology in the design, development, and delivery of assessments that are both accessible for individuals with disabilities and fair and valid for all test takers. These areas include (a) the integration of universal design and accessibility standards across item development and test delivery, (b) accounting for the interaction between accommodation use and item difficulty in adaptive assessments, and (c) ensuring that the use of computer-adaptive assessments for heterogeneous populations does not result in unintended consequences.

### Integration of Universal Design

Universal design has a lofty goal of creating items and tasks that are accessible to all test takers without the need for adjustment to testing conditions or format. Most advances in universal design of assessments have been focused on item development (e.g., simplified language) or on increasing access to testing accommodations embedded within the computer-delivery platform so that all students can use these tools. The integration of these item characteristics can present challenges when universally designed items are delivered on systems that do not have the capacity for accessibility features or when item features and delivery features are not cohesive. There are two situations in which these challenges are of the most immediate importance.

In the first situation, one vendor develops test items, and another vendor delivers these items. This situation often leads to a mismatch between the types of accessibility demonstrated by the items and interoperability with the delivery platform. Currently, it is common for item content to be delivered on testing platforms that do not support TTS or keyboard navigation (although this is changing rapidly). This situation precludes delivery of those accessibility features even if accessible item formats that can implement various accommodations according to the test taker's disability were created. The item author may follow the principles of universal design and implement the use of item tags and other item features that control how the item is formatted and delivered for each test taker. This work will be in vain, however, if the testing platform on which the items are administered has not been developed to make use of item-level features (e.g., using arrow keys to tab through item content, using TTS to hear content read aloud, or listening to the text descriptions of visual images are unavailable in a mouse-only system without TTS supports). One recommendation that should be explored is the integration of the IMS APIP standards for item content and the W3C WCAG standards for web delivery so that test content can be seamlessly transitioned to web delivery.

In the second situation (expected to be more common in the future), the testing platform may include a multitude of embedded supports for all students. For example, embedded supports such as on-demand audio to read aloud content can be made available to all test takers on a mathematics test rather than restricting these accommodations to individuals with documented disabilities. Likewise, the use of other tools (calculator, spellchecker, word prediction, and virtual protractor, ruler, highlighter, pencil, notepad, sticky notes) would be available to all students. This development, along with the use of a wide variety of new item types (e.g., drag and drop, highlighting in text, hotspots, simulations, automatically scored constructed-response items), will present unique challenges. As test items evolve, it is likely that there will be interactions between the embedded tools and the item-response format itself. Some of these interactions may be obvious, such as the need to turn off embedded supports that interfere with the construct being assessed. Others, however, may not be as clear. For example, the use of a virtual pencil to circle important content as a reading strategy may become confusing when the test taker is then asked to answer a constructed-response question (e.g., can students use the pencil tool to write their answers, or does the automated scoring engine require typed responses?). In addition, test takers may be confused if the tools disappear or reappear with every new item that is presented. Further, there are many questions remaining on the impact of multiple testing tools and the impact of turning some off at the item level. How many different embedded support tools should be available at once? Another important consideration is that some of these additional embedded support tools have accessibility challenges (e.g., a virtual protractor that requires a mouse to rotate is problematic for individuals who are blind or have fine motor impairments).

Finally, some testing accommodations (e.g., braille) will still remain as a feature only available to students who require this support, and not all items will be amenable to rendering in braille (particularly in a digital format). For example, some graphical features are still difficult to render, even with developments in electronic braille formats. Some assessment delivery platforms incorporating technology such as refreshable braille and on-demand embossing of braille are already available (e.g., OAKS Online Braille Interface; Oregon Department of Education, 2012); however, there are additional challenges in ensuring that item content can be rendered in refreshable braille, and there are additional steps required to emboss on demand, which can result in delays while testing, increases in the testing time, or distractions. For example, in mathematics, each item may need to be embossed and then delivered by the proctor to the test taker. Typically, the embosser must have its own room because it is loud and would distract test takers. It also adds a security step, because the embossed braille sheets must be secured but may become scattered or separated from other test materials and may not be remembered as being part of the testing material that needs to be secured and returned (unlike a whole test form). These are all challenges that will still need to be addressed in the future.

### Accounting for Divergent Response Profiles in CAT

In addition to the challenges of syncing item content with delivery, there are also challenges unique to CAT. One question that has not yet been thoroughly addressed focuses on how particular accommodations affect item responses for different individuals. It has been hypothesized that students with disabilities have divergent response profiles from those of students without disabilities. While in most cases a student might be expected to have relatively similar proficiency levels across subdomains of the full content domain being tested, students with disabilities may display mixed skill levels. This phenomenon is particularly likely to occur in students with learning disabilities (LD), for whom classification has historically been heavily influenced by divergent cognitive profiles (IQ-achievement discrepancy: U.S. Office of Education, 1977, p. G1082) or lower achievement levels in specific knowledge areas. Therefore, it is the divergence of displayed proficiency in some skill areas that leads to classification in the first place. The reauthorization of IDEA (2004) included alternative criteria for the identification of students with LD such as response to intervention (RTI) and strengths–weaknesses assessments that may lead to different classification than under discrepancy models (Fletcher, Coulter, Reschly, & Vaughn, 2004; Schultz, Simpson, & Lynch, 2006).

The nature of the specific learning disability also plays a role in what kinds of divergent effects are observed. Fletcher, Lyon, Fuchs, and Barnes (2007) defined five broad learning disabilities characterized by deficits in decoding, reading fluency, comprehension, math fluency, or writing. One implication is that students with LD may perform poorly on relatively easy test items in one area but well on relatively difficult items in a different part of the domain. The item-response models typically used for CAT assume a unidimensional latent ability trait. In order to capture varied proficiency in subdomains that are considered to be part of one larger domain, it may be necessary to use a more general model that can incorporate multidimensionality. If the unidimensional IRT model assumes that a test taker's item correct-response probabilities are all functions of the same underlying ability trait, and there are, in fact, multiple ability traits being displayed, then the CAT delivery method will be inefficient and will likely not be able to provide a precise measure of proficiency.

The potential presence of idiosyncratic knowledge patterns and the effect on the performance of CATs has been studied by researchers in various areas of educational research (see, e.g., Kingsbury & Houser, 2007). When using CAT, test taker item responses that vary greatly from the responses predicted by their proficiency estimates and the underlying model (e.g., correctly answering difficult items while incorrectly answering easier items) can be problematic in terms of item selection and scoring. Research on divergent profiles has provided evidence of idiosyncratic response patterns on a reading test for students with LD (Cromer & Wiener, 1966) and a mathematics test for students with LD (Stone & Davey, 2012), where, in both cases, performance was compared to that of students without LD. The analyses in the latter study examined differences in performance at the item-type level of the two groups when the groups were matched on a measure of proficiency. The results supported the hypothesis of differential performance in favor of students with LD taking the test with math-based modifications (e.g., calculator) on computation- or calculation-driven items when items could easily be solved using the calculator. In other words, students with LD were answering these items correctly more often than expected. This implies that there may be an interaction of the calculator accommodation and response, given proficiency, when items are amenable to being solved using a calculator. With the increased usage of a variety of accommodations by a heterogeneous population of students with disabilities, standardized tests delivered adaptively must be built to take diversity into account.

In some cases, a policy may be put in place that allows all students to use a particular accommodation if the accommodation removes access barriers when it is needed for one group (e.g., students with LD) and does not change the scores of the other group for whom it is not needed (e.g., students without LD). Such accommodations meet the requirements of the interaction hypothesis (see, e.g., Sireci, Scarpati, & Li, 2005). A weaker version is the differential boost hypothesis, which states that the effect for an appropriate accommodation on scores for students with LD must be significantly greater than that for the students without LD. The effects of various accommodations on performance for students with and without disabilities have been researched and debated extensively. This is a current hot topic as the consortia work to build consensus among states about which accommodation policies to implement. See, for example, Laitusis, Buzick, Stone, Hansen, and Hakkinen (2012) for a critical analysis of research on several accommodations for this purpose (audio presentation of reading or mathematics; refreshable braille, calculators, and American Sign Language for mathematics; American Sign Language and writing tools for English language arts).

When multiple accommodation profiles are allowed, a possible approach to accounting for the various profiles in practice would be to have multiple item-response models for each item by calibrating (or estimating) the item parameters using separate groups. This could lead to an item having different estimates of, for example, its difficulty or ability to discriminate between test takers of similar proficiency, likely leading to changes in when and how the item is selected for use for the different groups. However, typical IRT models require hundreds or thousands of test taker responses to each item being calibrated, depending on the number of parameters in the model. These sample sizes are difficult to obtain for some low-incidence disability populations. The use of common assessments as proposed by the major consortia (PARCC, Smarter Balanced Assessment Consortium[4]) may mitigate the issue of sample size by allowing for combined samples across states rather than within states. Few research studies have considered the specific challenges that might arise from including students with and without disabilities in the calibration process. However, Karkee, Lewis, Barton, and Haug (2003) performed two calibrations (with all students and without students with disabilities) taking state standards based assessments. While Karkee and colleagues did find significant differences between item parameter estimates in the two types of samples, the effects of these differences on resulting scores were negligible.

A further possibility would be to make the current estimation and selection algorithms more robust to error in the proficiency estimates. An experimentally designed study could focus on how much item responses vary, conditional on an external and stable measure of proficiency, due to the use of different accommodations. Such a study would allow psychometricians to determine the possible extent of instability in the proficiency estimates and identify items, item types, or item-accommodation combinations that may be problematic. However, a study of this sort would require large numbers of individuals in each disability-accommodation-proficiency category in order to accurately perform the calibrations. Additionally, students typically use bundles of accommodations (e.g., the read-aloud accommodation with extended time), requiring careful design in order to isolate the effects of particular accommodations.

### Unintended Consequences of Using CAT for Heterogeneous Populations

Adaptive-testing methods hold great promise for increasing measurement precision across a wider proficiency spectrum, allowing tests better to measure growth in K–12. However, it is important to ensure that the use of adaptive tests in heterogeneous populations taking the test under varying conditions does not cause unintended consequences. There are specific concerns related to the use of CAT for students with disabilities. As stated previously, CAT has the potential to target test items and conditions to students at an individual level. This is a major benefit of the adaptive testing mode, in that it allows for the administration of items that provide better information about test taker proficiency to comprise the test. However, the state accountability tests are designed to measure grade-level academic achievement. Some question whether it is possible to ascertain, with adequate precision, the proficiencies of students with disabilities at the lower end of a grade-level proficiency spectrum without including at least some off-grade-level items in the test. This brings about concerns regarding the meaning of resulting scores and whether scores based on mixed-grade-level content are comparable to scores based only on grade-level content. For example, the reliability of an on-grade-level score based on a reduced number of grade-level items may be questionable, because reliability tends to increase with the number of administered items that adequately measure the construct of interest (see, e.g., Traub & Rowley, 1991 for an overview). Psychometric targets with respect to performance at the required grade level may not be met without the administration of more items than would be desirable. Further, disability advocates have argued that adaptive tests should be designed to allow students with disabilities to respond to items that are cognitively complex even when they are statistically easier (Consortium for Citizens with Disabilities, 2012). While this approach is ideal, there may be practical limitations. Whether it will be possible to design such a test to meet all the other relevant constraints has yet to be seen.

Comparability is a key issue for adaptive testing. There are issues of comparability to related linear forms and comparability between tests that students are administered (Wang & Kolen, 2001). For some tests, students who need particular accommodations take a paper-based linear form instead of the computerized adaptive test. The reason is typically that the testing platform cannot incorporate and deliver the required accommodation. There is also a comparability issue between paper forms if, for example, graphs cannot be embossed or there is a difference in meaning between items delivered in two different conditions. This latter issue has been raised when the braille version includes or excludes information because of the type of representation used. Graphs and figures may be simplified when represented in braille form, reducing the amount of information provided. By way of contrast, a talking tablet that incorporates both braille and an audio accommodation may convey more information than is conveyed to students not using that format. Additionally, the use of contracted braille, in which individual letters may be represented by contractions, may be useful for braille readers who are proficient in its usage; however, the use of contracted braille may prove an obstacle for some test takers (see, e.g., Braille Authority of North America, 2010; Johnstone, Altman, Timmons, Thurlow, & Laitusis, 2009). This is another area in which tailored selection via the use of item-format tagging may provide benefits. Overall, comparability between adaptive forms is not a more severe or unusual issue, and adaptive testing may provide more control over comparability while increasing accessibility. However, score comparability is desirable, and these aspects must be considered.

**Summary**

Over the last decade, advances in technology have opened many opportunities for improving the accessibility of assessments for individuals with disabilities while also increasing engagement and precision of measurement through adaptive-testing models. These advances have included the integration of the principles of universal design into item authoring and the integration of assistive technologies into the development of CBT platforms. In addition, advances in adaptive testing have allowed improved measurement for a wider range of student achievement levels (not only typically developing students). These advances, however, come with additional challenges in integrating item content and item delivery systems, integrating information on accommodation research into adaptive-testing models, and ensuring that adaptive computer-delivered assessments do not have unintended consequences for students with disabilities. These challenges are all surmountable, and it is our hope that continued collaboration will result in future assessments that have achieved the goals of universal design while providing fair and valid assessments of *all* test takers' skills and abilities.

Note: This work is supported, in part, by the U.S. Department of Education, Institute of Education Sciences, National Center for Special Education Research under Grant No. R324A110088.

## Notes

1  www.w3.org/WAI
2  See http://iacat.org/node/442 for more details and an example.
3  http://caltesting.org/index.html
4  www.smarterbalanced.org/

## References

American Recovery and Reinvestment Act (ARRA) of 2009, Pub.L. No. 111–5, 123 Stat. 115, 516 (Feb. 19, 2009).

Americans with Disabilities Act of 1990, Pub.L. No. 101–336.

Assistive Technology Act of 2004, Pub.L. No. 108–364.

Betz, N. E., & Weiss, D. J. (1976). *Psychological results of immediate knowledge of results and adaptive ability testing.* Research Report 76–4. Minneapolis: University of Minnesota: Psychometric Methods Program.

Binet, A., & Simon, T. A. (1905). Méthode nouvelle pour le diagnostic du niveau intellectuel des anormaux. *L'Année Psychologique, 11*, 191–244.

Braille Authority of North America. (2010). *Guidelines and standards for tactile graphics, 2010*, Web Version. Retrieved from www.brailleauthority.org/tg/web-manual/index.html

California Department of Education, (2006). *California Standards Test (CST) technical report Spring 2006 administration.* Retrieved from www.cde.ca.gov/ta/tg/sr/documents/startechrpt06.pdf

Campbell, J. R., & Donahue, P. L. (1997). *Students selecting stories: The effects of choice in reading assessment.* Washington, DC: National Center for Education Statistics.

CAST. (2011). Universal design for learning guidelines version 2.0. Wakefield, MA: Author.

Consortium for Citizens with Disabilities. (2012). *Serving all students with a standards-based computer adaptive test.* Retrieved from www.c-c-d.org/fichiers/CCD_Computer_Adaptive_Testing_final.pdf

Cromer, W., & Wiener, M. (1966). Idiosyncratic response patterns among good and poor readers. *Journal of Consulting Psychology, 30*(1), 1–10.

Education for All Handicapped Children Act of 1975, Pub.L 94–142.

Elementary and Secondary Education Act of 1965, Pub.L. 89–10, 79 Stat. 27.

Fletcher, J. M., Coulter, W. A., Reschly, D. J., & Vaughn, S. (2004). Alternative approaches to the definition and identification of learning disabilities: Some questions and answers. *Annals of Dyslexia, 54*(2), 304–331.

Fletcher, J. M., Lyon, G. R., Fuchs, L., & Barnes, M. (2007). *Learning disabilities: From identification to intervention.* New York, NY: Guilford Press.

Gallagher, C. J. (2003). Reconciling a tradition of testing with a new learning paradigm. *Educational Psychology Review, 15*(1), 83–99.

Idaho State Department of Education. (2013). *Idaho Standards Achievement Tests spring 2013 technical report.* Retrieved from www.sde.idaho.gov/site/assessment/isat/docs/technicalReports/EID244_ISAT_Technical%20 Report_Final.pdf

IMS Global Learning Consortium. (2013). *Accessible Portable Item Protocol (APIP)*. Retrieved August 14, 2013, from www.imsglobal.org/apip/index.html

Individuals with Disabilities Education Act of 1990, Pub.L. 105–17, 20 U.S.C. §1400 *et seq.*

Individuals with Disabilities Education Improvement Act of 2004, Pub.L. 108–446.

Johnstone, C., Altman, J., Timmons, J., Thurlow, M., & Laitusis, C. (2009). *Field-based perspectives on technology assisted reading assessments: Results of an interview study with teachers of students with visual impairments (TVIs).* Minneapolis, MN: University of Minnesota, Technology Assisted Reading Assessment.

Karkee, T., Lewis, D. M., Barton, K., & Haug, C. (2003, April). *The effect of including or excluding students with testing accommodations on IRT calibrations.* Paper presented at the annual meeting of the National Council on Measurement in Education, Chicago, IL.

Kingsbury, G. G., & Houser, R. L. (2007). ICAT: An adaptive testing procedure to allow the identification of idiosyncratic knowledge patterns. In D. J. Weiss (Ed.), *Proceedings of the 2007 GMAC Conference on Computerized Adaptive Testing.* Retrieved October 1, 2009, from www.psych.umn.edu/psylabs/catcentral/pdf%20files/cat07Kingsbury.pdf

Laitusis, C., Buzick, H., Stone, E., Hansen, E., & Hakkinen, M. (2012). *Literature review of testing accommodations and accessibility tools for students with disabilities.* Retrieved from www.smarterbalanced.org/wordpress/ wp-content/uploads/2012/08/Smarter-Balanced-Students-with-Disabilities-Literature-Review.pdf

Mace, R. (June, 1998). *FAIA.* Presented at "Designing for the 21st Century: An International Conference on Universal Design," Presentation at FAIA, Hofstra University, Hempstead, NY. www.ncsu.edu/www/ncsu/design/sod5/ cud/about_us/usronmacespeech.htm

No Child Left Behind Act of 2001, Public Law No. 107–110, 115 Stat. 1425 (2002).

Powers, D., & Farnum, M. (1997). *Effects of mode of presentation on essay scores.* (ETS Research Mem. No. RM-08). Princeton, NJ: ETS.

Powers, D., Fowles, M. E., Farnum, M., & Ramsey, P. (1994). Will they think less of my handwritten essay if others word process theirs? Effect on essay scores of intermingling handwritten and word-processed essays. *Journal of Educational Measurement, 31*(3), 220–233.

Rehabilitation Act of 1973, Pub. L. No. 93–112, 87 Stat. 394, 29 U.S.C. § 701 *et seq.*

Russell, M., & Tao, W. (2004). Effects of handwriting and computer-print on composition scores: A follow-up to Powers, Fowles, Farnum, & Ramsey. *Practical Assessment, Research & Evaluation, 9*(1). Retrieved June 24, 2013, from http://PAREonline.net/getvn.asp?v=9&n=1

Schultz, E. K., Simpson, C. G., & Lynch, S. (2006). Specific learning disability identification: What constitutes a pattern of strengths and weaknesses? *Learning Disabilities, 18*(2), 87.

Sireci, S. G., Scarpati, S., & Li, S. (2005). Test accommodations for students with disabilities: An analysis of the interaction hypothesis. *Review of Educational Research, 75*, 457–490.

Stone, E., Cook, L. L., & Laitusis, C. C. (2013). *Assessing the adaptive elements of a test of reading comprehension for students with learning disabilities.* ETS Research Report 13–20. Princeton, NJ: ETS.

Stone, E., & Davey, T. (2011). *Computer-adaptive testing for students with disabilities: A review of the literature.* ETS Research Report 11–32. Princeton, NJ: ETS.

Stone, E., & Davey, T. (2012, April). *Item-bundle analysis to investigate problematic item types for students with disabilities taking computer-adaptive tests.* Paper presented at the annual meeting of the National Council on Measurement in Education, Vancouver, British Columbia, Canada.

Technology-Related Assistance for Individuals with Disabilities Act of 1988, P.L. 100–407.

Thompson, S. J., Johnstone, C. J., & Thurlow, M. L. (2002). Universal design applied to large scale assessments (Synthesis Report 44). Minneapolis, MN: University of Minnesota, National Center on Educational Outcomes. Retrieved from http://education.umn.edu/NCEO/OnlinePubs/Synthesis44.html

Thurlow, M. L., Quenemoen, R. F., & Lazarus, S. S. (2012). *Meeting the needs of special education students: Recommendations for the Race to the Top consortia and states.* Washington, DC: Arabella Advisors.

Traub, R. E., & Rowley, G. L. (1991). Understanding reliability. *Educational Measurement: Issues and Practice, 10*(1), 37–45.

Twenty-First Century Communications and Video Accessibility Act of 2010, Pub.L. 111–260.

U.S. Office of Education. (1977). Assistance to states for education for handicapped children: Procedures for evaluating specific learning disabilities. *Federal Register, 42*, G1082–G1085.

van der Linden, W. J. (2008). Some new developments in adaptive testing technology. *Zeitschrift für Psychologie/Journal of Psychology, 216*(1), 3–11.

Wang, T., & Kolen, M. J. (2001). Evaluating comparability in computerized adaptive testing: Issues, criteria and an example. *Journal of Educational Measurement, 38*(1), 19–49.

# 11
## Testing Technology and Its Effects on Test Security

David Foster

### Introduction

The use of technology in testing is often discussed in the context of test administration models (Drasgow, 2002; Drasgow, Luecht, & Bennett, 2006; Foster, 2013). At the most general level, there are two major categories of test-delivery models compared: paper-and-pencil tests and computerized tests. That is, the test is presented to the student either on a screen or on paper.[1] As with different ways of using paper to present test questions (e.g., booklet, collated sheets, etc.), today there are different types of screens on computer devices, such as desktop monitors, laptop monitors, tablet screens, and even smartphone screens (see Chernyshenko & Stark, this volume). The technology supporting the computerized, or technology-based tests, adds more complexity as to how the items on the screen actually get on the screen, how they adapt to different screen resolutions, whether scrolling is needed, and many other features. How items actually get to the screen is an important topic for computerized tests. Are the items coming from a local server, having been downloaded and stored on the server previously? Or are the items streaming from a continuous Internet connection? This difference and others, as they have evolved over the past two decades, have changed the terms we use to describe such testing. These terms are described in this section and will be used throughout the chapter.

As stated, terms important for this chapter refer to *the way tests are administered* rather than to the use of technology throughout the various steps of the test life cycle, including development of items and tests, collection of results, conducting statistical analysis, and reporting, among others. For coverage of these latter topics, the reader is referred to Drasgow, Luecht, and Bennett (2006). Paper materials are often also used in tests that mainly use technology for test administration. It is a rare and disciplined technology-based program that never prints out a paper version of items for review purposes or to provide a printed report. Similarly, paper-and-pencil tests will use computers and Internet technologies extensively in the development of paper-and-pencil tests and the booklets needed to deliver them.

Paper-and-Pencil Testing. Paper-and-pencil testing is a term referring to the traditional method of giving a test that is made of paper, often in the form of a booklet. It may include the use of machine-scorable answer sheets, also made of paper. The answer sheets are not always a necessary feature of a paper-and-pencil test, as "clicker" device technology is available that can collect the student responses. The tests themselves may also have been created and reviewed primarily on paper, although it is common today to create paper-and-pencil tests with the assistance of the computer or by using the Internet and then print them for test administration.

Computerized or Computer-Based Testing. In this chapter, the terms computerized and computer-based testing (CBT) will be used interchangeably and will refer to the use of a local server network, or manual-assist network,[2] to deliver tests to a desktop, laptop, or mobile device, usually within a testing center or school testing location (e.g., computer lab). These terms refer to a system in which prior to the launch of the test, the test content and other instructions are downloaded from the test program's servers[3] to the local server. During or after the exam, the same local network will collect the student responses and at some later point will transfer those data to the program's servers.

Internet Testing, Internet-Based Testing, or Online Testing. These terms are synonymous and refer to testing in which the Internet is the dominant technology for test administration. To be more specific, through a continuous Internet connection, the items are streamed as needed to the computer device used by the student. Each student response is also returned immediately through the Internet to a distant server. The difference between an Internet test and a computerized test, or CBT, is that for the latter, the test content is downloaded in its entirety prior to the beginning of the test administration event. This distinction is important, as seen in the difference between security threats discussed in what follows.

**Test Design Models**

Some terms have been used inconsistently to refer to test administration modes but in reality are test design models that take advantage of the computer technologies used to administer the tests.

*Computerized adaptive testing.* Computerized adaptive testing (CAT) is a term often used by testing professionals inappropriately, comparing CAT, a test design, to CBT. A CAT can actually be administered within a computerized/CBT system or as an online test or even noncomputerized adaptively as a paper-and-pencil test or in oral format.[4] For the computerized test or CBT, the entire pool of questions from which the CAT draws would be downloaded in advance, along with the testing software, and utilized during the exam. For a CAT delivered online, the item pool would remain at a remote server and items would be selected remotely and sent to a testing station at the time each item is selected for presentation to a student.

*Linear-on-the-Fly Test.* The linear-on-the-fly test (LOFT) is similar to a CAT in that it is a test design model, not a test administration mode. A LOFT pulls questions according to specific item presentation rules from a large pool of questions and can be administered as a CBT or online, depending on where the pool of questions resides and if the Internet is used to deliver each test question to the computing device.

*Fixed-Length Tests.* A fixed-length exam, similar to what is presented on a paper-and-pencil test, which may have a variety of test forms, can also be delivered as a computerized test or an online test.

There are many varieties of these basic test design models, the terms listed only being the more general and provided to illustrate the basic differences between them. See Drasgow, Luecht, and Bennett (2006) for a more complete review of many of these test design varieties.

*Technology-Based Testing.* To accommodate the need to be more general at times in this chapter, it will be valuable to refer to all of the test administration modes, with the exception of paper-and-pencil testing, as technology-based testing (TBT). This naming convention is used by the Council of Chief State School Officers and the Association of Test Publishers (2013).

## Technology Use in Educational Assessments

Which of the test administration modes and test design models listed are used for high-stakes educational testing purposes today? The answer: all of them! A large number educational tests are still presented in paper-and-pencil format to students as test booklets, often with answer sheets. Most statewide assessments given are still paper-and-pencil tests. Students also take some high-stakes tests on computers, some being delivered to a specific school testing location as a CBT, while others are presented online to more convenient and personal locations (e.g., a student's home). Some university courses, particularly online courses, use every mode as well for quizzes, midterm exams, and final exams, with the online method being naturally more compatible with the learning method. Some educational admissions tests are still paper and pencil (e.g., Law School Admissions Test, SAT and ACT), while others are computerized (e.g., Graduate Management Admissions Test and Graduate Record Exam). The United States government has funded (e.g., Race to the Top) consortia that have a mandate to provide technology-based tests for all states to use—to replace specific state assessments—by 2015. The relatively new organizations developing massively open online courses (MOOCs) are providing some of the end-of-course exams as computerized, using a computer lab or testing center network, or online. Most states and many school districts, if providing paper-and-pencil tests today, are researching and piloting the use of technology-based tests to be used in the near future.

Low-stakes educational tests are being administered most frequently as online tests, taking advantage of the convenience and low cost of Internet test administration. These tests serve the purposes of practice tests (for upcoming high-stakes tests), screening tests for job qualification or school admissions, and course quizzes. Often for these low-stakes tests, no student name is required and the scores are not reported, kept, or stored. Low-stakes testing on the Internet serves the valuable goals of informing students of their progress in a course of study or their readiness or preparedness for a high-stakes test without the need for the cost, security, and scheduling procedures that accompany high-stakes testing. Thousands of low-stakes educational tests can be found on hundreds of websites. Software programs are available that allow teachers to create and make available such tests.

It is clear that computer technology, including the Internet, has encouraged a move in education over the past decade away from paper-and-pencil testing to technology-based testing. Confusion still remains as to which configuration of technology will be used and when to make the move. Because technology changes so rapidly today, as soon as an educational organization decides on a path, new technology is introduced that creates reasonable doubt in the path chosen. When is the right time, then, to make the switch? Are there interim steps that can be taken? Is the state's (or district's or school's) technology capable of supporting the decision to move to a technology-based testing model? These are the right questions, but solid answers remain elusive, creating delays in decision making and implementation.

For large-scale educational testing efforts, the technology infrastructure needed to support the testing may not be in place. Challenges are created by not having enough computers or sufficient bandwidth or even enough electrical power outlets. There is also a technical support infrastructure that needs to be available to prepare the hardware and software in advance and be available to handle technical problems during the testing window. Also, from a psychometric perspective, there are concerns about administering the same tests to students using different devices with different computing performance and screen resolution, among other differences. Imagine one student taking a test on her smartphone, while a second student takes the same test on a computer in the school computer lab. Would the results be comparable? For questions like this, research is needed (see Way, Davis, Keng, & Strain-Seymour, this volume). The good news is that these problems and barriers have been recognized and that solutions are being created. But the issues remain today, and it is still possible to question the wisdom of quickly converting millions, perhaps hundreds of millions, of paper-and-pencil tests to technology-based tests.

For the purposes of this chapter, enough high-stakes educational testing programs are in place today using technology for test administration and test development to trigger every type of security concern that pertains to technology-based testing. The next section covers the reasons the increased use of technology is connected to increased test security risk.

### Reasons for Security Problems Specific to Technology-Based Testing

When new technologies began being used for test administration, new security threats began to appear. As a simple example, transmitting test files electronically to a test site instead of packaging booklets and answer sheets in boxes and shipping them creates the opportunity for someone to "hack" into the communication system and intercept the files.[5] Of course, the threat of theft or other forms of test fraud does not need to deter us from the benefits of using such technology but should instead cause us to evaluate the risks of such threats and implement security procedures, either preventing the threat or putting in place a defense that will detect an attack when it happens.

This section lists the reasons the use of technology to administer tests has introduced new threats and what those threats are. These reasons are inherent in the ways technology-based tests are used, and therefore the threats are difficult to avoid.

### Longer Testing Windows and On-Demand Testing

For some educational tests, including prominent examples such as college and graduate school admissions tests, students can schedule a time and date—within a specified testing period called a testing window—to take an exam at a time that is most convenient to them. Besides this strong advantage to students, the testing program is able to utilize limited technology resources (computer equipment, bandwidth, etc.) over a longer period, accommodating more students overall. It would be, otherwise, prohibitively difficult and expensive for testing programs to prepare testing locations to test all the students at the same time on the same day as would be done with a paper-and-pencil administration. As other educational testing programs move away from the paper-and-pencil testing models, they will need to determine the length of the window as they review the technology resources and locations available for testing.

What new security threat is present because of the use of a testing window instead of synchronous testing? The problem occurs because throughout the duration of a testing window, an exam is given at staggered times—with some tests scheduled at the beginning of the window and usually a large number just prior to the end of the window. With paper-and-pencil synchronized testing, it is difficult or even impossible for a student who just took an exam to memorize questions or capture them in some other way and share them with another student, because that second student is taking the test at the same time. Even with changes in time zones, it is impractical to share information from one student to another in a way that is useful. However, when the testing window is a couple of weeks or even a few days, students taking the test earlier in the window can capture the questions using a variety of methods and quickly share them with another student or a large number of other students in such a way that cheating using such preknowledge can be very effective.

It is not just students stealing questions that is of concern, and students may not even be the major source of this threat. Others, including teachers, school officials, government officials, and test-preparation companies, are able to benefit from the increased testing window length—if they are able to also capture the test content and use it to cheat. In a well-publicized incident (Davey & Nering, 2002), in 1994, Kaplan Educational Centers sent test takers to take the new computerized GRE exam published by ETS, asking them to memorize the exam questions they saw. After completing the tests, the individuals were debriefed, allowing the test preparation organization to capture as much of the new test as possible. Because the test was administered continuously in a testing window, later students could take advantage of knowing the questions they might see.

How might a short or long testing window contribute to test fraud on statewide educational assessments? With the expanded testing windows, teachers and school administrators that are today erasing wrong answers on answer sheets and replacing them with correct answers will simply use one of the many ways to record the questions presented to students taking earlier exams and use them to prepare students testing later in the window. If a computerized or CBT administration model is used, in which test content is downloaded to a school server prior to the beginning of the testing window, it is possible for someone to "hack" into the server and steal the test files that are stored there and all associated data (e.g., correct answer keys). More details on this method are in the next section, Electronic Download of Test Files.

Obviously, the longer the testing window, the more opportunities there are to capture and share test content effectively. When the window is very long, even indefinite, the availability of the questions remains useful to a large number of later test takers and may continuously reduce the value of the exam and resulting scores.

Reducing the size of the testing window is a possible solution but mostly ineffective. The ability to capture items and communicate them to others occurs very quickly across today's social networks. Returning to synchronous testing or reducing the length of the testing window may be impractical and also defeats the original advantages to both the testing program and students.

## Electronic Download of Test Files

Electronic distribution of test files lends itself to quick and sometimes easy technological ways of capturing the content—and the content is always 100% accurate. Since the late 1980s and continuing to the present time, computerized tests distributed as a set of computer files are typically downloaded from a server residing at the offices of the testing program (or a test administration contractor of the program) to a server at a testing center. The files are typically encrypted during the process. Besides the actual test questions, other relevant materials are usually included in the download, including scoring rules, answer keys, and relevant graphical, audio and video files, and so forth. The files may be sent a few hours to a few days before a particular test is scheduled to be taken and may remain at the site, stored on the server, as long as a testing window is open. It is at this step during transit, if encryption isn't employed, and during the length of time the files reside on a location's server that they are vulnerable to capture. In order to ensure the success of their efforts and to gain access to servers, pirates often collude with testing center personnel. With access to the server, they can capture the files, decrypt them if necessary, and put them into a format that can be quickly and easily sold on the Internet. This type of theft is particularly devastating to a program because the complete pool of items for the operational exam is stolen.

Test content pirates have effectively used this method for almost two decades—and continue to do so—to steal certification exams and sell them on the Internet. Foster and Zervos (2006) purchased hundreds of these certification test files from so-called braindump websites and compared them to the original test files. They were virtually identical, with most of the content matching between 99% and 100% *with the original published test files*. In 2009, Maynes (2009) analyzed the effects of this type of theft on certification programs. He states, "In a carefully constructed analysis . . . we found an astounding statistic with respect to braindump usage. Of 598 test takers on a very popular exam, we inferred statistically that more than 80% of them used braindump content." Using carefully constructed non-scored items seeded into the exam, Maynes determined statistically that only 7% would have passed—compared to the actual pass rate of 93%—if cheating using preknowledge from braindump sites had not been possible!

## Online Distribution of Test Content

Some testing programs use online testing to assess their students, which is defined as real-time streaming of test questions through a constantly available Internet connection. If unsecured and not encrypted, this stream of test data can be easily captured during transmission using any of several software programs, called "packet sniffers." The programs "watch" raw network traffic and can capture packets that fit certain criteria. This would allow the appropriate program to rebuild files those packets belong to. That the files were intercepted is unknown and can't be detected by either the sending or receiving computers.

Even if secure transmission protocols are followed (e.g., using SSL and its underlying shared encryption keys), the test content can still be at risk at the student's testing workstation in the browser. Remote access programs can access the student's workstation and view and capture whatever content the student is viewing. If the student is taking an online test, then the questions presented and answers made can be easily harvested.

This type of theft has little in common with stealing downloaded test content as described in the previous section. In order to capture the entire content of an exam, the thief has to remain online during the length of the exam. In addition, if the test is a CAT or LOFT, the thief will not be able to capture all the questions during a single exam session; he or she will have to repeat the process across many students, exposing the act of piracy for long periods of time. Plus, only exam questions and student answers will be harvested and not other information, such as answer keys.

## Internet Test Administration

The ubiquitous and inviting nature of the Internet encourages educational testing programs to administer high-stakes tests as conveniently and widely as possible, even exams with important consequences, without proper security in place. Often this is done in ignorance, believing that most students do not or will not cheat or that the existing security measures are effective. Unfortunately, it is a difficult process to determine how much cheating (or test content theft) is going on and who is doing it. It may be weeks or months before an obvious security breach occurs or comes to light.

As an example of the Internet allure, there are even models, termed "unproctored" online testing, that justify the wide distribution of an important online exam without security (Tippens et al., 2006). The most prominent model is widely used in the industrial/organizational psychology field, where job applicants take a screening exam to hopefully qualify for an interview for a limited number of positions. This screening exam requires no authentication or identification of the applicant, nor is there any monitoring of the exam or protection of the test content. Scores obtained are used to separate those individuals who qualified for the next step, perhaps an interview, and those who did not. According to proponents of the model, it works because of the threat of a verification test that the qualifying candidate may have to take at a later stage in the interviewing process. The threat of a verification test is intended to discourage applicants from cheating on the screening exam. No research has been reported indicating that the frequency of cheating is less on an nonsecure online exam when a verification test may be used.

In some educational settings, the model described or simply relying on the honesty of students may seem very attractive. It is a likely scenario for a teacher to ask students to complete a midterm or final exam online at their home, or other Internet-enabled location, over the weekend, reminding them of the honor code of not cheating they had agreed to at the beginning of the term. Or an organization providing online courses may simply let the students take the midterm or final exam without security in place. Because students can view the course content at home or at work, it is tempting to allow them to take the test in the same way—without proper security. Many online universities have the mistaken assumption that only a small, "acceptable percentage" of students cheat in university courses and that the set of test scores can be generally trusted.

## Test Question Overexposure

New technology-enabled test designs such as CAT increase exposure rates inordinately for some questions (Folk & Smith, 2002). Computerized adaptive tests select questions from the same pool of items when each new examinee takes the test. This results in both security advantages and disadvantages. The disadvantage is that many adaptive tests use algorithms that select the "best" questions to present to a test taker at any particular ability level. These questions are considered best by the program because they provide the most information about the test taker's ability when answered. If a question is psychometrically better than another for a subset of students, it may be selected more often than other questions and therefore becomes overexposed compared to other questions. The increased frequency becomes apparent, and such questions are targeted, stolen, and shared more often as a result (Davey & Nering, 2002). The security advantage of a CAT is that the majority of items are exposed less often than they would have been had the test been administered as a fixed-length traditional exam.

Item overexposure also occurs for test designs that use a cutscore to determine a pass/fail decision. Items continue to be presented to students even after a pass or fail decision has been made. With such TBTs, it is possible to determine when the test taker has answered enough questions to decide if the test has been passed or failed. At the point at which the pass/fail decision is certain, there is simply no reason to continue to present questions to the test taker. Every instance of item presentation after that point is an instance of overexposure.

Finally, our test session design may contribute to item overexposure. Most TBT engines have incorporated a feature of marking an item for later review. An item marked in this way can be revisited at a later point in the exam, usually at the end. This feature is similar to what a test taker is able to do if given a paper-and-pencil test, which is to move from page to page at will and review any question as often as desired. The security problem results from the fact that the test taker is able to manage a particular subset of questions that he or she can memorize in a more organized and efficient way during the exam. If these questions were reviewed and memorized at the end of an exam, it is much easier to leave the testing center and recall the items. Green (1988) recognized this potential security problem and suggested that for technology-based tests, the ability to return to previous questions can be removed. For some test designs, such as CATs, the ability to return and review questions is not recommended and is usually prohibited.

It is clear that test designs, test volumes, poor security practices, and other influences contribute to overexposure, exposure imbalances, and ultimately to disclosure to other students, who use the information to cheat on exams. Item exposure, overexposure, and disclosure are important topics that have not been researched and are not well understood. Exposure balancing among items on CATs has been researched and published extensively (e.g., Chen, Lei, & Liao, 2008; Hetter & Sympson, 1997; Stocking & Lewis, 1998).

**Testing Center Networks**

Testing center models developed in the late 1980s to accommodate the needs of technology-based testing modes. Existing educational institutions did not have (and, some would argue, still do not have) the capability to provide testing synchronously to a large number of students. The testing center models were developed to solve this general limitation, providing relatively close-by locations to which a student could travel and take the test. Typically, each center has a few workstations and a test administrator/proctor to provide intake process and security. Students can access a website or call a number to check for nearby locations and space availability and to schedule and pay for an exam. The testing center network model has worked well for educational admissions testing.

The security challenge occurs with testing center models when a conflict of interest exists. Some testing centers exist within the walls of educational institutions (e.g., Sylvan Learning Centers), and the educational centers in general have worked hard to create a barrier between the testing center activities and the learning or training activities. However, it is clear that an education center would benefit with additional business if it could show that its students perform better on tests after getting educational assistance from the other side of their business. Test administrators and proctors may receive or feel organizational pressure to "look the other way" when a security violation occurs or, worse yet, to inappropriately assist the student during the exam. Often, in educational settings, particularly in schools when paper-and-pencil assessments are given, teachers are assigned the task of monitoring the students during the exam. In testing centers, a student's teacher or instructor may be given the proctoring responsibility.

Testing centers, particularly those established as so-called franchised models, use part-time, voluntary, and inexperienced proctors to monitor the students. These proctors may not be able to recognize appropriate identification documents or may not understand the security rules of testing. In addition, they may not feel compelled to do anything if they see an infraction.

### Terminology and General Security Principles Test Fraud: Cheating and Test Theft

There are two distinct types of test fraud in high-stakes testing. *Cheating*, which is often used incorrectly as a synonym for all test fraud, is any effort that produces a test score higher than what is earned, either by oneself or on behalf of others. The act of *test theft* (or test piracy) is not concerned about obtaining a higher score but has as its goal the capture of some or all of the test content, including the items, the answers, and any other data (e.g., graphics) associated with the question. The theft or piracy of test content occurs for the purpose of sharing with or selling to others who will then use the preknowledge of test questions in order to cheat.

Test fraud is not always perpetrated by the examinee or even with his or her awareness. Much test fraud is managed and conducted by others, particularly in education, where the perpetrators may be teachers, principals, or other officials. In addition, many test takers may even be unaware that they are receiving inappropriate help or using preknowledge of actual test questions or that using such preknowledge is actually cheating.

### General Security Terminology

The terms "risk," "threat," "vulnerability," "breach," and others should be used carefully and precisely in order to understand and respond to security problems in educational high-stakes testing. This section provides a brief definition of each term along with examples.

I like the definition of *security* provided by Wikipedia (Wikipedia, 2013), which is, "Security is the degree of resistance to, or protection from, harm. It applies to any vulnerable and valuable asset." For educational high-stakes testing, the "vulnerable and valuable assets" referred to would be test content and test scores. Another point from the definition is that test security may only provide resistance to harm or damage and not total protection. Often, a security effort can be deemed successful if it reduces the likelihood of theft or cheating rather than preventing all of it.

A *threat* is a potential source of harm, such as the possibility of hacking into a scoring system by a student or company or copying by one student from another. An educational testing program should be aware of the threats and design the security system to thwart the more dangerous of them. Threats are divided into those for cheating and those for test theft. These are listed and described in more detail in a later section.

A *vulnerability* is a weakness in a test security system that can be exploited by a threat. All security systems for a high-stakes test have strengths and weaknesses. It is important for a testing program to be aware of the vulnerabilities or weaknesses and take efforts to strengthen them.

A *breach* is a successful attack by a threat and causes damage to the program. One student was able to copy from another. A test booklet has been stolen from a locked cabinet. A proctor helped a student cheat. Each breach causes damage, large or small.

*Risk* is a more complex term than the other three. Risk is defined as a combination of the likelihood of a breach and the likely amount of damage from the breach. High risk would be a very likely, very damaging breach, such as the successful theft of the entire test content. Low risk might be judged that single students will use a cheat sheet to cheat on an exam. Naturally, a testing program should use a limited security budget to target the threats that might result in a high-risk breach and spend less effort on those that are low risk. Risk is rarely calculated mathematically; however, most programs are aware of the more serious threats and the damage they might cause if successful. A reasonable allocation of security resources to protect against those threats is easily made.

These terms are used in the same way regardless of whether the tests are technology based or paper and pencil.

### Security Threats With Technology-Based Testing

In fighting test fraud, and in any other area where security is needed, half of the battle strategy is knowing what the dangers are. The other half is being able to do something about them. Security threats have been divided and categorized in many ways (Cizek, 1999; Cohen & Wollack, 2006), such as whether technology is used, whether the security problem occurred before or during testing, whether the test taker was involved or someone else, and so on. The definition of a threat was given earlier in this chapter as a potential source of danger. There are actually a large, perhaps unlimited number of specific threats, but they can be categorized more simply. Table 11.1 provides a list of six general cheating threats. Each of these categories is an inappropriate and perhaps illegal method that students and others use to increase a test score beyond what is deserved or earned. The table also provides the author's ranking as to the seriousness of the threat. The use of the ranking is to provide a first basis for evaluating the risk associated with a threat and subsequently allocating resources for defense or countermeasures.

Table 11.2 lists the stealing threats. There are six general categories of ways that individuals use to capture test content for the purposes of sharing with others, perhaps for financial gain.

*Risk Analysis.* For a particular testing program, after understanding the threats, both general (e.g., Tables 11.1 and 11.2) and specific, to the program, a risk analysis should be conducted to determine how to allocate security resources. An example may help to illustrate this point. A college instructor wants to provide the midterm exam to her students online but is worried about cheating. She isn't concerned that the students will use the textbook or Internet resources to help answer the questions because she has specifically encouraged the use of those materials. She is most concerned that a student will have someone else take the exam for him or her. The teacher would like to use the midterm exam in future semesters for the same course and wants to keep the material from being taken and shared with others. The cheating threat she is most concerned about is proxy test taking; the theft threats are those that capture the questions electronically using a camera or the copy/paste functionality in a browser. After the risk analysis, the professor needs to decide how each of those threats should be dealt with. Is there a way to neutralize or prevent the threat altogether? How can the students be deterred from using these methods? How can attempts to cheat or steal content be quickly detected and stopped? What vulnerabilities in her testing system will the students exploit? Figure 11.1 provides a high-level diagram of the options available to the professor once the threat has been identified and determined to have the potential for significant damage to the program.

Table 11.1 Types of Cheating

| Security Threat | Education Threat Ranking[6] | Description | Reasons for Ranking |
|---|---|---|---|
| Using Preexposure to Test Content | 1 | Obtaining and using information about the test, test questions and answers, before taking the test. | Low risk of detection. Exact content may be available. Difficult to tell final result from that of an honest test taker. |
| Using a Proxy to Take the Test | 2 | Hiring an expert or using a friend to take the test by proxy. | Medium risk of detection. Guaranteed higher score. May be expensive. |
| Receiving Help from a Person at the Testing Center, School or Other Location | 3 | Receiving answers to test questions from a person during or after the test. The person may be a proctor or simply allowed by the proctor to be in the room. Coaching by a knowledgeable person present, such as a teacher or instructor. Changing the responses on answer sheets after the test concludes. | Expert assistance. May involve additional collusion by proctors or administration staff. |
| Using Inappropriate Aids During the Test | 4 | Using one or more of many available inappropriate test aids that are used to provide assistance with test content or answers. | A variety of aids is available, most of which are very difficult to detect. Information may not be accurate. Moderate risk of detection. |
| Hacking Into Scoring Database to Raise Test Scores | 5 | Accessing the score database illegally and changing the score. | Low frequency and likelihood. Requires technical ability. Well-protected IT systems are difficult to access. |
| Copying from Another Person During the Test | 6 | Watching another person take the same test and copying the answers he or she provides. | Almost ineffective for technology-based tests, where usually only one question at a time is on the screen. Questions are also randomized. |

Table 11.2 Types of Test Theft

| Security Threat | Education Threat Ranking | Description | Reasons for Ranking |
|---|---|---|---|
| Capturing the Downloaded Test File | 1 | Capturing and decrypting downloaded test file or files during transmission. May benefit from collusion with someone at a testing location. | Exact content is captured. Easily made available and sold over the Internet. Quick turnaround. Low risk of detection. |
| Using Photography | 2 | Using a camera or cell phone to take a picture of each question during the test. | Exact content is captured. Medium risk of detection. Often will need collusion of proctor. |
| Electronically Copying the Test Session | 3 | Using Copy/Paste functionality or a digital recording device (e.g., TIVO) to capture the test material to a separate file. | Exact content is captured. Requires technology expertise. Medium risk of detection. May need collusion of testing center personnel. |

(*Continued*)

Table 11.2 (Continued)

| Security Threat | Education Threat Ranking | Description | Reasons for Ranking |
|---|---|---|---|
| Memorizing the Questions | 4 | Using memorization skills as test questions appear. Usually several individuals are assigned different blocks of questions. | Inexact content. Requires multiple confederates. Difficult to detect. |
| Transcribing the Questions Orally | 5 | Transcribing the text of the questions to an audio recording device during the test. | Easy to detect. Requires collusion of proctors or test administrators. |
| Colluding With an Insider | 6 | Obtaining a copy of the exam directly from a person working at the testing program or test administration services company. | Low frequency. Lack of opportunity for most thieves. |

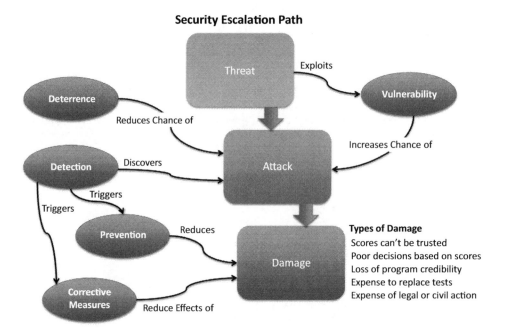

**Figure 11.1** Relationships between threats and methods to mitigate the threats

The professor has already completed a risk analysis and indicated the threats that lead to the greatest risk to her tests. She now needs to determine how to mitigate those threats. She can provide up-front deterrence, such as displaying rules, having students sign honor codes, and listing consequences. She can also put in place mechanisms to detect an attack, such as data forensics and monitors (e.g., proctors). If cheating or theft is discovered, she can move quickly to stop it and take corrective action to repair the damage. These latter steps will quickly reduce the impact of the attack. The next section lists several categories of methods that provide deterrent, detection, and corrective and preventative actions.

A testing program should be aware of the sensitizing effects of a breach on the risk analysis. Usually after a security breach, the source of the successful attack elevates that threat to the top position. This is illustrated by what happened after a man was caught in early 2012 taking the SAT on behalf of more than three dozen other individuals, some of them women. The College Board, the owner of the SAT, acknowledged the breach and quickly put in place measures to make sure that such an incident would be less likely in the future. With the proper government agencies, it began legal action against the proxy test taker. It changed the SAT policy and restricted a student's ability to take the exam to his or her own school. Stronger authentication procedures were also put in place. There are at least two lessons to be learned from this example. The first is that a risk analysis prior to the breach would likely have discovered the threat and instituted the procedures preventing the breach that did occur. The second lesson is that the breach and resulting actions by College Board may have left other threats unattended for a period of time. A risk analysis, conducted periodically, covering all threats including new ones would insure a balanced and more effective approach to managing test security.

### Solutions to Cheating and Theft Threats for Technology-Based Tests

Successfully combating the cheating on tests and test piracy is a multilevel activity. To use an obvious example, money in a bank is safeguarded at several levels. These levels include careful access controls and rules (e.g., username and strong passwords), keeping money in a strong safe, quick response by authorities in case of an attempted robbery, and criminal action after perpetrators are caught. In addition, the money may be "marked" in some way to detect when it is used to purchase goods; everyone working at the bank and law enforcement agencies is trained in what to do in the case of a potential or real robbery. The banking industry knows that a single security measure isn't going to reduce the frequency and success of attempted robberies; in fact, weak security would actually encourage more attempted thefts. The situation is no different with test security. A single security measure (e.g., proctoring) is not going to stop cheating or attempts to steal test content. In fact, just the opposite is true; relying too much on a single solution may actually increase attempts and their success. Several layers of security are necessary to protect test assets, which include the test content and the test scores. Each threat listed in Tables 11.1 and 11.2 can be countered or minimized in many ways. For example, consider a student who is paid by a test preparation company to memorize test questions during a computerized test administration. After the test, she attempts to recall as many questions and as much content for each question as possible. This is a challenging threat to deal with, as it is very hard to detect while it is occurring, but it can be defended against in several ways. Here is a partial list of things a testing program can do to discourage or prevent theft through memorization.

### *Ways to Mitigate Impact of the Threat of Test Theft through Memorization*

1. A policy prohibiting such behavior should be drafted and approved by the organization.
2. The policy, along with consequences for disobedience, should be read and agreed to by the student prior to the beginning of the exam. If the rule is not agreed to, the exam will simply not launch.

3. Test and item designs that make memorization and recall more challenging should be a routine part of item- and test-development practices.
4. A person memorizing exam content will not display normal patterns of responses and latencies of responding and may visit the review page more often than normal. Data forensics monitoring during the exam and post hoc may be effective in identifying a person memorizing questions.
5. Policies that provide authority to a trained and trusted proctor allowing the test to be suspended or cancelled would be effective.
6. The ability to mark and review questions during the exam can be disabled, reducing the opportunity for students to see questions many times or mass questions of particular content.
7. Legal action (civil or criminal) can be taken each time this type of behavior is detected and confirmed.

All of these actions, some of them, or additional ones can and should be taken if the threat of memorizing questions is judged to be very damaging and needs to be discouraged or stopped. It should be noted that most of these security solutions would not be available or possible if the student were taking a paper-and-pencil test.

This memorization example is approached in principle no differently from any other threat: Evaluate the potential damage (i.e., risk) from a successful attack by the source of the threat and then apply several layers of security resources appropriate to the level of risk.

The goal of this chapter is not to provide a specific solution or set of solutions to each threat but to educate regarding the various threats, point out the value of evaluating risk, and provide a framework for organizing security resources. This section has provided that framework, describing the various types and levels of solutions. Some solutions will be broad and encompassing (e.g., program security plan); others may be targeted at a specific threat (e.g., forensics similarity analysis).

Where can a program find recommended security solutions? Several U.S. and international organizations have provided guidelines or best practices specifically related to test security, many of which apply directly to technology-based testing. Here is a partial list that also includes a recent reference text (Wollack & Fremer, 2013) devoted entirely to test security:

- *Guidelines for Computer-Based Tests and Interpretations* (American Psychological Association, 1986)
- *Standards for Educational and Psychological Testing* (American Educational Research Association, American Psychological Association, and National Council on Measurement in Education, 1999)
- *Certification Testing on the Internet* (National Organization for Competency Assurance, 2001)
- *Ethical Principles of Psychologists and Code of Conduct*. Principle 9.11 Maintaining Test Security. Retrieved from www.apa.org/ethics/code2002.html (American Psychological Association, 2002)
- *Guidelines for Computer-Based Testing* (The Association of Test Publishers, 2002)
- *Guidance for Conformity to ANSI/ISO/IEC 17024: Requirement for Certification Program Security* (American National Standards Institute, 2006)
- *Test Security Standards* (Caveon Test Security, 2009)

- *Operational Best Practices for Statewide Large-Scale Assessment Programs* (The Council of Chief State School Officers and Association of Test Publishers, 2013)
- *Handbook of Test Security* (Wollack & Fremer, 2013)
- *The Security of Tests, Examinations, and Other Assessments* (International Test Commission, 2014)

These standards, best practices, and guidelines may be helpful as a testing program creates a security plan to deal with the threats it determines have the most potential for significant damage. Another recent source of security best practices for educational testing was published as a result of a symposium hosted by the U.S. National Center for Education Statistics (2012). The symposium focused on the prevention and detection of "irregularities" as well as how to respond in the event of a successful breach. It also included a section devoted specifically to technology-based tests.

As a more general perspective, there are several layers of security solutions that can be used to protect technology-based test content and the test scores they produce. See Foster (2013) for a review. The following sections present a general description of the various levels of security available to testing programs and a few examples to illustrate the range of solutions. Where available, references are provided to direct the reader to more detail and a broader set of solutions within that category.

### Organizational and Policy Solutions

It is axiomatic that great security begins with great planning. At a minimum, a testing organization needs a security plan, usually in the form of a handbook (see Fitzgerald & Mulkey, 2013 for more details). The plan would be signed off on by stakeholders and be revised regularly. It would include security policies that could be referenced when needed. The plan might provide for a security manager or director, along with a security committee to revise the plan and to review security incidents when they occur. The plan would provide details on how to effectively deal with the high-risk threats to program test security and to respond quickly to breaches when they occur.

Security planning would benefit from periodic independent test security audits, the results of which would indicate the program's security strengths and weaknesses. The program's plan could be adjusted to fix the vulnerabilities pointed out by the audit.

### Legal Solutions

Testing programs need to be aware of the value of legal solutions in the area of test security. This may take the form of civil or criminal action taken when a student or school administrator cheats on an exam. Or the program may need legal support for decisions such as score invalidations due to cheating. Setting up online student agreements, including the agreement not to disclose test content, would benefit from a legal review. Semko and Hunt (2013) review these benefits of legal support, among others. They also include an informative review of recent court cases involving test security issues and provide a perspective on how to better approach critical decisions, particularly score invalidation. Semko and Hunt also describe the legal remedies for test content that has been stolen, particularly invoking the provisions under copyright laws. They continue that topic with a description of successful efforts to protect a testing program's intellectual property, the test content.

### Test Administration Security Solutions

Proctoring, or monitoring of students while taking an exam, has never been an exact science. Often, volunteers are used in educational testing situations. If volunteers are not available or cannot be used, part-time, temporary workers are hired. They usually receive minimal training. Most recently, in statewide assessments, teachers serving as proctors have been found to have influenced student answers directly during the exam and afterward by tampering with the answer sheets. Clearly, better proctoring models are needed.

One new and increasingly popular proctoring model (Foster, Mattoon, & Shearer, 2009) is online proctoring, which involves trained and certified proctors viewing the students remotely and in real time through webcams. The proctors can generally detect the same types of efforts to cheat and steal test content that the in-classroom proctor can see but have the advantage of being completely objective relative to the test outcome. They can make decisions that a traditional proctor may not. Online proctors in some monitoring systems have the additional advantage of being able to control the student's exam software. That is, they can pause or suspend a test. If paused, the proctor will require the student to acknowledge the issue, put away any materials that are inappropriate, and acknowledge that further misbehavior would result in the possible cancellation of the exam or invalidation of the test score.

For technology-based tests, special care needs to take place to make sure that information is protected while files are downloaded and stored at a testing center server. In addition, for online tests and computerized tests, test content in transit needs to be encrypted and protected following best practices of information systems security.

### Test-Development Solutions

There are not many threats that occur during the activities of item and test development, but one is clearly apparent. Subject matter experts who author and/or review items may be exposed to the entire pool of items. More often, those review and authoring sessions rely on remote workers and conferencing technologies. Email systems may be used to send files back and forth. It is during all of these stages that the item pool is vulnerable to being stolen by one of the subject matter experts. A breach from this insider threat is a rare occurrence, but the results would be very damaging.

Routine background checks should be conducted on all contractors or employees involved in authoring or reviewing items. In addition, strong nondisclosure agreements should be in place. On-site authoring and review meetings would be better at making sure that test items were not exposed in a manner that can be captured to a personal laptop or memory stick. If contractors need to access a server remotely, good access-control methods should be in place, including usernames and passwords as well as login and logout times.

### Test- and Item-Design Solutions

Test designs that reduce exposure levels of items are better suited to counter threats of cheating and theft. A CAT item-selection algorithm can be very effective in discouraging theft and making limited preknowledge superfluous. Test-design considerations include the item selection method, the size of the item pool supporting all test designs, test-stopping rules, test time limits, use of breaks, mark-and-review feature in the testing system, and others.

Item designs that protect the content from theft and cheating are rare. In general, items that require the test taker to do more than recall a fact from memory may be more difficult to steal and share, but there is no research to support the assertion. Randomization of options for multiple-choice questions (plus randomization of the order of questions) has emerged as a recommended solution to prevent the threat of copying by one student from another during the exam. Impara and Foster (2006, p. 102) recommend that

> when there is no logical or numerical order, then response choices should be arranged randomly. Moreover, when multiple versions of a test are used in the same testing window (or when computerized testing is being done), the response choices can be randomized within and across test versions.

The innovative discrete-option multiple-choice (DOMC)[7] format can be used to protect test content and discourage cheating (Foster & Miller, 2009). The DOMC differs from the traditional multiple-choice format in that only one option is randomly picked and displayed at a time, along with YES and NO buttons. The student simply has to indicate if the option displayed is the correct one or not. The questions may continue to display options until the student answers the question correctly or incorrectly. Foster and Miller (2009) results showed that only about 2.54 options of those available were displayed on the average, with that average being less for more difficult questions. In addition to the obvious exposure advantage, students surveyed indicated that the question makes cheating and sharing items more difficult.

### Information Security Solutions

Information systems for all organizations are under constant attack by hackers and others. Every organization, including those associated with testing programs, understands that its information systems (e.g., networks, servers, workstations, users, communication systems, etc.) need to remain strong and up to -date. Companies exist that provide audits of an organization's information system security, including a service that attempts to breach current defenses. Reports from these efforts detail the strengths and weaknesses of a particular system and recommend changes where needed. As technology is changing more rapidly all the time, the need to stay current in this area is hard to overstate. Testing programs need to rely on competent contractors and have competent IT employees on staff.

Testing programs that use contract service providers for test development, test administration, and so forth need to evaluate the contractors' information systems security procedures.

### Internet Monitoring Solutions

It is important for testing programs to make sure that their test content is not being shared on the Internet, either in published form or through informal chats and forums. Visiting a popular website where students gather to talk about a test is important to make sure that question content is not discussed. If test content is discovered, the program can inform the webmaster that the information on the site is copyrighted and ask him or her to remove it. According to Zervos (2014), that simple act is often effective—most webmasters are happy to comply and are more careful to screen such content in the future.

For sites that benefit financially from selling or sharing inappropriate test information, more effort might be needed, such as sending cease-and-desist letters. If the test content has been properly copyrighted, a website may be in violation of the Digital Millennium Copyright Act, leading to further legal options. These options may be limited if the website is owned by companies outside the United States.

### *Data Analysis Solutions*

Data forensics analyses of student answers are often used for the statistical analysis of paper-and-pencil test results. The most common is the erasure analysis. Scanners can detect erasures on an answer sheet along with the final filled-in answer. If wrong-to-right erasures greatly outnumber right-to-wrong erasures, beyond a reasonable probability, the set of test results becomes suspect. Copying indices comparing the answer patterns of students sitting near each other during an exam are also able to indicate the presence of cheating.

For technology-based tests, erasure analyses are not possible, but patterns of similarity can be detected, perhaps indicating copying or collusion. An aberrant test result can also be detected if the pattern of responding is very different from the usual patterns, contingent on ability. Response time for each item and the total exam is a relatively unique measure for technology-based tests. Response time analyses can detect if a person is uninterested in or unmotivated to perform well on the exam. It can also provide evidence of aberrance to strangeness in the results. Cluster analysis of responses can detect if pairs or groups of students are colluding at a particular location or during a window for an online exam. This analysis is also helpful in detecting the operation of a proxy testing service.

Data forensics measures are useful to confirm that a security breach has occurred or to detect an unknown breach. Some programs run these statistical procedures as a matter of course, as a defense against unspecified attack. There is a U.S. national conference strictly devoted to the topic. Data forensics analyses that detect a problem in a set of data are not able to determine if the cause of the problem is actually cheating or test theft. Other explanations are available, such as student fatigue, lack of interest, illness, and so on. The focus on data forensics activities is not to detect test fraud but to determine which scores can be trusted and which should not be trusted.

With many of these solutions in place, the threats are mostly neutralized. The persistent cheaters and thieves may be successful, but by and large they will not be. However, new technologies or procedures could be developed to bypass security measures. The detection system, particularly the data forensics work, should be able to detect any new, unrecognized threats and alert the program. Investigative work should be able to determine the nature of the new threat.

## Conclusions

Technology-based tests have introduced some unique security concerns but, at the same time, have solved some. The advantages gained by using technology to administer exams are significant, including immediate scoring, more convenient testing locations, more efficient tests, better measurement of skills, and lower costs in many uses. These advances come at a time when those who would perpetrate test fraud have new technology tools as well, such as small, hard-to-detect digital photography and the Internet to help cheat and to share test content broadly. The advantages of technology for testing outweigh the disadvantages, so we move forward, considering now how to use smartphones and tablets as part of the assessment landscape. Because of all of these changes, along with the increased use of tests for educational accountability, the pressure to maintain good test security and even improve it is tremendous. Relying on methods that worked for decades for paper-and-pencil tests will simply not be sufficient. This chapter provides an overview of the security threats associated with technology-based tests and a model for setting up an effective defense. Standards, best practices, and guidelines for test security provided by industry organizations and associations will be helpful in this effort.

## Notes

1 One mostly ignored other "mode" of test administration is oral, when the test is presented orally by a test examiner to the student. There are some exams that still use this manual one-on-one method, although today's computers are capable of the delivery of oral-based items to the students.

2 At least one testing company downloads test content to a USB thumb drive that is then physically taken to and used at a testing workstation to provide the content and control for the test administration event. The process can be referred to as a manual-assist network, as the test taker needs to bring the thumb drive to the testing workstation.

3 The test content may be sent from servers belonging to an organization to which the testing program has contracted to assist in the test-administration process.

4 The combined paper-based and orally administered Stanford-Binet intelligence test is one that has been administered "adaptively" for many decades, long before the first CAT was introduced (1905).

5 Of course, a thief can intercept a shipment of test booklets, but the method of theft, hacking, is specific to electronic shipment, is peculiar to electronic test administration, and must be evaluated and countered.

6 These rankings are the author's and should be considered personal opinion. The ranking is for technology-based testing in education overall, not for individual uses of tests within education.

7 The DOMC item is patented by the author and is available by license.

## References

American Educational Research Association, American Psychological Association, & National Council on Measurement in Education. (1999). *Standards for educational and psychological testing*. Washington, DC: American Educational Research Association.

American National Standards Institute. (2007). *Guidance for conformity to ANSI/ISO/IEC 17024 requirements for certification program security*. Retrieved from http://publicaa.ansi.org/sites/apdl/Documents/Conformity%20 Assessment/Personnel%20Certifier%20Accreditation/Documents%20related%20to%20accreditation%20 under%20ANSI-ISO-IEC%2017024/Public%20Documents/ANSI-PCAC-GI-504.pdf.

American Psychological Association. (1986). *Guidelines for computer-based tests and interpretations*. Washington, DC: American Psychological Association.

American Psychological Association. (2002). *Ethical principles of psychologists and code of conduct*. Principle 9.11 Maintaining Test Security. Retrieved from www.apa.org/ethics/code2002.html

Association of Test Publishers. (2002). *Guidelines for computer-based testing*. Washington, DC: Association of Test Publishers, 2000.

Binet, A., & Simon, Th. A. (1905). Méthode nouvelle pour le diagnostic du niveau intellectuel des anormaux. *L'Année Psychologique, 11*, 191–244.

Caveon Test Security. (2009). *Test security standards*. Midvale, UT: Author.

Chen, S.-Y., Lei, P., & Liao, W.-H. (2008). Controlling item exposure and test overlap on the fly in computerized adaptive testing. *British Journal of Mathematical and Statistical Psychology, 61*, 471–492.

Cizek, G. J. (1999). *Cheating on tests: How to do it, detect it, and prevent it*. Mahwah, NJ: Lawrence Erlbaum Associates.

Cohen, A. S., & Wollack, J. A. (2006). Test administration, security, scoring, and reporting. In R. L. Brennan (Ed.), *Educational measurement* (4th ed., pp. 355–386). Westport, CT: American Council on Education/Praeger.

The Council of Chief State School Officers & Association of Test Publishers. (2013). *Operational best practices for statewide large-scale assessment programs*. Washington, DC: The Council of Chief State School Officers and Association of Test Publishers.

Davey, T., & Nering, M. (2002). Controlling item exposure and maintaining item security. In C. N. Mills, M. T. Potenza., J. J. Fremer, & W. C. Ward (Eds.), *Computer-based testing: Building the foundations for future assessments* (pp. 165–191). Mahwah, NJ: Lawrence Erlbaum Associates.

Drasgow, F. (2002). The work ahead: A psychometric infrastructure for computerized adaptive tests. In C. N. Mills, M. T. Potenza., J. J. Fremer, & W. C. Ward (Eds.), *Computer-based testing: Building the foundations for future assessments* (pp. 1–35). Mahwah, NJ: Lawrence Erlbaum Associates.

Drasgow, F., Luecht, R. M., & Bennett, R. (2006) Technology and testing. In R. L. Brennan (Ed.), *Educational measurement* (4th ed., pp. 471–455). Westport, CT: American Council on Education and Praeger Publishers.

Foster, D. (2013). Security issues in technology-based testing. In J. A. Wollack & J .J. Fremer (Eds.), *Handbook of test security* (pp. 39–83). New York: Routledge.

Foster, D. F., & Zervos, C. (2006). *The big heist: Internet braindump sites*. Poster presented at the annual conference of the Association of Test Publishers, Orlando, FL.

Green, B. F. (1988). Construct validity of computer-based tests. In H. Wainer & H. I. Braun (Eds.), *Test validity* (pp. 77–86). New York: Lawrence Erlbaum Associates.

Hetter, R. D., & Sympson, J. B. (1997). Item exposure control in the CAT-ASVAB. In W. A. Sands, B. K. Waters, & J. R. McBride (Eds.), *Computerized adaptive testing: From inquiry to operation* (pp. 141–144). Washington, DC: American Psychological Association.

Impara, J. C., & Foster, D. F. (2006). Item and test development strategies to minimize test fraud. In S. M. Downing & T. M. Haladyna (Eds.), *Handbook of test development* (pp. 91–114). Mahwah, NJ: Lawrence Erlbaum Associates.

International Test Commission. (2014). *The security of tests, examinations, and other assessments.* Retrieved from www.intestcom.org/guidelines/index.php

Maynes, D. (2009). *Caveon speaks out on IT exam security: The last five years.* Retrieved from http://caveon.com/articles/it_exam_security.htm

National Center for Educational Statistics. (2012). *Testing integrity symposium.* Proceedings retrieved from http://nces.ed.gov/pubsearch/pubsinfo.asp?pubid=2013454

National Organization for Competency Assurance (NOCA). (2001). *Certification testing on the Internet.* Washington, DC: Author.

Stocking, M. L., & Lewis, C. (1998). Controlling item exposure condition on ability in computerized adaptive testing. *Journal of Educational and Behavioral Statistics, 23,* 57–75.

Tippens, N. T., Beaty, J., Drasgow, F., Gibson, W. M., Pearlman, K., Segall, D. O., & Shepherd, W. (2006). Unproctored Internet testing in employment settings. *Personnel Psychology, 59*(1), 189–225.

Wikipedia. (2013). Security. Found at http://en.wikipedia.org/wiki/Security

Wollack, J. A., & Fremer, J. J. (2013). *Handbook of test security.* New York: Routledge.

# Commentary on Chapters 8–11: Technology and Test Administration
## *The Search for Validity*

**Kurt F. Geisinger**

The four preceding chapters by Chernyshenko and Stark; Foster; Luecht; and Stone, Laitusis, and Stone all deal with advances in technology and testing, especially test administration. Essentially, all are predicated on the need for test validity. That is, the goals of all four chapters do, at closer or more distant levels, relate to the need to be able to interpret scores resulting from an assessment appropriately. The four chapters, of course, address this most significant concern from very different perspectives, and all relate to the advance of technology.

At the 2014 International Test Commission biannual meetings in San Sebastian, Spain, about 50 professionals attended a 4-hour workshop on future issues in testing. Participants were asked how tests would be administered in 10 years, around 2024. Initially, no one responded, so the facilitator (the current author) directed the question to a specific participant with a long history of working in leadership positions in regard to computerized testing on both the Graduate Record Examination and the Certified Public Accountant tests, Dr. Craig Mills. Though somewhat reluctant to respond, Mills indicated that he expected that tests would be administered via tablets but cautioned that his answer was predicated on current technology and without conclusive knowledge of what the future would hold. His answer was top notch. The recent history of technological innovation reveals that predictions of the future are at best barely valid. An exemplar would be that of the Hayes Modem. Hayes Modem was the predominant modem company through the 1980s and early 1990s. This company was largely responsible for the development of the smart modem and was known for the quality of its workmanship; many modems today use technology based on what Hayes developed. Nevertheless, Hayes did not anticipate the capacity of modems to ever exceed a 2400 baud rate (through telephones), and in 1991, Supra Inc. introduced Supra-FAXModem 14400, a model that permitted baud rates of 14,400. Hayes experienced a steep decline in sales and finally declared bankruptcy in 1999. It can be seen that the future is hard to predict, especially when one technological development can upset one's well-informed prognostics, even by technological experts.

Each of the four preceding chapters has reviewed the recent past in regard to that chapter's theme, and the authors both describe and raise questions about current practice and needs for the future. A noteworthy credit to the chapter authors is that no chapter makes long-term predictions, since our aim is not to predict long into the future but to deal with issues that we face today and in the near future. Psychometricians in the field today, as well as those entering this exciting and rewarding field, must recognize that their work will change in the future and perhaps will continue to change ever more rapidly (Toffler, 1970).

The four chapters are described from the more general to the more specific, with Richard Luecht's chapter and the chapter by Chernyshenko and Stark being more general than the chapters by Foster and Stone and colleagues, both of which are more specific in scope. A presumption of all four chapters is that more and more tests in the future will be administered using technology, whether computer-based, tablet-based, or some other technology.

## The Four Chapters

Luecht traces the history of electronic testing from its beginnings in dedicated computer-based testing centers. Such centers were used by the two most significant first computerized tests: the Armed Forces Vocational Aptitude Battery (ASVAB) and the Graduate Record Examination (GRE). Today, these tests and many other admissions, licensure, and certification tests are administered by computers, and a great number of the states require part or all of their educational tests to be administered via computer or other technological devices. The two primary education consortia of the states developing Common Core assessments (PARCC and SBAC) are both planning to offer their tests of educational achievement (or accountability) via computers in the near future as this chapter is being written. Luecht provides a remarkable sense of the wide array of technological needs for operational administrations of such tests. Some readers may not know that there needs to be far more than software for test delivery and item analysis and other statistical analysis. Luecht offers a brief overview of the other systems needed, including item authoring, item banking, assessment delivery, score processing, and score reporting, among others. Some of these systems, like those related to digital data transmission, may not be known even to some experts in computer-based testing. He describes the need for complex databases that psychometricians and their technological support personnel need to understand so that the databases can serve multiple uses through restructuring. Perhaps the most valuable categorization provided in the chapter is the listing of the eight models of test delivery: preassembled linear tests, linear-on-the-fly examinations, item-level computer-adaptive tests, item-level stratified computer-adaptive tests, item-level sequential mastery tests, testlet-based computer-adaptive tests, testlet-based sequential mastery tests, and computer-adaptive multistage tests. The psychometric concerns with many of these models will likely drive psychometric research for at least the next decade. Some of this research will be theoretical, and other research will be more applied. Applied research may be deciding, for example, which model best meets the needs of specific testing programs. Luecht also makes the case that in the future, open-source software will be needed. Much as R has served a need for much statistical and psychometric analyses, this commenter agrees that the development of software for specialized uses will be expensive enough that open-source software would serve a significant balance for cost efficiency and utility.

Chernyshenko and Stark's chapter provides an introduction to the use of mobile devices to perform various psychological assessments. They define mobile devices as cell phones, tablets, and other truly portable devices. Specifically, desktop and even laptop computers were excluded. Their foci included both high-stakes and low-stakes assessments while considering three specific types of assessments: health assessments, learning assessments, and employment-selection assessments, referred to as mHealth, mLearning, and mWork, respectively. Of these, work assessment would appear to represent the highest stakes. Chernyshenko and Stark make an excellent case that tablets and perhaps even cell phones are wonderful devices, at least for lower-stakes assessments. Many physicians' offices now ask patients to complete a survey on a number of issues, including one's current health concerns, upon arriving at the physician's office. Why should these surveys not be performed prior to coming? Chernyshenko and Stark also provide a long listing of royalty-free measures that can be used diagnostically by psychologists, psychiatrists, and other physicians. Neuropsychological measures are also available for tablets and can be essentially self-administered and then interpreted by neuropsychologists. Computer-adaptive technology permits their use with some patients with mental health concerns and can even provide some self-monitoring steps. Yet the chapter authors do not believe that the tablets and other mobile devices are being used as fully as they could be; their technological strengths are not being fully utilized.

The use of these devices in mLearning permits assessments and monitoring of progress. Again, the author of the present review believes that these uses are perhaps best suited for formative purposes, whether for single students or whole classrooms, schools, or other groupings of students. In work settings, employment measures can be administered in either proctored or unproctored settings. Foster's chapter, discussed next in this review, provides clues about the interpretation and use of higher-stakes tests to ascertain that scores are valid, while Chernyshenko and Stark's chapter makes it clear that the administration of measures using these devices permits unparalleled assessments in one's natural environment, where one is likely to feel most at home. The chapter also describes the goals, strategies, and challenges of each of these uses of tests administered on mobile devices. It is clear, however, that a variety of research strategies are needed in regard to the administration of tests on mobile devices and that measures administered using different devices should be studied for equivalence. The reliability, validity, and fairness of such assessments also require further study, especially given that the experience using such devices may differ by groups.

The Foster chapter addresses questions of test security in a mobile testing environment where traditional proctoring is not generally possible. The chapter is a comprehensive but brief introduction to the need to ensure valid responding in tests, regardless of the stakes involved, and begins with a description of many kinds of tests from paper-and-pencil in-class tests through online tests and the security concerns. Effective unproctored online tests are more likely to be low-stakes tests. The present time period is one in which the nature and perhaps even the extent of cheating has increased. As pressures on school personnel rise when test results are used for accountability purposes, the tendency of educators to influence student responses inappropriately also increases. The theme of this chapter is that as new technology and techniques are being used to administer tests, new honesty threats are created. That is, new methods of cheating have emerged. For example, in windows (time frames) for which tests were administered to meet needs at fixed computer-based testing centers, people who took tests early in the window sometimes shared items with others. With differences across time zones, even when tests are administered on the same day, people who take the test in earlier time zones have provided information about the test to those taking the test at later (e.g., farther west) times. Sometimes test content is provided to others on websites, forcing test publishers to scan the Internet to determine if secure materials are being made inappropriately available. The probability of such exposure of test materials is made more likely as the number of times the item is used operationally increases, forcing test publishers to limit item exposure to test takers. If the Internet is used to transport test materials from a central test site to computer-based test centers, there is a possibility that the materials could be deliberately intercepted for devastating and invalidating purposes. This approach is simply test theft, the modern equivalent of breaking in to steal test materials. Nevertheless, more and more tests are being administered in "unproctored" online testing settings. In industry, unproctored assessments are typically screening measures that are taken prior to the possibility of an interview (Tippens, Beaty, Drasgow, Gibson, Pearlman, Segall, & Shepherd, 2006). Such assessments rarely mandate authentication or identification of the applicant and generally would require neither monitoring of the exam nor protection of the test content. In some educational settings, similar test administration procedures are followed, especially for lower-stakes tests. New techniques utilizing cameras and microphones for all test takers, with the microphone on throughout the assessment and the camera controlled by a distal proctor, are increasingly used but as yet rarely studied. Foster provides many approaches for reducing the ways that examinees can achieve inappropriate and invalid scores. What should be clear is that no one step can provide total security and that ongoing, informed procedures must be followed to reduce these risks, which literally have the possibility of invalidating scores in a broad-based manner. Test publishers are increasingly employing the techniques recommended by Foster.

The Stone, Laitusis, and Cook chapter focuses on the testing of individuals with disabilities, especially students with disabilities. The chapter traces the history of legislation as well as voluntary standards of practice that have permitted those with disabilities to access tests. They provide evidence that the population of students with disabilities is larger than many believe, indicating, for example, that in a California school testing, about 23% of test takers had disabilities and were given testing accommodations on that account. A point that they make several times relates to the belief that adaptive testing should, in principle, be a benefit for those individuals with disabilities in terms of their testing. Universal design is a general approach that has been developed in architecture to permit increased accessibility and is now being widely applied to test development and administration. The Assistive Technology Act of 2004 should help this process. A key is not permitting changes in testing procedure or accommodations that could impact the actual measurement of the construct being assessed. The approach taken by Stone and colleagues is that of differential psychology. They do not dichotomize people as those with disabilities and those without them but instead perceive continua along which people differ. As such, people vary in terms of how and how well they learn (strategically), how and how well they are able to express themselves and respond, and how and in what people choose to engage. The authors suggest that all these aspects are important in terms of accommodation. Therefore, one can imagine a reading test composed of pages from instruction manuals rather than fiction for students who are mostly interested in vocational concerns rather than college preparation.

Computer-based testing should be able to permit individual accommodations not only to meet legal and regulatory appropriateness but also to provide accommodations that permit people to be assessed as validly as possible. Standards for the assessment of individuals with disabilities are becoming more international as well, given that there are now standards for digital accessibility and Question and Test Interoperability (QTI) specifications that provide test-development and test-delivery vendors with standard XML language for describing questions and tests. In short, QTI provides a common language for authoring test items in a digital format (Stone et al., 2015, p. 15). Integration of universal design is the primary technique for so doing. Universal design should influence many aspects of test development and administration (including item development, platform development and use), test administration, test assembly, item selection (perhaps individualized), the nature of the questions implemented for specific students, and even score analysis. The chapter authors demonstrate, for example, that some students with learning disabilities (LD) may have strengths and weaknesses that differ from a typical model underlying the item-response theory upon which the test is built. The LD students may have strengths and weaknesses that differ from the population upon which the items were calibrated. Such responses may necessitate individualized or even special group performance interpretations. The perspective implied throughout the chapter is that appropriately testing students with disabilities includes more than simply providing accommodations. If the strategies provided in the chapter are followed, test scores and other results are much more likely to be validly interpreted.

## Summary and Future Directions

It is clear that psychometricians in the 21st century need to know a considerable amount about technology, including the different models that exist for providing tests that are built, delivered, scored, and analyzed technologically. To ensure that scores achieved are valid, much research will be required. Such research will need to compare different testing models and different technology to determine the comparability of scores. Some studies, for example, have found that taking a test on a laptop with the smaller screen and keyboard can make certain kinds of tests either slower or more difficult. Moreover, we must be certain that tablets (and other mobile devices) of different sizes and systems are comparable testing vehicles. Perhaps the most fundamental requirement for a valid score is that the person has taken the test in an honest manner. Some approaches to "beating the test" are not really dishonest, but they nevertheless negate the possibility of achieving a valid testing; when individuals memorize an essay and recall it on the test, that is not cheating per se, but it nevertheless does not provide a valid test of writing. Whether tests are fair to members of different groups, especially individuals with disabilities, needs to be determined via research. This concern relates to Messick's call for a review of the consequences of tests. (e.g., Messick, 1989). Other groups, such as those of low socioeconomic status (SES), immigrants, and individuals who have more limited access to technology, also need to be studied to see if technologically administered tests generate fair scores. There is much work to be performed, but that is what generates academic excitement. There is much learning to be had for all testing professionals, knowing that we cannot turn back the clock.

## References

Messick, S. (1989). Validity. In R. L. Linn (Ed.), *Educational measurement* (3rd ed., pp. 13–103). New York: American Council on Education and Macmillan.
Semko, J. A., & Hunt, R. (2013). Legal matters in test security. In J. A. Wollack & J. J. Fremer (Eds.), *Handbook of test security* (pp. 237–258). New York, Routledge.
Tippens, N. T., Beaty, J., Drasgow, F., Gibson, W. M., Pearlman, K., Segall, D. O., & Shepherd, W. (2006). Unproctored Internet testing in employment settings. *Personnel Psychology, 59*, 189–225.
Toffler, A. (1970). *Future shock*. New York: Bantam Books.
Zervos, C. (2014). Web administrators: The good, the bad and the ugly. Found at www.caveon.com/web-administrators-the-good-the-bad-and-the-ugly/

# 12

# From Standardization to Personalization
*The Comparability of Scores Based on Different Testing
Conditions, Modes, and Devices*

**Walter D. Way, Laurie L. Davis, Leslie Keng, and Ellen Strain-Seymour**

## Introduction

The logical progression of technology and the increased emphasis on fairness in testing are changing the traditional notions of standardized testing. Throughout its history, standardized testing has by definition implied a strict control over the testing formats and administration conditions. When multiple forms of tests are used, they are built to the same content and format specifications and the process of test equating is used to adjust for differences in form-to-form difficulty. Once a test has been developed and introduced, stability and consistency in structure and format over time are considered critical for meaningful longitudinal performance comparisons.

The introduction of computerized testing (also called computer-based and online testing in this chapter) in the late 20th century presented challenges to standardization because many testing programs that wished to introduce computerized testing were unable to offer it exclusively. The need to offer both computerized and paper-and-pencil versions of the same measures has been especially persistent in large-scale K–12 testing because of unevenness in available technology at the local school level (Bennett, 2003; Way & McClarty, 2012). Comparing scores and intended inferences across modes of administration has been shown to be challenging and is becoming even more complex as new technology-enhanced items (TEIs) are introduced into computer-based versions of tests (but not the corresponding paper versions) and as laptops and tablets become alternate input devices for assessment delivery.

Another evolution impacting large-scale standardized testing programs has been the increased participation of special populations, such as students with disabilities and English language learners. To better ensure that tests are accessible to these special populations, a continuum of testing adaptations is now offered, ranging from specially developed alternate assessments to modifications and accommodations of regular assessments. In particular, technology provides powerful new ways to design accessibility features and test administration accommodations for special-needs test takers. Although there is a large body of literature addressing questions related to how scores based on test administrations involving the use of these supports compare with test performance obtained under standard testing conditions, there are still many areas where findings are mixed and further research is needed (c.f., Laitusis, Buzick, Stone, Hansen, & Hakkinen, 2012; Pennock-Roman & Rivera, 2011).

In today's environment, standardized testing is more likely to be composed of a collection of testing variations than a single controlled venue. These variations are compelling because they can "personalize" the testing experience to the individual in ways that, ideally, maximize access to the content. Yet a multitude of variations in administration conditions may have unintended consequences if they alter the construct being measured. With technology advancing so quickly, it will be increasingly difficult for research about comparability of scores to keep up with the testing variations under which they will be obtained. How, then, should policymakers and testing professionals think about score comparability? Can broader inferences to inform decisions about testing variations be gleaned from existing research? Is there a sensible framework for considering comparability in this coming era of personalized testing? The purpose of this chapter is to address the comparability of test scores in the context of these evolving changes in the way large-scale testing is carried out.

There are four main sections to this chapter. We begin by discussing some background considerations related to the topic of test score comparability. Next, we review and discuss the rich research literature that has evolved over the past four decades addressing the comparability of scores between computer and paper test administration and between accommodated and nonaccommodated testing conditions. We then examine several emerging score comparability issues, in particular those associated with rapid advancements in technology such as the use of technology-enhanced items and administration using digital devices. Finally, we consider some principles and strategies for moving forward as large-scale testing programs evolve and change with the times.

## Background Considerations

Two consortia in the United States have developed assessments to measure the Common Core State Standards, and both of these consortia are directly confronting issues related to score comparability. The Smarter Balanced Assessment Consortium (SBAC) and the Partnership for Assessment of Readiness for College and Careers (PARCC) have each set forth hardware guidelines for their online tests that include desktop computers, laptop computers, and tablet computers. Each allows either keyboards or touch-screens as input devices for students responding to the tests. In addition, both consortia provide paper versions of their tests, even though their intention is to eventually offer online administrations only. Each has ambitious policies for offering technology-based accessibility features and accommodations as part of their online assessments. How should these consortia think about comparability under these circumstances?

Broadly speaking, there are two questions that focus consideration of comparability issues. First, does altering the mode or device used for the administration change the construct that is being assessed? Second, does altering the mode or device used for the assessment introduce construct-irrelevant variance? If the latter is true, technology, psychometric, training and/or administrative adjustments can be made that might reduce or eliminate the resulting lack of comparability. On the other hand, if the former is true, there is nothing that can be done to make scores directly comparable. Thus the issue of construct change versus construct-irrelevant variance has important implications for what to do going forward.

In the context of paper- versus computer-based testing, Bennett (2003) defined comparability as "the commonality of score meaning across testing conditions including delivery modes, computer platforms, and scoring presentation. When comparability exists, scores from different testing conditions can be used interchangeably" (p. 2). While predating the introduction of tablets and similar devices, Bennett's inclusion of computer platforms in his definition of comparability was prescient. However, his discussion of the topic did not anticipate the possibility of some test takers answering questions using a mouse and separate keyboard and others using their finger and a touch screen.

Winter (2010) observed that the equating literature distinguishes between "exchangeable" scores and "comparable" scores, associating the former with the conditions necessary for test equating and the latter with conditions associated with linking (c.f., Dorans & Walker, 2007). Winter proposed thinking about degree of comparability along two related dimensions, content and score level. Content comparability considers whether testing variations are composed of the same items, address the same test specifications, refer to the same underlying content standards, or merely measure the same content area. Score-level comparability considers the respective inferences made about raw scores, scale scores, or categorical classifications (e.g., achievement level or pass/fail status). Randall, Sireci, Li, and Kaira (2012) illustrated what might be an additional dimension to comparability evidence: invariance of test structure and item functioning across subgroups of test takers. Analyses of this type speak to the question of construct change (or difference).

How comparability is thought about clearly impacts the actions that might be taken in a testing program to address comparability. Returning to the plans of the SBAC and PARCC consortia, proposed methodologies to establish comparability seem to anticipate linking adjustments to account for different delivery modes but not necessarily for different administration platforms or conditions. For example, both SBAC and PARCC plan to examine comparability between online and paper formats. According to its website, SBAC "will conduct research and will perform equating studies to ensure that results are comparable across the two modes of assessment, and to put the paper-and-pencil forms onto the scale used for the online testing (SBAC, n.d.)." However, no mention of comparability with respect to devices is made. In a recent PARCC request for proposals, the following statement appeared: "Note that strict comparability (i.e., score interchangeability) across CBT and PPT is **not** a goal for PARCC; however, score interchangeability across CBT devices and input types **is** a goal" (State of Indiana, 2012).

The ways in which the consortia are planning to implement testing variations relate to associated content comparability claims. Both consortia are developing TEIs that are specifically designed for computer administration. Moreover, SBAC is utilizing computerized adaptive testing. These variations make it clear that different items will be used in different testing modes and, in the case of adaptive versus fixed-form SBAC test versions, that different test specifications will be followed in different testing modes. On the other hand, while the same items and content specifications will be measured across online variations introduced by different devices (e.g., desktop vs. laptop) and input types (e.g., keyboard vs. touch screen), these latter variations still raise many questions that the consortia will have to consider in supporting intended claims about score comparability.

As the body of knowledge and methodologies related to assessing comparability has grown and evolved, one lesson researchers have learned is that comparability is a multifaceted issue for which results and their implications are perpetually changing. This is becoming increasingly clear today in the context of such rapid evolutions in the technologies that are becoming available in educational settings as well as in daily life. The next two sections of this chapter trace this evolution of comparability research, as well as the new issues that are emerging with the introduction of new, technology-based testing variations.

### Evolution of Research Addressing Score Comparability

The main purpose of conducting research on score comparability on large-scale standardized tests is to help evaluate and support *fairness* in testing. One fundamental assumption underlying standardized testing is that all examinees take the test under conditions that are as similar as possible in order to yield comparable inferences. It would not be fair for factors such as the mode of administration or testing accommodations, which are not related to the intended measurement construct, to have a systematic influence (positive or negative) on the examinees' performance. It is therefore vital to the defensibility of a large-scale standardized testing program to provide evidence through comparability research showing that construct-irrelevant factors do not differentially impact how examinees perform on its tests.

There is a long history of research examining score comparability in standardized assessments. Comparability studies can be dated back over four decades when standardized intelligence tests, personality measures, and aptitude tests were administered in alternative modes besides the traditional paper-and-pencil format (see, for example, Dunn, Lushene, & O'Neil, 1972; Elwood, 1972; Hedl, O'Neil, & Hansen, 1971; Kiely, Zara, & Weiss, 1986; Scissons, 1976; Wildgrube, 1982). Mazzeo and Harvey (1988) provide a comprehensive summary of findings from studies comparing "automated and conventional" administration formats in the early days of score comparability research. Over the past two decades, due to the rapid advancement of technology, increased knowledge and emphasis on improving the test users' experience and the impetus to incorporate these innovations into standardized assessments, there has been a proliferation of research studies on score comparability across different modes of administration. Not surprisingly, the majority of the comparability studies have focused on the impact of administering an assessment across paper-and-pencil and computer-based testing modes.

### *Paper-and-Pencil Versus Computer-Based Testing*

Any difference found in test performance that is attributed to the mode of administration is often referred to as a *mode effect*. The importance of addressing mode effects is encapsulated in the professional testing standards (AERA, APA, NCME, 2014, c.f., Standards 9.7, 9.9), which emphasize the need for a sound rationale and empirical evidence supporting the reliability of scores and the validity of interpretations based on the scores when tests are given in multiple modes such as paper and pencil and on the computer. As such, comparability studies serve to not only identify potential mode effects but also to provide guidance or recommendations on how to account for them in the reporting of examinees' test scores and associated performance levels.

Various features and aspects of a test can lead to mode effects when it is administered as a paper-and-pencil and computer-based assessment. Kolen (1999) categorizes the potential sources of mode effect into four broad categories: test questions, test scoring, testing conditions, and examinee groups. Each of these categories is summarized as follows:

- *Test questions*. This includes any features of the test items that may lead to a difference in the examinee's experience across administration modes. Factors include whether the item requires scrolling, paging, geometric manipulation, or paper stimulus to respond correctly, the positioning of graphics in the item, length of reading passages, transferability of items across modes, and subtle item characteristics such as the layout of passages, location of line breaks, alignment of item with reading passage, and highlighting of relevant text (by underlining, by numbering, or with color) associated with the item.

- *Test scoring.* This category applies mainly to tests with constructed-response items and written compositions and includes characteristics such as the method of scoring (human vs. automated essay scoring), the representativeness of items used to train an automated scoring engine, and any differences in perceptions in human scorers between handwritten and computer-typed essay responses.
- *Testing condition.* This category includes factors such as whether the test is speeded, similarity between the mode of instruction and mode of assessment, and the various aspects of the computer-based testing interface (e.g., screen resolution, quality of tutorial, ease of navigation, availability and usability of computer-based tools).
- *Examinee groups.* This includes examinee-specific attributes such as degree of familiarity and comfort with computers, amount of exposure and experience with computer-based assessments, word-processing and typing skills, and opportunity to practice in the computer-based testing interface.

With these features in mind, a large number of comparability studies have been conducted on standardized assessments for a variety of content areas, grade levels, and item types over the past few decades. Several published studies (e.g., Kingston, 2009; Mead & Drasgow, 1993; Texas Education Agency, 2008; Wang, 2004; Wang, Jiao, Young, Brooks, & Olson, 2007, 2008; Winter, 2010) have attempted to summarize the findings and recommendations of various comparability studies meta-analytically only to arrive at mixed or inconsistent conclusions. Kingston (2009) suggested two reasons for these inconsistencies. The first may be attributable to the ever-changing landscape of technology, both software and hardware, and how it has impacted the development of computerized test administration systems. In fact, findings and recommendations from earlier comparability studies likely contributed to the improvement of item layouts and user interfaces for computer-based tests. These improvements, in turn, may have helped mitigate some of the mode effect found in earlier comparability studies. Another reason for the inconsistent comparability results may be the practical limitations of carrying out comparability studies in operational test administration settings. These limitations may impact the stability of study results and contribute to the inconsistent findings. Ideally, an experimental design in which a large number of examinees representative of the test-taking population could be randomly assigned to take test items in each of the modes. However, in practice, it is usually infeasible to do so in operational testing environments, especially if stakes such as high school graduation or grade promotion are associated with the test outcomes for examinees.

Consequently, another evolving line of research in score comparability is in the methodologies used to collect and analyze data in the various studies. For some studies, conditions were such that a common person (Horkay, Bennett, Allen, Kaplan, & Yan, 2006; Oregon Department of Education, 2007; Poggio, Glasnapp, Yang, & Poggio, 2005) or randomly equivalent groups (Bennett et al., 2008) designs were supportable for collecting data across testing modes. In many cases, however, data for comparability studies were collected using quasi-experimental designs. Such designs tend to be least burdensome on examinees as, unlike the common-person design, each examinee is only required to take the assessment in one of the modes. Also, unlike the randomly equivalent groups design, quasi-experimental designs do not require random assignment of examinees to the administration modes. Instead, equivalent groups are created after the data are collected using statistical techniques such as coarsened exact matching (Iacus, King, & Porro, 2011) or propensity score matching (Rosenbaum & Rubin, 1985). Several comparability studies involving statewide K–12 assessment have been conducted using a methodology known as matched samples comparability analysis (MSCA; Way, Davis, & Fitzpatrick, 2006; Way, Lin, & Kong, 2008; Way, Um, Lin, & McClarty, 2007), which is well suited for quasi-experimental designs and uses matching on a number of related examinee performance and demographic variables along with resampling techniques to create equivalent groups in each of the administration modes. Yu, Livingston, Larkin, and Bonett (2004), on the other hand, used propensity score matching on a large number of demographic variables to investigate comparability across paper- and computer-based assessments.

Once the data are collected, numerous analysis methods ranging from simple mean difference comparisons and correlations to approaches based on item response theory (IRT) can be used to evaluate comparability of test scores across testing modes. If mode effects are found to be significant in an operational test-administration setting, alternative scoring tables are usually generated using the results of comparability studies. Additional analyses at the item level can also be conducted using methods ranging from comparisons of classical item statistics such as $p$-values and response distributions to differential item functioning (DIF) and IRT parameter comparisons to help identify characteristics of test items that may contribute to mode effects. Results from item-level comparability studies are often used to inform item development guidelines for computer-based testing. Additionally, the issue of whether the mode of administration changes the construct that is being assessed has been examined in several research studies. The general finding across studies is that measurement invariance holds across computer-based and paper-and-pencil versions of assessments (e.g., Kim & Huynh, 2007; Randall, Kaira, & Sireci, 2010a, 2010b; Schweid & Sireci, 2010). These results imply that mode effects may be more attributable to construct-irrelevant variance. Administrative or statistical adjustments can therefore be made to mitigate or account for the lack of comparability. However, such studies generally considered computer-based and paper-and-pencil versions comprised of essentially the same item types and formats. When computer-based tests include technology-enhanced items that cannot be administered by paper and pencil, there may be more substantive reasons to attribute mode effects to differences in constructs measured.

In short, the product of more than four decades of investigations in the area of score comparability across paper- and computer-based assessments is an impressive body of research that includes findings across numerous content domains and item types, methodologies involving different data-collection designs and analysis techniques, and a continual interchange between study findings and operational test development that has helped identify and mitigate mode effects and improve the examinees' experience when taking computer-based assessments.

### Score Comparability With Testing Accommodations

Testing accommodations are features or processes that help provide equitable access to the content assessed on a test. Testing accommodations are often provided to examinees with specific impediments that make it difficult for them to access the tested content. For example, examinees with visual impairments could receive a braille version of the test, test takers with audio impairments could have their test questions signed, students with dyslexia could have their tests read aloud while also being given additional time for completion, and English language learners may be provided with linguistic accommodations such as access to bilingual dictionaries or glossaries, oral translation into their native language, or clarification in English (or the language of the assessment) by teachers or test administrators.

When implementing policies and procedures for testing accommodations, the comparability of test scores resulting from administering various accommodations should be studied and evaluated to help promote fairness in assessments. As one may surmise from the examples, the types of testing accommodation that could be provided are as myriad as the variety of special needs that may hinder an examinee from accessing the assessed content. Accommodations are also often customized to each individual examinee's needs such that different combinations of accommodations may be available to different test takers. Studying score comparability is therefore by no means a trivial research endeavor. Indeed, in comparison to the long history and large volume of comparability studies on testing mode, research focused on the comparability of various testing accommodations is still in its infancy. Studies that look at linguistic accommodations, for instance, have largely been conducted in the past decade (see, for example, Dolan, Murray, & Stangman, 2006; Duran, 2008; Kieffer, Lesaux, Rivera, & Francis, 2009; Pennock-Roman & Rivera, 2011, 2012; Sireci, Li, & Scarpati, 2003). The practical challenges faced by researchers of testing accommodations are usually due to the population of examinees who require them. The uniqueness of what each examinee needs can lead to small sample sizes and limits the generalizability of any findings.

The infusion of technology into testing accommodations adds yet another dimension to the complexity of evaluating score comparability. Many standardized testing programs have begun leveraging advancements in software and hardware technology, along with best practices in developing computer-based tests, to implement online accommodations in their tests. Examples of online accommodations include text-to-speech features (commonly found in GPS navigation systems) in which the computer can read aloud the test questions to examinees, built-in online dictionaries or glossaries that students can choose to activate while taking a computer-based test, or pop-up dialogs that include pictures or even animation that can help clarify the meaning of words or sentences in the test questions. As is the case with testing accommodations in general, research studying score comparability for tests with online accommodations is relatively new and somewhat limited. A handful of studies, for example, have examined the use of online clarification features, dictionaries, and glossaries (Abedi, 2009; Abedi, Courtney, & Leon, 2003; Abedi, Lord, Hofstetter, & Baker, 2000; Albus, Thurlow, & Bielinski, 2005; Kieffer, Lesaux, Rivera, & Francis, 2009; Pennock-Roman & Rivera, 2011).

The critical aspect underlying an evaluation of score comparability for any test accommodation is that the features of the accommodation should only remove the barriers that are preventing an examinee from accessing the tested content but not change the construct being measured. Thus, certain accommodations such as glossaries or clarifications may not be appropriate for reading assessments, where the goal is to assess an examinee's knowledge of vocabulary and comprehension. In practice, however, distinguishing whether an accommodation is helping examinees better access the content or affecting the underlying construct can be quite difficult. One methodological approach often used to help understand and disentangle these effects is referred to as the *interaction hypothesis* (Sireci, Li, & Scarpati, 2003; Zuriff, 2000). The interaction hypothesis states that if a testing accommodation is effective, then one should only observe an increase in test scores for the examinees that the accommodation is intended to help and not see a change in performance for other examinees. For example, if the text-to-speech accommodation is only intended to help special education students and English language learners, then one would expect to see improvements in test performance for those groups of examinees but not expect to find significant score differences for general education English-speaking students when they are tested with the text-to-speech feature. In general, the interaction hypothesis has been substantiated in comparability studies involving linguistic accommodations (Kieffer, Lesaux, Rivera, & Francis, 2009; Pennock-Roman & Rivera, 2011). Accommodations for students with disabilities, however, have been found to help both special education and general education examinees (Sireci, Li, & Scarpati, 2003).

### Lessons Learned

So what have we learned from the large body of research around score comparability? While findings from various comparability studies have not always been consistent, several themes have emerged identifying characteristics of assessments that likely contribute to mode effects. For example, test items often include content that cannot fit onto a single screen when given on a computer. Such an item would require examines to scroll through the passages and item stem and/or answer choices to read the entire content. In contrast, an examinee taking the same item on paper could likely read everything on a single page. Several comparability studies have found significant mode effects favoring the paper mode for items that require scrolling on the computer screen (Bergstrom, 1992; Bridgeman, Lennon, & Jackenthal, 2001; Choi & Tinkler, 2002; Higgins, Russell, & Hoffmann, 2005; Keng, McClarty, & Davis, 2008; O'Malley et al., 2005; Pommerich, 2004; Way, Davis, & Fitzpatrick, 2006). Another example is test items that require examinees to draw, label, or manipulate features (such as a figure or diagram) that are part of the item's content. Several studies have shown that such items also tend to be more difficult when administered on the computer (Greenwood et al., 2000; Keng, McClarty, & Davis, 2008; NAEP, 2001; Sandene et al., 2005). This is likely due to the fact that it is easier, or at least more familiar, for examinees to do graphing or geometric manipulation on paper than on the computer screen, if this is what they are accustomed to within the classroom. Additional characteristics specific to content areas (e.g., language arts, mathematics, science and social studies), item types (e.g., multiple choice vs. free response), examinee characteristics (e.g., technology fluency, keyboarding skills, experience with computer-based testing), and administration processes (e.g., testing interface, scorer perceptions) have been found to contribute to mode effects. For the interested reader, there are several literature reviews or reports (e.g., Kingston, 2009; Mead & Drasgow, 1993; Texas Education Agency, 2008; Wang, Jiao, Young, Brooks, & Olson, 2007, 2008; Winter, 2010) that summarize the findings and recommendations from years of score comparability research.

The findings and recommendations from comparability research have been instrumental in informing test-development guidelines and procedures for standardized assessments given across different modes of administration. In implementing the recommendations, researchers and practitioners have come to realize the importance of making the distinction between comparability of the *examinees' experience* versus comparability of the *test content*. The latter is a narrower and more literal interpretation of comparability that focuses on administering the tested content in the exact same layout and format across different modes. Doing so, however, may not always make sense. For example, the grid-in item type is often used on paper-and-pencil mathematics and science assessments in which examinees are required to grid or bubble in the numerical result of their computation. Testing programs that hold to the literal interpretation of comparability have designed the computer-based testing inter-face such that examinees need to click radio buttons to "grid" in their response, which one could argue is a more tedious task (and would make for a more challenging test-taking expe-rience) for examinees than simply typing in the numbers using the keyboard.

The plethora of digital devices and testing accommodations also adds an additional layer of complexity to score comparability. In fact, the definition of "computer-based testing" is a lot more nuanced now than it may have been even a decade ago. Basic characteristics such as screen or display size can vary so widely across digital devices that they could potentially impact score comparability within what is traditionally considered computer-based testing (Bridgeman, Lennon, & Jackenthal, 2001, 2003; Keng, Kong, & Bleil, 2011). Different input types such as external or onscreen keyboards, external mice or built-in touch pads, touch screens, and styluses may also affect score comparability for tests administered on computers. This expanded definition of computer-based testing also calls into question the research on whether altering the mode or device changes the construct being measured versus introduces construct-irrelevant variance. Because of the very different implications for each of these effects, further studies are warranted to inform the earlier findings.

Given these complexities, rather than holding to the literal and rigid dichotomy of "paper-and-pencil" versus "computer-based" testing in score comparability research, it may be advisable for research in this area to instead consider comparability of examinees' *experi-ence* across different potential test-taking configurations. The use of the term "experience" in this context acknowledges that exactitude in item layout or visual appearance across paper and computer delivery may be far less important than other experiential factors such as the ability to make marks on the item or to easily relocate content within a passage, even when the mechanisms to accomplish these actions may differ greatly across different delivery con-ditions. This paradigm shift in thinking about comparability and other emerging issues in score comparability are the focus of the next section in this chapter.

## Emerging Score Comparability Issues

As the pace of technological change increases, a host of issues threaten the standardization of test administration conditions and, therefore, the comparability of test scores from those administrations. On the one hand, technology enables us to measure things in ways we have not been able to previously and may, in fact, improve measurement accuracy and validity in some cases. On the other hand, the realities of updating school technology infrastructures to keep up with changing technologies almost guarantees that there will be a perpetual state of technological differences across students, schools, and states. How should we think about score comparability in this age of technological diversity?

### Technology-Enhanced Measures

Technology-enhanced items, or TEIs, are characterized by their use of technology to cap-ture and score student responses in computer-delivered tests in ways that extend beyond traditional selected-response or constructed-response items (Parshall, Davey, & Pashley, 2002; SBAC, 2012). The types of responses students might make to a TEI include such action verbs as "categorize," "connect," "create," "draw," "generate," "identify," "order," "match," "plot," "put," "rearrange," and "transform," which are generally perceived to measure a cognitively more complex skill level than is measured by traditional item types (SBAC, 2012). Direct observation of these types of higher-order skills in a paper-based assessment is limited both by the fixed nature of object presentation to students and by scoring costs. At best, these types of skills might be required as intermediate steps to answering a question, but they can only be observed indirectly and must be inferred through the students' selected response. Issues of comparability across testing mode are complicated when TEIs are included in the computer-based version of the test. Luecht and Camara (2011) state that it may be difficult to "equate" test forms in this case, as most TEI items are introduced for the express purpose of measuring something "different" than what can be measured through a multiple-choice item. As such, requiring strict comparability between paper and computer versions of a test may be inappropriate when TEIs are included in the computer-based version. A preferred strategy might be to establish a concordance between test scores on the two versions such that claims of score exchangeability are not implied.

While the threats to score comparability across devices are different than those across modes, comparability of TEIs across devices cannot simply be assumed, even though the same items and item types can be delivered to multiple computing platforms. The different response mechanisms available to students (mouse, touch screen, etc.) can influence the students' experience in responding such it may be easier or more difficult to "create," "draw," "match," "plot," and so on, depending on what device and response inputs a student is using. TEI interactions that were designed for and work well on a computer may be challenging to use in a touch screen environment. For example, Strain-Seymour, Craft, Davis, and Elbom (2013) discuss a drag-and-drop item type for which students were asked to place commas in the appropriate places in a sentence to make it grammatically correct. While students had little difficulty responding to this item when using a mouse on a computer, the drag-able commas and answer bays were so small that students' fingers completely obscured them when using a touch screen interface on a tablet. Students could not see if they had successfully grabbed a comma to drag with their finger and further could not see if they had placed the comma in the answer bay before lifting up their finger. The level of student frustration in attempting to answer this item was high, and many students left the item unanswered after multiple attempts. Yu, Lorié, and Sewall (2014) reported that more than half of students (52%) who tested on a tablet in a cognitive lab believed that performance tasks would take longer to complete on a tablet than on a computer, and nearly half (47%) indicated that they thought performance tasks were more difficult to complete on a tablet than on a computer. A more detailed discussion of factors that may influence comparability across devices is presented in what follows.

### Device Form Factor

The degree of comparability that might be expected of scores from different devices may depend to a large extent on the differences in device form factor (i.e., size, style, and shape as well as the layout and position of major functional components) and how students interact with the devices themselves. For example, as supported by previous research (Powers & Potenza, 1996), comparability between desktops and laptops can be expected to be relatively high because the form factors of the devices are fairly similar. Both desktops and laptops have physical keyboards (though they may vary in size and key positioning and spacing) that are positioned horizontally on a flat surface relative to a screen or monitor that is positioned vertically (though they may vary in size and flexibility in the degree of vertical placement).

Similarly, both are used with a mouse as the pointer input for selection (though they may vary in terms of whether the mouse pointer is controlled through an external mouse or a touch pad). Conversely, comparability between desktops and smartphones can be expected to be lower, as the form factors of the devices are relatively dissimilar. Unlike a desktop, a smartphone typically has a virtual keyboard that is overlaid on top of the small screen (typically 4–5 inches) when opened, expects touch input for selection, and may be flexibly used in a variety of hand-held positions and distances for viewing relative to the face. Thinking through how the form factor of a device influences how information is viewed and accessed by the student as well as how the student provides a response to a question is the logical first step in any evaluation of cross-device comparability.

The key differences across device form factors that are deserving of further analysis include screen size, ergonomics and positioning, touch-screen input, and keyboard functioning. Each of these differences along with its implications for comparability is addressed in more detail as follows.

**Screen Size.** Screen size is an important variable to consider in comparability because it can control the amount of information that can be seen at one time as well as how easily that information can be seen. Smaller screen sizes are more likely to introduce scrolling of items or passages, which has been consistently shown to lead to differences in item performance across testing modes. Screen size may also impact the ability of students to effectively read and comprehend passages on a device, as the readability of online text has been shown to be impacted by characteristics such as character (font) size, length of text, paging/scrolling, and amount of white space (Chaparro, Shaikh, & Baker, 2005).

A study by Bridgeman, Lennon, and Jackenthal (2001) that compared different computer monitor sizes indicated that the most critical factor was the amount of information available on screen without scrolling. While math scores appeared to be unaffected, lower scores were observed in verbal skills when smaller screen resolutions led to a lower percentage of the reading materials being visible at one time. Similarly, a study by Keng, Kong, and Bleil (2011) kept the amount of information shown on screen, the screen resolution, and the amount of scrolling constant across test conditions but varied screen sizes. The results showed no difference in student performance across test takers using netbooks and students using desktop and laptop computers. These two studies suggest that the amount of information available on screen at one time may be at least as important a factor as screen size, assuming that content is presented at a large enough size for basic legibility.

Most recently, Davis, Strain-Seymour, and Gay (2013) looked at student interactions with a 10-inch tablet and a 7-inch tablet for a small set of test questions. Students were asked to think aloud while working through the test questions on one tablet and, when finished, were presented with additional questions on the other tablet. Students generally found the 10-inch form factor to be acceptable for viewing and working with test content and found the smaller 7-inch form factor to be more challenging. While most students were able to read and complete the questions on the 7-inch tablet, many said that they thought they would have difficulty using the device for long reading passages, and many students tried to pinch and zoom to enlarge the text (a feature that was not enabled in this study). In addition, some questions were difficult to complete because the screen size was too small to accommodate the students' fingers on the area they were trying to manipulate. Although this was an issue observed with some questions for both sizes of tablets studied, it was exacerbated and observed more widely with the smaller tablet.

**Ergonomics and Positioning.** Desktops provide a limited range of user positions, with the most typical usage being from a seated position in front of a desk with the keyboard and screen tethered to the computer tower in front of the student. Laptops extend the range of user positions by integrating the computer processor into a compact and portable unit along with the keyboard and monitor. Laptops are portable and may be used on surfaces other than a desk (such as the user's lap) but tend to be used in similar seated positions as desktops in classroom settings. In contrast, most tablets weigh 1 to 2 pounds and are designed to be handheld, used in a flat position, placed in a docking station, or held upright by a foldable case. Smartphones are typically even lighter, weighing about 4 ounces on average and are primarily designed to be handheld. Unlike a desktop or laptop, a tablet or smartphone has no singular correct position, which is reinforced by reorientation of the on-screen image to portrait or landscape based on the position of the device. However, in a series of cognitive labs involving the presentation of assessment items, Davis and Strain-Seymour (2013a) found that the majority of students placed the tablets flat on the desk and leaned over them to view the screen despite being given no specific instruction on how to place or position the tablet. While students in these studies did not report physical discomfort, the time spent working with the tablets was relatively short (30–45 minutes). Some students speculated that they might suffer issues such as neck pain, thumb strain, or headache due to holding or viewing the tablet for longer periods of time. To the extent that students' choice of position with a device impacts their physical comfort in a test-taking situation, this could also impact their performance on a test relative to students testing with devices that support a more ergonomically sound posture. In another cognitive lab, Yu, Lorié, and Sewall (2014) observed that students' self-rated skill with the onscreen keyboard was related to their preference for positioning of the tablet. Students who rated themselves as having advanced typing skills with the onscreen keyboard tended to prefer to use the tablet in a flat position, whereas students who rated themselves as having beginner typing skills with the onscreen keyboard tended to prefer to use the tablet propped up at an angle.

**Touch-Screen Input.** While the touch-screen response mechanism of tablets and smartphones is intuitive and useful for a wide variety of input purposes, there are limitations relative to the level of precision obtainable for selection and manipulation of objects with a human finger. Touch-screen inputs are associated with high speed but reduced precision; they are typically faster than mouse inputs for targets that are larger than 3.2 mm, but the minimum target sizes for touch accuracy are between 10.5 and 26 mm, much larger than mouse targets, which tend to be more limited by human sight than by cursor accuracy (Forlines, Wigdor, Shen, & Balarkrishnan, 2007; Hall, Cunningham, Roache, & Cox, 1988; Meyer, Cohen, & Nilsen, 1994; Sears & Shneiderman, 1991; Vogel & Baudisch, 2007). Touch-screen input accuracy may suffer from spurious touches from holding the device and from occlusion when the finger blocks some part of the graphical interface (Holz & Baudisch, 2010).

Within studies of input devices such as touch screens, comparisons are made between the benefits of the immediacy of direct input, where moving onscreen objects resembles moving objects in the physical world, and those of mechanical intermediaries, such as the indirect input of a mouse. While speed, intuitiveness, and appropriateness for novices are benefits of direct input, mechanical intermediaries often extend human capability in some way (Hinckley & Wigdor, 2011). Similarly, touch-screen input is immediate and direct, while mouse input aids accuracy and allows one small movement to equate to movement of the cursor across a much larger screen distance.

While test content designed for delivery across touch-screen and nontouch devices should take these differences into account as much as possible, use of peripherals such as a stylus or tablet mouse may provide additional support for aiding student precision within a touch-screen environment. Tablet mice may be connected to a tablet via USB cable or Bluetooth and incorporate tablet-specific features such as use on almost any surface for portability and multidirection scrolling (see Microsoft's wedge mouse or Apple's magic mouse; Brown, 2012; Stern, 2010). Styluses are small, reasonably affordable, and resemble a pen or pencil, and while they are not technically more precise than a finger, they allow somewhat better visibility since the student's hand is not blocking the screen (Pogue, 2012). Observations suggest that preferences on using a stylus to respond to test items on a tablet seem to vary from student to student (Davis & Strain-Seymour, 2013; Yu, Lorié, & Sewall, 2014). Some students were very facile with the stylus and preferred the added element of precision that they perceived from using it. Others (typically younger elementary school students) had difficulty manipulating the stylus (pressing too hard, dragging the stylus as they lifted it from the screen, etc.) and felt they had more control by using their finger (Davis & Strain-Seymour, 2013).

An additional difference with touch-screen input is the absence of a mouse-controlled cursor. On a computer, a cursor can be moved without triggering an active selection state; cursor movement is differentiable from dragging. The cursor shows the user the precise location of the contact location before the user commits to an action via a mouse click (Buxton, 1990; Sutherland, 1964). A touch screen, on the other hand, does not have these two distinct motion-sensing states; pointing and selecting, moving and dragging are merged. No "hover" or "rollover" states as distinct from selection states can exist on a touch screen, which removes a commonly used avenue of user feedback within graphic user interfaces. Similarly, without a cursor, touch-screen interfaces cannot have cursor icons, which can be used to indicate state or how an object can be acted upon (Tilbrook, 1976).

**Keyboard Functioning.** Computer keyboards allow three states of interaction for students who are trained as touch typists—fingers can be off the keys, fingers can be resting on the keys without the keys depressed, or fingers can be depressing the keys. In contrast, touch-screen or onscreen keyboards do not allow students to rest their fingers on the characters without activating the keys, thereby eliminating the middle state, which makes it difficult for students to use keyboarding skills (Findlater & Wobbrock, 2012). For most students, typing speed and accuracy decreases and fatigue increases over longer periods of time with use of the onscreen keyboard, since it takes longer to convey their thoughts (Pisacreta, 2013; Sax, Lau, & Lawrence, 2011). In fact, most students either do not attempt keyboarding or quickly abandon it in favor of a one- or two-finger "hunt-and-peck" approach to typing on touch-screen tablets (Davis & Strain-Seymour, 2013b).

In addition to the basic text-entry issues, onscreen keyboards represent a different set of challenges than physical keyboards. First, students must know how to open and close the onscreen keyboards and be able to toggle between alpha and numeric keyboards, as not all keys are visible at once. Second, when open, the keyboard takes up screen real estate and often pushes content off the screen, forcing students to scroll up to locate information they wanted to reference in answering the question. As a result of these issues, testing programs may require the use of an external keyboard with a touch-screen tablet (PARCC, 2013; SBAC, 2013). However, external keyboards are not necessarily a panacea for these challenges. To begin with, there is a lot of variability in the types of external keyboards available for tablets, and not all will offer an experience that is similar to that of using a laptop or desktop keyboard (Frakes, 2013). Some students in the Davis and Strain-Seymour (2013b) studies also appeared to find it difficult to switch between using the external keyboard to type and using their finger to select text and place the cursor. One student characterized this drawback as "everything not being in one place." Last, use of the student's finger to place the cursor in the proper spot for editing text provides additional challenge, as students may have trouble getting the cursor to the right spot.

It should be noted, however, that many students in the Davis and Strain-Seymour (2013b) studies (especially younger ones who had not yet perfected keyboarding skills) expressed a preference for the onscreen keyboard. These students commented positively on features of onscreen keyboards not present with physical keyboards, such as haptic feedback (the key vibrating when touched) and other visual cues such as a glow or enlargement of a letter when touched. In fact, a study by Davis, Orr, Kong, and Lin (2014) in which students were asked to compose a short (approximately 250-word) essay on either a laptop, a tablet with external keyboard, or a tablet with the onscreen keyboard reported that the overwhelming majority (94%) of fifth-grade students found the onscreen keyboard either very easy or somewhat easy to use. While high school students in this study were less favorable toward the onscreen keyboard (only 71% found the onscreen keyboard either very easy or somewhat easy to use), the study found no differences in student essay scores for either fifth-grade or high school students across the three device conditions.

Interestingly, in their comparison of desktops and laptops, the one content area for which Powers and Potenza (1996) found differences was in writing, which they attributed to differences in the size of keyboards and layout of keys between the two devices. However, it is uncertain whether these differences would still be present now, nearly 20 years later. Certainly, text entry for touch-screen devices will likely continue to evolve over time as concepts such as adaptive keyboards, gestural input, selectable touch menus, Swype, split keyboards, and other innovative solutions present themselves (Findlater & Wobbrock, 2012; Pierce, 2012). Students' familiarity with and proficiency in working with text entry on touch-screen devices will similarly evolve. Testing programs with significant written components should monitor these developments closely and conduct research as appropriate to evaluate how these new text-entry methods and improved student familiarity with touch-screen text entry might impact comparability between computers and tablets.

**Touch Screen–Specific Features.** Touch-screen devices allow for certain interactions and experiences not available with computers. For example, pinch-and-zoom magnification, screen rotation (landscape to portrait), and autocorrect or autocomplete are all features common to tablets and smartphones but not frequently seen with computers. While not an inherent property of the touch interface, the purpose of these features is to offer alternative interactions to compensate for certain limitations of the device size and input mechanisms. The challenge for comparability occurs either when the features advantage or disadvantage users of the touch devices or when the features violate the measurement construct.

Students can use pinch-and-zoom magnification within a touch environment to enlarge portions of the screen and examine content in more detail. This might be viewed as a positive attribute in terms of overcoming the smaller screen size of tablets and smartphones and may be especially valuable for improving the readability of portions of text. However, it should be recognized that when a student zooms in, he or she is no longer able to view the item content in its entirety and may have to zoom back out to view information necessary to correctly answer the item. Additionally, while enlarging text may allow for better readability of the portion of the reading selection students are viewing, it may create other challenges for reading recall, as it is more difficult for students to retain their awareness of where information is "on the page" and to use other types of visual landmarks when zooming in and out.

Screen rotation from landscape to portrait is typically considered a positive attribute for tablet and smartphone applications. However, in considering issues of device comparability between tablets and computers in assessment settings, the differences inherent in how test content is displayed and viewed in a portrait versus a landscape orientation may create challenges. Computer monitors are typically (though not always) landscape orientation. Test content that is designed for computer delivery may not translate well to a portrait orientation on a tablet, as scrolling might be introduced, and long horizontal elements (like rulers or number lines) may not scale well. For this reason, testing programs may be better served by disabling screen rotation when presenting test items on tablets.

Autocorrect is similar to a spellcheck feature, which is present in most word processing software packages on computer. However, it is common for the online testing software not to include a spellcheck feature for writing assessments (just as dictionaries may not be allowed in a paper-based assessment of writing) when spelling is part of the construct being measured. However, as classroom instruction in writing becomes more integrated with technology and spelling becomes less a focus of evaluation for written composition, this may begin to change. Virginia and Oregon, for example, have both provided a spellcheck tool in their direct writing assessments since 2010 and 2011, respectively (Oregon Department of Education, 2010; Virginia Department of Education, 2010). In cases when spell check is available for students testing on computer, it is arguably appropriate to provide a similar capability for students testing on tablets.

Autocomplete goes a step beyond autocorrect and applies predictive algorithms to complete or suggest words to students based upon the first few letters typed. Given the limitations previously discussed with onscreen keyboards, this feature has some attraction relative to leveling the playing field with physical keyboards. However, this feature may go too far in providing assistance to students with word choice within their academic writing. Alternatively, it may disadvantage students, because it encourages them to pick words from a list without regard to their appropriateness in context.

### Rapid Evolution of Technology

While this section raises many questions about device comparability, it is important to keep in mind that the touch-screen technology for personal devices is relatively new (the first-generation iPad was not introduced until 2010), and research is only beginning to address how differences across these devices might impact comparability (see, for example, Olsen, 2014). What is clear is that the evolution of technology will only continue and that schools will continue to adopt different technologies in different time frames and will have little patience for a measurement field that is unprepared to accept these technologies for testing purposes. Establishing a framework and a process for evaluating new devices and new technologies is perhaps more important than understanding the impact to comparability of any specific device or technology. The final section of this chapter will attempt to lay out the important considerations for how to think about comparability as technology continues to evolve.

### Principles for Moving Forward

The confluence of adaptive testing, highly personalized accommodations, tests administered using a range of display and input devices, and greater complexity in technology-enhanced item types has moved us far from a traditional notion of comparability within which the same set of multiple-choice items are delivered on paper and on computer or a general test is altered to be made more accessible for students with special needs.

However, the fundamental concepts related to test validity still apply. For example, Kane (2006) discusses an argument-based approach to validity consisting of interpretive arguments and validity arguments. The interpretive argument outlines a rationale for making decisions or drawing conclusions about an observed performance by listing a series of inferences and corresponding assumptions. Clear and coherent interpretive arguments as related to comparability provide a foundation from which supporting documentation and research can be structured. The validity argument, then, provides the evaluation of the interpretive arguments. This conception of comparability as interpretive argument begins at the point of assessment design and development and fits well within the principles of evidence-centered design (ECD; c.f., Mislevy & Haertel, 2006). Kopriva (2010) makes this point in a summary discussion of comparability research:

> All in all, Evidence Centered Design can provide construct equivalent documentation, and this type of "conscious" design will also probably have an influence on producing "good enough" evidence of score equivalence. It can be used to identify where evidence needs to be collected, and what types of evidence might be viable and possibly necessary in making a strong argument that the inferences are comparable for everyone taking a test within the assessment system.
>
> (Kopriva, 2010, p. 239)

### Framing the Comparability Research Agenda

Although ECD provides a principled basis for approaching the increasingly complex issues of score comparability, it is perhaps too general to guide the necessary research agendas. A more specific context for formulating the interpretive arguments necessary for comparability might be Kolen's (1999) four categories for considering mode effects, described earlier in this chapter. In particular, the categories of test questions, test conditions, and examinee groups provide a useful structure for posing relevant comparability claims or questions. However, in order to use the structure, the potential for interplay across categories must be acknowledged. For instance, how a particular accommodation works with a given item type on a certain device could lead to a usability issue that only occurs with the alignment of these three variables.

We can take this even further and not just allow for contamination across these categories but *insist* upon it. If we arrange the categories of test questions, test conditions, and examinee groups into a three-dimensional matrix, we have a rich framework for investigating the new complexities of comparability (see Figure 12.1).

While it may be true that the absence of rollover effects and cursor icons on a tablet means less user feedback (which can compromise overall usability regardless of item type or examinee group), we cannot generally detect within cognitive labs a negative impact when a student is working with familiar item types. But consider, for instance, a particular examinee group: students with visual impairments, who tend to heavily utilize pinch-and-zoom functionality on tablets. Assume a test question goes beyond traditional interactivity and involves a multistep TEI format for graphing a solution set or constructing a graphic organizer. The

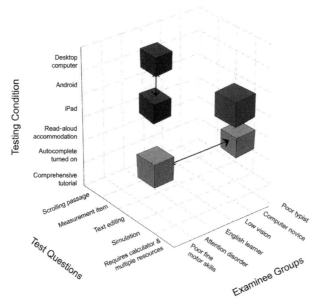

**Figure 12.1** Framework for Investigating Score Comparability

tablet, as a test condition, involves narrower avenues for user feedback, which is combined in this case with a zoomed-in view that might remove from view the full item context, instructions, and/or a button that becomes active after completion of a step. Under these conditions, it is conceivable that the same student might perform differently on that same item delivered via computer.

Table 12.1 provides an illustration of how research questions can be formulated in the context of this three-dimensional matrix. Imagine a research agenda that could investigate individual cells within this matrix to reveal problem areas. The goal would not be to identify needles in haystacks and oddities that pop up in the rarest of circumstances. Instead, the recognition of trends, patterns, and salient characteristics within this matrix signifying areas of vulnerability would be the desired outcome. In seeking out the appropriate methodologies for such analysis, we can again look to successful models from the past couple of decades of comparability gains. While psychometric research methods are typically highlighted within comparability research, the gains made as an industry to reduce mode effects have been a multidisciplinary endeavor. Causality theories for mode effects are often investigated through qualitative research, such as task analysis within cognitive laboratory contexts. Adjustments to computer-based testing interfaces as a way of addressing mode effects are typically informed by usability engineering, with usability studies employed to validate or compare interface revisions.

We can expect that navigating the new complexities of comparability will engage mixed methods to a greater degree than in the past. With so many variables in the mix, quantitative research agendas will be shaped and refined by the discoveries made through observation, focus groups, cognitive laboratories, and usability studies.

Table 12.1 Sample Comparability Research Questions

| Sample Comparability Research Questions | Research Methods |
| --- | --- |
| When content reflows to fill different amounts of available screen space, do the differences in line breaks, column widths, and/or amount of reading content seen on screen at once impact reading comprehension scores (*test questions*) across different devices (*testing condition*)? | Quantitative |
| Is scrolling easier on the tablet and familiarity with scrolling on the part of tablet users (*examinee groups*) such that prior psychometric guidelines around having the same amount of content visible across differently sized screens (*testing condition*) can be followed less strictly? | Quantitative |
| When math items, such as those involving complex algebraic equations (*test questions*), lend themselves to being worked through step by step, tracking one's work, are there differences between using a digital pencil tool on a tablet, a digital pencil tool on a computer, scratch paper provided with an online test, and the test booklet (*testing condition*)? Do the same conclusions hold true when the items involve coordinate grids and geometric figures that get directly marked on with a digital pencil or within a test booklet? | Cog Lab, Quantitative |
| When converting physical tools (*test questions*)—ruler, protractor, compass—to digital equivalents (*testing condition*), does the most valid approach involve verisimilitude in order to assess proper usage of these tools, or does the impossibility of matching the physical experience of such tool use and the disadvantage of manipulating these tools without the benefit of muscle memory suggest that making these tools easier to use and more true to their digital environment (e.g., a way to create, resize, and reposition a circle rather than swinging around the compass arm via the mouse) is a more valid and comparable approach? | Cog Lab, Quantitative |
| How extensive can online writing tools (*test questions*) become without compromising comparability with pencil-and-paper testing (*testing condition*)? For instance, should online environments incorporate spellcheck, autocorrect, table/chart creation, and advanced formatting? | Quantitative |
| How significant a factor is tablet familiarity (familiarity with a specific model and/or familiarity with touch screens in general; *examinee groups*) in comparability across computer and tablet conditions (*testing condition*)? | Cog Lab, Quantitative |
| To what degree will an accessibility solution for assessment rely on device-specific features (*testing condition*)? Are some tablet models more accessible than others (e.g., high-contrast mode on iOS but not Android and customized haptic feedback available natively on Android but not iOS)? | Device Review, Cog Lab |
| When complex TEIs are used (*test questions*), is the availability of a tutorial more critical for some populations (*examinee groups*)? | Cog Lab, Quantitative |
| Are any device- or operating system–specific features (*testing condition*) significant to comparability? For instance, do iOS text editing capabilities improve comparability between tablets and computers for writing tests (*test questions*)? | Cog Lab, Quantitative |
| To what degree are scores from tests delivered via hybrid devices that combine features of laptops and tablets comparable to scores from tests delivered via laptops? | Literature Review, Previous Research |

*(Continued)*

Table 12.1 (Continued)

| Sample Comparability Research Questions | Research Methods |
| --- | --- |
| What strategies are necessary to make simulations (*test questions*) accessible (*examinee groups*) on multiple devices (*testing condition*)? | Prototyping, Cog Lab |
| How does tab-based navigation on the computer compare to gesture-based navigation on a tablet (*testing condition*) in terms of the user experience for blind examinees (*examinee groups*)? Does one offer an advantage over the other, or are they similar enough that examinee familiarity and preference should be the determining factor when choosing the most appropriate device for an assessment? | Cog Lab, Time-on-Task Study |
| Will virtual keyboards, on-demand tactile onscreen keyboards, Swype-style keyboarding, and alternatives to Qwerty such as KALQ generate hardware- or software-specific definitions of keyboarding skills (*testing condition*) that need to be considered when investigating device comparability for writing (*test question*)? | Device Review, Cog Lab |

### Comparability and Interaction Effects

One analogy for thinking about impact of personalized testing and technology on comparability is the way that popular drugs are advertised. We all have seen commercials for new drugs that are supposed to help you sleep better or lower your blood pressure or help you be less anxious. These drugs typically have known potential side effects and interactions. The drug companies are required to communicate these side effects to consumers, and consumers are urged to consult with their doctors in considering whether they want to try the drug. Doctors utilize extensive databases to understand how different drugs interact with each other and especially under what conditions adverse effects may occur so they can be avoided.

Comparability in the context of different testing conditions, modes, and delivery devices might be thought of in a similar manner. That is, the comparability research agenda focuses on identifying those interactions among test questions, testing conditions, and examinee groups when assumptions of score comparability can be called into question. Test users are informed of these interactions and are encouraged or even directed to implement testing conditions for individuals so as to avoid them.

In some cases, it may be possible to correct for an interaction through statistical means, but this option becomes increasingly difficult as the interactions expand. For example, linking a paper version of a test that has alternate item types to substitute for the technology-enhanced items of the online version of the test may be feasible, but linking the paper version, the version presented on computer, and the versions presented on perhaps three or four different digital devices becomes unwieldy if not outright impossible. A better mechanism would be to synthesize usability research, cognitive labs, and small-scale data collections that might or might not involve the specific items and devices of the test in the field but would be similar enough to support interpretive arguments regarding the comparability of scores across conditions. However, many comparability studies and cognitive labs are not disseminated for a variety of reasons (e.g., inconclusive findings or assumptions about limited utility), which makes such research syntheses difficult. One implication of this is that the publication and research dissemination process for comparability studies may need to be considered in order for the field to keep abreast of emerging findings.

### Managing Complexity Through Simple Principles

Given a background of constantly changing technology, understanding, controlling, and/or adjusting for interaction effects across examinee groups, devices, and content characteristics to maintain comparability may seem so complex as to be unmanageable. It is therefore preferable to break this complexity down and attack it through practical strategies such as the conscious identification of possible threats to comparability starting at the earliest stages of test development.

Toward this end, some simple principles may have a significant impact in addressing comparability issues going forward. For instance, items, whether conventional or technology enhanced, should be available in their interactive form on a variety of devices at the earliest possible stage of item development. If particular combinations—some types of content, certain item interaction types, particular devices, the use of certain online tools, accessibility strategies, accommodations—may present usability challenges, the content developers may be in the best position to not only identify these problem areas but also correct them. Imagine an item writer who can author an item, immediately interact with it on his or her tablet, and evaluate it by envisioning test takers' experience of that item. When that same item is viewed by content reviewers on a variety of devices, further opportunities for detection and correction are created. Item-development guidelines can evolve with such exposure in a way that does not occur when the review of items does not involve their interactive form until the latest phases or when the range of devices used for such reviews is far narrower than what would be used in the classroom.

Other simple principles may relate to the design of the test-delivery environment and the involvement of the test-delivery system's user experience team in usability studies and other qualitative studies that take comparability into account. Such an applied research structure can lead to corrections for device-related usability problems long before they are field tested within the full test taker population. Similarly, recommendations and policies to limit ill-advised testing conditions can be made in partnership with test administrators and other personnel who can help enforce those policies. For instance, policies governing device familiarity (ideally fostered through routine classroom usage) can limit the adverse effects of device unfamiliarity and account in advance for certain student populations who may struggle with certain devices due to accessibility limitations or incompatibility with assistive technology. Device familiarity guidelines also help educators or students make better decisions when administration choices are available, such as whether to use a separate keyboard with a tablet.

### Summary and Conclusions

This chapter addressed the topic of score comparability in an era when technology is rapidly changing how large-scale standardized assessments are built and delivered. We have presented the problem of score comparability in this context and reviewed the research on comparability between paper-and-pencil and computer-based assessments as well as the comparability of accommodated tests with standard tests. We have also included research on emerging score comparability issues that have arisen with the advent of technology-enhanced measures and the use of tablets and other devices for test administration.

Because the pace of change in this area is so fast, much of the new research we have presented in this chapter will be outdated or supplanted very quickly. For example, as we write this chapter, we are not aware of any published large-scale studies examining test performance on computers versus tablets. However, we anticipate such research will be available by the time this book is published and that within 5 years, a great deal will be known about large-scale test delivery on tablets and similar devices. It is also likely that the use of technology will impact assessment design and delivery in ways that raise new questions about comparability of scores across new conditions for different examinee groups.

In this context, large-scale testing programs will be well served by the notion of comparability as interpretive argument that we have outlined in this chapter. Responsible use of technology in assessment will depend upon preserving claims regarding score comparability and the accumulation of principles and insights obtained from cumulative interdisciplinary research efforts.

## References

Abedi, J. (2009). Computer testing as a form of accommodation for English language learners. *Educational Assessment, 14*, 195–211.

Abedi, J., Courtney, M., & Leon, S. (2003). *Effectiveness and validity of accommodations for English language learners in large-scale assessments* (CSE Technical Report No. 608). Los Angeles, CA: National Center for Research on Evaluation, Standards, and Student Testing.

Abedi, J., Lord, C., Hofstetter, C., & Baker, E. (2000). Impact of accommodation strategies on English language learners' test performance. *Educational Measurement: Issues and Practice, 19*(3), 16–26.

Albus, D., Thurlow, M., & Bielinski, J. (2005). Reading test performance of English-language learners using an English dictionary. *Journal of Educational Research, 98*(4), 245–254.

American Educational Research Association (AERA), American Psychological Association (APA), & the National Council on Measurement in Education (NCME). (1999). *Standards for educational and psychological testing.* Washington, DC.

American Psychological Association Committee on Professional Standards and Committee on Psychological Tests and Assessments (APA). (1986). *Guidelines for computer-based tests and interpretations.* Washington, DC: Author.

Bennett, R.E. (2003). *Online assessment and the comparability of score meaning* (ETS-RM-03–05). Princeton, NJ: Educational Testing Service.

Bennett, R.E., Braswell, J., Oranje, A., Sandene, B., Kaplan, B., & Yan, F. (2008). Does it matter if I take my mathematics test on computer? A second empirical study of mode effects in NAEP. *Journal of Technology, Learning, and Assessment, 6*(9). Retrieved from www.jtla.org

Bergstrom, B. (1992). *Ability measure equivalence of computer adaptive and pencil and paper tests: A research synthesis.* Paper presented at the annual meeting of the American Educational Research Association, San Francisco, CA.

Bridgeman, B., Lennon, M.L., & Jackenthal, A. (2001). *Effects of screen size, screen resolution, and display rate on computer-based test performance* (ETS-RR-01–23). Princeton, NJ: Educational Testing Service.

Bridgeman, B., Lennon, M.L., & Jackenthal, A. (2003). Effects of screen size, screen resolution, and display rate on computer-based test performance. *Applied Measurement in Education, 16*(3), 191–205.

Brown, R. (2012, July). *Microsoft unveils tablet-friendly mice and keyboards (with hands-on).* Retrieved from http://reviews.cnet.com/8301-3134_7-57481956/microsoft-unveils-tablet-friendly-mice-and-keyboards-with-hands-on/

Buxton, W. (1990). The natural language of interaction: A perspective on non-verbal dialogues. In B. Laurel (Ed.), *The art of human–computer interface design* (pp. 405–416). Reading, MA: Addison-Wesley.

Chaparro, B.S., Shaikh, A.D., & Baker, J.R. (2005). Reading online text with a poor layout: Is performance worse? *Usability News, 7*(1). Available at: http://usabilitynews.org/reading-online-text-with-a-poor-layout-is-performance-worse/

Choi, S.W., & Tinkler, T. (2002). *Evaluating comparability of paper and computer-based assessment in a K–12 setting.* Paper presented at the Annual Meeting of the National Council on Measurement in Education, New Orleans, LA.

Davis, L.L., Orr, A., Kong, X., & Lin, C. (2014, April). *Assessing student writing on tablets.* Paper presented at the Annual Meeting of the National Council on Measurement in Education, Philadelphia, PA. Retrieved from http://researchnetwork.pearson.com/wp-content/uploads/NCME_Assessing-Student-Writing-on-Tablets_040414.pdf

Davis, L. L., & Strain-Seymour, E. (2013a). *Positioning and ergonomic considerations for tablet assessments*. Retrieved from http://researchnetwork.pearson.com/wp-content/uploads/Positioning.pdf

Davis, L. L., & Strain-Seymour, E. (2013b). *Keyboard interactions for tablet assessments*. Retrieved from http://researchnetwork.pearson.com/wp-content/uploads/Keyboard.pdf

Davis, L. L., Strain-Seymour, E., & Gay, H. (2013). *Testing on tablets: Part II of a series of usability studies on the use of tablets for K–12 assessment programs*. Retrieved from http://researchnetwork.pearson.com/wp-content/uploads/Testing-on-Tablets-Part-II_formatted.pdf

Dolan, R. P., Murray, E. A., Strangman, N. (2006). *Mathematics instruction and assessment for middle school students in the margins: Students with learning disabilities, students with mild mental retardation, and students who are English language learners*. Wakefield, MA: CAST.

Dorans, N. J., & Walker, M. E. (2007). Sizing up linkages. In N. J. Dorans, M. Pommerich, & P. W. Holland (Eds.), *Linking and aligning scores and scales* (pp. 179–198). New York: Springer-Verlag.

Dunn, T. G., Lushene, R. E., & O'Neil, H. F. (1972). Complete automation of the MMPI and a study of its response latencies. *Journal of Consulting and Clinical Psychology, 39*, 381–387.

Duran, R. P. (2008). Assessing English-language learners' achievement. *Review of Research in Education, 32*, 292–327.

Elwood, D. L. (1972). Test retest reliability and cost analyses of automated and face-to-face intelligence testing. *International Journal of Man-Machine Studies, 4*, 1–22.

Findlater, L., & Wobbrock, J. O. (2012). Plastic to pixels: In search of touch-typing touch-screen keyboards. *Interactions, 19*(3), 44–49.

Forlines, C., Wigdor, D., Shen, C., & Balakrishnan, R. (2007, May). *Direct-touch vs. mouse input for tabletop displays*. Paper presented at CHI, San Jose, CA.

Frakes, D. (2013, August). *Buying guide: Find the best iPad keyboard*. Retrieved from www.macworld.com/article/1164210/macworld_buying_guide_ipad_keyboards.html

Greenwood, L., Cole, U. M., McBride, F. V., Morrison, H., Cowan, P., & Lee, M. (2000). Can the same results be obtained using computer-mediated tests as for paper-based tests for National Curriculum assessment? *Proceedings of the International Conference on Mathematics/Science, Education and Technology, 2000*(1), 179–184.

Hall, A. D., Cunningham, J. B., Roache, R. P., & Cox, J. W. (1988). Factors affecting performance using touch-entry systems: Tactual recognition fields and system accuracy. *Journal of Applied Psychology, 73*, 711–720.

Hedl, J. J., O'Neil, H. F., & Hansen, D. N. (1971). *Computer-based intelligence testing*. Paper presented at annual meeting of the American Educational Research Association, February, New York, NY.

Higgins, J., Russell, M., & Hoffmann, T. (2005). Examining the effect of computer-based passage presentation on reading test performance. *Journal of Technology, Learning, and Assessment, 3*(4). Retrieved from www.jtla.org

Hinckley, K., & Wigdor, D. (2011). Input technologies and techniques. In A. Sears & J. A. Jacko (Eds.), *The human–computer interaction handbook: Fundamentals, evolving technologies and emerging applications* (pp. 161–176). Boca Raton, FL: CRC Press.

Holz, C., & Baudisch, P. (2010, April). The generalized perceived input point model and how to double touch accuracy by extracting fingerprints. In *Proceedings of the 28th international conference on human factors in computing systems* (pp. 581–590). New York, NY: Association for Computing Machinery.

Horkay, N., Bennett, R. E., Allen, N., Kaplan, B., & Yan, F. (2006). Does it matter if I take my writing test on computer? An empirical study of mode effects in NAEP. *Journal of Technology, Learning, and Assessment, 5*(2). Retrieved from www.jtla.org

Iacus, S. M., King, G., & Porro, G. (2011). Causal inference without balance checking: Coarsened exact matching. *Political Analysis*. Retrieved from http://j.mp/iUUwyH

Kane, M. T. (2006). Validation. In R. L. Brennan (Ed.), *Educational measurement* (4th ed., pp. 17–64). Washington, DC: The National Council on Measurement in Education & the American Council on Education.

Keng, L., Kong, X. J., & Bleil, B. (2011, April). *Does size matter? A study on the use of netbooks in K–12 assessment*. Paper presented at the annual meeting of the American Educational Research Association, New Orleans, LA.

Keng, L., McClarty, K. L., & Davis, L. L. (2008). Item-level comparative analysis of online and paper administrations of the Texas Assessment of Knowledge and Skills. *Applied Measurement in Education, 21*(3), 207–226.

Kieffer, M. J., Lesaux, N. K., Rivera, M., & Francis, D. J. (2009). Accommodations for English language learners on large-scale assessments: A meta-analysis on effectiveness and validity. *Review of Educational Research, 79*, 1168–1201.

Kiely, G. L., Zara, A. R., & Weiss, D. J. (1986). *Equivalence of computer and paper-and-pencil Armed Services Vocational Aptitude Battery tests*. Research Report No. AFHRL-TP-86-13. Brooks Air Force Base, TX: Air Force Human Resources Laboratory.

Kim, D.-H., & Huynh, H. (2007). Comparability of computer and paper-and-pencil versions of algebra and biology assessments. *The Journal of Technology, Learning, and Assessment, 6*(4). Retrieved from www.jtla.org

Kingston, N. M. (2009). Comparability of computer- and paper-administered multiple-choice tests for K–12 populations: A synthesis. *Applied Measurement in Education, 22*(1), 22–37.

Kolen, M. J. (1999). Threats to score comparability with applications to performance assessments and computerized adaptive tests. *Educational Assessment, 6*(2), 73–96.

Kopriva, R.J. (2010). Where are we and where could we go next? (pp. 233–248). In P.C. Winter (Ed.), *Evaluating the comparability of scores from achievement test variations.* Washington, D.C.: Council of Chief State School Officers. Retrieved from: http://www.ccsso.org/Documents/2010/Evaluating_the_Comparability_of_Scores_2010.pdf.

Laitusis, C., Buzick, H., Stone, E., Hansen, E., & Hakkinen, E. (2012). *Smarter Balanced Assessment Consortium: Literature review of testing accommodations and accessibility tools for students with disabilities.* Retrieved from www.smarterbalanced.org/wordpress/wp-content/uploads/2012/08/Smarter-Balanced-Students-with-Disabilities-Literature-Review.pdf

Luecht, R.M., & Camara, W.J. (2011). *Evidence and design implications required to support comparability claims.* Retrieved from www.parcconline.org/sites/parcc/files/PARCCWhitePaperRLuechtWCamara.pdf

Mazzeo, J., & Harvey, A.L. (1988). *The equivalence of scores from automated and conventional educational and psychological tests: A review of the literature* (ETS Report No. RR-88–21). Princeton, NJ: Educational Testing Service.

Mead, A.D., & Drasgow, F. (1993). Equivalence of computerized and paper-and-pencil cognitive ability tests: A meta-analysis. *Psychological Bulletin, 114,* 449–458.

Meyer, S., Cohen, O., & Nilsen, E. (1994, April). Device comparisons for goal-directed drawing tasks. In *Conference companion on human factors in computing systems* (pp. 251–252). New York, NY: Association for Computing Machinery.

Mislevy, R., & Haertel, G. (2006). Implications of evidence-centered design for educational testing. *Educational Measurement: Issues and Practice, 25*(4), 6–20.

NAEP. (April, 2001). *National Assessment of Educational Progress (NAEP) Technology-Based Assessment (TBA) Project Math Online (MOL) Pretest Report.* http://nces.ed.gov/nationsreportcard/pdf/studies/mol.pdf

O'Malley, K. J., Kirkpatrick, R., Sherwood, W., Burdick, H. J., Hsieh, M. C., & Sanford, E. E. (2005). *Comparability of a paper-based and computer-based reading test in early elementary grades.* Paper presented at the annual meeting of the American Educational Research Association, Montreal, Canada.

Olsen, J. B. (2014, April). *Score comparability for web- and iPad-delivered adaptive tests.* Paper presented at the Annual Meeting of the National Council on Measurement in Education, Philadelphia, PA.

Oregon Department of Education. (2010). ODE advisory panel recommendation to enable spell-check in Oregon's online writing assessment. Retrieved from www.ode.state.or.us/news/announcements/announcement.aspx?=6018

Oregon Department of Education. (2007). Comparability of student scores obtained from paper and computer administrations. Retrieved from www.ode.state.or.us

Parshall, C. G., Davey, T., & Pashley, P. J. (2002). Innovating item types for computerized testing. In W. J. van der Linden & C.A.W. Glas (Eds.), *Computerized adaptive testing: Theory and practice* (pp. 129–148). Norwell, MA: Kluwer.

Partnership for the Assessment of Readiness for College and Careers. (2013, February). *Technology Guidelines for PARCC assessments version 2.1—February 2013 Update.* Retrieved from www.parcconline.org/sites/parcc/files/PARCCTechnologyGuidelines2dot1_Feb2013Update.pdf

Pennock-Roman, M., & Rivera, C. (2011). Mean effects of test accommodations for ELLs and non-ELLs: A meta-analysis of experimental studies. *Educational Measurement: Issues and Practice, 30,* 10–28.

Pennock-Roman, M., & Rivera, C. (2012). *Smarter Balanced Assessment Consortium: Summary of literature on empirical studies of the validity and effectiveness of test accommodations for ELLs: 2005–2012.* Report prepared for Measured Progress by The George Washington University Center for Equity and Excellence in Education.

Pierce, M. (2012). Typing in the age of iPads. *THE Journal, 39*(3), 22–24. Retrieved from http://thejournal.com/articles/2012/04/10/typing-in-the-age-of-ipads.aspx?sc_lang=en

Pisacreta, D. (2013, June). *Comparison of a test delivered using an iPad versus a laptop computer: Usability study results.* Paper presented at the Council of Chief State School Officers (CCSSO) National Conference on Student Assessment (NCSA), National Harbor, MD.

Poggio, J., Glasnapp, D. R., Yang, X., & Poggio, A. J. (2005). A comparative evaluation of score results from computerized and paper and pencil mathematics testing in a large scale state assessment program. *Journal of Technology, Learning, and Assessment, 3*(6). Retrieved from www.jtla.org

Pogue, D. (2012, April). *On touch-screens rest your finger by using a stylus.* Retrieved from www.nytimes. com/2012/08/02/technology/personaltech/on-touch-screens-rest-your-finger-by-using-a-stylus-state-of-the-art.html?pagewanted=all&_r=0

Pommerich, M. (2004). Developing computerized versions of paper-and-pencil tests: Mode effects for passage-based tests. *Journal of Technology, Learning, and Assessment, 2*(6). Retrieved from www.jtla.org

Powers, D. E., & Potenza, M. T. (1996). *Comparability of testing using laptop and desktop computers* (ETS Report No. RR-96–15). Princeton, NJ: Educational Testing Service.

Randall, J., Kaira, L., & Sireci, S. G. (2010a). *Evaluating the comparability of paper and computer-based math and science tests within sex and socioeconomic groups: A multi-group confirmatory factor analysis.* Center for Educational Assessment, Research Report No 722. Amherst, MA: School of Education, University of Massachusetts.

Randall, J., Kaira, L., & Sireci, S. G. (2010b). *Evaluating the comparability of paper and computer-based math and science tests: A multi-group confirmatory factor analysis.* Center for Educational Assessment, Research Report No 724. Amherst, MA: School of Education, University of Massachusetts.

Randall, J., Sireci, S., Li, X., & Kaira, L. (2012). Evaluating the comparability of paper- and computer-based science tests across sex and SES groups. *Educational Measurement: Issues and Practice, 31*(4), 2–12.

Rosenbaum, P. R., & Rubin, D. B. (1985). Constructing a control group using multivariate matched sampling methods that incorporate the propensity score. *The American Statistician, 39*(1), 33–38.

Sandene, B., Horkay, N., Bennett, R., Allen, N., Braswell, J., Kaplan, B., & Oranje, A. (2005). *Online assessment in mathematics and writing: Reports from the NAEP technology-based assessment project.* Research and Development Series (NCES 2005-457). Washington, DC: U.S. Department of Education, National Center for Education Statistics.

Sax, C., Lau, H., & Lawrence, E. (2011, February). LiquidKeyboard: An ergonomic, adaptive QWERTY keyboard for touch-screens and surfaces. In *ICDS 2011, The Fifth International Conference on Digital Society* (pp. 117–122). Red Hook, NY: Curran Associates.

Schweid, J. A., & Sireci, S. G. (2010). *Evaluating the comparability of paper- and computer-based math and science tests: An MDS analysis.* Center for Educational Assessment, Research Report No 717. Amherst, MA: School of Education, University of Massachusetts.

Scissons, E. H. (1976). Computer administration of the California Psychological Inventory. *Measurement and Evaluation in Guidance, 9*(1), 22–25.

Sears, A., & Shneiderman, B. (1991). High precision touch-screens: Design strategies and comparisons with a mouse. *International Journal of Man-Machine Studies, 34*(4), 593–613.

Sireci, S. G., Li, S., & Scarpati, S. E. (2003). *The effects of test accommodations on test performance: A review of the literature.* Center for Educational Assessment, Research Report No 485. Amherst, MA: School of Education, University of Massachusetts.

Smarter Balanced Assessment Consortium. (2012). *Smarter Balanced Assessment Consortium: Technology enhanced item guidelines.* Retrieved from www.smarterbalanced.org/wordpress/wp-content/uploads/2012/05/TaskItem Specifications/TechnologyEnhancedItems/TechnologyEnhancedItemGuidelines.pdf

Smarter Balanced Assessment Consortium. (n.d.) Frequently asked questions. Retrieved from www.smarterbalan ced.org/resources-events/faqs/

Smarter Balanced Assessment Consortium (SBAC). (2013, February). *The Smarter Balanced technology strategy framework and system requirements specifications.* Retrieved from www.smarterbalanced.org/wordpress/wp-content/uploads/2011/12/Technology-Strategy-Framework-Executive-Summary_2-6-13.pdf

State of Indiana. (2012, December). Request for proposals 13–29: Solicitation for PARCC assessment administration. Retrieved from www.in.gov/idoa/proc/bids/RFP-13–29/

Stern, J. (2010, May). The mouse ain't dead . . . yet: Five of the best mice reviewed. Retrieved from www.engadget. com/2010/05/25/the-mouse-aint-dead-yet-five-of-the-best-mice-reviewed/

Strain-Seymour, E., Craft, J., Davis, L. L., & Elbom, J. (2013). *Testing on tablets: Part I of a series of usability studies on the use of tablets for K–12 assessment programs.* Retrieved from http://researchnetwork.pearson.com/wp-content/uploads/Testing-on-Tablets-PartI.pdf

Sutherland, I. E. (1964). Sketch pad a man-machine graphical communication system. In *Proceedings of the SHARE design automation workshop*: New York, NY: Association for Computing Machinery.

Texas Education Agency. (2008). *A review of literature on the comparability of scores obtained from examinees on computer-based and paper-based tests.* Retrieved from http://ritter.tea.state.tx.us/student.assessment/resources/techdigest/Technical_Reports/2008_literature_review_of_comparability_report.pdf

Tilbrook, D. M. (1976). *A newspaper pagination system.* Toronto: University of Toronto, Department of Computer Science.

Virginia Department of Education. (2010). *Frequently asked questions about Virginia's 2010 English standards of learning*. Retrieved from www.doe.virginia.gov/testing/sol/standards_docs/english/2010/faq_2010_english_sol.pdf

Vogel, D., & Baudisch, P. (2007, April). Shift: A technique for operating pen-based interfaces using touch. In *Proceedings of the SIGCHI conference on Human factors in computing systems* (pp. 657–666). New York, NY: Association for Computing Machinery.

Wang, S. (2004). *Online or paper: Does delivery affect results? Administration mode comparability study for Stanford Diagnostic Reading and Mathematics tests*. San Antonio, TX: Harcourt.

Wang, S., Jiao, H., Young, M. J., Brooks, T., & Olsen, J. (2007). A meta-analysis of testing mode effects in grade K–12 mathematics tests. *Educational and Psychological Measurement, 67*(2), 219–238.

Wang, S., Jiao, H., Young, M. J., Brooks, T., & Olsen, J. (2008). Comparability of computer-based and paper-and-pencil testing in K–12 reading assessments. *Educational and Psychological Measurement, 68*(1), 5–24.

Way, W. D., Davis, L. L., & Fitzpatrick, S. (2006, April). *Score comparability of online and paper administrations of the Texas Assessment of Knowledge and Skills*. Paper presented at the Annual Meeting of the National Council on Measurement in Education, San Francisco, CA. Retrieved from www.pearsonedmeasurement.com/downloads/research/RR_06_01.pdf

Way, W. D., Lin, C., & Kong, J. (2008, March). *Maintaining score equivalence as tests transition online: Issues, approaches, and trends*. Paper presented at the annual meeting of the National Council on Measurement in Education, New York, NY.

Way, W. D., & McClarty, K. L. (2012). Standard setting for computer-based assessments: A summary of mode comparability research and considerations. In G. J. Cizek (Ed.), *Setting performance standards* (pp. 451–466). New York: Routledge.

Way, W. D., Um, K., Lin, C., & McClarty, K. L. (2007, April). *An evaluation of a matched samples method for assessing the comparability of online and paper test performance*. Paper presented at the annual meeting of the National Council on Measurement in Education, Chicago, IL.

Wildgrube, W. (1982). Computerized testing in the German Federal Armed Forces: Empirical approaches. In D. J. Weiss (Ed.), *Item response theory and computerized adaptive testing conference proceedings* (pp. 353–359). Minneapolis, MN: University of Minnesota.

Winter, P. (2010). *Evaluating the comparability of scores from achievement test variations*. Council of Chief State School Officers: Washington, DC. Retrieved from www.ccsso.org/Documents/2010/Evaluating_the_Comparability_of_Scores_2010.pdf

Yu, L., Livingston, S. A., Larkin, K. C., & Bonett, J. (2004). *Investigating differences in examinee performance between computer-based and handwritten essays* (RR-04–18). Princeton, NJ: Educational Testing Service.

Yu, L., Lorié, W., & Sewall, L. (2014, April). *Testing on tablets*. Paper presented at the Annual Meeting of the National Council on Measurement in Education, Philadelphia, PA.

Zuriff, G. E. (2000). Extra examination time for students with learning disabilities: An examination of the maximum potential thesis. *Applied Measurement in Education, 13*(1), 99–117.

# 13
## Diagnostic Assessment
*Methods for the Reliable Measurement of Multidimensional Abilities*

Jonathan Templin

Educational measurement, like all scientific fields, is in a constant cycle of rediscovering, refining, and advancing theories to meet the challenges of the current times. Similarly, such a pattern can also be found in *diagnostic assessment*, an area that is also commonly referred to as *cognitive diagnosis* (e.g., Leighton & Gierl, 2007; Nichols, Chipman, & Brennan, 1995) or *diagnostic classification models* (DCMs; e.g., Rupp & Templin, 2008; Rupp, Templin, & Henson, 2010). Such models investigate the knowledge states of examinees via *diagnostic assessments* for the purpose of providing them with fine-grained feedback about their *multivariate profile of latent skills*, which have been called attributes, dispositions, or traits. Within this small yet growing corner of psychometrics, a particular set of statistical models with discrete (categorical) latent variables are used to obtain such multivariate attribute profiles of examinees, which are based on classifications of examinees into different latent classes.

Over the last 30 years, DCMs have evolved from a relatively small set of niche models to become larger and more mainstream in the psychometric community. Major differences between the current work in the area of DCMs and the work that was published early on in the field have been driven by two major aligned forces. The increase of computing power has made the estimation of complex models for large data sets feasible. Furthermore, there has been a renewed interest in using theories from cognitive sciences to explain the differential performance of examinees on highly specified assessments. In the beginning, this interest may have been fueled by a more rigorous look at empirically driven accountability systems, which set in motion a number of changes in educational systems all over the world. These changes have fundamentally shaped current theories and practices of educational measurement and stand to provide a solid backbone for measurement in the future.

In this chapter, I describe the current state of diagnostic models (henceforth called diagnostic classification models or DCMs) in educational measurement. I begin with a look at the statistical origins of DCMs in the literature of latent class models and trace some of the key methodological developments that have laid the foundation for the current state of the field. I then look at the current DCMs, showing how the field, having recently engaged in a process of unifying theory and practice surrounding DCMs with well-established statistical theories that sought to provide a measure of psychometric respectability and methodological rigor, is poised to reshape how educational measurement is conducted in both large- and small-scale settings.

## Conceptual and Statistical Foundations of DCMs

Before beginning the discussion of key methodological origins of DCMs, it is necessary to define the types of models incorporated into the term "DCMs." A variety of review articles for these models has recently appeared in the educational measurement literature (DiBello, Roussos, & Stout, 2007, Fu & Li 2007, Rupp & Templin, 2008). For readers who are interested in a comprehensive review of the current issues in diagnostic assessment in education, there is the edited volume by Leighton and Gierl (2007). For readers who are interested in a comprehensive introduction to DCMs more generally, there is the volume by Rupp and colleagues (2010). The perspective discussed in this chapter is strongly influenced by all of these works but places DCMs within a wider taxonomy of psychometric models and statistical techniques.

### A Definition of Modern DCMs

DCMs have alternatively been called *cognitive psychometric models* (e.g., Rupp, 2007), *cognitive diagnosis models* (e.g., Nichols, Chipman, & Brennan, 1995; Templin & Henson, 2006; see Nichols, 1994), *latent response models* (e.g., Maris, 1995), *restricted latent class models* (e.g., Haertel, 1989; Macready & Dayton, 1977), *multiple classification latent class models* (e.g., Maris, 1995, 1999), *structured located latent class models* (e.g., Xu & von Davier, 2008a, 2008b), and *structured item response theory models* (e.g., Mislevy, 2007; Rupp & Mislevy, 2007).

Clearly, each of these terms carries with it a particular connotation that highlights aspects of these models that are pertinent. Some definitions highlight their theoretical grounding, some their substantive purpose, and some their statistical properties. In keeping with the unification and broadening of methodologies that has taken place in the field, the term "DCMs" was chosen to separate the statistical methodology (i.e., the statistically driven classification of examinees) from a particular application type such as measuring component skills of an achievement test in an educational measurement setting. This was done, in part, as DCMs have utility beyond the measurement of response processes that are driven by information-processing views of cognition, as demonstrated by Templin and Henson (2006) within the context of a diagnostic assessment of psychological or psychiatric disorders. As such, here is an adaptation of a definition of DCMs (Rupp & Templin, 2008), which helps to set them apart from other statistical models with latent variables:

> DCMs are confirmatory multidimensional latent-variable models. Their loading structure / Q-matrix can be complex to reflect within-item multidimensionality or simply to reflect between-item multidimensionality. DCMs are suitable for modeling observable response variables with various scale types and distributions and contain discrete latent predictor variables. The latent predictor variables are combined by a series of linear-modeling effects that can result in compensatory and / or non-compensatory ways for predicting observable item responses. DCMs thus provide multivariate attribute profiles for examinees based on statistically-derived classifications. (p. 226)

This definition is helpful in distinguishing DCMs from multidimensional item response theory models (M-IRT; e.g., Ackerman, Gierl, & Walker, 2003) and multidimensional confirmatory factor analysis models (M-CFA) (e.g., McDonald, 1999).

Of all the definitional components, the most important is that DCMs are models that contain discrete latent variables that allow for statistically driven classifications of examinees, whereas M-IRT and M-CFA models contain continuous latent variables that purport to be on interval scales. Consequently, classifications of examinees are only possible through post-hoc procedures such as standard setting (e.g., Cizek, Bunch, & Koons, 2004; Zieky & Perie, 2006), which create cut-scores on the continuous scales apart from the scaling process. Like other multidimensional latent-variable models, however, DCMs have been constructed to measure multiple latent variables, creating multidimensional attribute profiles, even though these profiles are based on classifications. Driving this process is a specification of which attributes are measured by which items, which is typically called the *Q-matrix* in the DCM context. Although the term "Q-matrix" is conventionally used in the DCM literature and often attributed to Tatsuoka (1983), modern formulations of DCMs recognize that the Q-matrix is identical to a *factor pattern matrix* from M-CFA because it denotes which items "load" onto which discrete "factors." Unlike most other latent variable models, however, DCMs often feature latent variable interactions. In fact, most early DCMs are now recognized as having complex patterns of interacting latent traits. These latent variable interactions serve as the basis for understanding how latent variables are thought to be combined to produce item responses, broadening the practical appeal of their use.

### Evolutionary Lineages of Modern DCMs

The present formulation of DCMs within a unified statistical framework (presented in what follows) emanates from several different fields. Figure 13.1, adapted from Templin (2009), synthesizes where DCMs have evolved from, depicting the fields of mathematical psychology, clustering and classification methodology, and item response theory as being central to their growth as a modern modeling framework. Although the specifics of the methods depicted differ, each seeks the same goal: diagnosing the status of an examinee on the basis of observed response behavior, typically to a set of tasks on a diagnostic assessment.

Emanating from the domain of *mathematical psychology*, the knowledge space literature (e.g., Albert & Lukas, 1999; Doignon & Falmagne, 1998) describes a set of analytical methods for understanding how examinees acquire and retain knowledge about complex behavioral domains. A focus of this area of research is on the construction knowledge spaces through methods that are grounded in set theory and Boolean algebra with relatively close links to latent class models (Schrepp, 2005).

Aside from knowledge space theory, advances in DCMs can also be traced back to methodological advances in both *clustering and classification methodology* and IRT. Algorithmic classification techniques such as the *rule space methodology* (e.g., Tatsuoka, 1983, 1995, 2009), which has led to the *attribute hierarchy method* (AHM; e.g., Leighton, Gierl, & Hunka, 2004; Leighton, Cui, & Cor, 2009) served to supplement IRT analyses of data from tests assessments. In original development of these methods, examinees are classified based on the differences between their observed response patterns and the expected response patterns for examinees with a particular attribute profile given a particular Q-matrix. Classifications are done using specialized person-fit indices (e.g., Tatsuoka, 1996), likelihood functions (e.g.,

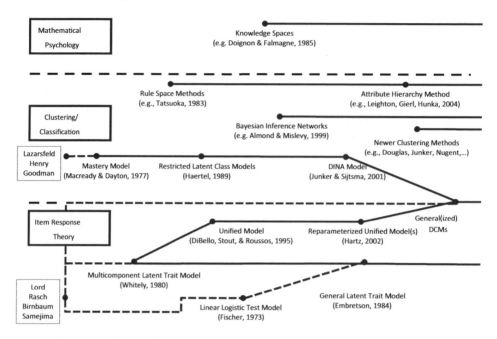

**Figure 13.1** Lineage of modern DCMs

Gierl, Leighton, & Hunka, 2008), or, more recently in AHM, neural networks (e.g., Gierl, Cui, & Hunka, 2008). Because of the algorithmic nature of these classification processes, analysts are able to classify examinees into high-dimensional attribute profiles (i.e., with more than 20 attributes).

Emanating from the rule space method but using test data directly, the partially ordered subset (or POSET) model formulations rely on latent class models and strictly ordered sets of attributes. More recently, researchers have begun to rediscover classical clustering techniques such as *K*-means clustering and hierarchical agglomerative clustering for purposes of classifying examinees with diagnostic assessment data (e.g., Chiu & Douglas, 2009; Nugent, Dean, Ayers, & Junker, 2009; Tatsuoka, 2002). From a fully parametric perspective, *Bayesian inference networks* (e.g., Almond, Mislevy, Steinberg, Yan, & Williamson, 2015) allow for the estimation of attribute profiles using a flexible model-based Bayesian estimation framework.

Within the item response theory framework, the roots of measurement models that use multivariate information about cognitive response processes to explain response behavior include Embretson's work on the *multicomponent latent trait model* (Whitely, 1980), a non-compensatory M-IRT model with continuous latent variables, and the *general latent trait model* (Embretson, 1984), which was inspired by the work of Fischer (1973) with the *linear logistic test model* (for a summary of research on this model see Fischer, 1997). Fischer's model had sought to decompose item difficulty as a function of item characteristics, thereby gaining additional explanatory information about item operating characteristics rather than examinees. These models became the inspiration for the *unified/fusion model* (DiBello, Stout, & Roussos, 1995) and the non-compensatory and compensatory versions of the *reparameterized unified model* (Hartz, 2002; Templin, 2006).

### General Latent Class Models as the Foundation for Modern DCMs

Statistically, there is a differentiation between latent class–based DCMs and other types of methods for cognitive diagnosis, as the latent-class based DCMs provide classifications directly from examinee data. To delineate latent class-based DCMs, I begin with the general latent class model (e.g., Goodman, 1974; Lazarsfeld & Henry, 1968; McCutcheon, 1987), which is a finite mixture model (e.g., McLachlan & Peel, 2000). Constrained versions of this model are used for examinee diagnosis. The general latent class likelihood of observing a particular pattern of responses $y_e$ for an examinee $e$ is:

$$P\left(\mathbf{Y}_e = \mathbf{y}_e\right) = \sum_{c=1}^{C} \nu_c \prod_{i=1}^{I} \pi_{ci}^{y_{ei}} \left(1 - \pi_{ci}\right)^{1-y_{ei}} \tag{1}$$

Here, the subscripts $c = 1,\dots.C$ represent the enumerated latent classes, items are indexed $i = 1,\dots,I$, and the dichotomously scored items are denoted $y_{ei}$. In examining Equation 1, there are two parameters of interest: $\pi_{ci}$, which is often referred to as the core of the measurement component linking observable item responses to the latent classes and $\nu_c$, which is often referred to as the structural component that provides the information of the distribution of examinees across classes from the sample. The $\pi_{ci}$ parameter is the probability an examinee who is a member of latent class $c$ answering item $i$ correctly, which is also known as a class-specific item difficulty (from classical test theory—the proportion of examinees from class $c$ answering item $i$ correctly). The likelihood for the measurement component of the model is a product across Bernoulli distributions for the $I$ items of the test, because item responses are assumed independent conditional upon the latent class of an examinee (also known as local independence, an often-assumed feature of psychometric models that, put another way, says the test measures only what is purported to be measured and nothing more).

The structural component of the general latent class model is represented by the $\nu_c$, which are also known to the mixture models community as the *mixing proportions*. These parameters, which sum to one, represent the probability that an examinee is a member of latent class $c$. As such, $\nu_c$ can also be interpreted as the *base-rate probability* of latent class membership in the population of examinees; for similar interpretational differences in IRT, see Holland (1990). Although it is not directly obvious from the statistical structure of the general latent class model, the structural model is analogous to structural models that form the basis of *structural equation modeling* (SEM; e.g., Kline, 2011) because it provides a model for the relationships among the latent variables. As this relationship is between categorical latent variables in general latent class models and DCMs, the exact specification of the structural model differs in these models from what is typically used in SEM.

### DCMs as Restricted Latent Class Models

DCMs are restricted latent class models as, for a test measuring $A$ dichotomous attributes, each of the possible $2^A$ attribute patterns is represented as a latent class. The class-specific item response probabilities, $\pi_{ci}$, are parameterized as functions of multiple discrete latent predictor variables. The specific combination of latent variables that are involved in the computation of $\pi_{ci}$ depends on the item–attribute relationships as specified in the Q-matrix for the assessment. As a result of the interaction between the Q-matrix and the latent class structure, the total number of latent classes in DCMs is specified **prior to an analysis**, which leads to equality restrictions of the general latent class model $\pi_{ci}$ item parameters across latent classes. DCMs, therefore, are *confirmatory latent class models*, where the attribute profile of each latent class is specified prior to fitting the DCM to response data. In the 1990s, the educational measurement literature witnessed a renewed interest in different ways in which the response functions for predicting how the $\pi_{ci}$ could be specified, which has resulted in a wide variety of seemingly different DCMs, all with different names but that all fit under a common framework.

### Recent Developments in Latent-Variable DCMs

In recent years, a shift has occurred in the field of DCMs, signaling the transition from a disconnected set of models to a unified framework for the specification, estimation, and fit assessment for the vast majority of DCMs. Researchers are able to articulate more explicitly how core DCMs can be distinguished by (a) the distributional type of the response variables they model, (b) the distributional type of the latent variables they contain, and (c) whether they constrain model parameters across items, across attributes, or neither (Rupp & Templin, 2008; Rupp et al., 2010). These developments in the area of modern DCMs mimic similar developments for other families of latent-variable models that are commonly used in educational measurement. Authors such as McDonald (1999) have summarized many theoretical relationships between IRT and CFA models, Brennan (2001) has summarized such relationships between latent-variable models in classical test theory and general linear models, and Raudenbush and Bryk (2002) have shown how IRT and CFA models can be specified as hierarchical linear models. Skrondal and Rabe-Hesketh (2004) have comprehensively synthesized the theory of various latent-variable models across a variety of traditional modeling frameworks in their landmark volume titled *Generalized Latent Variable Modeling: Multilevel, Longitudinal, and Structural Equation Models*.

### Modern DCMs in Generalized Linear and Nonlinear Mixed-Models Frameworks

Following the reviews in Skrondal and Rabe-Hesketh (2004) and Rijmen, Tuerlinckx, De Boeck, and Kuppens (2003), the modeling frameworks that unify a large variety of modern DCMs are typically labeled *generalized linear mixed models* (GLMM) and sometimes *nonlinear mixed models* (NLMM; e.g., Davidian & Giltinan, 1995; McCulloch & Searle, 2001; Verbeke & Molenberghs, 2000). More recently, Stroup (2012) noted the development of "doubly generalized" models where *both* the observed outcome/item and the latent/random effects could follow any type of parametric (or nonparametric) distribution, of which DCMs are a member. Several different GLMM parameterizations for the measurement component of DCMs have appeared in the educational and psychological measurement literature in recent years, most notably the *log-linear cognitive diagnosis model* or LCDM by Henson, Templin, and Willse (2009) and von Davier (2005). As originally described in the *general diagnostic model* of von Davier (2005), the concept is to map the categorical latent attribute variables onto the observable item responses through use of a *linear predictor* as commonly referred to in GLMMs. The model introduced by de la Torre (2011) replicated the LCDM by adding a general DCM that is equivalent to that of the LCDM, allowing the discussion of the LCDM to suffice for this chapter.

The *log-linear cognitive diagnosis model* provides a general parameterization of the item response probabilities in the measurement component for DCMs. Shown next is the original dichotomous item parameterization, which can be extended to a number of response types (e.g., Bozard, 2010; Templin & Bradshaw, 2013; Templin, Henson, Rupp, Jang, & Ahmed, 2008). For dichotomous items, the LCDM parameterization uses a logit or *log-odds link* to relate the linear predictor (the term in the exponent) to the item response probabilities $\pi_{ci}$:

$$\pi_{ci} = P(Y_{ci} = 1 | \boldsymbol{\alpha}_c) = \frac{\exp\left(\lambda_{i,0} + \boldsymbol{\lambda}_i^T \boldsymbol{h}(\boldsymbol{\alpha}_c, \boldsymbol{q}_i)\right)}{1 + \exp\left(\lambda_{i,0} + \boldsymbol{\lambda}_i^T \boldsymbol{h}(\boldsymbol{\alpha}_c, \boldsymbol{q}_i)\right)} \tag{2}$$

The first parameter in the linear predictor (i.e., the term in the exponent), $\lambda_{i,0}$, is the intercept parameter for item $i$. It represents the baseline log-odds of a correct response for examinees with attribute profiles where no measured attribute is mastered or possessed. The core component of the second part in the kernel, $\boldsymbol{h}(\boldsymbol{\alpha}_c, \boldsymbol{q}_i)$, is a linear (i.e., additive) "helper" function that contains indicators (binary 0/1 switches) that turn either on or off the possible parameters in the vector $\boldsymbol{\lambda}_i$.

To better understand how this linear combination functions, consider a test that measures three attributes, yielding a total of $2^3=8$ possible latent classes. Because the test measures three attributes, the Q-matrix entry for a given item is a row vector of zeroes and ones, where ones indicate the corresponding attribute in the column is measured by the item. With this example in mind, the terms in each of the set of attribute patterns, the possible set of item parameters, and the "helper" function are:

$$A = \begin{bmatrix} \alpha_1 \\ \alpha_2 \\ \alpha_3 \\ \alpha_4 \\ \alpha_5 \\ \alpha_6 \\ \alpha_7 \\ \alpha_8 \end{bmatrix} = \begin{bmatrix} [0,0,0] \\ [0,0,1] \\ [0,1,0] \\ [0,1,1] \\ [1,0,0] \\ [1,0,1] \\ [1,1,0] \\ [1,1,1] \end{bmatrix}; \lambda_i = \begin{bmatrix} \lambda_{i,1,(1)} \\ \lambda_{i,1,(2)} \\ \lambda_{i,1,(3)} \\ \lambda_{i,2,(1,2)} \\ \lambda_{i,2,(1,3)} \\ \lambda_{i,2,(2,3)} \\ \lambda_{i,3,(1,2,3)} \end{bmatrix};$$

$$\boldsymbol{h}(\boldsymbol{\alpha}_c, \boldsymbol{q}_i) = \begin{bmatrix} \alpha_{c1} \cdot q_{i1} \\ \alpha_{c2} \cdot q_{i2} \\ \alpha_{c3} \cdot q_{i3} \\ (\alpha_{c1} \cdot q_{i1})(\alpha_{c2} \cdot q_{i2}) \\ (\alpha_{c1} \cdot q_{i1})(\alpha_{c3} \cdot q_{i3}) \\ (\alpha_{c1} \cdot q_{i1})(\alpha_{c2} \cdot q_{i2})(\alpha_{c3} \cdot q_{i3}) \end{bmatrix} \tag{3}$$

The matrix $\mathbf{A}$ contains all possible vectors of attribute profiles $\boldsymbol{\alpha}_c$, where for this example $c = 1\ldots,8$. All attributes and Q-matrix entries are binary, making the elements of $\boldsymbol{h}(\boldsymbol{\alpha}_c, \boldsymbol{q}_i)$ binary indicators as well. Recall from earlier, the Q-matrix is the mechanism by which the attributes influencing item responses are delineated. Therefore, for a Q-matrix with $A$ attributes (here, three), the first $A$ elements of $\boldsymbol{h}(\boldsymbol{\alpha}_c, \boldsymbol{q}_i)$ represent the on/off switches for the $A$ possible main effect parameters (the first three rows in Equation 3). The second set of elements includes the on/off switches for all possible two-way interactions for items measuring two attributes. The remaining element of $h(\boldsymbol{\alpha}_c, \boldsymbol{q}_i)$ is the switch for a possible three-way interaction. For items measuring $A$ attributes, up to an $A$-way interaction is possible, if one can be estimated.

To further demonstrate the general model specification and estimation approach, consider an item that measures only two attributes, denoted $\alpha_1$ and $\alpha_2$. The corresponding row of the Q-matrix for this example item would then be $\boldsymbol{q}_i = [1,1,0]$ Given this item's Q-matrix entries indicating it measures attributes one and two, the "helper" function then becomes:

$$
\boldsymbol{h}(\boldsymbol{\alpha}_c, \boldsymbol{q}_i = \begin{bmatrix} 1 & 1 & 0 \end{bmatrix}) = \begin{bmatrix} \alpha_{c1} \cdot 1 \\ \alpha_{c2} \cdot 1 \\ \alpha_{c3} \cdot 0 \\ (\alpha_{c1} \cdot 1)(\alpha_{c2} \cdot 1) \\ (\alpha_{c1} \cdot 1)(\alpha_{c3} \cdot 0) \\ (\alpha_{c2} \cdot 1)(\alpha_{c3} \cdot 0) \\ (\alpha_{c1} \cdot 1)(\alpha_{c2} \cdot 1)(\alpha_{c3} \cdot 0) \end{bmatrix} = \begin{bmatrix} \alpha_{c1} \\ \alpha_{c2} \\ 0 \\ \alpha_{c1}\alpha_{c2} \\ 0 \\ 0 \\ 0 \end{bmatrix}
\tag{4}
$$

The on/off switches turn on any entry that contains attribute one by itself, attribute two by itself, or both attributes one and two as a pair. Similarly, the on/off switches turn off any entry that contains attribute three as that term in the Q-matrix is zero, leading to a zero entry in the "helper" function's result. The linear combination formed by $\boldsymbol{\alpha}_i^T \boldsymbol{h}(\pm_c, \boldsymbol{q}_i)$ results in an additive sum of the item parameters (the $\lambda_i$) and the attribute indicators, resembling the linear equation of an ANOVA model:

$$
\boldsymbol{\lambda}_i^T \boldsymbol{h}(\boldsymbol{\alpha}_c, \boldsymbol{q}_i = \begin{bmatrix} 1 & 1 & 0 \end{bmatrix}) = \begin{bmatrix} \lambda_{i,1,(1)} \\ \lambda_{i,1,(2)} \\ \lambda_{i,1,(3)} \\ \lambda_{i,2,(1,2)} \\ \lambda_{i,2,(1,3)} \\ \lambda_{i,2,(2,3)} \\ \lambda_{i,3,(1,2,3)} \end{bmatrix}^T \begin{bmatrix} \alpha_{c1} \\ \alpha_{c2} \\ 0 \\ \alpha_{c1}\alpha_{c2} \\ 0 \\ 0 \\ 0 \end{bmatrix}
\tag{5}
$$

$$
\lambda_{i,1,(1)}\alpha_{c1} + \lambda_{i,1,(2)}\alpha_{c2} + \lambda_{i,2,(1,2)}\alpha_{c1}\alpha_{c2}
\tag{6}
$$

Therefore, for a given examinee in latent class $c$ with attribute pattern $\boldsymbol{\alpha}_c$, the LCDM item response function for the this item is:

$$
\pi_{ci} = P(Y_{ci} = 1 \mid \boldsymbol{\alpha}_c) = \frac{\exp\left(\lambda_{i,0} + \lambda_{i,1,(1)}\alpha_{c1} + \lambda_{i,1,(2)}\alpha_{c2} + \lambda_{i,2,(1,2)}\alpha_{c1}\alpha_{c2}\right)}{1 + \exp\left(\lambda_{i,0} + \lambda_{i,1,(1)}\alpha_{c1} + \lambda_{i,1,(2)}\alpha_{c2} + \lambda_{i,2,(1,2)}\alpha_{c1}\alpha_{c2}\right)}
\tag{7}
$$

To illustrate the effect of the different model parameters on the item response probability, I use some hypothetical values for each. In particular, I set the intercept $\lambda_{i,0}=-2$, the main effect of attribute one $\lambda_{i,1(1)}=2$, the main effect of attribute two $\lambda_{i,1(2)}=1$, and the two-way interaction effect between attributes one and two $\lambda_{i,2,(1,2)}=2$. The intercept reflects the predicted log-odds of a correct response for examinees who do not possess either of the two measured attributes of the item (profiles $\alpha_1$ and $\alpha_2$ from Equation 3); because $\lambda_{i,0}=-2$, the probability of a correct response is:

$$\pi_{ci} = P\left(Y_{ci}=1 \mid \alpha_c = \alpha_1 \text{ or } \alpha_2\right) = \frac{\exp\left(\lambda_{i,0} + \lambda_{i,1,(1)}(0) + \lambda_{i,1,(2)}(0) + \lambda_{i,2,(1,2)}(0)(0)\right)}{1+\exp\left(\lambda_{i,0} + \lambda_{i,1,(1)}(0) + \lambda_{i,1,(2)}(0) + \lambda_{i,2,(1,2)}(0)(0)\right)} =$$

$$\frac{\exp\left(\lambda_{i,0}\right)}{1+\exp\left(\lambda_{i,0}\right)} = \frac{\exp(-2)}{1+\exp(-2)} = .12 \tag{8}$$

Because of our binary coding for attribute mastery status, this group is also called the "reference group" in a general linear modeling context, as all other parameters are specified and interpreted with respect to this group.

Examinees who possess the first attribute but not the second have a predicted log-odds of $\lambda_{i,0} + \lambda_{i,1,(1)} = -2 + 2 = 0$, giving an item response probability of .5. In this sense, for an item with a higher-level interaction, each main effect is conditional on the value of the other attributes being zero—called a conditional or "simple" main effect. Similarly, examinees who possess the second attribute but not the first have a predicted log-odds of $\lambda_{i,0} + \lambda_{i,1,(2)} = -2 + 1 = -1$ giving an item response probability of .27. Finally, examinees possessing both attributes have a predicted log-odds of $\lambda_{i,0} + \lambda_{i,1(1)} + \lambda_{i,1,(2)} + \lambda_{i,2,(1,2)} = 3$, with a corresponding item response probability of .95. The positive interaction effect indicates that the possession of both attributes provides an additional increase in the log-odds over what would be expected with possession of either of the two attributes marginally. It is the form of the interaction between latent variables that sets DCMs apart from other psychometric models in that most core DCMs provide for some type of latent variable interaction (see Henson et al., 2009; Rupp et al., 2010).

Figure 13.2 presents a plot of the linear predictor value and the item response probabilities, both shown for all four possible combinations of possession for each attribute (i.e., all four attribute profiles/latent classes). For this item, an investigation of the linear predictor of the LCDM proceeds similarly to how an investigation of a two-way analysis-of-variance (ANOVA) model would. The first plot in Figure 13.2 is like a treatment-means plot for two categorical design variables, showing the value of the linear predictor for each attribute combination. As in an ANOVA model, there is a visual indication of an interaction effect between the two attribute variables because the two lines in the plot are not parallel. The second panel in Figure 13.2 is of the item response function itself and is on the probability scale. In IRT models this plot is commonly referred to as the *item characteristic curve*, in the case of unidimensional models, or *item response surface*, in the case of multidimensional models. In these plots, the value of the latent predictor variable is plotted on the horizontal $X$-axis and the conditional item response probability is plotted on the vertical $Y$-axis. The analogous plot for DCMs, which are multidimensional latent-variable models, is called the *item characteristic bar chart* (Templin, 2009) as the latent predictor variables are no longer continuous.

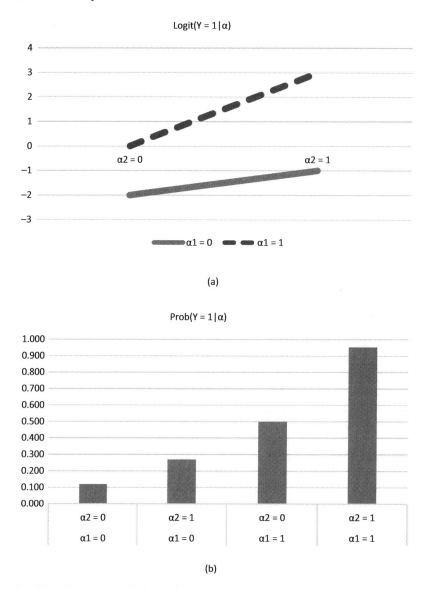

**Figure 13.2** LCDM item characteristic bar chart for sample item

The inclusion of item- and attribute-specific linear predictor parameters in the LCDM formulation makes the measurement component of the LCDM resemble that of a GLMM (see Stroup, 2012). As this is a general modeling framework, most features of GLMMs apply to the LCDM. For instance, statistical hypothesis tests for each model parameter come via asymptotic properties of marginal maximum likelihood estimators. Such tests allow analysts to eliminate unnecessary model parameters that are not significantly different from zero and therefore do not contribute to the reliable measurement of the attribute variables—such as removing nonsignificant interactions between attributes or removing an overspecified entry from the Q-matrix entirely by removing all nonsignificant main effects and interactions involving that attribute.

### Specifying Modern DCMs With the LCDM

Constraints can be placed on the LCDM parameters so that a number of previously defined DCMs can be obtained. The LCDM *subsumes* other DCMs, meaning that any analysis with the LCDM will fit the data *as well as* (in the worst case) *and likely better* than any other DCM. This represents a fundamental shift from previously established DCM practices of thinking "model-wise" in which the same restricted model applies to all items of a test to thinking "parameter-wise" within a broader modeling framework. Although these ideas are certainly not at all novel from traditional general or generalized linear modeling frameworks, they are novel for the field of DCMs. Prior to the advent of this generalized linear mixed-modeling approach, all items of a test had to follow one specific model, an implausible scenario under most conditions that frequently led to severe model–data misfit.

### Representing Core Modern DCMs With the LCDM

The LCDM subsumes many core DCMs in ways that allow for a greater understanding of the response processes that generate the item responses. To illustrate how core DCMs can be represented within the LCDM framework, I focus on two specific models with distinct structural characteristics, the noncompensatory *deterministic inputs noisy and-gate* or DINA model (Junker & Sijtsma, 2001) and its compensatory analog, the *deterministic inputs noisy or-gate* (DINO) model (Templin & Henson, 2006). The DINA model is colloquially called the "all-or-nothing" model because the DINA model distinguishes examinees with mastery of *all* measured attributes from those who lack at least one attribute. Likewise, the DINO model is called the "one-or-more" model because the DINO distinguishes examinees with mastery of one or more measured attributes on an item from those who have mastered none.

To show how the LCDM subsumes both of these basic DCMs, I will use the example with an item measuring two attributes that I used for the general LCDM formulation. In both the DINA and DINO models, examinees are placed into one of two groups per item, a "high-probability" group (characterized by one minus the slipping parameter for an item, $1-s_i$) and a "low-probability" group (characterized by the guessing parameter for an item, $g_i$). A general form for either model is:

$$\pi_{ci} = P\left(Y_{ci} = 1 \mid \delta_{ci}\right) = \left(1 - s_i\right)^{\delta_{ci}} g_i^{1-\delta_{ci}} \tag{9}$$

with $\delta_{ci} = \prod_{a=1}^{A} \alpha_{ca}^{q_{ia}}$ being the all-or-nothing on/off switch for the DINA model where $\delta_{ci}$ is one if an examinee from class $c$ has mastered all attributes measured by item $i$ and is zero otherwise. For the DINO model, the one-or-more on/off switch is $\delta = 1 - \prod_{a=1}^{A} (1 - \alpha_{ca})^{q_{ia}}$, where $\delta_{ci}$ is one when an examinee from class $c$ has mastered *at least* one attribute measured by the item and is zero otherwise. These functions are known as condensation functions (Maris, 1995, 1999). The two DINA/DINO item parameters can be expressed by LCDM parameters.

The DINA model representation of the example described previously can be obtained from the following LCDM parameterization:

$$g_i = \frac{\exp(\lambda_{i,0})}{1+\exp(\lambda_{i,0})}; (1-s_i) = \frac{\exp(\lambda_{i,0} + \lambda_{i,2,(1,2)}\alpha_{c1}\alpha_{c2})}{1+\exp(\lambda_{i,0} + \lambda_{i,2,(1,2)}\alpha_{c1}\alpha_{c2})} \tag{10}$$

In this model, the guessing parameter is the inverse log-odds function of only the intercept term because that is the only term relevant when no attribute has been mastered (where the DINA $\delta_{ci}=0$). The slipping parameter, however, is the inverse log-odds function of the intercept term *and* the highest-order interaction term present in the model (where the DINA $\delta_{ci}=1$). Because our hypothetical item measures only two attributes, the highest-order interaction is a two-way interaction. If more than two attributes were measured, this term would be the highest-order interaction with no lower-order interaction or main effects present. Thus, the DINA model represents an extreme form of a statistical model with an overadditive interaction and is analogous to an ANOVA model with *only* the highest-order interaction present *without* any lower order effects. In the classical general linear modeling literature (e.g., Kutner, Nachtsheim, Neter, & Li, 2005), such a model is generally ill advised, as the interaction can reflect the impact of lower-order interaction effects and main effects as well. Although it is theoretically possible that the DINA model may be an appropriate DCM for some items, it is unlikely to expect that it would fit all items on a diagnostic assessment.

Similarly, the DINO model representation of the example described previously can be obtained from the following LCDM parameterization:

$$g_i = \frac{\exp(\lambda_{i,0})}{1+\exp(\lambda_{i,0})}; (1-s_i) = \frac{\exp(\lambda_{i,0} + \lambda_{i,1}\alpha_{c1} + \lambda_{i,1}\alpha_{c2} - \lambda_{i,1}\alpha_{c1}\alpha_{c2})}{1+\exp(\lambda_{i,0} + \lambda_{i,2,(1,2)}\alpha_{c1}\alpha_{c2})} \tag{11}$$

Again, the guessing parameter is represented by the LCDM intercept (where the DINO $\delta_{ci}=0$). For the slipping parameter, there is only one $\lambda_{i,1}$ parameter estimated—only the sign changes depending on the effect (all of which where the DINO $\delta_{ci}=1$). The parameter allows for an increase in the log-odds when one attribute is possessed by an examinee. However, the increase in log-odds of any additional attributes possessed is cancelled out by the negative interaction effect. Therefore, the DINO model represents an extreme version of an underadditive model. Like the DINA model, it is theoretically possible that some items on a diagnostic assessment may follow such a structure, but it is implausible to expect that all items would adhere to this structure. Furthermore, DeCarlo (2011) has shown a number of identification issues for the DINA/DINO models that make their use questionable at best.

### Specifying Structural Models for Modern DCMs Within the LCDM Framework

To make the estimation of DCMs within a broader GLMM framework computationally more efficient for high-dimensional attribute spaces, linear model constraints can be imposed on the latent attribute structure as well. As authors such as Henson and Templin (2005) and Xu and von Davier (2008a) have shown, one can use a log-linear model for predicting the mixture proportions, $v_c$ and impose constraints or remove the interaction effect parameters to reduce the parametric complexity of the model without losing much precision. Similarly, one can estimate the proportions via a multivariate normal model for their tetrachoric correlation structure and impose higher-order factor models on the attribute space by structuring the tetrachoric correlation matrix appropriately (de la Torre & Douglas, 2004; Hartz, 2002; Templin & Henson, 2006). More information about the types and features of DCM structural models can be found in chapter 8 of Rupp and associates (2010).

It is also possible to reduce the parametric complexity by placing logical constraints on the latent classes, thereby reducing the total number of latent-class membership probabilities that need to be estimated. In the literature on DCMs, such constraints have been discussed under the label of *attribute hierarchies* to suggest that constraints could be guided by developmental theories of attribute acquisition (e.g., Leighton, Gierl, & Hunka, 2004; Tatsuoka, 1995). More recently, Templin and Bradshaw (2014) developed the *hierarchical diagnostic classification model* or HDCM to frame such hierarchies as analogous to ANOVA models with nested effects, providing a mechanism to test each hypothesized hierarchy in a model comparison.

### Estimation of Modern DCMs Within a Unified Framework

Before the recent developments that led to a unification of DCMs under a common GLMM framework for the measurement component, the wide-scale use of DCMs had been hampered by the fact that only disconnected software programs or estimation codes were available for different models (Rupp & Templin, 2008). Under a common GLMM framework for the measurement component, DCMs can now be estimated with relative ease with marginal maximum likelihood or within Bayesian estimation frameworks (see, e.g., Gelman, Carlin, Stern, & Rubin, 1995; Lynch, 2007). As with other statistical models, fully Bayesian estimation approaches allow researchers to incorporate theoretical knowledge about true parameter values into the estimation process. However, as the amount of data increases, the influence of this information rapidly decreases, and Bayesian estimation essentially becomes a mechanism for estimating complex models that could otherwise not be estimated at all.

Because DCMs are restricted latent class models, they can be estimated with any software program that allows for an estimation of mixture GLMMs with discrete latent variables, including the specification of various constraints on model parameters. For example, Templin and Hoffman (2013) and Rupp and colleagues (2010) have illustrated how DCMs can be estimated in Mplus (Muthén & Muthén, 1998–2013), which uses a frequentist estimation approach for item and structural parameters coupled with an empirical Bayes approach for the examinee parameters. Alternatively, one could use specialized programs for latent class analysis such as LatentGold (Vermunt & Magidson, 2015) or rely on noncommercial software that is available as a research license (see Rupp & Templin, 2008, for an overview). For researchers interested in investing time and effort to develop appropriate estimation code for statistical freeware, the programming environment *R* or, if a Bayesian approach is specifically desired, WinBugs would be suitable. More recently, FlexMIRT has incorporated the ability to efficiently model DCMs along with continuous latent variables (Cai, 2013).

### Motivations for Using Modern DCMs Over Continuous Latent-Variable Models

As discussed in this chapter, DCMs are very similar to other latent-variable models that are currently used by specialists in educational and psychological measurement. Motivations for use of DCMs have been limited in the past; however, recent research has demonstrated when such models can provide an added practical value for decision making. DCMs are not a statistical panacea that will solve all previously unresolved measurement challenges, but under the right conditions, they can provide a wealth of information for those interested in obtaining statistically driven classifications of examinees.

For instance, current educational measurement practice in the United States revolves around the administration of end-of-grade tests for the purposes of assessing whether students have achieved a certain level of proficiency within a domain, which is effectively a classification of learners into distinct mastery states. A debate on the relative merits of assigning proficiency classifications on the basis of end-of-grade tests for accountability purposes is beyond the scope of this chapter, but note that the process *could* be greatly improved by use of DCMs.

Research by Templin and Bradshaw (2013) has shown that the reliability of dichotomous attributes measured by DCMs is substantially higher than the reliability of similar continuous latent variable models due, to a large degree, to the discrete nature of the discrete latent variables. Specifically, the authors conducted a comparison of the reliability of a Rasch model with that of an analogous DCM. Under a Rasch model, a total of 34 items were required to reach a test-retest reliability of .80, 48 items were required to reach a test-retest reliability of .85, and 77 items were required to reach a test-retest reliability of .90. In contrast, the particular DCM in the study required only eight items to reach a reliability of .80, 10 items to reach a reliability of .85, and 13 items to reach a reliability of .90. In terms of assessment efficiency, these results showed that only $\frac{1}{3}$ of the items were required under a DCM to reach the same level of test-retest reliability as an existing end-of-grade test under a traditional IRT model for these data. These results suggest that if classification is the goal or if large numbers of traits must be estimated from a relatively small number of discrete items, then DCMs may be of use. At the same time, if there is no particular reporting preference for either continuous or discrete attribute profiles, then structurally similar M-IRT or M-CFA models and modern DCMs will provide results that are closely aligned (e.g., Haberman, von Davier, & Lee, 2008; Kunina, Rupp, & Wilhelm, 2009).

## Extending the Structure of Modern DCMs

The unified-mixture GLMM approach for specifying and estimating DCMs places them firmly into the psychometric taxonomy. In this section, I show how this approach affords additional flexibility for extending the core structures of DCMs to include additional explanatory variables and continuous latent variables, which are just beginning to be used by researchers.

### Extending the Structure of the Linear Predictor in the LCDM

I will denote a linear predictor for response variable $i$ for examinee $e$ by $\eta_{ei}$ to map the psychometric model onto the space of some parametric distribution. Here, the notation transitions away from the latent class-based notation with subscript $c$ because the general approach could include covariates that may differ across examinees from the same class. The linear predictor is a general placeholder that can take any real numbered value. It can be used in conjunction with differing link functions, thereby mapping the variables in the predictor onto the range of the mean of the hypothesized distribution of the item response (e.g., De Boeck & Wilson, 2004; Rijmen, Tuerlinckx, De Boeck, & Kuppens, 2003; Skrondal & Rabe-Hesketh, 2004).

One can then define a set of generalized latent variables for an examinee as elements of a vector $\gamma_e$, which could contain only categorical latent variables, as in prototypical DCMs, only continuous latent variables, as in M-IRT models, or a mix of categorical and continuous latent variables, as in newer extended DCMs (i.e., Bradshaw & Templin, 2013; Choi, 2010; or Henson, Templin, & Irwin, 2013; and Templin, Kingston, & Wang, 2011). Here, the notation continues to use an indicator matrix (i.e., Q-matrix or factor pattern matrix) to specify which latent variables are measured by each observed item, as indicated in $q_i$. One can also define a set of observed covariates collected in a matrix $\mathbf{X}_{ei}$ that are measured on examinee $e$ (examinee variables), item $i$ (item variables), or the interaction of examinee and item. These covariates are then related to person or item parameters via linear or nonlinear functions $g(\cdot)$ (see Dayton & Macready, 2002). In the context of certain item response GLMMs, approaches to modeling the influence of predictor variables on examinee and item parameters are also known as *explanatory item response modeling* (De Boeck & Wilson, 2004).

A general form of a latent variable model for the linear predictor is:

$$\eta_{ei} = \lambda_{0,i} + \boldsymbol{\lambda}_i^T \mathbf{h}\left(\boldsymbol{\gamma}_e, \boldsymbol{q}_i\right) + \boldsymbol{\beta}_i^T \mathbf{g}\left(\mathbf{X}_{ei}\right) \tag{12}$$

where the linear predictor parameters of the core LCDM formulation presented earlier are contained in $\boldsymbol{\lambda}_i^T$ and the linear predictor parameters for the covariates of the extended LCDM are contained in $\boldsymbol{\beta}_i^T$. Further extensions are also possible, for instance, for scale-type parameters.

As in GLMMs, the types and statistical distributions of the observed response variables that are modeled with the linear predictor predicate the choice of link function. For binary data, the *logit* or *log-odds link* is typically used so that the linear predictor models the log-odds of the probability of a correct response—the mean of the Bernoulli distribution. In this case, the distribution of error terms is fixed to be a logistic distribution with mean 0 and variance $\frac{\pi_i^2}{3}$ (see Hedeker & Gibbons, 2006). For continuous data, one could choose an *identity link*, which implies that the error terms have a normal distribution with some variance $\sigma_i^2$, also called the "unique variance" in the CFA literature. For count data, one could choose the *log link* by assuming a Poisson distribution of the response variables along with a scale factor for over/under-dispersion. A listing of commonly used link functions can be found in Skrondal and Rabe-Hesketh (2004).

The distribution of the discrete latent variables distinguishes DCMs from other latent-variable models with continuous latent variables. For instance, continuous latent variable models frequently assume that $\gamma_e$ is multivariate normally distributed with some multivariate mean vector—often fixed to a **0** vector—and associated covariance or correlation matrix $\Sigma$, depending on how the model is identified. For DCMs, however, the distribution of the latent variable is categorical. A convenient choice of distribution is the multivariate Bernoulli distribution (e.g., Maydeu-Olivares & Joe, 2005; Teugels, 1990), which assigns each possible sequence of binary outcomes its own probability. In the case of DCMs, each possible sequence of binary outcomes refers to a particular attribute profile/latent class $c$, and the distributional parameter for the multivariate Bernoulli distribution is the mixing proportion $\upsilon_c$.

As stated, a unified mixture GLMM framework for DCMs allows us to specify combinations of different types of latent variables as is done in both Henson, Templin, and Willse (2013) and Templin, Kingston, and Wang (2011). In both studies, the authors examined the structure of a large number of end-of-grade diagnostic assessments, both in reading and in mathematics, from a Midwestern state across several years. The authors applied a DCM that used the test blueprint from the end-of-grade assessment as the Q-matrix for a set of dichotomous attributes defined relative to a set of content standards. In addition to these variables, a continuous latent variable $\theta_e$ was measured on each item as well and included via a main effect $\lambda_{i,\theta}$, in the LCDM formulation, providing a bifactor DCM:

$$P\left(Y_{ei} = 1 | \boldsymbol{\alpha}_c, \theta_c\right) = \frac{\exp(\lambda_{i,0} + \lambda_{i,\theta}\theta_e + \boldsymbol{\lambda}_i^T \mathbf{h}\left(\boldsymbol{\alpha}_e, \boldsymbol{q}_i\right))}{1 + \exp(\lambda_{i,0} + \lambda_{i,\theta}\theta_e + \boldsymbol{\lambda}_i^T \mathbf{h}\left(\boldsymbol{\alpha}_e, \boldsymbol{q}_i\right))} \tag{13}$$

This model is graphically depicted in Figure 13.3 as a path diagram. The authors intended the model to resemble a hierarchical factors model (i.e., Thurstone, 1938), where the continuous latent variable represents a measure of "general intelligence" or "general ability on the subject area of a test." Had both the dichotomous latent attributes and continuous latent trait been observed instead of latent, this model would have been analogous to a linear models analysis of covariance model, but with a logistic link function for binary data. The authors found that the model that included the continuous higher-order factor fit statistically better than *any* other similar psychometric model (i.e., unidimensional IRT, M-IRT, higher-order M-IRT, or unstructured DCM) when information-based criteria for relative model–data fit were used. These results point to the power of combining predictor variables of different scale types. Because categorical latent variables cannot account for as much variability as continuous latent variables, they can be more easily estimated when a test is slightly more than unidimensional. A bifactor DCM can thus be seen as a means of capitalizing on information in the data set most efficiently: The dominant interindividual variation is reliably captured via a continuous unidimensional scale, while the secondary intraindividual variation beyond this dimension is reliably captured via the discrete multivariate attribute profile.

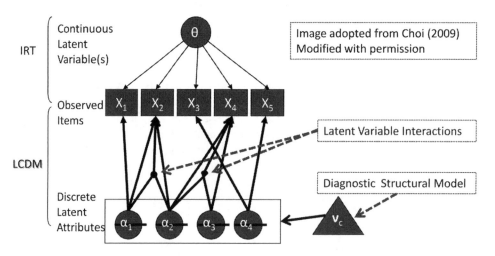

**Figure 13.3** Path diagram of bifactor DCM

## Concluding Remarks

The current state of the art in the field of DCMs should predominantly be comforting for researchers, because the field of educational and psychological measurement has amassed a rich resource library and practical expertise for tackling these challenges in other areas such as M-IRT and M-CFA specifically as well as GLMMs more generally. From a practitioner's viewpoint, the field has also articulated relatively comprehensive standards for inquiries into score reliability and inferential validation (e.g., American Educational Research Association, American Psychological Association, National Council on Measurement in Education, 1999), which await an adaptation to the area of DCMs.

In sum, DCMs have advanced a long way from their beginnings several decades ago. Although many challenges in their application still remain, I hope that by describing their place in the field of psychometrics in this chapter, I have demonstrated that they share much more similarities with related latent-variable modeling frameworks than is often suspected. In some ways, using DCMs presents a paradox. DCMs have been said to be models that allow for the accurate measurement of "fine-grained" skills (e.g., DiBello, Roussos, & Stout, 2007; Leighton & Gierl, 2007; Rupp & Templin, 2008). DCMs do so, however, by using coarse measures of latent characteristics—essentially partitioning each measured latent continuum into a few, typically two, categories. In so doing, DCMs increase the capacity to accurately measure multiple dimensions, yet they also lose the capacity to rank-order examinees more finely beyond assigning them to a few ordered categorical states. Thus, the successful application of DCMs is an important goal for the future of this field. Ultimately, the realized potential for their use will have to come from applications that can convincingly show that the types of inferences sought from diagnostic assessments can be most powerfully supported with these models.

If recent history is any indication, the future of DCMs will further make their form more practical, yielding perhaps bigger potential benefits for educational measurement as a whole. One area that may be particularly useful is that of the continued investigation of the bifactor DCM. In particular, this model may help large-scale assessment programs understand the features measured by the items of the test by combining the overall trait with specific attributes measured by sets of items. Further still, the advent of better multidimensional tests will hopefully lead to a better interweaving of testing with education, yielding better student outcomes.

## Note

This research was funded by National Science Foundation grants SES-1030337.

## References

Ackerman, T.A., Gierl, M.J., & Walker, C.M. (2003). Using multidimensional item response theory to evaluate educational and psychological tests. *Educational Measurement: Issues and Practice, 22*, 37–53.

Albert, D., & Lukas, J. (1999). *Knowledge spaces: Theories, empirical research, and applications.* Mahwah, NJ: Erlbaum.

Almond, R.G., Mislevy, R.J., Steinberg, L., Yan, D. & Williamson, D.M. (2015). *Bayes nets in educational assessment.* New York: Springer.

American Educational Research Association, American Psychological Association, National Council of Measurement in Education. (1999). *The standards for educational and psychological testing.* Washington, DC: AERA Publications.

Bozard, J.L. (2010). *Invariance testing in diagnostic classification models.* Unpublished master's thesis. The University of Georgia, Athens, GA.

Brennan, R.L. (2001). *Generalizability theory* (2nd ed.). New York: Springer.

Cai, L. (2013). flexMIRT version 2.00: A numerical engine for flexible multilevel multidimensional item analysis and test scoring. [Computer software]. Chapel Hill, NC: Vector Psychometric Group.

Chiu, C.-Y., Douglas, J., & Li, X. (2009). Cluster analysis for cognitive diagnosis: Theory and applications. *Psychometrika, 74*, 633–665.

Choi, H.-J. (2010). *A model that combines diagnostic classification assessment with mixture item response theory models.* Unpublished doctoral dissertation. The University of Georgia, Athens, GA.

Cizek, G.J., Bunch, M.B., & Koons, H. (2004). Setting performance standards: Contemporary methods. *Educational Measurement: Issues and Practice, 23*, 31–50.

Davidian, M., & Giltinan, D.M. (1995). *Nonlinear models for repeated measurement data.* London: Chapman & Hall.

Dayton, C.M., & Macready, G. (2002). Use of categorical and continuous covariates in latent class analysis. In J.A. Hagenaars & A.L. McCutcheon (Eds.), *Applied latent class analysis* (pp. 213–233). Cambridge, UK: Cambridge University Press.

De Boeck, P., & Wilson, M. (2004). *Explanatory item response theory models: A generalized linear and nonlinear approach.* New York: Springer.

de La Torre, J., & Douglas, J.A. (2004). Higher-order latent trait models for cognitive diagnosis. *Psychometrika, 69*, 333–353.

de la Torre, J. (2011). The generalized DINA model framework. *Psychometrika, 76*, 179–199.

DeCarlo, L.T. (2011). On the analysis of fraction subtraction data: The DINA model, classification, latent class sizes, and the Q-matrix. *Applied Psychological Measurement, 35*, 8–26.

DiBello, L., Roussos, L.A., & Stout, W. (2007). Review of cognitively diagnostic assessment and a summary of psychometric models. In C.V. Rao & S. Sinharay (Eds.), *Handbook of statistics (Vol. 26, Psychometrics;* pp. 979–1027). Amsterdam, Netherlands: Elsevier.

DiBello, L.V., Stout, W.F., & Roussos, L. (1995). Unified cognitive psychometric assessment likelihood-based classification techniques. In P.D. Nichols, S.F. Chipman, & R.L. Brennan (Eds.), *Cognitively diagnostic assessment* (pp. 361–390). Hillsdale, NJ: Erlbaum.

Doignon, J.P., & Falmagne, J.C. (1998). *Knowledge spaces.* Berlin, Germany: Springer.

Embretson, S.E. (1984). A general latent trait model for response processes. *Psychometrika, 49*, 175–186.

Fischer, G.H. (1973). The linear logistic test model as an instrument in educational research. *Acta Psychologica, 37*, 359–374.

Fischer, G.H. (1997). Unidimensional linear logistic Rasch models. In W.J. van der Linden & R.K. Hambleton (Eds.), *Handbook of modern item response theory* (pp. 221–224). New York: Springer.

Fu, J., & Li, Y. (2007, April). *An integrated review of cognitively diagnostic psychometric models.* Paper presented at the annual meeting of the National Council on Measurement in Education, Chicago, IL.

Gelman, A., Carlin, J.B., Stern, H.S., & Rubin, D.B. (1995). *Bayesian data analysis.* New York: Chapman & Hall.

Gierl, M., Cui, Y., & Hunka, S. (2008). Using connectionist models to evaluate examinees' response patterns on tests. *Journal of Modern Applied Statistical Methods, 7*, 234–245.

Gierl, M.J., Leighton, J.P., & Hunka, S.M. (2007). Using the attribute hierarchy method to make diagnostic inferences about examinees' cognitive skills. In J.P. Leighton & M.J. Gierl (Eds.), *Cognitive diagnostic assessment for education: Theory and applications* (pp. 242–274). Cambridge, UK: Cambridge University Press.

Goodman, L.A. (1974). Exploratory latent structure analysis using both identifiable and unidentifiable models. *Biometrika, 61*, 215–231.

Haberman, S.J., von Davier, M., & Lee, Yi-H. (2008). *Comparison of multidimensional item response models: Multivariate normal ability distributions versus multivariate polytomous ability distributions* (RR-08–45). Princeton, NJ: Educational Testing Service.

Haertel, E.H. (1989). Using restricted latent class models to map the skill structure of achievement items. *Journal of Educational Measurement, 26*, 301–323.

Hartz, S.M. (2002). *A Bayesian framework for the unified model for assessing cognitive abilities: Blending theory with practicality.* Unpublished doctoral dissertation. University of Illinois at Urbana-Champaign, Urbana-Champaign, IL.

Hedeker, D., & Gibbons, R.D. (2006). *Longitudinal data analysis.* New York: Wiley.

Henson, R., & Templin, J. (2005). *Hierarchical log-linear modeling of the joint skill distribution.* Unpublished manuscript. Champaign, IL: External Diagnostic Research Group.

Henson, R.A., Templin, J.L., & Willse, J.T. (2009). Defining a family of cognitive diagnosis models using log-linear models with latent variables. *Psychometrika, 74*, 191–210.

Henson, R. A., Templin, J., & Willse, J. T. (2013). *Adapting diagnostic classification models to better fit the structure of existing large scale tests.* Manuscript under review.

Junker, B. W., & Sijtsma, K. (2001). Cognitive assessment models with few assumptions, and connections with non-parametric item response theory. *Applied Psychological Measurement, 25,* 258–272.

Kline, R. B. (2011). *Principles and practice of structural equation modelling* (3rd ed.). New York: Guilford Press.

Kunina, O., Rupp, A. A., & Wilhelm, O. (2009). A practical illustration of multidimensional diagnostic skills profiling: Comparing results from confirmatory factor analysis and diagnostic classification models. *Studies in Educational Evaluation, 35,* 64–70.

Kutner, M. H., Nachtsheim, C. J., Neter, J., & Li, W. (2005). *Applied linear statistical models* (5th ed.). New York: McGraw-Hill.

Lazarsfeld, P. F., & Henry, N. W. (1968). *Latent structure analysis.* Boston: Houghton Mifflin Company.

Leighton, J., & Gierl, M. (2007). *Cognitive diagnostic assessment for education: Theory and applications.* Cambridge, UK: Cambridge University Press.

Leighton, J. P., Cui, Y., & Cor, M. K. (2009). Testing expert-based and student-based cognitive models: An application of the attribute hierarchy method and hierarchy consistency index. *Applied Measurement in Education, 22,* 229–254.

Leighton, J. P., & Gierl, M. J., & Hunka, S. M. (2004). The attribute hierarchy method for cognitive assessment: A variation on Tatsuoka's rule-space approach. *Journal of Educational Measurement, 41,* 205–237.

Lynch, S. (2007). *Introduction to applied Bayesian statistics and estimation for social scientists.* New York: Springer.

Macready, G. B., & Dayton, C. M. (1977). The use of probabilistic models in the assessment of mastery. *Journal of Educational Statistics, 2,* 99–120.

Maris, E. (1995). Psychometric latent response models. *Psychometrika, 60,* 523–547.

Maris, E. (1999). Estimating multiple classification latent class models. *Psychometrika, 64,* 187–212.

Maydeu-Olivares, A., & Joe, H. (2005). Limited- and full-information estimation and goodness-of-fit testing in 2n contingency tables: A unified framework. *Journal of the American Statistical Association, 100,* 1009–1020.

McCullough, P., & Searle, S. R. (2001). *Generalized, linear, and mixed models.* New York: Wiley.

McCutcheon, A. L. (1987). *Latent class analysis.* Newbury Park, CA: Sage.

McDonald, R. P. (1999). *Test theory: A unified treatment.* Mahwah, NJ: Erlbaum.

McLachlan, G., & Peel, D. (2000). *Finite mixture models.* New York: Wiley.

Mislevy, R. J. (2007). Cognitive psychology and educational assessment. In R. L. Brennan (Ed.), *Educational measurement* (4th ed.; pp. 257–305). Portsmouth, NH: Greenwood.

Muthén, L. K., & Muthén, B. O. (2013). Mplus [Computer software]. Los Angeles, CA: Muthén & Muthén.

Nichols, P. (1994). A guide for developing cognitively diagnostic assessments. *Review of Educational Research, 64,* 575–603.

Nichols, P. D., Chipman, S. F., & Brennan, R. L. (1995). *Cognitively diagnostic assessment.* Mahwah, NJ: Erlbaum.

Nugent, R., Dean, N., Ayers, B., & Junker, B. (2009, July). *Clustering in cognitive diagnosis: Some recent work and open questions.* Paper presented at the Cognitive Diagnosis Models Working Group at the SAMSI Summer Program in Psychometrics, Durham, NC.

Raudenbush, S. W., & Bryk, A. S. (2002). *Hierarchical linear models: Applications and data analysis methods* (2nd ed.). Newbury Park, CA: Sage.

Rijmen, F., Tuerlickx, F., De Boeck, P., & Kuppens, P. (2003). A nonlinear mixed model framework for item response theory. *Psychological Methods, 8,* 185–205.

Rupp, A. A. (2007). The answer is in the question: A guide for investigating the theoretical potentials and practical limitations of cognitive psychometric models. *International Journal of Testing, 7,* 95–125.

Rupp, A. A., & Mislevy, R. J. (2007). Cognitive foundations of structured item response theory models. In J. Leighton & M. J. Gierl (Eds.), *Cognitively diagnostic assessment for education: Theory and applications* (pp. 205–241). Cambridge, UK: Cambridge University Press.

Rupp, A. A., & Templin, J. (2008). Unique characteristics of cognitive diagnosis models: A comprehensive review of the current state of the art. *Measurement: Interdisciplinary Research and Perspectives, 6,* 219–262.

Rupp, A. A., Templin, J., & Henson, R. A. (2010). *Diagnostic measurement: Theory, methods, and applications.* New York: Guilford Press.

Schrepp, M. (2005). About the connection between knowledge structures and latent class models. *Methodology, 1,* 93–103.

Skrondal, A., & Rabe-Hesketh, S. (2004). *Generalized latent variable modeling: Multilevel, longitudinal, and structural equation models.* New York: Chapman & Hall/CRC.

Stroup, W.W. (2012). *General linear mixed models: Modern concepts, methods, and applications*. Boca Raton, FL: CRC Press.

Tatsuoka, C. (2002). Data-analytic methods for latent partially ordered classification models. *Journal of the Royal Statistical Society (Series C, Applied Statistics), 51,* 337–350.

Tatsuoka, K.K. (1983). Rule-space: An approach for dealing with misconceptions based on item response theory. *Journal of Educational Measurement, 20,* 345–354.

Tatsuoka, K.K. (1995). Architecture of knowledge structures and cognitive diagnosis: A statistical pattern recognition and classification approach. In P.D. Nichols, S.F. Chipman, & R.L. Brennan (Eds.), *Cognitively diagnostic assessment* (pp. 327–360). Hillsdale, NJ: Erlbaum.

Tatsuoka, K.K. (1996). Use of generalized person-fit indexes for statistical pattern classification. *Applied Measurement in Education, 9,* 65–75.

Tatsuoka, K.K. (2009). *Cognitive assessment: An introduction to the rule-space method*. Florence, KY: Routledge.

Templin, J. (2006). *CDM user's guide*. Unpublished manuscript, University of Kansas, Kansas, NE.

Templin, J. (2009, July). *On the origin of species: The evolution of diagnostic modeling within the psychometric taxonomy*. Paper presented at the annual International Meeting of the Psychometric Society (IMPS), Cambridge, UK.

Templin, J., & Bradshaw, L. (2013). Measuring the reliability of diagnostic classification model examinee estimates. *Journal of Classification, 30,* 251–275.

Templin, J., & Bradshaw, L. (2014). Hierarchical diagnostic classification models: A family of models for estimating and testing attribute hierarchies. *Psychometrika, 79,* 317–339.

Templin, J., & Bradshaw, L. (2013). Nominal response diagnostic classification models. Manuscript under revision.

Templin, J., & Henson, R.A. (2006). Measurement of psychological disorders using cognitive diagnosis models. *Psychological Methods, 11,* 287–305.

Templin, J., Henson, R., Rupp, A., Jang, E., & Ahmed, M. (2008, March). *Cognitive diagnosis models for nominal response data*. Paper presented at the annual meeting of the National Council on Measurement in Education in New York, NY.

Templin, J., & Hoffman, L. (2013). Obtaining diagnostic classification model estimates using Mplus. *Educational Measurement: Issues and Practice, 32*(2), 37–50.

Templin, J., Kingston, N., & Wang, W. (2011, October). *Psychometric issues in formative assessment: Measuring student learning throughout an academic year using interim assessments*. Invited talk for the 11th annual Maryland Assessment Conference in College Park, MD.

Teugels, J. (1990). Some representations of the multivariate Bernoulli and binomial distributions. *Journal of Multivariate Analysis, 32,* 256–268.

Thurstone, L.L. (1938). *Primary mental abilities*. Chicago, IL: University of Chicago Press.

Verbeke, G., & Molenberghs, G. (2000). *Linear mixed models for longitudinal data*. New York: Springer.

Vermunt, J.K., & Magidson, J. (2012). *Technical guide for Latent GOLD Choice 4.5: Basic and advanced*. Belmont, MA: Statistical Innovations.

von Davier, M. (2005). *A general diagnostic model applied to language testing data* (ETS Research Report RR-05-16).

Whitely, S.E. (1980). Multicomponent latent trait models for ability tests. *Psychometrika, 45,* 479–494.

Xu, X., & von Davier, M. (2008a). *Fitting the structured general diagnostic model to NAEP data* (RR-08–27). Princeton, NJ: Educational Testing Service.

Xu, X., & von Davier, M. (2008b). *Linking for the general diagnostic model* (RR-08–08). Princeton, NJ: Educational Testing Service.

Zieky, M., & Perie, M. (2006). *A primer on setting cut scores on tests of educational achievement*. Princeton, NJ: Educational Testing Service.

# 14
## Item Response Models for CBT

**Daniel Bolt**

Measurement models have historically provided the backbone to much of educational measurement practice. Many of the important questions of measurement are directly or indirectly answered through use of measurement models, questions such as: "How should a test performance be scored?," "How should the score scale be interpreted?," "How many items are sufficient?" or, "Are all subjects being equally measured by the test?" Models have also traditionally played an important role in how various aspects of the testing process are implemented, including how tests are constructed and administered, how scoring algorithms and metrics are defined and used, how measurement error is quantified, and how validation evidence is gathered.

Despite this historical importance, the role of measurement models has become even more prominent in the era of computer-based testing (CBT), where the computer administration and scoring of tests generally require model-based algorithms that can be implemented in real time. In CBT, measurement models thus define the actual mechanism by which measurement occurs. The advent of item response theory (IRT) models in this context can be attributed in large part to the central role of IRT in computerized adaptive testing (CAT). Through CAT, IRT models have dramatically increased measurement efficiency while also providing a metric by which persons administered entirely different test items can be scored and compared (Hambleton, 2006). Early conceptions of how IRT could be used in the context of CAT have developed in a number of different ways, many of which are documented in other chapters in this volume.

Given the importance of measurement models in CBT, it is appropriate that a volume on computer-based testing should devote specific attention to this topic. Indeed, a review of new and emerging measurement models and model developments provides one way of illustrating how the practice of measurement has evolved in the CBT era. This chapter seeks to highlight some of the unique types of IRT models that have emerged in support of CBT. Beyond simply describing the models, we seek to document some ways in which these developments have paralleled changes in the practice of measurement.

Many new modeling developments can be attributed to unique features of the CBT administration format. For example, relative to traditional paper–pencil tests, CBTs permit flexible test administration schedules and multiple, repeated assessments over time. Such flexibility comes at the cost of new item and test security concerns and the need to more closely monitor and attend to item exposure rates, for example. Large item banks are needed, banks that have in turn also afforded opportunities for new model-based methods for validating test items. The individualized tailoring of measurement instruments to improve efficiency can be achieved in different ways, some of which require consideration of new models. Models are also needed for automated scoring, including for item types that otherwise might have been human scored (e.g., essay items).

Other CBT–related features that have influenced IRT modeling relate to innovative item types and unique response formats. CBT also provides the ability to attend to new facets of performance, such as the sequence of steps or the amount of time used in solving an item, features that can be useful to attend to for scoring purposes. At the same time, the complexity of the person–computer interactions associated with many computer-based assessment tasks can also lead to challenges in which even the notion of "items" as traditionally defined may seem inappropriate.

The advent of CBT has likely also played an indirect role in still other areas of IRT model development. For example, formative assessment and diagnostic measurement, two contemporary measurement emphases, have been supported and advanced through CBT, often entailing new IRT models that relate directly to these goals.

As will be apparent, many of the new IRT modeling directions relax assumptions of Rasch, two-parameter logistic (2PL), and three-parameter logistic (3PL) models that have traditionally defined IRT. Specifically, the unidimensionality and local independence assumptions of these models are often unrealistic in CBT settings. As considered in a concluding section, the diversity of IRT and IRT–related models needed for CBT has led to new thinking about how IRT models function within a broader assessment framework.

Important supporting elements of IRT model development in CBT are advances in statistical computation, which have not only made more complex models computationally feasible but are also relatively easy to implement. In this regard, Bayesian estimation methods, such as Markov chain Monte Carlo methods, have become particularly appealing. The majority of new models presented in this chapter have found their implementation through such methods.

Perhaps the primary goal of this chapter is to generate an appreciation for the diversity of issues psychometricians must often attend to in applying IRT within CBT. As noted by Drasgow and Mattern (2006), it is often the need for appropriate psychometric models and techniques that represent a final obstacle to realization of the many innovations that can be achieved through CBT.

## IRT Models for Item Generation

A major challenge in CBT is the need for generating and calibrating large numbers of items. Much attention has been devoted to methods for automating an item-generation process (Bejar, 1996; see also Chapter 5 of this volume by Gierl, Lai, Fung, & Zheng). A common approach seeks to generate "clones" of an original item, whereby certain superficial elements of the original item (e.g., particular response options, the specific numbers used in an item stem) are substituted for by sampling from a set of predefined alternatives. IRT models that reflect this process are needed for at least a couple primary reasons. One reason is to help in defining item parameters for the generated items. Because very few persons are likely to be administered an exact replica of any given item, it is infeasible to calibrate the parameters for each generated item based on responses to only that item. However, the random sampling that occurs in cloning implies the item parameters can be viewed as random; viewing the item as a sample from a distribution provides a way of addressing the uncertainty of item parameters that need to be used for person scoring (Embretson, 1999). A second role for IRT models in this context is to help evaluate those elements of items within the item-generation process that affect its parameters and that should be accounted for either in the item-generation process or in relation to person scoring. Explanatory item response models (see De Boeck & Wilson, 2004), which can study how item characteristics influence item difficulty, for example, can thus help inform the item-generation process.

Item-generation models possess a hierarchical structure in which items can be viewed as nested within groups, often referred to as families. The defining features of a family are determined by a parent item, from which we might consider the other members of an item family (i.e., "item clones") as outcomes of an item-generation process. While in certain circumstances it might be reasonable to assume the parameters for items from a common family are the same across items (characterized as an "identical siblings" model—see Sinharay, Johnson, & Williamson, 2003), there will likely be some level of detectable variability of parameters across items within a family. Glas and van der Linden (2003) present a hierarchical item cloning model that portrays items (indexed $j$) as nested within families (indexed $p$), whereby each family is associated with a mean and covariance matrix representing the distribution of item parameters within the family. For example, at the level of the individual item (level 1), we might assume a three-parameter logistic model (3PL), whereby the probability of correct response from a person $i$ having ability level $\theta_i$ is given by

$$P\left(U_{ij_p} = 1 | \theta_i\right) = c_{j_p} + \left(1 - c_{j_p}\right) \frac{\exp\left[a_{j_p}\left(\theta_i - b_{j_p}\right)\right]}{1 + \exp\left[a_{j_p}\left(\theta_i - b_{j_p}\right)\right]}$$

where $a$, $b$, and $c$ denote the item discrimination, difficulty, and guessing parameters of the traditional 3PL model. At level 2, the multivariate distribution of item parameters within family $p$ (from which item $j$ has been selected) is characterized as:

$$\begin{bmatrix} a_{j_p} \\ b_{j_p} \\ c_{j_p} \end{bmatrix} \sim MVN\left(\mu_p, \Sigma_p\right).$$

Special cases and/or generalizations of this approach can be introduced by considering alternative level 1 models and/or different level 2 multivariate distributions. For example, a normal ogive model may be more convenient as a level 1 model for computational reasons. In addition, appropriate transformations of the item parameters (such as a log transformation of $a$ or a logit transformation of $c$) may be useful. Because the level-2 model implies an imperfect dependence among parameters across items within a family, the model has been called a "related siblings" model (see Sinharay et al., 2003).

A fundamental difference from traditional IRT calibrations is the estimation of the family parameters, $\mu_p, \Sigma_p$, in the hierarchical model as opposed to the parameters of the individual items. Glas and van der Linden (2003) present a marginal maximum likelihood algorithm that can be combined with a Bayesian method for estimating the family parameters; alternatively, Sinharay and colleagues 2003 demonstrate a full Bayesian approach. When applied in subsequent measurement applications, provided the items are selected randomly from within families, the effects of within-family variability on person scoring will become neutralized as more families (items) are sampled. It may thus become reasonable to ignore the potential biasing effects of the specific items chosen (e.g., being administered one of the more difficult items in an item family) when scoring persons if the number of items is large.

Once the mean and covariance matrix of an item family have been estimated, Glas and van der Linden (2003) show how an average information function, reflecting the information expected for a randomly chosen item, can be calculated for a family. This average can then provide a basis for how item families are selected in assembling a test. Sinharay and associates (2003) further illustrate the value in attending to the expected response functions (ERFs) of families, namely the expected scores for an item randomly sampled from a family. Assuming the within-family variability is reasonably low, use of the expected ERFs is argued to often be sufficient for purposes of person scoring. Figure 14.1 provides an illustration of ERFs for individual items, as well as an expected ERF, for three hypothetical item families. Johnson and Sinharay (2005) extended this approach to polytomously scored items, where ERFs seem particularly useful given the increased number of model parameters associated with polytomous items. The consequences of parameter variability are often difficult to evaluate with polytomous IRT models and are usually only meaningful in how they affect the ERFs.

More recent IRT modeling approaches have also attended to the distinguishing features of item families and the possibility of generating both item families as well as item clones within families. Geerlings, Glas, and van der Linden (2011) distinguish between "radicals," namely item features that significantly influence psychometric properties of items, and "incidentals," or item features that have a negligible effect. Radicals can be used to develop item-generation rules that define families. For example, Geerlings and colleagues (2011) illustrate a linear item cloning model (LICM) in which the mean item difficulty of a family is modeled as a linear function of radicals with specified design variables (weights) reflecting the frequency with which the radical is applied. The result is a two-level model similar to the Glas and van der Linden (2003) item cloning model but in which the family parameters $\mu_p, \Sigma_p$, are defined by the effects of the radicals, which then become the focus of estimation. Geerlings and colleagues

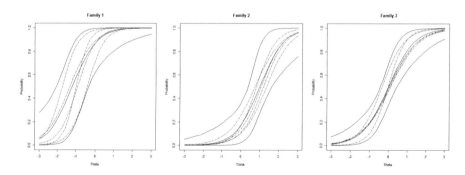

**Figure 14.1** Expected response functions and 95% confidence intervals, hypothetical item families

(2011) consider variants of the LICM in which the covariance matrix is assumed equal across families and the radicals only influence the family means. Geerlings, van der Linden, and Glas (2013) further explore the LICM in relation to alternative models as a basis for scoring persons.

An appealing feature of the LICM is its ability to model family effects using fewer parameters than there may be families. Besides the individual items, item families can also be viewed as random. One consideration in selecting among the item cloning and LICM models concerns the number of families desired for the item bank. Effective use of the LICM also requires an ability to distinguish radicals from incidentals.

Beyond their practical utility in item-generation contexts, models such as the LICM can also be used to validate items and item families. To the extent that cognitive theory may dictate how mean family difficulty should be affected by radicals, for example, the ability to confirm such effects using the LICM can be taken as evidence of validity. Applications of the model will thus be valuable not just in learning how to generate items but also in evaluating whether the generated items are functioning as intended.

## Models Related to Testlet-Based Administrations

Beyond the need for large item banks, CBT introduces other practical issues related to how items are administered. One concerns the administration of items in groups, or "testlets." There are a couple different motivations for this practice in CBT. A first motivation relates to the growing interest in administering multiple items around a common stimulus or problem-solving scenario. This practice becomes increasingly attractive in CBT, where it becomes easier to immerse an examinee in a complex problem-solving environment, for example, as will be considered more in the next section. A second motivation relates to perceived problems associated with a pure CAT in which tests are adaptively administered at the level of individual items. Wainer and Keily (1987) originally described several concerns with this approach, namely (1) context effects, (2) lack of robustness, and (3) alterations in item difficulty ordering. Context effects refer to the effects items may have on the functioning of later administered items, effects that are no longer balanced as in a traditional paper–pencil test on which the context is identical for all persons. Examples include effects related to item location, an item providing information of relevance (i.e., clues) for answering later items, or unbalanced content. The lack-of-robustness problem refers to the significant effects a single flawed item can have on the final result of a CAT administration, such as might be reflected by a miscoded or misread item. Finally, an item difficulty ordering, which is often present in traditional paper–pencil tests and can have positive confidence-building motivational effects (especially for persons of low ability), is often absent and certainly not uniform across persons in a traditional CAT.

By administering items in groups, or testlets, it becomes possible to control for context/location effects, balance item content, and even introduce an item difficulty ordering (Wainer, Bradlow, & Wang, 2007, chapter 4; Wainer & Keily, 1987). The result can be a form of multistage testing that maintains some of the advantages of paper–pencil testing (Hendrickson, 2007). As noted, the testlet concept in CBT also allows multiple items to be administered around a common stimulus. Such an approach offers the possibility of contextualizing items in a way that makes measurement more authentic, as may be particularly desirable for licensure/certification tests. Other simple examples are reading comprehension tests for which a number of different questions (items) organized around common reading passages could be administered. A shared concern under all of these scenarios is the likely presence of local dependence across items within a common testlet.

Various IRT models have been considered in the modeling of testlet-based tests. Wainer, Bradlow, and Du (2002; see also Wainer et al., 2007) introduced a 3PL testlet model in which the probability of correct item response is modeled as:

$$P\left(U_{ij(d)} = 1 \mid \theta_i, \gamma_{id}\right) = c_{j(d)} + \left(1 - c_{j(d)}\right) \frac{\exp\left[a_{j(d)}\left(\theta_i - b_{j(d)} - \gamma_{id}\right)\right]}{1 + \exp\left[a_{j(d)}\left(\theta_i - b_{j(d)} - \gamma_{id}\right)\right]}$$

where $\gamma_{id}$ represents a random person effect associated with testlet $d$ that is assumed Normal $(0, \sigma_d^2)$ and is uncorrelated across testlets. In the expression above, items (indexed as $j$) are nested within testlets (indexed as $d$); item difficulty, discrimination, and guessing vary at the item level. Through the testlet-specific random effects, the model can accommodate the increased statistical dependence commonly seen among items of a common testlet. The inclusion of the testlet effects thus avoids the underestimation of the standard errors of ability estimates that would occur if all items within a testlet were assumed locally independent. The model can also be generalized to accommodate items that are polytomously scored (Wainer et al., 2007). As the model only introduces parameters corresponding to the testlet effect variances, the cost in terms of added model complexity is not very substantial.

From one perspective, testlet effects can be viewed as additional trait dimensions. In this respect, testlet models can be viewed as special cases of a bifactor model (Gibbons & Hedeker, 1992). The bifactor model effectively allows items to have varying discrimination (factor loadings) with respect to testlet-defined factors. A graphical depiction of the bifactor model is shown in Figure 14.2. As seen in the figure, the bifactor model assumes each item measures a single general trait as well as a testlet (specific) factor that is uncorrelated with the general trait and all other testlet factors. Rijmen (2010) provides a discussion of the relationships between the testlet and bifactor models as well as multidimensional item response models, discussed further in the next section. Li, Bolt, and Fu (2006) provided an empirical comparison of testlet and bifactor models and found for their datasets that the bifactor models generally provided a better fit. In their examples, items from a common testlet frequently demonstrated varying levels of sensitivity to the testlet-specific dimensions depending on item type (e.g., vocabulary item types were less affected than inference item types on a reading comprehension test).

An alternative way of dealing with testlets is to model performances at the testlet level as opposed to item level. In this case, models for polytomously scored items can be applied to model testlet sum scores (Thissen, Steinberg, & Mooney, 1989). While such models effectively address the local dependence within testlets, they come at the cost of no longer providing information at the level of individual items. However, the loss of such information may not be important in many applications. Thus, the use of testlets in CBT has provided one motivation for consideration of polytomous IRT models. We consider polytomous IRT models in more detail in the next section.

It is important to acknowledge other variants of testlet-based administration that can impact IRT modeling. Keily and Wainer (1987) distinguish between linear and hierarchical testlets. Linear testlets refer to testlets in which each person is administered all items within the testlet. The previously described models for testlets apply to linear testlets. In a hierarchical testlet, items are administered in an individualized fashion within each testlet such that

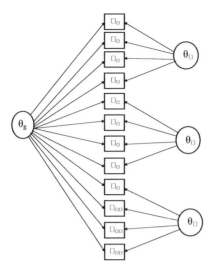

**Figure 14.2** Illustration of bifactor model

different items are administered depending on the pattern of responses given to prior items. This format leads to a unique outcome determined by the unique sequence of administered items combined with the correct/incorrect response to the final item. Partial hierarchical testlets are also possible, whereby persons can arrive at the same outcome through different pathways of administered items (such as when the same item is administered in response to a different pattern of previously administered items). This administration format raises the possibility that not just the correct/incorrect response to the final item, but also the particular pathway that led to that outcome, is relevant in estimating ability. Scalise and Wilson (2007) introduce an "iota model" that attends to such effects. The Scalise and Wilson model highlights the complexities that can be introduced in IRT modeling based not just on the use of testlets but also by how the items within testlets are administered. Such formats also bring testlet-based designs closer to the types of designs that can be used in e-learning contexts (Scalise & Wilson, 2007).

Clearly, testlet models offer attractive tools for addressing the desire to administer items in highly contextualized problem-solving environments. Such tests and associated models may also provide a mechanism by which novel forms of assessment, such as that needed in measuring learning that occurs in the context of educational computer-based games, may be realized (see, e.g., Rupp, Gushta, Mislevy, & Shaffer, 2010). Thus testlet models should remain an important area of IRT research related to CBT.

### Models for Innovative Item Types

One of the clear advantages of computer-based testing is its ability to accommodate a broader range of test item types than paper-and-pencil tests. As described in the previous section, the administration of groups of items around a common stimulus is one format that can be attractive in CBT. Chapter 3 of this volume describes many of the other recent advances in developing innovative item types. Parshall, Harmes, Davey, and Pashley (2010) list several dimensions along which such innovations have occurred (see also Drasgow & Mattern, 2006), specifically item format, response action, media inclusion, level of interactivity, and scoring method. Item types such as multiple-response, hotspot, fill-in-the-blank, and drag-and-drop items, among others, can often not only be efficiently implemented by computer but also have the potential to lead to richer descriptions of item performances (Becker, 2010). Advances in automated scoring (Clauser, Kane, & Swanson, 2002; Williamson, Xi, & Breyer, 2012) have also made many open-ended items, including essay-type items, a realistic item type for CBT.

While in some cases these item types can still be appropriately handled by traditional IRT models (i.e., when scored as binary, such as incorrect/correct), in many cases the items will be associated with more complex forms of scoring. In such cases, innovative item types in CBT often require alternative IRT models. In particular, polytomous IRT and multidimensional IRT models are often needed to accommodate such item types.

### Polytomous IRT models

The multicategory scoring of many innovative item types has made polytomous IRT models of significant value in CBT (Eggen, 2007). As CBT items frequently entail more complex responses, they can often also be scored in a more complex fashion than simply correct/incorrect. Because CBT items generally take more time to administer than traditional multiple-choice test items, it actually becomes a necessity that the items be scored using multiple score categories in order to attain a beneficial tradeoff in terms of measurement efficiency (Jiao, Liu, Haynie, Woo, & Gorham, 2012; Jodoin, 2003). In this regard, polytomous IRT models also are useful in evaluating the extent to which the innovative item types used in CBT are statistically improving measurement efficiency.

As an example of the use of polytomous models with a novel CBT item format, we consider a model presented by Attali (2011). Attali considers an item format in which persons continue to answer a multiple-choice item until the correct response is identified, a format that becomes easy to implement in CBT. A natural outcome to attend to with such items is the number of attempts the person makes before arriving at the correct answer. Attali (2011) applies Samejima's graded response model (GRM) in modeling such counts and is able through the model to quantify the increase in information provided by such items relative to items allowing only one attempt at a correct response.

Beyond the GRM, various other polytomous IRT models can be considered with CBT items. A discussion of these models and their differences has been provided by Dodd, de Ayala, and Koch (1995), and Nering and Ostini (2011). There are many dimensions along which such models can be compared/evaluated, including their representation of alternative response processes, that can make model selection difficult. It might be expected that in the advent of CBT, certain lesser-used models may in the future gain greater prominence given that new aspects of response process can be monitored. One example is Tutz's (1990) sequential response model (SRM) and its 2PL generalization presented by Mellenbergh (1995). Under the SRM, a person achieves a score of $k = 1, \ldots K$, on an item $j$ if item scoring is based on successful execution of an ordered sequence of steps, and exactly $k - 1$ of those steps are passed. If we assume that the probability that person $i$ successfully executes step $k$ is given by:

$$P\left(S_{ijk} = 1 | \theta_i\right) = \frac{\exp\left[a_j\left(\theta_i - b_{jk}\right)\right]}{1 + \exp\left[a_j\left(\theta_i - b_{jk}\right)\right]}$$

then the probability of obtaining an item score $k$ is given by

$$P\left(U_{ij} = k|\theta_i\right) = \left[1 - P\left(S_{ij,k+1} = 1|\theta_i\right)\right] \times \prod_{v=0}^{k} P\left(S_{ijv} = 1|\theta_i\right)$$

where $P(S_{ij0}=1|\theta_i)$ is set to 1.

One reason a model like the SRM may be useful with CBT is that it likely provides a good statistical representation of how certain hierarchical testlets may be administered, thus allowing the model to characterize testlet scores in a way that is also sensitive to performances on the individual items (i.e., steps). A second reason is that it will often be possible in CBT to more closely monitor person performance related to steps in solving an item, thus making the model more easily estimated in CBT than in paper–pencil applications. In general, the capacity to extract more information about item performances by computer also helps make aspects of response processes more salient, which can in turn be used to improve modeling (see Partchev & De Boeck, 2012, for a recent example involving response times) and therefore estimation of ability.

### Multidimensional IRT Models

A second category of IRT models of increased relevance in CBT consists of multidimensional IRT (MIRT; Reckase, 2009) models. In MIRT models, item scores are modeled as a function of multiple person abilities. For example, a common MIRT model for items scored as binary is the multidimensional logistic model (Reckase, 1985), where the probability of a correct response is expressed as:

$$P\left(U_{ij} = 1|\theta_{i1}, ..\theta_{in}\right) = c_j + \left(1 - c_j\right)\frac{\exp\left(a_{j1}\theta_{i1} + ... + a_{jn}\theta_{in} + d_j\right)}{1 + \exp\left(a_{j1}\theta_{i1} + ... + a_{jn}\theta_{in} + d_j\right)}$$

and where $\theta_{i1}, ..\theta_{in}$ denote $n$ latent abilities, $a_{j1}, ..., a_{jn}$ are their corresponding discrimination parameters, and $d_j$ is a multidimensional item difficulty parameter. While MIRT modeling introduces a number of additional complexities when used as a basis for CAT, there are at least a couple fundamental reasons multidimensional modeling can be attractive in that context. As described by Segall (1996), one reason relates to content coverage. By viewing content areas as corresponding to distinct but correlated ability dimensions, a multidimensional framework makes it possible to administer items so as to ensure adequate content coverage while also allowing the correlations between dimensions to inform how items are selected across content areas. This becomes even more significant when the content areas vary in item difficulty (Segall, 1996). A second reason relates to improved estimation of ability (or, alternatively, increased measurement efficiency). By estimating several abilities simultaneously, it becomes possible in a Bayesian fashion to use the correlations between dimensions to improve ability estimates for each individual dimension. Segall (1996) and Luecht (1996) have demonstrated how the use of multidimensional item selection and scoring techniques generally provides comparable subscore reliability estimates with approximately a third fewer items than when applying strictly unidimensional methods (see also Segall, 2010).

In many measurement settings, despite the known presence of multiple ability dimensions in the data, it may only be of interest to estimate a single ability (e.g., a "general ability factor") for score reporting. In such cases, the use of a multidimensional IRT model can still provide a necessary tool for appropriately addressing patterns in the statistical dependencies among items and interpreting latent statistical dimensions in the data. For example, van der Linden (1999) illustrated a multidimensional adaptive testing method that seeks to estimate a single composite score (see also Segall, 2001). An appreciation of such applications is important, as there may often not be sufficient reliabilities at the subscore level to support the report of multiple subscores (see Sinharay, Puhan, & Haberman, 2010), even though a multidimensional model will be useful in application.

Finally, relative to separate unidimensional calibrations, multidimensional models are attractive in their ability to accommodate individual items that may simultaneously measure multiple abilities. As a result, a test need not be restricted to test items that possess a "simple structure" form of multidimensionality where each item measures only one skill. For example, often it is attractive in CBT to administer items that require integration of skills in solving an item.

Other complex issues associated with use of multidimensional CAT using multidimensional models are beyond the scope of this chapter and are discussed further by Segall (2010). Substantial progress in recent years has been made in addressing obstacles to multidimensional CAT, in part due to increased computer speed. In addition, some recent advances in the estimation of MIRT models have been presented by Beguin and Glas (2001), Cai (2010a, 2010b), and Edwards (2010).

Future IRT modeling within CBT will likely focus more on multidimensional models. One issue concerns the nature of the interaction assumed between the multiple abilities. Most work in the area of multidimensional IRT has focused on models that assume disjunctive (additive) interactions between abilities, such as the Reckase (1985) model mentioned previously. However, models for conjunctive (multiplicative) interactions have also been proposed (e.g., Embretson, 1980). Such models can be particularly useful for diagnostic measurement, where particular skill deficiencies can often be more easily identified when the skill requirements of items interact in a noncompensatory fashion. In the Embretson (1980) model, for example, the probability of item correctness is modeled as:

$$P\left(U_{ij} = 1 | \theta_{i1}, ..\theta_{in}\right) = \prod_{v=1}^{n} \frac{\exp\left(\theta_{iv} - b_{jv}\right)}{1 + \exp\left(\theta_{iv} - b_{jv}\right)}$$

where $b_{j1}, ...,b_{ji}$ now denote dimension-specific difficulty parameters. The model can be viewed as the product of Rasch-modeled components in which each component involves a different ability. As for the Tutz and Mellenbergh models described earlier, an appealing feature of the Embretson model is its clear connection to a response process that might be more easily monitored in CBT.

Beyond the need for appropriate models are also appropriate design considerations for tests. Even tests intended to measure varied skills can often yield data structures that appear largely unidimensional. At times, such results may be due to high intercorrelations among the skills. In other cases, it may reflect a strong sequencing with respect to the difficulty requirements of the items in relation to the measured skills. Consideration of such issues in the test design stage, with the later role of IRT models in mind, is clearly important.

## Models Related to Item and Test Compromise

Another set of challenges related to CBT is the increased potential for test compromise. Due to flexible administration times and repeated testings, there is greater opportunity for items to be exposed prior to a test administration. This can occur when a prior examinee shares information with a future examinee or through coordinated efforts among groups of persons in identifying and sharing large collections of items. Several models have been developed to measure and account for such effects. The important roles of such models and methods in CBT are highlighted by the dedication of entire conferences to these issues over the past 2 years.

Segall (2002) proposed a model in which both items and persons are characterized by test compromise parameters. Segall's model assumes items can be categorized as previously exposed (i.e., Type I) items versus never previously exposed (i.e., Type II) items, with at least some items being of Type II. Person parameters include an ability ($\theta$), as in traditional IRT models, and an item preview dimension ($\omega$) that represents the person's level of exposure to Type I items. All items are characterized by traditional item discrimination ($a$) and difficulty parameters ($b$) in relation to $\theta$, while Type I items are also characterized by slope ($\alpha$) and intercept ($\beta$) parameters in relation to the influence of $\omega$. The occurrence of a correct item response is determined by either (1) knowing the correct answer as a result of ability or (2) answering correctly due to having been exposed to the item, the latter being relevant only for Type I items. The model can thus be viewed as a type of multidimensional IRT model in which the statistical identification of parameters is made possible by the existence of Type II items.

Besides providing a way of measuring exposure with respect to persons and items, one of the advantages of the Segall (2002) model is its capacity to evaluate the consequences of item exposure. Specifically, the model can be used to quantify the gain experienced by a given person to a given item that reflects the biasing effects of exposure. For example, a correct response due to exposure will matter more for an item the person would have otherwise been expected to answer incorrectly. When such biases are accumulated across items, it also becomes possible to evaluate the consequences of exposure at the test score level.

A related model to the Segall (2002) model was presented by McLeod, Lewis, and Thissen (2003). Like the Segall model, the McLeod and associates model assumes a person's response to an item reflects the person being in either an exposure (i.e., "memorization") state or a problem-solving state. The resulting model is a modified 3PL model in which the lower asymptote (c) parameter represents the joint effects of guessing and memorization. Unlike the Segall model, the McLeod and associates model does not assume a separate person parameter related to exposure; rather, it is used to identify the relative likelihood that a given response pattern reflects a person who was responding with item preknowledge. Consequently, the model can be viewed as a tool whose primary focus is the detection of person-level exposure (i.e., preknowledge), analogous to how person-fit/appropriateness measure indices are used (i.e., Drasgow, Levine, & McLaughlin, 1987).

Two other models related to item exposure and cheating have been presented by Segall (2004) and Shu, Henson, and Luecht (2013). In the Segall (2004) model, the process by which informants share items with a focal examinee is modeled, providing a mechanism by which to explain why some items are more subject to compromise than others. The Shu and colleagues (2013) model portrays item compromise using a mixture IRT model, whereby latent classes of persons are distinguished according to whether they engage in cheating behavior.

Variability in response behavior to exposed versus nonexposed (secure) items in a cheating class is statistically handled by attaching a unique (higher) ability parameter to persons who engage in cheating with respect to items that have been exposed. Like the McLeod and associates approach, the Shu and colleagues model is primarily motivated by interest in identifying persons that have cheated.

It seems clear that one distinguishing feature among models of item exposure relates to their primary intended purpose. As described by Segall (2002), there are a variety of potential motivations for this form of modeling. One objective may be to identify optimal item replenishment schedules, in which case a model can help to identify relationships between item exposure rates and compromise effects. Another objective might be to evaluate the prevalence of cheating in a population. When compromise effects are measured at the item level, a model can also be used to identify individual items that appear to have been compromised. Finally, models such as Segall's (2002) provide a tool by which person ability estimates could potentially be purified of cheating effects.

### Models That Attend to Response Times

One unique form of information that can be easily recorded by computer is the response time to an item. Attending to response times can serve a variety of practical purposes. Response times can help inform about the quality of items, such as their validity, and can also provide collateral information of relevance to estimating item parameters, such as item difficulty. With respect to persons, response times can also aid in the detection of cheating, speededness, or guessing behavior, and can also serve as an indirect indicator of ability. In terms of test administration, response time data may also be useful in test-construction decisions or in selecting among items for CAT, especially when time limits of some kind are imposed on the test.

Models of response time have long been of interest in psychometrics, and various approaches to the use of response times in IRT have been considered. van der Linden (2009) provides a recent review. He distinguishes models that treat item correctness and response time as separate outcomes (e.g., Rasch, 1960) versus models that integrate these components by either using response time in the modeling of response correctness (e.g., Roskam, 1987) or response correctness in modeling response time (e.g., Thissen, 1983). Following a review of these and other approaches, van der Linden (2009; see also van der Linden, 2011) outlines a number of conclusions that can be derived concerning psychometric models that attend simultaneously to response correctness and response time. One implication is that response times in a measurement context are only meaningful when interpreted in relation to both characteristics of the items (i.e., the labor required by the item) and persons (i.e., the average speed at which a person works). Consistent with the assumption of a constant ability for a person across items, it may be psychometrically reasonable to assume a person proceeds through the test at constant speed; likewise, invariant item difficulty across persons suggests constant labor requirements. Both response times and response correctness can then be viewed as random variables with distinct distributions, with expected response times being a function of item (labor) and person (speed) parameters that are distinct from corresponding parameters related to correctness (i.e., item difficulty and person ability parameters). Perhaps counterintuitively, when viewed in this way, van der Linden (2009) argues that it can be reasonable to assume conditional independence between the response times and item scores, both within an item and across items. This allows the commonly cited speed–accuracy tradeoff to be considered as a within-person phenomenon that may or may not also be manifest in between-person correlations between person and item parameters.

In this context, van der Linden (2007) proposed a hierarchical model for item responses and response times. The model is composed of distinct components for response times and item correctness and introduces models for each of these components. In van der Linden's example, the correctness of response can be portrayed using the traditional 3PL model:

$$P\left(U_{ij} = 1 | \theta_i\right) = c_j + \left(1 - c_j\right) \frac{\exp\left[a_j\left(\theta_i - b_j\right)\right]}{1 + \exp\left[a_j\left(\theta_i - b_j\right)\right]}$$

while response time can be characterized in terms of a lognormal distribution:

$$\ln T_{ij} = \beta_j - \tau_i + \varepsilon_{ij}, \quad \varepsilon_{ij} \sim N\left(0, \alpha_j^{-2}\right)$$

where $\beta_j$ denotes an item labor intensity parameter for item $j$, $\tau_i$ denotes a speed parameter for person $i$, and $\varepsilon_{ij}$ is a random error term. As a consequence, both response correctness and response speed are characterized with respect to person as well as item parameters. Both response correctness and response time are jointly analyzed in the model, and both are treated as outcomes.

Figure 14.3 provides a conceptual illustration of the model. Within this framework, the specific choices of models for response correctness and response time can be adapted. Part of the value in specifying such a model follows from the capacity to study correlations between either person or item parameters across these two model parts, that is, the extent to which person ability correlates with person speed and/or item difficulty correlates with item labor intensity. van der Linden (2009, p. 267) reports on the correlational outcomes observed with the hierarchical model when applied with various real assessments. The general conclusion is that positive correlations between difficulty and labor intensity parameters tend to be rather consistent, but the correlations between person speed and ability parameters are quite variable, sometimes positive and sometimes negative. Such variability may reflect how good time-management skills (likely possessed by higher-ability persons) may imply varying levels of speed depending on the test and time limit constraints of the test. In this context, Klein Entink, Fox, and van der Linden (2009) have further extended the model to include person covariates to explore and interpret the correlational structure that may exist between person ability and speed. Other extensions, such as models that accommodate different subpopulations of persons implementing different problem-solving strategies (as might manifest in both differential profiles of response correctness and response time) or different group structures among items, may also be possible.

The van der Linden hierarchical model seems useful as a general framework for thinking about how other aspects of item performances (beyond response time) might be simultaneously incorporated into assessment. As noted earlier, the capacity of the computer to incorporate a variety of features of item performance may also lead to the study of other outcomes that can be similarly analyzed along with response correctness.

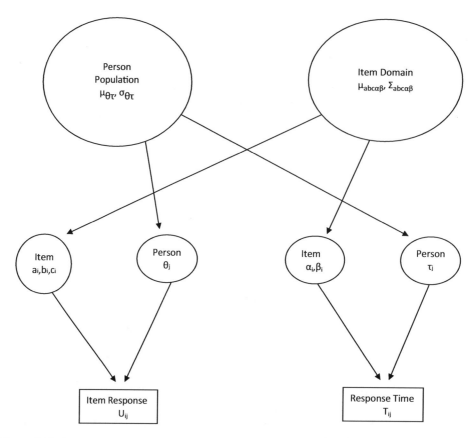

**Figure 14.3** Conceptual illustration of van der Linden (2007) hierarchical framework for modeling speed and accuracy on test items

### Looking Forward

While IRT models have evolved in a number of interesting ways in relation to CBT, there remain many directions for future work. We consider in this last section some of the more general ways in which IRT modeling has been impacted by CBT, ways that seem likely to influence future applications and extensions of IRT.

First is the growing role of *random item IRT* models. By random, we imply the item as being viewed as a sampled unit from a population, with interest focused on characteristics of the population (e.g., mean and variance). Clearly issues related to automatic item generation and the use of item families in the context of CBT have played a role. De Boeck (2008) describes some of the general issues motivating this form of modeling and its implications for psychometric analyses, including, for example, how differential item functioning analyses are conducted and interpreted. Prior work has also illustrated the usefulness of this form of modeling in learning about how item predictors influence the psychometric characteristics of items (e.g., De Boeck & Wilson, 2004), which, as noted earlier, can be useful in item validity studies. Models such as the linear logistic test model (LLTM; Fischer, 1973) when extended to include item residuals (Rijmen & De Boeck, 2002) allow useful inferences to be drawn regarding the effects of particular item features on characteristics such as item difficulty. These models are made much more practical in CBT settings due to the large number of items that are often available for analysis.

A related but separate motivation for random item IRT modeling is its emphasis on test performances in relation to a much larger domain of behaviors that are ultimately of interest. Whereas the previous application uses random effects to account for the uncertainty of item parameters, the latter scenario considers items as samples from a population (De Boeck, 2008). Along these lines, Briggs and Wilson (2007) consider some potential connections between IRT and generalizability theory, where item effects can be portrayed as facets (possibly random) whose variance can be quantified and used to inform the design of assessments, for example. When different items are administered to different persons (and/or different items to the same person) over time, CBT naturally encourages thinking of test performances in relation to a domain (population of items) from which even a large item bank would be viewed as a sample.

Future work in this area may help in uncovering other advantages of the random item perspective, as well as additional generalizations of IRT models that include random item effects. One issue is the need for appropriate estimation methods that can handle crossed (random person-by-random item) effects; some progress has been made in this area (e.g., Cho & Rabe-Hesketh, 2011). Due to the item sampling procedures inherent in using methods such as CAT or other forms of CBT, as well as the ability to test persons repeatedly using different forms, CBT will likely provide an excellent context for further development of such models.

Another promising area of IRT model development relates to models that deal explicitly with repeated measures and assessment of change (see, for example, Rijmen, De Boeck, & VanderMaas, 2005). One of the clear advantages of CBT is the capacity for more frequent testing of persons, such as in progress-monitoring applications. With computers, it also becomes possible to integrate testing and assessment within intelligent tutoring or e-learning environments, where changes in ability are occurring over the course of a single assessment. Both types of applications emphasize the person in terms of their acquisition of proficiency over time, as opposed to viewing proficiency as a static trait. Such applications require models that can be used to evaluate items in terms of new characteristics, most notably their sensitivity to change and/or their potential to instill learning. Such models can also capitalize on known information about skill acquisition, as might be informed by theories of learning progressions related to the skills of interest.

Finally, we note that a consistent element to all of the models in this chapter is their responsiveness to either tasks of increased complexity or new information that is accessible in computer testing applications. As noted, these changes make questionable those models that assume measurement of a single proficiency and that require local independence across individual items. In many cases, it may even be unrealistic to characterize aspects of performance in relation to "items," such as in computer-based simulations where sequences of behavior are of greater interest than any single action. Thus another important area of work of relevance in CBT relates less to the development of new models but rather to how IRT models are thought about and used within a broader assessment framework. Mislevy, Steinberg, and Almond (2003) discuss some implications of evidence-centered design principles in how IRT models are understood to function as evidence models, whereby data are used toward making inferences about person ability. This broader assessment framework emphasizes the integration of many other elements (e.g., the structure of proficiencies, the design of tasks) in this process. Such a framework discourages an "off-the-shelf" approach to how IRT models are used in the context of CBT but rather a more thoughtful consideration of a number of other elements. In this context, graphical models (Almond & Mislevy, 1999) provide a framework in which IRT models can be seen as a special case that applies when certain structures of proficiency, certain forms of evidence, and certain tasks are used in an assessment context. Much like the response time models described earlier in the chapter, one might anticipate generalizations of IRT models that can accommodate other aspects of performance. Such applications would seem to require an even greater role for the psychometrician in the assessment process.

The computer is offering much exciting future work within the field of psychometrics, particularly for those who like to think creatively about the use of models in assessment contexts. As experience with this mode of administration accumulates and new dimensions of its use become better understood, we would expect that newer, increasingly diverse, and likely specialized forms of IRT models will continue to be needed.

## References

Almond, R. G., & Mislevy, R. J. (1999). Graphical models and computerized adaptive testing. *Applied Psychological Measurement*, 23(3), 223–237.

Attali, Y. (2011). Immediate feedback and the opportunity to revise answers: Application of a graded response IRT model. *Applied Psychological Measurement*, 35, 472–479.

Becker, K. A. (2010, April). *The care and feeding of innovative items*. Paper presented at the Annual Meeting of the National Council on Measurement in Education (NCME), Denver, CO.

Béguin, A. A., & Glas, C. A. (2001). MCMC estimation and some model-fit analysis of multidimensional IRT models. *Psychometrika*, 66(4), 541–561.

Bejar, I. I. (1996). *Generative response modeling: Leveraging the computer as a test delivery medium* (ETS RR-96–13). Princeton, NJ: Educational Testing Service.

Briggs, D. C., & Wilson, M. (2007). Generalizability in item response modeling. *Journal of Educational Measurement*, 44, 131–155.

Cai, L. (2010a). A two-tier full-information item factor analysis model with applications. *Psychometrika*, 75(4), 581–612.

Cai, L. (2010b). High-dimensional exploratory item factor analysis by a Metropolis–Hastings Robbins–Monro algorithm. *Psychometrika*, 75(1), 33–57.

Cho, S. J., & Rabe-Hesketh, S. (2011). Alternating imputation posterior estimation of models with crossed random effects. *Computational Statistics & Data Analysis*, 55(1), 12–25.

Clauser, B. E., Kane, M. T., & Swanson, D. B. (2002). Validity issues for performance-based tests scored with computer-automated scoring systems. *Applied Measurement in Education*, 15, 413–432.

De Boeck, P. (2008). Random item IRT models. *Psychometrika*, 73, 533–559.

De Boeck, P., & Wilson, M. (Eds.). (2004). *Explanatory item response models: A generalized linear and nonlinear approach*. New York: Springer.

Dodd, B. G., De Ayala, R. J., & Koch, W. R. (1995). Computerized adaptive testing with polytomous items. *Applied Psychological Measurement*, 19(1), 5–22.

Drasgow, F., Levine, M. V., & McLaughlin, M. E. (1987). Detecting inappropriate test scores with optimal and practical appropriateness indices. *Applied Psychological Measurement*, 11(1), 59–79.

Drasgow, F., & Mattern, K. (2006). New tests and new items: Opportunities and issues. In D. Bartram & R. K. Hambleton (Eds.), *Computer-based testing and the Internet: Issues and advances* (pp. 59–75). New York: Wiley.

Edwards, M. C. (2010). A Markov chain Monte Carlo approach to confirmatory item factor analysis. *Psychometrika*, 75, 474–497.

Eggen, T. J. H. M. (2007). Choices in CAT models in the context of educational testing. In D. J. Weiss (Ed.), *Proceedings of the 2007 GMAC Conference on Computerized Adaptive Testing*.

Embretson, S. (1980). Multicomponent latent trait models for ability tests. *Psychometrika*, 45(4), 479–494.

Embretson, S. E. (1999). Generating items during testing: Psychometric issues and models. *Psychometrika*, 64, 407–433.

Fischer, G. H. (1973). The linear logistic test model as an instrument in educational research. *Acta Psychologica*, 37(6), 359–374.

Geerlings, H., Glas, C.A.W., & van der Linden, W.J. (2011). Modeling rule-based item generation. *Psychometrika, 76*, 337–359.

Geerlings, H., van der Linden, W.J., & Glas, C.A.W. (2013). Optimal test design with rule-based item generation. *Applied Psychological Measurement, 37*(2), 140–161.

Gibbons, R.D., & Hedeker, D.R. (1992). Full-information item bi-factor analysis. *Psychometrika, 57*(3), 423–436.

Glas, C.A.W., & van der Linden, W.J. (2003). Computerized adaptive testing with item clones. *Applied Psychological Measurement, 27*, 247–261.

Hambleton, R.K. (2006). Psychometric models, test designs and item types for the next generation of educational and psychological tests. In D. Bartram & R. K. Hambleton (Eds.), *Computer-based testing and the internet: issues and advances* (pp. 77–90). New York: Wiley.

Hendrickson, A. (2007). An NCME instructional module on multistage testing. *Educational Measurement: Issues & Practice, 26*, 44–52.

Jiao, H., Liu, J., Haynie, K., Woo, A., & Gorham, J. (2012). Comparison between dichotomous and polytomous scoring of innovative items in a large-scale computerized adaptive test. *Educational and Psychological Measurement, 72*(3), 493–509.

Jodoin, M.G. (2003). Measurement efficiency of innovative item formats in computer-based testing. *Journal of Educational Measurement, 40*, 1–15.

Johnson, M.S., & Sinharay, S. (2005). Calibration of polytomous item families using Bayesian hierarchical modeling. *Applied Psychological Measurement, 29*, 369–400.

Klein Entink, R.H., Fox, J.P., & van der Linden, W.J. (2009). A multivariate multilevel approach to the modeling of accuracy and speed of test takers. *Psychometrika, 74*, 21–48.

Li, Y., Bolt, D.M., & Fu, J. (2006). A comparison of alternative models for testlets. *Applied Psychological Measurement, 30*, 3–21.

Luecht, R.M. (1996). Multidimensional computerized adaptive testing in a certification or licensure context. *Applied Psychological Measurement, 20*(4), 389–404.

McLeod, L., Lewis, C., & Thissen, D. (2003). A Bayesian method for the detection of item preknowledge in computerized adaptive testing. *Applied Psychological Measurement, 27*, 121–137.

Mellenbergh, G.J. (1995). Conceptual notes on models for discrete polytomous item responses. *Applied Psychological Measurement, 19*, 91–100.

Mislevy, R.J., Steinberg, L.S., & Almond, R.G. (2003). Focus article: On the structure of educational assessments. *Measurement: Interdisciplinary Research and Perspectives, 1*(1), 3–62.

Nering, M.L., & Ostini, R. (Eds.). (2011). *Handbook of polytomous item response theory models*. New York: Taylor & Francis.

Parshall, C.G., Harmes, J.C., Davey, T., & Pashley, P.J. (2010). Innovative items for computerized testing. In W.J. van der Linden & C.A.W. Glas (Eds.), *Elements of adaptive testing* (pp. 215–230). New York: Springer.

Partchev, I., & De Boeck, P. (2012). Can fast and slow intelligence be differentiated? *Intelligence, 40*(1), 23–32.

Rasch, G. (1960). Studies in mathematical psychology: I. Probabilistic models for some intelligence and attainment tests. Oxford, UK: Nielsen & Lyd-ische.

Reckase, M.D. (1985). The difficulty of test items that measure more than one ability. *Applied Psychological Measurement, 9*(4), 401–412.

Reckase, M.D. (2009). *Multidimensional item response theory*. New York: Springer.

Rijmen, F. (2010). Formal relations and an empirical comparison among the bi-factor, the testlet, and a second-order multidimensional IRT model. *Journal of Educational Measurement, 47*, 361–372.

Rijmen, F., & De Boeck, P. (2002). The random weights linear logistic test model. *Applied Psychological Measurement, 26*(3), 271–285.

Rijmen, F., De Boeck, P., & vanderMaas, H.L.J. (2005). An IRT model with a parameter-driven process for change. *Psychometrika, 70*, 651–669.

Roskam, E.E. (1987). Toward a psychometric theory of intelligence. In E.E. Roskam & R. Suck (Eds.), *Progress in mathematical psychology* (pp. 151–171). Amsterdam: North-Holland.

Rupp, A.A., Gushta, M., Mislevy, R.J., & Shaffer, D.W. (2010). Evidence-centered design of epistemic games: Measurement principles for complex learning environments. *The Journal of Technology, Learning and Assessment, 8*(4), 4–47.

Scalise, K., & Wilson, M. (2007). *Bundle models for computer adaptive testing in e-learning assessment*. Paper presented at the 2007 Graduate Management Admission Council (GMAC) Conference on Computerized Adaptive Testing, Minneapolis, MN.

Segall, D.O. (1996). Multidimensional adaptive testing. *Psychometrika, 61*, 331–354.

Segall, D.O. (2001). General ability measurement: An application of multidimensional item response theory. *Psychometrika, 66*, 79–97.

Segall, D.O. (2002). An item response model for characterizing test compromise. *Journal of Educational and Behavioral Statistics, 27*, 163–179.

Segall, D.O. (2004). A sharing item response model for computerized adaptive testing. *Journal of Educational and Behavioral Statistics, 29*, 439–460.

Segall, D.O. (2010). Principles of multidimensional adaptive testing. In In W.J. van der Linden & C.A.W. Glas (Eds.), *Elements of adaptive testing* (pp. 57–75). New York: Springer.

Shu, Z., Henson, R., & Luecht, R. (2013). Using deterministic, gated item response model to detect cheating due to item compromise. *Psychometrika, 78*(3), 481–497.

Sinharay, S., Johnson, M.S., & Williamson, D.M. (2003). Calibrating item families and summarizing the results using family expected score functions. *Journal of Educational and Behavioral Statistics, 28*, 295–313.

Sinharay, S., Puhan, G., & Haberman, S.J. (2010). Reporting diagnostic scores in educational testing: Temptations, pitfalls, and some solutions. *Multivariate Behavioral Research, 45*(3), 553–573.

Thissen, D. (1983). Timed testing: An approach using item response theory. In D. Weiss (Ed.), *New horizons in testing: Latent trait test theory and computerized adaptive testing* (pp. 179–203). New York: Academic Press.

Thissen, D., Steinberg, L., & Mooney, J.A. (1989). Trace lines for testlets: A use of multiple-categorical-response models. *Journal of Educational Measurement, 26*, 247–260.

Tutz, G. (1990). Sequential item response models with an ordered response. *British Journal of Mathematical and Statistical Psychology, 43*, 39–55.

van der Linden, W.J. (1999). Multidimensional adaptive testing with a minimum error-variance criterion. *Journal of Educational and Behavioral Statistics, 24*(4), 398–412.

van der Linden, W.J. (2007). A hierarchical framework for modeling speed and accuracy on test items. *Psychometrika, 72*, 287–308.

van der Linden, W.J. (2009). Conceptual issues in response time modeling. *Journal of Educational Measurement, 46*, 247–272.

van der Linden, W.J. (2011). Modeling response times with latent variables: Principles and applications. *Psychological test and assessment modeling, 53*, 334–358.

Wainer, H., & Keily, G.L. (1987). Item clusters and computerized adaptive testing: A case for testlets. *Journal of Educational Measurement, 24*, 185–201.

Wainer, H., Bradlow, E.T., & Du, Z. (2002). Testlet response theory: An analog for the 3PL model useful in testlet-based adaptive testing. In W.J. van der Linden & C.A.W. Glas (Eds), *Computerized adaptive testing: theory and practice* (pp. 245–269). Dordrecht, The Netherlands: Kluwer Academic Publishers.

Wainer, H., Bradlow, E.T., & Wang, X. (2007). *Testlet response theory and its applications*. Cambridge, MA: Cambridge University Press.

Williamson, D.M., Xi, X., & Breyer, F.J. (2012). A framework for evaluation and use of automated scoring. *Educational Measurement: Issues & Practice, 31*, 2–13.

# 15

# Using Prizes to Facilitate Change in Educational Assessment

**Mark D. Shermis and Jaison Morgan**

## Introduction

### Trajectories of Computerized Adaptive Testing and Automated Essay Scoring

In this chapter, we discuss one approach to fostering change in educational assessment, the use of incentives to stimulate solutions for assessment challenges that are not adequately solved. We document three studies, two involving prizes that examine the performance of machine scoring with that of trained human raters for both essay and short-answer performance assessments. The results from the three studies suggest that well-managed incentives can permit the leveraging of resources to spur innovation at an efficient cost. Moreover, the use of carefully designed prizes can result in more transparent and open communication in which competitors *actually help each other* find optimal solutions. The result here might be viewed as a case study on how to foster innovation in educational assessment.

To begin with, we examine the histories of two different measurement technologies—computerized adaptive testing (CAT) and automated essay scoring (AES)—both of which were "ideas" in the mid 1960s and had working models by the mid 1970s. The two technologies then diverged. Due to its open-source nature, CAT was extensively researched by academic investigators during the 1980s and 1990s, whereas the proprietary nature of AES limited research and its general acceptability. Today CAT (or its variations) is a common approach to testing, whereas AES has had only limited application. We then discuss why prizes might work in the context of educational assessment.

### Computerized Adaptive Testing (CAT)

In a formal sense, adaptive testing has been around since the beginning of the 20th century with the publication of the first Binet-Simon Test (1906; Binet & Simon, 1916), later the Stanford-Binet Intelligence Scale (Terman, 1916). Under specific guidelines, the test administrator could begin and end with items more appropriate to the intelligence level of the individual being tested. It did not require that all items be given to all examinees. One of the earlier computerized adaptive tests was developed by David Weiss at the University of Minnesota (Vale & Weiss, 1975; Weiss, 1973). It employed a mainframe computer and stradaptive testing model that used "peaked tests" developed under classical test theory to branch examinees to appropriate performance levels (Lord, Novick, & Birnbaum, 1968).

More commonly, computerized adaptive tests (CAT) refer to item response theory assessments that are based on the performance level of the examinee (Weiss, 1985). CATs work in the following fashion: After the examinee responds to each item, his/her ability estimate is updated and an item most appropriate to the new estimated ability is selected from a pool of items (Birnbaum, 1968; Lord, 1980). If an examinee is performing well on an ability test, the items will become progressively harder. If the examinee responses are incorrect, the subsequent items will be easier. For personality assessments, the items endorsed will lead to the administration of additional items that reflect more or less of the trait being assessed, depending on the direction of the endorsement.

Weiss and his colleagues at the University of Minnesota are often credited for developing CAT routines that were made available for researchers to use at no or a modest cost (e.g., MicroCAT; Assessment Systems Corporation, 1985). This early work made the CAT routines accessible to researchers for experimentation and further development (Ho & Hsu, 1989). While commercial vendors were busy developing their own systems (Schaeffer, 1995), academic researchers were nevertheless able to continue research in the field. During the 1980s and 1990s, the annual conventions of the National Council on Measurement in Education, the American Educational Research Association, and the American Psychological Association were full of papers addressing CAT and related issues such as item banking, branching strategies, item calibration methods, paper-and-pencil equivalency, bias, and the like. Moreover, under the organization of David Weiss, the Office of Naval Research sponsored productive CAT conferences in 1975, 1977, 1979, and 1985.

Early large-scale uses of CAT took the form of applications for military selection (Moreno, Wetzel, McBride, & Weiss, 1984; Segall & Moreno, 1999) and school counseling (McBride, 1986). Today, CAT or its derivatives are employed in a wide range of educational, personnel, and licensing settings. For example, Luecht and Sirici (2011) point out that the technology is used for testing programs such as the ACCUPLACER postsecondary placement exams (College Board, 1993), the Graduate Record Exam (now a multistage computer-adaptive test; Eignor, Way, Stocking, & Steffen, 1993), the Measures of Academic Progress (Northwest Evaluation Association, 2005), and several other licensure and certification exams such as the Uniform CPA Examination (accountancy certification; AICPA Examinations Team, 2010). It continues to be studied in a wide variety of educational and industrial settings (Luecht & Sireci, 2011; Sands, Waters, & McBride, 1997).

Early CAT research focused on the nature of the algorithms (Wainer, Dorans, Flaugher, Green, & Mislevy, 2000). So, for instance, approaches that employed maximum likelihood calculations, which seemed to be the most efficient, required that the individual get at least one item correct and one item incorrect before an ability estimate could be computed. So these algorithms sometimes started by giving examinees an easy item that they would answer correctly and then branched a difficult item in hopes of an incorrect answer. While this was a good strategy for the algorithm, it was unusually startling for the examinee, and hybrid models were developed to address this challenge (e.g., starting off with a less efficient Bayesian model and then switching to maximum likelihood after the right/wrong state had been achieved). Currently, there are a variety of algorithms in computerized adaptive testing from which to select (Luecht & Sireci, 2011).

Another line of inquiry had to do with the nature of the item banks (Stocking & Swanson, 1998). If examinees enter the test with the same initial ability estimate, then the CAT algorithms tend to use the same items so that only 30 to 40% of the items in the bank are used (Luecht & Sireci, 2011). Consequently, research on how to better utilize the item banks emerged with suggestions for covering a greater range of items. For example, randomly selecting an item from a range of difficulty/discrimination levels rather than selecting the *best* item was one solution. Moreover, some tests required that specific content be covered even though the items weren't necessarily ideal in estimating the ability level of the student. This line of inquiry comes under the subcategory of "exposure control" (Revuelta & Ponsoda, 1998).

Test item security is a topic that cuts across all types of testing but is particularly sensitive in CAT because of the exposure control issue cited (Way, 1998). Most testing companies monitor exposure rates of items and look for changes in item difficulty over time. If the difficulty rate decreases significantly, one possibility is that the item has been compromised and needs to be retired. Some testing companies monitor external websites where items might be shared among test takers. In order to reduce the probability of this occurring, many CATs have multiple "forms" via which only certain items from the item bank will be used in a given time period or window.

The main point to be made here is that while CAT research continues to explore and expand the boundaries of adaptive assessments, the topic has been openly explored for about 40 years. A recent check of Google Scholar lists more than 200,000 references on the topic. Specific references to *automated essay scoring* number at about 25,000.

### Automated Essay Scoring (AES)

In 1966, Ellis Page wrote on "The imminence of grading essays by computer" in a landmark *Phi Delta Kappan* article (Page, 1966). The article, greeted with considerable skepticism, predicted the coming of automated essay grading—the capacity of the computer to score extended written responses. Nevertheless, Page and his colleagues at the University of Connecticut produced a stable version of Project Essay Grade (PEG), a FORTRAN-based program that successfully evaluated English written prose (Ajay, Tillett, & Page, 1973). Given the context and the type of data to which his team had access (e.g., short college-level essays), PEG performed remarkably well. The 1973 study predated the entrance of high-stakes state-administered accountability assessments at United States public schools, a period in which exact agreement rates for human raters were in the low .70s. Prior to that time, it was common to see trained raters achieving agreement rates in the low to mid .60s (Page, 2003). Even so, PEG was able to perform as well as and sometimes better than the interrater performance of two trained human raters (Page & Petersen, 1995). As impressive as the technology performance was at the time, it was not long lasting due to some significant limitations, including a lack of computer access and a time-consuming method for data entry (i.e., tape or punched cards).

By the early 1990s, the advances of the Internet and word processing had sufficiently unfolded, and electronic processing and evaluation of student-written papers became a real possibility. Page and his colleagues began to update the FORTRAN-coded PEG and convert it to the C programming language (Page, Lavoie, & Keith, 1996). The program still processed the text in batch mode. The original version of PEG used only limited natural language processing (NLP) elements as part of its repertoire (Ajay et al., 1973). The text was parsed and classified into language components, such as part of speech, word length, and word functions; PEG would count key words and make its predictions based on the patterns of language that human raters valued or devalued in making their score assignments. Page classified these counts into three categories: simple, deceptively simple, and sophisticated. An example of a simple count would be the number of adjectives in an essay. Empirically, writers tend to be rewarded by human raters for using more adjectives (Page, Keith, & Lavoie, 1995).

A deceptively simple count might be the number of words in an essay. Longer essays tend to be assigned higher scores by human raters. However, Page found that the relationship between the number of words used and the score assignment was not linear but rather logarithmic. That is, essay length is factored in by human raters up to some threshold and then becomes less important as they focus on other aspects of the writing. Breland, Bonner, and Kubota (1995) also noted that essay word count was correlated with human score, consistent with a PEG feature, specifically the fourth root of the number of words in an essay.

A sophisticated count would be attending to words that are proxies for something that might have greater meaning. For example, a count of the word "because" may not be important in and of itself, but as a discourse connector, it serves as a proxy for sentence complexity. Human raters tend to reward more complex sentences (Page & Petersen, 1995).

In 1998, a web interface was added to PEG that permitted students to enter their essays remotely (Shermis, Mzumara, Kiger, & Marsiglio, 1998; Shermis, Mzumara, Olson, & Harrington, 2001). This new capability had few word processing features other than the basic editing of text, but it meant that student writers could enter their responses from anywhere in the world. After they clicked a "submit" button, the essay would be processed by a PEG server and would return a score assigned by PEG. It would also store the results in a database that could later be retrieved for analysis.

At about the same time, Vantage Learning released its first version of its Intellimetric™ scoring engine (Elliot, 1999). The Intellimetric scoring engine used empirical relationships to derive its predictive models but also incorporated elements, computational linguistics, and classification (Elliot, 2003). The Intellimetric scoring engine analyzes more than 300 semantic, syntactic, and discourse level features that fall into five major categories: focus and utility, development and elaboration, organization and structure, sentence structure, and mechanics and conventions. It was the first scoring engine to be marketed with an electronic portfolio, MyAccess!™, where students could store past work. The portfolio system also provided writing aids, sophisticated word-processing capabilities, and analytics for teachers to monitor student writing progress.

The original PEG and Intellimetric scoring engines could provide assessments of content, but only in an indirect way. That is, using a list of key words and synonyms, one could determine the frequency with which a candidate essay employed the same terminology as that drawn from an expert list or from a normative model. Intelligent Essay Assessor's primary evaluation is based on the essay's content using a technique known as latent semantic analysis (LSA) (Landauer, Foltz, & Laham, 1998; Landauer, Laham, & Foltz, 2003). LSA is a corpus-based statistical modeling approach that uses large corpora to model word usage. LSA generates information about statistical word usage in a document without regard to word ordering. This information for a single document is compared to other documents to determine the similarity between that source document and a large set of reference documents (e.g., usually a set of essays that have both text and rater scores but can be composed of other materials such as knowledge bases or textbooks) in terms of vocabulary use. LSA modeling requires a very large corpus of reference documents (several thousand) to reliably model a given domain. The underlying claim is that if LSA determines that two documents are similar with regard to word usage, then they are likely to be semantically similar (i.e., have the same meaning). In the context of essay scoring, LSA is trained on reference documents in a particular domain, such as textbook passages and/or human-scored essay responses to an essay topic. This training creates a semantic representation of topical knowledge. This method focuses on essay content and can be used to score essays that respond to opinion or fact-based topics.

E-rater™ represents the first hybrid approach that leveraged NLP–derived linguistic properties in texts that were aligned with human scoring rubric criteria and empirical relationships between human ratings (Attali & Burstein, 2006; Burstein et al., 1998). E-rater features aligned with human scoring criteria included features related to writing conventions, sentence variety, topical vocabulary usage, sophistication of vocabulary, and organization and development. The system can also identify anomalous essays, for example, essays that appear to be off-topic. E-rater was the first system to be used in a large-scale, high-stakes assessment setting with the Graduate Management Admissions Test. In addition to assessment settings, e-rater features were also used in one of the first instructional settings, Criterion®, to provide individualized feedback for student writers, directing students' attention to areas of success or improvement (Burstein, Chodorow, & Leacock, 2004).

### Trademark Hindrances to Development and Competition

Of critical importance is that CAT began as an open system that was available to researchers for investigation, expansion, and study. During the 1980s and 1990s, numerous papers were delivered on the topic at NCME, AERA, and APA, as well as in conferences in Europe and Asia. Topics included the development of different CAT techniques, item calibration, reliability and validity of the scores using the methodology, comparisons with paper-and-pencil tests, differential impact, and assessments of using CAT for high-stakes testing. In this sense, no stone was left unturned, as the scientific community had the opportunity to take the scoring software and test its limits in both a theoretical and an applied way. In contrast, AES was a closed system, available only to those that held the trademarks to the systems. Some vendors (e.g., ETS) published the results of their work but only described their systems at a general level (Williamson, 2009). Academic researchers had a limited capacity to study the proprietary technology because the systems were protected by trademarks and intellectual copyright. The lack of access, research, and competitive development most likely stunted the growth and acceptance of the methodology as a mainstream technology in educational assessment.

### The Race to the Top

A new generation of measurement instruments is being developed for use in the United States as part of the Race to the Top assessments. These instruments will be based on the instructional goals of Common Core State Standards that articulate the required proficiencies for United States students to be "college ready" by the time they graduate from high school (Porter, McMaken, Hwang, & Yang, 2011). These new assessments will likely rely less on multiple-choice questions and use performance measures that more closely match the construct under investigation. The move to Common Core State Standards in the United States represents a significant departure from a curricular structure that heretofore has been driven by individual states.

Over the past 30 years, the high-stakes assessments associated with most state objectives have been calibrated to the minimal standards for exiting high school. These standards have not been universal and vary from state to state. In the area of high-stakes state writing assessment, writing objectives can range from the summarization of reading material to the ability to create prose of a particular genre to the mastery of a particular writing form. Writing assessment practices also differ from state to state, including the amount and type of writing expected, types of rubrics used, scoring and adjudication protocols, the number and qualifications of raters employed, quality-assurance practices, and the reporting of results (Shermis & Hamner, 2013).

In part because of the emphasis on minimum competency and the varied nature of what a state might emphasize in its high-stakes testing programs, there grew a widening pool of college students who had the skill set to graduate from high school yet had to enroll in remedial college classes because that skill set did not include the higher-order knowledge or skills required to perform well in entry-level college classes (Attewell, Lavin, Domina, & Levey, 2006), where the curriculum is typically based on the standards of the discipline's national organizations (Dossey, Halvorsen, & McCrone, 2008). The two major Race to the Top consortia (Partnership for Assessment of Readiness for College and Careers, PARCC, and SMARTER Balanced Assessment Consortia, Smarter Balanced) and their 35 subscriber states intend to change that pattern by having all students—even those who may wish to pursue a vocational track—work toward college readiness rather than a mastery of basic high school skills (Tucker, 2009).

With regard to assessments in English language arts and in many of the science areas, this shift will mean more writing. For instance, students might be given an array of articles in geology to read and then respond to an essay prompt that addresses some conclusion that they might make based on the articles. The essay might ask the student to explain a rationale for a conclusion or to cite evidence in support of an argument. Part of the current debate in planning the new instruments is whether this performance assessment is really a writing task (where the emphasis is on writing ability), reading comprehension (where the emphasis is on understanding the content), or one of critical thinking (where the emphasis is on synthesizing and evaluating information; Shermis, 2014). Two of these options are consistent with Weigle's distinctions regarding the multiple purposes of assessment, assessing writing (AW) and assessing content through writing (ACW; Weigle, 2013; Weir, 2005). In many cases, the student will be asked to produce a written artifact that must be evaluated—and to do so numerous times throughout the academic year. The sheer number of written responses for high-stakes summative assessments across the grade levels makes it challenging and cost ineffective to have human raters exclusively score the assessments. For example, the state of Florida has approximately 180,000 students in each grade level. If each student produced five essays per year, the state would be required to conduct almost 11 million reviews, raising questions as to the feasibility of recruiting a sufficient number of qualified human graders to provide final scores, read reliably, in a timely manner across the entirety of the United States. The goals of the consortia have been to strongly encourage the development and use of machine scoring algorithms in order to make it possible to score such volumes in a timely and cost-effective manner.

In 2011, the William and Flora Hewlett Foundation (Hewlett), a grant-making organization supporting the work of the consortia, set out to deliver a new set of incentives to test the limits of machine scoring and its use within the newly conceived assessments. The program was named the Automated Student Assessment Prize (ASAP), in part to underscore the sense of urgency regarding whether or not those technologies could perform sufficiently before exposing them to such a wide range of students. ASAP is akin to the Ansari X Prize for space competition in which the X Prize Foundation offered a $10,000,000 prize for the first nongovernment organization to launch a reusable manned spacecraft into space twice within 2 weeks. It was modeled after early-20th-century aviation prizes, and aimed to spur development of low-cost space flight (Kay, 2011). Neither Hewlett nor those responsible for designing ASAP expressed any bias or preference toward the outcome of the study, only that it was essential to better understand AES capabilities under fair, open, and transparent scrutiny, a challenge that had historically been limited by the proprietary nature of the software. The incentives were designed to attract the current commercial providers, only those capable of servicing the needs of large-scale state assessments, to predict the scores of previously state-administered responses on student tests. In parallel, ASAP included a public competition, in which $100,000 of cash rewards were offered to data scientists capable of producing new AES machine scoring algorithms, with the intent that those new approaches might meet or exceed the established standard in the private demonstrations and thereby push the industry to consider different methodologies adopted in the public competition. A fuller description of the ASAP competition is given in Shermis (2014).

Prior to ASAP, various conferences and organizations had arranged similar but limited demonstrations of AES performance, but none of those had aligned with the pending demands for such services. The timing of the consortia's announcements to consider AES as a solution for deeper measures of student learning and in a more cost effective and efficient way, as well as the relationship between Hewlett and the Consortia, were one of the key differentiators and one of the primary levers for securing the participation of those private vendors. Absent those pressures, it is unclear whether the vendors would have committed to such a head-to-head comparison. Similarly, as the public competition was unveiled, cash rewards were made available from a total pool of $100,000 to the competitors. However, when surveyed, participants in the public competition consistently revealed that motivations to improve the current state of public education through machine scoring and predictive modeling outnumbered interests strictly confined to financial compensation. In both cases, the timing and purpose of the competition proved instrumental in attracting a broad range of players (Shermis, 2014).

In terms of funding, CAT was reasonably well supported from the Office of Naval Research. As noted before with ASVAB application, the benefits to the military for shorter testing times were potentially significant, and research on the testing algorithms had the potential to pay off in palpable ways. Moreover, the Institute for Educational Studies (and its predecessors) along with the National Science Foundation has provided federal support for years. In contrast, the focus of military support for automated essay scoring has been in simplifying technical manuals for those working on military equipment. One application of some AES algorithms is to locate specific topics and provide wording alternatives for complex language (Foltz & Landauer, 2002).

### Why Prizes Might Work

In their report to the Hewlett Foundation, Morgan, Shermis, Van Deventer, and Vander Ark (2013) list four reasons the use of prize inducements might promote advancements in educational assessment:

1. Leverage Funds—Prizes motivate participants to invest time and energy in solving a problem they might not otherwise consider. Prizes are usually performance based and only paid out once a viable solution is demonstrated.

2. Mobilize Talent—Prizes spark the interest of diverse groups of professionals and students. Many prizes are won by scientists several degrees of separation from the subject sector. Prizes are an extremely efficient strategy for mobilizing diverse talent impossible to locate using conventional approaches.

3. Innovate—The cross-pollination of participants from different backgrounds and with different skill sets unleashes creativity, allowing problem solvers to generate fresh ideas. The use of leader boards and discussion tools promotes transparency and competition, but it also inspires collaboration and innovative discovery.

4. Influence—The results of prize competitions can garner public attention and influence key decision makers. Good prizes result in newsworthy mobilization and breakthrough outcomes that result in press coverage that can be worth more than the prize purse (Morgan et al., 2013, p. 7).

While the use of prizes to recognize accomplishments in education has been a long-established practice, the use of prize inducements has a shorter history. Most prize inducements have been set for technological developments, and the research has shown mixed results.

## Method

The Common Core State Standards Initiative has brought to the surface the need for students to be able to handle a variety of writing tasks, and there is a focus on students' ability to produce a variety of essay types, that is, to write in different genres. It is clear that AES, in its current state, does not have the capacity to analyze the breadth of linguistic and pragmatic forms that are found across the anticipated array of genres students will need to produce. To address this concern as part of its "deeper learning" agenda, Hewlett's commitment to the ASAP program of research should be perceived as a sponsored series of investigations to ascertain how well machine-scored essays compared to their human-rated counterparts. This question was addressed in two parts, first as a demonstration among the leading commercial providers of those services and then as an open competition for which cash prizes were awarded.

The vendor demonstration compared eight commercial vendors and one university laboratory's performance on automated essay scoring with that of human raters (Shermis & Hamner, 2012, 2013). That study employed eight different essay sets drawn from six states representing the PARCC and Smarter Balanced consortia. In the first study, four of the essays were "source based," meaning that students were asked to read an artifact (source document) and then respond with an essay. The remaining four essay tasks reflected more traditional writing prompts (i.e., narrative, descriptive, persuasive). A pool of 22,029 essays was randomly divided into three sets, stratified by task: a *training set* ($n = 13,336$) was available to vendors for one month to model the data, and a test set was provided at the conclusion of the training period, for which they were required to make score predictions within a 59-hour window. The training set included two human rater scores, an adjudicated score, and the text of the essay. The *test set* included only the text of the essay. Six of the eight essays were transcribed from handwritten documents using one of two transcription services. Transcription accuracy rates were estimated to be greater than 98%. The challenge to the nine teams was to predict the human resolved score for each essay. A third *validation set* was also randomly selected but not used in the first study. It was reserved for a public competition (described in what follows) and included both scores for and text of the essays.

Performance on the first study was evaluated on seven different measures (Shermis & Hamner, 2012, 2013). The first two measures reflected the distributional properties of the essay score: means and standard deviations. The remaining five measures addressed how well the machine scores agreed with those actually assigned by the human raters contracted by the state departments of education. These included exact agreement, exact+adjacent agreement, kappa, quadratic weighted kappa, and the Pearson product–moment correlation. The automated essay scoring engines performed well on the distributional measures. With a high degree of consistency, all nine demonstrators were able to replicate the means and standard deviations for the scores assigned by the state departments of education. With regard to agreement measures, there was some variability, but the automated essay scoring engines performed well on three of the five measures (exact+adjacent agreement, quadratic weighted kappa, correlation). Vendors achieved a top mark of $k_w = .78$, while human raters achieved an average of $k_w = .74$. On the two measures where the performance was not as high (exact agreement and kappa), there was also high variability among the human raters. The conclusion of that study was that with additional work, automated essay scoring could be a viable solution in some aspects of evaluating high-stakes long-form writing assessments (e.g., as a second reader).

The second study was similar to the first except that it was run as a public competition on the Kaggle platform (www.kaggle.com), a web-based platform for data prediction competitions where organizations can post data for analysis to data scientists throughout the world (Burstein et al., 2004; Ho & Hsu, 1989). This competition used quadratic weighted kappa as the sole evaluation criterion and challenged data scientists to maximize the value of this agreement measure with human scores. The prizes for the top performers on this metric were $60,000 for first place, $30,000 for second place, and $10,000 for third place. As such, this challenge was presented as a data modeling competition (onward Kaggle Inc., 2010).

The goal of the public competition was to ascertain whether data scientists employing new methodologies, such as those used in building predictive models for stock market prices, weather patterns, glacial drift, and other fields of scientific study disparate to NLP, LSA, and related machine scoring disciplines, could produce results in a faster and more effective way than the current standards. Also, the goal included encouraging and making available to the existing commercial vendors those new programming approaches in order to improve the overall state of the industry. The public competition, which ran in parallel to the commercial demonstration, involved 159 teams of data scientists from around the world.

There were minor but important differences between the commercial demonstration and the public competition. First, the data scientists had approximately 3 months to create and train their engines rather than the 1 month allocated to the commercial vendors (who had existing scoring engines). In this process, they used the same training data that the vendors used, with the exception that the data provided to the public competitors had to undergo an anonymization step. This was intended to address concerns that individual students might be identified from details of their essays used in the competition despite the fact that all of the prompts were designed to elicit either factual or innocuous information.

In order to assess the suitability of the anonymized data for evaluating automated essay scoring systems, a small internal study was completed with the LightSIDE engine to determine the degree to which there might be differences. LightSIDE is an open-source scoring engine developed at Carnegie Mellon University and was included along with the commercial vendors in the first study. In that study, the engine demonstrated a high agreement with human ratings but had no NLP capabilities. The analysis was performed because it was suspected that the anonymized data might be harder to model than the original data since they would contain less-specific information. However, the LightSIDE model showed only a slight drop across the data sets in quadratic weighted kappa from .763 to .759, which, based on a $t$-test, was not statistically significant ($p = .15$). While the data anonymization process therefore seems not to have substantially impeded the ability of machine-learning based systems to model human scores on this data set, it may have had the effect of making it more difficult for participants to develop features related to deeper aspects of writing ability (Shermis, Lottridge, & Mayfield, 2014). Since content words were replaced with meaningless symbols in the process, the grammatical structures and meaning relationships within each essay were certainly made less accessible, even to human readers.

The top three public competitors achieved average quadratic weighted kappas of 0.814, 0.808, and 0.806 on the test set. As a comparison, the highest overall vendor performance in the first study obtained an average quadratic weighted kappa of .78, and human raters averaged about 0.75. The first-place team consisted of three members: a particle physics engineer from Oxford, a German computer scientist, and a weather analyst working in Washington, DC, at the National Oceanic and Atmospheric Administration (NOAA). The individual members of those competing teams were introduced to the commercial providers, including the open-source code offered through LightSIDE. Subsequently, many of those individuals were either employed or consulted with the private vendors, and those relationships have led to important development in the field of automated student assessment through machine scoring. In fact, one company that employed a Phase I winning team member went on to participate and win the second phase of ASAP as a result of that collaboration. An inspection of the winning software code from the open competition showed that many of the innovative approaches included using existing techniques but in unique and previously unconsidered ways.

The findings of this study are limited by the fact that the tasks investigated were not designed with automated scoring in mind. Rather, because these tasks were taken from preexisting state assessments, they were developed to conform with standard human rating practices. Furthermore, the study relied on a single statistical evaluation criterion of agreement with human ratings and did not incorporate external validation measures, an assessment of fairness, or any evaluation of the construct relevance of the features used by particular models. The focus on agreement with human ratings alone may have encouraged participants to rely on proxies that are not clearly construct related, and future research will be needed to assess the generalizability of the approaches developed.

Phase II of ASAP then compared short-form constructed responses evaluated both by human raters and machine scoring algorithms (Shermis, 2014). The study focused on a public competition administered again on the Kaggle platform, in which both public competitors and commercial vendors vied to develop machine scoring algorithms that would match or exceed the performance of human raters in a summative high-stakes testing environment. Data ($N = 27,485$ essays) were drawn from three different PARCC and Smarter Balanced states, employed 10 different prompts that addressed content mastery from varying domains in the curriculum, and were drawn from Grade 8 and 10 assessments. Samples ranging in size from 2,130 to 2,999 responses per task were randomly selected from the data sets provided by the states and then randomly divided into three sets: a *training set*, a *test set*, and a *validation set*. The *training set* was used by the participants to create their scoring models and consisted of a score assigned by a human rater and the text of the response. The test set consisted of essay text only and was used as part of a blind test for the score model predictions. During the course of the competition, participants could submit interim results on the validation set (or public leaderboard data set) and receive feedback on how well their models were performing compared to those of the other teams. The leaderboard essentially served as a dashboard that indicated how much progress was being made among the competing teams. The distribution of the samples was split in the following approximate proportions: 60% training sample, 20% public leaderboard, 20% private leaderboard sample. Teams had 10 weeks to create and test their model predictions during the training and public leaderboard phases. They had 5 days to optimize their prediction models for the *test set*. Results showed that on five of seven measures (two distribution measures and five agreement measures), the machine scoring algorithms reasonably approximated the characteristics of human ratings, though none of the algorithms matched or exceeded human benchmarks. In Phase I of the ASAP competition (automated essay scoring), human benchmarks for agreement were matched or exceeded on some of the data sets used in that study. The study provided recommendations on approaches to task design that might improve machine scoring performance but recommended that machine scoring be limited for the time being to use as a "read behind" or in low-stakes environments.

As with the ASAP essay scoring challenge, two limitations should be mentioned in connection with the research design of the short-answer scoring phase. Again, the tasks investigated were not designed with automated scoring in mind, with the consequence that better performance might be observed if tasks were better suited to the technology. And the evaluation criteria for the study were narrowly focused on human agreement, so that the validity and construct relevance of model components cannot be established.

**Summary**

So, what happened? Phase I was broken into two parts—first a vendor demonstration on essay scoring and then an international public competition using the same data. The vendors, some of whom have been working in the automated essay scoring space for 15 years, were able to achieve a top agreement rate of .78 on quadratic weighted kappa. The public competitors had two and one-half months to formulate their prediction models and achieved a top agreement rate of .81 on the same measure. In the second competition, vendors and the data scientists competed side by side on developing code to predict scores for short-answer responses. While the machine scoring algorithms achieved a quadratic weighted kappa of .76, the human benchmark was very high at .90. The results of all three studies are illustrated in Figure 15.1. For Phase II, the winners (all five of them) were required to reveal their source code and to publish papers describing their technical approach. Though the official winner of ASAP Phase II was a previously unknown undergraduate student from the University of New Orleans, the unofficial winner was a collaboration between a commercial vendor and one of the public winners from the first (essay) competition (i.e., the team would not reveal its source code and therefore was not qualified to win cash prizes). Source code from the top public competitors remains available for public download, opening up research and investigation into AES that had previously not been available.

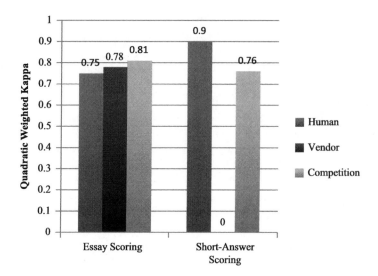

**Figure 15.1** Results from the essay demonstration, public competition, and short-answer competition on quadratic weighted kappa

## Conclusion

The three studies conducted on behalf of the two major Race to the Top consortia produced valuable information regarding the viability of machine scoring for the next generation of assessments associated with the Common Core State Standards. This information has been factored into their testing specifications. From an innovation standpoint, the ASAP prizes appeared to have impacted the factors associated with prize results.

*Leveraging Funds.* Prizes motivate participants to invest time and energy in a problem they might not otherwise tackle. And because they're working toward a deadline, participants quickly dive into the work, spending tens of hours if not hundreds of hours of their personal time. Based on competitor reports, we conservatively estimate that the 250 participants in Phase I of ASAP invested time worth more than $7.5 million, and the 187 participants in Phase II invested $4.7 million to win a combined purse of $200,000—a total of more than $12 million in research and development time within two 3-month time periods. The nine organizations participating in the private vendor demonstrations collectively spent an additional $200,000 to demonstrate the current capabilities of their software. There is simply no other philanthropic strategy that can induce the same level of short-term leverage.

*Mobilize Talent.* The Kaggle, Inc. website notes that "By exposing the problem to a large number of participants trying different techniques, competitions can very quickly advance the frontier of what's possible using a given dataset." Prizes create opportunities for smart people to apply their skills and knowledge to complex problems.

A research fellow in glaciology, a teaching assistant in Slovenia, and an actuary all competed in the ASAP. Data scientists from around the globe—in Poland, Singapore, Australia, London, and elsewhere—registered for the competition, downloaded the data, and designed algorithms to score student responses. Individuals competed on their own, but more often than not, participants organized teams that met in the discussion forums. For Phase I, a British particle physicist, a data analyst for the National Weather Service in Washington, DC, and a graduate student from Germany comprised the first-place team.

Certainly the cash reward is a motivator, but there's more to it than just the money. Well-constructed prizes create interesting challenges. The Kaggle leaderboard recognizes status among a global community. ASAP winners said they like to solve puzzles and contribute to the greater good.

*Innovate.* Prizes spur innovation. The different backgrounds, education, and skill sets of the competitors enrich the field to which they're applying their knowledge. One of the earliest prizes, the Longitude Prize of 1714, sought a solution to the problem of measuring longitude at sea. It's likely that the British Parliament, the sponsors of the prize, assumed that an astronomer or cartographer would come up with the answer. No one expected that John Harrison, a British clockmaker, would create the marine chronometer.

The important lesson is that most innovation is translational—something that worked in one field may work in another. The question is how to expose cross-discipline and cross-sector innovation. Prizes are an efficient means of promoting translational innovation.

Data scientists and statisticians in the open competitions deployed different scoring strategies from the natural language processing approach typically taken by vendors in the field. Some of the winners from ASAP Phase I are already helping some of the big testing companies improve their services. In Phase II, short-answer scoring, competitors were required to open source their code and provide instruction manuals with the goal that others will continue to build on their successes.

*Influence.* Both phases of ASAP have been developed with the support of and with the intent to benefit PARCC and SBAC, the Race to the Top state testing consortia that rolled out new online tests in 2014–2015. Both consortia aim to offer much higher-quality assessments than are common today but at much lower prices. To accomplish these objectives, the consortia plan to incorporate scoring solutions similar to those used to license doctors (United States Medical Licensing Exam) and admit students to graduate schools.

Prior to ASAP, it was unknown how these systems compared to human graders. In its role as a fair and impartial arbiter of machine scoring systems, ASAP encouraged the participation of major vendors in these competitions and introduced them to new talent, resulting in significant breakthroughs in scoring technology. The results of both competitions gained the attention of national news organizations, including National Public Radio and the *New York Times.*

Additionally, ASAP has been able to address some of the criticisms leveled at these systems. Common complaints include the ability of students to "game" the software, getting a good score just by writing a longer essay, and the concern that machine scoring can't address specific content. By designing prizes to examine those questions, ASAP has helped the consortia understand the current capabilities of machine scoring.

Prizes allow organizations an opportunity to highlight both weaknesses and strengths in a particular field and share the results of the work with a broader community (Morgan et al., 2013, pp. 7–10).

Well-constructed prizes mobilize global talent and spur innovation. A college student from Ecuador competed against some of the best testing companies in the world after 10 weeks of work. Young individuals from Slovenia to Singapore, from Pittsburgh to Poland poured hundreds of hours a week into the competition, hoping to see their names creep up a leaderboard. Winners from Phase I teamed up with a testing company for Phase II to edge out the rest of the competition.

There are a number of challenges that lie ahead for automated essay scoring—the technology is by no means perfect. One challenge is that it is reasonably possible to "game" the scoring engines. That is, it is possible to write a bad essay that gets a good score. However, the research to date suggests that one has to be a good writer to write the bad essay that gets a good score. But the fact that it is possible to do presents a challenge of face validity for the technology. The Hewlett Prize didn't address so-called bad faith essays since all the high-stakes essays used in that competition had already been cleaned of such artifacts. One can imagine another prize in which the scoring algorithms are equipped to score such documents or at least identify them for exclusive human rater review. There are other possibilities for such work in other areas of psychometrics. For example, prizes might be held for innovative item types or the thwarting of security breaches. Moreover, the focus of the competition was on summative essays, not formative ones. While AES has been applied to formative assessments, much work needs to be done to demonstrate the construct validity of this particular application (Bennett & Gitomer, 2009).

In sum, prizes can work.

## Note

Most of the research reported in this chapter was done while the senior author was at the University of Akron. This work was supported through funding from the William and Flora Hewlett Foundation. The opinions expressed in this chapter are those of the authors and do not necessarily represent the policy or views of the William and Flora Hewlett Foundation or its board of directors. The authors would like to thank Tom Vander Ark (OpenEd Solutions) and Lynn Van Deventer (the Common Pool) for their tireless efforts in executing the studies associated with this chapter and Sharon Apel-Bursky for her background research. Correspondence concerning this chapter should be addressed to Mark D. Shermis, 2700 Bay Area Blvd., University of Houston–Clear Lake, Houston, TX 77058–1098. Electronic mail may be sent via Internet to mshermis@uhcl.edu.

## References

AICPA Examinations Team. (2010). *Uniform CPA examination scoring and administration report 2009* (limited distribution). Ewing, NJ: AICPA.

Ajay, H. B., Tillett, P. I., & Page, E. B. (1973). *Analysis of essays by computer (AEC-II)*. Washington, DC: U.S. Department of Health, Education, and Welfare, Office of Education, National Center for Educational Research and Development.

Assessment Systems Corporation. (1985). *User's manual for the MicroCAT (trademark) testing system*. St. Paul, MN: Defense Technical Information Center.

Attali, Y., & Burstein, J. (2006). Automated essay scoring with e-rater V.2. *Journal of Technology, Learning, and Assessment, 4*. Available from http://jtla.bc.edu

Attewell, P., Lavin, D., Domina, T., & Levey, T. (2006). New evidence on college remediation. *The Journal of Higher Education, 55*(5), 886–924.

Bennett, R. E., & Gitomer, D. H. (2009). Transforming K–12 assessment: Integrating accountability testing, formative assessment and professional support. In C. Wyatt-Smith & J. Cumming (Eds.), *Educational assessment in the 21st century* (pp. 43–61). New York: Springer.

Binet, A., & Simon, T. (1916). *The development of intelligence in children: The Binet-Simon Scale*. Baltimore, MD: Williams & Wilkins.

Birnbaum, A. (1968). Estimation of an ability. In F. M. Lord & M. R. Novick (Eds.), *Statistical theories of mental test scores* (pp. 423–479). Reading, MA: Addison-Wesley.

Breland, H. M., Bonner, M. W., & Kubota, M. (1995). *Factors in performance on brief, impromptu essay examinations*. College Board Report No. 95–4. New York: College Entrance Examination Board.

Burstein, J., Chodorow, M., & Leacock, C. (2004). Automated essay evaluation: The Criterion Online writing service. *AI Magazine, 25*(3), 27–36.

Burstein, J., Kukich, J., Wolff, S., Lu, C., Chodorow, M., Braden-Harder, L., & Harris, M. D. (1998). Automated scoring using a hybrid feature identification technique. In *Proceedings of the 36th Annual Meeting of the Association for Computational Linguistics and 17th International Conference on Computational Linguistics*. Montrèal, Canada, & New Brunswick, NJ: Association for Computational Linguistics.

College Board. (1993). *ACCUPLACER(R): Computerized placement tests: Technical data supplement*. New York: College Board.

Dossey, John A., Halvorsen, Katherine, & McCrone, Sharon. (2008). *Mathematics education in the United States—2008: A capsule summary fact book written for the Eleventh International Congress on Mathematical Education (ICME-11)*. Monterrey, Mexico: National Council of Teachers of Mathematics.

Eignor, D.R., Way, W.D., Stocking, M.L., & Steffen, M. (1993). *Case studies in computer adaptive test design through simulation*. Princeton, NJ: Educational Testing Service.

Elliot, S. M. (1999). *Construct validity of IntelliMetricTM with international assessment*. Yardley, PA: Vantage Technologies.

Elliot, S.M. (2003). Intellimetric: From here to validity. In M.D. Shermis & J. Burstein (Eds.), *Automated essay scoring: A cross-disciplinary approach* (pp. 71–86). Mahwah, NJ: Lawrence Erlbaum Associates, Inc.

Foltz, P.W., & Landauer, T.K. (2002). The supermanual interactive electronic technical manual. In *Proceedings of the Interservice/Industry Training, Simulation & Education Conference (I/ITSEC)*. Orlando, FL, & Arlington, VA: National Training and Simulation Association.

Ho, R.-G., & Hsu, T.C. (1989). A comparison of three adaptive testing strategies using MicroCAT. Paper presented at the annual meeting of the American Educational Research Association. San Francisco, CA.

Kay, L. (2011). *Managing innovation prizes in government*. Washington, DC: IBM Center for the Business of Government.

Landauer, T.K., Foltz, P.W., & Laham, D. (1998). Introduction to latent semantic analysis. *Discourse Processes, 25*(2–3), 259–284.

Landauer, T.K., Laham, D., & Foltz, P.W. (2003). Automated scoring and annotation of essays with the Intelligent Essay Assessor. In M.D. Shermis & J. Burstein (Eds.), *Automated essay scoring: A cross-disciplinary perspective* (pp. 87–112). Mahwah, NJ: Lawrence Erlbaum Associates, Inc.

Lord, F.M. (1980). Applications of item response theory to practical testing problems. New York: Routledge.

Lord, F. M, Novick, M.R., & Birnbaum, A. (1968). *Statistical theories of mental test scores* (Vol. 47). Reading, MA: Addison-Wesley.

Luecht, R., & Sireci, S.G. (2011). *A review of models for computer-based testing*. New York: College Board.

McBride, J.R. (1986). *A computerized adaptive edition of the Differential Aptitude Tests*. Paper presented at the annual meetings of the American Psychological Association, Washington, DC.

Moreno, K.E., Wetzel, C.D., McBride, J.R., & Weiss, D.J. (1984). Relationship between corresponding Armed Services Vocational Aptitude Battery (ASVAB) and computerized adaptive testing (CAT) subtests. *Applied Psychological Measurement, 8*(2), 155–163.

Morgan, J., Shermis, M.D., Van Deventer, L., & Vander Ark, T. (2013). *Automated Student Assessment Prize: Phase 1 & Phase 2: A case study to promote focused innovation in student writing assessment*. Seattle, WA: Getting Smart.

Northwest Evaluation Association. (2005). *Technical manual: For use with the Measures of Academic Progress and Achievement Level tests*. Lake Oswego, OR: Northwest Evaluation Association.

onward Kaggle Inc. (2010). Home Page. Retrieved July 18, 2012, from www.kaggle.com

Page, E.B. (1966). The imminence of grading essays by computer. *Phi Delta Kappan, 48*, 238–243.

Page, E.B. (2003). Project Essay Grade: PEG. In M.D. Shermis & J. Burstein (Eds.), *Automated essay scoring: A cross-disciplinary perspective* (pp. 43–54). Mahwah, NJ: Lawrence Erlbaum Associates, Inc.

Page, E.B., Keith, T., & Lavoie, M.J. (1995, August). Construct validity in the computer grading of essays. Paper presented at the annual meetings of the American Psychological Association, New York, NY.

Page, E.B., Lavoie, M.J., & Keith, T.Z. (1996, April). Computer grading of essay traits in student writing. Paper presented at the annual meetings of the American Psychological Association, New York, NY.

Page, E.B., & Petersen, N.S. (1995). The computer moves into essay grading: Updating the ancient test. *Phi Delta Kappan, 76*(7), 561–565.

Porter, A., McMaken, J., Hwang, J., & Yang, R. (2011). Common Core Standards: The new U.S. intended curriculum. *Educational Researcher, 40*(3), 103–116.

Revuelta, J., & Ponsoda, V. (1998). A comparison of item exposure control methods in computerized adaptive testing. *Journal of Educational Measurement, 35*(4), 311–327.

Sands, W. A, Waters, B. K, & McBride, J.R. (1997). *Computerized adaptive testing: From inquiry to operation*. Washington, DC: American Psychological Association.

Schaeffer, G.A. (1995). *The introduction and comparability of the computer adaptive GRE general test* (GRE Board Professional Report No. 88–08aP). Princeton, NJ: Educational Testing Service.

Segall, D.O., & Moreno, K.E. (1999). Development of the computerized adaptive testing version of the Armed Services Vocational Battery. In F. Drasgow & J.B. Olson-Buchanan (Eds.), *Innovations in computerized assessment* (pp. 35–66). Mahwah, NJ: Lawrence Erlbaum Associates, Inc.

Shermis, M.D. (2014). State-of-the-art automated essay scoring: A United States demonstration and competition, results, and future directions. *Assessing Writing, 20*, 53–76.

Shermis, M.D., & Hamner, B. (2012). Contrasting state-of-the-art automated scoring of essays: Analysis. Paper presented at the annual meeting of the National Council on Measurement in Education, Vancouver, BC.

Shermis, M.D., & Hamner, B. (2013). Contrasting state-of-the-art automated scoring of essays. In M.D. Shermis & J. Burstein (Eds.), *Handbook of automated essay evaluation: Current applications and new directions* (pp. 313–346). New York: Routledge.

Shermis, M.D., Lottridge, S.M., & Mayfield, E. (2014). *The impact of anonymization for automated essay scoring.* Paper presented at the National Council on Measurement in Education, Philadelphia, PA.

Shermis, M.D., Mzumara, H.R., Kiger, B.S., & Marsiglio, C. (1998). *The Testing Center annual report 1998.* Indianapolis, IN: IUPUI Testing Center.

Shermis, M.D., Mzumara, H.R., Olson, J., & Harrington, S. (2001). On-line grading of student essays: PEG goes on the web at IUPUI. *Assessment and Evaluation in Higher Education, 26*(3), 247–259.

Stocking, M.L., & Swanson, L. (1998). Optimal design of item banks for computerized adaptive tests. *Applied Psychological Measurement, 22*(3), 271–279.

Terman, L.M. (1916). *The measurement of intelligence: An explanation of and a complete guide for the use of the Stanford revision and extension of the Binet-Simon intelligence scale.* New York: Houghton Mifflin.

Tucker, B. (2009). The next generation of testing. *Multiple Measures, 67*(3), 48–53.

Vale, C.D., & Weiss, D.J. (1975). *A study of computer-administered stradaptive ability testing* (RR 75-4). Minneapolis, MN: Psychometric Methods Program, Department of Psychology, University of Minnesota.

Wainer, H., Dorans, N.J., Flaugher, R., Green, B.F., & Mislevy, R.J. (2000). *Computerized adaptive testing: A primer.* New York: Routledge.

Way, W.D. (1998). Protecting the integrity of computerized testing item pools. *Educational Measurement: Issues and Practice, 17*(4), 17–27.

Weigle, S.C. (2013). English language learners and automated scoring of essays: Critical considerations. *Assessing Writing, 18,* 85–99.

Weir, C.J. (2005). Limitations of the Common European Framework for developing comparable examinations and tests. *Language Testing, 22*(3), 261–300.

Weiss, D.J. (1973). *The stratified adaptive computerized ability test* (RR 73-3). Minneapolis, MN: Psychometric Methods Program, Department of Psychology, University of Minnesota.

Weiss, D.J. (1985). Adaptive testing by computer. *Journal of Consulting and Clinical Psychology, 53*(6), 774.

Williamson, D.M. (2009). *A framework for implementing automated scoring.* Paper presented at the American Educational Research Association, San Diego, CA.

# Commentary on Chapters 12–15: Future Directions
## Challenge and Opportunity

**Edward Haertel**

At the beginning of the 20th century, even as the foundations of modern measurement theory were being laid, A.A. Michelson (1903, pp. 23–24) famously wrote that "The more important fundamental laws and facts of physical science have all been discovered, and these are now so firmly established that the possibility of their ever being supplanted in consequence of new discoveries is exceedingly remote. Nevertheless, it has been found that there are apparent exceptions to most of these laws, and this is particularly true when the observations are pressed to a limit . . . such that extreme cases can be examined." He went on to suggest that future discoveries "must be looked for in the sixth place of decimals." Michelson was not suggesting that all that remained for physics was to measure physical constants more and more precisely. Rather, his point was that the path to discovery of new natural phenomena and the growth of scientific knowledge was by way of continued refinements of physical measurements.

As with physics more than a century ago, general models and methods for educational measurement are by now well worked out. The statistical frameworks of classical test theory, generalizability theory, and the simpler models of item response theory, as well as theoretical frameworks guiding test design and the validation of test score uses and interpretations, are not likely to be swept aside anytime soon. But, as with physics since Michelson's time, increasing refinements raise new questions and bring new opportunities for further research and improvement. In educational measurement, these refinements are made possible by new technologies, including new modes of data acquisition, interactive assessment formats, vastly increased computational power, more sophisticated algorithms, and more rapid and efficient dissemination of new information and discoveries. The four chapters in this final section of *Technology in Testing: Measurement Issues* survey significant areas at the frontiers of contemporary measurement, describing just four points on the ever-expanding periphery of the field. As shown in these chapters, new technologies are already supporting better practice in educational measurement. These include more responsive accommodation to the needs of individual learners, more detailed and specific interpretations of examinees' measured capabilities, incorporation of different kinds of information (e.g., response latencies) into measurement models, and, in support of all these goals, enhanced communication and collaboration among measurement professionals around the world.

In Chapter 12, Way, Davis, Keng, and Strain-Seymour consider some implications of technology for score comparability and offer a useful framework for future investigation as both item formats and varieties of interactive devices evolve. Measurement requires systematic observation of performance under controlled conditions, but it has long been recognized that the greatest possible uniformity in testing conditions may not afford the most accurate and comparable measurement for all examinees. As measurement theory and practice have progressed, there has been a trend toward greater flexibility in accommodating the particular circumstances of different test takers. The word "personalization" in the title of this chapter highlights movement beyond testing accommodations for differentially abled examinees toward a recognition that all examinees may be at their best using those interactive technologies with which they are most familiar, be they laptops, tablet devices, or even smartphones. As test developers respond to customer demands for assessments delivered on a greater range of devices, increased personalization becomes possible. This movement brings new technical challenges, but also the potential for increased validity, as the technology used in the test setting comes to resemble more closely the technology available in the classroom or the workplace. Greater costs of development and validation for assessments delivered on multiple devices may be offset by savings realized when testing can be done using whatever technology is readily available.

In Chapter 13, Templin offers a comprehensive and informative history and overview of diagnostic classification models (DCMs), especially the *log-linear cognitive diagnosis model* (LCDM), which subsumes many earlier DCMs as special cases. His discussion clarifies the tradeoff, in choosing among statistical models for item response data, between fine-grained ranking of examinees with respect to one or a few broad characteristics versus coarser measurement with respect to a larger set of dimensions, with skill profiles across those dimensions represented by discrete latent classes. For many important instructional applications, using DCMs to measure multiple skills may yield more useful information than simpler IRT models. Such applications include not only formative assessment in classrooms but also modeling student proficiencies in real time to guide interactive educational software, as well as comparison and evaluation of curriculum materials. DCMs will be most useful when applied to tests designed from the outset to differentiate among specific student misconceptions or skill profiles. Thus, as a conceptual tool, the DCM modeling framework may also lead to more refined specification of measured constructs and improved test design.

In Chapter 14, Bolt considers various ways in which computer-based testing (CBT) has spurred new developments in IRT. Chapter 14 addresses a range of concerns beyond the obvious requirement for item-selection algorithms for computerized adaptive testing. CBT brings with it demands for very large item pools, especially where item exposure and test security are concerns. Thus, CBT has been one driver for the development of IRT models for item cloning, especially the linear item cloning model (LICM). Concern over context effects, balanced content coverage, and the use of multiple items associated with the same rich stimulus have prompted applications of testlet-based administrations in CBT, with associated statistical models. Innovative item types used in CBT may call for polytomous or multidimensional IRT applications. Bolt also briefly surveys models incorporating parameters for item exposure and examinee cheating, useful for detecting and investigating test compromise in CBT applications. Finally, Chapter 14 takes up response-time modeling, summarizing models in which examinees are characterized by both ability and rate of work. In the early days of IRT, with only a few models to choose from, testing experts sought to build tests so as to avoid violations of model assumptions. As shown by Bolt's thoughtful review, the world has changed. Relaxing assumptions such as local independence, CBT test designers today enjoy much greater freedom and flexibility in test design, as new psychometric tools appropriate for such tests become available.

In Chapter 15, Shermis and Morgan discuss the trajectories of technical developments in computerized adaptive testing (CAT) versus automatic essay scoring (AES) and propose that progress was less rapid in AES in part because much of the early research and development work was proprietary. In support of this hypothesis, they describe the dramatic success of the two Hewlett-sponsored competitions offering monetary prizes for the most successful open-source programs developed for essay and for constructed-response scoring. In addition to generating publicity and attracting new talent to work on these problems, the prizes also led to significant borrowing from other academic fields in which machine learning algorithms have been employed for different purposes. The authors suggest additional measurement challenges for which similar competitions might be of similar value.

Much progress has been made, but further challenges remain. For various reasons, progress has been more rapid in the large-scale, on-demand summative assessment of student learning than in the fine-grained formative assessment of day-to-day work in classrooms. Increased customization, more complex and interactive item types, greater use of machine-scorable free-response formats, and DCMs may support better formative assessments of student learning, providing teachers with more timely, reliable, and useful information about students' individual trajectories toward mastery of intended learning outcomes. Still further, well-intentioned critics have asked repeatedly why large-scale assessment systems cannot capitalize on the information provided by students' classroom work, thereby rendering assessments more "authentic" and at the same time reducing overall testing burden. Ultimately, if curriculum-embedded formative assessments can be linked to multidimensional models of student proficiency, these ongoing assessments of students' classroom activities might in turn support broader summative descriptions of their longer-term achievement outcomes.

When there are stakes attached to test performance, what is not tested may not be taught. So long as external assessments fall short of assessing the full range of intended learning outcomes, instructional time and resources will likely be allocated disproportionately to the measured subset of learning goals. Thus, the impression lingers that "put crudely, we start out with the intention of making the important measurable, and end up making the measurable important" (Wiliam, 1998, p. 1). With new measurement technologies, the field is poised to make great strides toward better measurement of the full range of complex and meaningful learning outcomes, providing information that can both inform and motivate better instruction for all learners.

## References

Michelson, A.A. (1903). *Light waves and their uses* (The decennial publications of the University of Chicago, Second Series, Volume III). Chicago: University of Chicago Press.

Wiliam, D. (1998, July). *The validity of teachers' assessments.* Paper presented to Working Group 6 (Research on the Psychology of Mathematics Teacher Development) of the 22nd annual conference of the International Group for the Psychology of Mathematics Education, Stellenbosch, South Africa. Retrieved from www.dylanwiliam. org/Dylan_Wiliams_website/Papers_files/PME%2022%20WG6%20paper.doc

# Index